To our students—past, present, and future—from whom we have learned and continue to learn much about international organizations and the politics and processes of global governance

International Organizations

FOURTH EDITION

International Organizations

The Politics and Processes of Global Governance

Margaret P. Karns,
Tana Johnson, and
Karen A. Mingst

LYNNE
RIENNER
PUBLISHERS

BOULDER
LONDON

Published in the United States of America in 2024 by
Lynne Rienner Publishers, Inc.
1800 30th Street, Suite 314, Boulder, Colorado 80301
www.rienner.com

and in the United Kingdom by
Lynne Rienner Publishers, Inc.
1 Bedford Row, London WC1R 4BU
www.eurospanbookstore.com/rienner

Library of Congress Cataloging-in-Publication Data
Names: Karns, Margaret P., author. | Johnson, Tana, author. | Mingst, Karen
    A., 1947– author.
Title: International organizations : the politics and processes of global
    governance / Margaret P. Karns, Tana Johnson, Karen A. Mingst.
Description: Fourth edition. | Boudler, Colorado: Lynne Rienner Publishers,
    Inc., 2023. | Includes bibliographical references and index. | Summary:
    "A comprehensive, in-depth examination of the full range of
    international organizations"— Provided by publisher.
Identifiers: LCCN 2023018743 (print) | LCCN 2023018744 (ebook) | ISBN
    9781685859794 (paperback) | ISBN 9781685859800 (ebook)
Subjects: LCSH: International agencies. | International organization.
Classification: LCC JZ4850 .K37 2024 (print) | LCC JZ4850 (ebook) | DDC
    341.2—dc23/eng/20230420
LC record available at https://lccn.loc.gov/2023018743
LC ebook record available at https://lccn.loc.gov/2023018744

British Cataloguing in Publication Data
A Cataloguing in Publication record for this book
is available from the British Library.

Printed and bound in the United States of America

The paper used in this publication meets the requirements
of the American National Standard for Permanence of
Paper for Printed Library Materials Z39.48-1992.

5 4 3 2 1

Contents

Illustrations

Preface

IN RECENT YEARS, THE POLITICS AND PROCESSES OF GLOBAL GOVERNANCE have become increasingly complex as the varieties of international organizations and other actors have multiplied and challenges have mounted. Many of the ideas we tried to express in the first edition of this book in 2004 have continued to develop. In the years since the third edition appeared in 2015, the world has changed immensely, and there has been an astonishing amount of new scholarship in several areas.

This new edition has been thoroughly updated to take into account recent developments, shifting power relations (especially between the United States and China), and current scholarship. It includes newer theoretical approaches such as postcolonialism and highlights the continuing importance of regional organizations with a new section on the Arctic Council. We have added a chapter on human security, covering health (including the Covid-19 pandemic), food (including the 2022–2023 global food crisis), migration and refugees, and human trafficking. Russia's 2022 invasion of Ukraine is covered in the peace and security chapter, with a case study of the documentation in real time of war crimes in Ukraine and the war's effects on global food security. We delve into the impact of populist nationalism in several parts of the world, issues relating to digital currencies, the roles of both social media and traditional media, and the significance of the youth climate-justice movement. The book continues to be informed by familiar and emerging theories of international relations and organization.

As we wrote in the preface to the first edition of *International Organizations*, when Lynne Rienner calls and invites you to write a book, the invitation is hard to resist, particularly when it comes with passion, enthusiasm, and encouragement. Lynne was patient then and through the second and third editions, and particularly so with this fourth edition when life got in the way of our ability to push forward with revisions. We thank her for all the support that she has provided.

With Lynne's encouragement, we welcomed Tana Johnson as coauthor for this fourth edition, and some of the changes in the book reflect her fresh thinking. Karen Mingst has largely (but fortunately not entirely) stepped back from active involvement in the project. Coordination among three authors can be a challenge, and in keeping with the book's subject, we have had to develop new habits of cooperation.

We have incurred a debt to our students, who have given us feedback on what worked and what did not in previous editions. We are grateful to the many colleagues around the world who contributed ideas and feedback, helping us to refine our thinking and improve the volume. We owe special thanks to students who have worked with Margaret Karns at the University of Massachusetts, Boston (Margaret Hassey, Michael Cole, Rebecca Yemo, Jean-Pierre Murray, Krystal-Gayle O'Neill, Kuntala Bandyopadhyay, Carlos Perez Espitia, Dennis Jjuuko, and Prince De Makele Mounguembou) and students who have worked with Tana Johnson at Duke University (Liza Becker) and the University of Wisconsin (Laura Downer, Yena Kim, Hana Livingston, Stephanie Mertens, Hasaan Parker, Megan Shaw, Muhammad Shayan, Phelan Simkus, and Hannah Tuttle). To all students and colleagues who have participated in discussions of our ideas but are not named here, we also say thanks.

Portions of Chapters 3–4 and 7–11 are drawn from Karen A. Mingst, Margaret P. Karns, and Alynna J. Lyon, *The United Nations in the 21st Century*, 6th ed. (New York: Taylor & Francis, 2022). We are particularly grateful for Alynna Lyon's contributions to the material on the United Nations and peace and security. This material is included with permission of Routledge/Taylor & Francis.

No project like this is possible without the support of friends and families, who bear the burden of long hours, weeks, and months of concentrated labor. To you, we express our deepest thanks.

—*Margaret Karns,*
Tana Johnson, and
Karen Mingst

1

Why Global Governance?

THE GROWING EVIDENCE OF CLIMATE CHANGE, THE DISRUPTIONS CAUSED by the global Covid-19 pandemic, the increasing challenges of migration in several parts of the world, the rapid emergence of China as a superpower, and the shock of Russia's 2022 invasion of Ukraine have brought home to people around the world the urgency and complexity of the global governance challenges we face today. Against this backdrop remain the persistent issues of nuclear weapons proliferation, large-scale humanitarian crises affecting global food supply, deep poverty and economic inequality in many parts of the world, and continuing threats to basic human rights and human security. Confronting these seemingly intractable challenges are a variety of international actors, institutions, and processes that over more than a century now have come to form what we call global governance.

None of these problems can be solved by sovereign states acting alone. All require cooperation of some sort among states and the growing number of nonstate actors; many require the active participation of ordinary citizens; some demand the establishment of new international mechanisms for monitoring or negotiating new international rules; and most require the refinement of means for securing states' and other actors' compliance. Many contemporary problems also call for new types of partnerships—some between existing organizations such as the United Nations (UN) and the African Union (AU) in the Sahel; others involve public–private partnerships such as the one between the UN and the Bill and Melinda Gates Foundation to address various international health issues. In short, there is a wide variety of cross-border issues and problems that require governance. Sometimes the need is truly global in scope, as with pandemics and climate change. In other cases, the governance problem is specific to a region or group of countries, as with the need to manage an international river or regional migration surge. Sometimes, a problem cannot be neatly classified, as with the Arctic, where the nexus of issues posed by climate change affects not just states, species, and peoples but significant parts of the whole world. As Bruce Jentleson (2012: 145) has noted, "The need for global governance is not an if question. It is a how question." But what do we mean by global governance?

What Is Global Governance?

In 2005, two international relations scholars noted that the idea of global governance had attained "near-celebrity status" (Barnett and Duvall 2005:1), but almost two decades later its meaning is still contested. Sometimes the term *global governance* has been used as a synonym for international organizations. More often, it is used to capture the complexity and dynamism of the collective efforts by states and an increasing variety of nonstate actors to identify, understand, and address various issues and problems in today's turbulent world. In 1995, the Commission on Global Governance, an independent group of prominent international figures, published a report on what reforms in modes of international cooperation were called for by global changes after the end of the Cold War. The commission defined governance as "the sum of the many ways individuals and institutions, public and private, manage their common affairs. It is a continuing process through which conflicting or diverse interests may be accommodated and cooperative action may be taken. It includes formal . . . as well as informal arrangements that people and institutions have agreed to or perceive to be in their interest" (Commission on Global Governance 1995: 2).

But what is the relationship between governance and government? While clearly related, the two concepts are not identical. As James Rosenau (1992: 4) put it:

> Both refer to purposive behavior, to goal-oriented activities, to systems of rule; but government suggests activities that are backed by formal authority, by police powers to insure the implementation of duly constituted policies, whereas governance refers to activities backed by shared goals that may or may not derive from legal and formally prescribed responsibilities and that do not necessarily rely on police powers to overcome defiance and attain compliance. Governance, in other words, is a more encompassing phenomenon than government. It embraces governmental institutions, but it also subsumes informal, nongovernmental mechanisms whereby those persons and organizations within its purview move ahead, satisfy their needs, and fulfill their wants.

Thus, global governance is not global government; it is not a single world order; there is no top-down, hierarchical structure of authority, but power and authority in global governance are both present in varying ways and to varying degrees. Reviewing the evolution of the concept, Thomas Weiss and Rorden Wilkinson (2014: 211) conclude, "We understand global governance as the sum of the informal and formal ideas, values, norms, procedures, and institutions that help all actors—states, IGOs, civil society, and TNCs [transnational corporations]—identify, understand, and address transboundary problems." It therefore encompasses international law and international organizations created by states, but goes well beyond them. It is "the collective effort by sovereign states, international organizations, and other nonstate actors to address common challenges and seize opportunities that transcend national frontiers. . . . [It is] an ungainly patchwork of formal and informal institutions" (Patrick 2014: 59).

To some, global governance is only linked to the post–Cold War international order; others speak of patterns of governance in different historical orders; still others conceive of it as an evolving set of institutions, rules, patterns of interaction, actors, and processes. For some scholars, global governance only includes institutions, processes, and policies that are truly global in scope. Others, most notably Amitav Acharya (2016a) argue that global governance includes not only formal and informal global intergovernmental institutions and policies, but also regional and multistakeholder ones with local and domestic politics in states often playing a key role in influencing states' willingness and ability to commit.

Analyzing the varieties of global governance and the actors in the politics and processes that have shaped them is the central purpose of this book. We show why, if one wants to understand collective global efforts to solve those "problems without passports," it is no longer enough to look just at international organizations created by states. Although states retain their sovereignty and still exercise coercive power, global governance increasingly rests on other bases of authority. Thus, the study of this phenomenon requires exploring not only the forms it can take, the politics and processes by which it has developed, the actors who play various roles, and the relationships among them but also the forms and patterns of both power and authority. As the title of one book conveys, "Who governs the globe?" is an essential question to answer, as are the questions of "who gets what?," "who benefits?," and with what consequences (Avant, Finnemore, and Sell 2010b).

Part of the value, then, of the concept "global governance" is how it enables us to look at the long-term process of organizing collective efforts to deal with shared problems—that is, the process of international organization—past, present, and future (Claude 1964: 4).

Global governance is incredibly complex, and no single book can cover it all. For the sake of manageability, we focus primarily on interstate varieties of global governance, particularly on global and regional intergovernmental organizations (IGOs), while also showing where and how various types of nonstate actors (NSAs) play important roles. We introduce networks, forms of private governance, and public–private partnerships, but leave these largely to others to elaborate. Because global governance is dynamic, we identify changes in governance needs and approaches over time.

Why the Growing Need for Global Governance?

The emergence of the concept of global governance in the 1990s accompanied the growing awareness of a number of systemic changes happening in the world, the rapid proliferation of new issues and actors, and the inadequacy of existing international organizations (particularly the United Nations) to address many problems. These changes have included globalization, technological advances, the growth of transnationalism, changing relations among the great powers, the growing awareness of global environmental problems, and the proliferation of NSAs. Separately and collectively, they have fundamentally altered global politics and contributed to the increased need for global governance.

Globalization

In the 1990s, what initially appeared to be simply growing interdependence among states and peoples became something much more fundamental—a complex multidimensional process of economic, cultural, and social change. Particularly noticeable was the rapid pace of change, the compression of time and space, and the scale and scope of interconnectedness. There are many definitions of *globalization*. Some focus on political, societal, and cultural integration, whereas others point more specifically to the economic integration of markets through trade, capital flows, and flows of technology and workers. By the early 2000s, most observers agreed that globalization had become unprecedented in the degree to which markets, cultures, peoples, and states had become linked, thanks to changes in technology, transportation, and communications that sped up the movement of ideas, goods, news, capital, technology, and people.

Globalization has spurred proliferating networks of nongovernmental organizations (NGOs) and financial markets, linking like-minded people and investors, as well as the unwelcome, often illegal actors—terrorists and drug traffickers. It has contributed to the homogenization of culture with the global spread of ideas and popular culture.

Globalization has also led to the reassertion of ethnicity and nationalism in many parts of the world. The ways global events can have local consequences and local events can have global consequences mean that crises in one region can affect jobs, production, personal savings, and investment elsewhere. Civil wars and conflicts in some of the world's poorest regions, such as Yemen, Afghanistan, and Mali, ripple outward through the flows of asylum seekers and migrants to richer countries.

The effects of globalization change the significance of borders of states and the very nature of world politics. They mean that states no longer have a monopoly on power and authority. They increase the recognition of transnational problems that require global regulation in some form. The consequence has been a huge growth in transnational, regional, and global forms of public and private rulemaking and regulation since the early 1990s. This includes expanded jurisdiction of existing IGOs like the International Maritime Organization; networks of cooperation among government agencies, such as the Financial Action Task Force, that link government experts on money laundering; and private standard-setting initiatives such as that by the Forest Stewardship Council.

Although globalization affects all spheres of human activity, not all are equally affected. It has deepened global inequality between the haves and have-nots, especially those living on less than $1.90 a day—the UN's 2022 benchmark for extreme poverty. It has created winners and losers between countries and within countries. As UN Secretary-General Kofi Annan noted in 2000, "The central challenge . . . is to ensure that globalization becomes a positive force for all the world's people, instead of leaving billions of them behind in squalor" (2000: 6).

Increasing globalization is not inevitable, however. In the 2020s, there is growing discussion of the possibility of decreasing globalization or even deglobalization. In some areas, populism has risen in response to globalization with a rejection of traditional elites, a turn toward authoritarianism, and decreased support for international cooperation. During the Covid-19 pandemic, people in many parts of the world became aware of how globalization had created complex global supply chains between producers of various goods in different parts of the world, the manufacturers dependent on those goods, and consumers. When those supply chains were disrupted by the closing of national borders, the health of people and nations was jeopardized. Russia's invasion of Ukraine in 2022 severed many economic and other links between that country and the rest of the world, showing that country's vulnerability as a result of its integration in the global economy. The war in Ukraine also revealed the high global dependence on grain and fertilizer from Russia and Ukraine and, hence, the war's severe effects on food security.

Although globalization now appears to be evolving in unpredictable ways, it is closely linked to the revolution in global communications and transport which owes much to technological changes.

Technological Changes

Globalization would not have been possible without major technological changes in transport and communications that allow the movement of people and goods rapidly over great distances and move information, images, written words, and sound by telephone, Internet, television networks, and various forms of social media. Today's container ships and tankers carry many times the tonnage faster and at lower cost than ever before. The ease and lower cost of contemporary jet travel have contributed to the flow of international tourists. In 2012, the number of tourists worldwide passed the 1 billion mark for the first time; it reached 1.5 billion in 2019 according to the World Tourism Organization. The figure was just 25 million in 1952.

Technological advances in communication from the mid-nineteenth-century development of the telegraph to the telephone, radio, film, television, photocopying, satellite communications, faxing, cell phones, the internet, email, and social media have had an enormous impact on global politics and governance. In 2021, the International Telecommunication Union (ITU) reported that an estimated 63 percent of the world's population was using the internet—an increase of 17 percent since 2019. The number of cell or mobile phone subscriptions in the world reached 8 billion in 2021, and the ITU noted that no technology had ever spread this rapidly, especially among the rural poor. Transnational communications allow citizens all over the world to exchange ideas and information and to mobilize like-minded people in support of a particular cause in real time. The cascade of events from Tunisia to Egypt to Yemen, Jordan, Bahrain, Morocco, Libya, and Syria during the Arab Spring uprisings in 2011 owed much to people's use of social media and the inability of authoritarian governments to block the flow of images and information. A similar cascade of events and worldwide mobilization occurred in 2019 with the Black Lives Matter protests that started in the United States. Both the transportation and communications revolutions have aided the formation of transnational networks and social movements.

Expanding Transnationalism
Among the effects of globalization across issues and technological changes is the growth of transnationalism—the networks and connections through which individuals and various types of nonstate actors work together across state borders. It is exhibited in the activities of global civil society, international NGOs, transnational advocacy networks, and transnational social movements.

Beginning in the late 1980s and 1990s, the spread of democracy bolstered the growth of civil society in countries where restrictions on citizens' groups were lifted. Civil society groups created coalitions from the local to the global across a wide range of issues, including the environment, human rights, economic development, and security. The result has been a dramatic rise in transnational activities and corresponding demands for representation in processes of global governance. Various types of transnational groups are discussed further in Chapter 6, but it is important to note that the democratization trend was reversed in the second decade of the twenty-first century, and the consequences for transnationalism remain to be seen as of this writing.

Changing Great Power Relations
Finally, transformations in the international political system, most notably changing great power relationships, are responsible for the increased need

for global governance. Beginning with the collapse of Soviet-supported communist governments in Central Europe in 1989 and 1990 and the disintegration of the Soviet Union itself in 1991 into fifteen separate, independent states, the end of the Cold War marked the beginning of a new era. The international system shifted from a bipolar structure to a post–Cold War structure that was simultaneously unipolar, dominated by a single superpower (the United States) and a nonpolar, networked system of a globalizing world. For a brief period of time, US hegemony reasserted itself. But that period also saw the end of superpower support for many weak states in Asia and Africa, unleashing a string of deadly conflicts and related humanitarian crises in the former Yugoslavia, Somalia, Afghanistan, and elsewhere. These produced increased demands for new forms of conflict resolution, including UN peacekeeping and postconflict peacebuilding. The system changes opened new political space for states and NSAs—space for pursuing new types of cooperation in ending those conflicts, expanding the scope and reach of human rights norms, pursuing ambitious goals for development, and governing growing trade and investment flows. In short, it produced a series of new governance challenges and possibilities for developing new forms of governance.

Thirty years after the Cold War's end, the world has a new global superpower that is challenging the dominance of the United States. The rise of China is nothing short of remarkable, including its dramatic economic growth to become the world's second largest economy and its expanded investment in its military capabilities. With its greater self-confidence under the leadership of President Xi Jinping since 2012, China has played a much more assertive international role, competing with the United States for influence and global leadership more broadly. Through its Belt and Road Initiative (BRI), China is supporting major infrastructure projects in many countries and regions. It also created the Asian Infrastructure Investment Bank (AIIB), which is seen as a rival to the World Bank, and it has become far more active within the UN system, seeking top positions in a number of UN agencies and other international organizations. China sees itself as a model for many developing countries, but also wants to assume a greater role in international organizations and become not just a "rules-taker" but a "rules-maker" (Economy 2022: 172). In various ways, China has been using both soft and hard power to follow through on Xi Jinping's pledge for China "to lead in the reform of the global governance system" while continuing to assert the primacy of the sovereignty and noninterference norms that allow all countries to determine their political and economic paths. While arguing the need for change—especially to give China and other emerging economies more say in international institutions and norms—China is mindful that it owes much to the US-led systems of international norms, rules, and institutions for its own rise (Economy 2022: 172).

The growing competition between the United States and China has major implications for the future of global governance. Complicating the picture, however, is Russia—the former superpower—which shares China's antipathy for the United States and whose 2022 invasion of Ukraine violated one of the fundamental rules of the post–World War II US-led international order: the rule against using military force to change borders. Whether these geopolitical shifts portend something like a new Cold War or renewal of the original one (some asserted it never fully ended) or something else again will undoubtedly influence the future shape of global governance. The need for governance that can manage these geopolitical shifts and competition is significant, and the Russian invasion of Ukraine, for example, has triggered new demands to address the fundamental inadequacy and unrepresentativeness of the UN Security Council. The makeup of the council and the provision for five permanent members with veto power was realistic in 1945 as the only way to ensure that both the United States and Soviet Union accepted the creation of the United Nations. The makeup of the Security Council has long been unrepresentative of the UN's full membership and demands for change, especially from countries in the Global South, are hardly new, as is discussed in Chapter 4.

Other needs for global governance arise in relation to specific issues and problems, such as growing numbers of humanitarian crises and complex intrastate conflicts like in Yemen and the Sahel; demands to address gender inequality and gender-based violence; surges in numbers of refugees, displaced persons, and migrants in many areas of the world; an epidemic (Ebola in West Africa in 2014) and a global pandemic (Covid-19) within six years of each other; and the existential challenge of climate change. As Acharya (2016a: 4–5) argues, "Global governance institutions and processes are what their demanders make of them. New areas of demand . . . explain not only the creation of new norms and institutions, but also add diversity to the overall architecture of global governance." He further asserts that there is a relationship between demand and the design of elements of global governance, including membership, scope, mandate, and decision-making rules.

The six issue area chapters of this book examine the changing nature of each issue area, the relevant key global and regional IGOs, and other types of governance structures, the roles of state and nonstate actors, and the evolution of key aspects of governance. The increased need and demand for global governance magnify the importance of multilateralism as a core process and the importance of leadership and different strategies used by states and nonstate actors. One key way multilateralism has changed is with the expansion of the number and kinds of actors participating. As Deborah Avant, Martha Finnemore, and Susan Sell (2010c: 7) note, "knowing global needs is rarely enough to explain how and why a particular governance outcome was chosen." Yet the expansion in the numbers and types of actors, along with the number of different governance structures and the varying agendas of different actors can make the complexity of global governance difficult to sort out.

Actors in Global Governance

The complexity of global governance is a function not only of its many forms but also of its many actors. To be sure, states are central actors in IGOs and in many other forms of global governance, but IGO bureaucracies, treaty secretariats, NGOs, multinational corporations (MNCs), scientific experts, civil society groups, international credit-rating agencies, think tanks, major foundations, networks, public–private partnerships, private military and security companies, as well as transnational criminal and drug-trafficking networks are among the many NSAs (see Figure 1.1). As Dingwerth and Pattberg (2006: 191) put it, "In essence, global governance implies a multi-actor perspective on world politics." Still, "the novelty is not simply the increase in numbers but also the ability of nonstate actors to take part in steering the political system" (Biermann and Pattberg 2012: 6). Thus, studying actors in global governance means examining the nature and degree of various actors' participation in different issue areas, their relative power and authority, and in some cases their domestic politics and institutions.

States

States continue to be key actors in global governance. States alone have sovereignty, which has historically given them authority over their own territory and people and over the powers delegated to international institutions. To be sure, today's reality is that sovereignty is compromised by the weakness of many states; by globalization, the Internet, and social media; by conditionality on international aid; and by the influences of international norms and NSAs such as banks, global financial markets, and NGOs. Traditionally, states have been the primary sources of IGOs' funding and military capabilities for multilateral peacekeeping and peace enforcement. They create international law and norms and determine their effectiveness through their compliance or failure to comply. States are still also a primary locus of many people's identities.

Because the more than 190 states in the international system vary so

Figure 1.1
Actors in Global Governance

- States and their subnational and local jurisdictions
- IGOs and their bureaucracies
- NGOs and civil society groups
- Experts and epistemic communities
- Networks and partnerships
- Multinational corporations
- Private foundations

dramatically, however, their relative importance in global governance varies. Large, powerful states are more likely to play greater roles than are smaller, less powerful states. Yet small states and middle powers can also be sources of important global governance initiatives, the classic case being Malta, whose permanent representative to the UN in 1967, Arvid Pardo, made his tiny island nation's mark by getting the General Assembly to adopt the norm of the seabed and other global commons areas as "the common heritage of mankind." With significant shifts in the relative power of major states now under way, patterns that have prevailed in the past are changing, making the future difficult to predict.

Historically, the United States used its dominant position after World War II to shape much of the structure and rules of the postwar international system, including the liberal international economic order. Because it used its hard material power and its soft power of attraction and persuasion to promote the principles of multilateralism and compromise and to promote liberal ideas, scholars refer to US hegemony in characterizing the US role. IGOs offered a way to create structures compatible with American notions of political order and through which to promote US political and economic interests as well as ideas and values. Although domestic support for such institutions was not necessarily ensured, governmental and public commitment have generally been strong in the United States and many other countries. The predominance of Americans in many IGO secretariats and the relatively large share of operating and program funding contributed by the United States has reinforced US influence over the policies and programs of many IGOs.

Nonetheless, the history of the United States and international commitments is a mixed one, as shown by the US rejection of membership in the League of Nations in 1921, of the proposed International Trade Organization in 1948, of the UN Convention on the Law of the Sea in 1982, and of the International Criminal Court (ICC) and the Comprehensive Test Ban Treaty in 1998. Since 1972, the United States has used its veto in the UN Security Council more than any of the other four permanent members. The US Congress withheld full payment of dues to the UN from 1985 to 2000 and held up reform of the International Monetary Fund (IMF) between 2010 and 2015.

To be sure, US hegemony was challenged throughout the Cold War by the Soviet Union and its allies and by the rise of nationalism among states in Africa, Asia, and the Caribbean that gained their independence from European colonial rule in the 1950s and 1960s. It has also been challenged by the country's own quasi-imperial overstretch and wars in Vietnam, Iraq, Afghanistan, and the global war on terror, which have drained resources and cost the United States legitimacy among friends and allies. Still, the international order that US hegemony created persists.

Yet today, the United States cannot shape global governance alone. As one journalist commented in 2011: "The United States still has formidable strengths. . . . But America will never again experience the global dominance it enjoyed in the 17 years between the Soviet Union's collapse in 1991 and the financial crisis of 2008. Those days are over" (Rachman 2011: 63). Under the administration of President Donald J. Trump, the United States severely undermined its power and influence in global governance with open criticisms of the UN, withdrawal from the 2015 Paris Climate Agreement, the Iran Nuclear Agreement, the UN Educational, Scientific, and Cultural Organization (UNESCO), and even the World Health Organization (WHO) during the Covid-19 pandemic, and the president's personal disdain for multilateralism. Although the administration of President Joseph Biden signaled renewed support for the UN, the Paris Climate Agreement, the WHO, and multilateralism in general, others' faith in US credibility and reliability remains severely damaged.

One of the most extraordinary shifts in world politics in recent years is the rise of China. It is a shift that became more marked with the 2020 pandemic when China moved quickly to position itself as a global leader in pandemic response. With the rapid growth of its economic importance in the world and greater self-confidence under the leadership of President Xi Jinping since 2012, China is now actively challenging the United States and Western dominance in many global institutions. In the UN, for example, China has rapidly increased the number of its nationals serving in various posts and, as of 2021, there were four UN specialized agencies headed by Chinese nationals—more than by any other of the five permanent members of the Security Council (P-5). As the second largest economy since 2013; a major donor to the World Bank; a major investor in Asia, Latin America, and Africa through its Belt and Road Initiative; the second largest contributor to the UN regular budget and peacekeeping expenses; and the world's largest emitter of carbon dioxide, China is a key actor in global governance.

Before 2022, Russia also sought to restore its position as a major player thirty years after the Soviet Union's dissolution and the collapse of Russia's economy in the 1990s, which diminished its power. What type of player it will be depends in part on the outcome of the war in Ukraine. India and Brazil are assertive emerging powers. Together with China, they blocked continuation of the World Trade Organization (WTO) Doha negotiations in 2008 on the issue of the right of developing countries to resist liberalization of trade in agricultural products. Brazil and India are active contenders for permanent seats on the UN Security Council. India has long refused to participate in treaties such as the Nuclear Non-Proliferation Treaty that it regards as discriminating against newer nuclear weapon states. Likewise, Brazil resisted US efforts to create the Free Trade Area of the Americas.

Middle-power states have traditionally played a particularly important role in international institutions, often acting in concert in the UN and other IGOs, taking initiatives on arms control, human rights, and other issues. Argentina, Australia, Canada, the Netherlands, Nigeria, Norway, and Sweden are known for their commitment to multilateralism, ability to forge compromises, and support for reform in the international system. The Nordic countries (Denmark, Finland, Iceland, Norway, and Sweden), together with the Netherlands have traditionally been major contributors to UN peacekeeping operations; they have met or exceeded development assistance targets; and they have provided about 10 percent of all UN leadership positions. Although they have exemplified Western values, "their effectiveness and reputation within the UN have rested on a perception . . . as being *different* from the rest of the West (or North)" (Laatikainen 2006: 77). The essence of the role of middle powers lies in the importance of secondary players both as followers and leaders in international politics. In a time when power and influence in the world are shifting, fostering cooperation in the future is likely to require leadership based not only on military capability and economic strength but also on diplomatic skill and policy initiatives—strengths that middle and emerging powers as well as small and developing states can contribute.

For the large number of less developed, small, and weak states, power and influence generally come only insofar as they are able to form coalitions that enlarge their voices and offer opportunities to set global agendas and link issues of importance to them. IGOs provide valuable arenas for this and for international recognition and legitimacy. By forming and working through various coalitions, small and developing countries have endeavored to shape the agendas, priorities, and programs of many IGOs with varying degrees of success. The Group of 77 (G-77) has been a major vehicle for developing countries to push their development and trade-related interests since the mid-1960s. Similarly, the thirty-nine-member Alliance of Small Island States (AOSIS) has been an important voice on the issue of global climate change. Small and less powerful states also often pick and choose the issues of greatest priority around which to focus their limited resources. Given the large number of IGOs, they may seek to take an issue of particular interest to the body most favorable to their interests—a phenomenon known as forum shopping. By analyzing the roles of small states in global governance, one can discover how skillful use of multilateral diplomacy, coalitions, and networks can alter the power equation, leading to outcomes that serve the interests of people, groups, and states that are not generally considered powerful.

Although states are still regarded as central to maintaining order in the world, since 1990 a number of countries have been sources of disorder due to their inability to perform most basic functions. Hence, problems emanating from weak, failing, and failed states have become global governance challenges. They include spillover in the form of refugees from civil wars, famine, and conflicts; terrorist groups such as al-Qaeda in the Maghreb that exploit the weakness of states surrounding the Sahara; weak states such as the Democratic Republic of Congo, South Sudan, and Mali that are unable to protect their citizens and rely on UN peacekeeping operations to provide some measure of security. State capability also includes the ability to comply with international rules; track infectious diseases; take effective measures to reduce carbon dioxide emissions; limit trafficking in sex, organs, drugs, and arms; and promote human well-being so that people do not feel compelled to migrate elsewhere in search of a better life.

States, however, may not act with one voice in global governance. Increasingly, provincial, state, and local governments, especially in democratic countries with federal forms of government, are involved in international economic negotiations and in implementing environmental regulations and human rights initiatives, acting independently and occasionally at odds with their national governments. Mayors of large cities now meet periodically at global conferences, becoming subnational actors in global governance. Similarly, transgovernmental networks of government officials—police investigators, financial regulators, judges, and legislators—provide a means of exchanging information, tracking money laundering and terrorist financing, coordinating cross-border law enforcement, expanding the reach of environmental and food safety regulations, and providing training programs and technical assistance to counterparts (Slaughter 2004: 2–4). Such networks are part of the multilevel character of global governance. As Frank Biermann and Philipp Pattberg (2012: 13) put it, "Global standards need to be implemented and put into practice locally, and global norm setting requires local decision-making and implementation . . . with the potential of conflicts and synergies between different levels of regulatory activity." Chapters 9 and 10 examine some examples.

Intergovernmental Organizations

IGOs are organizations that include at least three states as members, have activities in several states, and are created through a formal intergovernmental agreement such as a treaty, charter, or statute. They also have headquarters, executive heads, bureaucracies, and budgets. Over 260 IGOs ranging in size from 3 members (the US-Mexico-Canada Agreement) to more than 190 members (the Universal Postal Union) exist. Members may come primarily from one geographic region (as in the case of the Organization of American States) or from all geographic regions (as in the case of the World Bank). Although some IGOs are designed to achieve a single purpose (such as the Organization of Petroleum Exporting Countries), others have been developed for multiple tasks (such as the UN and African

Union). The majority of IGOs are regional or subregional, with a commonality of interest motivating states to cooperate on issues directly affecting them. Among the universe of IGOs, most are small in membership and designed to address specific functions. Most have been formed since World War II, and Europe, among the different regions, has the densest concentration of IGOs (see Figure 1.2).

IGOs are recognized subjects of international law, with separate standing from their member states. In a 1949 advisory opinion, *Reparations for Injuries Suffered in the Service of the United Nations*, the International Court of Justice (ICJ) concluded: "The Organization [the United Nations] was intended to exercise and enjoy, and is in fact exercising and enjoying, functions and rights which can only be explained on the basis of international personality and the capacity to operate upon an international plane. It is at present the supreme type of international organization, and it could not carry out the intentions of its founders if it was devoid of international personality."

International relations scholars have long viewed IGOs primarily as agents of their member states and focused on their structural attributes, decisionmaking processes, and programs. After all, IGOs are formed by states, and states grant IGOs responsibilities and authority to act. Yet increasingly, IGOs have also been seen as actors in their own right, because their secretariat members play key but often invisible roles in persuading member states to act, coordinating the efforts of different groups, providing the diplomatic skills to secure agreements, and ensuring the effectiveness of programs (Mathiason 2007). These include senior officials such as the UN

Figure 1.2   Classifying Types of IGOs

	Examples
Geographic Scope	
Global	United Nations, World Health Organization, World Trade Organization
Regional	Association of Southeast Asian Nations, African Union, European Union
Subregional	Economic Community of West African States, Gulf Cooperation Council
Purpose	
General	Organization of American States, United Nations
Specialized	International Labour Organization, World Health Organization, World Trade Organization

Secretary-General (UNSG) and their deputy, under- and assistant secretaries-general, and the UNSG's special representatives (SRSGs); the directors-general of organizations such as the WHO and WTO; the heads of UN funds and programs, such as the executive director of the World Food Programme (WFP) and the UN High Commissioners for Refugees and Human Rights (UNHCR and UNHCHR); the president of the World Bank; the executive director of the IMF; the secretary-general of the Organization of American States; and the president of the European Commission. These people "will generally possess an identity that is distinct from that of any other entity and an interest in promoting the well-being of the organization and its membership" (Duffield 2007: 13). Stories are legion about the roles secretariat officials have played in achieving international trade agreements, cease-fires in wars, governments' agreement to revise their development strategies to meet international guidelines, organizational reforms, and even the creation of new IGOs (Johnson 2014).

Like other bureaucracies, IGO secretariats often do much more than their member states may have intended. Because many (but not all) IGO bureaucrats are international civil servants rather than individuals seconded to a secretariat from national governments, they tend to take their responsibilities seriously and work hard "to promote what they see as 'good policy' or to protect it from states that have competing interests" (Barnett and Finnemore 2004: 5). IGO bureaucracies also tend to develop their own organizational cultures—sometimes based on the professional backgrounds of many staff members (e.g., public health, finance)—and this can influence how they define issues and what types of policy solutions they recommend. They must respond to new challenges and crises, provide policy options for member states, determine how to carry out vague mandates, reform themselves, and formulate new tasks and procedures. For example, the UN Secretariat created peacekeeping at the height of the Cold War and later devised postconflict peacebuilding operations that include a wide variety of tasks from electoral assistance to police and court reform. IGOs have resources, including money, food, weapons, and expertise. Many IGO bureaucracies play important roles in analyzing and interpreting information, giving it meaning that can prompt action. To some extent, IGOs "help determine the kind of world that is to be governed and set the agenda for global governance" (Barnett and Finnemore 2004: 7).

Thus, IGO bureaucracies are not just tools of states. They are also purposive actors that have power to influence world events. Their authority, and that of bureaucracies generally, "lies in their ability to present themselves as impersonal and neutral—as not exercising power but instead serving others" (Barnett and Finnemore 2004: 21). The need to be seen in this way is crucial for the credibility of the UN Secretariat or the EU Commission, for example. But there is also significant evidence of IGOs doing something that "wasn't specifically tasked to them . . . [and] outside any reasonable notion of delegated discretion" (Oestreich 2012: 11). This theory of IGO agency and its implications is discussed further in Chapter 2.

To be sure, not all IGOs are alike, as we shall examine in later chapters. Their authority and autonomy as actors in global governance vary significantly in kind and degree. Like domestic bureaucracies, international bureaucracies may use inaction as a way to avoid doing something they oppose. IGOs may also act against the interests and preferences of strong or weak states (and their secretaries-general may suffer retaliation as a result); they may form partnerships with nonstate actors, other IGOs, and select states to pursue or protect certain policies; and they may attempt to persuade states to change their behavior—for example, by reducing corruption, eliminating food subsidies, or turning over war criminals for prosecution by the International Criminal Court.

Not only do IGOs have secretariats, but so also do a large number of international treaties, particularly in global environmental governance where there is no strong, central IGO. The size of these secretariats varies; that of the UN Framework Convention on Climate Change is quite large; others have just a few staff members. Their roles as autonomous actors include generating and disseminating knowledge, framing the definitions of problems and identifying solutions, influencing negotiations through their ideas and expertise, and helping states with treaty implementation (Biermann and Siebenhüner 2013: 149–152). The autonomous influence of the international secretariats of IGOs and treaty regimes varies widely, as it does with all bureaucracies. A major study of environmental bureaucracies has found that the type of problem is a key factor; people and procedures are two other important factors (Campe 2009: 149–152).

International courts are distinctive forms of international organization but are not necessarily seen as IGOs. They have proliferated in recent years, with the creation of nineteen since 1990, creating what one scholar refers to as the "judicialization" of international relations and global governance (Alter 2013). Their roles include dispute settlement, constitutional review, administrative review, enforcement, and providing advisory opinions to the UN in the case of the International Court of Justice (ICJ). Two courts—the Permanent Court of Arbitration and the International Centre for the Settlement of Investment Disputes in the World Bank system—are specifically arbitral bodies, that is, cases are decided by arbitration panels. As with IGOs, there are debates over whether international courts are agents of states or "trustees of the law" with legal and political authority as well as autonomy. Many newer courts provide access for nonstate actors, including NGOs.

Nongovernmental Organizations and Civil Society
Like IGOs, NGOs are key actors in global governance, playing a number of roles. The growth of NGOs and NGO networks since the 1980s has been a

major factor in their increasing involvement in governance at all levels, from global to local. Increasingly, global governance is marked by various types of interactions between IGOs and NGOs.

NGOs are private voluntary organizations whose members are individuals or associations that come together to achieve a common purpose. Some are formed to advocate a particular cause, such as human rights, peace, or environmental protection. Others are established to provide services such as disaster relief, humanitarian aid in war-torn societies, or development assistance. Some are in reality government-organized groups (dubbed GONGOs). Scholars and analysts distinguish between not-for-profit groups (the vast majority) and for-profit corporations; it is also common to treat terrorist, criminal, and drug trafficking groups—the bad side of nonstate actors—separately, as discussed in Chapter 6.

NGOs along with civil society groups are increasingly active today at all levels of human society and governance, from local or grassroots communities to national and international politics. Many national-level groups, often called interest or pressure groups, are now linked to counterpart groups in other countries through networks or federations. International nongovernmental organizations (INGOs), like IGOs, may draw their members from more than one country, and they may have very specific functions or be multifunctional. The big INGOs, along with transnational advocacy networks (TANs) such as the Coalition to Ban Landmines, that bring together many smaller groups are among the most visible NGO actors in global governance. Their roles have been particularly important in expanding human rights and humanitarian and environmental law.

The estimates of numbers of NGOs vary enormously, although the majority—millions—are national-based organizations. In 2020, the UN recognized over 22,000 international NGOs with an international dimension in terms of membership or commitment to conduct activities in several states. Of those, more than 4,000 enjoy a consultative status within the UN. Many large INGOs are transnational federations involving formal, long-term links among national groups. Examples include the International Federation of Red Cross and Red Crescent Societies, Oxfam, Médecins Sans Frontières (Doctors Without Borders), the World Wildlife Fund, Transparency International (the leading NGO fighting corruption worldwide), Human Rights Watch, and Amnesty International. The Union of International Associations (UIA) based in Brussels maintains the most comprehensive directory of all IOs, both NGOs and IGOs.

Most of the thousands of grassroots groups in countries around the world are not part of formal networks but may have informal links to large international human rights and development NGOs like Human Rights Watch and CARE, from which they obtain funding for local programs or training assistance. The links between grassroots groups and INGOs are key to activities such as promoting population control, women's empowerment, healthcare, respect for human rights, and environmental protection. Because these relationships often involve large, Northern-dominated NGOs and Southern grass-roots groups, there is a concern about the dependence they foster. Since the early 1990s, the internet, e-mail, fax, and various forms of social media have been valuable tools for NGO mobilization and autonomy, enabling them to access areas that governments and IGOs may be slow to reach.

NGOs are key sources of information and technical expertise on a wide variety of international issues, from the environment to human rights and corruption. They are frequently key actors in raising awareness of and helping frame issues. Thus, landmines came to be seen as a humanitarian rather than an arms control issue, for example (Thakur and Maley 1999). They lobby for policy changes by states, IGOs, and corporations; along with civil society groups, they mount mass demonstrations around major international meetings such as the 2021 UN conference on climate change in Glasgow. They contribute to international adjudication by submitting friend-of-the-court briefs to international criminal tribunals, such as those for the former Yugoslavia and Rwanda, and to trade and investment tribunals. Many NGOs have participated at least indirectly in UN-sponsored global conferences and international negotiations, raising issues and submitting documents. In some cases, they have contributed treaty language, such as with the UN Convention to Combat Desertification (1996) and the Rome Statute of the International Criminal Court (2002). They also play important roles in monitoring states' and corporations' implementation of human rights norms and environmental regulations.

We explore the diversity and global governance activities of NGOs and other nonstate actors in Chapter 6, as well as in the issue chapters.

Experts and Epistemic Communities

In a world whose problems seem to grow steadily more complex, knowledge and expertise are critical to governance efforts. There is a need to understand the science behind environmental problems such as climate change, ozone depletion, and declining fish stocks as a basis for considering policy options. Cost-effective alternatives must be developed for fuels that emit carbon dioxide if there is to be political support for making policy changes and new rules. Thus, experts from governmental agencies, research institutes, private industries, and universities around the world have increasingly been drawn into international efforts to deal with various issues. For example, in the UN's early years, statisticians and economists developed the System of National Accounts, which provides the basis for standardizing how countries calculate GDP and other core statistics that serve as a means of measuring economic performance (Jolly, Emmerij, and Weiss 2009: 42). The technical committees of the International Organization for Standardization (ISO), for example, are entirely composed of experts. Often experts may be part of transnational networks and participate in international conferences and negotiations, laying out the state of scientific knowledge, framing issues for debate, and proposing possible solutions. Since 1988, hundreds of scientists from around the world have participated on the Intergovernmental Panel on Climate Change, whose policy-neutral reports have provided key inputs for global climate change negotiations and sought to raise awareness of the rapid climate-related changes taking place and their likely future effects. Chapter 10 elaborates more on other examples of expert groups and networks in environmental politics—knowledge-based actors that scholars often refer to as "epistemic communities."

Networks and Partnerships

Networks have become ubiquitous since the 1970s, when Robert Keohane and Joseph Nye (1971) first pointed out the importance of regular interactions of governmental and nongovernmental actors across national boundaries. Subsequently, other scholars have explored the existence of various types of networks, and their power, roles, and policy inputs. For example, Anne-Marie Slaughter (2004) examined the importance of transgovernmental networks of police, judges, regulators, finance ministers, and legislators as central actors in many forms of global governance. Some scholars have focused primarily on networks and information sharing; others were focused on enforcement, such as with environmental regulations; and still others have looked at how networks have solved problems related to harmonization of regulations. Margaret Keck and Kathryn Sikkink (1998), among others, have looked at TANs.

Analytically, networks can be examined as both actors and structures. As actors, they may be defined as an organizational form consciously created by any set of actors that pursue "repeated, enduring exchange relations with one another . . . [yet] lack a legitimate organization authority to arbitrate and resolve disputes that may arise during the exchange" (quoted in Kahler 2009: 5). Networks are distinguished by their voluntary nature, the central role of information and learning, their ability to generate trust among participants, and their lack of hierarchy (Sikkink 2009: 230). Networks' success depends on their ability to promote and sustain collective action, add new members, and adapt. Their effectiveness will also vary by issue area, their "centrality" to an issue, and the politics of a given issue, as Charli Carpenter's work (2014) on "lost causes" has shown. As noted previously, TANs are a particular form of network active in global governance, for example, in setting and monitoring human rights standards. Illicit networks such as transnational criminal organizations are targets of governance efforts to control money laundering and other illegal activities; whereas transgovernmental networks allow government officials to share regulatory approaches, provide technical assistance, and harmonize approaches to problems.

Partnerships—particularly what are called public–private partnerships (PPPs) such as those between various UN agencies and private foundations or corporations—have also become increasingly common as actors and particularly as forms of global governance that Liliana Andonova (2017: 6) describes as "a specific new organizational form" transforming multilateralism in the twenty-first century. They bring together expertise and resources, combining the public mandates of IGOs with the market or norm-based steering mechanisms in what she sees as qualitatively different arrangements between states and NSAs. PPPs resemble networks in that they are voluntary arrangements and offer greater flexibility than legalized arrangements, can change rapidly, and are also not without problems. Some, such as the UN Global Compact and the Global Fund to Fight AIDS, Tuberculosis and Malaria have their own secretariats. Catia Gregoratti (2014: 311) notes how partnerships between the UN and businesses have "refashioned not only ideas of how development should be achieved and who should deliver it but also the institutional architecture of the UN itself." Partnerships involving UN agencies and private corporations and foundations and have become widespread in areas of development, health, women, and children. Their functions range from advocacy, policy development, developing standards of conduct, and business development to providing information, funding, goods, and services. With the UN's 2015 adoption of the Sustainable Development Goals, a variety of multistakeholder partnerships have been formed to carry out the ambitious agenda (Beisheim and Simon 2018). See Chapters 8 and 11 for further discussion of partnerships.

Multinational Corporations

Multinational corporations or MNCs are a particular form of NSA organized to conduct for-profit business transactions and operations across the borders of three or more states. They are companies based in one state with affiliated branches or subsidiaries and activities in other states and can take many different forms, from Levi's subcontracting jean production to Nepalese factories to Royal Dutch Shell's operations in Nigeria and Goldman Sachs's global operations. By choosing where to invest (or not to invest), MNCs shape the economic development opportunities of communities, countries, and entire regions such as Africa, where for a long time foreign investment lagged behind that of other regions.

Since the 1970s, MNCs have "profoundly altered the structure and functioning of the global economy" (Gilpin 2001: 290). They control resources far greater than those of many states and have taken an active and often direct role in influencing international environmental decisionmaking (Biermann and Pattberg 2012: 8). Globalization of markets and production in industries such as banking and automobiles has challenged corporate leaders and managers to govern these complex structures and posed problems for states and local governments losing their connection to and control of these larger corporate networks. Corporate choices about investment have also changed the landscape of development assistance. Far more funding for development today comes from private investment capital than from bilateral, government-to-government aid, or from multilateral aid through the UN and other IGOs.

In short, MNCs are important global governance actors. Today they number more than 60,000 depending on one's definition. They are involved in 50 percent of the world's trade and represent about 40 percent of the value in Western stock markets. About 10 percent of the largest MNCs generate 80 percent of the world's total profits. In 2020, the Fortune Global 500 list showed that for the first time China had the largest number with 124 MNCs, while the United States was home to 121 (Kennedy 2020). Given the economic power of MNCs, it is not surprising that their activities have long raised questions. How can they best be regulated—through new forms of international rules or codes of conduct, or through private, industry-developed mechanisms? How can they be mobilized for economic development in collaboration with international agencies and NGOs? How can less developed countries be assured that powerful MNCs will not interfere in their domestic affairs, challenge their sovereignty, destroy their resources and environment, and relegate them to permanent dependency? MNCs are particularly important actors in addressing trade, labor, and environmental issues such as ozone depletion and climate change. It was in recognition of the need to regulate corporate behavior and engage MNCs as positive contributors to global governance that UN Secretary-General Kofi Annan initiated the UN Global Compact on Corporate Responsibility in 1999, which now encompasses more than 21,000 companies in more than 160 countries, an innovation that is discussed further in Chapter 8.

*   *   *

The various actors in global governance cannot be analyzed in isolation from one another. They play varying roles, with different degrees of power, authority, and effectiveness. Sometimes, they compete for scarce resources, international standing, and legitimacy. At other times, their activities complement one another. Increasingly, they are linked in complex networks and partnerships. Subsequent chapters explore these roles and relationships further.

Processes of Global Governance: Multilateralism Matters

Understanding the nature of multilateral diplomacy is essential to understanding how IGOs and informal groupings of states function, how nonstate actors have become involved in governance processes, and how different kinds of outcomes come about. Yet the practice of multilateral diplomacy has deep historical roots, as examined in Chapter 3. What matters here is that the Latin American states with support from the United States played key roles in expanding the scope of who could participate, gaining recognition of the equal status and votes of states large and small, and creating a norm of universal participation based on sovereign equality. They were also instrumental in introducing practices of voting, majority rule, regular meetings, and a secretariat to support them, which were all drawn from their experience with a series of inter-American conferences in the late nineteenth century (Finnemore and Jurkovich 2014).

Multilateralism generally refers to a group of states coordinating their relations according to certain principles, with the expectation that each will benefit in the long run (Ruggie 1993). For example, the principle of nondiscrimination governing the global trade system's most favored nation principle prohibits countries from discriminating against imports from other countries that produce the same product. In collective security arrangements, participants must respond to an attack on one country as if it were an attack on all. The process is one which in the words of Vincent Pouliot (2011: 19) involves an "inclusive, institutionalized and principled form of political dialogue" with inherent benefits. It is critical to global governance because it is how "things get done. Thus, it is not just the number and type of parties that matters. It is also the rules of conduct, openness of debate, and greater legitimacy that come from having more participants, including small states, marginalized groups, and all types of actors that can "help mitigate the discriminatory exercise of arbitrary power" (Pouliot 2011: 20). From his perspective, multilateralism is "a functional imperative" because of the transnational nature of contemporary problems and hence needs to include a "host" of actors.

The question whether the practice of multilateralism is linked with US hegemony after World War II is contentious. John Ruggie (1982), for one, has suggested that it is, while Amitav Acharya (2014: 54) suggests that weaker states have used multilateral approaches that are suited to their specific goals and identities and, in the process, either excluded stronger powers or socialized them into locally developed norms. It is noteworthy that China under President Xi Jinping has become a major proponent of multilateralism.

What makes multilateralism in the twenty-first century different from multilateralism in the nineteenth century and at the end of World War II is its complexity, numbers of participants, and diversity of voices. There are now literally scores of participants. States alone have almost quadrupled in number since 1945. The first sessions of the UN General Assembly now look like cozy, intimate gatherings. Other types of actors add to the complexity, as do various coalitions of states. As one observer notes: "Large numbers . . . introduce a qualitatively different kind of diplomacy in international politics. The hallmark of this diplomacy is that it occurs between groups or coalitions of state actors" (Hampson 1995: 4). In addition, a central issue for many IGOs today is how to do a better job of incorporating NGOs, civil society groups, and other NSAs into processes of global governing, since "securing agreement of government officials is not enough to permit the smooth running of these institutions" (O'Brien et al. 2000: 208). Diplomats—the representatives of states—need to engage in "network diplomacy" with this variety of players, not just with fellow diplomats, with diplomacy becoming an exercise in "complexity management" (Heine 2013: 62).

Greater numbers of players (and coalitions of players) mean multiple interests, with multiple rules, issues, and hierarchies that are constantly in flux. These all complicate the processes of multilateral diplomacy and negotiation—of finding common ground for reaching agreements on collective action, norms, or rules. Managing complexity has become a key challenge for diplomats and other participants in multilateral settings. For example, UN-sponsored conferences such as the 2021 Glasgow conference (discussed further in Chapter 10) have several thousand delegates from 193 member countries, speaking through interpreters in English, French, Russian, Chinese, Spanish, and Arabic. Hundreds of NGOs and numerous private citizens are interested in what happens and are active around the official sessions, trying to influence delegates.

Although the universe of multilateral diplomacy is complex, there is actually a high degree of similarity in the structures of most IGOs and in the types of decisionmaking processes used. We look here at key patterns in how decisions get made in multilateral bodies including IGOs.

How Do Decisions Get Made?

Historically, because IGOs are created by states, the principle of sovereign equality has dictated one-state, one-vote decisionmaking. Indeed, until well into the twentieth century, all decisions had to be unanimous, as states would not accept the concept of majority decisionmaking. This is often cited as one of the sources of failure for the League of Nations.

An alternative principle accords greater weight to some states on the basis of population or wealth and results in weighted or qualified voting. In the IMF and World Bank, for example, votes are weighted according to financial contribution. In the EU's Council of Ministers, qualified majority voting applies to issues where the EU has supranational authority over member states. The number of votes for each state is based on population; the number of votes required to pass legislation ensures that the largest states must have support of some smaller states; and neither the smaller states alone nor fewer than three large states can block action. Another form of qualified majority voting prevails in the UN Security Council, where the five permanent members each have a veto and all must concur (or not object) for decisions to be made.

Since the 1980s, much of the decisionmaking in the UN General Assembly, Security Council, and other bodies, as well as in global conferences, the WTO, and many other multilateral settings has taken the form of consensus that does not require unanimity. It depends on states deciding not to block action, and it often means that outcomes represent the least common denominator—that is, more general wording and fewer tough demands on states to act. "Pressure toward consensus," Courtney Smith (1999: 173) notes, "now dominates almost all multilateral efforts at global problem solving." Key variables in achieving consensus among multiple actors with diverse interests are leadership; small, formal negotiating groups; issue characteristics (including issue salience to different actors); various actor attributes such as economic or military power or ability to serve as brokers; the amount and quality of informal contacts among actors; and personal attributes of participants such as intelligence, tolerance, patience, reputation, negotiating skills, creativity, and linguistic versatility. Let us look briefly at two of these: leadership and actor strategies.

Leadership

Leadership in multilateral diplomacy can come from diverse sources: powerful and not-so-powerful states, a coalition of states, an NGO or coalition of NGOs, a skillful individual diplomat, or an IGO bureaucrat. Leadership can involve framing an issue in a way that garners strong support for action or coming up with a compromise that secures agreement on a new international trade agreement; it may involve the skill of negotiating a treaty text acceptable to industry, NGOs, and key governments. It may be the efforts of a coalition of NGOs and college students publicizing an issue such as sweatshops and pressuring companies to change their behavior. It may involve a government's (or any other actor's) willingness to act first—to commit monetary resources to a program or military forces for enforcement, change trade laws, or commit to significant carbon dioxide emissions reductions, as Presidents Barack Obama and Xi Jinping did ahead of the 2015 UN climate change conference in Paris. Leadership in multilateral diplomacy can also come from a prominent official such as the UNSG or the UN Environment Programme's executive director who prods various actors to do something.

Increasingly, we see women among the leaders in global governance in senior official positions in governments and IGOs and as permanent representatives of their countries in the UN and other IGOs, but it has taken a major push for gender equality in IGOs and countries for this to occur. Although the numbers of women in official leadership positions have certainly increased, they remain relatively small but are complemented by women exercising leadership through NGOs and social movements on various issues (Haack and Karns 2023).

Historically, the United States provided much of the leadership for multilateralism after World War II, using its position as the dominant, hegemonic power to shape the structure of the system, including establishing many IGOs, such as the UN, the Bretton Woods institutions, the International Atomic Energy Agency (IAEA), and the liberal international trade regime centered first in the General Agreement on Tariffs and Trade and later in the WTO. This enabled the United States to use IGOs as instruments of its national policies and to create institutions and rules compatible with its interests and values. The wisdom of this approach as then–US Senator Barack Obama put it in 2007 was to recognize that "instead of constraining our power, these institutions magnified it" (Obama 2007).

As geopolitical shifts are taking place, the United States has found itself stretched thin and less willing and able to lead at the same time. As a result, Bruce Jentleson (2012: 141) notes, "there is much less deference to US preferences and privileges." Now, even more than in the past, leadership in global governance may come from disparate sources, including NSAs, or be absent altogether. Increasingly, China has sought to place its officials in senior IGO positions, as noted earlier. It has also worked to reframe established liberal norms on security and development particularly with regard to peacekeeping and peacebuilding, shifting as one scholar describes from being a "norms taker" to a "norms maker" (Alden and Large 2015). One measure of Russia's loss of influence and potential for leadership following its 2022 invasion of Ukraine was the failure of its candidate for the governing board of the International Civil Aviation Organization to gain enough votes for reelection. Likewise, there are increasing challenges to the "lock" other major powers have long had on certain posts such as the United States has, for example, on the World Bank presidency. In an encouraging sign of greater diversity, in 2023, African women held a number of senior posts, including the executive directorships of the WTO, the UN Fund for Population Activities, and the UN Global Compact, and Deputy Secretary-General of the UN.

Actor Strategies

The nature of multilateral arenas means that actors cannot just present their individual positions on an issue and then sit down. Delegates must actively engage in efforts to discern the flexibility or rigidity of others' positions on particular issues. They must build personal relationships to establish the trust that is essential to working together. Some states, NGOs, and other actors will take a stronger interest in particular topics than others; some will come with specific proposals, push to get them on the agenda and then work to mobilize support; some will be represented by individuals with greater expertise than others on a topic or more skill in drafting compromise language; some will be represented by people with little or no experience in multilateral diplomacy while others have long experience and great skill in negotiating across cultures, which is an inherent part of multilateral diplomacy. Some actors' positions will matter more than those of others, because of their relative power in the international system, in a specific region, or on a particular issue. The face-to-face interactions of the individuals representing participating states (and groups) are what caucusing is all about, even in an age of online communication. It may take place at the back of the UN General Assembly, in the delegates' dining room, at diplomatic receptions, in the restrooms, or in the corridors surrounding the official meeting place. In short, those actors that pursue well-thought-out strategies for taking advantage of multilateral arenas and diplomacy are more likely to be successful in securing their aims.

One actor strategy that is a hallmark of multilateral diplomacy is the formation of groups or coalitions of states. States can pool their votes, power, and resources to try to obtain a better outcome than they might by going it alone. Early in the UN's history, for example, regional groups formed to elect nonpermanent members of the Security Council and other bodies. The Cold War produced competing groups under the leadership of the Soviet Union and United States, plus the Non-Aligned Movement. Latin American, African, and Asian states formed the G-77 in 1964 to promote their shared interests as developing countries. In short, group diplomacy is pervasive throughout much of the UN system and in regional organizations and the WTO. Coalitions and groups are discussed further in Chapter 4.

Group members must negotiate among themselves to agree on a common position, maintain cohesion, prevent defections to rival coalitions, and choose representatives to bargain on their behalf. Small states or middle powers often play key roles in bridging the positions of different groups of states. For example, during the Uruguay Round of international trade negotiations in the early 1990s, a group of countries called the Cairns Group, led by Canada, Australia, and Argentina, helped resolve sharp disagreements between the United States and the EU over agricultural trade. A variation on coalition building, especially for nonstate actors, as discussed earlier, is the creation of networks to expand their reach and link various groups with shared concerns and awareness that common goals cannot be achieved on their own. Networking has been used extensively by TANs for a variety of issues and problems, from promoting the rights of women and stopping the construction of large dams to addressing the governance challenges of HIV/AIDS.

The proliferation of international forums means that states and nonstate actors can often "shop" for the forum best suited to take an issue. Although some issues logically belong only within the relevant specialized IGO, the increasing interrelatedness of many issues makes the neat compartmental-ization of these IGOs often outdated. For example, a labor issue could be raised in the International Labour Organization, the WTO, or the EU. Health issues could be raised in the WHO, the World Bank, the UN Joint Programme on HIV/AIDS, the Bill and Melinda Gates Foundation, or the Global Fund to Fight AIDS, Tuberculosis, and Malaria. Despite consensus that African states should resolve regional conflicts in an African organiza-tion, such as the AU or the Economic Community of West African States, some African states have preferred to take disputes to the UN, where they hope to gain more support for their cause.

In reality, actor strategies in global governance bear strong resem-blance to common governance and policymaking actions. These include framing an issue, agenda-setting, advocacy, and mobilizing support through coalition-building. There are rich global governance-related literatures on each of these topics that illumine the variety of actors in global governance and the roles they play in various institutions and processes through which some issues get attention and action and some do not, some policy options get on the table and some do not. They show how different governance problems are defined and potential solutions are identified and how support for and against issues and potential solutions are mobilized. For example, some of this work has been inspired by Keck and Sikkink's (1998) book on transnational advocacy networks followed more recently by Carpenter's (2014; Carpenter et al. 2014) work on advocacy, agenda-setting, gatekeep-ers, issue adoption, and lost causes. Examining these actor strategies in global governance means thinking about it in terms of policy processes, not institutional structures or elements of governance, such as law, rules, norms, and programs, important as these are. We discuss these processes further in Chapter 6.

The Varieties of Global Governance

Global governance encompasses a variety of cooperative problem-solving arrangements and activities that states and other actors undertake in an effort to resolve conflicts, serve common purposes, and overcome ineffi-ciencies in situations of interdependent choice. These forms include a wide variety of international organizations (IOs), both IGOs and NGOs; less for-mal groupings of states such as various "Gs", clubs, and friends groups; international rules, regulations, standards, and laws, as well as norms or "soft law"; international regimes in which the rules, norms, and structures in a specific issue area are linked together; ad hoc arrangements and con-ferences; private governance arrangements; and public–private partnerships such as the UN Global Compact and Partnerships for Sustainable Develop-ment (see Figure 1.3). The varieties have proliferated, complicating efforts to create neat categories. Where scholars in the past identified international regimes governing issues such as nuclear nonproliferation, now there are a number of "regime complexes," that is, "networks of three or more international regimes that relate to a common subject matter" such as food security (Orsini, Morin, and Young 2013: 29). Let us look briefly at these varieties of global governance.

Key Structures and Mechanisms: IGOs

IGOs provide the central core of formal multilateral machinery that constitutes the "architecture of global governance" (Cooper and Thakur 2014: 265). Since the late nineteenth century , more and more IGOs have been created to perform more and more tasks. They serve many functions, including collecting information and monitoring trends (as in the case of the UNEP), delivering services and aid (UNHCR), and providing forums for intergovernmental bargaining (the EU) and adjudicating disputes (the ICJ and other courts). They have helped states form stable habits of cooperation through regular meetings, information-gathering and analysis, and dispute settlement, as well as operational activities (see Figure 1.4). They enhance individual and collective welfare. They have provided modes of governance in the evolution of the world economy since 1850 (Murphy 1994). They also "construct the social world in which cooperation and choice take place" and "help define the interests that states and other actors come to hold" (Barnett and Finnemore 2005: 162). A further function of IGOs and particularly of the UN has been the development of key ideas and concepts about security (e.g., the concept of human security) and economic and social development (human and sustainable development). As the authors of the final volume of the United Nations Intellectual History Project conclude, ideas are among the most significant contributions the UN has made to the world and to human progress. The UN has generated ideas, provided a forum for debate, given ideas legitimacy, promoted their adoption for policy, generated resources for implementing and monitoring progress, and sometimes even buried ideas (Jolly, Emmerij, and Weiss 2009: 34–35).

Figure 1.3
Varieties of Global Governance

- International structures and mechanisms (formal and informal) IGOs: global, regional, other; NGOs; networks, and partnerships
- International rules and laws, multilateral agreements; customary practices; judicial decisions, regulatory standards
- International norms or "soft law;" framework agreements; select UN resolutions
- International regimes and regime complexes
- Ad hoc groups, arrangements, and global conferences
- Private and hybrid public–private governance

How IGOs serve their various functions varies across organizations. IOs differ in membership. They vary by the scope of the subject and rules. They differ in the amount of resources available and by level and degree of bureaucratization as well as in their effectiveness.

Why do states join such organizations? Why do they choose to act and cooperate through formal IGOs? Kenneth Abbott and Duncan Snidal (1998: 4–5) suggest that IGOs "allow for the centralization of collective activities through a concrete and stable organizational structure and a supportive administrative apparatus. These increase the efficiency of collective activities and enhance the organization's ability to affect the understand-

Figure 1.4
IGO Functions

- Informational: gathering, analyzing, and disseminating data
- Forum: providing place for exchange of views and decisionmaking
- Normative: defining standards of behavior
- Rule creation: drafting legally binding treaties
- Rule supervision: monitoring compliance with rules, adjudicating disputes, taking enforcement measures
- Operational: allocating resources, providing technical assistance and relief, deploying forces
- Idea generation

ings, environment, and interests of states." Thus, states join to participate in a stable negotiating forum, permitting rapid reactions in times of crisis. They join IGOs to negotiate and implement agreements that reflect their own interests and those of the larger community. They participate to provide mechanisms for dispute resolution. They join to take advantage of centralized organization in implementing collective tasks. By participating, they seek a voice in international debates on important issues as well as a say on critical norms of behavior. They also frequently agree to delegate program implementation to international bureaucrats. Yet states maintain their sovereignty and varying degrees of independence of action.

IGOs not only create opportunities for their member states, they also exercise influence and impose constraints on their member states' policies and processes. IGOs affect member states by setting international and national agendas, forcing governments to take positions on issues. They subject states' behavior to surveillance through information-sharing and monitoring such as the Universal Periodic Review process created by the UN Human Rights Council in 2006 (discussed in Chapter 9). IGOs encourage states to develop specialized decisionmaking and implementation processes to facilitate and coordinate IGO participation. They embody or facilitate the creation of principles, norms, and rules of behavior with which states must align their policies if they wish to benefit from reciprocity. For example, as described in Chapter 8, China's admission to the WTO required extensive governmental reforms.

Most countries perceive that there are benefits to participating in IGOs even when it is costly. South Africa never withdrew from the UN over the long years when it was repeatedly condemned for its policies of apartheid. Iraq did not withdraw from the UN when it was subjected to more than a decade of stringent sanctions. China spent fourteen years negotiating the terms of its entry into the international trade system and undertaking changes in laws and policies required to comply with WTO rules. Twelve countries joined the EU between 2004 and 2007, despite the extensive and costly changes required. The United States is one of the very few countries that have withdrawn from IGOs to demonstrate their unhappiness with an organization's actions.

Although the earliest IGOs were established in the nineteenth century, there was a veritable explosion of IGOs in the twentieth century, as discussed in Chapter 3. Since the 1960s, there has also been a growing phenomenon of IGOs creating other IGOs. One study found that IGO birthrates "correlate positively with the number of states in the international system," but found death rates of IGOs low (Cupitt, Whitlock, and Whitlock 1997: 16). A more recent study found that around 38 percent of IGOs have now become so-called zombies—they continue to act but have made no progress on achieving their mandates. Another 10 percent are essentially dead, existing in name but having no visible level of activity (Gray 2018).

NGOs

The governance functions of NGOs parallel many functions provided by IGOs. In general, however, NGOs can be divided into service and advocacy groups. The latter provide processes at many levels to pressure or persuade individuals, governments, IGOs, corporations, and other actors to improve human rights, protect the environment, tackle corruption, ban landmines, or intervene in conflicts such as Syria's civil war. The Geneva Conventions delegate legal responsibility for humanitarian law to the International Committee of the Red Cross. Some IGOs, such as the ILO, the World Tourism Organization, and the UN Joint Programme on HIV/AIDS, provide for NGO roles in their governance. The Final Outcome of the 1992 UN Conference on the Environment and Development in Rio de Janeiro recommended that NGOs participate at all levels in implementation. As a result of global trends to privatize activities previously controlled by governments, services once provided by governments or IGOs are now often contracted out to NGOs, which have also become critical partners for UN and other IGO programs, funds, and agencies in delivering disaster relief, running refugee camps, administering development programs, delivering food aid to areas of famine, and working to protect the environment. They are important forms of global governance because of how they enable individuals to "act publicly" (Kaldor 2003: 585). Likewise, their "voluntary, local, and issue-specific character . . . [and the networks they create] make them a useful link between the subnational community and national and international communities and institutions" (Ku and Diehl 2006: 171). In this sense, they function as transmission belts among multiple levels of governance.

Rule-Based Governance:
International Rules, Standards, and Law

The scope of what is generally known as public international law has expanded tremendously since the 1960s. Although the Statute of the ICJ recognizes five sources of international law (treaties or conventions, customary practice, the writings of legal scholars, judicial decisions, and general principles of law), much of the growth has been in treaty law. At the conclusion of the twentieth century, for example, there were a total of 82,000 publicized international agreements, including the Vienna Convention on Treaties; conventions on ozone, climate change, and whaling; law of the sea; humanitarian law (the Geneva Conventions); human rights law; trade law; and intellectual property law, as well as arms control agreements (Johnston 1997). By far the largest number of new multilateral agreements deals with economic issues. Treaty-based law is particularly valued, but customary practice persists as an important source of new law, particularly because of the long time it takes to negotiate and ratify agreements involving many states.

For purposes of global governance, one major limitation of public international law is that it applies only to states, except for war crimes and crimes against humanity. At present, only EU treaties can be used directly to bind individuals, MNCs, NGOs, paramilitary forces, terrorists, or international criminals. Treaties can, however, establish norms (sometimes referred to as soft law) that states are expected to observe and, where possible, enforce against NSAs.

Another problem in the eyes of many is the limited international enforcement mechanisms and the role of self-interest in shaping states' decisions about whether to accept treaties and other forms of international rules. International law traditionally left it to states to use "self-help" to secure compliance. Both the UN Charter and EU treaties provide enforcement mechanisms, primarily in the form of sanctions, although the threat of sanctions is not necessarily a strong motivator for states to comply with international rules.

Even without enforcement mechanisms, as Louis Henkin (1979: 47) concluded, "Almost all nations observe almost all principles of international law and almost all of their obligations almost all of the time." What explains this mostly compliant behavior? Legal experts cite different factors: coincidence with national interest and basic efficiency (Chayes and Chayes 1995), the value of preserving one's reputation for law-abiding behavior (Brewster 2013), and the value of the benefits of reciprocity. Peer pressure and persuasion from other states and domestic or transnational pressures from NGOs may also induce compliance (Ratner 2013).

Yet not all states comply with all international law. Noncompliance can be explained by the ambiguity of treaty language, for example (Chayes and Chayes 1995). For weaker and developing countries, failure to comply can be a consequence of inadequate local expertise, resources, or governmental capacity to do what is required for compliance. In many states, domestic politics may play a major role in determining their willingness or ability to comply with international law. That has certainly been a major factor for the United States in the failure of the Senate to ratify a number of treaties. Yet as Jana von Stein (2013) has noted, noncompliance is a spectrum not a dichotomy. And, as Beth Simmons (2009) has shown, compliance with international human rights treaties largely depends on the citizens of states since they have the most incentive to hold their governments to human rights commitments through domestic mechanisms. She also emphasizes that actual improvements in human rights are more important than technical, legal compliance with treaties.

Global and regional organizations incorporate different levels of legal commitments. The EU has its own legal system that lies between traditional national legal systems and international law, with the Court of Justice of the EU to interpret it and enforce judgments against member states. EU law is discussed more in Chapter 5, as the EU has a high level of legal obligation or legalization, relatively high levels of precision (rules tend to be clearly defined), and high levels of delegation (authority granted to third parties for implementation). Because of this, the EU has played a key role in setting legal standards across a variety of issue areas that are followed not only in the EU but around the world (Bradford 2020). Other IGOs and regional integration arrangements lie between the extremes of legalization, where actors combine and invoke varying degrees of obligation, precision, and delegation to create varying blends of politics and law (Abbott et al. 2000).

Beyond public international law and EU law is a wide range of international standard-setting and rulemaking, both public and private, that forms an important part of global governance. States, corporations, and standards-setting bodies such as the International Organization for Standardization, which is itself a network of standards-setting bodies and discussed further in Chapter 3, all contribute. In other examples, the WHO manages the International Health Regulations and the Food and Agriculture Organization oversees the Codex Alimentarius, both of which are sources of rules and standards. Even the UN Security Council contributes through its rulemaking on antiterrorism and nuclear nonproliferation.

The largest number of these rules and standards are outputs of private sector bodies that create international product standards on everything from the strength of steel and the specifications that enable nuts and bolts to connect to the dimensions of cargo containers. Clearly, the major impetus for setting and complying with these standards are economics and market access for private companies (Büthe and Mattli 2011; Gadinis 2015). Since the creation of the WTO in 1995, an added stimulus has come from the WTO Agreement on Technical Barriers to Trade and the obligations of all WTO members to use international standards as the technical basis for domestic laws and regulations. Also important are what one scholar has called "informal rules" (Tieku 2019) and what others would call soft law or norms.

International Norms or "Soft Law"

Since the late 1980s, scholars have increasingly recognized the importance of norms as another variety of global governance. Norms are shared expectations or understandings regarding standards of appropriate behavior for various actors, particularly states. They range from the norm that states are obligated to carry out treaties they ratify (*pacta sunt servanda*) to the expectation that combatants will not target civilians. Norms vary in strength and determining whether one exists involves ascertaining whether states perceive that a certain practice is obligatory or expected. Some norms are so internalized in states that they are difficult to recognize unless a violation occurs. Still others are weak, contested, or "emerging." The importance of norms has emerged from early work on human rights and humanitarian norms, chemical and nuclear weapons taboos, and the "polluter pays" principle with regard to the environment. It was the work of Martha Finnemore and Kathryn Sikkink (1998) that first explored how norms emerge and spread through their articulation of the concepts of "norm life cycles" and "norm cascades," as well as "norm entrepreneurs" and "norm internalization." For Acharya (2004, 2014) norms take on a regional character, exploring the question of why some transnational ideas and norms find more acceptance in some locales than in others, providing important insights on norm diffusion. Two points bear emphasizing: first, norms are works in progress that can encompass different meanings and reflect power relations; second, how norms are framed can be critically important to whether and how they take hold and spread, how they are adopted in different parts of the world, how much they matter, and whether they erode over time.

Many norms are incorporated into international legal conventions and referred to as soft law. Examples include human rights and labor rights norms, the concept of the global commons applied to the high seas, outer space, and polar regions, and the concept of sustainable development. The debate over the status of the concept of "responsibility to protect" as a norm is discussed in Chapter 7. Other forms of soft law include codes of conduct, world conference declarations, and certain UN resolutions such as the 1970 General Assembly Resolution 2749 that recognized the high seas, outer space, and polar regions as forming the common heritage of mankind.

In environmental law, we can see the evolution of norms, soft law, and law over time. An initial framework convention often sets forth norms and principles that states agree on, but no concrete actions are mentioned. As scientific understanding of the problem improves, the political environment changes, and technology provides new possible solutions leading states, key corporations, and other interested actors may agree on specific, binding steps to be taken. Protocols are used to supplement the initial framework convention and form the "hard" law. Negotiations often follow to make explicit that hard law establishing state obligations to take urgently needed action to reduce emissions. Soft law is easier to negotiate and more flexible, and it leaves open the possibility of negotiating hard law in the future. Soft law can also be a means of linking international law to private entities, including individuals and MNCs, such as through codes of practice of corporate social responsibility.

International Regimes and Regime Complexes

Since the 1980s, scholars have used the concept of international regimes to understand governance where principles, norms, rules, and decisionmaking procedures are linked in a particular issue area. Where international regimes exist, such as for nuclear weapons proliferation, whaling, health, and food aid, participating states and other international actors recognize the existence of certain obligations and feel compelled to honor them. Because this is "governance without government," they comply based on an acceptance of the legitimacy of the rules and underlying norms and the validity of the decisionmaking procedures. They expect other states and actors also to comply and use relevant dispute settlement procedures to resolve conflicts.

International regimes encompass rules and norms, as well as the practices of actors that show how their expectations converge and their acceptance of and compliance with rules. IGO decisionmaking procedures, bureaucracies, budgets, headquarters, and legal personality may be part of a given issue area, but individual IGOs, by themselves, do not constitute a regime. Some issues, such as nuclear accidents that trigger widespread nuclear fallout (e.g., the 1986 Chernobyl disaster), do not need a formal organization that functions regardless of whether there is an accident. Ad hoc arrangements for decisionmaking and taking action when an accident occurs can be coupled with existing rules and norms. The regime for nuclear weapons proliferation, however, includes the inspection machinery and safeguard systems of the International Atomic Energy Agency, the export controls of the Nuclear Suppliers Group, and the Nuclear Non-Proliferation Treaty, the Comprehensive Test Ban Treaty (which is observed even though it is not yet fully in effect), the UN Security Council's enforcement powers, and the IAEA's technical assistance programs to non–nuclear weapon countries for developing peaceful uses of nuclear energy. In issue areas where regimes exist, they constitute the core global governance.

Scholars have also identified a number of what are called "regime complexes." These are defined as "an array of partially overlapping and nonhierarchical institutions governing a particular issue area" (Raustiala and Victor 2004: 278–279). The complexity arises from the lack of hierarchy and overlaps in membership, mandates, and rules, which can lead to uncertainty about which rules and interpretations of rules prevail and the potential for decisions in one body to undermine or influence decisions in another (Alter and Raustiala 2018). It can create opportunities for forum shopping, that is, for states to seek the forum likely to be most favorable to their preferences and for conflicts over interpretations of rules and competing authority claims.

The global refugee regime complex, explored further in Chapter 11, is one example. Its elemental regimes include the refugee regime centered around the UNHCR, the human rights regime centered around the international human rights conventions and the UN Office of the High Commissioner for Human Rights, the humanitarian regime that includes the UN Office for Coordination of Humanitarian Affairs, and the labor migration regime based on International Labour Organization conventions. Because of the complexity, what becomes problematic is not only that elemental regimes overlap, but as Betts (2013) notes, relevant actors are in different agencies that have different mandates, memberships, decisionmaking processes, and dynamics with different sources of authority. Other examples include the food security, maritime piracy, and international forest regime complexes.

The value of the regime complex concept is that it captures the reality that "Global problems increasingly overlap and intersect. As new problems emerge on the international agenda, they often are fit into preexisting institutions and agreements"; these arrangements "rarely occur on a blank slate" (Alter and Raustiala 2018: 337). A regime complex is often an almost inevitable result of broader international relations trends: the density of international agreements and international organizations; the ease of creating something new instead of reforming something that already exists; the inevitability of shifts in power and preferences as well as the emergence of new problems, demands for greater representation, and some degree of confusion. Indeed, regime complexity makes it harder to understand the global governance of some issues and requires more than just mapping a complex to discover how institutions and outcomes have evolved, how states and other actors have adapted their strategies given the complexity, and who have been winners and losers.

Groups and Global Conferences

As multilateralism has become the dominant practice in international affairs, other less formal forms of global governance have emerged—some more institutionalized than others. These include various intergovernmental arrangements and groups that lack the legal formality of charters or treaties such as UN-sponsored global conferences, panels, forums, and commissions.

The first of the Gs was the G-77, formed by developing countries of Africa, Asia, and Latin America in 1964 in conjunction with the establishment of the United Nations Conference on Trade and Development. For many years, it operated as a unified bloc constituting more than two-thirds of the UN's membership. It is still active today, but less cohesive, as member country interests have diverged.

The Group of Seven (G-7) began in the mid-1970s when summit meetings of governmental leaders were not yet common practice and major changes in international economic relations suggested the value of periodic, informal gatherings. These later evolved into a regular arrangement, including annual summits, but not a formal IGO. The G-7's agenda grew well beyond macroeconomic policy coordination, as discussed further in Chapter 8. From 1992 to 2014, Russia joined the group for noneconomic discussions, thus creating the Group of Eight (G-8), which dealt with issues surrounding the Cold War's end, the rising threat of terrorism, and so on. That ended with Russia's annexation of Crimea in 2014.

In 1999, the Group of 20 (G-20) was created as a forum for economic policy discussions among the finance ministers and central bank governors of advanced and emerging market countries. It includes nineteen states and the EU, with the World Bank and IMF participating on an ex officio basis. Today, the G-20 members represent 90 percent of world GDP, 80 percent of world trade, and two-thirds of world population. Little known until the 2008–2009 global financial crisis, when US president George W. Bush convened the first summit meeting, it now convenes annually at the summit level. Like the G-7, it does not have a permanent secretariat. The G-20 welcomed the African Union in 2023 and is discussed in Chapter 8.

Within and outside the UN system, various ad hoc multilateral "contact" and "friends" groups have been formed to harness multilateral diplomatic efforts to address specific problems. The first contact group was formed in the late 1970s to secure the independence of Southwest Africa, which was originally a German colony, then a League of Nations mandate territory administered by South Africa, but not given independence or converted to a UN trusteeship after World War II (Karns 1987). After nearly ten years of diplomacy, it gained independence as Namibia in 1990. Other contact groups have formed, for example, to aid the search for peace in Central America in the late 1980s and in the former Yugoslavia in the 1990s, and to marshal assistance for Ukraine in 2022.

Another type of governance entity is the not-for-profit World Economic Forum—an international organization (not IGO) that promotes public–private cooperation. It hosts an annual gathering of government, business, and other elites each year in Davos, Switzerland.

Since the 1970s, the UN has convened many global conferences and, more recently, summits on topics ranging from the environment, food supply, population, and women's rights to water supplies, children, and desertification. There was a large cluster of these conferences in the 1970s and another in the 1990s, with a lull in the 1980s and an effort to scale back since 2000. These conferences have spawned complex multilateral diplomacy, with NGOs, scientific experts, corporations, and interested individuals trying to influence outcomes, but often have been disappointing because their outcomes represent the least common denominator of agreement among the large number of participants, of whom only states actually have a formal say.

UN conferences like the Summit for Children (New York, 1990), the Earth Summit (Rio, 1992), and the four World Conferences on Women (1975, 1980, 1985, 1995) have been important global political processes for addressing interdependence issues. Cumulatively, the conferences have also bolstered understanding of the linkages among issues such as environmental protection, equal rights (especially for women), poverty elimination, and participation of local communities. They are discussed in Chapter 4.

Private Governance

Private governance is a growing phenomenon that involves authoritative decisionmaking in areas where states have not acted, or have chosen not to exercise authority, or where states have themselves been ineffective in the exercise of authority. A variety of private transnational regulatory organizations, for example, have been established and governed by actors from business, civil society, and other sectors to set a wide range of voluntary standards for corporations and other entities on issues ranging from workers' rights to climate change. These entities also promote, monitor, and enforce standards. Operating through markets, they rely on incentives such as consumer demand, reputational benefits, reduced transactional costs, and avoidance of mandatory regulations (Abbott, Green, and Keohane 2016: 2) Other examples of private governance and governors include international accounting standards set by the International Accounting Standards Board; the private bond-rating agencies, such as Moody's Investors Service and Standard & Poor's Ratings Group, whose rules can shape government actions through a threatened drop in a country's rating; International Chamber of Commerce rules and actions; initiatives to establish social and environmental certifications for certain products, such as the those of Fairtrade International and the Forest Stewardship Council, through which major corporations and advocacy groups collaborate; and labor standards in a single multinational firm, such as Nike or Ford.

Private authorities are not inherently good or bad, but they have some advantages and disadvantages. Abbott, Green, and Keohane (2016), for example, have compared the ways private governance initiatives can more quickly identify and fill governance gaps (and fill niches blocked by lack of agreement among states) as well as provide opportunities for NSA participation.

They also find such initiatives less resilient than IGOs, vulnerable to changes in circumstances, and less predictable.

Occasionally, however, global corporations may be more powerful than some international organizations in their ability to "more effectively sanction and govern network members" (May 2018: 348).

Public–Private Partnerships

Since the late 1980s, the variety of public–private partnerships involving the UN and most of its specialized agencies, funds, and programs, including the UN Development Programme, the World Bank, the UN Children's Fund, and the UNEP, has mushroomed with the recognition that such partnerships can contribute to achieving internationally agreed development goals. UNSG Kofi Annan's Global Compact initiative, created in 1999, was an important step, as was the 2002 World Summit on Sustainable Development in Johannesburg, which called for creating partnerships for sustainable development. Partnerships have become a major source of funding and have influenced ideas of how development should be achieved and who should deliver it, as well as the architecture of the UN itself (Gregoratti 2014: 311). Some are large, institutionalized, multistakeholder arrangements; others are more temporary with fewer actors. Not all are about donating money; they may involve mobilizing corporate knowledge, personnel, and expertise to achieve policy objectives. These partnerships represent a more decentralized form of governance, one that is also networked, flexible, and voluntary (Andonova 2017). Public–private partnerships such as Goldman Sachs 10000 Women global initiative and the EU Directive on gender balance in decisionmaking positions, for example, have served as vehicles for promoting gender equality in businesses and governments (Prügl and True 2014).

Although the newer forms of global governance vary in scope, effectiveness, and durability, as discussed in later chapters, those that do not involve states have begun to raise troubling questions of legitimacy. We explore this issue in Chapter 12.

The Politics and Effectiveness of Global Governance

The politics of global governance reflects "struggles over wealth, power, and knowledge" in the world (Murphy 2000: 798) and over "the global structures, processes, and institutions that shape the fates and life chances of actors around the world" (Barnett and Duval 2005: 7–8). Thus, although power relationships among states still matter, so do the resources and actions of a host of NSAs, including international organizations. Among the central issues, then, are who gets to participate in decisionmaking, whose voices get heard, who gets excluded at what price, and whose interests do certain institutions privilege. Power matters, as do authority, legitimacy, and accountability. As with all types of governance, effectiveness, or the ability to deliver public goods and to make a difference, matters.

Power: Who Gets What? Who Benefits? Who Loses?

At one time, the politics of global governance seemed to be about US power and hegemony. To be sure, US power and preferences shaped (and continue to influence) many pieces of global governance, including the UN and the liberal international economic system. Following the Cold War's end and the dissolution of the Soviet Union, the United States emerged as the sole superpower; its economy drove globalization, and democracy seemed to be spreading everywhere. Yet beginning with the contested invasion of Iraq in 2003, US power and influence in the world have substantially declined. Even before then, the unilateralist policies of the George W. Bush administration were leading small, middle-power, and larger states to take initiatives without US participation, let alone leadership, such as with the International Criminal Court, the Kyoto Protocol, and the convention banning antipersonnel landmines.

Today, there are many indicators that the United States is no longer at the center of global politics in the way it once was, and there are "more states with more relations with one another on a wider range of issues than ever before" (Jentleson 2012: 135). Two factors in particular stand out. One is the rapid rise of China as a superpower competing with the United States in ways the former Soviet Union never did. The other explanation is rooted in US domestic politics: the impact of the Trump administration in denigrating the value of allies, international institutions (including the UN), and multilateralism in general and touting "America first." Although his successor, President Biden, announced that "America is back," what was damaged is not easily repaired, especially after the precipitous US withdrawal from Afghanistan in 2021. Increasingly, global politics is being seen as multipolar with Russia, China, and the United States increasingly in competition with one another, while others such as India, Brazil, and South Africa are declining to take sides. This all makes for a world in which the politics of different issues and of governance is pluralized. It is also making for a world in which multilateralism is increasingly challenged.

Global governance arrangements exist because states and other actors create them and imbue them with power, authority, and legitimacy and deem them valuable for performing certain tasks and serving certain needs and interests. Yet IGOs are not just passive structures and agents of states. As Michael Barnett and Martha Finnemore (2005: 162) have argued, they have power "both because of their form (as rational-legal bureaucracies) and because of their (liberal) goals," as well as the authority that derives from goals that are "widely viewed as desirable and legitimate." They can exercise "compulsory power" through the use of material resources like humanitarian relief, food, peacekeepers, weapons, and sanctions, as well as normative resources such as naming and shaming, spreading global values and norms such as gender equality, or inculcating "best practices." IGO secretariats' set agendas of meetings and conferences, structure options for Security Council debates, and classify and organize information, whether on types of economies, what is a genocide, or who is a refugee. These all constitute "institutional power." A third type of IGO power, "productive power," is that of determining the existence of a problem such as internally displaced persons (as differentiated from refugees who cross national borders), defining it, proposing solutions, and persuading other actors to accept those solutions (Barnett and Finnemore 2005).

The power of NSAs also can be derived from various material resources as well as symbolic and normative resources. Transnational advocacy groups, civil society organizations, and NGOs of all stripes have shown the many ways they can marshal the resources inherent in naming and shaming to pressure MNCs and governments of targeted states to change their behavior.

Power, whether in global or local governance, is intimately linked to authority and legitimacy. IGOs can exercise power largely because they are generally recognized to have legitimate authority, just as states whose governments are recognized as legitimate are recognized by other states and accepted as members of IGOs. Understanding the nature and types of authority and legitimacy in global governance is part of the puzzle.

Authority and Legitimacy: Who Governs and On What Basis?

Historically, states were the only entities thought to have authority in international politics due to their sovereignty, and the only authority IGOs had was assumed to be that delegated by states, and thus it was subject to withdrawal. In recent years, there has been more attention given to issues of authority and legitimacy with gradual recognition of the varied bases of authority and legitimacy in global governance.

Many commentators agree that authority is derived from the consent of and deference by others "based on the acceptance of a decision or an interpretation because it comes from a certain source. It is a belief in certain qualities of an authority which make subordinates adapt their beliefs and behavior" (Zürn 2018: 38). Compliance is not automatic, though. As Barnett and Finnnemore (2004: 20–21) emphasized, "Actors might recognize an authority's judgment as legitimate but still follow an alternative course of action for some other set of reasons." With their particular interest in international organization bureaucracies, they argue that "authority provides the substance of which IOs are made . . . and bureaucracy is the embodiment of rational-legal authority . . . a form of authority that modernity views as particularly legitimate and good." They note, however, that bureaucracies must be able to "present themselves . . . as not exercising power but instead serving others."

A somewhat broader view of authority is presented by Avant, Finnemore, and Sell (2010c) in their book *Who Governs the Globe?* where they posit five bases of authority: institutional, delegated, expert, principled, and capacity-based. The first is derived from the rules and purposes of an institution, whether an IGO such as the IMF or a credit-rating agency such as Moody's. The second is the primary basis of IGO authority: delegated authority from member states for certain tasks, such as peacekeeping. The third derives from the need for certain tasks to be done by those with specialized knowledge about them, for example, the medical and public health experts in the WHO. That expertise influences how staff see the world and define issues, what policy options are considered, and the very culture of the institution. The fourth base—principled or moral authority—reflects the fact that many IGOs and NGOs are created precisely to serve or protect a set of principles, morals, or values, such as peace, women's rights, disarmament, or environmental protection. Finally, demonstrated ability to accomplish tasks such as alleviating extreme poverty is a further basis of authority.

Yet why do the powerful and not-so-powerful actors in global governance decide to cooperate, accept, and defer to the authority of at least some IGOs? Why do actors obey rules in the absence of coercion or change their behavior when shamed by a transnational advocacy group or accept the authority of the ICJ or a private credit-rating agency? The decision to comply with rules, norms, and law fundamentally rests on legitimacy defined as "the belief by an actor that a rule or institution ought to be obeyed" (Hurd 2007: 30). Such a belief affects behavior, Ian Hurd adds, because "the decision whether to comply is no longer motivated by the simple fear of retribution or by a calculation of self-interest but instead by an internal sense of rightness and obligation."

A key aspect of legitimacy is membership in the international community, whose system of multilateral, reciprocal interactions helps validate its members, institutions, and rules. As Thomas Franck (1990: 205) has noted, "It is because states constitute a community that legitimacy has the power to influence their conduct." IGOs, like the UN, are perceived as legitimate to the extent that they are created and function according to certain principles of right process, such as one state, one vote. The UN Security Council's legitimacy as the core institution in the international system imbued with authority to authorize the use of force derives from the widespread acceptance of that role, as we examine in Chapter 4.

As political theorists have long noted, flags and rituals are important symbols of legitimate authority. Thus, UN peacekeepers' blue helmets symbolize the UN's authority and the international community's recognition of their legitimacy to act. When the Security Council refused to approve the US military operation in Iraq in 2003, it denied the United States the symbols of legitimacy and affected how the mission was regarded by much of the world. Likewise, the strong General Assembly votes condemning Russia's 2022 invasion of Ukraine were a clear signal to Russia of the world's opprobrium. The very first symbol of legitimate international authority was the red cross (and later the red crescent)—the emblem adopted by the International Committee of the Red Cross after its founding in 1863 as the first emergency humanitarian organization.

Legitimacy is also increasingly tied to other considerations, including whether NSAs and civil society have a voice and can participate. Yet for NGOs, IGOs, and other actors, their legitimacy is based not only on participation but also on their responsiveness, transparency, and accountability.

Accountability: Who Is Accountable to Whom and How?

As a result of the diffusion of domestic democratic norms into the international arena, virtually all global governance actors have faced growing demands for greater accountability and transparency. Some of these demands come from NGOs and civil society groups; others come from democratic governments, major donors, and major borrowers. There is no single, widely accepted definition of accountability, however. At its core is the idea of account-giving—reporting, measuring, justifying, and explaining actions. For some, accountability involves a set of standards for evaluating the behavior of public entities. How responsive and responsible are they? Do they act in a fair and equitable manner? For others, accountability is defined in terms of mechanisms that involve obligations to explain and justify conduct (Schillemans and Bovens 2011: 4–5).

The question is, therefore, to whom, for what, and by what mechanisms various global governance actors are accountable. Are IGOs accountable only to their member states, for example? To their major donors? To development aid recipients? Trying to satisfy both donors and recipients may satisfy neither. Tamar Gutner (2010), for example, showed that trying to get the IMF involved with the UN's Millennium Development Goals and poverty reduction was a poor fit with that institution's expertise, reducing the ability of anyone to hold it accountable. To whom are NGOs accountable? Clifford Bob (2010: 200), for example, argues that advocacy groups are held accountable in democratic states primarily by the domestic laws that regulate their activities, since dissatisfied members can simply leave the organization. What about expert groups or private governance arrangements? The fact that many global governance actors, including most IGOs, have multiple constituencies, are responsible for multiple tasks, and face multiple demands and points of view makes them vulnerable to what some scholars have called "multiple accountabilities disorder" (Schillemans and Bovens 2011).

There are various ways through which actors may be held accountable, ranging from hierarchical and fiscal accountability to peer and public reputational accountability (Grant and Keohane 2005). Transparency is also critical to achieving accountability, that is, making information about organizational actions open to public scrutiny (Grigorescu 2007: 626). For IGOs, issues of accountability and transparency frequently hinge on whether conferences and meetings are open to the public or closed and operating more like private clubs. This is why some institutions have established mechanisms for accountability, such as the World Bank's Inspection Panel and the UN's Office of Internal Oversight Services. In other situations, an ad hoc body may be created to investigate a particular problem, as in the case of the independent inquiry committee (the Volcker Committee) that investigated possible malfeasance in the UN's Oil-for-Food Programme in Iraq in 2005. NGOs and member states often play key roles in pushing for such IGO accountability and transparency. Ensuring international accountability, however, is still relatively haphazard and less likely to constrain more powerful actors. Lack of transparency may adversely affect not only legitimacy and compliance but also the efficacy of all kinds of institutions. An ongoing challenge for global governance in the future, then, is how to increase transparency and accountability of the varieties of governance without undermining the very conditions that enable deal-making and cooperation.

Effectiveness: How Do We Know What Works? How Do We Measure Success and Failure?

The task of assessing effectiveness is one of the central challenges in public policymaking. What are the outcomes of rules and actions? How are people actually affected? Is security increased, are health and well-being improved, is poverty reduced, is environmental degradation slowed, and sustainable development advanced? To assess effectiveness we need to go beyond formal compliance. Indeed, "Agreements themselves may not be ambitious enough to provide more than temporary or cosmetic relief of global problems" (Simmons and de Jonge Oudraat 2001: 13–14).

The key questions are: What works? For whom does it work? Who does what to translate agreements into action, including incorporating norms into domestic laws? Which techniques or mechanisms work best to get actors to change their behavior, and what are the reactions to noncompliance? What types of incentives or technical assistance to developing countries will enable them to comply with environmental rules? How and when are diplomacy or public shaming, economic sanctions, or military force most likely to secure compliance? When are particular types of peace operations most likely to secure, keep, or build conditions of lasting peace? With all the advances in what Jacqueline Best (2017) calls "measurement-driven governance" and Hans Krause Hansen and Tony Porter (2017) call "big data," what are the consequences? Does this narrow the focus only to what can be counted? Does the Human Development Index or the Gender Equality Index really tell us what is happening to the quality of people's lives around the world? Are states motivated by being ranked and graded as some scholars suggest (Davis et al. 2012; Cooley and Snyder 2015)? Who should be held accountable for the validity of such rankings as Nikhil Gutta (2012) asks? We address these issues in Chapters 7 through 12, but despite decades of global governance initiatives across multiple issue areas, we still do not have answers to some of these questions.

* * *

The challenges of global governance, then, include a wide variety of international policy problems and issues that require governance, not all of which are necessarily global in scope. Rather, what we see are multilevel, often diffuse varieties of governance with many different actors playing key roles alongside states. The need and demand for more global governance is clearly rising; the processes are complex; the politics is an ongoing struggle to influence "who gets what" and "who benefits"; and the issues of legitimacy, accountability, and effectiveness require constant attention. Effectiveness and success depend on whom you ask. Most important, we should not assume that all global governance is necessarily good. As Inis Claude Jr. (1988: 142) noted many years ago, "I must question the assumption of the normative superiority of collective policy, the view that one can have greater confidence in the wisdom and the moral quality of decisions made by a collectivity concerning the use of power and other resources than in the quality of policies set and followed by individual states."

Suggested Further Reading

Acharya, Amitav, ed. (2016) *Why Govern? Rethinking Demand and Progress in Global Governance*. New York: Cambridge University Press.

Avant, Deborah D., Martha Finnemore, and Susan K. Sell, eds. (2010) *Who Governs the Globe?* New York: Cambridge University Press.

Barnett, Michael, and Raymond Duvall, eds. (2005) *Power in Global Governance*. New York: Cambridge University Press.

Grigorescu, Alexandru. (2020) *The Ebb and Flow of Global Governance: Intergovernmentalism versus Nongovernmentalism in World Politics*. Cambridge: Cambridge University Press.

Johnson, Tana. (2015) *Organizational Progeny: Why Governments Are Losing Control over the Proliferating Structures of Global Governance*. New York: Oxford University Press.

Weiss, Thomas G., and Rorden Wilkinson, eds. (2023) *International Organizations and Global Governance*, 3rd ed. New York: Routledge.

2

Theories of Global Governance

SCHOLARS USE THEORIES TO DESCRIBE, EXPLAIN, AND PREDICT VARIOUS aspects of international relations. Each is based on a set of key ideas about the nature and roles of individuals, conceptions of the state, sovereignty, and interactions among states and other actors, as well as conceptions about the international system.

The principal goal of theory is to simplify and clarify what matters most. Although scholars may disagree about what to include and what to leave out, they leave it to the consumers of theoretical work to decide whether the choices are reasonable and whether they help explain real-world events.

An important debate in international relations (IR) theory generally is whether one should focus on measuring and explaining human behavior and institutions objectively through positivist or rationalist theory, or whether one should instead focus on interpreting the language and symbols of social interaction through constructivist or nonrationalist theory. This is especially relevant to global governance, since values, rules, and identities play important roles alongside more traditional factors, such as economic and military capability and interests. Although the debate tends to polarize scholars, each approach and method provides a useful lens for studying global governance (Fearon and Wendt 2002).

Rationalist theories identify links between antecedents, called independent variables, and outcomes, referred to as dependent variables. From theory, propositions are hypothesized and tested by observations in the real world. For example, functionalist theory proposes that international organizations tend to grow from a more narrow and technical focus to broader and more political undertakings. This insight has been tested against the development of European regionalism and the history of the creation of UN specialized agencies through careful tracing of processes and detailed case studies of particular institutions.

In contrast, constructivism and most critical theories are not testable in the same ways. Instead, they are critiqued with reference to whether the propositions are internally logical or help elucidate the true nature of international institutions. Drawing on the work of sociologists, many social constructivists argue that actors' identities and interests are the product of debate and interaction.

In this chapter, we briefly discuss five major theories—liberalism, realism, social constructivism, critical theories, and feminist and postcolonial theories—with particular attention to what each says about global governance and international cooperation. We depart from traditional approaches by discussing liberalism before realism because liberalism has long been the dominant theoretical approach of most scholars of international organizations and global governance. One of the persistent puzzles, however, is the neglect of multilateralism in all international relations theories. It is a puzzle that motivated James Caporaso (1993: 51) to ask why the concept has not "played a more prominent role . . . [since] the prima facie case for the importance of multilateral activity in the international realm would seem great." He was quick to make clear that he was not arguing that multilateral activities and organizations have been ignored. Rather, his point is that multilateralism "is not extensively employed as a theoretical category and that it is rarely used as an explanatory concept" (53). Thus, readers should not expect to find mention of the concept in our discussion of the five major theories.

Liberalism

Liberal theory in the classical tradition holds that human nature is basically good, social progress is possible, and human behavior is malleable and perfectible through institutions. Injustice, aggression, and war are products of inadequate or corrupt social institutions and of misunderstanding among leaders. They are not inevitable, but can be eliminated through collective or multilateral action and institutional reform. The expansion of human freedom is a core liberal belief that can be achieved through democracy and market capitalism.

The roots of liberalism are found in the seventeenth-century Grotian tradition, the eighteenth-century Enlightenment, nineteenth-century political and economic liberalism, and twentieth-century Wilsonian idealism. The Grotian tradition developed from the writings of Hugo Grotius (1583–1645), a Dutch legal scholar. Just before the European states' challenge to universal religious authority in the Peace of Westphalia (1648), Grotius asserted that all international relations were subject to the rule of law—the law of nations and the law of nature. He rejected the idea that states can do whatever they want and that war is their supreme right. Grotius believed that states, like people, are basically rational and law-abiding.

The Enlightenment's contribution to liberalism rests on Greek ideas that individuals are rational beings and have the capacity to improve their condition by creating a just society. If a just society is not attained, the fault rests with inadequate institutions. The writings of Immanuel Kant (1724–1804) reflect these core Enlightenment beliefs with their extensive treatment of the relationship between democracy and peace. Kant was among the first thinkers to articulate this connection and the possibility of "perpetual peace" among democratic states. The liberal theory of democratic peace does not mean that democratic states would refrain from war in their relations with nondemocratic states, but Kant argued that in a "pacific union," free democratic states would retain their sovereignty while working to avoid war.

Nineteenth-century liberalism linked the rationalism of the Enlightenment and the growing faith in modernization through the scientific and Industrial Revolution to promoting democracy and free trade. Adam Smith (d. 1790) and Jeremy Bentham (1748–1832) believed that free trade would create interdependencies that would raise the cost of war and reward fair cooperation and competition with peace, prosperity, and greater justice. This strand of liberalism forms the basis for economic liberalism, whose core belief is the power of free markets to stimulate economic growth and maximize economic welfare. To this end, governments must permit free economic intercourse.

The beliefs of US president Woodrow Wilson—captured best in the "Fourteen Points," on which the Versailles Treaty ending World War I and the Covenant of the League of Nations were based—formed a core of twentieth-century liberalism. Wilson envisioned that creating a system of collective security, promoting self-determination of peoples, and eliminating power politics could prevent war. The League of Nations illustrated the importance that liberals put on international institutions for collective problem solving. Early twentieth-century liberals were strong advocates of international law, arbitration, and courts to promote cooperation and guarantee peace. Because of their faith in human reason and progress, they were often labeled "idealists." With the League of Nations' failure to prevent World War II and the Cold War, liberalism and idealism came under intense criticism from realist theorists.

For liberals, states are the most important actors, but they are pluralistic, not unitary actors. That is, moral and ethical principles, power relations among domestic and transnational groups, and changing international conditions shape states' interests and policies. There is no single definition of states' national interests; instead, states vary in their goals, and their interests change. Liberals also recognize that nonstate actors and transnational and transgovernmental groups play important roles in IR.

Liberals view the international system as a context in which multiple interactions occur and various actors "learn" from their interactions, rather than a structure of relationships based on the distribution of power among states and a fixed concept of state sovereignty. Power matters, but it is exercised in this framework of rules and institutions, which also makes international cooperation possible. Second, liberals expect mutual interests to increase with greater interdependence, knowledge, communication, and the spread of democratic values. This will promote greater cooperation and thereby peace, welfare, and justice. Third, liberals view domestic politics in states as playing an important role in shaping states' policies, preferences, and actions. Hence, when states' political systems are similar (for liberals, this means democratic), their preferences are more likely to be compatible and cooperation is more likely. Finally, liberals view intergovernmental organizations (IGOs) as arenas where states interact and cooperate to solve common problems and international law is a major instrument for framing and maintaining order in the international system.

For liberals, then, IGOs play a number of key roles, including contributing to habits of cooperation and serving as arenas for negotiating and developing coalitions. They are a primary means for mitigating the danger of war, promoting the development of shared norms, and enhancing order. Their operational activities help address substantive international problems and may form parts of international regimes as discussed in Chapter 1. They can be used by states as instruments of foreign policy or to constrain the behavior of others.

Finally, a new strain of liberal theory has developed since the 1990s that draws attention to the role of women in global governance as both an independent and a dependent variable. Positivist feminist theorists argue that most IR theory, including liberal theory, has ignored the place of women. For international organization scholars, this means paying more attention to the role of women in international institutions as leaders, staffers, permanent representatives of states, and lobbyists with nongovernmental organizations (NGOs). Historically women have been poorly represented in the halls of power; they were virtually absent from the League of Nations and only recently have they held more senior positions at the United Nations (Chapter 4).

Liberal feminists also call for increased attention to developing organizational policies that affect women, especially the role of women in economic development; women as victims of crime, violence, and discrimination; and women in situations of armed conflict. Yet women are not just victims; they are important actors, and feminist theorists have pushed hard in recent years to promote acceptance of this view.

Core liberal beliefs in the roots of cooperation and roles of international institutions have been challenged since the 1970s by so-called neoliberal institutionalists. Their ideas form an important variant on liberal theory.

Neoliberal Institutionalism or Neoliberalism
In the 1970s, liberalism experienced a revival after the preeminence of realism during the Cold War. Increasing international interdependence and

heightened awareness of the sensitivities and vulnerabilities that characterize interdependence were major factors boosting this revival. Robert Keohane and Joseph Nye's book *Power and Interdependence* (1977), which outlined how international institutions constituted an important response to conditions of complex interdependence, had a major influence. Some neoliberal institutionalists suggest that states are attracted to efficiency, expertise, and other benefits from cooperating through international institutions—especially if there is not much concern about some states benefiting even more than others (Snidal 1991). They take a state-centric view of IR and believe that states have incentives to cooperate because they seek to maximize absolute gains. As a result, cooperation is common (not a rare exception), with institutions providing a means for states to solve collective action problems.

The 1970s and early 1980s presented a puzzle for neoliberals. Given the major international economic dislocations resulting from the collapse of the Bretton Woods arrangements for international monetary relations, increasing developing economy debt, and the decline in US economic power relative to Europe and Japan, why did the post–World War II institutions for economic cooperation (such as the International Monetary Fund [IMF] and General Agreement on Tariffs and Trade [GATT]) not collapse? Keohane's influential book *After Hegemony* (1984) answered this question by emphasizing the effects of institutions and practices on state behavior, including their willingness to cooperate.

Thus, according to neoliberal institutionalists, states that have continuous interactions with each other choose to cooperate because they realize that they will have future interactions with the same actors. Continuous interactions also serve as the motivation for states to create international institutions, which in turn moderate state behavior, provide a context for bargaining and mechanisms for reducing cheating by monitoring behavior, and facilitate transparency of the actions of all. International institutions provide focal points for coordination and make state commitments more credible by specifying what is expected, thereby encouraging states to establish reputations for compliance. They are an efficient solution to problems of coordination because they provide information that aids decision-making and reduces the transaction costs for achieving agreement among large numbers of states (Keohane and Martin 1995). States benefit because institutions do things for members that cannot be accomplished unilaterally. Thus, institutions have important and independent effects on interstate interactions by providing information and by framing actions, but they do not necessarily affect states' underlying motivations.

Neoliberals recognize that not all efforts to cooperate will yield good results. Cooperation can aid the few at the expense of the many and accentuate or mitigate injustice. Some neoliberals have been more willing than earlier liberals to address issues of power. To explain the creation of the post–World War II network of international economic institutions and shared standards for liberalizing trade and capital flows, neoliberal institutionalists such as Robert Keohane (1984) and John Gerard Ruggie (1982) focused on the role of the United States as a hegemonic state, the particular character of the order it created (embedded liberalism), and the joint gains it offered the Europeans and Japanese for cooperating.

Liberalism and neoliberalism have spawned several middle-level theories—middle-level because they are not "grand" theories that attempt to explain IR more generally. They provide additional dimensions for explaining international cooperative behavior. These include functionalism, regime theory, rational design, and collective goods theory.

Functionalism

Functionalism is rooted in the belief that governance arrangements such as IGOs arise out of basic or functional needs of people and states. Functionalists also assert that international economic and social cooperation is a prerequisite for political cooperation and eliminating war, whose causes (in their view) lie in ignorance, poverty, hunger, and disease.

As articulated by David Mitrany in *A Working Peace System* (1946: 7), the task of functionalism is "not how to keep the nations peacefully apart but how to bring them actively together." He foresaw "a spreading web of international activities and agencies, in which and through which the interests and life of all nations would be gradually integrated" (14). Not all functionalists share this vision, but they do share a belief that it is possible to bypass political rivalries of states and build habits of cooperation in nonpolitical economic spheres. Increasing amounts of such cooperation will expand these cooperative interactions and build a base of common values, eventually spilling over into cooperation in political and military affairs. A key aspect of this process is the role of technical experts and the assumption that these experts will lose their close identification with their own states and develop new allegiances to like-minded individuals around the world. The form that specific functional organizations take is determined by the problem to be solved; that is, form follows function.

Functionalism is applicable at both regional and global levels and has been important in explaining the evolution of the European Union as a process of integration (discussed further in Chapter 5). The "father of Europe," Jean Monnet, believed that nationalism could be weakened and war in Europe made unthinkable in the long run by taking practical steps toward economic integration that would ultimately advance a European political union. The success of the European Coal and Steel Community, proposed by Monnet, led to the creation of the European Atomic Energy Community to manage peaceful uses of atomic energy and to the European Economic Community, with its common market and many facets of practical cooperation.

Functional theory fell short in its prediction that such cooperation would spill over in a deterministic way from the economic area into areas of national security. Although most analysts would credit European integration with making the region a "zone of peace," achieving common foreign and security policy has proved particularly difficult for EU members. In 2022, faced with Russia's invasion of Ukraine, EU members rapidly agreed on a set of collective responses, including providing arms to Ukraine and cutting their use of Russian oil and gas. That initial unity, however, is likely to be severely tested the longer the war continues. In fact, so-called neo-functionalists such as Ernst Haas (1964) theorized that the processes and dynamics of cooperation are not automatic. At key points, political decisions are needed, and these may or may not be taken, as the evolution of European integration has borne out.

Functionalist theory also helps us understand the development of early IGOs such as the Universal Postal Union and Commission for Navigation on the Rhine River, as well as the specialized agencies of the UN system such as the World Health Organization, UN Children's Fund, the Food and Agriculture Organization, and the International Labour Organization. These are discussed in Chapter 3 and later chapters.

Harold Jacobson, William Reisinger, and Todd Mathers (1986) tested key propositions of functionalism as an explanation for the phenomenon of IGO development and found that the overwhelming number of IGOs could be classified as functional. That is, they have specific mandates, links to economic or technical issues, and limited memberships, often related to geographic region. They and Tana Johnson (2014) have shown that the majority of IGOs created since 1960 have been established by other IGOs and show increasing differentiation of functions.

Functionalism fails to address a number of key questions, such as how can all causes of war be alleviated and whether habits of economic and social cooperation transfer to political areas. In fact, the European integration process since 1950 has shown the degree to which functionalists underestimated the strength of state sovereignty and national loyalties. Despite these limitations, functionalism has proven a useful theoretical approach for understanding IGOs and the cooperation many IGOs foster in economic and social issue areas.

International Regimes

A second important middle-level theory in liberalism emerged with the adaptation from international law of the concept of international regimes (introduced in Chapter 1). Defined as "sets of implicit or explicit principles, norms, rules, and decisionmaking procedures around which actors' expectations converge in a given issue area" (Krasner 1982: 1), regime theory has enabled scholars to theorize and analyze the totality of global governance in specific issue areas. It has thereby brought greater recognition among international organization scholars that international law consists not only of formal rules but also norms and soft law that over time may be codified and sometimes institutionalized in IGOs. As Andreas Hasenclever, Peter Mayer, and Volker Rittberger (2000: 3) succinctly summarize: regimes are deliberately constructed, partial international orders on either a regional or a global scale.

Regime theory has been shaped not only by liberalism and neoliberalism but also by realism and neorealism. Some regime theorists have focused on the role of power relations among states in shaping regimes, particularly the role of a hegemonic state such as the United States (or the United Kingdom in the nineteenth century). Others recognize how common interests aid states in enhancing transparency and reducing uncertainty in their environment. Regime theorists have also used constructivist approaches to focus on social relations and the ways the strong patterns of interaction often found in an international regime can affect state interests (Hasenclever, Mayer, and Rittberger 2000). Regime theory has thus been useful in explaining how regimes are created and maintained and how, why, and when they change.

Regime theorists have focused on IGO roles in the creation and maintenance of regimes, while being careful not to equate an IGO with the existence of a regime. By themselves, IGOs do not constitute a regime, but their charters may incorporate principles, norms, rules, decisionmaking processes, and functions that formalize these aspects of a regime. An IGO's decisionmaking processes may be used by member states for further norm and rule creation, for rule enforcement and dispute settlement, for providing collective goods, and for supporting operational activities. Thus, IGOs are one way that habits of cooperation are sustained and expanded.

Identifying international regimes in different issue areas enables scholars to discuss the interactions not only between states and IGOs but also between various IGOs, between IGOs and NGOs, and among noninstitutionalized rules and procedures that have developed over time. Regimes enable scholars to examine informal patterns and ad hoc groupings that enhance international cooperation.

In recent years, as discussed in Chapter 1, scholars have also explored regime complexes in issue areas where multiple regimes overlap, often with conflicting norms, rules, and procedures, such as in food security and human mobility (discussed in Chapter 11). Despite inherent ambiguities, regime theory and the study of international regimes and regime complexes have helped link international institutions and governance by establishing that governance involves more than just IGOs.

Rational Design

Another middle-level theory in liberalism is rational design, a variant that offers insights into why the structures of IGOs vary (or are similar). During the 1990s, there was considerable debate among regime theorists and other liberal scholars regarding the reasons certain types of organizations had particular distinguishing characteristics. A response came from those scholars versed in the rational choice approach to decisionmaking, a simplified and abstract description of players' goals and constraints to predict types of agreements. Barbara Koremenos, Charles Lipson, and Duncan Snidal (2001) offered propositions linking different characteristics of organizations. For example, where an issue involves distributing benefits and costs fairly, organizational membership is apt to be larger. When there are doubts about what other states will do in the future, organizational decisionmaking will tend to be centralized; it will be more decentralized when a few states are negotiating over a narrow range of issues. Likewise, compliance with rules will be easier to enforce if organizations are narrowly focused. When efficiency in making decisions in crisis situations is needed—as in the case of the UN Security Council and a major threat to international peace—small size (i.e., fewer member states) is preferred. This is discussed further in Chapter 4 in connection with debates about Security Council reform.

Rational design theorists applaud the theory's ability to explain many outcomes with a few independent variables. The theory holds up fairly well when tested against actual events. For example, participation in the nuclear nonproliferation regime requires states to accept inspections, a deliberate strategy to reduce uncertainty and defection. Rational design theory has also shown why institutions like the European Common Market—the forerunner of the EU—were heavily centralized but flexible (Oatley 2001).

Critics of rational design raise many questions, however. During negotiations leading to the creation of a new institution, they argue that the decisions are nested in larger political structures and arrangements that are the products of other decisions. Furthermore, it is not easy to know where to start, which decisions matter most, or where the application of power matters most (Duffield 2003). In short, rational design provides little accounting for historical contingencies, accidents, miscalculations, or future possibilities.

One recent variant of rational design incorporates elements of functionalism, in what Jonas Tallberg and colleagues (2013) call rational functionalism, to address the relationship between states, international organizations, and transnational actors. They argue that states and IGO bureaucracies are rational actors that make deliberate choices about access for nonstate actors based on their assessments of what "functional benefits those actors may be able to bring to the organization" (29).

Collective or Public Goods Theory

Another approach in liberalism to explaining governance and cooperation has involved the application of collective or public goods theory. Biologist Garrett Hardin, in his article "The Tragedy of the Commons" (1968), tells the story of a group of herders who share a common grazing area. Each herder finds it economically rational to increase the size of his herd, allowing him to sell more in the market and return more profits. Yet if all herders follow what is individually rational behavior, the group loses; too many animals graze the land and the quality of the pasture deteriorates, which leads to decreased output for all. As each person rationally attempts to maximize his own gain, the collectivity suffers, and eventually all individuals suffer. What Hardin describes—the common grazing area—is a collective good available to all members of the group, regardless of individual contribution.

In the global context, collective or public goods include the "natural commons," such as the high seas, atmosphere, ozone shield, and Antarctica, which have been recognized as the common heritage of humankind since the late 1960s and are not under the sovereignty of any state. More controversial are contemporary concerns about major tropical forest regions, such as in the Amazon and Indonesia, the deforestation of which is now recognized as a major threat to the health of the planet. Collective goods include "human-made global commons" (Kaul 2000: 300) such as universal norms and principles and the internet, as well as "global conditions" ranging from peace and financial stability to environmental sustainability and freedom from poverty.

The use of collective goods involves activities and choices that are interdependent. Decisions by one or a few states have unanticipated negative effects for others. For example, if developed economies had not agreed in the 1980s to discontinue the production and sale of chlorofluorocarbons, this would have affected all countries through long-term depletion of the ozone layer (Chapter 10). With collective goods, market mechanisms are inadequate and alternative forms of governance are needed. A central concern in collective or public goods theory revolves around the question of who provides the public goods. Without some kind of collective action mechanisms, there is a risk that such goods will not be adequately provided. Once they are, the goods exist and all can enjoy them, which creates the problem of free-riding.

Collective goods are easier to provide in small groups than in large groups. Mancur Olson, in *The Logic of Collective Action* (1968: 35), argues that "the larger the group, the farther it will fall short of providing an optimal amount of a collective good." Free-riding and defection are harder to conceal and easier to punish if the group is small.

One alternative is to force nations or peoples to govern collective goods by establishing international organizations with effective police powers that coerce states or individuals to act in a mutually beneficial manner. Elinor Ostrom (1990), however, suggests that the most effective management may be self-governance, with private agents acting as enforcers. Individuals or groups make binding contracts to commit themselves to cooperative strategies and use the enforcers to monitor each other and report infractions.

In short, collective goods theory can be used to explain the role of international agreements, IGOs, and certain international regimes in relation to various collective goods. It is also useful in investigating gaps in international efforts to deal with policy issues.

Thus, collective or public goods theorists, along with other liberal theorists, see IGOs, international law, and international regimes playing a variety of roles in facilitating cooperation and managing public goods in different issue areas. This includes creating some degree of shared interests and providing forums for international cooperation. These contrast with those of realists, who are primarily interested in states' exercise of power and pursuit of national interests. Given those interests, cooperation may not be possible, and effective global governance is unlikely.

Realism

A product of a long philosophical and historical tradition, realism in its various forms is based on the assumption that individuals act rationally to protect their own interests. In the international system, realists see states as the primary actors that act in a unitary way (i.e., domestic politics do not really matter) in pursuit of their national interests, which are generally defined in terms of maximizing power and security relative to other states. States coexist in an anarchic international system characterized by the absence of an authoritative hierarchy. As a result, they must rely primarily on themselves to manage their insecurity through balance of power and deterrence. Because realists see each state as primarily concerned with acquiring more power relative to other states, competition between states is keen, and realists see little basis for cooperation.

For most realists, in the absence of international authority, there are few rules or norms that restrain states, although Hans Morgenthau, generally regarded as the father of modern realism, included chapters on international morality, law, and government in his pathbreaking textbook *Politics Among Nations*. In his view (1967: 219–220): "The main function of these normative systems has been to keep aspirations for power within socially tolerable bounds. . . . Morality, mores, and law intervene in order to protect society against disruption and the individual against enslavement and extinction." But Morgenthau suggested that there had been a weakening of these moral limitations from earlier times, when there was a cohesive international society bound together through elite ties and common morality. Thus, international law and government, in his view, are largely weak and ineffective. For him, international organizations are a tool of states to be used when desired; they can increase or decrease the power of states, but they do not affect the basic characteristics of the international system. Because they reflect the distribution of power among states, they are no more than the sum of their member states. In fact, they are susceptible to manipulation by the great powers. Thus, realists have generally believed that international organizations have no independent effect on state behavior or world politics in general. Still, like Morgenthau, Hedley Bull (1977) in his book *The Anarchical Society: A Study of Order in World Politics* clearly recognized that the nature of anarchy in the international system was not without a degree of order.

Most realist theorists, therefore, do not claim that international cooperation is impossible, only that there are few incentives for states to enter into international arrangements. Since international institutions and agreements have no enforcement power, they have no authority and hence no real power (Gruber 2000). Realists generally do not see nonstate actors such as NGOs and multinational corporations (MNCs) as independent actors in international politics. If they have a role, they tend to support the power and interests of states. To most realists, deterrence and balance of power have proven more effective in maintaining peace than have international institutions.

Deterrence and balance of power are not necessarily static, and the international system may be more dynamic than many realists recognize. One variant of realism—power transition theory—has gained renewed attention with China's rapid rise in the twenty-first century. Kenneth Organski (1968: 338–376), for example, posits that fluctuations in the major determinants of national power, particularly the uneven processes of industrialization, have in the past and can in the future lead to changes in power distribution in the system. Power transition theory helps explain the United Kingdom's rise to dominance in the international system during the nineteenth century as the first country to undergo industrialization and political modernization. Now China's rise challenges the world order that the United States has dominated since 1945, and President Xi Jinping has been clear about his intent, as Elizabeth Economy (2022: 8) notes, to lead "in transforming the institutions, norms, and values that govern relations among international actors, as well as China's place within that system." Power transition theory's emphasis on power positionality is related to a more recent strand of realism: structural or neorealism.

Neorealism or Structural Realism

Among the variants of realism, the most prominent is neorealism, or structural realism, which owes much to Kenneth Waltz's *Theory of International Politics* (1979). The core difference between traditional realists and neorealists lies in the emphasis on the structure of the international system for explaining world politics. The system's structure is determined by the ordering principle, namely, the absence of overarching authority (anarchy) and the distribution of capabilities (power) among states. What matters are states' material capabilities; state identities and interests are largely given and fixed. Anarchy poses a severe constraint on state behavior. But how it is defined, and how much of a constraint it imposes on the possibilities for cooperation and international order, are matters of dispute and some confusion among both neorealists and neoliberals (Baldwin 1993). This has important implications for theorizing about global governance, since most definitions involve questions of government, authority, and governance in some way. Likewise, the way the power distribution shapes state behavior and provides order in international politics, either through balances of power or through a hierarchy of relations between states with unequal power, underscores that order is less a product of state actions, much less of international institutions, than a product of system structure.

In neorealist theory, the possibilities for international cooperation are logically slim, but not impossible. As Waltz (1979: 105) posits, "When faced with the possibility of cooperating for mutual gain, states that feel insecure must ask how the gain will be divided . . . 'Who will gain more?' . . . Even the prospect of large absolute gains for both parties does not elicit their cooperation so long as each fears how the other will use its increased capabilities." Some neorealists believe that relative gains may be more important in security matters than in economic issues, making cooperation more difficult to achieve, harder to maintain, and more dependent on states' power on those issues (Lipson 1984: 15–18). Since anarchy fuels insecurity, states are wary of becoming too dependent on others, preferring greater control and increased capabilities.

Many neorealists recognize the emergence of international regimes and institutions but believe that their importance has been exaggerated. Others, such as John Mearsheimer, are not just skeptical about international institutions, but outright disdainful. In his view, institutions are merely arenas for pursuing power relationships. They have "minimal influence on state behavior and thus hold little promise for promoting stability in the post–Cold War world" (Mearsheimer 1994–1995: 7). Although not all neorealists would go as far as this, many clearly believe that international institutions do not have independent effects worth studying. Although there are many criticisms of neorealism's inability to explain system change and failure to incorporate variables other than the structure of the international system, it continues to have a strong influence on IR scholars.

Strategic or Rational Choice Theory

Two middle-level theories derived from realism that have addressed issues of international cooperation more directly are strategic or rational choice and hegemonic stability theory. Strategic or rational choice theory has enjoyed wide usage in political science and economics. It assumes that preferences are deduced from objective and material conditions of states.

Predicated on the view that markets are the most efficient mechanism of human behavior, strategic choice theorists often use the language of microeconomic theory to explain state choices. They also acknowledge that market imperfections may arise. Information may be incomplete, or transaction costs may be too high. Then organizations and institutions can play key roles. They may also act as constraints on choice.

Lloyd Gruber (2000) is one scholar who is intrigued by the fact that states find it rational to take part in international arrangements, even though they would prefer the original, precooperation status quo. He argues that states fear being left behind; they want to join the bandwagon, even when it is not directly in their best interests. Hence, they may believe that the status quo—not participating in such agreements—is not an option and agree to conform to the rules of the game.

Key to rational or strategic choice theory is the assumption that state actions are based on rational calculations about subjective expected utility based on estimates of others' capabilities and likely intentions. From this perspective, Keohane (1993: 288) suggests, "international institutions exist largely because they facilitate self-interested cooperation by reducing uncertainty, thus stabilizing expectations." An analysis of rational state action in Europe, for example, must take Europe's many international institutions into account.

Theories of Hegemonic Stability and Great Power Concerts

Middle-level hegemonic stability theory is rooted in the realist tradition but was developed in the 1970s and 1980s to answer the question of how the liberal open world economy was created and has been maintained. The theory's answer is that this has occurred through the power and leadership of a dominant or hegemonic state that uses its position in a liberal international economy in particular ways. As Robert Gilpin (1987: 72) noted, "Hegemony without a liberal commitment to the market economy is more likely to lead to imperial systems and the imposition of political and economic restrictions on lesser powers."

Hegemonic stability theory is based on the premise that an open market economy is a collective or public good (Kindleberger 1973) that cannot be sustained without the actions of a dominant economy. When there is a predominant state with "control over raw materials, control over sources of capital, control over markets, and competitive advantages in the production of highly valued goods" (Keohane 1984: 32), it has the means to exercise leadership over other economies and to use its economic power for leverage over other states. If such a dominant power is committed to an open, liberal world economy based on nondiscrimination and free markets, it can use its position to guarantee provision of the collective good—an open trading system and stable monetary system. In doing so, it must perform several tasks, including creating norms and rules, preventing cheating and free-riding, encouraging others to share the costs of maintaining the system, managing the monetary system, using its own dynamism as an engine of growth for the rest of the system, and responding to crises. As strategic choice theorists would argue, the hegemon may also be engaging in behavior that perpetuates its power and position.

To date, there are only two examples of such hegemonic leadership. The first occurred during the nineteenth century, when the United Kingdom used its dominant position to create an era of free trade among major economic powers. The second began after World War II, when the United States established the Bretton Woods system to promote international trade and investment. An important part of its role has been the willingness to pay the costs to make its vision of a liberal economic order a reality (discussed in Chapter 8).

Some have questioned whether a theory based on two cases is sufficient to explain why a dominant state would undertake a leadership role or be committed to liberal values. These have depended, Ruggie (1982) noted, on the particular hegemon's "social purpose" and commitment to "embedded liberalism."

The persistence of the liberal international economic order in the face of the economic dislocations of the 1970s and 1980s led Keohane (1984) to explore the consequences of declining hegemony. He found that, in a view compatible with the liberal institutionalist position, cooperation may persist, even if the hegemon's power declines and it is not performing a leadership role. A residue of common interests and the norms of the regime help maintain it, for "regimes are more readily maintained than established" (Kindleberger 1986: 8). Such views have contributed significantly to understanding the bases of states' choices and the role of power, especially hegemonic power, in the creation of international regimes.

Although most realists have little to say about the varieties of global governance, more recent work on hegemonic stability and great power behavior evidences cross-fertilization among different theories. These approaches lead researchers to look at the role of dominant states in global governance outcomes, and how other actors affect governance processes. The benefits of cross-fertilization—in this case, from sociology—are evident when we examine the contribution of constructivism to global governance.

Social Constructivism

Since the 1990s, social constructivism has been particularly important for studying global governance, most notably the role of norms and institutions. Although there are many variants, all constructivists agree that the behavior of individuals, states, and other actors is shaped by shared beliefs, socially constructed rules, and cultural practices. They argue that what actors do, how they interrelate, and how others interpret their behavior create and can change the meaning of norms. The approach has deep roots in sociology and social theory.

At the core of constructivist approaches is a concern with identity and interests and how these can change—a belief that ideas, values, norms, and shared beliefs matter, that how individuals talk about the world shapes practices, and that humans are capable of changing the world by changing ideas. Whereas realists treat states' interests and identity as given, constructivists believe they are socially constructed—that is, influenced by culture, norms, ideas, and domestic and international interactions. Thus, after World War II Germany reoriented its identity to multilateralism, joining the North Atlantic Treaty Organization and European institutions with US encouragement. For constructivists, then, states do not have identities or national interests before interactions with others. As Alexander Wendt (1995: 81) explains, "the social construction of international politics is to analyze how processes of interaction produce and reproduce the social structures—cooperative or conflictual—that shape actors' identities and interests and the significance of their material contexts."

Constructivists put a great deal of importance on institutions as embodied in norms, practices, and formal organizations. The most important institution in international society is sovereignty because it determines the identity of states. Yet constructivists criticize those who see sovereignty as unchanging and point to various transformations in understandings of sovereignty. To illustrate how sovereignty determines the identity of states, however, one need only consider how states such as Somalia retain their statehood and continue to be members of IGOs even when they are widely seen as "failed" for their inability to control their borders and govern their people.

Among the key norms affecting state behavior is multilateralism. In *Multilateralism Matters*, Ruggie (1993) and others examine how the shared expectations surrounding this norm affect the behavior of states. Other studies have examined the influence of norms and principled beliefs on international outcomes, including the evolution of the international human rights regime (Risse, Ropp, and Sikkink 1999), the spread of weapons taboos (Tannenwald 2007), and humanitarian intervention (Finnemore 2003).

In examining international organizations, constructivists seek to uncover the social content of organizations, the dominant norms that govern behavior and shape interests, and how these interests influence actors. International organizations may serve as agents of social construction, as norm entrepreneurs trying to change social understandings (Finnemore and Sikkink 2001). They can be teachers and creators of norms, socializing states to accept new values and political goals (Finnemore 1996b). The UN

Educational, Scientific, and Cultural Organization, for example, "taught" developing states the relevance of establishing science bureaucracies as a necessary component of being a modern state. The World Bank put the concept of poverty alleviation on international and national agendas in the late 1960s as it "sold" poverty alleviation to members through a mixture of persuasion and coercion, in the process redefining what states were supposed to do to ameliorate the situation.

For constructivists, then, IGOs have real power. Michael Barnett and Martha Finnemore (2005: 162), for example, argue that IGOs "construct the social world in which cooperation and choice take place. They help define the interests that states and other actors come to hold and do so in ways compatible with liberalism and a liberal global order. These are important exercises of power." With respect to the role of IGO bureaucracies, Barnett and Finnemore note that the authority of these organizations and their secretariats "lies in their ability to present themselves as impersonal and neutral—as not exercising power but instead serving others" (2004: 21).

Some constructivists have focused on the potential of international organizations such as the European Union to socialize individual policymakers and states. Jeffrey Checkel (2005), for example, explores the different mechanisms, including strategic calculation, role-playing, and normative suasion, that connect organizations to socializing outcomes. When the norms of the institution become deeply rooted and thus internalized, actors' identities can be transformed and interests changed.

Thus, to constructivists, international organizations are purposive actors with independent effects on international relations. They have been important to the processes of changing understandings and behavior with respect to poverty, humanitarianism, colonialism, slavery, environmentally sustainable development, and other problems. Although most constructivists have focused on positive outcomes such as decolonization, human rights norms, and poverty alleviation, others have reminded us that IGOs may also be dysfunctional and act contrary to the interests of their members. They may pursue particularistic goals, competing over turf, budgets, and staff. They may have bureaucratic cultures that tolerate inefficient practices, lack accountability, and engage in mission-defeating behaviors (Barnett and Finnemore 1999).

Critical Theories

There is another set of IR theories that challenge conventional wisdom and offer alternative frameworks for understanding the world. They fall under an amorphous category labeled "critical theories." Critical theorists seek to understand the making of history—the forces that transform history. Among the most prominent are Marxist and neo-Marxist theories, and their derivative, dependency theory. Those rooted in Marxism share a historicism that drives questions of how the present international order came into being and what forces are at work to change it. Other critical theories reflect the rise of feminist perspectives on the importance of the roles of women in the world and how social (and political) structures may reflect deep-seated masculine dominance. Still others identify as postcolonial theorists emphasizing how colonialism and postcolonialism affect present-day structures and institutions. Understanding how structural changes occur and the role of social forces is central to these critical theories.

Marxist and Neo-Marxist Theories

Although Marxism was discredited with the demise of the Soviet Union and the triumph of capitalism, it is still an important perspective for describing the hierarchy in the international system and the role of economics in determining that hierarchy. It still influences the thinking of many in the developing world, whose colonial past and experience with capitalism are characterized by poverty and economic disadvantage. Marxist and neo-Marxist critical theories contribute important perspectives to understanding IR and global governance through frameworks for linking politics, economics, social forces, and structures of order.

Like realism and liberalism, Marxism comprises a set of core ideas that unite its variants. These include a grounding in historical analysis, the primacy of economic forces in explaining political and social phenomena, the central role of the production process, the particular character of capitalism as a global mode of production, and the importance of social or economic class in defining actors. The evolution of the production process is a basis for explaining the relationship between production, social relations, and power. According to Karl Marx (1818–1883), a clash would inevitably occur between the capitalist class (the bourgeoisie) and the workers (the proletariat). From that class struggle would come a new social order. Interpreting this in the context of international relations, Robert Cox (1986: 220) noted: "Changes in the organization of production generate new social forces which, in turn, bring about changes in the structure of states and . . . [alter] the problematic of world order."

Marxist views of the structure of the global system, and hence of global governance, are rooted in these ideas about the relationships of class, the capitalist mode of production, and power. The hierarchical structure is a by-product of the spread of global capitalism that privileges some states, organizations, groups, and individuals and imposes significant constraints on others. Thus, developed countries have expanded economically (and in an earlier era politically, through imperialism), enabling them to sell goods and export surplus wealth they could not absorb at home. Simultaneously, developing countries have become increasingly constrained and dependent on the actions of the developed.

Variants of Marxism emphasize the techniques of domination and suppression that arise from the uneven economic development inherent in the capitalist system. The influence of an Italian Marxist, Antonio Gramsci (1891–1937), on critical theorists and some neoliberal institutionalists, however, has been considerable, given Gramsci's interpretation of hegemony as a relationship of consent to political and ideological leadership, not domination by force. Thus Cox (1992b: 140) argued that the foundation of hegemonic order "derives from the ways of doing and thinking of the dominant social strata of the dominant state or states . . . [with] the acquiescence of the dominant social strata of other states."

These views have important implications for neo-Marxist theorizing about contemporary global governance. For example, in Craig Murphy's view (2000: 799), global governance is "a predictable institutional response not to the interests of a fully formed class, but to the overall logic of industrial capitalism." Robert Cox (1986) and Stephen Gill (1994) have emphasized the importance of "globalizing elites" in the restructuring of the global political economy and global governance. These elites are found in the key economic institutions (the IMF, the World Trade Organization, and World Bank), in finance ministries of G-7 countries, in the headquarters of MNCs, in private IR councils (e.g., the US-based Council on Foreign Relations), and in major business schools. True to a classical Marxist dialectical process, transnational social forces backing neoliberalism are increasingly challenged by those resisting globalization, as well as by environmental, feminist, and other social movements that in Murphy's (2000) view constitute a new locus for class analysis and a potential source of future change.

Marxists and neo-Marxists view international law and organizations as products of dominant states, dominant ideas, and the interests of the capitalist class. Some view them as instruments of capitalist domination imposed on others. The Gramscian view sees international organizations as a means to get others to consent to domination through shared ideas. Murphy (1994) argues that they have been instrumental in the development of the modern capitalist state by facilitating industrial change and the development of liberal ideology. Cox (1992a: 3) also sees them as being concerned with "longer-term questions of global structural change and . . . how international organizations . . . can help shape that change in a consensually desirable direction."

Marxists and neo-Marxists are almost uniformly normative in their orientation. They see capitalism as "bad," its structure and mode of production as exploitative. They have clear positions about what should be done to ameliorate inequities. Thus, they are proponents of major structural change in international relations.

Dependency Theory
Dependency theorists—particularly those writing in the 1950s from Latin America, such as Raul Prebisch, Enzo Faletto, Fernando Henrique Cardoso,

and Andre Gunder Frank—sought to understand why development was benefiting rich Northern countries, rather than the poorer South, and why that gap was widening. They hypothesized that the basic terms of trade were unequal between the developing and the developed world, partially as a consequence of colonialism and neocolonialism, and partially because MNCs and international banks based in developed countries were hamstringing dependent states. The latter organizations were thought to help establish and maintain dependency relations. They were also viewed as agents of penetration, not benign actors (as liberals would characterize them) nor as marginal actors (as realists believe). Dependency theorists argue that public and private international organizations can forge transnational relationships with elites in the developing economies (the "comprador class"), linking domestic elites in exploiter and exploited countries in a symbiotic relationship.

Many dependency theorists argued that the solution was to disengage national economies from the international economy, foster industrial growth in the South through import substitution, protect internal markets from competition, and seek major changes in international economic institutions. Only when countries in the South had reached a certain level of development could they fully participate in the international economy. These views had strong appeal and shaped the agenda of developing countries in the United Nations during the 1960s and 1970s. In essence, dependency theorists argued that development could not take place without fundamental changes in international economic relations to redress inequalities of power and wealth.

Dependency theorists share the view of other Marxist-derived theories that international organizations are generally the tools of capitalist classes and states. Likewise, MNCs have been viewed as instruments of capitalist exploitation and mechanisms of domination that perpetuate underdevelopment.

Even with the demise of the Soviet Union in the 1990s, Marxism and its variants did not vanish. Some aspects of these critical theories have permeated debates over globalization, particularly among opponents of globalization, including those who oppose corporate control over the economy and those who are trying to strengthen protection for workers, small farmers, poor people, and women. Stagnating economic and social conditions and the widening inequality globally have also fueled renewed interest in the perspectives that critical theories offer. There is also strong evidence that Chinese policies are heavily influenced by Marxist theory.

Critical Feminism
Among the strains of critical theory are feminists who argue that studying gender involves more than just counting women in elite positions or programs targeting women. Gender permeates all international structures. International relations, with its emphasis on states and international organ-

izations, diplomacy and war, historically ignored the roles of homes, families, communities, ordinary people, and women. Studying international relations as exclusively the public domain means that a whole range of private human activity is simply ignored, even though it is at the heart of development, human rights, human security, and identity (Peterson 2003).

Critical feminists are especially interested in highlighting how contemporary international economic rules—as enforced by the wealthiest states, the IMF, private bond-rating agencies such as Standard & Poor's, and private investors generally—create a unique burden on women. During the Covid-19 pandemic, feminist scholars called attention to the undue burdens borne by women as a result of lockdowns, virtual schooling for children, and so on. They argue that a neoliberal capitalist model of economic governance puts pressure on states to reduce social spending and reduce protections on local goods from foreign competition, with the immediate result that the poor are exposed to the ravages of global competition.

Critical theorists see women as particularly vulnerable to exploitation when the public sector fails to provide essential services or is adversely affected by globalization. They point to the fact that the overwhelming majority of trafficked persons are women. Women experience a double exploitation because of how the world economy is defined and managed. Even the "mainstreaming of women" in development programs, as advocated by liberal feminists, is often overwhelmed, they argue, by the grand strategy of promoting economic liberalization and austerity (True 2011).

Skeptics, including other feminists, have challenged the tone of some critical feminist writing, arguing that the exploitative structures they describe are not automatically the fault of men, but both women and men are part of the problem and part of the solution. In particular, neoliberal economists emphasize the importance of market forces as a means of disciplining profligate states and promoting the efficient use of resources, both of which will benefit all citizens, including women.

Postcolonial Theory

Another critical theory—postcolonialism—is an outgrowth of the decolonization of much of the world in the 1950s and 1960s, and in some ways it is a tool to critique other IR theories. It is a way of understanding the world and illuminating the effects of both colonization and decolonization. Postcolonial scholars argue that today's international organizations are reflections of the colonial past (Hanchey 2018). The UN, for example, is seen as a venue for the continuation of domination, intervention, and exploitation for the former colonial powers of the Global North, given that some founders were the major colonial powers at the time. Its activities as well as those of other international organizations are derided as neocolonial (Wickens and Sandline 2007). Postcolonialists suggest that to critically examine the still largely Eurocentric international system, there needs to be recognition of how the former colonial powers continue to dominate the UN and many other IGOs and NGOs (Seth 2011).

Securitization Studies

Another critical theory, securitization studies, primarily focuses on a critique of the increasing role of security in public policy. This began with criticisms of the military-industrial complex in the 1940s and concerns that states were exaggerating security threats to feed the financial needs of those involved in producing weapons (Lasswell 1941). Following the September 11, 2001, terror attacks on the United States, scholarship linking migration and security ballooned with the concern that migration could be a conduit for terrorism (Rudolph 2003; Tirman 2004). Although certain issues clearly have a security dimension, securitization scholars assert that states and international organizations seek to exercise increasing control over their political environment by defining certain issues (such as health, food, and migration) as a matter of security. In so doing, they remove the object from traditional political constraints and exert extraordinary powers in its defense (Buzan, Waever, and de Wilde 1998).

Critical security studies, as Murray (2022: 20) notes in reference to migration, "elucidates how human security challenges are linked to the social construction of migration as a security threat. It problematizes the migration-security nexus by rejecting the assumption that security is objective and identifiable, and that migration poses an inherent threat to what some scholars call 'ontological security.'" These studies tend to cluster into one of two approaches. The Copenhagen School primarily emphasizes securitization as a discursive process of threat construction (Buzan, Waever, and de Wilde 1998), while the Paris School links the discursive processes to institutional practices, such as government bureaucracies' tendencies to categorize and label migrants to justify certain policies such as border controls adopted for security reasons (Squire and Huysman 2017).

Securitization studies have become relevant to global governance and international organization with the emergence of the concept of "human security" as an umbrella for categorizing a variety of issues from hunger (food insecurity) to health, climate change, human trafficking, and migration. One indication of this is the chapter in this book dedicated to these human security issues (Chapter 11).

Proclaiming an issue a matter of human security demands a person or organization with legal or moral authority and a capacity to act on the statement. Although governments and IGOs—including the UN, the UN Office of Drugs and Crime, and the EU—have portrayed the effort to limit human and drug trafficking in some parts of the world as a way to promote security, the rhetoric has not always been accepted by local authorities (Jackson 2006).

Determining what is a threat to security also involves defining what is threatened (a state? a region? the planet? a large number of people?). It also requires addressing how societies, states, IGOs, NGOs, or other entities should respond to such threats. How IGOs in particular respond is likely to be shaped by the nature of the processes, cultures, and dynamics in these organizations. We turn to look at a group of theories that aim to analyze and explain these processes.

Theories of Organizational Interactions

Interstate relations are not the only interactions that are important for understanding international cooperation and global governance. Relevant middle-level theories that provide insights for studying interactions among the various global governance actors and in specific organizations have been drawn from sociology and economics. These theories see organizations as actors making choices that are influenced by their bureaucratic routines and cultures and interacting with their environments, including other organizations and their member states.

Interorganizational Processes

The proliferation of actors in global governance has made it imperative to study interorganizational relations. Sociologists have long contended that for all types of organizations, the most important part of the environment is their cooperative and conflictual relations with other organizations. Organizational interdependence emerges from the shared need for resources (money, specialized skills, and markets), overlapping missions, or the desire to add new specialties at lower cost. In response, organizations may innovate to exclude rivals or increase coordination and cooperation. Thus, interorganization theorists examine how and why organizations, often working in the same environment or on the same type of problems, may both clash and cooperate.

Interorganization theorists are also interested in the dependence of one organization on another. For example, the UN Security Council needs resources and information to fulfill its mission, and this dependence limits its autonomy. Similarly, the regional development banks may depend on the World Bank for cofinancing large projects, setting development priorities, and technical expertise. In the 1980s, the African Development Bank found itself subservient to the World Bank, having fewer economic resources and a less visible field presence and being the last to be repaid. This dependence was reinforced by the attitude of the African countries (Mingst 1987: 291).

Coordination problems between and among IGOs, such as those among economic and social agencies in the UN system, or among NGOs such as the humanitarian relief groups, form another group of interorganizational problems. Chapter 4 explores how the UN Economic and Social Council was intended to play a central coordinating role for the system but has lacked the resources and clout to do so effectively. Humanitarian crises in the 1990s and the problem of too many groups trying to help led to the creation of the UN Office for Coordination of Humanitarian Affairs in 1998 as the lead humanitarian agency coordinating efforts in the field. The number and scale of contemporary humanitarian crises ranging from the conflicts in Yemen, Ukraine, and Mali to the persistent floods of migrants in the Americas and the Mediterranean require enormous coordination efforts with the UN system, between UN-related organizations and the EU, and with a multitude of humanitarian NGOs.

Networks

Part of understanding how organizations interact is recognizing that they may do so within broader networks. The concept of networks comes from sociology, but it has been appropriated into thinking about global governance. Harold Jacobson was the first to identify the relevance of networks for the field, as was reflected in the title of his groundbreaking textbook *Networks of Interdependence: International Organizations and the Global Political System* (1984). The sociological literature on networks examines the various links between organizations and individuals (private and public), domestically and internationally. Often there is a linchpin organization in the network, an organization able to mobilize coalitions on particular issues or control the process of bargaining. Such organizations have seldom been delegated such authority but are able to legitimate their actions with respect to the specific issue area (Jönsson 1986).

Various types of networks (as introduced in Chapter 1) are examined in this book. Anne-Marie Slaughter (2004), for example, looks at networks of government officials, judges, legislators, and police that make up what she calls the "new world order." Miles Kahler (2009: 3) examines networks as both structures and actors in global governance and networked politics as "new forms of governance in international relations." Anna Ohanyan (2012: 372, 377) links network theory and sociological institutionalism in a theoretical approach for studying NGOs and their positive or negative agency that she calls "network institutionalism." She argues that the network approach "is a useful bridge between the NGO studies and dominant IR theories that generally treat NGOs as inconsequential and marginal in world politics" (372). Network structure, she notes, matters in "shaping the extent of NGO autonomy and agency . . . [while] network institutionalism focuses on the network position of an NGO as an important variable that can explain the extent of NGO agency in world politics" (377).

Transnational advocacy networks have become increasingly important to global governance (Chapter 6). Such networks share "the centrality of values or principled ideas, the belief that individuals can make a difference, the creative use of information, and the employment by nongovernmental actors of sophisticated political strategies in targeting their campaigns"; they are "bound together by shared values, a common discourse, and dense exchanges of information and services" (Keck and Sikkink 1998: 2). These networks also try to set the terms of international and domestic debate, influence international and state-level policy outcomes, and alter the behavior of states, international organizations, and other interested parties. The International Campaign to Ban Landmines is a prominent example of a transnational advocacy network from the late 1990s; a contemporary example is the International Campaign to Abolish Nuclear Weapons. Both are discussed in Chapter 7. The human rights, environmental, and women's movements further illustrate the phenomenon. Network analysis encompasses international and domestic actors and processes and examines how individuals and groups are linked and what strategies they use to promote their goals.

Principal-Agent (PA) Theory

PA theory is particularly important for analyzing the relationship between IGOs and their member states as well as between decisionmaking bodies in IGOs and their secretariats or bureaucrats. This theory originated in economists' work on the theory of the firm, which was adopted by those studying US government bureaucracies and more recently has been adapted to the study of IGOs and NGOs. PA theorists posit that principals (that is, decisionmakers) delegate authority to an agent (e.g., a bureaucracy), empowering the agent to act on behalf of the principals. Principals delegate such authority for a number of reasons: to benefit from the agent's specialized knowledge, enhance certitude, resolve disputes, or enhance their own credibility. But principals need to be careful of the agents taking independent actions that the principals do not approve. Much of the PA literature discusses how principals control agents (establishing rules, monitoring and reporting, using checks and balances) and how agents can become independent, autonomous actors.

Scholars of IGOs and NGOs have turned to PA theory to examine how states as collective principals delegate authority and control to IGOs and how the agents (IGOs and NGOs) can exert autonomy (Hawkins et al. 2006; Oestreich 2012). The theory has been used to show how agents interpret mandates, reinterpret rules, expand permeability to third parties, and create barriers to principals' monitoring. Much of this literature has focused on the UN Secretary-General, the IMF, the World Bank, and the EU.

In using PA theory to look at NGOs, some have found that NGOs may be crucial intermediaries between states and IGOs but not independent actors that change preferences (Lake and McCubbins 2006: 341, 368). Others suggest the ways that NGOs have agency—the ability to choose among different courses of action, learn from experience, and effect change, which may be independent from states and also dysfunctional (Cooley and Ron 2002).

Like social constructivists, PA theorists are concerned with examining the degree of independence and autonomy of international organizations and their bureaucrats. Although social constructivists explain some cases of IGO autonomy by referring to the authority and expertise of their bureaucracies, PA theorists find that principals will endeavor to limit their agents' autonomy and that agents act rationally and strategically when they try to expand their authority. PA theory ties closely to another group of theories looking at intraorganizational processes.

Intraorganizational Processes

This group of middle-level theories focuses on what happens in organizations themselves. Two have particular relevance for the study of international organizations: theories of organizational culture and theories of organizational adaptation and learning.

Organizational culture. Over time, organizations tend to develop cultures of their own, independent from and different than the cultures of their members. In the 1970s, sociologists and anthropologists began to study these cultures rather than seeing organizations only as technical, rational, impersonal mechanisms. During the 1980s, it became popular to think of organizations as autonomous sites of power with their own particular cultures, norms, and values. Thus, organizations might become agents themselves, not just structures through which actors operate. Organization theorists created typologies of organizational cultures and showed how these can change over time (Hawkins 1997).

International organization scholars, particularly constructivists, have borrowed the notion of organizational culture, believing that "the rules, rituals, and beliefs that are embedded in the organization (and its subunits) . . . [have] important consequences for the way individuals who inhabit that organization make sense of the world" (Barnett and Finnemore 1999: 719). For example, the practice of UN peacekeeping includes sets of rules designed to maximize the probability of success. Those rules, including requirements of consent and impartiality, became embedded in the peacekeeping culture of the UN Secretariat and have provided an explanation for why the UN Secretariat misperceived the unfolding genocide in Rwanda in 1994 (Barnett and Finnemore 2004). The World Bank has been shown to have a distinctive organizational culture, since many of its professional staff have graduate degrees in economics or finance from US or UK institutions (Weaver 2008: 77). Organizational cultures, then, can explain some organizational behaviors, although they can also be subject to change over time.

Organizational adaptation and learning. Organization theorists have been particularly interested in examining how organizations evolve. Ernst Haas (1990) delineates two such processes. In the first, organizations adapt by adding new activities to their agendas without actually examining or changing underlying bases of the organization and its values. The organization muddles through and change occurs incrementally. Such was the case when the UN took on added peacekeeping tasks in the early 1990s, including election monitoring, humanitarian aid delivery, and protection of populations threatened by ethnic cleansing and genocide. Only with the failures in Somalia and Bosnia (discussed in Chapter 7) did the UN Secretariat and member states look seriously at the lessons to be learned from the incremental, unplanned changes.

The second kind of change process is based on the premise that organizations can, in fact, learn. With learning, members or staff question earlier beliefs and develop new processes. Thus, learning involves redefinition of organizational purposes, reconceptualization of problems, articulation of new ends, and organizational change based on new, underlying consensual knowledge. Such has been the case with the evolution of World Bank programs from an initial emphasis on infrastructure projects to poverty alleviation and good governance (Chapter 8). The Security Council's adoption of Resolution 1325 on women, peace, and security in 2001 required significant organizational learning and adaptation to implement the Women, Peace, and Security Agenda (Chapter 7). Similarly, following problems with the global response to the 2014–2015 Ebola epidemic in West Africa (Chapter 11), the World Health Organization endeavored to change its procedures for declaring a health crisis of international concern. Other examples abound.

Organizational theories from sociology and economics enable us to probe deeper into international organizations by helping us understand the interorganizational and intraorganizational processes. Increasingly, scholars are using multiple theoretical perspectives, enhancing our knowledge in new ways.

IR Theory and Global Governance

Subsequent chapters use these various theories when appropriate. In Chapters 3 and 5, functionalism explains much of the history of UN specialized agencies and the EU. In Chapters 7 through 11, specific international regimes are examined, along with their major principles, rules, and decision-making processes and the cultures of related IGOs, various networks, and intraorganizational processes. Case studies help illustrate how different theories are used by international organization scholars. In Chapter 7, realist theory helps us understand the difficulties that international institutions have in addressing threats to states' peace and security and most particularly with Russia's 2022 invasion of Ukraine. Chapter 8 considers how hegemonic stability and critical theories have influenced analysis of economic governance issues. In Chapter 9, liberal theory and constructivism contribute to our understanding of the evolution of human rights norms and efforts to promote greater respect for those norms. In Chapter 10, collective goods theory forms a central focus for analyzing international efforts to address environmental problems. In Chapter 11, constructivism and securitization theories are key to analyzing human security governance. Throughout the book, middle-level interorganizational and intraorganizational theories help us understand how different international organizations function and the connections among different actors and their roles.

These theories also are linked to a variety of research methods used by scholars to study international organizations and global governance. We have not discussed these methods in detail, but the books and articles from which we draw have utilized both long-established and newer methods from the social sciences and humanities. As the editors of the first book focusing on research methods for IOs note, "many IO scholars have recently called for a renewal in the way IOs are approached, stressing the need for innovative tools to capture the intergovernmental and transnational world . . . the same scholars have highlighted the difficulty to conduct research on IOs, due to the need for 'discretion' and access barriers" (Badache, Kimber, and Maertens 2023: ix). Potential methods have expanded greatly—from traditional archival work, participant observation, and analyses of UN roll call voting to newer possibilities such as focus groups, virtual interviews, infographics, and analyses of social media. Therefore, we challenge you, our readers, not only to "think theoretically" about IOs and global governance, but to be creative in devising methods for your studies.

Suggested Further Reading

Badache, Fanny, Leah R. Kimber, and Lucile Maertens, eds. (2023) *International Organizations and Research Methods: An Introduction*. Ann Arbor, MI: University of Michigan Press.

Barkin, J. Samuel. (2013) *International Organization: Theories and Institutions*, 2nd edition. New York: Palgrave Macmillan.

Barnett, Michael, and Martha Finnemore. (2004) *Rules for the World: International Organizations in Global Politics*. Ithaca, NY: Cornell University Press.

Hawkins, Darren G., David A. Lake, Daniel L. Nielson, and Michael J. Tierney, eds. (2006) *Delegation and Agency in International Organizations*. Cambridge: Cambridge University Press.

Rai, Shirin M., and Georgina Waylen, eds. (2008) *Global Governance: Feminist Perspectives*. New York: Palgrave Macmillan.

Rittberger, Volker, ed., with Peter Mayer. (1993) *Regime Theory and International Relations*. Oxford: Clarendon.

Young, Robert J. C. (2001) *Postcolonialism: An Historical Introduction*. London: Blackwell.

Wendt, Alexander. (1999) *Social Theory of International Politics*. Cambridge: Cambridge University Press.

3

International Organizations and the Foundations of Global Governance

THE ANTECEDENTS FOR CONTEMPORARY INTERNATIONAL ORGANIZATIONS and global governance lie in early efforts by political communities to establish norms and rules for interacting with their neighbors. The Greek city-states sought to establish permanent protective alliances to address conflict issues and follow established rules. The Hanseatic League (1200s–1400s) was formed to facilitate trade and the interaction among a group of Northern European cities on the Baltic and North Seas. Similarly, the Kingdom of Naples and Sicily, the Papal States, and the city-states of Florence, Venice, and Milan established a system for regularizing diplomacy and commercial interaction in the fourteenth and fifteenth centuries. Many of these early practices persisted as the contemporary state system evolved, providing some foundation for the later development of more institutionalized forms of governance.

The State System and Its Weaknesses: The Process of International Organization

International relations (IR) scholars date the contemporary state system from 1648, when the Treaty of Westphalia ended the Thirty Years War. Although most of the more than 100 articles of the treaty dealt with allocating the spoils of war, other provisions proved groundbreaking. Articles 64, 65, and 67 established several key principles of a new state system: territorial sovereignty; the right of the state (prince or ruler) to choose its religion and determine its own domestic policies; and the prohibition of interference from supranational authorities like the Catholic Church or Holy Roman Empire. The treaty marked the end of rule by religious authority in Europe and the emergence of secular states. With secular authority came the principle of the territorial integrity of states that were legally equal and sovereign participants in the international system.

73

Sovereignty was (and remains) the core concept in this state system. As French philosopher Jean Bodin (1530–1596) put it, sovereignty is "the distinguishing mark of the sovereign that he cannot in any way be subject to the commands of another, for it is he who makes law for the subject, abrogates law already made, and amends obsolete law" (1967: 25). Although there is no supreme arbiter among states, Bodin acknowledged that sovereignty may be limited by divine law or natural law, by the type of regime, or even by promises to the people.

During this period, Hugo Grotius, the early Dutch legal scholar discussed in Chapter 2, rejected the concept that states have complete freedom to do whatever they wish. Thus, even in the seventeenth century, the meaning of state sovereignty was contested. More recently, Stephen Krasner (1993: 235) has argued: "The actual content of sovereignty, the scope of authority that states can exercise, has always been contested. The basic organizing principle of sovereignty—exclusive control over territory—has been persistently challenged by the creation of new institutional forms that better meet specific national needs." Although breaches of sovereignty occur continuously through treaties, contracts, coercion, and imposition, Krasner asserts that there is no alternative conception of international system organization. Other scholars, such as James Rosenau (1997: 217–236) see states as vulnerable to demands from below—decentralizing tendencies, including domestic constituencies and nonstate actors—and from above, including globalization processes and international organizations. They have to contend with a variety of new actors and processes that confound and constrain them, limiting authority and challenging the notion of state sovereignty, and hence the state system based on that principle. Noting shifting interpretations of sovereignty in the 1990s, UN Secretary-General Kofi Annan stated in his 1999 annual address to the UN General Assembly, "State sovereignty, in its most basic sense, is being redefined by the forces of globalization and international cooperation" (Annan 1999). Kalevi Holsti (2004: 138), however, has pointed out, that "state capacity in the contemporary world varies greatly from the very weak to the very strong. But that does not make them less or more sovereign."

One significant indicator of the continuing importance of sovereignty is the importance that states attach to borders not just as "jurisdictional divisions," according to Beth Simmons (2019: 257), but as "institutions of governance." She notes how much more important border security and states' physical presence at borders have become in many parts of the world; how much more of the world's population now lives near border crossings; and how much borders matter with regard to legal and illicit movement of goods, people, terrorists, and traffickers. In short, Simmons argues (2019: 266), "Governing borders has become a complex matter," one for which there is limited public international law and increasingly dense state practice.

States' attachment to sovereignty and their borders may be strong, but the weaknesses of the state system became increasingly apparent during the nineteenth century with growing international trade, migration, democratization, technological innovation, and other developments that increased interdependence and highlighted the limitations imposed by state sovereignty. These changes gave rise to the process of international organization—the historical process that "represents a secular trend toward the systematic development of an enterprising quest for political means of making the world safe for human habitation" (Claude 1964: 405). The concrete manifestations of that process, which continues today, have been the creation of international organizations, including intergovernmental and nongovernmental organizations.

This chapter provides a historical overview of the process of international organization since the mid-nineteenth century. The process has been propelled and shaped by the weaknesses of the state system and by major power wars, technological changes, European imperialism, economic development and growing interdependence associated with industrial capitalism, and now globalization. It has also been shaped by the decolonization process that ended European and US imperial rule in Latin America, Asia, and Africa, and the emergence of a host of governance challenges in the late twentieth and early twenty-first centuries. Subsequent chapters provide greater depth on the UN system, regional organizations, and nongovernmental organizations (NGOs).

Early Governance Innovations: The Legacy of the Nineteenth Century

In the nineteenth century, the process of international organization was stimulated by several key trends. Napoleon's defeat in 1815 ended the upheavals that followed the French Revolution and Napoleon's effort to create a French empire in Europe. The emergence of five major European powers—Austria-Hungary, Great Britain, France, Prussia, and Russia—ushered in an era of relative peace that lasted for almost a century. Industrialization, beginning in England, spread to all parts of the continent, resulting in expanded commerce and trade among the European countries and between European states and their colonies. Technological innovations such as the telegraph gave rise to practical problems in interstate relations and the need to establish common standards. State-to-state interactions became more frequent and intense, while the spread of democratic ideas empowered people to organize nongovernmental groups to address humanitarian needs, workers' rights, and private business interests.

In a pioneering textbook on international organization, *Swords into Plowshares,* Inis Claude (1964) described three major innovations of governance that emerged in the nineteenth century: the Concert of Europe, public international unions, and the Hague Conferences. Recent histories, some inspired by efforts to "globalize" the study of IR, have added more complexity to the story (Acharya 2016a; Acharya and Buzan 2017). We now know more about the contributions of actors in the Global South, the intertwined development of international civil society and transnational movements with that of IOs, and the importance of the concept of internationalism as a kind of ideological framework (Helleiner 2014; Herren 2016).

The Concert of Europe

In Inis Claude's (1964) telling, the first IO–related innovation was the Concert of Europe, established in 1815—a group of major European powers making systemwide decisions by negotiation and consensus. Members agreed to coordinate behavior based on certain rights and responsibilities, with expectations of diffuse reciprocity. They still operated as separate states and societies, but in a framework of rules and consultation without creating a formal organization.

The concert system involved periodic multilateral meetings among the major European powers for settling problems and coordinating actions. Meeting over thirty times in the century before World War I, the major powers constituted a club of the like-minded, dictating the conditions of entry for other would-be participants. They legitimated the independence of new European states, such as Belgium and Greece in the 1820s. At the last of the concert meetings, which took place in Berlin in 1878, they divided up the previously uncolonized parts of Africa, extending the reach of European imperialism.

Although these meetings were not institutionalized and included no explicit mechanism for implementing collective action, they solidified important practices that later IOs followed. These included multilateral consultation, collective diplomacy, and special status for "great powers." As Claude (1964: 22) summarizes, "The Concert system was the manifestation of a rudimentary but growing sense of interdependence and community of interest among the states of Europe." Such a community of interest was a vital prerequisite for modern international organizations and broader global governance.

The idea of mutual consultations among major powers and special responsibilities, necessitated by a growing community of interests, was the inspiration for the League of Nations Council, the UN Security Council, and the concept of permanent members with the special privilege of veto power. It can be seen in the Group of Seven, established in the 1970s to coordinate the macroeconomic policies of the seven major developed states.

Public International Unions and Other Specialized Bodies

Public international unions were the second important nineteenth-century organizational innovation. The European states established a number of agencies to deal with problems stemming from the Industrial Revolution, expanding commerce, communications, and technological innovation. These involved such concerns as health standards for travelers, shipping rules on the Rhine and other rivers, access to ports, the movement of increased mail volumes, and the cross-boundary usage of the newly invented telegraph.

Many of these practical problems of expanding international relations among states proved amenable to resolution with intergovernmental cooperation. The International Telegraph Union (ITU) was formed in 1865 and the Universal Postal Union (UPU) in 1874; each was instrumental in facilitating communication, transportation, trade, and industrial development. With growing levels of interdependence, the European states found it necessary to cooperate on a voluntary basis to accomplish nonpolitical tasks. Almost immediately, these began to include non-European states (and some then colonial territories, such as India and Egypt).

Because the ITU and UPU were among the first intergovernmental organizations (IGOs) to be established, they set a number of precedents. Both were based on international conventions that called for periodic conferences of parties to the conventions. The delegates, however, came from telegraph and postal administrations of the parties, not ministries of foreign affairs—establishing the pattern of involving technical experts when dealing with technical matters. Thus, multilateral diplomacy was no longer the exclusive domain of traditional diplomats. Both organizations, along with subsequent public international unions, established international bureaus or secretariats composed of permanent staff hired from various countries. They also created councils consisting of representatives of a few selected members to function as policy directorates on behalf of the organization in the intervals between general conferences. As Claude (1964: 32) notes, "Thus was established the structural pattern of bureau, council, and conference which, with many elaborations but few deviations, serves as the blueprint of international organization today." In addition, the public unions developed techniques for multilateral conventions—lawmaking or rulemaking treaties—through periodic revisions of the regulations. Thus, public international unions and organizations dedicated to defined nonpolitical tasks gave rise to functionalism and specialized IGOs helping states deal with practical problems in their international relations, as discussed in Chapter 2.

Alongside the public international unions, other bodies were established to facilitate cooperation of experts from different nations, including the regular flow of information. Examples include the International Geodetic Commission established after a conference in Berlin in 1864 to connect geodetic experts responsible for surveying and mapping. The International Office of Public Hygiène was founded in 1907 as the first health-related international institution concerned with the spread of human, animal, and plant diseases.

The Hague System

The third governance innovation in the nineteenth century was the concept of generalized conferences in which all states were invited to participate in problem solving. In 1899 and 1907, Czar Nicholas II of Russia convened two conferences in The Hague (Netherlands), involving both European and non-European states, to think proactively about what methods states should have available to prevent war and under what conditions arbitration, negotiation, and legal recourse would be appropriate (Aldrich and Chinkin 2000). Exploring such issues in the absence of a crisis was a novelty. In fact, universal participation of states was not yet a norm.

As Finnemore and Jurkovich (2014: 362) recount, "The Hague Conferences . . . mark an important inflection point in the evolution of expectations about participation and shared governance. . . . Of particular significance was the fact that while the number of European delegates remained roughly the same between the first and second Hague Conferences, participation from the Global South (particularly Latin America) expanded dramatically." All of the Latin American states were invited in 1907, and nineteen attended. Thereafter, broad participation became the norm, carrying over what Finnemore and Jurkovich point out had been the practice among the Latin American states since their first conference in 1826. Accompanying this were expectations of sovereign equality among states, recurring conferences, the practice of majority voting on resolutions, the creation of a secretariat to collect and distribute information as well as a governing board to meet between plenary meetings, and the understanding that states could only be legally bound with their consent. Today, we take these things for granted as core elements of international organization and multilateralism, but we need to acknowledge their roots in the Americas and the pressure for inclusion that made change possible (Finnemore and Jurkovich 2014: 369).

The Hague Conferences created the Convention for the Pacific Settlement of International Disputes, ad hoc international commissions of inquiry, and the Permanent Court of Arbitration (PCA). The latter grew out of the widespread practice of inserting clauses into treaties calling for arbitration should disputes arise among parties. The PCA, composed of jurists selected by each country from which members of arbitral tribunals are chosen, remains in existence and has been used extensively for handling boundary, investment, and other disputes involving states, corporations, and other nonstate actors, including the recent dispute between the Philippines and China over claims in the South China Sea.

The Hague Conferences produced several major procedural innovations. The Latin American states' pressure, supported by the United States, resulted in twenty-six states participating in the first conference, including China, Siam, the Ottoman Empire, Mexico, and Japan. The second conference had forty-five participating states. Thus, what had been largely a European state system until the end of the nineteenth century became a truly international system at the beginning of the twentieth. For the first time, participants elected chairs, organized committees, and took roll-call votes, all of which became permanent features of twentieth-century organizations. The Hague Conferences also promoted the novel ideas of common interests of humankind and the codification of international law.

With the outbreak of World War I in 1914, a third Hague Conference was never convened. But the first two, along with numerous other conferences held during the nineteenth century, represented the first collective efforts to address problems of war, emergencies, and issues arising from new technologies and greater commerce on a regular, universal basis.

Nineteenth-century innovations therefore established vital foundations for the development of twentieth-century IGOs and the broader notion of global governance in the twenty-first century. States established new approaches to dealing with problems of joint concern, including the great power multilateralism of the concert system, the functional and specialized public international unions, and the broader participation and legalistic institutions of the Hague system.

Alongside the development of these foundations for IGOs, there were also important nongovernmental initiatives, including international peace societies, the International Committee of the Red Cross, the international labor movement, and the International Chamber of Commerce. This history is discussed further in Chapter 6. The nongovernmental effort to develop international standards for everything from nuts and bolts to telecommunication frequencies and shipping containers led to the 1946 creation of the International Organization for Standardization (ISO) and is covered later in this chapter. One further late nineteenth-century IO development was the creation of the Inter-Parliamentary Union in 1889. It continues to bring parliamentarians from 179 countries together in regular conferences to support the development of international law, promote democratic governance and accountability, and promote gender parity in legislatures today.

Craig Murphy (1994) makes a somewhat different argument than Claude and others about the nineteenth-century transportation, communication, standards, monetary, and trade organizations. From the standpoint of international political economy, he argues, rather than being responses to economic developments, these specialized IOs were designed to facilitate the creation of larger market areas in which industrial goods could be sold. Their promoters believed that what we now call economic globalization would benefit everyone (Murphy 1994).

The institutional arrangements of the nineteenth century proved inadequate for preventing war among the major European powers in the twentieth century, however. High levels of interdependence and cooperation in numerous areas of interest did not prevent World War I, illuminating the weaknesses and shortcomings of the arrangements and the state system. Yet the war had barely begun when private groups and prominent people in Europe and the United States began to plan a more permanent framework to prevent future wars. NGOs such as the League to Enforce Peace in the United States and the League of Nations Society and Fabians in the United Kingdom played active roles in pushing for the creation of a new IGO and drafting plans for it. French and British government committees were appointed to consider the form of a new institution. US President Woodrow Wilson based his own proposal for a permanent IGO on some of these plans. The resulting League of Nations expanded on those nineteenth-century foundations and set many important precedents.

The League of Nations

League principles. The League of Nations first and foremost reflected the environment in which it was conceived. Ten of the League Covenant's twenty-six provisions focused on preventing war. Two basic principles were paramount: member states agreed to respect and preserve the territorial integrity and political independence of states, and members agreed to try different methods of dispute settlement. Failing that, the League was given the power under Article 16 to enforce settlements through sanctions. The second principle was firmly embedded in the proposition of collective security: that aggression by one state should be countered by all acting together as a "league of nations."

Although the Covenant's primary focus was on maintaining peace, it also recognized the desirability of economic and social cooperation, but established no machinery for carrying out such activities except in providing for one or more organizations to secure "fair and humane conditions of labour for men, women and children" (Article 23). The Covenant also envisioned the desirability of bringing all public international unions under the League's direction, but this did not happen.

League organs. The Covenant of the League of Nations established three permanent organs—the Council, Assembly, and Secretariat—and two autonomous organizations, the Permanent Court of International Justice (PCIJ) and the International Labour Organization (ILO). The Council was composed of four permanent members (United Kingdom, France, Italy, and Japan) and four elected members. Because the Covenant permitted the Council and Assembly to change both categories of membership, membership varied between eight and fifteen states. For example, Germany gained permanent Council membership when it joined the League in 1926, as did the Soviet Union in 1934. The failure of the United States to ratify the Treaty of Versailles after World War I meant that it never assumed its seat.

The Council was to settle disputes, enforce sanctions, supervise mandates, formulate disarmament plans, approve Secretariat appointments, and implement peaceful settlements. League members agreed to submit disputes to arbitration, adjudication, or the Council if they could not reach negotiated agreements. They agreed also to register all treaties with the League Secretariat (thus eliminating secret agreements). If states resorted to war, the Council had the authority under Article 16 to apply diplomatic and economic sanctions, but the requirement of unanimity made action very difficult to achieve. The Council was clearly a remnant of the European concert system.

The League's Assembly was a quasi-legislative body that met annually and consisted of representatives of all member states (sixty at the peak), each with one vote. It was authorized to admit new members, approve the budget, elect the nonpermanent members to the Council, and act on matters referred by the Council. Beginning with its first session in 1919, the Assembly established a number of precedents, such as requiring the League's secretary-general to submit an annual report on the activities of the organization, engaging in general debate involving speeches by heads of delegations, and creating six committees to consider important matters between annual sessions (all practices continued by the UN General Assembly). Decisions in committees were by majority, in contrast to decisions in the Assembly itself, which required unanimity. Strict unanimity was tempered by special procedures requiring less-than-majority votes. In practice, states generally preferred to abstain rather than block action. In addition to the main committees, the Assembly set up various other advisory committees dealing with health, drug traffic, slavery, trafficking in women, child welfare, transit, economics and finance, and intellectual cooperation. At the time, the League's Assembly was considered quite revolutionary, and over time its activities drew even more attention than the Council.

The Covenant established the Secretariat but provided few instructions on its responsibilities. More a clearinghouse for relevant information, the Secretariat had little independent authority. Still, it became the first truly international civil service, with its members independent of the member states. The first League secretary-general, Sir Eric Drummond (who served 1919–1933), was considered an excellent administrator who chose not to undertake political initiatives and, by playing a limited role, avoided the kinds of political pressures to which later UN Secretaries-General have been subject. The Secretariat provided coordination for some twenty organizations that were affiliated with the League, including the Health Organization, the Mandates Commission, the ILO, and the PCIJ.

Successes and failures. The League enjoyed a number of successes, many of them concerned with European territorial issues. It conducted plebiscites in Silesia and the Saar and then demarcated the German–Polish border. It settled several territorial disputes, including those between Finland and Russia and Bulgaria and Greece. In the latter case, the Council agreed to send military observers to oversee a cease-fire and troop withdrawal and established a commission of inquiry to recommend terms of settlement—all precedents the UN later adopted.

The League established the mandate system under which former German colonies in Africa and the Pacific and non-Turkish territories of the former Ottoman Empire were administered by the United Kingdom, France, South Africa, Belgium, Australia, New Zealand, and Japan under the League's supervision. The League's Mandates Commission, composed of nongovernmental representatives, reviewed annual reports submitted by the colonial powers about conditions in the mandates.

Most important, the League was the first permanent international organization of a general political nature with continuously functioning political, economic, social, judicial, and administrative machinery. It embodied the idea that the international community could and should act against international lawbreakers and promote cooperation on a wide range of problems.

Overall, the League fell far short of expectations, however. As LeRoy Bennett (1995: 41) put it, "As long as all members realized mutual advantages through cooperation, the League provided them with a useful avenue for achieving their common goals." When Japan, Italy, and Germany challenged the status quo, he added, "the League mirrored the lack of cooperative will among its members." The failure to act when Japan invaded Manchuria in 1931 pointed to the Council's refusal to take decisive action and the unwillingness of either the United Kingdom or France to institute military action or economic sanctions. The Council's delayed response to Italy's 1935 invasion of Ethiopia, a League member, further undermined its legitimacy. Fifty of the fifty-four members of the League Assembly concurred with cutting off credit to the Italian economy and stopping arms sales, but these measures were insufficient to make Italy retreat, and by 1936 all sanctions against Italy were abandoned. The League neither intervened in the Spanish civil war nor opposed Hitler's remilitarization of the Rhineland and occupation of Austria and Czechoslovakia. With the great powers unwilling to uphold the League's principles, its power and legitimacy deteriorated.

The League of Nations was also unable to respond to the Great Depression of the 1930s. Proposals to reorganize the League's structures to address economic and social issues, including human rights, did not come to fruition, but did influence the drafting of the United Nations Charter a decade later.

In sum, the League's close association with the unjust peace of World War I and the Treaty of Versailles hamstrung the organization from the outset. The absence of the United States from League membership proved a critical weakness, but it was the unwillingness of other major powers, most notably the United Kingdom and France, to uphold the League's principles and to respond to overt aggression by Japan, Italy, and Germany that doomed the League as an instrument of collective security. Some also argue that the very idea of collective security was overly idealistic in a world of sovereign states. The Covenant itself contained a number of gaps, although none could be considered fatal flaws.

Between 1935 and 1939, many members withdrew, and the League was silent during the six years of World War II from 1939 to 1945. Its members convened one final time in April 1946 to terminate the organization and transfer its assets to the new United Nations.

The Emergence of a Common Core of IGO Structures

Despite its shortcomings, the League represented an important step forward in the process of international organization and in global governance. Thus, early in World War II, many people recognized the need to begin planning for a new organization, one whose scope was greater than the League's. Planning began shortly after the United States entered the war in 1941 and built on the lessons of the League in laying the groundwork for the United Nations (Grigorescu 2005). Even before the war ended, a number of new specialized international organizations were established, including the Food and Agriculture Organization (FAO), the UN Relief and Rehabilitation Agency, the World Bank, and the International Monetary Fund (IMF). Shortly after World War II, still other IGOs were established in a number of regions around the world.

Over time, it became evident that one of the major trends of the twentieth century was the development of numerous IOs small and large; general purpose and specialized; intergovernmental and nongovernmental; global, regional, and transregional to serve disparate goals and manage various needs, as shown in Figure 3.1.

Cumulatively, precedents set by the Concert of Europe, the public international unions, the Hague Conferences, the inter-American states, and the League of Nations established the basic structural forms for the majority of international organizations, particularly IGOs. These include a limited membership council; an assembly of all member states wherein each state has one vote—signifying the internationalization of the democratic principle of equal representation of all members, regardless of size, wealth, or power; and a secretariat to provide administrative services, implement programs, and serve as institutional continuity. The councils in some IGOs, however, such as the UN Security Council, the European Union Council, and the executive boards of the World Bank and IMF, operate with weighted or qualified voting, such as the five Security Council permanent members' veto power. Still, not all full-membership entities labeled "assembly" or "general assembly" or "conference" are alike. Although many are like the League Assembly in being made up of representatives of all member states, some, like the African Union's Assembly of Heads of State and

Figure 3.1   Twentieth-Century Growth Patterns of IGOs and INGOs

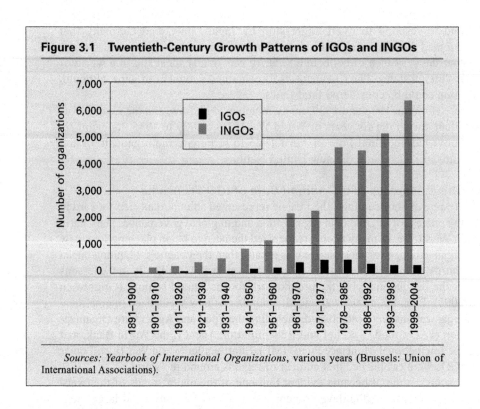

Sources: Yearbook of International Organizations, various years (Brussels: Union of International Associations).

Government—are entities that function at the summit level only. Among regional organizations, only the Organization of American States has a general assembly modeled on the League and UN assemblies. A number of regional organizations such as the North Atlantic Treaty Organization, the European Union, and African Union have parliamentary bodies, although they differ in fundamental ways. Some also have judicial bodies, as discussed later in the chapter.

The secretariats of these IGOs, like bureaucracies more generally, tend to share certain characteristics. They derive authority in performing "duties of office" from their rational-legal character and their expertise; they derive legitimacy from the moral purposes of the organization and from their claims to neutrality, impartiality, and objectivity; and they derive power from their missions of serving others. In many IGOs, the secretariats are staffed by technocrats—people with specialized training and knowledge who shape policy options consistent with that expertise. That professional training along with norms and occupational cultures tend to shape the way they see the world and to "influence what problems are visible to staff and what range of solutions are entertained" (Barnett and Finnemore 2005: 174; Piiparinen 2016).

Thus, as one studies various IGOs, one sees commonalities in structures, decisionmaking processes, and some functions, such as assemblies approving organizational budgets and electing executive heads. Yet one must be attuned to the differences between and among organizations and specific entities. As illustrated earlier, use of the word "assembly" does not necessarily mean that two entities with the same name in different organizations will have the same composition or functions.

Subsequent sections of this chapter briefly examine the establishment of the United Nations, the expansion of functional and specialized organizations within and outside the UN system, and the growth of international courts. Chapter 4 provides a more detailed look at the UN, and regional and transregional organizations are the subject of Chapter 5.

The UN System

The establishment of the United Nations in the closing days of World War II was an affirmation of the desire of war-weary nations for a general international organization that could help them avoid future conflicts and promote international economic and social cooperation. In many important ways, the UN structure was patterned after the League of Nations, with changes made where lessons had been learned. For example, the League's Council could act only with unanimous agreement; the UN Security Council, while requiring the support of all five permanent members, needs only a majority of the nonpermanent members to take action. The UN Charter also built on lessons from the public international unions, conference diplomacy, and Hague Conference dispute settlement mechanisms.

The Atlantic Charter of August 14, 1941—a joint declaration by US president Franklin Roosevelt and British prime minister Winston Churchill calling for collaboration on economic issues and a permanent system of security—was the foundation for the "Declaration by the United Nations" in January 1942. Twenty-six nations affirmed the principles of the Atlantic Charter and agreed to create a new universal organization to replace the League of Nations. The UN Charter was drafted in two sets of meetings between August and October 1944 at Dumbarton Oaks in Washington, DC. The participants agreed that the organization would be based on the principle of the sovereign equality of members, with all "peace-loving" states eligible for membership, thereby excluding the Axis powers—Germany, Italy, Japan, and Spain. It was further agreed (though not without some strong dissension) that decisions on security issues would require unanimity of the permanent members of the Security Council, the great powers. There was consensus on broadening the scope of the new organization beyond that of the League, and President Roosevelt early on sought to ensure domestic support for US participation.

When the United Nations Conference on International Organization convened in San Francisco on April 25, 1945, delegates from the fifty participating states modified and finalized what had already been negotiated among the great powers. Among them were a small number of women, including seven Latin American women who pushed successfully for provisions on human rights and women's rights in the UN Charter (Dietrichson and Sator 2022). On July 28, 1945, with Senate approval, the United States became the first country to ratify the Charter. It took only three months for a sufficient number of countries to ratify the document. As one conference participant noted after the Charter was signed: "One of the most significant features was the demonstration of the large area of agreement which existed from the start among the 50 nations. . . . Not a single reservation was made to the charter when it was adopted. . . . The conference will long stand as one of the landmarks in international diplomacy" (Padelford 1945). Historically, the emphasis in accounts of the UN's founding has been on the roles of the major powers and countries in the Global North. Recent work has shown the influence of delegations from the Global South, including the nineteen independent Latin American countries that made up the largest voting bloc, plus three from Africa, seven from the Middle East, and three from Asia (Weiss and Roy 2016; Dietrichson and Sator 2022).

Four of the UN's principal organs were patterned after those of the League of Nations: the Security Council, General Assembly, Secretariat, and International Court of Justice (ICJ). The UN Charter remedied a major gap in the League Covenant by creating the Economic and Social Council (ECOSOC) and it carried the mandates system forward under the Trusteeship Council. As Chapter 4 explores in depth, the UN is a complex system with many parts and many functions, making it the centerpiece of global governance since its inception, despite its many weaknesses. Other IGOs have been created within the UN system, such as the UN Conference on Trade and Development, the UN Children's Fund, and the International Atomic Energy Agency, as well as countless programs, funds, commissions, and committees. It has sponsored global conferences and summits; it serves as a catalyst for global policy networks and has increasingly established partnerships with nonstate actors.

Among the core elements of the UN system are a number of specialized agencies, including the first two public international unions: the ITU and UPU. There are now several related organizations, among them the World Trade Organization (WTO) and the International Organization for Migration (IOM).

The Expansion of Functional and Specialized Organizations

The establishment of single-function IGOs to address specific issues such as health, economics, trade, labor issues, and environmental threats mirrors a pattern carried over from national governments. Over time, new organizations have been created to address more specialized problems in response to new issues and unmet needs. Thus, the numbers of functional and specialized IGOs have increased exponentially since the mid-nineteenth century.

In line with functionalist theory, functional organizations were once perceived to be nonpolitical, with technical experts working out solutions to problems among the member states. Staying above politics is not always possible, however, since the issues such IGOs deal with are not merely technical but can touch at the core of state sovereignty and deeply political concerns, especially as rules and regulations expand. Nonetheless, they retain their functional, specialized character and are important elements of global governance, forming the institutional core for governance activities on a particular set of issues.

The founders of the UN envisaged that functional agencies would play key roles in activities aimed at economic and social advancement. As a result, Articles 57 and 63 of the UN Charter call for the affiliation with the UN of specialized organizations established by separate intergovernmental agreements with "wide international responsibility" in economics, health, food, educational, and cultural fields. Today, the seventeen specialized agencies are formally affiliated with the UN through agreements with ECOSOC and the General Assembly. Like the UN itself, they have global rather than regional responsibilities, but separate charters, memberships, budgets, and secretariats as well as their own interests and constituencies. (See Chapter 4 for further discussion and Figure 4.2 for a full list of UN specialized and related agencies.) There are a significant number of functional organizations in the UN system that are not classified as specialized agencies, as they have been established by the UN itself and report to the Security Council or General Assembly. There are also a wide variety of other specialized functional organizations outside the UN system. Some are regional in scope; others have been formed by countries with shared interests in specific issues. Figure 3.2 lists some of the variety of functional organizations.

The evolution of governance and core functional IGOs in four areas of activity are discussed here, with others discussed in subsequent chapters. Efforts to address health, communications, and labor issues began in the nineteenth century, and those for economic, agriculture, and food issues developed during the twentieth century. In addition, we look at the standardization movement that began in the nineteenth century and the creation of the International Organization for Standardization—an IO, not an IGO—after World War II.

Health and the World Health Organization

One of the oldest areas of functional activity is health, an issue that respects no national boundaries. In medieval times, as trade expanded between Europe and East Asia, epidemics followed trade routes. European discovery

> **Figure 3.2**
> **Functional Intergovernmental**
> **Organizations (selected)**
>
> *Functional Organizations within
> the United Nations System*
> • Food and Agriculture
>   Organization
>   International Atomic Energy
>   Agency
> • International Civil Aviation
>   Organization
> • International Labour Organization
> • International Maritime
>   Organization
> • International Telecommunications
>   Union
> • UN High Commissioner for
>   Refugees
> • Universal Postal Union
> • World Health Organization
> • World Meteorological
>   Organization
>
> *Other Functional Organizations*
> • International Coffee Organization
> • International Whaling Commission
> • Northwest Atlantic Fisheries
>   Organization
> • Organization of Petroleum
>   Exporting Countries
>
> *Regional Functional Organizations*
> • African Development Bank
> • Arab Monetary Fund
> • Economic Community of
>   West African States
> • European Central Bank
> • Mekong River Commission
> • Pan American Health
>   Organization

of the Americas brought diseases like smallpox, measles, and yellow fever to the Western Hemisphere. Increased trade and travel in nineteenth-century Europe accelerated the spread of deadly diseases across national borders and populations. Clearly, no single state could solve health problems alone. Cooperation was required.

In response to a cholera outbreak in Europe, the first International Sanitary Conference was convened in Paris in 1851 to develop a collective response based on increased knowledge about public health and medicine and improvements in sanitation. Between 1851 and 1903, eleven such conferences were convened to develop procedures to prevent the spread of contagious and infectious diseases.

In 1907 the Office International d'Hygiène Publique was created with a mandate to disseminate information on communicable diseases, such as cholera, plague, and yellow fever. More than a decade later, at the request of the League of Nations Council, an international health conference met to prepare for a permanent international health organization. The Office did not become part of this new health organization but remained a distinct entity with its own secretariat.

In 1948, a single health organization, the World Health Organization (WHO), came into being as a UN specialized agency. The principal decisionmaking body is the World Health Assembly (WHA), which is composed of delegations from its 194 member states, the majority of whom are medical doctors or come from health or related government ministries. This reflects the pattern set by the ITU and UPU as the first public international unions and gives meetings a professional atmosphere that differs greatly from that of the UN General Assembly. Each country has one vote, and decisions are made either by simple majority or by a two-thirds majority for important questions. The WHA meets annually in contrast to the assemblies and conferences of many other functional organizations. As the WHO's legislative body, it approves international regulations concerning sanitary and quarantine requirements and standards for diagnostic procedures, as well as for biological, pharmaceutical, and other products; it controls the WHO's budget, appoints the director-general, elects members of the Executive Board, adopts agreements, and sets goals and policies.

The Executive Board is a smaller group of thirty-four technically qualified individuals elected by the WHA for three-year terms. By "gentlemen's agreement," at least three of the UN Security Council members are supposed to be represented. The board sets WHA agendas and resolutions to be considered and oversees implementation of WHA decisions and policies. The WHO's Secretariat, located in Geneva, has several key roles: carrying out the programs the WHA has approved (often in partnerships with national health ministries, NGOs, research centers, etc.), providing technical guidance and support as a global hub of scientific and technical expertise, and coordinating responses to international health emergencies. The WHO has the distinction of having been the very first UN specialized agency with a woman director-general—former Norwegian prime minister Gro Harlem Brundtland, who served from 1998 to 2003.

The WHO is a quintessential functionalist organization and is one of the largest of the UN specialized agencies in terms of both membership (194 members), staff (7,000 in 150 countries), and budget ($5.84 billion in 2020–2021), a sign of the universality of health concerns. In contrast to many UN agencies, a significant portion of its funding comes from states' voluntary contributions (in addition to their assessed contributions) and from private donors, such as the Bill and Melinda Gates Foundation. These are known as extrabudgetary funds and are generally designated for specific purposes, such as polio eradication or HIV/AIDS programs. The World Bank has been a major funder of the WHO's budget and programs since the late 1980s. WHO is also one of the more decentralized functional organizations, having six regional offices (Africa, Americas, Southeast Asia, Europe, Eastern Mediterranean, Western Pacific) with significant autonomy to adopt their own programs, select their own directors, and control their own budgets. With the director-general, other WHO officials, and many WHA delegates being medical doctors and public health experts, they form a strong epistemic community based on their technical expertise and training. The WHO is involved in partnerships with other IGOs, such as UNICEF and the World Bank, as well as private partners such as the Gates Foundation and NGOs. These include the Global Vaccine Alliance (GAVI) and the Global Fund to Fight AIDS, Tuberculosis and Malaria.

The WHO's activities today include four major areas: containing the spread of communicable diseases; disease eradication; standard-setting and norm creation; and noncommunicable diseases, often called lifestyle-related health issues. Of these, disease eradication remains its most important activity.

In 1951, the WHO approved the International Sanitary Regulations, which were renamed the International Health Regulations (IHR) in a 1969 revision. They constitute the only international treaty that "explicitly regulates a state's obligations to the international community on the spread of infectious diseases." They also established the WHO as the "repository of all required disease surveillance information" (Youde 2012: 147). Initially, the IHR required states to report outbreaks of four communicable diseases (yellow fever, cholera, plague, and smallpox) and take appropriate measures to contain any outbreak without impeding international travel and commerce. Over time, governments often failed to report outbreaks in a timely manner or underreported the number of cases, fearing condemnation and adverse economic consequences such as loss of tourism revenue, although some failures were the result of limited resources. Smallpox was removed in 1981 after its successful eradication.

Globalization, however, has had a dramatic effect on the transmission, incidence, and vulnerability of individuals and communities to disease through migration, air transport, trade, and troop movements, including of UN peacekeepers. During the 1980s and 1990s, new diseases emerged that were not covered under the IHR, such as Ebola, West Nile virus, and HIV/AIDS. Older diseases thought to be under control, such as tuberculosis, reemerged in different, often drug-resistant forms. New threats to health arose with incidents of bioterrorism, such as the Tokyo sarin nerve gas attack in 1995 and the US anthrax scare in 2001. At the same time, the internet, cell phones, and other technologies have facilitated faster and better information about outbreaks that countries might once have been able to hide. This made it imperative to enable the WHO to receive reports of outbreaks from non-state actors in addition to governments and to make determinations if an event constitutes a public health emergency of international concern.

In 1995, the WHA requested the director-general to undertake a major revision of the IHR to make them more relevant to contemporary health threats and more effective. The negotiations took almost a decade, concluding in 2005, and the revised IHR took effect in 2007. Key changes included a wider range of public health risks so that rather than listing a set of specific diseases that should be reported, the IHR now refer to all events "posing a serious and direct threat to the health of human populations" (Article 1.1). This makes them more flexible and relevant to future public health threats. Particularly important is the WHO's ability to receive and act on information from nongovernmental sources. The IHR require member states (194 plus 2 territories as of late 2020) to assess their own surveillance and response systems and implement plans to ensure core capacities. There is also explicit recognition of the human right to health in connection with public health emergencies. Yet the regulations did not come with financial resources to support implementation; as some critics have charged, they perpetuated the link between health and an "absence of disease" framework rather than promoting a broader concept of health and the factors that support it (Youde 2012: 128–129). Furthermore, the revised IHR did not eliminate problems with states' transparency, as was evident in 2020 when the Chinese government initially suppressed information on the coronavirus outbreak (discussed further in Chapter 11).

One of the WHO's greatest accomplishments was the successful eradication of smallpox in 1980—the only human disease to be fully eradicated thus far. The campaign against malaria and polio has built on that success and demonstrates the important role of partnerships in WHO's current activities. Rotary International and the Bill and Melinda Gates Foundation have been particularly important for this campaign along with UNICEF, the Global Vaccine Alliance, and the US Centers for Disease Control and Prevention. The goal of polio eradication was close to realization in 2006, but local resistance to vaccination in Nigeria led to outbreaks that subsequently spread to neighboring countries, South Asia, and Syria.

In its third major area of activity, standard-setting and norm creation, the WHO has set standards for air pollution and drinking water. As early as 1970, the WHA approved guidelines for drug manufacturing, covering such issues as labeling, potency, purity, and safety, at the urging of developing countries concerned about the quality of imported drugs and pharmaceutical company exports of inferior ones. The WHO has also dealt with the pharmaceutical industry on the issues of pricing for antiretroviral AIDS drugs in poor countries and on the issue of vaccine distribution in the Covid-19 pandemic. The issue of accessibility, quality, and affordability of drugs in developing countries is an ongoing issue that overlaps with WTO-related issues of intellectual property rights and generic drugs. Another area of WHO standard-setting and norm creation was the Health for All by 2000 program initiated with the 1978 Alma Ata Declaration that called for acceptance of health as a public good, universal access to essential medicines, and nondiscrimination in care provision.

In 2003, the WHA approved the Framework Convention on Tobacco Control. This marked a major step in its fourth area of activity—noncommunicable diseases or lifestyle-related health issues. Key among them is its campaign against smoking and tobacco, which the *World Health Report 2003* named as the world's leading cause of preventable deaths—an estimated 5 million and mostly in developing areas by that time since consumption had dropped significantly in developed countries (Youde 2012: 41–42). Not surprisingly, the campaign encountered stiff opposition from the large tobacco companies and initially from the United States. The story of the choice to negotiate a framework convention and the extensive NGO activity on the issue is discussed in Chapter 6. The convention bans advertising of tobacco products, requires health warnings on packaging, and creates broader liability for manufacturers. It took effect in 2005 and had been ratified by 182 parties as of 2023 (the United States, Indonesia, and Argentina are the three largest nonratifiers.)

The convention is the very first case of the WHO using the authority granted by Article 19 of its constitution to adopt a global health treaty, and it has subsequently been complemented by the Protocol to Eliminate Illicit Trade in Tobacco Products, concluded in 2012. Implementation has been slow, however, and smoking rates continue to rise in developing countries. The marketing restrictions have not been implemented and generally there is a loss of momentum on the issue.

The WHO continues to be the key IGO in global health governance. We look further at its critical role in Chapter 11, including how it handled major outbreaks of communicable diseases—Ebola in West Africa in 2014 and the global Covid-19 pandemic.

Telecommunications

Like health issues, telecommunication services have changed dramatically, from the invention of the telegraph and telephone in the nineteenth century to radio, computers, satellites, and internet in the twentieth century and various social media in the early twenty-first century. The founding of the International Telegraph Union in 1865 enabled people to communicate through one international network. But as that network has changed and new types of communication devices have developed, the successor organization, the ITU, which merged with the International Radio Union in 1932, rests on informal understandings rather than formal legal edicts. These include open access to outer space and the radio spectrum of airspace and the principle of prior use. States must respect use of specific frequencies and not transmit on them, but states also have a right to exclude foreign firms from their telecommunications industries, establishing the basis of a legal monopoly. Most telecommunications norms must be deduced from various agreements, statements, and the behavior of state and industry officials.

As in the health arena, where multiple governance structures interact, the ITU is one among many public and private bodies focusing on communications. It devotes significant attention to ensuring technical standards for various technologies and preventing interference in radio transmissions. The ITU works with the International Organization for Standardization and the International Electrotechnical Commission, which are both nongovernmental entities, and with a group of regional bodies under the Global Standards Cooperation Group in setting these technical standards.

The ITU along with the UPU pioneered a number of structures for specialized, functional IGOs. These include the predominance of technical experts among the member state delegates to periodic conferences and in the bureau (secretariat). ITU administrative conferences, held every three to four years, deal with technical issues, while plenipotentiary conferences, held every four years, establish budgets and elect administrative council members, the secretary-general and deputy secretary-general, sector bureau directors, and members of the Radio Regulations Board. They may also revise the ITU Convention, approve strategic plans, and deal with any other questions that arise.

The exponential growth of the internet has played a major role in globalization and the diffusion of ideas, culture, and technology. The internet has also raised a host of governance issues and the need for new sets of rules and new types of authorities to enforce those rules. What makes it a striking case in global governance is the predominance of private authorities and modes of governance, not the ITU. During the internet's early years, the rules were the product of a small epistemic community of technologically sophisticated users and, for a long time, internet governance involved just one key actor, the Internet Corporation for Assigned Names and Numbers (ICAAN). This is a California-based nonprofit group that manages the internet's address system, allocating domain names, establishing rules for reallocation of names, and setting regulations for selling domain names.

Not surprisingly, as the use of the internet spread, different views emerged over who should be included in its governance, whether it should be the responsibility of governments or shared among a number of stakeholders, including the private sector, the technical community, civil society, and governments. The ITU plays a role, but it is not a central one as the multistakeholder model has largely prevailed. In 2003 and 2005, the UN convened the World Summit on the Information Society (WSIS), bringing together all the key stakeholders to address a broad range of internet-related issues.

The WSIS brought to a head the debate over who should govern the internet. Civil society actors fought to broaden the issue of internet infrastructure and governance to questions of development and equity for developing countries and for ensuring that the interests of humans get equal voice with those of governments and commercial entities (Carr 2018: 747–748). Not surprisingly, some governments argued against ceding authority to a foreign private actor (particularly one based in the United States), the technical community, or civil society on the grounds that internet governance was the responsibility of governments. The final outcome was the creation of the Internet Governance Forum, a multistakeholder arena in the UN system. The forum includes an advisory group with members from governments, the commercial private sector, and public civil society organizations whose task is to discuss issues of internet governance. The forum is convened by the UN Secretary-General and meets annually. In 2015, its mandate was extended for another ten years.

The ITU coordinates a number of WSIS follow-up activities, including maintaining a database of information and communication technology initiatives. It is also a platform for discussions on the management of domain names and addresses. Consistent with its earlier role in telecommunication standardization, it works on standardizing broadband and cable networks and the interoperability of various types of networks. The ITU also works to improve internet access in developing countries, recognizing how the internet has become a key form of public infrastructure around the world.

The origins, functions, and nature of other functional organizations tend to reflect the nature of the issues they were established to address. In that regard, the history of the International Labour Organization is quite different from that of either the WHO or the ITU.

Labor Issues and the ILO

The origins of the ILO can also be traced to the nineteenth century, when growing problems with industrialization drove two industrialists, Welshman Robert Owen and Frenchman Daniel Legrand, to advocate an organization to protect workers from abuses. Long factory hours, poor working conditions, and low wages led to the formation of labor unions to advance workers' rights. In 1913, the International Federation of Trade Unions was founded to address these grievances on a transnational basis. With the expansion of the right to vote in many European countries, labor assumed growing political importance, and Owen and Legrand's ideas led to adoption of the ILO constitution in 1919 by the Paris Peace Conference, based on the belief that world peace could only be accomplished by attention to social justice (see Murphy 1994). Thus, the ILO became an autonomous organization within the League of Nations structure, an institutional model used for other functional organizations related to the United Nations.

Important principles articulated in the preamble to the ILO constitution detail the humanitarian, political, and economic motivations for its establishment. The first is based on the humanitarian recognition that "conditions of labour exist involving . . . injustice, hardship and privation to large numbers of people." Such persistent injustices pose a political threat, with the potential to upset international peace and harmony. Second, there is an economic implication that "the failure of any nation to adopt humane conditions of labour is an obstacle in the way of other nations which desire to improve the conditions in their own countries." Ironically, organized labor, while agreeing with the general goals, actually opposed the establishment of the ILO, believing that the organization as proposed was too weak and lacked the capacity to set labor standards.

Setting standards for treatment of workers with international conventions is the ILO's major activity. Between 1919 and 1939, the ILO approved sixty-seven conventions, covering such issues as hours of work, maternity protection, minimum age, and old-age insurance. In 1926 it was the first international organization to establish procedures for monitoring human rights in states—in this case, workers' rights. In 1926 it also instituted the system of annual meetings of the Committee of Experts to examine state reports on treaty implementation.

The ILO had concluded more than 190 conventions and supplementary protocols, of which 155 had received sufficient ratifications to come into force as of 2023. It has also made more than 200 nonbinding recommendations. Among the eleven conventions and protocols designated "fundamental" are those concerning elimination of forced and compulsory labor, freedom of association and the right to collective bargaining, elimination of discrimination in employment, occupational health and safety, and the abolition of child labor. As of 2023, 120 states had ratified all of these fundamental conventions; the United States had ratified only two (the conventions banning forced labor and child labor) while China had ratified seven. The United Kingdom and Germany have ratified ten; Japan has ratified eight; Russia has ratified all eleven. Four conventions are designated as "priority" instruments and referred to as "governance" conventions because of their importance to the international labor standards system. The most recent convention (no. 190) deals with workers' right to be treated with respect at work, an issue that was highlighted during the Covid-19 pandemic when many health workers experience harassment and even violence at work, including from patients. In many countries, the international labor codes on such issues as the right to organize and bargain, the ban on slavery and forced labor, the regulation of hours of work, agreements about wages, and workers' compensation and safety are translated directly into domestic law.

The ILO, headquartered in Geneva, Switzerland, became a UN specialized agency in 1946. It accomplishes its work through three major bodies—the International Labour Conference, the Governing Body, and the International Labour Office—each of which includes a tripartite representation structure involving government officials, employers, and workers. This integration of governmental and nongovernmental representatives is a unique approach not seen in any other IGO. During the Cold War, the tripartite structure was controversial, since in communist states there was no clear differentiation between government, management, and labor. Since the 1990s, the tripartite structure has become controversial again with the declining numbers of people in labor unions and the increasing number of NGOs advocating on behalf of nonunionized workers, offering policy advice, and playing key monitoring roles. Yet NGOs have no official position in the structure, and the labor unions do not want to share power. Thus, while the tripartite structure provides greater representation, there are tensions between these different parts of civil society.

The International Labour Conference is the ILO's main decisionmaking body. It meets annually, with each of its 187 member states represented by four individuals: two government officials, and one each from labor and management. The conference, with each person voting independently, sets international labor standards, adopts the budget, and hears compliance reports compiled by the Committee of Experts.

The Governing Body, the executive arm, establishes programs and the budget and elects the director-general. It is composed of fifty-six members representing twenty-eight governments, fourteen employers, and fourteen worker groups. Ten "states of chief industrial importance" (Brazil, China, France, Germany, India, Italy, Japan, Russia, the United Kingdom, and the United States) are ensured governmental seats; the other government members are elected by the International Labour Conference every three years. Employer and worker members are elected by their constituent groups.

The International Labour Office forms a permanent secretariat under the leadership of the director-general, who serves a five-year renewable term. While the ILO employs about 3,300 people, many are outside of Geneva in its 5 regional and 107 field offices.

Among functional organizations, the ILO is regarded as having the most effective system of monitoring states' compliance with conventions, one that has served as a model for other entities in monitoring human rights more generally. Governments are required to report on practices covered under the various ILO conventions; ILO staff then prepare comments for the Committee of Experts and may use direct contacts, reports of other UN bodies, and reports from employer and worker groups to supplement government reports. The findings of the Committee of Experts, although not binding on states, are then conveyed to a conference committee for a final report. In some cases, the ILO may form a commission of inquiry consisting of three independent members to undertake an investigation of a complaint of persistent noncompliance and to recommend measures to be taken to address the problem. Thirteen such commissions have been established over the ILO's history. In 1998, for example, a commission of inquiry found that Myanmar had not complied with the forced labor conventions, which led to condemnation and denial of ILO development funds. In 2000, Article 33 was invoked for the first time with a request to the International Labour Conference to take measures against Myanmar. The norm, however, is not to use coercive measures but to work with the country in question and offer technical assistance programs to facilitate compliance. A complaint in 2015, for example, concerned Venezuela's failure to comply with the conventions on minimum wages, freedom of association and right to organize, and International Labour Standards. Another example in 2022–2023 concerned violations of labor rules for workers at the World Cup soccer facilities in Qatar.

Although ILO processes have not substantially changed over time, the organization's jurisdiction has broadened. Initially, the dominant focus was on standards to improve the working conditions of male wage labor. Standards were expanded to include occupational health and safety. In recent years, the ILO has approved conventions for previously unrepresented and often nonorganized workers: women, migrant and domestic workers, and Indigenous and tribal peoples. The platform of action labeled "Decent Work" aims to address the inequalities resulting from globalization by focusing on job creation, rights at work, social protection and dialogue, and gender equality.

The ILO continues to be the primary specialized, functional organization devoted to labor issues and standards. It is the primary source of data on trends in wages and employment, including child labor and work from home. Increasingly, labor issues have come to overlap with trade issues and the work of the WTO. A number of states and NGOs have argued that trade rules and labor standards should be linked. Yet many developing countries do not want to erode their competitive advantage, namely, cheap labor. To them, the proper forum for dealing with labor issues is the ILO. Still, two regional organizations have linked trade and labor issues: the European Union, which has a long and successful history of addressing labor rights while expanding its common and then single market, and the North American Free Trade Agreement, which has a side agreement on labor issues, the North American Agreement on Labor Cooperation.

Although there is a long history of international governance efforts on labor issues, other areas of economic activity have only been the subject of international cooperation since the end of World War II. We look here at the foundations of international economic governance laid in the 1940s.

As the Industrial Revolution expanded, the need for managing increased trade, capital flows, and price fluctuations in raw materials grew. Some initiatives were private, some were public. During the 1920s and early 1930s, industry-based cartels for selected industrial products and commodities such as tin and natural rubber were created to coordinate product outputs and control prices; many became successful at price-fixing and market-allocation schemes.

Neither private cartels nor governments were able to control the effects of the Great Depression of the 1930s. Not only were millions of people out of work and impoverished in the United States and Europe, but the prices of most raw materials plummeted, causing the people in Europe's African and Asian colonies and in the independent countries of Latin America to suffer greatly. Governments, starting with the United States in its Smoot-Hawley Tariff Act of 1930, adopted "beggar thy neighbor" policies, raising barriers to imports and causing world trade to collapse. As noted earlier in the chapter, the League of Nations was not set up to deal with economic issues. Efforts to initiate international cooperation as the depression unfolded failed, at least in part because the United States was unwilling to participate.

Faced with economic collapse, a number of US and UK economists realized during the 1930s that international institutions were needed to help countries with balance-of-payments difficulties, to provide stable exchange rates and economic assistance, and to promote nondiscrimination in and reciprocal lowering of barriers to trade. The idea of an international institution to mobilize foreign assistance to support economic development of poorer countries, however, came from several sources as more recent scholarship has shown. One was US President Franklin Roosevelt's Good Neighbor Policy toward Latin America in the 1930s and the negotiations to create an inter-American bank to promote economic development in that region. A further inspiration came from Sun Yat-sen, leader of China's 1911 revolution, who proposed an International Development Organization in 1918 and whose idea was promoted by the Chinese delegation to the Bretton Woods conference. From these roots, the norm that international institutions should support the economic development of poorer countries was born (Helleiner 2014). The dual role envisioned for the World Bank is still reflected in its official name and acronym: the International Bank for Reconstruction and Development (IBRD).

Recognizing the importance of reducing barriers to the flow of goods and capital and the value of international economic cooperation for its own well-being, the United States furnished the vision of an open international economy, the leadership to establish institutions, and the money to assist others. Henry Dexter White, chief international economist at the US Treasury from 1942 to 1944, and UK economist John Maynard Keynes presented competing plans for economic governance at a conference held in Bretton Woods, New Hampshire, in 1944. In an effort to provide an independent, countervailing balance to US economic power, Keynes proposed a world central bank capable of regulating the flow of credit; he also favored creating a new international currency to facilitate lending to countries experiencing liquidity problems. White argued for a weaker agency that would promote the growth of international trade but preserve the central role of the US dollar in the international economy.

White's plan prevailed. The newly formed International Monetary Fund (IMF) would not be a world central bank but would promote economic growth by providing financial stability for countries facing short-term balance-of-payments difficulties and thereby stimulating international trade. Over time, the US view about conditionality for assistance also prevailed and was greatly strengthened in the 1980s (see Chapter 8).

Ideas about how governance of trade should proceed also differed. At the Bretton Woods conference, a comprehensive body, the International Trade Organization (ITO), was proposed to provide a general framework for trade rules and a venue for ongoing trade discussions. One contentious issue concerned the special problem of commodities. The British, under

Keynes's influence, argued for international government-controlled buffer stocks of commodities to reduce detrimental price volatility. The United States opposed all such schemes. The details were left to the Havana Conference in 1948, when the charter for the proposed International Trade Organization (ITO) was to be approved.

At the Havana Conference, other major differences surfaced. The United States favored extensive trade liberalization, while the Europeans, including the British, were more concerned with retaining their special preferential arrangements with their colonies and former colonies. Many developing countries, absent from earlier negotiations, took a strong stance in favor of schemes protecting commodity exporters. Cuba, Colombia, and El Salvador played key roles, advocating such policies as unilateral producer actions. The efforts of the developing countries failed, however, and the industrialized countries won, agreeing only to limited producer and consumer schemes in which voting power was equally balanced. Also absent was any discussion of the idea that trading schemes should be used as a way to transfer economic resources from the rich to the poor countries.

Such key differences, coupled with major opposition from a coalition of protectionists and free-traders in the US Congress and lack of enthusiasm in other industrialized countries, led to the failure of the ITO before it was even established. The Havana Charter was never ratified. Instead, twenty-three of the participants in the ITO negotiations developed the General Agreement on Tariffs and Trade (GATT). As discussed in Chapter 8, the GATT became the major venue for trade negotiations from 1949 to 1995, when the WTO was created with infrastructure for dispute settlement that goes far beyond anything envisaged in the 1940s.

The three Bretton Woods institutions were designed to address systemic weaknesses in economic governance and promote a liberal economic order. The World Bank and IMF are UN specialized agencies, as are the International Finance Corporation and International Development Association, but until the late 1990s they operated largely independent of the UN system. The WTO is not a specialized agency; it is a related organization, and thereby its director-general participates in the UN Chief Executives Board—the entity for coordinating the disparate agencies in the UN system. The evolving governance roles of the World Bank, IMF, and GATT/WTO and their institutional structures are discussed in depth in Chapter 8, along with other elements of global economic governance.

The Food and Agriculture Organization and International Food Regime

Efforts to create an international organization for food and agriculture first began in the late nineteenth century. An international conference was held in 1905 in Rome that led to creation of the International Institute for Agriculture, patterned after other early IGOs with a general assembly of member states (forty), a bureau, a secretary-general, and bureaus of Agriculture Intelligence and Plant Diseases, General Statistics, and Economic and Social Institutions. The institute published the first agricultural census in 1930 and provided crop reports and statistics on imports and exports that affected the prices of agricultural staples. Recognizing the importance of rebuilding agriculture and food supplies at the end of World War II, the United States hosted the UN Food and Agricultural Conference in 1943 (even before the UN's own creation), which then led to the creation of the Food and Agriculture Organization (FAO) as one of the first UN specialized agencies in 1945.

The FAO's purposes include increasing agricultural productivity to eliminate hunger and improve nutrition, addressing problems of surpluses and shortages, establishing common standards, and harmonizing national agricultural policies with free trade principles. Based in Rome, it carries out basic research through a series of research centers around the world and acts as an information center for agricultural activities, including fisheries and forestry. Its experts—agricultural experts, nutritionists, economists, and social scientists—provide policy and technical assistance to improve agriculture and food supplies, eliminate hunger and food insecurity, make agriculture more productive and sustainable, reduce rural poverty, and protect livelihoods from natural and other disasters. The FAO monitors global food and agricultural systems, providing early warning on diseases and pests such as the 2020 locust plague, and promoting proper nutrition.

From the 1950s to the 1970s, the FAO supported the development and dissemination of high-yield strains of rice and other grains, along with fertilizers, pesticides, and technical assistance, producing the Green Revolution for developing countries with large increases in yields, especially in Mexico and India. Despite these initiatives, a major food crisis erupted in the 1970s, undermining the FAO's reputation. In response, the UN organized the first World Food Conference in 1974, which led to a number of reforms to bolster production and distribution. There was a substantial decentralization of the FAO through the creation of country offices, and the International Fund for Agricultural Development (IFAD) was created in 1977 to focus specifically on the rural extreme poor. It functions like a multilateral development bank in providing grants and low-interest loans to improve agricultural methods in rural areas, including critical ancillary activities such as financial services and off-farm employment. It is also a UN specialized agency.

The FAO and IFAD are complemented by a third entity in the international food regime: the World Food Programme (WFP), created in 1963 to provide food aid to disaster-stricken areas, refugees, displaced people, and war zones as well as severely impoverished and malnourished populations. It, too, is a specialized agency. Since the 1980s, the programmatic thrust of the UN system's food and agricultural agencies has been to promote sustainable agricultural practices, rural development, and alleviation of acute and chronic hunger. All of these are reflected in the two series of development-related goals the UN has established since 2000: the Millennium Development Goals (2000–2015) and the Sustainable Development Goals (2015–2030). These goals and the food institutions are discussed in Chapter 8.

As the UN's operational arm in food assistance, the WFP is the primary responder to food emergencies accompanying natural disasters, war, and famine around the world. Some have called it the world's largest humanitarian organization. Its mission includes short-term aid and aid in more protracted situations as well as for development. At the beginning of 2020, before the Covid-19 pandemic struck, some 690 million people around the world were estimated to go hungry, with another 135 million in 55 countries (more than half in Africa) on the brink of starvation. Some 43.3 million people in fifty-one countries in 2022 faced food emergencies with the top ones being Afghanistan, Somalia, Ethiopia, the Democratic Republic of Congo, Yemen, and South Sudan. The WFP is critical for addressing food security issues and is discussed further in Chapter 11.

Somewhat like the WHO, the WFP relies heavily on voluntary contributions of money and surplus food from UN member states, other UN funds and agencies, private foundations, and other donors. Eighty percent of its budget comes from just ten major donor states, including the United States, Germany, the United Kingdom, EU, and Scandinavian countries. In 2020, it had more than 17,000 employees involved in field activities in more than ninety countries, often risking their lives in areas of conflict. The organization has ships, planes, and trucks to manage food deliveries (World Food Programme 2020). It partners with more than 3,000 local and international NGOs, and community-based organizations to distribute food. Because much of its work involves providing food aid in humanitarian crises, the WFP works closely with the UN High Commissioner for Refugees and the UN Office for the Coordination of Humanitarian Affairs, as well as the other food institutions.

The FAO, IFAD, and WFP are connected to many other organizations— some global, some regional, some general-purpose, many very specialized, and some private. These include the Agriculture and Development Assistance Committee of the Organisation for Economic Co-operation and Development as well as the WTO and the WHO, all of which have specific interests and responsibilities that link them to the food regime. The Codex Alimentarius Commission, established by the FAO in 1961, sets guidelines, international standards, and codes of practice relating to food safety and pesticide residues to protect consumers' health and ensure fair practices in international agricultural trade.

In addition, there are private actors, such as international and national research institutes and foundations and a host of NGOs. The Consultative

Group on International Agricultural Research, created in 1972, coordinates and oversees the work of fifteen research centers such as the International Rice Research Institute, based in the Philippines. The Bill and Melinda Gates Foundation and the Howard G. Buffett Foundation are funding the WFP to buy surplus crops from poor farmers in Africa and Central America to feed recipients facing hunger and starvation. This "purchase for progress" project is intended to help developing-country farmers produce more food and sell it in some of the poorest regions of the world (Wroughton 2008).

The multiplicity of organizations in the food regime has produced overlap in responsibilities and some confusion, hence the calls for improving global governance for food security. The result is a "regime complex" discussed in Chapter 11. We turn to look at a very different specialized organization, the ISO—a private international organization, not an IGO.

The Standardization Movement and the ISO: Private International Standard Setting

As discussed in Chapter 1, rulemaking is an important part of global governance with public international law being a critical part and the UN playing an important part in its creation since 1945. However, much of the international economic activity, particularly trade and globalization as we have known it since the 1990s, would not have occurred if it were not for the creation of many internationally agreed-on standards for everything from screw threads, nuts, and bolts to shipping containers. These have been and are the work of global networks of private standard-setting bodies and technical committees—forms of international organization that are quite different from the UN and its functional and specialized agencies. They include the International Accounting Standards Board, the International Organization of Securities Commissions, the International Financial Reporting Standards, the International Electrotechnical Commission, the International Social and Environmental Accreditation and Labeling Alliance, and the ISO.

Industrial and fundamental (i.e., weights and measures) standard-setting dates from the mid-nineteenth-century when industrialization created a need for common units of measurement, measurement tools, product and performance standards, such as for steel rails, steam boilers, and reinforced concrete and the national and cross-national interoperability of things like railroad gauges, telegraph, telephone and electrical power grids, nuts, bolts, and screws. As Yates and Murphy (2019: 105–106) note, democratic governments in particular were reluctant to deal with industrial standards unless there were serious threats to public safety; the main impetus came from engineering associations and committees of technical experts in various fields who saw themselves as serving a larger public interest that would benefit humanity as a whole. Since 1880, the process has been private, voluntary, deliberative, consensus-based, and largely invisible, producing what

Yates and Murphy (2019: 2) call "a critical infrastructure for the global economy." They conclude that the history of global standard-setting has been marked not only by the technical expertise of those involved but also by their commitment. It is "the history of a social movement, a standardization movement that has ebbed and flowed since the late nineteenth century" (11). The "infrastructure" the movement has created consists of documents that define "specific qualities of products, technical processes, or (more recently) organizational practices" (9).

The standardization movement's initial focus was on national standards and the creation of national standard-setting bodies in industrialized ecountries. After World War II, the second period focused on international standardization and included the creation of the ISO in 1947 and the encouragement to developing countries to create their own bodies. As the use of computers and the internet grew beginning in the late 1980s, new types of multistakeholder standard-setting bodies emerged, and work spread to emerging areas of environmental management systems, quality assurance standards, and social responsibility.

Mark Mazower (2012: 102) calls the ISO "perhaps *the* most influential private organization in the contemporary world, with a vast and largely invisible influence over most aspects of how we live, from the shape of our household appliances to the colors and smells that surround us." In effect, it is an organization of organizations, including the national standard-setting entities in its member countries that are themselves made up of still more organizations and committees. One might think of the ISO as a network of networks and also as a "bridge between the public and private sectors" (Mazower 2012: 44).

The ISO has 165 members. Headquartered in Geneva, Switzerland, it has produced some 20,000 standards through the work of numerous technical committees composed of national delegates from industrial trade associations, professional and technical societies, governments and regulatory agencies, and relevant NGOs. Some aspects look like other international organizations because there is a secretary-general, a council, a president, two vice presidents, a small secretariat, and an annual meeting of member bodies. The secretariats for the committees are provided on a rotating basis by one of the ISO member bodies. Meetings are often virtual or scattered around the world if in person. There are advisory groups to address coordination issues across industrial sectors and a technical management board, made up of the ten most influential standard-setting bodies, that has agenda-setting power. At the heart of the ISO's operation is the recognition of the need for coordination and some standards along with the acceptance of consensus as the mode of decisionmaking and voluntary cooperation as the basis for enforcement and compliance, reinforced by national laws requiring the adoption of international standards. An added motivation for accepting ISO standards is the incorporation of some standards into WTO rules and the demand for goods meeting internationally accepted standards. Since the 1960s, a further motivation has come from the creation and enlargement of the European Common Market and, since 1990, the EU single market. Not surprisingly, as Murphy and Yates (2009: 29) note, "a small group of ISO member bodies, mostly in Europe but also Japan and the United States, plays a disproportionate role within the organization."

International Courts for Adjudication and Dispute Settlement

As illustrated by the foregoing snapshots of the ITU, WHO, the ILO, the Bretton Woods institutions, the FAO and international food regime, and the ISO, the development of specialized and functional organizations has been a key trend in the evolution of elements of global governance. Similarly, institutions for international adjudication were first created by the Hague Conferences of 1899 and 1907 and thus began another trend, one that has led to the creation of a growing variety of international courts for dispute settlement.

The second Hague Conference, in 1907, established the Permanent Court of Arbitration as discussed earlier—the first standing institution to settle international disputes through binding decisions based on international law. This laid the foundations for the PCIJ under the League of Nations and its successor, the ICJ. Over the century since its founding, there has been an increasing legalization of international issues, a corresponding increase in international courts, and an increased willingness by developing countries and nonstate actors (especially since the end of the Cold War) to use international judicial bodies. There are now more than twenty permanent judicial institutions and approximately seventy other international institutions that exercise judicial or quasi-judicial functions (Project on International Courts and Tribunals, www.pict-pcti.org). This represents a substantial shift in what Karen Alter (2014: 4–5) refers to as the "new international judicial architecture," wherein courts are not only resolving interstate disputes but also assessing state compliance with international law and reviewing the legal validity of state and international legislative and administrative acts. Many of what she calls new-style courts have compulsory jurisdiction and allow nonstate actors to initiate litigation. That makes them "new political actors on the domestic and international stage" who because of their international nature, can "circumvent domestic legal and political barriers and to create legal change across borders." Their legal nature allows them, Alter adds, to "provoke political change through legal reinterpretation and . . . to harness multilateral resources to knit together broader constituencies of support." Equally significant is the volume of binding rulings issued by the growing number of international courts—some 37,000, more than 90 percent of which have been issued since 1990.

Older-style international courts and newer ones are both characterized by the independence of their judges, whose power comes from their mandate to interpret international law. They adjudicate disputes between two or more entities, at least one of which is a state or IGO, using established rules of procedure, and provide a legally binding ruling (Alter 2014: 70). Figure 3.3 illustrates the number and the variety of contemporary international courts.

From the PCIJ to the ICJ

Article 14 of the Covenant of the League of Nations established the PCIJ. Judges representing major world legal systems were elected by the League's Council and Assembly. Unlike arbitral tribunals, the PCIJ was permanent, rules were fixed in advance, judgments were binding on parties, and proceedings were public. It could provide advisory opinions as well as binding decisions. However, the PCIJ was never integrated into the League. States could participate in one and not the other. Thus, the United States was a party to the PCIJ beginning in 1931, but not a League member. Between 1922 and 1940, the PCIJ decided twenty-nine contentious cases between states and handed down twenty-seven advisory opinions. Hundreds

---

Figure 3.3   Selected International and Regional Courts (with dates of operation)

Courts with Universal Scope
- International Court of Justice (1946–)
- International Criminal Court (2002–)
- International Tribunal for the Law of the Sea (1982–)
- Permanent Court of Arbitration (1899–)
- World Bank Centre for the Settlement of Investment Disputes (1966–)
- World Trade Organization Dispute Settlement Unit (includes the Dispute Settlement Body and the Appellate Body) (1995–)

Ad Hoc Criminal Tribunals
- International Criminal Tribunal for Rwanda (1995–2012)
- International Criminal Tribunal for the Former Yugoslavia (1995–2017)

Regional Courts
- African Court of Justice and Human Rights (2004–)
- Court of Justice of the Andean Community (1996–)
- Court of Justice of the European Union (1952–)
- Economic Community of West African States Court of Justice (1991–)

Specialized Regional Courts
- Court of Justice of the Common Market for Eastern and Southern Africa (1994–)
- European Court of Human Rights (1959–)
- Inter-American Court of Human Rights (1979–)

Private International Arbitration
- International Chamber of Commerce International Court of Arbitration (1923–)
- London Court of International Arbitration (1883–)

of treaties and conventions conferred jurisdiction on it to settle disputes among parties. Many PCIJ decisions helped clarify key issues of international law and laid a solid foundation for its successor, the ICJ, which refers directly to PCIJ decisions and procedures in conducting its business.

The ICJ, with fifteen justices headquartered in The Hague, Netherlands, is a major organ of the United Nations. All members of the United Nations are therefore parties to the ICJ Statute. As the judicial arm of the United Nations, the ICJ shares responsibility with the other major organs for ensuring that the principles of the UN Charter are followed. Like the PCIJ, the ICJ affords member states an impartial body for settling legal disputes and gives advisory opinions on legal questions referred to it by international agencies. The ICJ is discussed in more detail in Chapter 4.

Regional Courts

With the growth of regional organizations (see Chapter 5), there has been a corresponding proliferation of regional courts and judicial-like bodies, most of which deal with economic or human rights issues. The Court of Justice of the European Union is a key part of the European Union—the most legalized of all IGOs—and a key actor in Europe's process of integration over almost six decades. It has the power to interpret the various EU treaties and secondary legislation, as well as to rule on disputes between individuals, corporations, states, and EU institutions. The Court of Justice is also one of the most active international courts, issuing hundreds of binding rulings each year. It is discussed further in Chapter 5.

As Figure 3.2 makes clear, Africa, Latin America, and Europe all have a variety of regional courts. All three regions have human rights courts and all have multiple economic courts. The absence of courts in the Middle East and Asia is noteworthy.

Many regional courts fit the description of new-style international courts, as they have compulsory jurisdiction and provide access for nonstate actors, such as private litigants and supranational prosecutorial bodies (Alter 2014: 82). The former has been accomplished by making jurisdiction a condition of community membership rather than an opt-in or opt-out choice as it is for the ICJ. As Alter (2014: 86) notes, many of these courts have undergone significant design changes since 1990. For example, the Economic Community of West African States Court of Justice was originally established to address economic issues, but in 2005 it gained jurisdiction over human rights violations and now provides direct access for private litigants.

Specialized Courts and Tribunals

Among the specialized international courts are the ad hoc criminal tribunals for the former Yugoslavia and Rwanda, established by the UN Security Council in the 1990s, and the International Criminal Court, which came into existence in 2002 (both discussed in Chapter 9). Some special courts and tribunals are tied to UN specialized agencies, such as the ILO's Administrative Tribunal and the World Bank's International Centre for the Settlement of Investment Disputes (ICSID). The International Tribunal for the Law of the Sea was established by the UN Convention on the Law of the Sea to adjudicate disputes relating to that convention. It is open to state parties to the convention and nonstate entities, such as IGOs and state and private enterprises. In 2014, the Permanent Court of International Arbitration ruled that the Philippines could take its case disputing China's territorial claims in the South China Sea to the Law of the Sea Tribunal, despite China's refusal to participate in legal proceedings.

The ICSID and the WTO's Dispute Settlement Body are particularly noteworthy. The former is an autonomous World Bank entity that provides facilities for dispute arbitration between member countries and investors who are citizens of other member countries. Submission of disputes is voluntary, but once the parties agree to arbitration, neither may withdraw consent. Often agreements between host countries and investors include a provision stipulating that disputes will be sent to the ICSID. In recent years, the number of cases submitted to the ICSID has increased significantly, and its activities have expanded to include consultations with governments on investment and arbitration law. The WTO's dispute settlement procedures are discussed in Chapter 8.

Private International Adjudication

As economic globalization has broadened and deepened, cross-border trade and investment disputes have become more common. Although there are intergovernmental institutions for settling such disputes, such as the ICSID, the growth of these disputes has led to the establishment of private settlement approaches. There are upward of a hundred different forums, with caseloads doubling every year.

Generally, private arbitration procedures are flexible, with rules established for each case. Naturally, proceedings are held in private, and the awards are confidential. The London Court of International Arbitration is one of the oldest such bodies, established in 1892. Its main function is to select arbitrators for private parties requesting arbitration. Among such groups, the most active is the International Chamber of Commerce's International Court of Arbitration, dating from 1923. It has handled more than 19,000 cases since its founding, involving parties and arbitrators from 180 countries. In 2012, almost 500 cases were adjudicated by arbitrators drawn from seventy-six countries. Increased international and regional adjudication reflects several trends: (1) international law's expansion into domains previously subject only to state jurisdiction; (2) state and nonstate actors' willingness to expand the availability and jurisdiction of courts and tribunals; (3)

the growth of regional economic arrangements and transactions that require adjudication; and (4) massive human rights violations in post–Cold War conflicts that drove the creation of arrangements for dealing with war crimes and crimes against humanity. As one legal analyst, Cesare Romano (1999: 709), concludes, "The enormous expansion and transformation of the international judiciary is the single most important development of the post–Cold War age."

* * *

The foundations of contemporary institutions of global governance have evolved over time, from states and a rudimentary set of international rules to an increasingly complex network of international organizations. As we have explored in this chapter, the nineteenth century set a series of precedents for the development of IGOs. The twentieth century was marked by the rapid proliferation of IGOs and international adjudicatory institutions. The twenty-first century is already noted for the further evolution and proliferation of these and new types of institutions to meet the growing needs for global governance. The center for much of that activity is still the United Nations system to which we turn in Chapter 4.

Suggested Further Reading

Claude, Inis L., Jr. (1964) *Swords into Plowshares: The Problems and Progress of International Organization*, 3rd ed. New York: Random House.

Cogan, Jacob Katz, Ian Hurd, and Ian Johnstone, eds. (2016) *The Oxford Handbook of International Organizations*. New York: Oxford University Press.

Northledge, F. S. (1986) *The League of Nations: Its Life and Times, 1920–1946*. New York: Holmes and Meier.

Reinalda, Bob. (2021) *International Secretariats: Two Centuries of International Civil Servants and Secretariats*. New York: Routledge.

Squatrito, Theresa, Oran R. Young, Andreas Follesdal, and Geir Ulfstein. (2018) *The Performance of International Courts and Tribunals*. New York: Cambridge University Press.

Yates, JoAnn, and Craig Murphy. (2019) *Engineering Rules: Global Standard-Setting Since 1880*. Baltimore, MD: Johns Hopkins University Press.

4

The United Nations:
Centerpiece of
Global Governance

THE UNITED NATIONS HAS BEEN THE CENTERPIECE OF GLOBAL GOVERN-
ance since the end of World War II. It is the only intergovernmental organization (IGO) with global scope and nearly universal membership with an
agenda encompassing the broadest range of governance issues. The UN is a
complex system with many pieces. One of its functions is creating international law, norms, and principles. It has created other IGOs within the UN
system such as the UN Environment Programme (UNEP), as well as countless funds, committees, and programs; it has sponsored global conferences and
summits. It serves as a catalyst for global policy networks and partnerships
with other actors. In short, the UN is the central site for multilateral diplomacy, and the UN General Assembly is center stage. Its three weeks of general
debate at the opening of each fall assembly session draw foreign ministers and
heads of state from many countries to take advantage of the opportunity to
address all the nations of the world and engage in intensive diplomacy.

The UN Security Council is the core of the global security system and
is the primary legitimizer of actions dealing with threats to peace and security. This is what made the 2002–2003 debate over war against Iraq so
important. Would the Council endorse a US-led preventive war or not?
Since the end of the Cold War, the Security Council has redefined security
threats to include systematic human rights violations, genocide, massive
refugee flows, and HIV/AIDS. It has acted as an international regulatory
and legislative authority by imposing sanctions, creating war crimes tribunals, and responding to terrorism and nuclear weapons proliferation, creating new obligations for member states. In 2011, when the Council authorized the use of force to protect Libyan civilians, many observers cheered
what seemed to be a greater willingness to intervene in humanitarian crises.
Its failure to adopt any resolution during the first three years of the Syrian
civil war, with its huge loss of civilian lives and flow of refugees into

neighboring countries, however, made clear that inconsistency on intervention issues was still the norm. Likewise, the Council's inability to respond to Russia's 2022 invasion of Ukraine underscored its limitations.

The UN's importance, especially the relative importance of the Security Council and General Assembly, have risen and fallen over the years as world politics affected the organization. The approval of the ambitious Sustainable Development Goals (SDGs) in 2015 along with the Paris Climate Agreement that year seemed to affirm the UN's continuing role as the centerpiece of global governance. Yet on its seventy-fifth anniversary in 2020, the UN struggled to meet the many ongoing challenges of threats to peace and security, lagging development, human rights violations, and environmental degradation.

The UN Charter and Key Principles

The UN Charter expresses the hopes and aspirations of the UN's founders for a better world, lessons from the League of Nations, and the realities that states were able to agree on in 1945. As discussed in Chapter 3, several key principles undergird the UN's structure and operation and represent fundamental legal obligations of all members. These are contained in Article 2 of the Charter as well as in other provisions (see Figure 4.1).

The most fundamental principle is the sovereign equality of member states, which means that states do not recognize any higher governing authority. Equality refers to states' legal status, not their size, military power, or wealth, making Russia, Lithuania, China, and Singapore equals. This is the basis for each state having one vote in the General Assembly. Inequality is also part of the UN framework, embodied in the permanent membership and veto power of five states (the P-5) in the Security Council.

Closely related to the UN's primary goal of maintaining peace and security are the twin principles that all member states shall (1) refrain from the threat or use of force against the territorial integrity or political independence of any state, or in any manner inconsistent with UN purposes; and (2) settle their international disputes by peaceful means. On many occasions since the UN's founding, however, states have failed to honor these principles and have failed to submit their disputes to the UN for settlement. Members accept the obligation to support enforcement actions such as economic sanctions and refrain from giving assistance to states that are the objects of UN preventive or enforcement action. They have the collective responsibility to ensure that nonmember states act in accordance with these principles as necessary for maintaining international peace and security. A further key principle is the obligation of member states to fulfill in good faith all the obligations they assume under the Charter. This affirms a fundamental norm of all international law and treaties: *pacta sunt ser-*

Figure 4.1 Key UN Charter Provisions

Chapter I: Purposes and Principles

Art. 2(3): All Members shall settle their international disputes by peaceful means.

Art. 2(4): All Members shall refrain in their international relations from the threat or use of force against the territorial integrity or political independence of any state.

Art. 2(7): Nothing contained in the present Charter shall authorize the United Nations to intervene in matters which are essentially within the domestic jurisdiction of any state.

Chapter VI: Pacific Settlement of Disputes

Art. 33(1): The parties to any dispute . . . shall, first of all, seek a solution by negotiation, enquiry, mediation, conciliation, arbitration, judicial settlement, resort to regional agencies or arrangements, or other peaceful means of their own choice.

Chapter VII: Action with Respect to Threats to the Peace, Breaches of the Peace, and Acts of Aggression

Art. 39: The Security Council shall determine the existence of any threat to the peace, breach of the peace, or act of aggression.

Art. 41: The Security Council may decide what measures not involving the use of armed force are to be employed. . . . These may include complete or partial interruption of economic relations . . . and other means of communication, and the severance of diplomatic relations.

Art. 42: Should the Security Council consider that measures provided for in Article 41 would be inadequate or have proved to be inadequate, it may take such action by air, sea, or land forces as may be necessary to maintain or restore international peace and security.

Art. 51: Nothing in the present Charter shall impair the inherent right of individual or collective self-defence if an armed attack occurs against a Member of the UN.

Chapter VIII: Regional Arrangements

Art. 52: Nothing in the present Charter precludes the existence of regional arrangements or agencies for dealing with such matters relating to the maintenance of international peace and security.

Art. 53: The Security Council shall . . . utilize such regional arrangements or agencies for enforcement action under its authority. But no enforcement action shall be taken under regional arrangements or by regional agencies without the authorization of the Security Council.

---

vanda, treaties must be carried out. Among these obligations is payment of assessed annual contributions (dues) to the organization.

The final principle in Article 2 addresses the limits on the jurisdiction of the UN and underscores the long-standing norm of nonintervention in the domestic affairs of states, but it provides a key exception for enforcement actions. Who decides what is an international and what is a domestic problem? Since the UN's founding in 1945, the scope of what is considered "international" has broadened with UN involvement in human rights, development, humanitarian crises, environmental degradation, and broad issues of human security. Since the Cold War's end in 1991, many UN peacekeeping operations have involved intrastate rather than interstate conflicts, in other words conflicts within rather than between states. The UN's founders recognized the tension between the commitment to act collectively against a member state and the affirmation of state sovereignty represented in the nonintervention principle. They could not foresee the dilemmas that changing definitions of security, ethnic conflicts, humanitarian crises, failed states, and terrorism would pose. Human rights might well be seen as a matter of domestic jurisdiction, but the Preamble and Article 1 of the UN Charter both contain references to human rights and obligate states to show "respect for the principle of equal rights and self-determination of peoples." Hence, discussions of human rights have always been regarded as legitimate international rather than solely domestic concerns. Actions to promote or enforce human rights norms have been much more controversial.

In Article 51, the Charter affirms states' "right of individual or collective self-defence" against armed attack. Thus, states are not required to wait for the UN to act before undertaking measures in their own (and others') defense. They are obligated to report their responses under Chapter VIII, Article 52, and they may create regional defense and other arrangements. Unsurprisingly, the self-defense principle has led to many debates over who initiated hostilities and who was the victim of aggression. For example, in the Arab-Israeli conflict, was it Israel or the Arab states that first used force? In the debate over going to war against Iraq in 2003, did Iraq possess weapons of mass destruction, and did these pose a sufficient threat to the United States and other countries to justify war? A special committee labored for many years over the problem of defining aggression before concluding that the Security Council has the ultimate responsibility to determine what are acts of aggression. A 2010 amendment to the Rome Statute of the International Criminal Court, however, defined the crime of aggression as "the use of armed force by a State against the sovereignty, territorial integrity or political independence of another State, or in any other manner inconsistent with the Charter of the United Nations."

The Principal Organs of the United Nations

The structure of the UN as outlined in the Charter includes six principal bodies: the General Assembly, the Security Council, the Economic and Social Council (ECOSOC), the Secretariat, the International Court of Justice (ICJ), and the Trusteeship Council. Each organ has changed over time, responding to external realities, internal pressures, and interactions with other agencies. As a complex system of organizations, the UN extends well beyond these six organs. Among the affiliated organizations are the seventeen independently established specialized agencies, ranging from the World Health Organization (WHO), the Food and Agriculture Organization

(FAO), and the International Labour Organization (ILO) to the International Monetary Fund (IMF) and the World Bank (but not the World Trade Organization which is considered a "related organization"), as introduced in Chapter 3. In addition, the General Assembly, Security Council, and ECOSOC have used their powers to create a large number of subsidiary bodies, programs, and funds, illustrating the phenomenon of "IGOs creating other IGOs" (Jacobson 1984: 39). Figure 4.2 captures the complexity of the UN system. In the sections that follow, we discuss how the six major UN organs have evolved in practice and some of their political dynamics.

The General Assembly

The UN General Assembly, like the League of Nations Assembly, was designed as the general debate arena where all UN members would be equally represented according to a one state, one vote formula. It is the organization's hub, with a diverse agenda and the responsibility of coordinating and supervising subsidiary bodies but with power only to make recommendations to members, except on internal matters such as elections and the budget. It has exclusive competence over the latter, giving it a measure of surveillance and control over all UN programs and subsidiary bodies. The Assembly also has important elective functions: admitting states to UN membership; electing the nonpermanent members of the Security Council, ECOSOC, and the Trusteeship Council; appointing judges to the ICJ; and appointing the UN Secretary-General on the recommendation of the Security Council. It also grants observer status to nonmember states and international organizations, such as for the Holy See (the Vatican), the International Committee of the Red Cross, and many regional and other IGOs. In 2012, reflecting the frustration of a majority of UN members and the Palestinian people at the failure of efforts to negotiate an end to the Israeli-Palestinian conflict and create an independent Palestinian state, the Assembly voted to upgrade the Palestinian Authority's status from "nonmember observer entity" to "nonmember observer state," a recognition of de facto sovereign statehood.

In many ways, the General Assembly comes closer than any other international body to embodying what is often called the "international community." To paraphrase Shakespeare, if "all the world's a stage," the UN General Assembly is center stage—a stage particularly important for small states such as Costa Rica, Fiji, Malta, Singapore, and Zambia.

The General Assembly can consider any matter in the purview of the UN Charter (Article 10); although its recommendations are nonbinding, the number of items on the Assembly's agenda has continually grown over the years, from 46 in 1946 to more than 150 in recent years. Many items are repeated year after year with no effort at review. They range from various conflict situations, such as the Israeli-Palestinian conflict, to arms control, development, poverty eradication, global resource management, human

Figure 4.2   The United Nations System

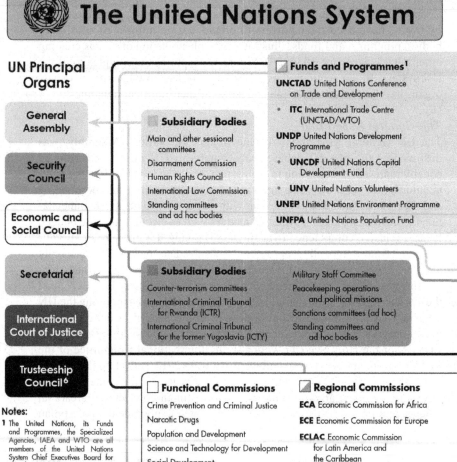

The United Nations System

UN Principal Organs

General Assembly

Security Council

Economic and Social Council

Secretariat

International Court of Justice

Trusteeship Council⁶

Subsidiary Bodies

Main and other sessional committees

Disarmament Commission

Human Rights Council

International Law Commission

Standing committees and ad hoc bodies

Subsidiary Bodies

Counter-terrorism committees

International Criminal Tribunal for Rwanda (ICTR)

International Criminal Tribunal for the former Yugoslavia (ICTY)

Military Staff Committee

Peacekeeping operations and political missions

Sanctions committees (ad hoc)

Standing committees and ad hoc bodies

Funds and Programmes¹

UNCTAD United Nations Conference on Trade and Development

- **ITC** International Trade Centre (UNCTAD/WTO)

UNDP United Nations Development Programme

- **UNCDF** United Nations Capital Development Fund
- **UNV** United Nations Volunteers

UNEP United Nations Environment Programme

UNFPA United Nations Population Fund

Functional Commissions

Crime Prevention and Criminal Justice

Narcotic Drugs

Population and Development

Science and Technology for Development

Social Development

Statistics

Status of Women

Sustainable Development

United Nations Forum on Forests

Regional Commissions

ECA Economic Commission for Africa

ECE Economic Commission for Europe

ECLAC Economic Commission for Latin America and the Caribbean

ESCAP Economic and Social Commission for Asia and the Pacific

ESCWA Economic and Social Commission for Western Asia

Departments and Offices

EOSG Executive Office of the Secretary-General

DESA Department of Economic and Social Affairs

DFS Department of Field Support

DGACM Department for General Assembly and Conference Management

DM Department of Management

DPA Department of Political Affairs

DPI Department of Public Information

DPKO Department of Peacekeeping Operations

DSS Department of Safety and Security

OCHA Office for the Coordination of Humanitarian Affairs

OHCHR Office of the United Nations High Commissioner for Human Rights

Notes:

1 The United Nations, its Funds and Programmes, the Specialized Agencies, IAEA and WTO are all members of the United Nations System Chief Executives Board for Coordination (CEB).

2 UNRWA and UNIDIR report only to the General Assembly (GA).

3 IAEA reports to the Security Council and the GA.

4 WTO has no reporting obligation to the GA, but contributes on an ad hoc basis to GA and Economic and Social Council (ECOSOC) work on, inter alia, finance and development issues.

5 Specialized Agencies are autonomous organizations whose work is coordinated through ECOSOC (intergovernmental level) and CEB (inter-secretariat level).

6 The Trusteeship Council suspended operation on 1 November 1994, as on 1 October 1994 Palau, the last United Nations Trust Territory, became independent.

This is not an official document of the United Nations, nor is it intended to be all inclusive.

UN-HABITAT United Nations Human Settlements Programme

UNHCR Office of the United Nations High Commissioner for Refugees

UNICEF United Nations Children's Fund

UNODC United Nations Office on Drugs and Crime

UNRWA[2] United Nations Relief and Works Agency for Palestine Refugees in the Near East

UN-Women United Nations Entity for Gender Equality and the Empowerment of Women

WFP World Food Programme

▨ Research and Training Institutes

UNICRI United Nations Interregional Crime and Justice Research Institute

UNIDIR[2] United Nations Institute for Disarmament Research

UNITAR United Nations Institute for Training and Research

UNRISD United Nations Research Institute for Social Development

UNSSC United Nations System Staff College

UNU United Nations University

▨ Other Entities

UNAIDS Joint United Nations Programme on HIV/AIDS

UNISDR United Nations International Strategy for Disaster Reduction

UNOPS United Nations Office for Project Services

Related Organizations

CTBTO Preparatory Commission Preparatory Commission for the Comprehensive Nuclear-Test-Ban Treaty Organization

IAEA[1,3] International Atomic Energy Agency

OPCW Organisation for the Prohibition of Chemical Weapons

WTO[1,4] World Trade Organization

◣ Advisory Subsidiary Body

Peacebuilding Commission

▨ Specialized Agencies[1,5]

FAO Food and Agriculture Organization of the United Nations

ICAO International Civil Aviation Organization

IFAD International Fund for Agricultural Development

ILO International Labour Organization

IMF International Monetary Fund

IMO International Maritime Organization

ITU International Telecommunication Union

UNESCO United Nations Educational, Scientific and Cultural Organization

UNIDO United Nations Industrial Development Organization

UNWTO World Tourism Organization

UPU Universal Postal Union

WHO World Health Organization

WIPO World Intellectual Property Organization

WMO World Meteorological Organization

World Bank Group

- **IBRD** International Bank for Reconstruction and Development
- **ICSID** International Centre for Settlement of Investment Disputes
- **IDA** International Development Association
- **IFC** International Finance Corporation
- **MIGA** Multilateral Investment Guarantee Agency

▨ Other Bodies

Committee for Development Policy

Committee of Experts on Public Administration

Committee on Non-Governmental Organizations

Permanent Forum on Indigenous Issues

United Nations Group of Experts on Geographical Names

Other sessional and standing committees and expert, ad hoc and related bodies

OIOS Office of Internal Oversight Services

OLA Office of Legal Affairs

OSAA Office of the Special Adviser on Africa

SRSG/CAAC Office of the Special Representative of the Secretary-General for Children and Armed Conflict

SRSG/SVC Office of the Special Representative of the Secretary-General on Sexual Violence in Conflict

UNODA Office for Disarmament Affairs

UNOG United Nations Office at Geneva

UN-OHRLLS Office of the High Representative for the Least Developed Countries, Landlocked Developing Countries and Small Island Developing States

UNON United Nations Office at Nairobi

UNOV United Nations Office at Vienna

Published by the United Nations Department of Public Information DPI/2470 rev.3—13-38229—August 2013 rights, advancement of women, international justice and law, reports from other UN organs, follow-up to UN-sponsored conferences, administrative matters, and the UN's finances. Resolutions may be aimed at individual member states, nonmembers, the Security Council or other organs, the Secretary-General, or even the Assembly itself.

Although the Security Council is the primary organ for dealing with threats to international peace and security, the Assembly can make inquiries and studies with respect to conflicts (Articles 13–14), it may discuss a situation and make recommendations if the Security Council is not exercising its functions (Articles 11–12), and it has the right to be kept informed by the Security Council and the Secretary-General (Articles 10–12). The "Uniting for Peace" resolution, passed during the Korean War in 1950, ignited controversy, however, over the respective roles of the two bodies. Under the resolution, the General Assembly claimed authority to recommend collective measures when the Security Council was deadlocked by a veto. It was subsequently used to deal with crises in Suez and Hungary (1956), the Middle East (1958, 1967, 1980, 1982), the Congo (1960), and the war in Ukraine (2022). In all, eleven emergency special sessions of the Assembly have dealt with threats to international peace when the Security Council was deadlocked. The eleventh was convened in 2022 after Russia's invasion of Ukraine.

In 1962, in the *Certain Expenses of the United Nations* case (ICJ Advisory Opinion 1962), the ICJ was asked to give an advisory opinion on whether the General Assembly had the authority to authorize peacekeeping operations (the opinion was affirmative). Since the early 1990s, however, the permanent members of the Security Council have tacitly agreed that only the Security Council should authorize the use of armed force. Still, when the Security Council fails to act because of one or more P-5 vetoes, the General Assembly can give voice to international sentiment, as it did in 2014 on Russia's takeover of Crimea, in 2016 on violations of international law in Syria, in 2021 with a resolution condemning the lethal violence used by Myanmar's armed forces against peaceful demonstrators, and in 2022 to condemn Russia's annexation of portions of Ukraine. In general, the Assembly is a cumbersome body for dealing with delicate situations of peace and security. It is most useful for the symbolic politics of agenda-setting and mustering large majorities in support of resolutions.

The UN Charter also entrusted the General Assembly with an important role in developing international law (Article 13). Although the Assembly is not a world legislature, its resolutions may lay the basis for new international law by articulating new principles, such as one that called the seas the "common heritage of mankind," and new concepts like sustainable development. These are often the basis for soft law—norms that represent a widespread international consensus but may not (yet) be embodied in "hard" or treaty form—and may (or may not) then be embodied in multilateral norm- or law-creating treaties and conventions drafted under General Assembly authorization. For example, the "common heritage" principle was incorporated into the 1967 Treaty on Outer Space and 1982 Convention on Law of the Sea. The 2005 World Summit endorsed the emerging norm of states' responsibility to protect their own people and the international community's responsibility to act when governments fail to protect vulnerable people. This responsibility to protect norm (R2P), as it has become known, was the basis for the Security Council's 2011 decision to authorize the use of force to protect Libya's civilian population and is discussed further later in this chapter. Over time, the General Assembly has produced many multilateral lawmaking treaties, including the 1961 Vienna Convention on Diplomatic Relations, the 1969 Vienna Convention on the Law of Treaties, the 1968 Treaty on the Non-Proliferation of Nuclear Weapons, the 1994 Convention on the Safety of United Nations and Associated Personnel, and the 2017 Treaty on the Prohibition of Nuclear Weapons. Assembly resolutions have also approved all the major international human rights conventions, most of which were drafted in the former Commission on Human Rights, which was replaced in 2006 by the Human Rights Council, which reports to the General Assembly.

Finally, the General Assembly shares responsibilities for Charter revision with the Security Council. The Assembly can propose amendments with a two-thirds majority; two-thirds of the member states, including the P-5, must then ratify the changes. The General Assembly and Security Council together may call a general conference for the purpose of Charter review. To date, there have been only two instances of Charter amendment, both enlarging the membership of the Security Council and ECOSOC.

How the General Assembly functions. Regular annual meetings of the General Assembly are held for three months (or longer) each fall and begin with a "general debate" period when heads of state, prime ministers, and foreign ministers by the score come to New York to speak before the Assembly. In addition, there have been thirty-two special sessions called to deal with specific problems (e.g., financial and budgetary problems in 1963, development and international economic cooperation in 1975, disarmament in 1978, HIV/AIDS in 2001, Covid-19 in 2020, and challenges to prevent and combat corruption in 2021). These special sessions should not be confused with the emergency special sessions convened under a "Uniting for Peace" resolution.

The bulk of the General Assembly's work occurs in six functional committees: the Disarmament and International Security Committee (the First Committee); the Economic and Financial Committee (the Second Committee); the Social, Humanitarian, and Cultural Committee (the Third Committee); the

Special Political and Decolonization Committee (the Fourth Committee); the Administrative and Budgetary Committee (the Fifth Committee); and the Legal Committee (the Sixth Committee). All six are committees of the whole, exact duplications of the plenary Assembly. The Assembly has created other, smaller committees to carry out specific tasks, such as studying a question (e.g., the ad hoc Committee on International Terrorism) or framing proposals and monitoring (e.g., the Committee on Peaceful Uses of Outer Space, the Disarmament Commission). The Sixth Committee and the International Law Commission, an elected group of thirty-four jurists nominated by UN member states, have responsibility for drafting international conventions to carry out the Assembly's mission of "encouraging the progressive development of international law and its codification" (Article 13).

Each year, the General Assembly elects a president and seventeen vice presidents who serve for that session. By tradition, presidents tend to come from small and middle-power states, and often from developing countries. Only on four occasions (1953, 1969, 2006, and 2018) has a woman been elected. The president's powers are limited but allow much to be accomplished through personal influence and political skills in guiding the work of the Assembly, averting crises, bringing parties into agreement, ensuring that procedures are respected, and accelerating the cumbersome agenda.

Key to the General Assembly's functioning are member states' delegations. The UN Charter provides that each member can have no more than five representatives in the Assembly, but Assembly rules have permitted five alternates and unlimited advisers and technical experts. The practice of establishing permanent missions and ambassadors began with the League of Nations. Although missions are mandatory for Security Council members, who must be able to meet immediately in the event of an emergency, the practice became common for most member states with the establishment of UN headquarters in New York in 1948. Missions vary in size from about 150 personnel (the US mission) to a single person of diplomatic rank. Small and poor states often combine their UN mission with their embassy in Washington, DC, to save money; most states' missions grow significantly during the fall Assembly sessions, sometimes including a few parliamentarians or legislators. (The US House and Senate alternate in having representatives on the US delegation to the General Assembly each year.)

Delegates attend General Assembly and committee sessions, participate in efforts to shape agendas and debate, and represent national interests. Expertise and skill in multilateral diplomacy matter and enable some delegates to be more influential than others. Because almost all countries of the world are represented at the annual Assembly sessions, there are many opportunities for informal bilateral and multilateral contacts, which countries may use to deal with issues outside the Assembly's agenda. UN diplomats have to deal with a huge spectrum of issues and many different viewpoints and policies. During the regular Assembly sessions, the social obligations of endless receptions, which would be considered politically incorrect not to attend, can be exhausting. Because it can take a long time for a new delegate to learn the ropes and become effective, it is not uncommon for some delegates to serve for many years. The United States, however, tends to rotate its foreign service officers at the UN mission frequently, demonstrating that experience in multilateral diplomacy is not valued highly.

Ties between UN missions and home governments vary from loose to tight. Some delegations have considerable autonomy in dealing with the various issues on Assembly agendas and determining how best to represent their countries' interests. Others operate on a "tighter leash" and must seek instructions from their capitals on what strategies to use and how to vote on given resolutions.

Decisionmaking in the General Assembly. Early in UN history, states from the same geographic region or with shared economic or political interests formed coalitions to shape common positions on particular issues and control blocs of votes. Several factors led to the development of these groups. First, the Charter specified that in electing the nonpermanent members of the Security Council, the General Assembly give consideration to "equitable geographical distribution," but offered no guidance on how to do so or what the appropriate geographic groups should be. The five recognized regional groups of states are Western European and Other (includes the United States, Israel, Japan, and Canada), Eastern European, African, Latin American and Caribbean, and Asian. Each regional group determines the rules and procedures for selecting candidates for Security Council or ECOSOC seats and which candidates to support for the ICJ or Secretary-General.

A second factor in the emergence of caucusing groups is the principle of one state, one vote. General Assembly decisions are made by a majority (either simple or two-thirds under specified circumstances, such as elections and questions of peace and security). As a result, a stable coalition of states comprising a majority of members, like a majority political party or coalition of parties in a legislature, can control most decisions. Coalitions in the UN have tended to persist for long periods and correspond with major substantive divisions in the General Assembly. The two longest-standing divisions have been the East–West one, defined largely by Cold War issues, and the North–South division, related to development issues.

During the Cold War, Eastern European states voted consistently with the Soviet Union, as did many nominally nonaligned states. The Western European, Latin American, and British Commonwealth states voted closely with the United States on Cold War–related issues and often on human rights and internal UN administration. Colonial and economic questions, however, divided this US-dominated coalition. By 1960, the United States could no longer muster a simple majority because of the influx of new African and Asian states. Since the Cold War's end, Russia and other Eastern European states have tended to vote with the Western European states or a larger "Northern" group.

The North–South division has centered on economic inequalities and development, colonialism and decolonization, and great power military capabilities. In the 1950s, developing countries were fragmented into the Afro-Asian group, the Latin American group, and the Non-Aligned Movement (NAM). With the creation of the UN Conference on Trade and Development (UNCTAD) in 1964, they formed the Group of 77 (G-77), and UNCTAD's own system of group negotiation reinforced their tendency to operate as a unified bloc that constituted more than two-thirds of the UN's membership. Beginning in the early 1970s, the G-77 "could, and did, steer the United Nations in directions that it wanted to move, it could, and did, commit the United Nations to principles that it wanted to legitimize, and it could, and did, demand global actions conducive to its interests. The Group of 77 ultimately could not enforce compliance with its demands, but it could bring attention to them and impressively argue for their rectitude" (Puchala and Coate 1989: 53).

Although the North–South divide persists, the G-77's cohesion has eroded since the late 1980s. The South is now splintered between a number of more developed countries, such as Brazil, China, India, Malaysia, Mexico, and South Africa; a large number of very poor countries; and others in between. The developed countries, however, have never been as cohesive as the countries of the South. Many European states have been more supportive of developing countries' concerns than has the United States, weakening the North's ability to operate as a coalition in responding to the South.

Other caucusing groups in the UN include the Afro-Asian group, French-speaking and English-speaking African countries, the Association of Southeast Asian Nations, the NAM, the Organisation of Islamic Cooperation, the Alliance of Small Island States, and the European Union (see Figure 4.3). The level of activity and cohesion in these groups depends on the issue, as do the processes by which they formulate common positions. The EU has a formalized process of continual consultation among its twenty-seven member states and for delegating responsibility for enunciating common policies. Other groups rely on formal and informal meetings of delegates. The Alliance of Small Island States, a grouping of thirty-nine small island and low-lying coastal developing states that share similar development challenges and concerns about climate change, has created its own NGO (Islands First) to assist with research and lobbying; it operates out of its chairman's permanent mission.

Although coalitions and blocs emerged in response to the UN's provisions for elections and voting, most General Assembly decisionmaking is done by consensus—that is, by acclamation or acquiescence without a formal vote. In this case, the Assembly president consults with delegations and then announces that a resolution is adopted. Consensus, therefore, refers to a decision "supported by, or at least not objectionable to, all parties involved" (Smith 2006: 218). When the Assembly does vote, Article 18, paragraph 2 of the UN Charter specifies that it use a simple majority of those states "present and voting" to decide all questions other than "important questions" dealing with peace and security, elections, budget, and admission or suspension of members. One study showed that only one-third of Assembly decisions between the first and sixty-fourth sessions involved recorded votes, with the highest percentage of these occurring in the 1980s on Middle East issues (Hug 2012). Coalitions and blocs are as active in trying to forge consensus as they are in marshaling votes, but the outcome is less divisive because states' individual positions are not revealed as in a roll call vote.

The General Assembly's shifting agendas and relevance. Politics in the General Assembly mirrors world

Figure 4.3
Caucusing Groups in the United Nations (number of member states)

Regional Electoral Groups
- African Group (54)
- Asia-Pacific Group (55)
- Eastern European States Group (23)
- Group of Latin American and Caribbean States (33)
- Western European and Other Group (28)

Selected Other Regional and Multilateral Caucusing Groups[a]
- African Union (55)
- Alliance of Small Island States (39)
- Association of Southeast Asian Nations (10)
- Brazil, Russia, India, China, and South Africa (5)
- Cairns Group (20)
- Caribbean Community (15)
- European Union (27)
- Group of 77 and China (~134)
- New Agenda Coalition (6)
- Nonaligned Movement (ca. 120)
- Nordic Group (5)
- Organisation of Islamic Cooperation (57)

Source: https://www.un.org/dgacm/en/content/regional-groups for the electoral groups. Various sources for the selected caucusing groups.
Note: a. In addition to the groups listed here, there are several "friends" groups such as the Friends of R2P and the Friends of Women, Peace, and Security.

politics, but not always the realities of power, given the principle of one state, one vote. The Assembly is *the* place to set the agendas of world politics, to get ideas endorsed or condemned, actions taken or rejected. Any state can propose an agenda item. In the 1960s, UN membership increased dramatically (see Figure 4.4) with the end of European colonial rule in Africa and Asia, a process of largely peaceful transformation in which the UN played a significant role. The membership change had a particular influence on the General Assembly's agendas and voting patterns. From the early 1960s to the mid-1980s, the G-77 endeavored to use its two-thirds majority in the Assembly to achieve a number of goals, especially the proposed New International Economic Order (Chapter 8). That pattern shifted in the mid-1980s with the eroding consensus in the G-77, changes in Soviet and US policies that increased the Security Council's role, and the increased importance of the IMF and World Bank for dealing with debt and development issues. The result has been a steady decline in the Assembly's role.

Today, the North–South divide persists around issues of economic inequality and development, self-determination (particularly for Palestine), and great power military capabilities. But human security issues, including human rights, development, international security, migration, global inequalities, and the environment, are often very divisive, as are questions of political rights, state sovereignty, and UN intervention. On these issues, while the North–South divide is still salient, there are more crosscutting currents.

Many criticisms of the UN are really criticisms of the General Assembly. The number of resolutions passed by the Assembly has steadily increased over time, from about 119 annually during the first five years to a peak of 360 each year in 2001–2002, when efforts to reduce the number began. The seventy-fifth Assembly, in 2020, approved 269 resolutions. Over the years, many resolutions have passed with little concern for imple-

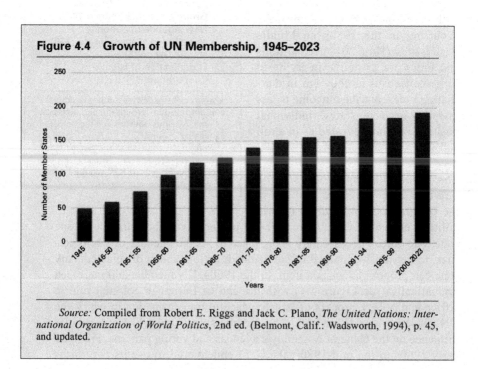

Figure 4.4 Growth of UN Membership, 1945–2023

Source: Compiled from Robert E. Riggs and Jack C. Plano, *The United Nations: International Organization of World Politics*, 2nd ed. (Belmont, Calif.: Wadsworth, 1994), p. 45, and updated.

mentation. Many are "ritual resolutions" that appear annually on agenda items, such as the right to development or the situation in the Palestinian territories, and are formulated in very general terms, thus masking dissent that would be evident if the wording were more specific.

After the end of the Cold War, the General Assembly was marginalized as the epicenter of UN activity shifted to the Security Council and Secretariat, much to the dismay of the South, which preferred more consultation between the General Assembly and Security Council on peace and security issues. With increasing tensions among the major powers, especially the United States, Russia, and China, the General Assembly has again become an important forum for marshaling international opprobrium with the Security Council stymied by P-5 vetoes.

Unquestionably, the General Assembly needs reform and revitalization. There has been some progress since the mid-1980s in reducing the agenda and number of resolutions as well as requiring explicit renewal of programs or funds based on continuing relevance and effectiveness. Changes, however, require the concurrence of a majority of states.

The Security Council

Under Article 24 of the UN Charter, the Security Council has primary responsibility for maintenance of international peace and security and the authority to act on behalf of all members of the United Nations. Provisions for carrying out this role are spelled out in Chapters VI and VII (see Figure 4.1). Chapter VI provides a wide range of techniques to investigate disputes and help parties achieve peaceful settlement. Chapter VII specifies the Security Council's authority to commit all UN members to take enforcement measures, such as sanctions or military force. Before 1990, the Security Council used its enforcement powers under Chapter VII on only two occasions, relying on the mechanisms in Chapter VI to respond to conflicts during the Cold War years. For example, before 1992, all UN peacekeeping forces were authorized under Chapter VI. Since then, the Security Council's use of Chapter VII, including its provisions for economic sanctions and military enforcement action, has increased dramatically, and most peacekeeping operations now carry Chapter VII authority (discussed further in Chapter 7).

The Security Council was kept small to facilitate more efficient (i.e., swifter) decisionmaking in dealing with threats to international peace and security. It is the only UN body that has both permanent and nonpermanent members. The five permanent members—the United States, the United Kingdom, France, Russia (successor state to the seat of the Soviet Union in 1992), and the People's Republic of China (which replaced the Republic of China in 1971)—are key to Security Council decisionmaking, since each has veto power. The nonpermanent members, originally six in number and expanded to ten in 1965, are elected by the General Assembly for staggered two-year terms after nomination by one of the five regional groups. At least four nonpermanent members must vote in favor of a resolution for it to pass. Under current rules, no country may serve successive terms as a nonpermanent member. Five of the nonpermanent seats go to Africa and Asia, two each to Latin America and Western Europe, and one to Eastern Europe. As of 2020, there were sixty-three member states that had never been elected to one of the nonpermanent seats. They included many small states as well as Israel, Iceland, and Afghanistan. One difficulty is that Council members must keep representatives in New York at all times, which can be an expensive burden for small states.

The designation of permanent members reflected the distribution of military power in 1945 and the desire to ensure the UN's ability to respond quickly and decisively to any aggression. Neither the United States nor the Soviet Union would have accepted UN membership without veto power. The veto also reflected a realistic acceptance by others that the UN could not undertake enforcement action either against its strongest members or without their concurrence, but the veto has always been controversial among small states and middle powers. Since the Security Council represents less than 8 percent of the total UN membership, its composition is clearly outdated and discussion of "equitable representation" is a major reform issue.

The Security Council differs from the General Assembly and ECOSOC in that it has no regular schedule of meetings or agenda; historically, it has met and acted only in response to specific conflicts and crises. Any state, including non-UN members, has the right to bring issues before the Security Council, although there is no guarantee of action. The Secretary-General can also bring a matter to the Council's attention. In 2000, the Security Council presidents initiated so-called thematic meetings to address issues such as HIV/AIDS as a threat to peace, child soldiers, cooperation between the UN and regional organizations under Chapter VIII of the Charter, the role of women in peace and security, protection of civilians, small arms, and in October 2022 during the presidency of Gabon, the financing of armed groups and terrorists through illicit trafficking of Africa's natural resources. As the topics suggest, this approach has become important to addressing broader issues of human (rather than just state) security.

Nonmembers may attend formal meetings and address the Council on request when they have an interest in a particular issue. States that contribute peacekeeping troops now regularly participate in informal consultations with the Council, as do the heads of the International Committee of the Red Cross, other NGOs, and other individuals with relevant expertise under what is known as the Arria formula, named for Venezuelan Ambassador Diego Arria, who first applied it in 1992. Thirty-two such meetings—a record—were convened in 2021. The Council members have visited countries and conflict areas for fact-finding, supporting peace agreements, and mediation efforts. In short, "the Security Council is not a sealed chamber, deaf to voices and immune to pressure from beyond its walls" (Johnstone 2008: 88–89).

Much of the diplomacy and negotiation relating to the Council's work takes place in informal consultations such as those among the P-5, with troop contributors, Secretariat officials, and nonstate actors. Although there have long been complaints about the Council's working methods, in actuality it has "continued to be the most adaptable international body, at times capable of modifying its methods of work literally on the spot" (*Security Council Report* 2014). The Council presidency rotates monthly (by alphabetical order of country names) among the fifteen members, and presidents play an active role in facilitating discussions and consensus building, determining when the members are ready to reach a decision and hence when to convene a formal meeting, plus conferring with the Secretary-General. It has also become common for presidents to use their month in office to highlight a particular theme in an open debate, with the country's president or prime minister sometimes chairing the meeting.

In conjunction with its actions on terrorism, nuclear weapons proliferation, and targeted sanctions since the 1990s, the work of the Security Council also occurs in the Counter-Terrorism Committee, the Non-Proliferation Committee, working groups, and sanctions committees, whose tasks include monitoring reports, managing exemptions, and managing designation lists. The committees are often assisted by panels of experts and monitoring groups that are recruited from lists maintained by the Secretariat; they are chaired by one of the ten nonpermanent member states and operate on the basis of consensus. The Council's work also includes overseeing all UN peacekeeping operations and political missions.

In addition to its responsibilities under the Charter for maintaining international security, the Council participates in the election of the Secretary-General, justices to the ICJ, and new UN members in collaboration with the General Assembly. During the 1940s the Council held approximately 130 meetings a year. This frequency diminished during the Cold War; in 1959, for example, only five meetings were held. Since the early 1990s, the frequency of meetings has steadily risen, with 291 in 2022; often the number of private meetings and informal consultations is even greater. As of mid-2022, the Council had approved over 2,600 resolutions since its inception and issued hundreds of presidential statements that summarized the outcomes of meetings where no resolutions were acted on. The majority of both have come since 1990. With increasing tensions among the P-5 countries, however, the number of resolutions and presidential statements has dropped, with just six approved by late 2022. Council members failed to pass resolutions on the Covid-19 pandemic and on humanitarian access to Syria. Given the lack of consensus among the P-5, the United Kingdom initiated informal "sofa talks" in an effort to encourage more consultations.

The veto power of the P-5 has long been controversial. It was a particular problem during the Cold War, when the Soviet Union employed it frequently to block action on many peace and security issues and to block admission of Western-supported new members and nominees for Secretary-General. The United States did not exercise its veto until the 1970s, reflecting its early dominance and many friends. Thereafter, the United States used its veto more than any other permanent member until 2012 (see Table 4.1 for a summary of vetoes cast). The majority of US vetoes have been cast on resolutions relating to the Arab-Israeli-Palestinian conflict and in defense of Israel. China took advantage of the precedent that allowed abstentions not to be counted as negative votes (i.e., vetoes) to abstain a total of twenty-seven times between 1990 and 1996 on a series of enforcement measures (including those against Iraq), thus registering its disagreement but not blocking action. Between 2011 and 2020, Russia and China jointly exercised their vetoes on nine occasions to block Council action, mostly on the civil war in Syria, including on humanitarian access, reflecting their shared concerns regarding sovereignty, nonintervention, and US dominance. Not surprisingly, Russia exercised its veto on the situation in Ukraine following its 2014 seizure of Crimea and on four occasions in 2022 after its invasion of Ukraine. It is important to recognize that vetoes are

Table 4.1   Vetoes in the Security Council, 1946–2022

Period	China[a]	France	Britain	US	USSR/ Russia	Total
1946–1955	1	2	—	—	80	83
1956–1965	0	2	3	—	26	31
1966–1975	2	2	10	12	7	33
1976–1985	0	9	11	34	6	60
1986–1995	0	3	8	24	2	37
1996–2005	2	0	0	10	1	13
2006–2011	2	0	0	3	3	8
2012–2022	11	0	0	3	25	39
Total	18	18	32	86	150	304

Sources: Data compiled from www.globalpolicy.org/images/pdfs/Z/Tables_and_Charts/useofveto.pdf; www.un.org/Depts/dhl/resguide/scact2011.htm; http://research.un.org/en/docs/sc/quick; and https://www.securitycouncilreport.org/atf/cf/%7B65BFCF9B-6D27-4E9C-8CD3-CF6E4FF96FF9%7D/working_methods_theveto-6.pdf.

Notes: a. Between 1946 and 1971, the Chinese seat on the Security Council was occupied by the Republic of China (Taiwan), which used the veto only once (to block Mongolia's application for membership in 1955). The first veto exercised by the present occupant, the People's Republic of China, therefore did not occur until August 25, 1972.

only exercised when other council members insist on a vote on a draft resolution that they know a P-5 member objects to and will likely veto (Luck 2016: 202). What changed in 2022 was that the General Assembly approved a procedure that now requires the Assembly to meet within ten days of the exercise of a veto by one of the P-5 (Resolution 76/262). This meant that Russia faced overwhelming votes in the Assembly against its actions on four occasions.

Although literature on the UN has long emphasized the P-5 members' veto power as an important part of decisionmaking in the Security Council, the reality is that in recent years the Council has been divided on only a limited number of issues and otherwise operates largely by consensus. Presidential statements and press statements reflect Council agreement; the sanctions committees and working groups operate by consensus; even most resolutions are adopted by consensus. A 2014 *Security Council Report* (2014b) concluded that although there may be a premium on consensus, the downside is that "in pursuing resolutions with strict consensus . . . stronger language is lost."

The Cold War made Security Council actions on peace and security threats extremely problematic. Some conflicts, such as the French and US wars in Vietnam and Soviet interventions in Czechoslovakia and Hungary, were never brought to the UN. A UN response to North Korea's invasion of South Korea in 1950 was possible only because the Soviet Union was boycotting the Security Council at the time and the General Assembly used the Uniting for Peace resolution to act. Although Cold War politics often sidelined the Security Council, it has been recognized at least since the mid-1960s that the Council has the power of "collective legitimation" on behalf of a large part of the international community (Claude 1967; Voeten 2005).

In the late 1980s, the Security Council's activity, power, and prestige increased dramatically. Major shifts in Soviet foreign policy led to closer P-5 cooperation and a succession of breakthroughs in regional conflicts, including the Iran-Iraq War and conflicts in Afghanistan, Central America, Namibia, and Cambodia. The number of Security Council meetings per year rose, and the Council initiated the practices of informal, private consultations and decisionmaking by consensus. In the confrontation with Iraq after its invasion of Kuwait in 1990, the strength of agreement among both the P-5 and the nonpermanent members of the Council was unprecedented.

Beginning in 1990, the Security Council took action on more armed conflicts (particularly intrastate conflicts), made more decisions under Chapter VII of the UN Charter, authorized more peacekeeping operations, and imposed more types of sanctions in more situations than ever before. It took the unprecedented step of creating ad hoc war crimes tribunals to prosecute individuals responsible for genocide and war crimes in Rwanda, the former Yugoslavia, and Sierra Leone and made referrals to the International Criminal

Court, established in 2002. It authorized NATO bombing against Bosnian Serb forces in Bosnia in 1995 and UN-administered protectorates in Kosovo and East Timor. It expanded definitions of threats to peace to include terrorism even before the September 11, 2001 attacks and thereafter approved Resolution 1373, which requires all member states to adopt antiterrorism measures outlined in the International Convention for the Suppression of the Financing of Terrorism. It has attempted to prevent Iran, North Korea, and other actors from acquiring nuclear weapons, and approved Resolution 1540 (2004), which obligates states to establish domestic controls to prevent proliferation of weapons of mass destruction to state or nonstate actors.

In 2000, after heavy lobbying by women's groups and staff from the UN Development Fund for Women (UNIFEM), the council adopted Resolution 1325 on women, peace, and security or WPS—a major step in the direction of incorporating women and women's roles in peace operations, mediation, and peace negotiations. It has also taken a more proactive approach to protecting civilians in drafting the mandates of peace operations. It authorized military action to the latter end in Libya and for cross-border humanitarian assistance in Syria. Unquestionably, the inability of Security Council members to agree on action to halt the conflict in Syria or even for a long period to agree on a humanitarian assistance mission, however, demonstrated the Council's impotence in the face of great power opposition.

The creation of various monitoring bodies since 1990 marked a sharp departure from earlier actions of the Security Council and demonstrated a degree of learning regarding how best to frame and target sanctions, for example, and how to improve their effectiveness. The use of such regulative and legislative authority over UN members, and the Council's intrusive sanctions and weapons inspection regimes for Iraq (discussed in Chapter 7), led Canadian diplomat David Malone (2006: 173) to call this "a movement toward a regulatory approach to international peace and security." Likewise, the Council's overall activism since Iraq's invasion of Kuwait in 1990 has underscored the view that it is "the most relevant international institution for granting or withholding collective legitimation for international war" and for the use of armed force more generally (Hurd 2007: 124). Furthermore, Ian Hurd (2008b: 35) argues that the case of US war against Iraq in 2003 showed "that even powerful states were forced to frame their policies around the existence of the Council. Both coalitions of states, pro- and anti-invasion . . . accepted that Council approval was a powerful resource for states, and so they fought to either win it or withhold it from the other." Despite concerns at the time that the Council was a failed body, both sides saw the legitimacy of its authority at stake.

The Charter clearly endows the Council with a great deal of formal power and authority over questions of international peace and security. Yet the use of that authority is problematic, scholars note, given the "contradiction between international commitment and state sovereignty," particularly the traditional assumption that international obligations are binding only with states' consent (Hurd 2007: 5). Searching for evidence of the Council's authority for the post–9/11 antiterrorism actions mandated in Resolution 1373, for example, Bruce Cronin and Ian Hurd (2008: 201) confirm: "It is not the act of issuing these mandatory declarations that offers evidence of increased authority, but, rather, the fact that most member states accepted the *right* of the Council to do so."

The Council's refusal to approve the US war against Iraq in 2003 reinforced its perceived authority. Russia's about-face when the Council-authorized NATO intervention in Libya turned into regime change rather than just protection of civilians, along with Russia and China's use of their veto power to block action in Syria, however, underscores the difficulty of addressing threats to domestic peace and security. In short, when there is P-5 consensus, action can be taken; when the Security Council is divided, the result is stasis. The P-5 are increasingly divided with the growing tensions between the United States, China, and Russia with some commentators describing it as a new "cold war." Russia's presence on the Council after its 2022 invasion of Ukraine and the doubly awkward situation when it assumed its rotation as president of the Council in April 2023 have provoked renewed debate about the Council's efficacy.

In short, the UN Charter gives the Security Council enormous formal power, but does not give it direct control over the means to use that power. The Council depends on the voluntary cooperation of states and their willingness to contribute to peacekeeping missions, enforce sanctions, pay their dues, and support enforcement actions either under UN command or by a coalition of the willing with sufficient highly trained military personnel and material. Most important, states' voluntary compliance depends on their perceptions of the legitimacy of the Council and its actions—its symbolic power (Hurd 2002: 35). As the case of the United States and Iraq in 2003 demonstrated, even powerful states may work hard to use that symbolic power to serve their interests.

The increased Security Council activity since 1990 has led many UN members to push strongly for reform in the Council's membership so that it better reflects the world of today, not the world of 1945. This debate, which we take up later in this chapter, concerns how to make the Council function more effectively and how to ensure the continuing legitimacy of its authority.

ECOSOC

Although the sections of the UN Charter (Chapters IX and X) that deal with ECOSOC are short and very general, this is the most complex part of the UN system. ECOSOC is the UN's central forum for addressing international economic and social issues, and its purposes range from promoting higher standards of living to identifying solutions to economic, social, and health problems and "encouraging universal respect for human rights and fundamental freedoms." The activities it oversees encompass more than 70 percent of human and financial resources of the UN system. The founders of the UN envisioned that the various specialized agencies, ranging from the ILO, WHO, and FAO to the World Bank and IMF, would play primary roles in operational activities devoted to economic and social advancement, with ECOSOC responsible for coordinating those activities. Hence the Charter speaks of ECOSOC's functions in terms of that coordination, and in terms of undertaking research and preparing reports on economic and social issues, making recommendations, preparing conventions (treaties), convening conferences, and consulting with NGOs. Of those tasks, coordination has proven the most problematic, since a myriad of activities lie outside the effective jurisdiction of ECOSOC. Through consultative status with ECOSOC, more than 6,000 NGOs have official relationships with the UN and its activities as of 2022 (see Chapter 6 for further discussion).

ECOSOC's membership has been expanded through two Charter amendments. The original eighteen members were increased to twenty-seven in 1965 and to fifty-four in 1973. Members are elected by the General Assembly to three-year terms based on nominations by the regional blocs. Motivated by recognition that states with the ability to pay should be continuously represented, the P-5 and major developed countries such as Germany and Japan have been regularly reelected. ECOSOC acts through decisions and resolutions, many of which are approved by consensus or simple majority votes. None are binding on member states or on the specialized agencies, however. Recommendations and multilateral conventions drafted by ECOSOC require General Assembly approval (and in the case of conventions, ratification by member states).

ECOSOC holds one four-week substantive meeting each year, alternating between UN headquarters in New York and Geneva, where several of the specialized agencies and other programs are headquartered. It also hosts a number of other meetings, including an annual meeting with finance ministers heading key committees in the World Bank and IMF plus many short sessions, panel discussions, and preparatory meetings. The annual session is now divided into five segments: high-level, coordination, operational activities, humanitarian affairs, and general. The high-level segment includes the High-Level Political Forum on Sustainable Development (HLPF) established in 2012 as a multistakeholder forum focusing on integrating various dimensions of sustainable development and implementing the SDGs approved in 2015. The HLPF is responsible for the Annual Ministerial Review, created in 2007, to assess the state of implementation of international development goals, including the Millennium Development Goals and, since 2015, the SDGs. In addition, the biennial Development Cooperation Forum brings together all relevant actors for dialogue on issues relating to development cooperation, such as financing, different types of partnerships, and accountability. Meetings include member states, all relevant UN institutions, civil society groups, and the private sector.

The activities that ECOSOC is expected to coordinate are spread among many subsidiary bodies (such as expert and working groups composed of independent experts and consultants), eight functional commissions, five regional commissions, and the seventeen specialized agencies. A number of entities created by the General Assembly, such as the UN Development Programme (UNDP), the UN Fund for Population Activities (UNFPA), United Nations Children's Fund (UNICEF), and the World Food Programme (WFP), report to both the General Assembly and ECOSOC, compounding the complexity. The scope of ECOSOC's agenda includes topics ranging from housing, literacy, and the environment to narcotic drug control, refugees, statistics, and the rights of Indigenous peoples. Development is by far the largest subject area.

The specialized agencies and their relationship to ECOSOC. Several of the specialized agencies, including the ILO, Universal Postal Union, and World Meteorological Organization, predate the UN itself, as discussed in Chapter 3. Article 57 of the UN Charter laid out the broad terms under which these agencies were to be brought into relationship with the UN. The first agreement, with the ILO, provided a model for others, although the system of weighted voting in the Bretton Woods institutions distinguishes them from other agencies. The agreements cover such things as exchange of information and documents, treatment to be given by agencies to recommendations from the UN organs, and cooperation in personnel, statistical services, and budgetary arrangements. Among the factors that complicate the relationship of specialized agencies to ECOSOC is geographical dispersal. The ILO, International Telecommunication Union (ITU), World Intellectual Property Organization, and WHO are headquartered in Geneva, but the FAO is in Rome, the UN Educational, Scientific, and Cultural Organization (UNESCO) is in Paris, the International Civil Aviation Organization (ICAO) is in Montreal, the IMF and World Bank are in Washington, DC, and the International Maritime Organization (IMO) is in London. In the field, each agency has often had its own separate building and staff. This dispersal affects efficiency, budgets, and coordination.

Historically, the specialized agencies and particularly the Bretton Woods institutions have operated quite independently of ECOSOC and the rest of the UN system. Since directors-general of the agencies have the same diplomatic rank as the UN Secretary-General, they have often perceived themselves as operating their own fiefdoms. How can one achieve an integrated international program when different agencies, with their own administration and objectives, are carrying out similar activities? The ILO is illustrative. Its activities include employment promotion, vocational guidance, social security, safety and health, labor laws and relations, and rural institutions. These overlap with the FAO's concern with land reform, UNESCO's mandate in education, the WHO's focus on health standards, and the UN Industrial Development Organization's concern with manpower in small industries. The result is constant coordination problems. Since 1998, ECOSOC has hosted annual meetings of finance ministers and officials from the World Bank, IMF, World Trade Organization, and UNCTAD to improve interactions among these institutions and coordinate financing for development. Likewise, in the late 1990s, resident directors of the World Bank and IMF began cooperating more with other UN agency personnel working in developing countries. In 2008, the high-level UN Development Group was merged into the Chief Executives Board for Coordination, which is discussed later.

Functional commissions. Part of ECOSOC's work is done in eight functional commissions: Social Development, Narcotic Drugs, the Status of Women, Science and Technology for Development, Population and Development, Crime Prevention and Criminal Justice, Statistics, and Forests. The Commission on Statistics reflects the importance of statistical studies and analysis to economic and social programs and the major contribution the UN system makes annually to governments, researchers, and students worldwide through its statistical studies. The wide range of data on social and economic conditions that have been gathered over the years is vital for dealing with various global problems. For example, when the General Assembly inaugurated the first Development Decade in 1961, women were among the groups singled out for development funds, even though there were no data on the economic status of women at the time. Only with the 1991 publication of the first edition of *The World's Women*, compiled under the auspices of the Commission on the Status of Women (CSW), were data finally available to inform policymaking on issues relating to women around the world. As Michael Ward (2004: 2) concludes in his book *Quantifying the World*, "The creation of a universally acknowledged statistical system and of a general framework guiding the collection and compilation of data according to recognized professional standards, both internationally and nationally, has been one of the great and mostly unsung successes of the UN organization."

The CSW was established in 1946 to prepare recommendations and reports concerning the promotion of women's political, economic, social, and educational rights and concerning any problems requiring immediate attention. It drafted several conventions on women's political and marital rights as well as the Declaration on the Elimination of Discrimination Against Women, adopted by the General Assembly in 1967, and the Convention on the Elimination of All Forms of Discrimination Against Women (CEDAW), which was approved in 1979 and entered into force in 1981. The 1995 Fourth World Conference on Women in Beijing gave the CSW a central role in monitoring implementation of the Beijing Platform for Action under the broad mandate of achieving gender equality and empowerment of women—a mandate broadened in follow-up special sessions of the General Assembly, including most recently at the Beijing+25 session in 2020. CSW sessions focus on specific themes such as gender equality; violence against girls; access of women and girls to education, science, and technology; and empowerment of rural women. The CSW has forty-five members, who are elected by ECOSOC for four-year terms, and it meets annually with active participation from NGO representatives.

Until 2006, one of the most active commissions was the Commission on Human Rights. All of the UN-initiated declarations and conventions on human rights up to that point were products of this body's work. After the 2005 World Summit, the General Assembly created the Human Rights Council in 2006, which has assumed many of the former commission's responsibilities but reports to the Assembly rather than ECOSOC (see Chapter 10 for further details).

Regional commissions. Since 1947, ECOSOC has created five regional commissions. These are designed to stimulate regional approaches to development with studies and initiatives to promote projects based on the rationale that cooperation among countries in a given geographic area would benefit all. With the current focus on the SDGs across the entire UN system, they provide venues for implementing and coordinating discussions about global goals in specific regions. They are discussed further in Chapter 8.

Field activities. One of the major aspects of the UN's proliferating economic and social activities has been the growth of operational field activities, especially technical assistance. Through various programs, including the UNDP, created in 1965, and through specialized agencies such as the WHO, the FAO, and UNESCO, the UN disburses funds and expertise to developing countries to train people and introduce new technologies. Coordinating these activities in the field is a large part of ECOSOC's challenge.

Coordination is inherently difficult in any complex organization, and national governments have their own problems in this regard. Indeed, one analyst has argued that ECOSOC's problems are attributable in part to "the absence of coordination at the national level in regard to international policies and programmes" (Taylor 2000: 108). The steady expansion of UN economic and social activities over more than seventy-five years has made ECOSOC's mandate almost impossible to fulfill, leading to persistent but largely unsuccessful calls for reform discussed later in this chapter.

The Secretariat

In 2019, the UN Secretariat comprised about 37,000 professional and clerical staff based in New York, Geneva, Vienna, Nairobi, and field operations around the world, not including the secretariats of the specialized agencies or military and civilian personnel in UN peace operations. These international civil servants are individuals who, though nationals of member states, represent the international community. Many are also technocrats—individuals with specialized training and knowledge. As Barnett and Finnemore (2005: 174) note, "Professional training, norms, and occupational cultures strongly shape the way [these] experts view the world. They influence what problems are visible to staff and what range of solutions are entertained."

The earliest IGO secretariats were established by the Universal Postal Union and International Telegraph Union in the 1860s and 1870s, but their members were not independent of national governments. The League of Nations established the first truly international secretariat and set the precedent for secretariat personnel to remain impartial or neutral in serving the organization as a whole. Member states were expected to respect the international character and responsibilities of the staff, regardless of their nationality. This practice carried over to the UN and the specialized agencies, with UN Secretariat members recruited from an ever broader geographic base as the membership expanded. Secretariat members are not expected to give up their national loyalty but to refrain from promoting national interests—a sometimes difficult task in a world of strong nationalisms. Articles 100 and 101 deal with the Secretariat's internationalism and independence. Personnel for all but the most senior posts are recruited from the broad UN membership and are advanced over time on the basis of merit and seniority, mindful of geographic distribution and with increasing attention to gender balance in recent years.

While the General Assembly, Security Council, and ECOSOC provide arenas where member states debate issues and make recommendations and decisions, the UN Secretariat, including the Secretary-General and senior leadership, form the "second" UN. They wield significant influence within the UN itself and occasionally over member states. The Secretary-General in particular has contributed to the emergence of the UN as an autonomous actor in global governance and world politics.

The Secretary-General. The position of the UN Secretary-General (UNSG) has been called "one of the most ill-defined: a combination of chief administrative officer of the United Nations and global diplomat with a fat portfolio whose pages are blank" (Hall 1994: 22). The UNSG is the manager of the organization, responsible for providing leadership to the Secretariat, preparing the UN's budget, submitting an annual report to the General Assembly, and overseeing studies conducted at the request of the other major organs. Article 99 of the UN Charter authorizes the Secretary-General to present to the Security Council issues that threaten international peace. This provides the legal basis for the UNSG's authority and ability to be an independent actor. The UNSG also commands moral authority as "the representative of the community's interests or the defender of the values of the international community" (Barnett and Finnemore 2004: 23).

Over time, UNSGs have often (but not always) come to play significant political roles as spokespersons for the organization; as conveners of expert groups, commissions, and panels to frame issues, marshal research, and outline choices; as mediators drawing on the Charter's spirit as the basis for taking initiatives; and as "guardians of the Charter" (Ravndal 2020). Yet the Secretary-General must simultaneously meet the demands of two constituencies—member states and the Secretariat itself. States elect the UN's chief administrator and do not want to be either upstaged or publicly opposed by the person in that position. This is particularly true for the P-5. As chief executive officer, the UNSG also has to have good personnel management and budgetary skills. The balancing act is not always easy.

The Secretary-General holds office for a five-year renewable term on recommendation by the Security Council and election by two-thirds of the General Assembly. The process of nomination is intensely political and secretive, with the P-5 having key input because of their veto power. In fact, as Chesterman (2015: 507–508) notes, the P-5 have shown a distinct preference for an individual accustomed "to taking orders rather than giving them—someone who will be more 'secretary' than 'general.'" In 1996, the United States strongly opposed the reelection of Boutros Boutros-Ghali, for example, forcing member states to agree on an alternate candidate, Kofi Annan. Efforts to establish a better means of selecting this global leader have been unsuccessful thus far, but in 2015 the General Assembly took the unusual step of unanimously passing a resolution (A/RES/69/321) calling for a more open and transparent selection process to allow all member states to review information on candidates and meet and question them. The push to name a woman to the post got a boost with language that referred to the need for "gender and geographical balance while meeting the highest possible requirements." This followed the 1 for 7 Billion civil society campaign to open the selection process in 2016 where seven of the thirteen final candidates were women. There is no rule that the post must rotate among geographic groups, but not surprisingly, those elected have tended to come from relatively small states (see Figure 4.5).

The UNSGs have been a key factor in the UN's emergence as an autonomous actor in world politics, thereby making the organization something more than just a forum for multilateral diplomacy. The effectiveness of the Secretariat depends heavily on the UNSG's leadership and on the

Figure 4.5   UN Secretaries-General (1946–present)

Secretary-General	Nationality	Dates of Service
Trygve Lie	Norway	1946–1953
Dag Hammarskjöld	Sweden	1953–1961
U Thant	Burma	1961–1971
Kurt Waldheim	Austria	1972–1981
Javier Pérez de Cuéllar	Peru	1982–1991
Boutros Boutros-Ghali	Egypt	1992–1996
Kofi Annan	Ghana	1997–2006
Ban Ki-moon	Republic of Korea	2007–2016
António Guterres	Portugal	2017–

"competence, capability, and general character of any Secretary-General" (Jonah 2007: 170). Hence, personality, experience, and skills matter. Kent Kille (2006), for example, describes three key leadership styles of Secretaries-General: manager, strategist, and visionary. From the standpoint of international relations theories, UNSGs are generally analyzed as an agent, with member states (and sometimes the Secretariat itself) being the principals, but there is also ample evidence of them as autonomous actors, with that autonomy constrained on occasion.

Since 1945, successive UNSGs have taken advantage of opportunities for initiatives, applied flexible interpretations of Charter provisions, and sought mandates from UN policy organs as necessary. They have developed their own political roles and that of the institution. Their personalities and interpretation of the Charter, as well as world events, affect the power, resources, and importance of the position at any given time. Trygve Lie, the first UNSG, created the precedent of using the UNSG's annual report to the General Assembly to comment on the state of the world and share his opinion on issues. Among his successors, Dag Hammarskjöld, used this to introduce the term "preventive diplomacy," while Kofi Annan commented on changing interpretations of state sovereignty. António Guterres has been particularly noted for his gender parity strategy (discussed below).

The UNSG is well placed to serve as a neutral communications channel and intermediary for the global community. While representing the institution, he or she can act independently of the policy organs even when resolutions have condemned a party to a dispute, maintaining lines of communication and representing the institution's commitment to peaceful settlement and alleviation of human suffering. Over time, UNSGs have used a variety of methods to maintain peace, from fact-finding and using their "good offices" to employing "groups of friends" (Whitfield 2007). For example, Dag Hammarskjöld articulated principles for UN involvement in peacekeeping and for an international civil service. Javier Pérez de Cuéllar epitomized the ideal intermediary using a persistent, low-key approach to the Falklands/Malvinas War, the Iran-Iraq War, and the conflicts in Cyprus, Namibia, Afghanistan, and Central America. Increasingly, UNSG's have appointed special representatives (SRSGs) to fulfill various roles in conjunction with UN peace operations and to promote action on various thematic issues—a development that, as Manuel Fröhlich (2013: 232) notes, "underscores the fact or the ambition that, at times, [international organizations] act in their own right."

Secretaries-General have also played the role of norm entrepreneurs. For example, Boutros-Ghali and Annan both encouraged the development of the UN's role in promoting democratic governance (Johnstone 2007; Haack and Kille 2012). Following NATO's intervention in Kosovo in 1999 without Security Council authorization but in support of the emerging norm of humanitarian intervention, Annan chose to speak directly to the meaning of state sovereignty, recognizing "rights beyond borders" (UN 1999a).

A key resource for UNSGs is the power of persuasion. The "force" of majorities behind resolutions may lend greater legitimacy to initiatives, though it may not ensure any greater degree of success. Autonomy is also key to the UNSG's influence. For example, during the Security Council's 2002–2003 debate over Iraq's failure to disarm and cooperate with UN inspections and whether to authorize a US-led war, Kofi Annan steered an independent course by pushing for Iraqi compliance, Security Council unity, and peace, preserving his ability to serve as a neutral intermediary.

As U Thant stated: "The Secretary-General must always be prepared to take an initiative, no matter what the consequences to him or his office may be, if he sincerely believes that it might make the difference between peace and war" (quoted in Young 1967: 284). Secretary-General Boutros Boutros-Ghali demonstrated the limits of autonomy. As one commentator described: "He saw an opening for the UN in the post–Cold War disarray and plunged: prodding the United States to send thousands of American soldiers to rescue Somalis from famine; urging the United Nations into new terrain in Cambodia, Bosnia and Haiti" (Preston 1994: 10–11). His activism and his antagonistic relationship with the United States, however, led to his defeat for a second term in 1996.

Kofi Annan was the first Secretary-General from within the UN bureaucracy and the first one from Africa. He proved even more of an activist than his predecessor, winning the 2001 Nobel Peace Prize for himself and the UN. He carried out extensive administrative and budgetary reforms, including creating the office of deputy secretary-general and appointing the first woman to hold high office in the UN—Louise Fréchette of Canada. He initiated steps to strengthen liaisons with NGOs and regional IGOs, dialogue with major business leaders, and reach out to the US Congress, an important step given Congress's refusal to appropriate full funding for US dues to the UN for much of the 1990s.

Annan was widely respected and was reelected by acclamation in 2001. He used his "bully pulpit" to take initiatives on a wide variety of issues from HIV/AIDS and the Millennium Development Goals to the Global Compact on Corporate Responsibility. He commissioned independent reports on the UN's failures in the 1995 massacre in the UN-declared safe area of Srebrenica, the 1994 Rwandan genocide, and the 2003 attack on UN personnel in Iraq. His public acceptance of blame was "nothing short of revolutionary at the United Nations" (quoted in Crossette 1999: A8).

Still, the latter part of Annan's tenure was marred by scandals over the Oil-for-Food Programme with Iraq and sexual misconduct of peacekeepers in the Democratic Republic of Congo. He devoted considerable energy to trying to secure reforms at the time of the UN's sixtieth anniversary in 2005, even though these initiatives usually come from member states (Luck 2005). Yet, even activist UNSGs can find their influence limited. As Mark Malloch Brown (2008: 10), former administrator of UNDP and later *chef de cabinet* to Kofi Annan, remarked: "I found when it came to management and budgetary matters that the secretary-general was less influential than I had been as administrator of UNDP. Whereas I had had a cooperative board that was not infected by bitter political confrontation, he was hostage to intergovernmental warfare."

Ban Ki-moon, the Republic of Korea's former foreign minister and a career diplomat, succeeded Annan in January 2007 and was the second Asian to lead the UN. In pressing for management reform, he appointed a significant number of women to various posts and oversaw the creation of UN Women in 2010 from four small UN programs. He reorganized the Departments of Peacekeeping Operations and Political Affairs. He was criticized, however, for the long delay in speaking out about the atrocities in the Syrian civil war. He also refused to take responsibility on behalf of the institution for the cholera epidemic in Haiti that was linked to UN peacekeepers. When Ban was reelected for a second term in 2012, one journalist remarked, "while Ban has been a letdown on many fronts, it's worth asking whether anyone else could have done better—at least on Syria. . . . The fact is that when the great powers squabble, there's little that anyone in the organization can accomplish, be they competent or not. . . . The big powers, tired of locking horns with Annan, wanted someone bland and pliable to replace him, and the colorless South Korean fit the bill" (Tepperman 2013). In his last year in office, Ban earned kudos for his leadership in steering the 2015 Paris Climate Conference to a successful conclusion.

Given the active campaign in 2016 to elect a woman, António Guterres, the ninth UNSG and former prime minister of Portugal, unsurprisingly spoke of the importance of gender equality in his opening speech. He appointed an all-women team of top advisers in 2017, achieved the milestone of full gender equality in the UN's senior management in early 2018, and pushed to appoint an equal or greater number of women than men to other Secretariat posts to reduce the Secretariat's gender gap. Guterres has also made reforms to strengthen the UN's capacity for conflict prevention and protection of civilians top priorities. He has faced daunting challenges in mobilizing states and other actors to address climate change, the Covid-19 pandemic, the needs of more than 70 million refugees and forcibly displaced people around the world, Russia's invasion of Ukraine, and other problems amid rising tensions among the great powers. Guterres faced no serious opposition to his reelection in 2021.

Conflict-related SRSGs are now appointed in conjunction with all UN peace operations; from the earliest times, SRSGs have also served as mediators, exercising significant independent influence. Among the most notable have been Sérgio Viera de Mello, who served successively in Lebanon, Kosovo, East Timor, and Iraq, where he died in the 2003 bombing of UN headquarters in Baghdad; Martti Ahtisaari, winner of the 2008 Nobel Peace Prize, who served as SRSG in Namibia and Kosovo; and Lakhdar Brahimi, who served on thirteen occasions, including in Haiti, South Africa, Afghanistan, Iraq, and Syria.

Thematic SRSGs have dealt with a wide range of topics, ranging from the impact of armed conflict on children and HIV/AIDS in Africa to the Millennium Development Goals, the Global Compact on Corporate Responsibility, migration, and sexual violence in conflict. They represent the UNSG by "becoming a presence themselves—not necessarily with office space in New York, but certainly as a distinct voice and promoters of ideas in direct consultation with diplomats and the media as well as with governments, relevant agencies, and NGOs worldwide" (Fröhlich 2014: 186). In short, SRSGs have a degree of leeway for action that allows them to exercise leadership, speak for the UNSG, and help in the exercise of that office.

The makeup and functions of the Secretariat. The UN Secretariat and the secretariats of the specialized agencies share some of the characteristics of bureaucracies more generally. They derive authority from their rational-legal character and from their expertise; they derive legitimacy from the moral purposes of the organization and from their claims to neutrality, impartiality, and objectivity; they derive power from their missions of serving others. Their work often has little to do with the symbolic politics of the General Assembly or the high-politics debates of the Security Council. It involves the implementation of the economic, humanitarian, and social programs as well as peace operations, which represent much of the UN's tangible contribution to fulfilling the promises of its Charter. The Secretariat is also responsible for gathering statistical data, preparing studies and reports, servicing meetings, preparing documentation, and providing translations of speeches, debates, and documents in the UN's six official languages.

The UN Secretariat includes both professional and general services staffs, and the high-level posts of under- and assistant secretaries-general; departments such as political affairs, peacekeeping, and General Assembly and Conference Management; the offices of the high commissioners for refugees and human rights and the coordinator of humanitarian affairs; and programs and funds such as UNDP, UNICEF, and UN Women (see Figure 4.1 for details on the organization of the Secretariat). Top-level posts are appointed by the UNSG based on nominations and political pressures from member governments. Three norms now govern these appointments: equitable geographic representation that assures countries in the Global South that top posts do not go only to individuals from the Global North; professional qualification to ensure that individuals are appropriately qualified; and, most recently, gender parity to boost the number of women in UN senior leadership.

Among past Secretariat reforms have been the creation of the post of Deputy Secretary-General (DSG) in 1997 and a more cabinet-style of management in 2005. The Senior Management Group, chaired by the UNSG, brings together leaders of UN departments, offices, funds, and programs in regular meetings, including video conferences with UN offices around the world. It is a forum for policy-related matters, planning, and information-sharing with respect to emerging challenges and crosscutting issues. The DSG is tasked with many of the administrative responsibilities and managing Secretariat operations. UNSG Guterres specifically charged DSG Amina Mohammed with overseeing the implementation of the SDGs. The Chief Executives Board, which includes the executive heads of thirty-one UN specialized agencies, funds, and programs, meets twice a year (virtually) under the Secretary-General's chairmanship to facilitate coordination across the UN system.

The UN's bureaucrats play a significant role in shaping the agendas of meetings and in managing the technical and support functions required by a large multinational and multilingual organization. The ways professional staff understand particular conflict situations can also influence how member states view them. For example, Barnett and Finnemore (2004: 151–152) showed how UN staff defined the situation in Rwanda in 1994 as a civil war and failed to see that the unfolding genocide was quite different from violence against civilians in other ethnic conflicts. They noted, "The rules of peacekeeping . . . [at that time] prohibited peacekeeping in a civil war and in the absence of a stable cease-fire." Thus, the UN's failure to stop the genocide in Rwanda was "the predictable result of an organizational culture that shaped how the UN evaluated and responded to violent crises." Examples of Secretariat influence in defining issues can be drawn from other UN agencies. The influence of liberal economists in the IMF and World Bank has long been noted as a major factor shaping how those institutions' bureaucracies think about and address development issues and financial crises.

As discussed in Chapter 3, IGOs, including the UN, have a history of creating other IGOs, but the impetus for creating new entities has often come from within the UN Secretariat, with bureaucrats having a major hand in the design. Examples include the Intergovernmental Panel on Climate Change, which UNEP bureaucrats designed to get around opposition from key member states; the UNDP; and the WFP (Johnson 2014). In short, there is a good deal of evidence that the professional staff of the UN Secretariat and its many agencies, funds, and programs are often independent actors in the UN system, influencing agendas, shaping specific policy proposals, and even pushing for the creation of new entities.

Whereas women have always made up the majority of the UN's general services staff (as translators, secretaries, etc.), the gender composition of the UN's professional staff has been an issue since the 1970s when pressure from within the Secretariat first required the UNSG to provide information annually on women's employment in the UN system. The result was clear evidence of the exclusion of women. Furthermore, women have predominantly held positions relating to low politics and "soft" issues, such as social welfare, human rights, the environment, and health, rather than the "hard," high-politics issues of security, trade, finance, and agriculture (Haack 2014). One particularly notable exception has been the IMF with first Christine Lagarde as managing director from 2011 to 2019 followed by Kristalina Georgieva. It has taken extensive efforts from UN staff and the CSW, from civil society activists, the women's movement, and the two most recent UNSGs to change that picture, as shown in Figure 4.6 (Haack, Karns, and Murray 2022).

As noted earlier, UNSG Guterres earned high praise after announcing his Gender Parity Strategy in 2017 and even more praise when he achieved that goal in his Senior Management Group in early 2018, including three women in his top staff. Yet the pattern in leadership positions across the UN system continues to be largely male-dominated with just ten women among the thirty-one members of the Chief Executives Board as of late 2022 including only three women heading specialized agencies (UNESCO, ICAO, and the IMF).

Over time, the UN Secretariat has been criticized for lapses in its neutrality, duplication of tasks, and poor management practices. Member states share blame with UNSGs and staff for the problems and the proliferation of entities. General Assembly and Security Council resolutions may be vague and unrealistic; objectives often depend on member governments' actions and other factors to be fulfilled; since the UN is a political organization, the Secretariat is subject to interference from member states. Indeed, many member states do not necessarily want the UN to have an

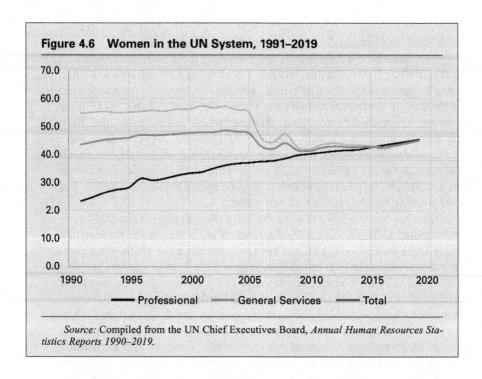

Figure 4.6 Women in the UN System, 1991–2019

Source: Compiled from the UN Chief Executives Board, *Annual Human Resources Statistics Reports 1990–2019.*

effective Secretariat and Secretary-General, since that could diminish their own ability to control what the UN does. We discuss other aspects of Secretariat reform later in the chapter.

The International Court of Justice

As the judicial arm of the United Nations, the ICJ shares responsibility with the other major organs for ensuring that the principles of the Charter are followed. Its special role is providing states with an impartial body for settling legal disputes in accordance with international law (so-called contentious cases) and giving advisory opinions on legal questions referred to it by the General Assembly, Security Council, and specialized agencies.

The General Assembly and Security Council have joint roles in electing the fifteen judges, who serve nine-year terms (five are elected every three years). Judges must have qualifications befitting appointment to the highest judicial body in their home country and recognized competence in international law. Together they represent the major legal systems of the world, but they act independently of their national affiliations, using different sources of law (set forth in Article 38 of the ICJ Statute) as the basis for judgments. Their deliberations take place in private, their decisions are decided by majority vote, and decisions include the reasons on which they are based.

The ICJ has noncompulsory jurisdiction, meaning that parties to a dispute (states only) must all agree to submit a case to the court; there is no way to force a party to appear before the court, but once states agree to ICJ jurisdiction, they are legally bound to follow the decision. With no executive to enforce decisions, however, enforcement depends on voluntary state compliance, the perceived legitimacy of the court's actions, and the "power of shame" if states fail to comply with a judgment.

The issue of the court's jurisdiction has been particularly vexing. Article 36.2 of the ICJ Statute—the Optional Clause—gives states the opportunity to declare that they recognize ICJ jurisdiction as compulsory. States that sign this clause agree to accept the court's jurisdiction in all legal disputes, or they may agree to accept the court's jurisdiction as compulsory only for disputes with other states that have also accepted compulsory jurisdiction. The clause was tested in 1984 when Nicaragua initiated proceedings against the United States for mining its harbors and undermining its government and economy (ICJ Contentious Case 1984b). The United States disputed the court's jurisdiction on the grounds that Nicaragua had not accepted compulsory ICJ jurisdiction and even had it done so, the issues were political, not legal. The ICJ ruled against the United States. In response, President Ronald Reagan terminated US acceptance of the court's compulsory jurisdiction in October 1985.

The ICJ had 182 contentious cases brought before it between 1946 and 2022. In the past, the court was never heavily burdened, but its caseload has increased substantially. In the 1970s it averaged one or two pending cases; between 1990 and 1997 that number increased to nine then thirteen pending cases; and in 2022 there were eighteen cases on the docket. In addition, between 1946 and 2022 the court issued twenty-seven advisory opinions. The increased caseload is a result in part of greater trust in the court by developing countries after the Nicaragua case showed in 1986 that a small, developing country could win a judicial victory over a major power (the United States). An added factor has been the option of using a chamber of five justices to hear and determine cases by summary procedure, potentially speeding up what is often a very lengthy process. Noting that this option has been used for a number of complex territorial dispute cases, such as that involving the Gulf of Maine (ICJ Contentious Case 1984a), J. G. Merrills (2011: 139) notes that "states also see the chambers procedures as a way of having cases which raise highly technical issues heard by small tribunals selected for their expertise."

Only rarely have ICJ cases dealt with major political issues of the day, since few states want to trust a legal judgment for settlement of a largely political issue, although Ukraine filed a case against Russia in 2022 for violations of the genocide convention. Several cases addressed decolonization questions, including in Namibia and Western Sahara (ICJ Advisory Opinions

1971, 1975). There have been a growing number of cases involving territorial disputes, including delimitation of the North Sea continental shelf, fisheries jurisdiction in the previously mentioned Gulf of Maine, and the maritime boundary between Cameroon and Nigeria (ICJ Contentious Cases 1969, 1984a, 2002). A number of pending cases concern maritime delimitation in the Caribbean Sea and Pacific Ocean. The court has also ruled on the legality of nuclear tests (ICJ Contentious Case 1974 [Nuclear Tests Cases]), and on hostage taking (ICJ Contentious Case 1980 [Case Concerning US Diplomatic and Consular Staff in Tehran]), environmental protection (ICJ Contentious Case 1997 [Case Concerning the Gabcikovo-Nagymaros Project]), and genocide (ICJ Contentious Case 2007 [The Application of the Genocide Convention in the Conflict between Bosnia-Herzegovina and the former Yugoslavia]). The case involving genocide brought by The Gambia against Myanmar is discussed in Chapter 9.

Among the ICJ advisory opinions are several on legal issues relating to the functioning of the UN. These include the opinion concerning reparation for injuries suffered during UN service, in which the UN's international legal personality was clarified; the opinion on the issue of reservations to multilateral treaties; the opinion that declared peacekeeping expenses to be part of the fiscal obligations of member states; and the immunity from legal process of a special rapporteur of the Commission on Human Rights (see, respectively, ICJ Advisory Opinions 1949, 1951, 1962, 1999). In the first one, the United Nations was accorded the right to seek payment from a state held responsible for the injury or death of a UN employee. With this case, the ICJ established that it had the power to interpret the UN Charter, which was not expressly conferred on it by the Charter or by the court's own statute or rules. Two more recent advisory opinions concerned the legal consequences of the construction of the barrier wall in the occupied Palestinian territories and the accordance with international law of Kosovo's unilateral declaration of independence (ICJ Advisory Opinions 2004, 2010). Both represented more political issues and were requested by the General Assembly. In 2019, the court provided an advisory opinion to the General Assembly on the legal consequences of the separation of the Chagos Archipelago from Mauritius at the time of its independence in 1965. In 2023, the Pacific island state of Vanuatu persuaded the General Assembly to seek an advisory opinion on whether governments have "legal obligations" to protect people from climate hazards and whether failure to meet those obligations could bring "legal consequences" (Birnbaum 2023) The ICJ's opinion could have significance for efforts to address climate change.

When dealing with the UN Charter and the legality of acts of other UN organs, the ICJ, in the words of Justice Mohammed Bedjaoui, has shown "discretion, measure, modesty, restraint, caution, sometimes even humility" (quoted in Ramcharan 2000: 183). In the 1949 *Reparation for Injury* case, the court took an activist approach to its powers, but in its 1971 advisory opinion on Namibia, it took a narrower view that it did not have power to review actions by the General Assembly and Security Council. In 1992 the court took a narrow view of its role when asked by Libya to authorize provisional measures after the Security Council threatened it with sanctions unless it extradited nationals accused of participation in the Lockerbie bombing of Pan Am Flight 103 (ICJ Contentious Case 1992).

The ICJ is limited by the fact that only states can bring contentious cases. This excludes the court from dealing with contemporary disputes involving states and nonstate actors, such as terrorist and paramilitary groups, NGOs, and private corporations, and explains why Karen Alter (2014) refers to the ICJ as an "old-style" court in contrast to newer courts discussed in Chapter 3. In addition, what she calls "new-style" international courts have far-reaching compulsory jurisdiction and may perform judicial roles other than dispute settlement, such as administrative review, enforcement, and constitutional review. Furthermore, while judicial decisions are sources of international law under the ICJ Statute, Article 38.1(d) provides that the "decision of the Court has no binding force except as between the parties and in respect of that particular case." In other words, state sovereignty limits the applicability of ICJ judgments, unlike the judgments of national courts in some countries, which use precedents from prior cases to shape judgments and thus the substance and interpretation of law. In reality, the ICJ has used many principles from earlier cases to decide later ones. This contributes to greater consistency in its decisions and more respect for its ability to contribute to the progressive development of international law. The ICJ also draws increasingly from decisions rendered by national and regional courts in an effort to give the impression of a unified field of international legal jurisprudence.

Past assessments of the court frequently dwelt on its relatively light caseload and slow processes, but others have stressed its contributions to "the process of systematizing, consolidating, codifying and progressively developing international law" (Ramcharan 2000: 177). Using the contentious case involving a territorial dispute between Qatar and Bahrain, Alter (2014: 177) notes how, despite lengthy proceedings, the ICJ could issue "a binding compromise under the guise of a legal solution" to address a long-standing dispute that had eluded resolution. The outcome benefited the economic development of both parties. Thus, the ICJ has been important to the constitutional development of global governance and complementary to the UN's political organs in its role.

It is important to note that there are a number of other international tribunals in the UN system, as briefly discussed in Chapter 3. Some are tied to specialized agencies such as the ILO Administrative Tribunal and the International Centre for the Settlement of Investment Disputes in the World Bank system. The UN Convention on the Law of the Sea, concluded in 1982, established the Law of the Sea Tribunal. In Chapter 9, we look at the ad hoc war crimes tribunals created by the Security Council in the 1990s and the International Criminal Court, which is a related organization of the UN.

The Trusteeship Council

The UN Trusteeship Council was established to oversee the administration of the non-self-governing trust territories that carried over from the mandate system of the League of Nations. These were former German colonies, mostly in Africa, that were placed under the League-supervised control of other powers (United Kingdom, France, Belgium, South Africa, and Japan) because they were deemed unprepared for self-determination or independence. After World War II, the mandates for Lebanon, Syria, Jordan, and Iraq were terminated, and each was granted independence. The United Kingdom turned the Palestine mandate over to the UN in 1947 when it was unable to cope with rising conflict between Arabs and Jews. The eleven UN trust territories also included Pacific islands that the United States liberated from Japan during World War II. The council's supervisory activities included reporting on the status of the people in the territories and conducting periodic visits to the territories.

At the initial Trusteeship Council session in 1947, Secretary-General Trygve Lie stated that the goal for the trust territories was full statehood. Thus, when the council ended the agreement for the Trust Territory of the Pacific Islands in 1993, it no longer had any responsibilities. For almost fifty years, the council and its system of supervision provided a model for the peaceful transition to independence for other colonial and dependent peoples, thus playing a role in the remarkable process of decolonization during the 1950s and 1960s.

The Trusteeship Council no longer meets in annual sessions. Without a UN Charter amendment abolishing it, there have been proposals for new functions, such as giving the council responsibility for monitoring conditions affecting the global commons (seas, seabed, and outer space). Another called for using it to assist "failed states."

Global Conferences and Summits

Multilateral global conferences date back to the period after World War I when the League of Nations convened conferences on economic affairs and disarmament. Since the late 1960s, the UN has sponsored global conferences and summit meetings of heads of state and government on topics ranging from the environment, food supply, population, and women's rights, to children, water supplies, racism, and climate change, as shown in Table 4.2. Often, these are intended to focus international attention on new or persisting problems and bring together diverse constituencies to develop programs of action. They are ad hoc events, convened at the request of one or more countries, and authorized by the General Assembly or ECOSOC,

Table 4.2 Selected UN-Sponsored Global Conferences and Summits

Topic	Global Conference	Summit
Aging	1982, 2002	
Agrarian reform and rural development	1989, 2006	
Biodiversity	2021	
Children		1990
Climate	1979, 1990, 2007, 2010	2009, 2015, 2019
Education for sustainable development	2009	
Environment	1972, 2013	
Environment and sustainable development	1992, 2012	
Financing for development		2002, 2008, 2019
Food	1974, 2002	1996, 2009, 2021
Habitat (human settlement)	1976, 1996, 2016	
Human rights	1968, 1993	
Law of the sea	1958, 1973–1982	
Least-developed countries	1981, 1990, 2001, 2011	
Population	1974, 1984, 1994, 2014	
Racism	1987, 2001, 2009	
Refugees and migrants		2016
Sustainable development		2002, 2015, 2019
Sustainable development of small island states	1994, 2005, 2014	
Ocean	2017, 2022	
UN reform, new millennium challenges		2000, 2005
Women	1975, 1980, 1985, 1995	2015

with all member states eligible to attend. Names can be deceiving, and this is particularly true for those events since 1990 called "summits" in which the sessions for heads of state and government last one or two days and may or may not be accompanied by a conference running two to six weeks. There was a large cluster of global conferences in the 1970s and another in the 1990s, with a lull in the 1980s and an effort to scale back after 2000.

The UN conferences and summits serve a variety of purposes. For one, they are efforts to raise global consciousness about a particular problem, how it is defined, and how it might be addressed. This means educating publics and government officials; generating new information; and developing soft law, new norms, principles, and international standards. They may highlight gaps in existing international institutions, create new forums for debate and consensus building, and "set in motion a process whereby governments make commitments and can be held accountable" (Schechter 2005: 9). The early environmental and women's conferences, in particular, led governments to create national bodies to address the issues.

Many of these events provide opportunities for participation and input from scientific and other expert groups, NGOs, and private corporations. The global conferences (but not necessarily summits) have often involved two conferences in the same location—the official conference with UN member states and a parallel NGO-organized conference. The 1972 UN Conference on the Human Environment in Stockholm included 114 UN member states and more than 250 NGOs in the parallel Environment Forum. The 2002 Johannesburg Summit on Sustainable Development was attended by approximately 21,000 accredited people, including representatives of 191 states and some 3,200 representatives of NGOs and other groups. The 2017 Ocean Conference included researchers, members of the business community, and celebrities such as Leonardo DiCaprio, who helped raise the profile of the event. These parallel conferences contributed greatly to the growth of NGOs and civil society as participants in global governance; they have also helped increase understanding of the links among issues as seemingly disparate as environmental protection, human rights (especially for women), poverty alleviation, and development and trade. We look at NGO participation in the global conferences in Chapter 6.

Global conferences typically involve extensive preparatory processes, including in-depth studies by experts and preparatory meetings, convened by committees known as "prepcoms" and involving NGOs and states. This is where decisions are made on many key agenda items, experts are brought in, and NGO roles at the conference itself are determined. There may also be regional meetings to build consensus on proposed conference outcomes. The background studies can also serve as wake-up calls, such as when studies before the 1982 World Assembly on Aging showed that developing countries would face challenges of aging populations in less than fifty years.

The outcomes of global conferences generally include declarations and action plans. Several conferences in the 1970s also led to new institutions, among them the UNEP and the UN Development Fund for Women. The 1992 UN Conference on the Environment and Development charged NGOs with key roles in implementing goals. The Platform of Action approved at the 1995 Fourth World Conference on Women, in Beijing, called for "empowering women" through access to economic resources. The 2017 Ocean Conference's action plan called for a trust fund to support ocean conservation, reduction of single-use plastics, restoration of fish stocks, and protection of tidal marshes and coral reefs. Later chapters analyze the outcomes of UN conferences in specific issue areas, but by one assessment, the "conferences are one of the main devices . . . that are used to spawn, nurture, and massage new ideas as well as to nudge governments, international secretariats, and international civil service to alter their conceptions and policies" (Emmerij, Jolly, and Weiss 2001: 89).

Critics from across the political spectrum have argued that the large global conferences are too unwieldy, often duplicate the work of other bodies, and are an inefficient way to identify problems and solutions. In 2003, the General Assembly voted to end the practice. As a result, many subsequent major UN-sponsored gatherings have been summits, rather than global conferences, often convened for only one or two days immediately before the fall General Assembly session. For example, the Millennium Summit in 2000 focused on mobilizing agreement on the eight Millennium Development Goals, thus deliberately addressing the need to integrate the development-related goals of several separate conferences. At the 2005 World Summit, various UN reform proposals were the central focus. Although leaders failed to act on Security Council reform, they approved the creation of the Peacebuilding Commission and the Human Rights Council to replace the Commission on Human Rights, approved language endorsing the responsibility to protect, condemned terrorism "in all its forms and manifestations," and recognized the serious challenge posed by climate change (Annan 2005). UNSG Ban Ki-moon convened the Climate Summit in 2014 to galvanize action on the problem of climate change. In 2019, the Youth Climate Action Summit brought young people from over 140 countries to discuss their views on climate change ahead of the leaders' summit. In 2020, UNSG Guterres convened a summit on the twenty-fifth anniversary of the Beijing women's conference.

A second type of UN-sponsored global conference has been used to negotiate major law-creating treaties. The first such conference was the UN Conference on the Law of the Sea (UNCLOS), convened from 1973 to 1982 with over 160 governments engaged in complex negotiations. The Law of the Sea Convention, concluded in 1982, came into effect in 1994 and has since been ratified by 168 states. A similar process began in 2007 for a successor agreement to the 1992 UN Framework Convention on Climate Change (UNFCCC) and 1997 Kyoto Protocol. These negotiations included only those states that were parties to the UNFCCC and are discussed in Chapter 10.

In short, UN-sponsored conferences and summits are an integral part of global governance, not just stand-alone events tied to the UN. As broader political processes, the conferences have mobilized energies and attention in a way that established institutions cannot. They have pushed different parts of the UN system to change, although the record of implementation is uneven and much depends on NGOs' ability to pressure governments to live up to their commitments. Summits can boost implementation through peer pressure on leaders to pledge their countries' cooperation. Still, some view large conferences as unwieldy, duplicating the work of other bodies, and an inefficient way to identify problems spotty and identify solutions.

Persistent Organizational Problems and the Need for Reform

Over the UN's seven-decade history, there have been many efforts at reform. Indeed, one longtime observer called this "a constant refrain . . . never finished, never perfected" (Luck 2007: 653). In the 1970s, the focus was on improving coordination of economic and social programs in the UN system; in the 1980s, calls for financial reforms dominated the agenda. Since the early 1990s, managerial reforms, improving the UN's ability to support peace operations, and gender equality in the Secretariat have been key issues. Security Council reform is a recurring major issue. In 2018, UNSG Guterres used the annual *Report of the Secretary-General on the work of the Organization* to call for a reform effort that "aims at making the Organization more effective, nimble, field focused and efficient to serve Member States and their populations." He noted, "This is the first time that the United Nations has embarked on a reform agenda of this scale" (UN 2018: 72).

To some extent, the UN is still hamstrung by pre–Cold War structures, redundant agencies, inadequate personnel policies, lack of accountability and transparency, limited resources, and the inability to meet the needs of a changing world. The composition of the Security Council is particularly problematic as it reflects the world of 1945, not the world of today. As one former UN official has noted, "The world wants more of the UN, and the organization is only able to deliver less" (Brown 2008: 3).

How can UN reform occur? First, changes in the major organs require amending the Charter. Like many constitutions, the UN Charter was designed to be difficult to amend. Under Articles 108 and 109, amendments must be approved and ratified by two-thirds of the member states, including the P-5. The principal reform that would require amendment is changing the size and composition of the Security Council. This also is the most controversial reform. Thus far, this has happened only on two occasions. In 1963, the membership of the Security Council was increased from eleven to fifteen, its voting majority changed from seven to nine, and ECOSOC was enlarged from eighteen to twenty-seven members. In 1971, ECOSOC was expanded to fifty-four members.

Many changes can and have been accomplished without amending the UN Charter, however. This includes the creation of new entities such as the Peacebuilding Commission (2006) and the UNEP Assembly (2013) to meet new demands; addressing coordination, management, transparency, and accountability issues; and terminating bodies that have outlived their usefulness, such as the Commission on Sustainable Development (2012). In 1997, UNSG Kofi Annan merged three departments into one Department of Economic and Social Affairs and all of the Geneva-based human rights programs into the single office of the UN High Commissioner for Human Rights. He reduced the size of the UN Secretariat by almost 4,000;

created the post of DSG; grouped the central offices into five executive groups, with their heads forming a cabinet; and promoted the idea of UN "houses" in developing countries to bring UN development agencies and programs together. Ban Ki-moon restructured support for peacekeeping operations by creating a new Department of Field Support while retaining the planning and strategy functions in the Department of Peace Operations. He also consolidated four agencies dealing with gender issues into UN Women.

The primary obstacles to UN reform are not procedural but political, however. There are deep disagreements among the UN's members. All want to steer the organization in directions congruent with their objectives or prevent it from infringing on their interests. Everyone agrees that the UN needs reforming, but they disagree about the kind of reform needed and the purpose. Developed countries want more productivity and efficiency from the UN Secretariat, reductions in programs and activities, elimination of overlap, improved management, and better coordination. Developing countries are interested in greater economic and political equity through redistribution of resources and enhanced participation in key decisionmaking. They want more power in the system and more programs oriented toward development. They fear management reforms that would cost them their share of plum secretariat jobs and the loss of favored programs. NGOs want a UN more open and accountable to civil society, allowing them more input and participation. In short, most reform proposals have hidden political agendas and policy goals. We focus on four issues: Security Council reform, Secretariat reform, financing, and integrating nonstate actors.

Structural Reform of the Security Council

The key ingredients for serious UN reform, as a former UN official notes, "require major concessions from powerful and weak countries alike" and a willingness to "rise above their own current sense of entrenched rights and privileges and find a grand bargain" (Brown 2008: 6, 8). Nowhere is this more true than with Security Council reform. Efforts to use anniversaries of the UN's founding (such as in 1995, 2005, and 2015) to galvanize major changes have largely failed. Because Russia's 2022 invasion of Ukraine was such a blatant violation of the UN Charter, it provoked numerous calls for UN reform, including of Security Council membership and permanent members' veto power.

Virtually everyone agrees that more states should be added to the Security Council. The permanent members underrepresent the majority of the world's population; Europe is overrepresented at the expense of Latin America, Africa, and Asia; China is the only developing and Asian country, although its self-identification is increasingly dubious given that its economy is now second to the United States; Germany and Japan contribute more financially than do Russia, the United Kingdom, and France, yet have no guaranteed role. India's economy has now surpassed that of the United Kingdom. In addition to geopolitical and systemic changes, there is greater normative value placed on diversity, equity, and representation today than in 1945. As Ian Hurd (2008a: 201) notes, "changing the formal membership . . . is a necessary step to increasing, or to halting the loss of, the legitimacy of the Council and of its resolutions." Some have referred to this as a means of "decolonizing" the UN (Ryder, Baisch, and Eguegu 2020). Thus, the first key issue is the size and composition of the Council's membership. If its size is increased to enhance its representativeness, how can it still be kept small enough to ensure efficiency?

A second issue concerns whether to continue the distinction between permanent and nonpermanent members. Closely related is the question of whether new permanent members will have veto power. Some proposals would give no veto power to the new permanent members; others would limit veto power of all permanent members to Chapter VII decisions; still others would grant veto power comparable to what the P-5 currently enjoy; others would eliminate the veto entirely on the grounds that it is undemocratic. The latter is a nonstarter for the current permanent members, and the United Kingdom and France are hardly eager to give up their seats. However, having more permanent members with veto power would likely increase the potential for blockage.

Resolving the issues of representation and permanent membership has proven impossible so far. There is no agreement on what process or formula should be used to determine who would get new permanent seats. There are three likely African candidates: Nigeria, Egypt, and South Africa. Countries such as Italy and Pakistan that know a rival is more likely to be a candidate (Germany and India, respectively) tend to oppose adding permanent seats. China opposes seats for Japan and India and prefers to keep the Council small and maintain the veto. Brazil, India, Germany, and Japan publicly campaigned for permanent seats in advance of the 2005 sixtieth anniversary World Summit, and Secretary-General Annan also pushed hard for action, yet those efforts came to naught. Some observers have even suggested that any new Security Council members not be states at all but regional bodies. This could mean replacing France with a rotating EU seat (something the European Parliament has already endorsed) and including the African Union and other bodies. The issues in the debate over reforming the Security Council's composition are summarized in Figure 4.7.

In short, there is no agreement precisely because the issue of Security Council representation is so important. The lesson is also that major reforms like this are likely to come only at glacial speed and when world events create the motivation and political will for agreement on change. Russia's invasion of Ukraine—a blatant violation of the Charter—provoked

---

Figure 4.7   The Debate over Security Council Reform (selected proposals)

Issue:

Membership and Terms

- Council needs greater representation of Africa, Asia, and Latin America
- Permanent members should better reflect geopolitics and economics

Proposals

- Increase permanent seats (proposals range from 3 to 11)
- Increase nonpermanent seats (proposals range from 1 to 13)
- Allow nonpermanent members to run for second term

Veto Power

- Require two vetoes to block a resolution
- Eliminate entirely from Permanent Five (P-5)
- Reduce scope for its use to Chapter VII decisions
- Limit its use in cases of mass atrocities
- Keep current P-5, but no veto for new permanent members
- Give all permanent members veto power

Efficiency

- Size should be large enough to allow greater representation, but small enough to preserve the ability to act. Proposals are 20–25 members.

Who Decides:

- Reform of Council membership requires Charter amendment, which takes a vote of two-thirds of the General Assembly members and must be "ratified in accordance with their respective constitutional processes by two-thirds of the members of the UN, including all the permanent members of the Security Council" (Chapter XVIII, Article 108).

Reforms in methods of work may be made by the Security Council itself.

---

renewed discussion of the issue and action by the General Assembly to require the Assembly to meet within ten days of the use of the veto.

With respect to increasing the transparency and efficiency of the Security Council's work, there have been a number of changes, as discussed earlier, including consultations with countries that contribute troops and matériel to peacekeeping operations and with NGOs through Arria formula meetings. More meetings are open, especially at early stages of deliberation, and the Security Council now provides more information on the nature of discussions and what resulted.

Even with representation issues unresolved, the Security Council retains a high degree of legitimacy. States still want to become nonpermanent members (although Saudi Arabia declined a seat in 2013 to protest the Council's failure to resolve the Syrian crisis and Iranian nuclear situation). Participation is seen as a mark of status and prestige for a state and its diplomats. The Council has authorized new peacekeeping operations, including with enforcement powers (discussed in Chapter 7) and has been called on to address new types of security threats. It continues to be seen as the most authoritative body in the UN. Even if the Council's composition were changed, other persistent problems, namely, coordination of the array of different agencies and programs in the UN system and improving management, would still need to be addressed.

Secretariat Reform

There are three major Secretariat reform issues. One is the problem of its size; the second concerns its management and efficiency; and the third is the problem of multiple agencies engaged in similar tasks with inadequate coordination. The last issue has plagued the UN system almost from the beginning in part because the founders designed the organization to be decentralized to increase the capacity of different groups to participate while minimizing the potential for politicization.

The UN Secretariat grew almost constantly from its founding to a high point of 41,400 people in 2014. By 2020, this had dropped to about 37,000. This growth stemmed from the expansion of UN membership and the proliferation of programs and activities, ranging from peacekeeping missions to technical assistance. As the bureaucracy expanded, charges of political bias and administrative inefficiency surfaced, with the United States being particularly vocal as the UN's largest contributor. Studies conducted by the UN and some member states came to similar conclusions about the expansion of programs with little consideration for financial commitments, coordination, and weak to nonexistent program evaluation.

The first five UNSGs paid little attention to internal management of the Secretariat and had little incentive for change. Only in the 1990s did the UN implement management systems such as program reviews, internal audits, performance evaluations of staff, and effective recruitment and promotion practices. Even then, developed countries were more concerned than developing countries about effective management, financial control, and clear objectives. After all, they were paying the largest shares of the bills.

When Kofi Annan became Secretary-General in 1997, he was pressured by the United States in particular to reduce the size of the Secretariat by 25 percent and implement other reforms. In his "quiet revolution," thirty departments were grouped into four sectoral areas (peace and security, humanitarian affairs, development, and economic and social affairs); some departments were merged; administrative costs were cut, and a code of staff conduct was developed. In 2002, Annan instituted a new system for recruiting, placing, and promoting staff that emphasized merit, competence, and accountability over tenure and precedent. In addition, a number of reforms were undertaken to support peacekeeping operations.

The latter part of Kofi Annan's tenure as Secretary-General was marred by a series of scandals that raised issues of mismanagement and accountability, prodding more reforms. As a result, the Secretariat introduced measures to improve the performance of senior management, including monitoring individual performance and policies covering fraud, corruption, financial disclosure, and procurement contracts. It alsocreated a new Office of Internal Oversight Services, with operational independence.

Clearly, Secretariat reform is an ongoing process if the UN's bureaucracy is to grow in capacity, adapt its management and working procedures, and maintain its effectiveness, accountability, and legitimacy. One important aspect of this has been the push since the late 1990s to increase the presence of women in the professional staff, particularly in higher level positions.

The problem of multiple agencies engaged in similar tasks has plagued the UN system from the beginning. The founders designed the organization to be decentralized because this would increase the capacity of different groups to participate while minimizing politicization. The lack of coordination among different agencies, programs, and funds in the areas of economic and social development and in response to humanitarian crises, however, has been particularly problematic. Numerous reports over the years have produced recommendations for improving ECOSOC's effectiveness as the coordinating agency, but the challenges to accomplishing this have proved persistent.

The problems of coordination and management in humanitarian crises are illustrative. Historically, there has been a functional division of responsibilities among UN agencies: the UN High Commissioner for Refugees (UNHCR) creates and manages refugee camps, UNICEF handles water and sanitation, the WFP is responsible for food supplies and logistics, and WHO handles health needs. In emergencies, there are scores of NGOs that vary in size and resources, have different cultures and philosophies, and often resist efforts to harmonize activities. In some situations, there may also be UN peacekeepers present. The UN Office for the Coordination of Humanitarian Affairs was created in 1998 in the context of the several complex humanitarian crises of the 1990s in an effort to remedy the coordination problem. It is headed by an undersecretary-general and responsible for coordinating all emergency relief in and outside the UN system. Just creating a UN office for coordination does not guarantee cooperation by all actors. Other UN agencies and NGOs may resist relinquishing their independence and compete for a share of the action.

Within the UN's development system, activities are heavily influenced by the major contributors and their tendency to earmark a significant proportion of their contributions, particularly for the UNDP, to reflect their own agendas. As Stephen Browne (2022) notes, this "undermines the system further" because it leads the agency and its staff to seek funding from many different sources, including large corporations, simply to support established programs, also making their "permanent preoccupation . . . finding money." As a result, he adds, "Fellow organizations in the UN are regarded as rivals rather than as potential collaborators."

When Guterres took office in 2017, he created an ambitious "United to Reform" agenda that included three pillars: development, management, and peace and security. In addition to his Gender Parity Strategy, the initiative included restructuring some departments and creating the Departments of Operational Support and Management Strategy, Policy and Compliance to improve coherence, program delivery, transparency, and accountability. The reforms also called for enhanced partnerships with international financial institutions, civil society, the private sector, and regional organizations.

As with any large, complex bureaucracy or set of bureaucracies, change is difficult and likely to be more incremental than fundamental. So it is with the UN Secretariat, but it is essential if the UN is to grow in capacity, adapt its management and working procedures, and maintain its effectiveness and legitimacy.

Financing is another persistent problem for the UN. More than "mere housekeeping," one observer suggests, "some of the most contentious political struggles that have wracked and at times imperiled the organization have swirled around its financing" (Laurenti 2007: 675).

Financing

The UN has long had financial problems since it has no independent source of money and depends almost entirely on its member states for assessed and voluntary contributions. In recent years, partnerships with major philanthropists such as the Bill and Melinda Gates Foundation and some corporations have bolstered funding for specific areas like health and food relief, but these are relatively small relative to the UN's total budget and needs. As with Security Council reform, there has been no shortage of proposals for changing structures and methods of financing and for enhancing oversight and efficient use of resources. Although reform in UN financing does not require Charter amendment, it does require support from a majority of member states and, most important, support of the UN's major contributing states. If the UN's largest contributor, the United States, opposes adoption of the UN budget unless changes are made, as happened in the 1980s, 1990s, and again in 2005, it can provoke a financing crisis for the organization unless a compromise is found.

Like the UN system itself, the UN's budget is complex. The regular budget covers its administrative machinery, major organs, and their auxiliary agencies and programs. It grew from less than $20 million in 1946 to more than $3.0 billion in 2020. Peacekeeping expenses constitute a separate budget ($6.5 billion in 2020), and the specialized agencies all have separate budgets. The three types of budget expenditures are funded by member states' assessments according to a formula based on ability to pay. Many specialized agencies, funds, and programs, including UNICEF, UNDP, WFP, WHO, and UNHCR, depend on states' and private donors' voluntary contributions. Table 4.3 illustrates the relative size of both assessed and voluntary contributions for each of these three categories of budget expenditure between 1986 and 2020. The fluctuation of peacekeeping costs since 1990 is particularly notable. Also evident are the effects of the major powers' insistence on "no growth" in the UN's regular budget in the late 1990s. Before then, UN budgets had grown with membership increases, new programs and agencies, inflation, and currency rate fluctuations.

The formulas for member states' assessed contributions for both the regular budget and peacekeeping operations are reevaluated every three years. The General Assembly's Committee on Contributions considers national income, per capita income, any economic dislocations (such as from war), and members' ability to obtain foreign currencies. Initially, the highest rate (for the United States) was set at 40 percent of the UN budget. The minimum rate was 0.04 percent for states with the most limited means. Over time, these have been adjusted, with the US share reduced to 25 percent in 1972 and 22 percent in 1995, and the minimum reduced to 0.01 percent in 1978 and 0.0001 percent in 1997. For example, between 1985 and 2000, Japan's share increased significantly, from 11.82 percent to 20.57 percent,

Table 4.3   UN System Expenditures (in US$ millions), 1971–2020

| | Assessed Contributions | | | | Voluntary Contributions | | |
	Regular	Peace-keeping	Agencies	Total Assessed	Selected UN Programmes and Funds	Specialized Agencies	Total Voluntary
1971	157	24	213	394	584	182	766
1980	534	141	792	1467	2558	734	4,759
1990	791	464	1,378	2,633	3,790	1,347	5,317
2000	1,089	1,800	1,766	4,655	5,681	1,406	7,087
2010	2,167	7,594	2,587	12,348	17,170	3,653	20,823
2015	2,771	8,158	2,537	13,466	21,177	4,249	25,426
2017[a]	2,578	7,300	2,517	12,395	23,905	4,171	28,076
2020	3,073	6,580	NA	NA	NA	NA	NA

Source: "Total UN System Contributions, 1971–2017," https://archive.globalpolicy.org/images/pdfs/Total_UN_System_Contributions.pdf, "Budgetary and financial situation of the organizations of the United Nations system," https://digitallibrary.un.org/record/3887718?ln=en. Note that General Assembly resolution 72/266 A shifted the budget cycle to annual on a trial basis, beginning with the program budget for 2020.
Note: a. Year with most recent data on all voluntary contributions.

while the Soviet/Russian figure declined from 11.98 percent to 1.15 percent, reflecting Russia's reduced size and economic difficulties. Between 1995 and 2005, China saw its assessment triple, from 0.72 to 2.05 percent; by 2020, it reached 12 percent. Figure 4.8 shows the scale of assessments for major contributors and the majority of UN members for 2021. Ten states contribute 69 percent of the UN's regular budget, and the other 183 UN members together contribute 31 percent.

Not surprisingly, states frequently fail to pay their assessments for reasons ranging from budget technicalities, poverty, or politics, including unhappiness with the UN in general or with specific programs and activities. The result has been periodic financial crises. In 2019 the UNSG released a statement citing "the worst cash crisis facing the United Nations in nearly a decade" as only 70 percent of the total assessment from member states had been paid, resulting in a $1.3 billion shortfall. The only sanction provided by the UN Charter, in Article 19, is denial of voting privileges in the General Assembly if a member falls more than two years in arrears.

The first UN financing crisis arose in the early 1960s over peacekeeping operations in the Congo and Middle East, when the Soviet Union, other communist countries, and France refused to pay their share of assessments because, in their view, peacekeeping authorized by the General Assembly was illegal. The ICJ's *Certain Expenses* opinion (ICJ Advisory Opinion 1962) confirmed the legality of the General Assembly's action and the obligation of members to pay. The second crisis arose in the 1980s, when the US Congress withheld part of the US dues because of dissatisfaction with the politicization of many UN agencies, with UN administration and management in general, and with the size of the US assessment relative to that of other wealthy states. An agreement was worked out that gave the major donors increased power to review programs and establish priorities for use of financial resources.

In the late 1990s, the UN faced another serious financial crisis with member states owing over $2.5 billion for current and past assessments. The United States owed $1.6 billion, two-thirds of the total due. The arrearages (unpaid assessments or debts) illustrated the tension between demands for governance and institutional weakness arising from states' unwillingness (in the case of the United States) or inability (in the case of many states in economic crisis) to pay their assessed contributions. The crisis was partially resolved by an agreement to reduce the US assessments for the regular budget and peacekeeping and payment of all arrears by 2003, subject to certain conditions (Karns and Mingst 2002). The financing problem and the problem of US nonpayment persist, however. In mid-2020, the United States again owed a significant portion of the total $3.74 billion in arrearages that forced the UN to impose a temporary hiring freeze, among other steps.

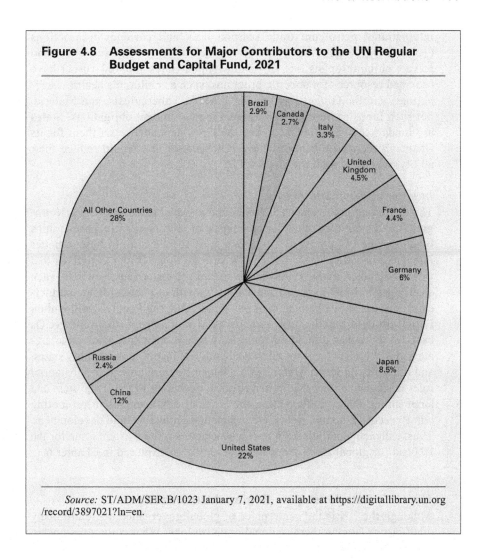

Figure 4.8 Assessments for Major Contributors to the UN Regular Budget and Capital Fund, 2021

Brazil 2.9%
Canada 2.7%
Italy 3.3%
United Kingdom 4.5%
France 4.4%
Germany 6%
Japan 8.5%
United States 22%
China 12%
Russia 2.4%
All Other Countries 28%

Source: ST/ADM/SER.B/1023 January 7, 2021, available at https://digitallibrary.un.org /record/3897021?ln=en.

There has been no shortage of proposals for changes to deal with the UN's persistent financing problems. All seek to provide a steady and predictable flow of resources for peacekeeping, economic, and social activities—revenues that would be independent of states in particular. As Thomas Weiss (2009: 196) notes, "Allowing the UN to manage such independent revenues would alleviate the world organization's reliance on member-states' largesse and permit a more rational and less agency-driven agenda regarding priorities and resource availabilities." Among the ideas that have been mentioned are international taxes on arms sales, international air travel, international petroleum trade (carbon tax), and currency transactions (Tobin tax). Pledges from corporations such as Winterthur and Pfizer and private philanthropists like Bill and Melinda Gates and Ted Turner have provided resources for specific programs, such as children's health, vaccinations, and the Global Fund to Fight AIDS, Tuberculosis, and Malaria, but such funds cannot be used to meet regular budget obligations. States are fundamentally reluctant to see the UN's dependence on them for its financing reduced too much, however, because that would reduce their ability to control what the UN does.

Integrating Nonstate Actors

The increasing involvement of NGOs and private businesses with UN programs and activities and various types of public–private partnerships involving the UN points to a fourth area of needed reform: how to better integrate nonstate actors into the UN system. Some of the initiatives that were undertaken in the 1990s in this regard are discussed elsewhere, such as changes in NGO participation and the growth in public–private partnerships, discussed in Chapters 6 and 8–11. In 2000, the People's Millennium Forum brought together representatives of more than a thousand NGOs based in more than a hundred countries where participants resolved to create a global civil society forum to deal with UN institutions, member states, and other institutions (Alger 2007). Nonstate actors now play substantial roles in supplementing the limited financial resources of the UN system and augmenting and complementing the work of UN agencies in promoting human security, human rights, environmental protection, and development. Thus, enhancing participation by nonstate actors is a persistent issue for the UN and for global governance more generally, as explored in Chapter 6.

The UN's Relationship to Regional Organizations

Although the UN is the centerpiece of global governance, there are many other pieces, among them regional organizations. What is the relationship between the UN as a global IGO and various regional IGOs? When the UN was created in 1945, there were virtually no regional IGOs in existence. The Organization of American States, the Council of Europe, NATO, and the Arab League were all created between 1945 and 1950. Nonetheless, among the UN's founders there was a tension between the principles of globalism and regionalism. The UK Foreign Office was more interested in regional spheres of influence and order, while US President Franklin Roosevelt was an advocate of a universal or global organization. The debate was framed almost exclusively in terms of security, and as a result the provisions of Chapter VIII of the UN Charter refer to regional security arrangements. The Charter is silent on broader roles for regional organizations, such as promoting economic and social cooperation, and on how these might be linked to UN activities.

Although Article 52 legitimates the existence and operation of regional alliances and encourages regional efforts to settle local disputes peacefully, it very clearly gives the UN Security Council (under Articles 24, 34, and 35) primary responsibility for maintaining international peace and security. The Council has sole authority to authorize the use of force and obligate member states to undertake sanctions, except in situations where states may exercise their right of self-defense individually or collectively (Article 51). The Council may use regional security agencies for enforcement action under its authority, but "no enforcement action shall be taken under regional arrangements or by regional agencies without the authorization of the Security Council" (Article 53). Regional organizations are to inform the Security Council of any activities planned or undertaken to maintain international peace and security (Article 54).

The Charter does not define the regional entities referred to in Chapter VIII, nor does it indicate how such entities are to relate to the UN, thus leaving issues of responsibility and legitimacy unresolved. For much of the Cold War, this was unimportant, but the situation changed dramatically when the UN became overburdened in the 1990s by post–Cold War regional, intrastate, ethnic conflicts; collapsing states; and demands for peace operations. Since then, extensive ties have been developed with various regional organizations for addressing issues of peace and security, including a few joint peace operations (discussed in Chapter 7), but also humanitarian crises, including the Covid-19 pandemic. There are also arrangements for coordinating the work of the regional development banks with UN development agencies and the World Bank, for example. Recognizing the necessity of approaching many economic and social problems in regional contexts, ECOSOC early on created five regional economic commissions to mesh their work with that of other programs. Some of these arrangements are discussed in Chapter 8.

Today, regionalism and globalism coexist with minimal friction outside the security area, and regional organizations have become increasingly important pieces of the global governance puzzle.

Suggested Further Reading

Chesterman, Simon, ed. (2007) *Secretary or General? The UN Secretary-General in World Politics*. New York: Cambridge University Press.

Cronin, Bruce, and Ian Hurd, eds. (2008) *The UN Security Council and the Politics of International Authority*. New York: Routledge.

Jolly, Richard, Louis Emmerij, and Thomas G. Weiss. (2009) *The United Nations: A History of Ideas and Their Future*. Bloomington: Indiana University Press.

Mingst, Karen A., Margaret P. Karns, and Alynna J. Lyon. (2022) *The United Nations in the 21st Century*, 6th ed. New York: Taylor & Francis.

von Einsiedel, Sebastian, David M. Malone, and Bruno Stagno Ugarte, eds. (2016) *The UN Security Council in the 21st Century*. Boulder, CO: Lynne Rienner.

Weiss, Thomas G., and Sam Daws, eds. (2020) *The Oxford Handbook on the United Nations*, 2nd ed. New York: Oxford University Press.

Weiss, Thomas G., and Ramesh Thakur. (2010) *Global Governance and the UN: An Unfinished Journey*. Bloomington: Indiana University Press.

5

Regional
Organizations

REGIONS AND REGIONAL ORGANIZATIONS HAVE EMERGED AS MAJOR PARTS
of international politics. Hence, the study of international organizations and
global governance includes the many regional and subregional organizations
in Europe, Asia, Africa, the Middle East, the Americas, and the Arctic; their
efforts to address security, economic, environmental, human rights, and human
security issues; and the interactions between and among global and regional
organizations. Comparative regionalism—the study of the processes surrounding the creation of and interactions among regional organizations and
their design and functioning—has become a field of study in its own right.

Early political and economic communities were regional, given the limits of trade and communications, and Chapter VIII of the UN Charter envisaged regional security arrangements, a number of which were created in the
early years after World War II. Although there is no similar Charter provision
with respect to regional economic and social cooperation, the UN Economic
and Social Council (ECOSOC) created regional economic commissions very
early after it came into existence, and regional development banks were
established in the 1950s, 1960s, and 1990s. Today, there is a strong sense of
regionalism as a level of governance in the world along with the global and
local, and of the potentially "productive partnership between these different
levels" (Hurrell 2007: 141) as well as between and among different regions
and regional organizations.

Regional organizations can be categorized along the same lines as global
organizations: general purpose, peace and security, economic, functional,
and technical. Many are predominantly economic, created to improve economic growth, development, and well-being by lowering barriers to trade in
goods and services and capital flows. Regional trade agreements, in particular, have proliferated in recent years, (Chapter 8). There are also regional
human rights and environmental institutions, some of which are discussed in
Chapters 9 and 10.

Regions vary widely in terms of the scope of regionalism and regional organizations, their institutional forms, membership, and identity. The sharpest contrast is between Europe (especially the European Union) and Asia. Europe has developed formal bureaucratic-legalistic institutions, including courts with enforcement powers, qualified majority voting procedures, extensive transparency and monitoring, a dense legal system of rules and regulations, and significant intrusions on the sovereignty of member states. Regionalism in Asia is more informal and nonlegalistic, involving consensus decisionmaking, informal agreements, limited commitments by states, and strong adherence to the norm of noninterference in countries' internal affairs. Africa has an extensive set of institutions, but they are relatively weak because of member states' limited resources and reluctance to accept intrusions on sovereignty. Regions also vary in the extent to which member states share a sense of identity. Studies of comparative regionalism analyze the causes of these variations, the dynamics of the processes by which regions rise and decline, and how differences in the context, scope, structures, and shared identity of regional governance arrangements correlate with effectiveness.

Rationalist theories, particularly realism and liberalism (especially its functionalist variant), have long dominated theorizing on regionalism. Constructivism has had a significant effect since the mid-1990s in identifying the roles of norms, ideas, and identity in shaping regionalism and as a way to measure outcomes of regionalism. As Alice Ba (2014: 312) noted: "Theories have generally not been sufficiently inclusive of the world's full range of experiences and conditions and how such differences might bear on the form and purpose of regional organizations outside the Euro-American zone, as well as the analytic categories, concepts, and processes that theorists draw upon and highlight to understand and explain them." Similarly, Amitav Acharya (2016b), noting the wide variations among regionalisms in the non-Western world, has questioned whether theories and approaches developed in earlier periods (especially in the European context) can apply to contemporary shifts in world politics.

This chapter examines some of the major factors and theories regarding the roots and dynamics of regionalism, as well as the major institutions and dynamics in six regions of the world: Europe, Latin America, Asia, Africa, the Middle East, and the Arctic. Regional groups' activities with respect to security, economic well-being and development, human rights, and the environment are discussed in the chapters dealing with these issue areas.

The Roots and Dynamics of Regionalism

The idea that states in a certain geographic area can more easily and effectively address common economic and security problems because they are closer to the problems and are presumed to share some background and approaches is not the only motivation for the development of regionalism. It is a dynamic process often involving the development of intraregional interdependence along with creating regional norms, building regional institutions, and fostering a degree of regional identity among states and peoples in a given area (Acharya 2012: 26). Where early post–World War II regional initiatives tended to focus on trade liberalization and managing interstate conflict, later, especially non-Western regionalism, has focused more on preserving state sovereignty and limiting the influence of major powers from outside the region and those within, that is, the noninterference norm. It has also prioritized economic development along with less formal institutions and processes, smaller bureaucracies, consensus decisionmaking, and no formal dispute settlement mechanisms (Acharya 2016b: 117).

Regionalism is not necessarily a one-way process, as the sense of region-ness, the degree of commitment to common policies, and effectiveness of institutions can decline over time. Regionalism is dynamic, so new challenges and issues can and have resulted in significant shifts in regional institutions. Scholars have debated the question of how much diffusion has taken place across regions. That is, to what extent has there been either a deliberate effort by some regional organizations, especially those in the Global North, or a process by which regionalism, including institutional designs and governance of specific policy areas, has been fostered elsewhere in the world. Thomas Risse (2016: 3) has argued that the dynamics are "primarily determined by indirect mechanisms of emulation rather than by direct—'sender-driven'—influence mechanisms." Certainly, there has been some "lesson drawing" and "normative emulation" in his view with the EU being a major source (if not stimulus) for diffusion of the idea of regionalism and regional cooperation; of specific designs for regional organizations such as regional courts and parliamentary bodies; and of regional governance regarding specific policy areas. Before proceeding, we need to address the question of how regions are defined.

Defining a Region

Traditional definitions of regionalism assumed that the participating states shared geographical proximity; some cultural, linguistic, and historical heritage; and a degree of mutual interdependence. The constructivist approach posits that a region is a social and political construction with various concepts, metaphors, and practices determining how the region is defined and who is included and excluded (Acharya 1997). This view emphasizes that regions are *made*; it is less static in that it acknowledges how identity, norms, and meaning can change over time. Another approach defines regions in terms of nonterritorial, functional factors such as transnational capitalist processes, the environment (e.g., acid rain), or identity groups (Väyrynen 2003: 27).

The lack of agreement on the definition of regions means there is no single guide to identifying their boundaries. Instead, decisions as to what constitutes a particular region reflect the perceptions, prejudices, or desires of those states that constitute a core group for regional initiatives. They form in effect an "in-group" that subsequently determines whether to accept any "outsiders." What is now the EU began with six member states in Western Europe. Today it has twenty-seven members that span the continent. Turkey's application for membership has challenged the definition of "Europe," because Turkey is a predominantly Muslim country with a weak democratic system straddling Europe and Western Asia. In the absence of a pan-Asian organization, India has been excluded from the predominantly Southeast and East Asian regional initiatives—the Association of Southeast Asian Nations (ASEAN) and Asia Pacific Economic Cooperation (APEC).

Most regions are marked today by multiple organizations with overlapping memberships. Where several coexist in the same geographic and political space, they may be viewed as concentric circles or nested regimes (see Figure 5.1).

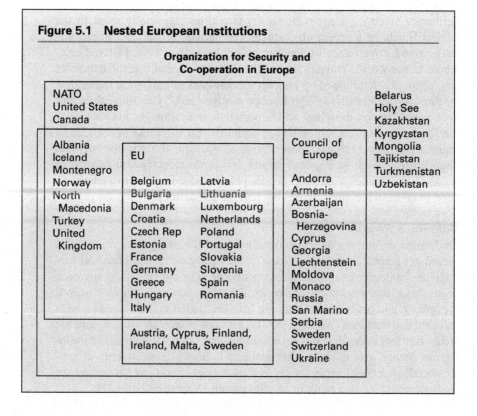

Figure 5.1   Nested European Institutions

Organization for Security and Co-operation in Europe

NATO
United States
Canada

Albania
Iceland
Montenegro
Norway
North
  Macedonia
Turkey
United
  Kingdom

EU

Belgium   Latvia
Bulgaria   Lithuania
Denmark   Luxembourg
Croatia   Netherlands
Czech Rep   Poland
Estonia   Portugal
France   Slovakia
Germany   Slovenia
Greece   Spain
Hungary   Romania
Italy

Austria, Cyprus, Finland,
Ireland, Malta, Sweden

Council of
Europe

Andorra
Armenia
Azerbaijan
Bosnia-
  Herzegovina
Cyprus
Georgia
Liechtenstein
Moldova
Monaco
Russia
San Marino
Serbia
Sweden
Switzerland
Ukraine

Belarus
Holy See
Kazakhstan
Kyrgyzstan
Mongolia
Tajikistan
Turkmenistan
Uzbekistan

One additional feature of "new regionalism" is the growth of nonstate and civil society activities as part of the dynamics within regions. These include anti-Americanism in regions such as Latin America and Europe, anti-Japanese and anti-Chinese protests, and Chinese production networks in Asia. Such "societal resistance to regional powers," Acharya (2007a: 649) notes, "could be inspired by local resentment against their economic and political dominance. It could also represent a reaction led by civil society actors, against globalization (and its regional variant, regionalization)."

Political Factors Driving Regionalism

Regardless of the theoretical approach one takes, regionalism does not just happen. Deliberate policy choices by states' leaders or perhaps more accurately by their policy elites are key to expanding economic or political activity among a group of states to reap anticipated benefits. Among the political factors linked to the development of regionalism are power dynamics, identity (or shared perception of a definable region) and ideology, internal and external threats, domestic politics, and leadership. In democratic systems, public support can also be key.

Power dynamics. Power dynamics can play a significant role through pivotal regional powers such as Indonesia in ASEAN and Egypt in the Arab League, or through the efforts of great or hegemonic powers to create and shape regional orders. Regionalism in Europe, Latin America, and Asia, for example, has been strongly influenced by US preferences. In the European case, the United States supported early regional initiatives as imperative to resisting communism during the Cold War. Latin American countries saw regionalism as a way to counter US influence. In the Asian case, the United States preferred bilateral relationships over multilateral regionalism (Katzenstein 2005). The creation of the ASEAN Regional Forum (ARF) in the 1990s was an effort by the Southeast Asian states to engage both China and the United States in "a system of regional order . . . thereby dampening not only their mutual rivalry but also their dominance over the weaker states of the region" (Acharya 2007a: 648). Future Asian regionalism will clearly be influenced by the growing geopolitical competition associated with the rise of China and by India's choices. While power dynamics matter, identity and ideology in the region are also important.

Identity and ideology. A number of studies have focused on identity, or shared perception of being part of a definable region, as a key factor in the definition of region and development of regionalism. Acharya (2012: 23) argues that "as with nation-states, regions may be 'imagined' and 'socially constructed.'" He stresses that "territorial proximity and functional interactions are by themselves inadequate to constitute a region in the absence of an 'idea of the region,' whether conceived from inside or out." In other words, "regional coherence and identity are not givens, but result primarily from self-conscious socialization among the leaders and peoples of a region." Much of his and others' work has analyzed how the ASEAN states constructed their sense of regional identity by elaborating key ideas and processes often described as the "ASEAN Way." Yet as constructivists posit, national and regional identities are subject to reinterpretation and change, making it "possible for former enemies to become friends and for security communities to replace historical patterns of anarchy and disorder" (Acharya 2007a: 636). The prime example of this phenomenon is Germany's transformation from enemy to core member of multiple European organizations.

Ideology can be a factor that brings states together in a regional organization. Both NATO (North Atlantic Treaty Organization) and the EU are based on liberal ideology, while many non-Western regional organizations were and still are based on anticolonialism, nonintervention, and ideologies of pan-Arabism (the Arab League) and pan-Africanism (the Organization of African Unity [OAU] and now the African Union [AU]). Like identity, ideologies can change. In the 1990s, for example, the Organization of American States (OAS) embraced liberal democracy, along with a shift from nonintervention to democracy promotion and protection, and regional trade arrangements in many regions now embrace liberal economics. Börzel and Risse (2016) note the need to account for "autocratic regionalism," such as evidenced in the Shanghai Cooperation Organization (SCO) formed by Russia and China in the late 1990s. Still, shared identity or ideology alone cannot bring about a regional security community. Such entities and other types of regional organizations tend to arise out of external or internal threats.

Internal and external threats. A shared sense of external or internal threat can be a key political factor that drives states toward closer regional cooperation. The Cold War threat of communism, and especially of Soviet expansion, was a powerful impetus to regionalism in Western Europe in the 1950s and 1960s. It was directly responsible for the creation of NATO (1949) and part of the rationale behind the European Community's formation. Other Cold War regional alliances included the Rio Pact (1947), the Southeast Asian Treaty Organization (1954), and the Warsaw Treaty Organization (1955). European integration was also driven by the desire to contain German nationalism by enmeshing that country in tight links with France and other neighboring states. Cold War competition between the United States and the Soviet Union for influence in non-Western countries contributed to regionalisms that sought to bolster states' sovereignty and autonomy. Thus, the US presence in Southeast Asia during the Vietnam War played a major role in the formation of ASEAN. In the Middle East, the 1979 Iranian Revolution and the war between Iran and Iraq in the 1980s were seen as threats by the tiny Persian Gulf states that established the Gulf Cooperation Council (GCC) in 1981.

The Cold War's end in 1990 reshaped many regional organizations. Not only did Soviet-dominated institutions die, but the loss of the Soviet threat required a fundamental rethinking of NATO's purpose and a redefinition of the memberships and activities of other European organizations. Threats or the absence of threats clearly overlap with power dynamics, since resistance to outside or regional powers often plays a role in regionalism. Fear of a resurgent Japan has been one of the deterrents to Asian regionalism, for example, and shared hostility to the state of Israel has been a major source of unity for the Arab League. Anti-Americanism fueled by resentment of US dominance has contributed to challenges to the US role in Latin America, Asia, the Middle East, and Europe. This is evident in the EU's effort to create a self-defense force separate from NATO and in Venezuela's efforts to create a "Bank of the South" as an alternate regional financing institution to the Inter-American Development Bank, International Monetary Fund, and World Bank, which are all seen as US-dominated. China's increasing assertiveness is having significant effects on ASEAN. Similarly, Russia's 2022 invasion of Ukraine bolstered NATO solidarity and propelled EU members to agree to a number of steps they had previously resisted.

Economic crises are another form of threat that has increased countries' perceptions of the need for closer regional cooperation. The 1997–1998 Asian financial crisis and China's increasing share of foreign direct investment , for example, contributed to a sharpened awareness that ASEAN needed to develop its capacity to deal with financial and monetary vulnerability. The prolonged failure to advance trade liberalization under the World Trade Organization since the late 1990s, and attendant fear that rival trade blocs would limit market access, led to the proliferation of regional and bilateral free trade agreements (Chapter 8). In Africa, conflicts, humanitarian disasters, pandemics, and political and economic failures contributed to the reorganization of the OAU into the AU in 2002 in an effort to strengthen regional cooperation. Today, however, complex transnational threats such as terrorism, environmental degradation and climate change, migration and refugee flows, drug trafficking, and crime challenge traditional definitions of regions and of security itself (explored further in Chapter 11).

Domestic politics. State structures and regime types matter with respect to regional governance initiatives. Where states in a region have similar types of political and economic institutions, it will be easier to reach agreement on regional arrangements, and such arrangements are likely to be more effective. The EU is a prime example of this, in that all member states are democracies. ASEAN illustrates the difficulty that regional organizations encounter when there are wide variations among members' political systems, from communist regimes (Vietnam and Laos) to authoritarian governments (Myanmar and Cambodia) to democratic states punctuated by military rule (Thailand). In two regions—Africa and Latin America—the desire to address the problem of unconstitutional changes of government have led the AU and the OAS to create regional mechanisms for addressing military coups and initiatives by political leaders to remain in office after their terms expire. Both are discussed later in this chapter.

In addition, the nature of domestic coalitions and their strategies toward other states affect the structure of regional order. Solingen (1998), for example, argues that it takes a strong domestic political coalition, including strong export-oriented manufacturing industries, to support closer economic integration and the tough decisions to open borders to trade that will subject locally owned companies to outside competition. This was the case with South America's Common Market of the South (Mercosur). Likewise, pressures from a transnational coalition of European firms in favor of a European market were important to completing the EU single market in 1992. The strong "pro-regional" identity of elites who worked to build community and generate public support for closer regional integration has been an important factor in many EU countries (Börzel and Risse 2016). In contrast, protecting sovereignty and domestic regimes have often been foremost among the concerns of domestic coalitions, elites, and individual leaders in Africa, Asia, and the Middle East, ensuring that those regional institutions are weaker and often less effective.

Regional arrangements can also affect domestic politics, creating commitments that governments may find helpful for resisting demands of domestic groups. A preferential trade agreement, for example, can aid a government in locking in liberal economic reforms (Mansfield and Milner 1999: 605). It may also give a federal government enhanced power over its states and provinces, as the North American Free Trade Agreement (NAFTA) has done in Canada and the United States.

Leadership. Regionalism does not just happen. Deliberate policy choices by states and their leaders are key to increasing the flow of economic and political activities. Jean Monnet and Robert Schuman were among those visionary post–World War II Europeans who conceived of a united Europe, along with leaders of France and West Germany, who were each instrumental in the birth of postwar European regionalism. Indonesia played a lead role for ASEAN, while Australia and Japan did so for APEC, Egypt and Gamal Abdel Nasser for the Arab League, and Venezuela and Colombia for the Andean Pact. The United States provided leadership for NATO and the OAS, but it was Canada that proposed the Canada-US Free Trade Agreement, the predecessor of NAFTA.

Economic Factors Driving Regionalism

High levels of economic interdependence, most notably trade and investment flows, the complementarity of economies and policies, the availability of compensatory mechanisms for integration in developing countries, and the desire to stimulate trade and attract foreign investment by creating a larger market are commonly linked to regional economic initiatives. There is also debate among scholars of comparative regionalism about the relative importance of intraregional economic interdependence (Ravenhill 2001; Börzel and Risse 2016). Interdependence increases the costs generated by lack of coordinated national policies because it raises the sensitivity of economic events in one country to what is happening with its trading partners. It is the foundation of the functionalist theory of regional integration that is now seen as largely applicable to Western Europe and the EU's early development. Tanja Börzel and Thomas Risse (2016) argue, however, that regional institutions where states pool and delegate authority are the result of factors other than intraregional economic interdependence such as security interdependence. They note that ASEAN and Mercosur show medium levels of economic interdependence but limited delegation. In contrast, they characterize sub-Saharan Africa and Latin America and the Caribbean as having higher levels of pooling and delegation but low intraregional trade, while North America shows high interdependence and low pooling and delegation to NAFTA.

Since 1990, economic globalization has stimulated regional integration in a variety of ways. The globalization of foreign direct investment has deepened regional integration in Europe. Elsewhere, states have adopted regionalism as a strategy to counter the adverse effects of globalization. The New Partnership for Africa's Development (NEPAD) represented an attempt to counter Africa's increasing marginalization in an era of globalization. As our discussion shows, economic factors and prospects of higher material well-being alone have rarely sufficed as a basis for successful regional cooperation.

In short, economic interconnectedness does not necessarily lead countries in a geographical area to see themselves as part of a region or to think in terms of regional cooperation. John Ravenhill (2001: 14–15) concluded: "No clear correlation exists between levels of interdependence between specific economies, measured by the relative importance of bilateral trade flows, and the emergence of economic regionalism . . . [and] no critical threshold of regional economic interdependence exists below which regionalism never occurs and beyond which such collaboration always takes place."

Comparing Regions

By examining some of the major regional organizations, we will see more clearly how history, culture, domestic politics, and other factors have facilitated or impeded the growth of regional institutions. Comparing these institutions will also illuminate some of the similarities and differences in their design and the degree to which member states have agreed to transfer some of their authority to regional bodies—variously described as pooling or delegating. Some indicators include majority decisionmaking versus consensus or unanimity and delegating some authority to supranational bodies such as courts. Where similarities exist among certain regional bodies, that may well reflect the diffusion of institutional designs. Some examples of this include more than ten copies of the European Court of Justice (Alter and Hooghe 2016) and the spread of regional parliamentary bodies (Rüland and Bechle 2014). Börzel and Risse (2019: 1244) also describe diffusion as "a powerful explanation for the supply of regional integration," along with the role of elites in both Latin America and sub-Saharan Africa where economic interdependence has been low.

* * *

In the next six sections, we provide short overviews of the organizations in each geographic region and a more in-depth examination of one major regional organization. We start with Europe, where regionalism has progressed the furthest and which has sometimes been seen as a model for regional organizations elsewhere.

Europe's Regional Organizations

Since World War II, European states have established a dense network of regional organizations to address security, economic, and other needs. In the Cold War years, the Iron Curtain formed a sharp boundary line between two sets of organizations. In Eastern Europe, states under Soviet domination joined together in the Warsaw Pact for common defense and in the Council of Mutual Economic Assistance to manage their economic relations. In Western Europe, with strong support from the United States, the Organisation for European Economic Cooperation (OEEC) was established in 1948 to administer US Marshall Plan aid and to lower trade and currency barriers; NATO was established in 1949 with US and Canadian participation as a military alliance to defend against perceived threats from the Soviet Union. The Europeans created the Council of Europe in 1949, a multipurpose organization "to achieve a greater unity among its Members for the purpose of safeguarding and realizing the ideals and principles which are their common heritage and facilitating their economic and social progress" (Council of Europe, Statute 2, Article 1).

Very shortly, the perceived shortcomings of the OEEC and Council of Europe led six countries (France, West Germany, the Netherlands, Belgium,

Luxembourg, and Italy) to begin a process of deeper integration with a new set of institutions, starting with the European Coal and Steel Community (ECSC) in 1952. This was followed by the European Atomic Energy Community (Euratom) and European Economic Community (EEC, also known as the European Community or Common Market) in 1958. The integration process continues today as the European Union. The Western European Union was established in 1954 to provide a framework for German rearmament, and the European Free Trade Association was established in 1960 for states that chose not to join the Common Market.

During the period of détente between East and West in the 1970s, the Conference on Security and Cooperation in Europe (or Helsinki Conference) was established, bringing together countries from Eastern and Western Europe (plus the United States and Soviet Union). It was succeeded by the Organization of Security and Co-operation in Europe (OSCE) in 1990.

The Warsaw Pact and the Council of Mutual Economic Assistance disbanded in 1991 with the collapse of communist governments in Central and Eastern Europe and the dissolution of the Soviet Union. Eleven former members are now members of NATO and the EU. The Cold War's end transformed the landscape and its dense set of nested institutions (shown in Figure 5.1). Russia's efforts in recent years to re-create links with parts of the former Soviet Union and its invasion of Ukraine in 2022 continue to affect that landscape. This section examines three of the European organizations: NATO, the OSCE, and the EU.

The North Atlantic Treaty Organization

NATO is the most highly organized regional security organization in the world. It began as a Cold War military alliance, designed, in the words of its first secretary-general, Lord Hastings Ismay, "to keep the Americans in, the Russians out, and the Germans down" (quoted in Schimmelfennig 2007: 145). It has long been far more than just a treaty of alliance. Since 1991, it has enlarged its membership to thirty (see Figure 5.1) and created partnerships with several Mediterranean and Eurasian states, including Russia for a time. Even as it debated its post–Cold War mission, NATO became involved in operations on the periphery of Europe—first in Bosnia and Herzegovina, then in Kosovo, and subsequently in Afghanistan, Iraq, Sudan, and Libya as well as antipiracy operations off the coast of Somalia. With Russia's annexation of Crimea in 2014, President Vladimir Putin's claim of a right to intervene on behalf of Russian-speakers, and the invasion of Ukraine in 2022, NATO has returned to its priority of collective territorial defense of its European members, with Russia as the primary threat. Finland was admitted as a member in 2023, while Sweden's application was stalled by Turkey and Hungary, but both countries saw Russia's 2022 invasion as a reason to give up their long-standing neutrality.

At the core of the 1948 North Atlantic Treaty is the agreement in Article 5 "that an armed attack against one or more of them [the parties to the treaty] in Europe or North America shall be considered an attack against them all," obligating all member states to assist the member attacked when the state consents. The first time this was invoked in more than fifty years, however, was after the September 11, 2001, terrorist attacks on the United States. NATO is also firmly grounded in a liberal theory of peace, as the treaty's preamble states that members "are determined to safeguard the freedom, common heritage and civilization of their peoples, founded on the principles of democracy, individual liberty, and the rule of law."

Structure. NATO's principal organ is the North Atlantic Council, which meets at least twice yearly at the ministerial level (i.e., ministers of foreign affairs or defense) and weekly at the ambassadorial level at its headquarters in Brussels. Periodically, the council meets at the summit level (i.e., heads of government and state) to provide strategic direction, launch new initiatives, and build partnerships with non-NATO members. Decisions tend to be made on the basis of consensus, with members having a de facto veto. The NATO secretary-general chairs the council in addition to preparing budgets, arranging meeting agendas, supervising the secretariat, and representing the organization in relations with governments and other international organizations. A large number of committees handle defense planning, political affairs, armaments, air space, and communications. The NATO Parliamentary Assembly, comprising 269 legislators from member countries and partner states, links the alliance with legislatures and, through them, with citizens.

The NATO Military Committee, composed of chiefs of staff or their representatives from member countries, oversees NATO's elaborate integrated military command structure and missions. The position of Supreme Allied Commander Europe has traditionally been held by a senior US military officer. Supreme Headquarters Allied Powers Europe, located in Mons, Belgium, is responsible for all alliance operations. The renewed sense of Russia as an adversary has led NATO members, particularly Germany, to increase their commitments to the alliance, including the size of their national defense budgets—a long-standing issue. Along with NATO's integrated military command structure, there is a complex structure of civilian and military consultation, cooperation, and coordination, plus agreements on members' force levels and defense expenditures. Forces are maintained in Western Europe, the Atlantic, and the Mediterranean, and efforts have been made over many years to coordinate equipment specifications and training to ensure their interoperability (e.g., that Dutch, French, or German artillery can use US ammunition). Despite the integrated command structure, military forces remain under command of their national officers.

Key issues. One long-standing issue has been the US commitment to European defense and the degree to which the United States and Europe agree on security priorities. The US tendency to inform allies of policy changes only after decisions have been made in Washington, rather than consulting with them beforehand, is a recurring source of tension. A second key issue is burden-sharing. The United States has frequently complained about the Europeans paying and doing too little to maintain their defense capabilities (a classic free-rider problem). In 2014, members pledged that within a decade their respective defense spending would reach the goal of 2 percent of national GDP, and 2022 marked eight years of increased spending.

As noted already, the end of the Cold War made NATO an organization in search of a new role with debates over enlargement to incorporate former Soviet bloc countries in Eastern and Central Europe; the scope and nature of its mission inside and outside Europe; and over its relationship with Russia. Behind the issue of enlargement was the belief that the values uniting the alliance for more than fifty years—democracy, the rule of law, and individual liberties—were keys to lasting peace and security in the Euro-Atlantic region. Although NATO members worked hard to convince Russia that expansion was not a threat, Russia fiercely opposed enlargement. Even so, between 1997 and 2020, NATO admitted fourteen countries, starting with Poland, the Czech Republic, and Hungary and concluding with North Macedonia. Yet enlargement was not accompanied by either enhanced military capabilities or a new shared security vision.

Between 1994 and 2014, there were efforts to build constructive relations with Russia, including creating a mechanism for regular consultations and cooperation regarding a wide range of issues, such as transparency of military doctrines and nuclear safety. Nevertheless, Russia continued to perceive NATO as an anti-Russian military alliance. NATO's intervention in Kosovo in 1999 without UN Security Council approval only fed Russian fears, as did its involvement in the UN-sanctioned intervention in Libya in 2011. Georgia's and Ukraine's applications for NATO membership after Russia's invasion of Georgia in 2008 added fuel to the fire and contributed to the 2014 and 2022 crises over Ukraine.

New post–Cold War roles: Former Yugoslavia and the Balkans. The conflicts in the former Yugoslavia in the early 1990s drew NATO into its first military operation to enforce the UN Security Council–authorized arms embargo, no-fly zone, and bombing of Bosnian Serb installations. The latter action helped shift the military balance in Bosnia and led to peace negotiations. Under the 1995 Dayton Accords, NATO then undertook major peacekeeping and peacebuilding responsibilities, providing the majority of Implementation Force troops. These troops were succeeded by the Stabilization Force from 1996 to 2004, after which the EU took over. In 1999,

NATO conducted a seventy-eight-day bombing campaign against the Federal Republic of Yugoslavia (Serbia) and then provided the majority of troops for the UN-authorized Kosovo Force from 1999 to the present. These activities are discussed further in Chapter 7.

Afghanistan and the war on terrorism. The September 11, 2001, terrorist attacks on the United States led NATO members to express their solidarity by invoking Article 5 of the North Atlantic Treaty for the first time. With the US declaration of a global war against terrorism, NATO moved to adapt to this new security environment and enhance its operational capabilities. In 2003, NATO assumed command of the UN-sanctioned International Security Assistance Force (ISAF) in Afghanistan—its first operation outside of Europe. By the end of 2008, NATO had more than 50,000 troops in Afghanistan assisting the Afghan government in extending its authority throughout the country, conducting operations against the resurgent Taliban and al-Qaeda, and supporting the Afghan army. Because the mission was controversial among the European allies, US officials repeatedly had to make the case for why European security was linked to NATO's success in stabilizing Afghanistan. Following the end of ISAF in 2014, NATO and US forces continued to assist the Afghan National Security Forces under the US-Afghan Bilateral Security Agreement and the NATO Status of Forces Agreement until the abrupt US withdrawal in 2021. Terrorism in its various forms, however, remains a key focus for NATO.

Iraq, Darfur, Somalia, Libya. In four other situations outside Europe, NATO forces have had varying degrees of involvement since 2003. The 2003 Iraq War sharply divided the NATO allies, creating a crisis in the alliance. European members refused US requests for limited support; three countries blocked planning for NATO support of its own member, Turkey, and for any official NATO presence in Iraq. However, the alliance did have a role in training and assisting the Iraqi army from 2004 to 2011. It has supported AU peacekeeping missions in the Darfur region of Sudan and in Somalia, principally by providing airlifts for AU peacekeepers. In addition, NATO ships have patrolled waters off the Horn of Africa to combat piracy.

NATO's role in toppling the Muammar Qaddafi regime in Libya in 2011 was more extensive and controversial. Under two UN Security Council Resolutions, NATO enforced a no-fly zone and arms embargo as well as undertaking air and naval strikes against Libyan forces attacking civilians and civilian-populated areas. By one set of measures, the operation saved tens of thousands of lives and "enabled the Libyan opposition to overthrow one of the world's longest-ruling dictators . . . without a single allied casualty" (Daalder and Stavridis 2012: 2). By other measures, NATO's operation amounted to war, not a humanitarian intervention, in the eyes of many. (For further discussion, see Chapter 7.)

The Libyan operation, involving eighteen countries (fourteen NATO members and four partners), demonstrated NATO's unique ability to respond quickly and effectively to crises, thanks to its unified command structure and capability of planning and executing complex operations. It was also indicative of tensions within the alliance in that fourteen member countries did not participate. And it highlighted the burden-sharing problem of European underinvestment in defense capabilities as the United States provided 75 percent of the intelligence and surveillance data, 75 percent of the refueling planes, and much of the ammunition (Daalder and Stavridis 2012: 6).

NATO and Russia's 2022 invasion of Ukraine. NATO's eastward expansion since the mid-1990s brought it directly to Russia's borders, and the possibility of Ukraine becoming a member of NATO was seen as a contributing factor to Russian President Vladimir Putin's decision to invade Ukraine in early 2022. The effect on NATO has been substantial. First, Russia's aggression posed the greatest threat to Euro-Atlantic security since the height of the Cold War. Second, the war led NATO leaders to agree to deploy new battle groups to four Eastern European countries (Bulgaria, Hungary, Romania, and Slovakia) and strengthen those already in Poland, Estonia, Latvia, and Lithuania. Third, two longtime neutral countries— Sweden and Finland—were prompted to apply for NATO membership. Finland has the longest border with Russia of any country in Europe. Germany and other countries increased their defense spending and NATO commitments in response to the new threat. Germany also was prompted to undertake some fundamental rethinking of its foreign policy, including its energy dependence on Russia, its policy on exporting arms, and its commitment to European defense. NATO allies also adopted a variety of economic sanctions against Russia and provided extensive military support to Ukraine as well as financial and humanitarian aid.

* * *

NATO presents the unusual case of an international organization whose original purpose disappeared for a time, challenging it to transform itself, with a variation of the original purpose reappearing thirty years later. Beginning with events in Crimea and Ukraine in 2014 and magnified by Russia's 2022 invasion, issues of alliance commitment have become primary again, and NATO members face a complex security environment. The invasion of Ukraine once again has made Russia the major threat to European security, although the perception of that threat is strongest among the Central and Eastern European members. Terrorism continues to be a threat to security; China's rise has implications for the alliance; and increasingly sophisticated cyber and hybrid threats along with technological changes and growth of artificial intelligence require fresh thinking. It is also important to bear in mind that NATO is not just a European organization. Canada and the United States are members, and the latter has dominated NATO for all of its history with the Europeans fundamentally dependent on it for leadership, its strategic nuclear capabilities, and the presence of its troops on European soil. It has often been difficult for the European states without that American role to forge a common course of action on security issues, which has made free-riding an easier course. This helps explain the coexistence of NATO with other European security-related organizations, such as the Organization for Security and Co-operation in Europe (OSCE).

The Organization for Security and Co-operation in Europe

The OSCE is the broadest organization in the European security architecture, with fifty-seven member states in Europe and Central Asia, plus the United States and Canada. It has evolved since it replaced the Conference on Security and Co-operation in Europe in 1990 into an instrument for broadly defined security cooperation and coordination and conflict prevention and resolution. The normative core for the OSCE-based security regime was established in the Helsinki Final Act of 1975. This contained a set of ten principles governing interstate relations, including refraining from the threat or use of force, inviolability of frontiers, peaceful settlement of disputes, respect for human rights and fundamental freedoms, self-determination of peoples, and cooperation among states. The Cold War's end in 1990 and pressures for independence from groups and regions in the former Soviet Union and former Yugoslavia led to strengthening of confidence-building measures, transparency, democratization, and minority rights protections and the creation of a more formal IGO.

A secretariat, parliamentary assembly, and permanent council were established in 1990 along with various centers and offices for human rights and democracy, national minorities, arms control, and counterterrorism, as well as transnational crime and trafficking in drugs, arms, and people. The OSCE is particularly noted for its work in organizing, supervising, and monitoring electoral processes and its efforts to protect human and minority rights. It has trained police in Croatia, Serbia, Kyrgyzstan, and Azerbaijan; negotiated a cease-fire in Chechnya; mediated agreements between governments and secessionist regions in Moldova, Azerbaijan, Georgia, and Tajikistan; and undertaken conflict prevention, election and cease-fire monitoring in Ukraine between 2014 and 2022. It has been a major partner of the UN Mission in Kosovo, where its responsibilities have included development of civil society, human rights protection, and establishing a judicial system.

The OSCE has often come under fire from Russia and other states, however, for what is seen as too exclusive a focus on countries "east of Vienna" and for applying uneven standards in its election monitoring and human rights promotion (Ghébali 2005: 14). Consequently, Russia and some Central Asian states have limited OSCE election observation.

While the activities of the OSCE overlap with those of NATO, the Council of Europe, and the EU, it occupies a niche because of its broad membership and its long-term field missions in parts of the former Soviet Union and Yugoslavia. There is both cooperation and competition with the European Union, the strongest regional organization.

The European Union

The EU is a unique IGO that is deeply institutionalized and legalized and involves far more commitment from its member states and loss of sovereignty than any other IGO. Whereas the initial steps involved only six Western European states, as of 2022 twenty-seven countries are full members. The EU's development embodies a process of integration, where steps taken in one area have spilled over into others over time. It has exemplified both functionalism and neofunctionalism. It encompasses aspects of both supranationalism (sometimes referred to as federalism) and intergovernmentalism, where member states retain primary responsibility for decisionmaking. Thus, its development has involved widening membership and deepening ties among the member states, integrating economies and societies more closely, and expanding the authority of community institutions over the member states. Much of the policymaking in Europe today is common or EU policy, made in Brussels through EU institutions. The EU affects the daily lives of its more than 447 million citizens, most of whom can now move freely between member states and carry EU passports. The EU commanded 14.9 percent of world GDP in 2022 and citizens in nineteen member countries use the euro as their currency.

The EU's development has transformed governance in Europe, influencing everything from regulations on the habitat of birds to voting in the World Trade Organization; with its own legal system, parliament, bureaucracy, currency, and court, its complex institutions resemble those of nation-states. It has also altered global politics and governance with the joint actions and common policies of EU members. The process of European integration is attributable to a complex set of factors but is not irreversible, as Britain's withdrawal from the EU in 2020 demonstrated. Likewise, the EU's efforts to solidify democracy in its Eastern European member countries have been challenged by steps toward more authoritarianism in Poland and Hungary.

Historical overview of European integration. Regional political and economic integration in (Western) Europe is the result of several factors. For one, European leaders at the end of World War II sought to find ways to overcome the national rivalries that had led to two devastating wars in the first half of the twentieth century. In addition, the United States was committed to promoting democracy and an open international economic system to replace the protectionism, competitive currency devaluations, and other policies that had marked the rivalries among European powers (and excluded US businesses from European markets). The Soviet threat added impetus to strengthening the war-weakened countries, as did internal threats from strong communist political parties in France and Italy. A desire to enmesh the Germans in international agreements that would prevent them from posing future threats to European security was another motivating factor. The United States added incentives through Marshall Plan requirements that the European governments cooperate in developing plans for utilizing aid, formulate a joint effort rather than submitting separate national requests, and create an international organization to administer the aid to the sixteen participating countries.

Visionary Europeans such as Jean Monnet and Alcide De Gasperi, who dreamed of a "United States of Europe," also contributed. Thus, security threats, economic incentives, and visions all played a part. So did economic interests of powerful sectors, particularly in the French and German economies (notably heavy industry and agriculture), along with trends in the post–World War II international economy (notably rising trade and capital flows among the industrialized countries), which led governments to look for ways to respond to new opportunities for promoting economic gains.

The European Coal and Steel Community (ECSC). The birth of European integration occurred in May 1950 with a proposal by French foreign minister Robert Schuman to place Franco-German coal and steel production under a common "high authority." This meant accepting recently defeated Germany as an economic equal and handing over authority for both countries' key coal and steel industries to a supranational authority. Schuman provided a concrete step for turning vague dreams into reality, but in the key economic sector that supported war-making capability (arms industries)—a strategy that accorded well with neofunctionalist theory. The result was the ECSC, established in 1951 with six member states (France, Germany, Italy, Belgium, Luxembourg, and the Netherlands). The United Kingdom rejected an invitation to join because of strong sentiments in both major political parties against loss of sovereignty and national control over coal and steel.

Illustrating the classic dynamic of functionalism, the ECSC was successful enough in boosting coal and steel production that the six member states agreed in 1958 to expand their cooperation under Euratom and the EEC or Common Market. The founding documents of these three organizations form the constitutional basis of the European Union. The governing institutions of the three have since been merged. Two other integrating organizations were proposed in the 1950s but rejected: the European Defence Community and European Political Community.

The Treaties of Rome: Euratom and the common market. The Treaties of Rome (1958) represented recognition that the community could not develop the coal and steel sectors in isolation from other economic sectors. One treaty committed members to creating a common market over a period of twelve years by removing all restrictions on internal trade; a common external tariff; reducing barriers to free movement of people, services, and capital; the development of common agricultural and transport policies; and establishing the European Social Fund and European Investment Bank. The second treaty created Euratom to establish a common market for atomic energy.

Although there were certainly tensions among the members and between governments and the community institutions, there was remarkably rapid progress in taking significant steps toward achieving a common market. In 1962, the Common Agricultural Policy (CAP) came into existence, with a single market for farm products and guaranteed prices for farmers. In the 1960s, the members also began the arduous process of harmonizing various health, safety, and consumer protection standards and regulations, as well as easing the barriers to movement of workers among member countries. In 1968, two years ahead of schedule, they completed an industrial customs union and had removed enough internal barriers to trade to agree on a common external tariff with nonmember countries and form a single negotiating party in international trade talks. In 1969, governments agreed on the principles of economic and monetary union, which were regarded as essential for achieving political union, although the sovereignty that would be lost was difficult for them to contemplate at the time. Despite disagreement over whether economic or monetary union should come first, they agreed to begin efforts toward controlling exchange-rate fluctuations and coordinating their national economic policies.

Enlargement. Slow economic growth in the 1970s stalled any deepening of European integration, but in 1973, the community's first enlargement took place with the accession of the United Kingdom, Ireland, and Denmark (Norwegian voters rejected the accession agreement their government had signed). Later in the 1970s, a strong desire to bolster the new democracies in Greece, Spain, and Portugal provided motivation for their accession. The addition of Ireland and three Southern European countries introduced a much wider disparity among members' levels of economic development than existed with the original six or with the United Kingdom and Denmark, however.

In 1994, the decision was made to admit Finland, Sweden, and Austria. In anticipation of further enlargements to former Soviet bloc states in Eastern

Europe, the European Council delineated conditions for new members, including respect for democracy, rule of law, human rights, protection of minorities, a functioning market economy, and a demonstrated capacity to implement past and future EU rules and legislation. These so-called Copenhagen conditions have provided benchmarks for candidate countries and incentives for making the requisite changes in their economies, political systems, and laws. Three further enlargements, in 2004, 2007, and 2013, brought in eleven Eastern European and two Mediterranean countries. Table 5.1 offers details on some consequences of the seven enlargements.

The EU now encompasses much of the continent and far greater diversity than ever before. For the thirteen newer members, EU membership has meant adhering to some 80,000 pages of EU laws and regulations accumulated over five decades of the integration process. Although all members won special concessions and extra time to phase in the EU's extensive environmental legislation, they had to wait seven to ten years before getting full benefits such as free movement of labor and agricultural subsidies. Still, the requirements for accession provided a powerful incentive for governments to change. The disparities and tensions between older and newer members, however, have created a number of issues, including the need for reforming institutional structures. In addition, with Brexit and the United Kingdom's withdrawal from the EU, the organization has actually shrunk and, although

Table 5.1 EU Enlargements

	Original Members (1958)	First (1973)	Second (1981)	Third (1986)	Fourth (1995)	Fifth (2004)	Sixth (2007)	Seventh (2013)
Member states	Belgium France Germany Italy Luxembourg Netherlands	United Kingdom Ireland Denmark	Greece	Spain Portugal	Austria Finland Sweden	Cyprus Czech Rep. Estonia Hungary Latvia Lithuania Malta Poland Slovakia Slovenia	Bulgaria Romania	Croatia
Population	185m	273m	287m	338m	370m	450m	493m	506m
Seats in European Parliament	142	273	287	338	370	732	785	766
Number of member states	6	9	10	12	15	25	27	28

there are a number of candidate countries, there are serious questions about whether there will be future EU enlargements. We look at the Brexit process and consequences for the EU below, along with the challenges posed by Poland's and Hungary's shifts away from democratic norms.

Deepening integration. The process of deepening European integration has entailed completing the creation of a single market, expanding the range of common policies, establishing the EU itself, and instituting a monetary union and the single currency. It has involved four additional treaties and several institutional changes and is still widely viewed as an elite-driven process that has proved increasingly controversial.

In 1987, European Community members adopted the Single European Act (SEA) and the goal of completing a single market by the end of 1992. This meant a complicated process of removing remaining physical, fiscal, and technical barriers to trade; harmonizing different national health, food-processing, and other standards; varying levels of indirect taxation such as value-added taxes; and removing barriers to movement of peoples, such as professional licensing requirements. The changes allowed banks and companies to do business throughout the community; allowed EC residents to live, work, and draw pensions anywhere in the EC; ended monopolies in sectors such as electricity and telecommunications; and included institutional changes, such as greater power for the European Parliament (EP).

Even before the SEA's 1992 deadline for completing the single market, the then twelve members signed the Maastricht Treaty on European Union, calling for "an ever closer union among the peoples of Europe." The original European Community became one of three pillars of the new EU. The second pillar comprises common foreign and security policy (CFSP), and the third includes justice and home affairs—new areas of common policy. The second and third pillars, however, largely remain matters for individual governments or intergovernmental agreement. The Maastricht Treaty also included an agreement to institute a single European currency in 1999.

Difficulties in securing ratification of the Maastricht Treaty showed that not all of Europe's citizens accepted deepening integration. Danish voters rejected it in a referendum and, only after agreement was reached that Denmark could opt out of certain provisions in the treaty was it passed. The treaty was also put to a referendum in France, where it narrowly passed.

Three subsequent treaties have dealt with enlargement and institutional reform. The 1997 Treaty of Amsterdam came into force in 1999, giving a green light to further enlargement and dealing with issues such as social policy, immigration, asylum, the environment, and consumer protection. The 2003 Treaty of Nice brought changes important to an enlarged and more democratic EU such as increasing the number of seats in the EP, modifying the EU's system of qualified majority voting, and limiting the number of commissioners to one per state. The 2007 Treaty of Lisbon was designed to improve the efficiency of EU institutions and provide the EU with international legal personality, enabling it to sign international treaties or be a member of other IGOs, and made the EU Charter of Rights legally binding on members. The Treaty of Lisbon was rejected by Ireland's voters in 2008 but approved in 2009 after changes were made. Figure 5.2 provides a timeline for and summarizes key parts of the European integration process.

Structure. The current structure of EU institutions, including the European Council, the European Commission, the Council of the European Union, the European Parliament, and the European Court of Justice, is shown in Figure 5.3. Some of the institutions embody intergovernmentalism, where members retain more voice; some exemplify supranationalism, with the authority to impose rules and judgments on member states.

The European Commission. The European Commission is the supranational, executive, and bureaucratic body of the EU and the engine for integration. It has the exclusive responsibility for initiating new community laws and advancing the goals of the treaties. In this respect, it is "the conscience of the European Union because it is designed to look after the good of the whole, which no one government or group of governments could do alone" (Ginsberg 2007: 165). The Commission works with national bureaucracies to ensure that states implement policies and legislation; it represents the EU in international trade negotiations and at the UN, draws up the budget and spends funds approved, and can promulgate regulations on

---

Figure 5.2　Timeline of European Integration

Year	Event
1951	European Coal and Steel Community created (six members)
1957	Treaties of Rome establish European Economic Community and European Atomic Energy Community (six members)
1962	Common Agricultural Policy launched
1968	Completion of customs union
1970	Launch of European political cooperation
1979	First direct elections for European Parliament
1986	Single European Act launches single market
1992	Maastricht Treaty on European Union (three pillars)
1997	Treaty of Amsterdam authorizes further enlargement
2002	Launch of single currency (euro)
2003	Treaty of Nice brings institutional reforms
2009	Treaty of Lisbon authorizes constitutional changes

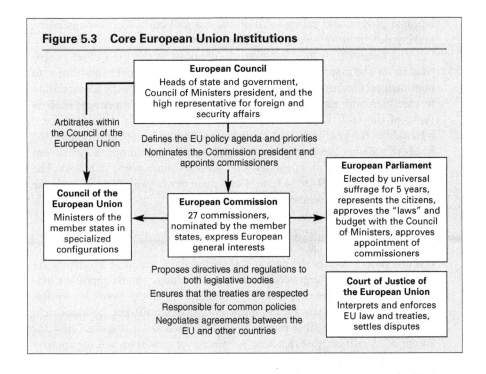

Figure 5.3 Core European Union Institutions

European Council

Heads of state and government, Council of Ministers president, and the high representative for foreign and security affairs

Arbitrates within the Council of the European Union

Defines the EU policy agenda and priorities
Nominates the Commission president and appoints commissioners

Council of the European Union

Ministers of the member states in specialized configurations

European Commission

27 commissioners, nominated by the member states, express European general interests

European Parliament

Elected by universal suffrage for 5 years, represents the citizens, approves the "laws" and budget with the Council of Ministers, approves appointment of commissioners

Proposes directives and regulations to both legislative bodies
Ensures that the treaties are respected
Responsible for common policies
Negotiates agreements between the EU and other countries

Court of Justice of the European Union

Interprets and enforces EU law and treaties, settles disputes

technical matters that are binding on states. The Commission also plays a key role in the enforcement of EU law, with the right to warn states when they are violating treaty obligations, publicize states' failure to implement EU law, initiate legal action in the Court of Justice against them, and impose sanctions or fines if law is not being implemented.

The Commission is led by a group of twenty-seven commissioners who are nominated by national governments (one per member state) in consultation with the Commission president for five-year renewable terms. They are not national representatives and may not be removed by their national governments. Instead, they are expected to act in the interests of the EU as a whole and according to the letter and spirit of the founding treaties. The Commission as a whole is approved by and accountable to the EP, which may also censure and remove the entire commission, but not individual commissioners. Most commissioners are responsible for one or more particular policy areas (known as directorates-general) and for supervising the work of some 33,000 civil servants ("Eurocrats"), aided by their respective personal staffs or cabinets. The directorates include all major policy areas of the EU, ranging from agriculture and the internal market to competition policy, justice and home affairs, external relations, regional policy, trade, and environment and energy. The Commission functions much like a national government cabinet and on the basis of collective responsibility, making decisions by consensus or simple majority.

The president of the Commission functions as the EU's chief executive. He or she assigns the portfolios of other commissioners and can veto nominations for commissioners. The president represents the Commission in meetings with national governments and at summit meetings, such as those of the G-7. Like commissioners, the president is appointed for a renewable five-year term and is nominated by the European Council (the heads of member governments) and approved by the European Parliament (EP). Many Commission presidents have been former prime ministers. The president for the 2019–2024 term, Ursula von der Leyen of Germany, is the first woman to serve in the post.

The Council of the European Union. The EU's Council of the European Union is made up of national government ministers who make decisions on law and policy, and in the past it was called the Council of Ministers. As such, it represents intergovernmentalism. The Council must approve Commission proposals for new laws in conjunction with the European Parliament. Historically, it was far more powerful than the EP, but the Maastricht Treaty increased the EP's power so that the two share responsibility for accepting, modifying, or rejecting proposals for new laws and for approving the EU budget. In addition, the Council has executive functions with respect to common foreign, security, and defense policy; coordination policies; judicial cooperation; and concluding treaties on the EU's behalf. It can also request the Commission to conduct studies and initiate proposals.

The Council of the European Union is made up of one government minister per state, with the composition changing based on the subject under consideration (foreign, economic, agriculture, competition policy, etc.). In effect, the Council comprises multiple councils (ten in all) responsible for specific policy areas. The frequency and importance of meetings depend on the degree to which member states have transferred policymaking authority to the EU. Agriculture and fisheries ministers, for example, meet monthly to deal with issues of commodity prices and subsidy levels, whereas transport, education, and environment ministers meet only a few times a year, since these areas are still largely the domain of national governments. With efforts to increase common foreign, security, and defense policy since 1992, the foreign ministers have met more frequently.

The presidency of the Council of the European Union rotates every six months by country, and along with the Commission president, the Council president represents the EU at many major international meetings. The two roles tend to form a co-executive. Continuity between presidents and support for the council are provided by the Committee of Permanent Representatives (COREPER), which comprises the ambassadors of member states in

Brussels and other senior officials. COREPER actually negotiates agreements on all policy initiatives except the most contentious issues.

The Council uses different voting systems depending on the policy areas and political sensitivity of the subject. Unanimity is required for foreign, security, and defense policy, as it is for changes to the treaties, enlargement, and taxation. Some fifty policy areas are decided by qualified majority voting more akin to a double majority requiring 55 percent of the member states representing at least 65 percent of the EU population voting in favor. In reality, most Council decisions are taken by consensus, without a formal vote.

Because the members of the Council of the European Union are national political figures, the dynamics of the council are inevitably influenced by national interests, the stability of a national government, the ideology of members, and their relative authority.

The European Council or EU Summit. The European Council came into existence in 1974 when member-state heads of state and government (prime ministers and presidents) agreed to hold regular summit meetings to give greater political direction to broad policy priorities. The European Council convenes four or more times a year. Although it generally does not get involved in details of legislation and policymaking, it has been the key body for major EU initiatives, such as concluding the single market, monetary union, enlargement, foreign policy issues, constitutional reform, and migration.

The 1987 Single European Act gave legal status to the European Council; the Treaty of Lisbon created the post of president, elected by the Council for a two-and-a-half-year term, renewable once, and responsible for organizing and hosting Council summits and working to build consensus among its members. Council makeup includes the heads of state and government, the European Council president, and the president of the European Commission. The high representative for foreign affairs and security policy and the president of the European Central Bank may also be included but are not members. The advantages of the European Council include its flexibility given the lack of rules and separate bureaucracy, its informality and absence of formal agendas, and its ability to delegate to other institutions and focus on the big picture (McCormick and Olsen 2014: 179).

The European Parliament. The EP is the voice of EU citizens as the only EU body that is directly elected by voters in the member states (since 1979). Yet it is little known or understood. It consists of 705 members elected for five-year renewable terms, with seats allocated according to member states' population. This makes it one of the largest legislative bodies in the world and unwieldy because of its size, twenty-three official languages, and three venues: Strasbourg for plenary sessions, Brussels for committee meetings, and Luxembourg, where staff have their offices.

Members are seated by political group, not by national delegations, as the rules of procedure strongly encourage the formation of transnational political groups. Eight party groups span the left-right ideological spectrum of European politics from pro- to anti-European. As of the 2019 EP elections, the three largest groups are the Socialist Group on the left, the European People's Party Group on the right, and Renew Euro, a liberal, pro-Europe group, in the center. The growth of green, nationalist, populist, and Euroskeptic parties in various European countries is evident in the EP as well. Despite ideological differences, party groups frequently share common interests on particular issues and in promoting the EP's influence within the EU.

The Parliament's role has expanded over time with members using arguments about democratic accountability to gain greater legislative and supervisory responsibilities. Its input into the lawmaking process was successively expanded by the SEA, Maastricht, Amsterdam, and Lisbon treaties such that it now shares legislative and budgetary powers with the Council of the European Union on many issues, which forces the Commission to take the parliament's opinions more seriously. The Commission, however, has the sole power to propose new laws and policies. Interest groups now pay more attention to the EP to influence the shape of legislation, whereas once they directed most of their efforts at the Commission. But low voter turnout in EP direct elections underscores voters' sense that it still does not affect their lives very much.

The Court of Justice of the European Union (CJEU), formerly the European Court of Justice (ECJ). What makes the CJEU's role unique among international judicial bodies is that EU treaties are legally enforceable documents, unlike the UN Charter. They create legal obligations that the CJEU has the responsibility to interpret and enforce from its seat in Luxembourg. The court has the power to rule on the constitutionality of all EU law, provide advisory opinions to national courts in cases where there are questions about compatibility of national and EU law, and settle disputes involving other EU institutions, member states, individuals, or corporations. It is therefore a supranational institution along with the Commission. Member states are obligated to uphold European law and enforce CJEU decisions.

The ECJ was established in 1952 and is composed of twenty-seven judges appointed by member states for six-year renewable terms, plus a registrar and eleven advocates-general who ease the court's burden by reviewing cases coming to the court and providing what are, in effect, preliminary opinions that may be accepted or rejected by the full court. The court may sit in full (*en banc*) or in smaller chambers (ten as of 2022). Court rules require that cases brought by member states be heard by the full court. In the civil law tradition, decisions are generally announced without indicating any dissenting opinions. There is no appeal. In 1989, to respond to a rising case-load and allow the judges to concentrate on fundamental tasks, the Court of First Instance (now called the General Court) was established to deal with all cases brought by individuals and companies, with the exception of cases dealing with trade defense issues, such as antidumping. Thus, this court hears competition cases and disputes over technical legislation and questions of fact. In 2005, the EU Civil Service Tribunal took over all cases involving disputes between the EU institutions and their staff, such as those involving gender discrimination and application of staff regulations.

ECJ/CJEU cases fall into two broad categories: preliminary rulings in which the court is advising national courts and tribunals on how points of national law relate to EU law, and direct actions brought by an individual, corporation, member state, or EU institution. Direct actions include cases brought by the European Commission against a member state for failure to fulfill an obligation and cases brought by individuals, corporations, member states, or an EU institution seeking to annul an EU law on the grounds that it is illegal or seeking action against an EU institution for failure to act in accord with the treaties. Virtually every member state has been brought before the court at least once—and some several hundred times—for failure to fulfill obligations. A 1964 landmark case (*Flaminio Costa v. Enel*) established the supremacy of EU law over national law even when it conflicts with the latter (ECJ 1964). In 2020, the CJEU in *Commission v. Hungary* found that Hungary had violated the General Agreement on Trade in Services and the EU Charter on Fundamental Rights when it imposed novel requirements on foreign universities operating in Hungary (CJEU 2020).

The ECJ/CJEU has had an essential role in promoting European regional integration and governance by determining the EU's character and extending the reach of EU law, especially in cases related to the single market, such as *Cassis de Dijon*, in which the court ruled that products meeting one country's standards could not be barred from sale in another (ECJ 1979). Since 1954, it has issued more than 42,000 judgments. Cases cover subjects from trade issues to agricultural policy questions, environmental law, consumer safety regulations, freedom of movement for workers, and equal treatment for women. It has played a particularly strong role in the development of EU social rights and law, as well as EU power over member states' tax policy. In 1995, the court upheld freedom of movement for workers by overturning Belgian soccer rules that made it difficult for a Belgian player to transfer to a French club (ECJ 1995). In 2022, the CJEU ruled for the first time on domestic workers and held that their exclusion from access to social security benefits constituted indirect discrimination on the basis of sex because it affected women almost exclusively (CJEU 2022).

The ECJ/CJEU's success and the corresponding development of EU law has hinged on the willingness of national courts to seek and abide by preliminary rulings, and the court's efforts through direct actions to get member states to fulfill their legal obligations under the treaties. No member state has refused to accept a major ECJ ruling, but there have been many cases of delayed implementation. The court has the power to impose fines on states for refusing to act on its rulings, and the Commission may initiate infringement proceedings with the CJEU, which can lead to a fine or imposition of sanctions, measures that other international courts do not have the authority to undertake. States do criticize rulings that they view as hostile to their national interests, but the court's success (and power) can also be attributed to its actions vis-à-vis other EU institutions. The ECJ helped expand the EP's powers by ruling that the latter could bring community acts for judicial review. Representing supranationalism over the intergovernmentalism of the Council of the EU, the court has played a key role in European regionalism and the development of the EU legal order.

EU law is more than the decisions of the ECJ/CJEU, however. There are laws in the form of regulations issued by the Council of Ministers alone, by the Council and the Parliament together, or by the Commission alone (depending on the applicable section of the treaties and date). There are Commission directives that specify results to be achieved, such as competition policy or air pollution standards, but leave the means to member states. There are also decisions that are binding measures issued to specific parties, such as to block a merger between two companies. EU law represents a distinctive legal system, lying between traditional national (or municipal) legal systems and international law, with a powerful court to interpret the law and enforce judgments against member states. As William Phelan (2012: 375) points out, "all Member States must comply with all compulsory and automatically applied EU obligations addressed to them. . . . It is thus an obligation that is *not conditional* on other states' behavior." In sum, then, EU law represents the pooled sovereignty that characterizes the EU and is an important aspect of what makes the EU very different from other international organizations.

Other EU institutions. In addition to the Commission, Council of the European Union, European Council, Parliament, and Court of Justice, the EU has a variety of specialized institutions and agencies that have been created over the years as the scope of European integration and needs have required. These include the European Police Office, or Europol, to facilitate police cooperation since the opening of borders between member states; the European Central Bank, created in 1998 in conjunction with the creation of the single currency and catapulted to greater visibility since the eurozone crisis in 2008 (see Chapter 8); and the European Investment Bank, set up in 1958 to provide long-term finance for capital development projects.

EU common policies. Beginning with trade and agriculture, the EU has moved progressively into more and more areas of policy, ranging from fisheries and food safety to transport, competition, social policy, regional development, monetary policy and common currency, environment, justice and home affairs, external relations, human rights, and migration. Three different approaches have been used to advance common policies: mutual recognition of different national standards, community directives establishing standards frameworks, and harmonization of standards (the most difficult, because this requires agreeing on a new common set of standards). Chapter 8 addresses policies associated with the single market, agriculture, and monetary union as well as the Eurozone crisis (2008–2012). EU environmental policy is discussed in Chapter 10; Chapter 11 touches on Justice and Home Affairs and the EU's handling of the 2015 refugee crisis as well as the continuing problem of migration (Ceccorulli 2021). We briefly focus here on social policy and on common foreign and security policy (CFSP). Social policy illustrates an area where the EU's supranational powers are evident. EU CFSP illustrates intergovernmentalism.

Social policy. EU social policy, along with regional development policy, aims to address social and economic inequalities within and among the member states through regulations on markets and working conditions along with cash transfers and services. It arises from the long history of social welfare policies in most EU member countries and encompasses workers' rights, equal pay for men and women, workers' freedom of movement within the EU, and working and living conditions. The most active proponents have been European labor unions, social democratic parties, the Commission, and Court of Justice. The opponents include businesses and conservative political parties who argue that high labor costs reduce European company competitiveness.

The ECJ confirmed equal pay and coordination of social security systems in decisions on the case of *Defenne* in 1971, 1976, and 1978, for example. The Commission then actively promoted common social policy beginning in the 1980s because of concerns for the social dimensions of the single market, such as the consequences of workers' mobility and variations in social security benefits and wages. Social policy was a key part of the 1986 SEA and a separate Charter of Social Rights, which was adopted in 1989 by eleven of the twelve members. It was subsequently incorporated into the Maastricht Treaty and the Treaty of Amsterdam. Provisions were added for EU action against discrimination based on age, gender, disability, ethnicity, belief, race, and sexual orientation. Efforts have also been under way since 1987 to make European university education more compatible and to encourage educational exchanges and the transfer of credits through the Erasmus Program. These changes have greatly increased the mobility of European university students. One persistent social policy problem is the discrepancies between the wealthier core and northern countries and the poorer regions in southern countries, including Greece, Italy, Portugal, and Spain, and the former communist countries in the east, which have few social protections.

CFSP. After achieving the initial customs union and common external tariff in 1968, the European Community began negotiating as a single entity in international trade negotiations under the General Agreement on Tariffs and Trade. In 1970, it initiated foreign policy coordination under what was called European Political Cooperation with the situation in the Middle East between Israel and the Palestinians being a particular shared concern, one that persists with the EU speaking out on behalf of Palestinian rights and a two-state solution to the Israeli-Palestinian conflict.

The end of the Cold War and the 1992 Maastricht Treaty provided the impetus and legal basis for making common foreign policy part of the EU integration process and for enhancing the EU's role as a global actor. Building on that, the 1997 Treaty of Amsterdam established the position of High Representative for Common Foreign and Security Policy and the legal basis for addressing conflict management and humanitarian aid. In a further step, the 2003 Treaty of Nice created Common Security and Defence Policy (CSDP) as a separate policy area and the Political and Security Committee composed of member states' foreign ministers to deal with civil and military crises. The 2009 Lisbon Treaty further strengthened the institutional bases for CFSP by creating the European External Action Service (EEAS)— the EU's foreign or diplomatic corps—and by giving the EU international legal personality to enter into treaties. It also empowered the High Representative to conduct negotiations with nonmember entities, make policy proposals to the Council, and call extraordinary meetings.

Still, the EU has faced difficulties in acting rapidly, effectively, and with one voice amid crises such as the wars in the former Yugoslavia in the 1990s, the Iraq war in 2003, the 2011 Syrian and Libyan crises, and Russia's 2014 annexation of Ukraine. The chief problem is that CFSP is a policy area that remains strictly intergovernmental with unanimity required for action. Even qualified majority voting would strengthen the EU's ability to respond, especially in crisis situations. Efforts to change this have met resistance particularly from smaller countries who fear that their national interests would not be protected without a veto and from some key officials who see the work of achieving unity as a source of EU strength. The reality is that member states continue to run their own foreign policies and are not always committed to joint action (Lehne 2022). They bring different histories, geographical locations, memberships in other IGOs, and perceptions of security threats that complicate reaching consensus for a common foreign policy. Although Russia's 2022 invasion of Ukraine changed this somewhat, until then, there was a debate between western and eastern member states over whether Russia's actions and policies or conflicts in the Middle East and the influx of migrants and refugees represented the greatest threats (Paats 2021: 53).

The primary decisionmaking body for CFSP is the European Council. The Treaty of Lisbon gave the Council's president authority to represent the EU with nonmember states on issues of common policy. This includes representing the EU in the G-7, for example. The day-to-day work is led by the High Representative and supported by the EEAS and operational missions which are part of the Commission. The High Representative also serves as vice-president of the Commission. The CJEU and EP have limited roles in CFSP. The court's role relates to the legality of decisions to mandate sanctions; the EP's role includes nonbinding resolutions and budgetary allocations for staffing and various activities. In addition to the High Representative, there are four commissioners who are responsible for enlargement negotiations, trade, international cooperation and development, and humanitarian aid and crisis management.

Among the EU foreign policy objectives since the late 1980s have been strengthening multilateralism; preserving international peace and security; strengthening democracy, human rights, and good governance; and contributing to conflict prevention and settlement (GLOBSEC Policy Institute 2019). In 2003, although the US invasion of Iraq divided EU members, the Council set three core objectives in the first European Security Strategy: addressing security threats, enhancing security in the EU's neighborhood, and promoting multilateralism (GLOBSEC Policy Institute 2019: 6). In 2016, a further sharpening took the form of the EU Global Strategy. Among the priorities are counterterrorism, cybersecurity, and energy security; "building state and societal resilience to the East and South of the EU"; an integrated approach to conflicts at all stages; promoting and supporting "cooperative regional orders"; and contributing to global governance, including UN reform, implementing EU commitments on sustainable development and climate change, and investing in UN peacebuilding.

As of 2022, the EU had supported twenty-one common security and defense (CSDP) missions, including military training in Mali, Somalia, and the Central African Republic; security sector reform missions in Iraq and Ukraine; peace enforcement in the Democratic Republic of Congo; Mediterranean naval forces dealing with migrants; antipiracy efforts off Somalia; and two missions in the Palestinian territories. It also had CFSP special representatives working in Bosnia, Central Asia, the Horn of Africa, Kosovo, the Sahel, and Georgia. The EU has an extensive web of relationships with individual countries through its Neighborhood Policy and with other regional groupings, such as ASEAN and the AU. The Commission has missions in many capitals and at the United Nations. Other countries maintain diplomatic representatives in Brussels.

What, then, does the record of EU CFSP and CSDP look like? The EU failed to prevent war in Yugoslavia in 1991–1992, despite having assumed primary responsibility for dealing with the situation with the blessing of the UN and the United States. Since then, however, its capabilities for humanitarian, peacekeeping, peace enforcement, and antipiracy operations have enabled it to play an increasingly active role on a wide range of issues. Taking members' individual contributions and the EU contribution together, the EU is the largest contributor to the UN and contributes the majority of global development aid. It is also a major source of humanitarian relief aid through UN agencies and NGOs. It has strongly supported the International Criminal Court and is a leading proponent of global environmental cooperation, democracy promotion, human rights, nonproliferation of weapons of mass destruction, and antiterrorism efforts. The first person to serve as High Representative, Catherine Ashton, led the six-party negotiations with Iran over its nuclear program that concluded with the 2015 agreement. As discussed further in Chapter 7, the EU has also employed various types of sanctions, most notably in response to Russia's 2014 annexation of Crimea and 2022 invasion of Ukraine.

Readers may well wonder about the relationship between the EU and NATO, whose memberships heavily overlap, as shown in Figure 5.1. CSDP is meant to be complementary to NATO and involve different functions, such as low-level crisis management, policing, training, and security sector reform in the Global South. NATO continues to bear the primary responsibility for Europe's defense as long as the United States remains committed to Europe. To be sure, there are debates about this relationship and possible changes where the Europeans might assume greater responsibilities in NATO and merge CSDP with it, allowing the United States to focus more on other areas of the world (Howarth 2020: 326). Thus far, there have been few efforts to rationalize the two.

Russia's invasion of Ukraine was a wake-up call for EU members. As one author noted, "To begin with the shock has been intellectual. The Russian threat has often been overlooked, relegated, underestimated, at least in Western Europe. . . . At worst, Russia could only be a marginally disruptive regional power, with a GDP lower than that of the Benelux countries!" (Cirbirski 2022). The EU's response was quick and united, including an unprecedented set of sanctions, €500 million provided through the European Peace Facility for arming the Ukrainian forces, and funds for refugee assistance. Germany for the first time announced an increase in its defense spending to more than the NATO-mandated 2 percent of its GDP and pledged €100 million to modernize its own army. Shortly thereafter, Finland and Sweden—long-time neutrals—announced their intention to apply for membership in NATO as noted earlier.

On March 11, 2022, in a summit meeting convened by French President Emmanuel Macron as president of the EU Council, the EU leaders declared "Ukraine is part of our European family," condemned Russia's "unprovoked and unjustified" actions, and called for immediate and unconditional withdrawal of all forces and a series of other actions, including protection of refugees and prompt consideration of Ukraine's application for EU membership (EU Council 2022). The declaration also acknowledged the problems posed by Europe's dependency on Russian oil, gas, and coal—problems that challenge the EU and its member governments going forward. Still, the Council extended the sanctions that had been in place since Russia's 2014 annexation of Crimea and added further measures affecting financial, trade, energy, transport, technology, and defense sectors. These included the closure of EU air space and ports to Russian-owned and -registered ships and aircraft; diplomatic and visa measures; and sanctions against more than a thousand individuals and entities.

Over time, the development of EU foreign policy has reflected the evolving habits of cooperation of the members, their learning from past mistakes (such as in the former Yugoslavia in the 1990s and in response to Russia's actions since 2014), and their willingness to create new capabilities and procedures to make their policies more effective.

Contemporary challenges to European integration. Since the 1950s, the pattern of European regionalism was one of both widening and deepening integration among the countries that have become part of the EU. The appeal of joining the EU clearly remains strong, as there were seven candidate countries in 2022 (Albania, Moldova, the Republic of North Macedonia, Montenegro, Serbia, Turkey, and Ukraine). To be sure, there have always been differences in states' positions on specific aspects of widening and deepening. Denmark and the United Kingdom long opposed more supranationalism or federalism, and the European Monetary Union (which these countries both opted out of). The 2009–2013 Eurozone crisis led to tensions between the most heavily indebted countries (Greece, Spain, Portugal, Cyprus, and Ireland) and the European Central Bank and German government over demands for austerity (Chapter 8). The 2015 refugee migration crisis similarly led to significant tensions among EU member states.

In 2014, the EP elections demonstrated the rising opposition to the EU in all member states except the Netherlands. Not until the 2016 Brexit referendum in the United Kingdom, however, had the citizens of a member state voted for their government to withdraw from the EU. The subsequent four years of negotiations over the terms of withdrawal revealed the extent of legal, economic, and social integration and the challenges of disentangling.

The Brexit process required the major EU institutions to develop guidelines for negotiating with the United Kingdom, subject to European Council and EP approval. The Commission was tasked with the actual negotiations. One key consideration was to make the terms of agreement with the United Kingdom tough enough to discourage other member states from considering withdrawal. Among the major issues were the UK's financial obligations to the EU; future relations between the EU and UK; the rights and legal status of EU residents in the UK; and the border between the UK and EU in Ireland (between Northern Ireland, which is part of the United Kingdom, and the Republic of Ireland, which is an EU member). Difficulties on the UK side required three extensions of the negotiations before the official withdrawal finally took place on January 31, 2020.

The consequences of Brexit are still unfolding. One immediate result was the creation of new nontariff barriers to UK–EU trade, including customs requirements, higher transport costs, and more difficulties in crossing borders. (Tariffs and quotas were banned.) UK and EU citizens have lost the freedom to travel without barriers for pleasure, work, and settlement. The United Kingdom has experienced significant labor shortages with workers from the continent no longer able to freely enter the country. The EU has lost one-sixth of its economic power and a very significant part of the foreign and security policy "weight" it enjoyed as a result of the UK's global influence. It also has a budget financing gap that means higher contributions for the remaining twenty-seven members. Trade for both entities has decreased; relations remain strained, especially because the issue of the border between Northern Ireland and Ireland was only resolved in March 2023. The parties did agree, however, to maintain common standards in a number of areas of social policy, especially workers' rights and on environmental policy. (For more details on the Brexit process and consequences, see Fabbrini 2020; De Ville and Siles-Brügge 2019).

The United Kingdom's withdrawal was one type of challenge to European integration. A very different challenge has come from developments since 2010 in Poland and Hungary and, to a lesser extent, the Czech Republic, Romania, and Slovenia that have weakened their democratic institutions and undermined the rule of law—which are fundamental EU values and requirements of member states. Hungary is widely viewed as having become more authoritarian under its right-wing prime minister, Viktor Orbán, who came to power in 2010 and has taken steps to weaken key institutions (including the judiciary) and freedom of the media, for example. Poland's removal of its human rights ombudsman, curtailment of the independence of judges, and Constitutional Tribunal's 2021 ruling on the supremacy of the Polish constitution over EU law were seen as deliberate noncompliance and "democratic backsliding" (Priebus 2022: 4).

As one scholar notes, "noncompliance with primary and secondary law is a regular feature of EU governance . . . a persistent and systematic breach of the EU's fundamental values . . . is qualitatively distinct" (Priebus 2022: 3). The 1997 Treaty of Amsterdam that authorized further enlargement and included a provision on the principles of democratic governance such as rule of law and a respect for personal freedoms (Article 2) also provided a procedure (Article 7) by which the European Council can suspend certain rights of a member state found in violation of those principles. Utilizing this provision has been seen as "a nuclear option" and difficult to implement, however, to be used only as a last resort (Zamęcki and Glied 2020: 62).

As a result of concerns about Hungary and Poland, the Commission created several new instruments, including the Justice Scoreboard and the Annual Rule of Law Review Mechanism adopted in 2013 and 2014 in an effort to restore compliance and prevent similar developments in other member states. After Poland and Hungary defied CJEU rulings, the Council determined in 2017 that the situation in Poland constituted a serious breach, which made it the first country subjected to the Article 7 procedure. A similar determination was made about Hungary in 2018. In 2020, the European Parliament voted to request the Council to continue the Article 7 proceedings by preparing specific recommendations for Poland and Hungary, setting deadlines for compliance, and considering tying future EU funding to compliance with rule of law. In 2021, the CJEU cut billions of euros of funds to Poland and Hungary and later ordered Poland to pay €70 million in fines for failing to reverse its illegal disciplinary regime for judges. In 2023, the CJEU ruled that Poland's 2019 justice reform infringed EU law, upholding the earlier Commission decision that the Polish Supreme Court lacked independence and impartiality. These challenges are not likely to be resolved quickly.

Is Europe a Model for Other Regions?

Theories of regional organization have long been influenced by the European experience and European integration theory. As Andrew Moravcsik (1998: 500) noted, the EU has served as "a laboratory in which to investigate a series of common political phenomena developed further in Europe than elsewhere on the globe." There is no question that countries in other regions have often viewed developments in Europe as a potential model to follow as later sections of this chapter will show. Yet the circumstances that supported the development of European regional governance, particularly European integration as it progressed from the ECSC to the EU, cannot be and have not been duplicated elsewhere. Many Asian leaders have strongly rejected the European model as inappropriate. Nevertheless, people in other regions continue to use the European experience as a benchmark and guide for one model of regional governance even as there are challenges in Europe itself to that model.

Regional Organizations in the Americas

Evolution of Regionalism in the Americas

Some of the earliest regional initiatives took place in the Western Hemisphere in the nineteenth century. In 1889, the first of nine International Conferences of American States created the International Union of American Republics (renamed the Pan American Union in 1910). The last of these conferences, in 1948, established the Organization of American States (OAS) as the primary forum for inter-American cooperation. In a separate initiative, the Inter-American Treaty of Reciprocal Assistance (Rio Treaty) was signed in 1947. This is a far more limited collective defense arrangement than NATO, as the Latin American governments refused to accept joint command of military forces or any binding obligation to use force without their explicit consent (Article 20). The Summit of the Americas process, begun in the 1990s, brings together the heads of state and government from the region every two to four years (minus Cuba in many years) to focus on hemispheric issues. Its meetings are serviced by the OAS Secretariat. Since the 1950s, there have also been a variety of initiatives for regional and subregional cooperation and, in some cases, integration among groups of states in North, Central, South America, and the Caribbean.

The Americas, therefore, have seen two approaches: hemispheric regionalism or pan-Americanism, encompassing the whole Western Hemisphere, and regional/subregional cooperation and economic integration initiatives among various groupings of countries. As a result, the definition of the region depends on whether one is looking at the entire Western Hemisphere or at Latin America and the Caribbean. Both approaches have eschewed EU-style supranationalism in favor of intergovernmentalism. Both are marked by the differing visions of the United States and the Latin American states. Whereas the United States has historically been interested in the security of the region, Latin Americans have seen unity as the most effective way to pursue their interests, including protection against US dominance. Many Latin American nations historically opposed ceding any authority to an organization in which the United States was a member. The coexistence of these approaches reflects the most significant characteristic of the Americas: the enormous disparity in size, power, and economic wealth between the United States and all other states.

Over time, several political factors have driven regionalism in different parts of the Americas. These include efforts to build and retain power as a region and in multilateral and global arenas, including gaining access to Northern and global markets; promoting more democratic regimes; presidential diplomacy, especially by Latin American presidents; and competition among countries for regional leadership. Occasionally, regional initiatives also have been tools to support countries' domestic structural reforms and, after the 1990s, reactions to the US-led neoliberal agenda. The EU has sometimes been seen as a model for development, cooperation, and trade with some evidence of active EU efforts to support some initiatives (Bianculli 2016).

Regionalism in the Americas since the end of World War II is often described in terms of four periods or waves. The first period (1945–1980) was one in which the OAS played "an important role in promoting a dialogue between the countries of the Americas, without economic intentions or integrationist prerogatives" (Mariano, Bressan, and Luciano 2021: 2). Latin American and Caribbean initiatives during this period were nonetheless inspired by the developments in Europe to adopt a functionalist model of regional integration to promote trade and industrial development through import substitution in a number of regional experiments.

In the 1990s, the Cold War's end, settlements of the Central American conflicts of the 1980s, and the end of ideological conflict led to a second period that was particularly conducive to regional political and economic cooperation (Nolte 2021: 183–184). Other contributing factors included the move from authoritarian regimes to democracy in all Latin American countries except Cuba; the acceptance by most governments of neoliberal market capitalism; the effects of globalization, including Latin American countries' fear of being marginalized in the world economy; and a new security agenda of transnational problems, including drug trafficking and environmental concerns. Several new subregional Latin American economic blocs were created in this period including the North American Free Trade Agreement (NAFTA), the Southern Common Market (Mercosur), and, at the hemispheric level, the US-backed Free Trade Agreement of the Americas (FTAA).

The first decade of the 2000s brought a third period, including changes prompted by the Latin Americans' rejection of neoliberalism and the rise of leftist governments, including the election of President Hugo Chávez in Venezuela in 1998 who rejected neoliberalism and US involvement (Petersen and Schulz 2018: 106). There was also more NGO and civil society activity at the regional level and the emergence of what scholars have variously called "posthegemonic" or "postliberal" regionalism (Tussie and Riggirozzi 2012). This included the creation of the Union of South American Nations (UNASUR) promoted by Brazil; the Bolivarian Alliance for the Peoples of Our Americas, promoted by Venezuela, and the Community of Latin American and Caribbean States. These provided new "spaces" for South American and Latin American political and functional cooperation (Briceño-Ruiz 2018) with initiatives focusing on economic integration, poverty, inequality, and regional stability. They were intergovernmental, not integrationist; more fragmented; and less focused on institutionalization— that is, "regionalism light," in the words of one scholar (Nolte 2021: 185). An added factor since 2000 has been the general neglect of the region by the United States. The result has strengthened cooperation in South America, Latin America more broadly, and the Caribbean, leading to what José Briceño-Ruiz (2018: 576) calls the gradual "construction of South America as an international region."

The fourth period since 2010 has seen the retraction and fragmentation of regionalism in Latin America. Illiberal governments have challenged democracy, regionalism, and multilateralism more generally. There have been consultations and agreements, but little strengthening of existing institutions. In fact, one characteristic of the years between 2004 and 2012—overlapping the third and fourth periods—is the many summits among Latin American presidents. This includes a grand total of 144 in nine years, 29 of them among South American leaders, 18 among Caribbean leaders, and 52 among Central American leaders (Nolte 2021: 181). Whether this was a positive and productive thing is a matter of debate. Some scholars note that the summit diplomacy facilitated trust and political agreements; others argue that it aided crisis management; still others see it as indicating the dysfunctionality of other aspects of regionalism (Mace et al. 2016). The dramatic decrease in summits since 2012 is seen by some as indicative of a crisis in Latin American regionalism. As Nolte (2021: 182) notes, "Presidential activism had been necessary to overcome some of the structural constraints of Latin American regionalism." The crisis deepened with the Covid-19 pandemic, which came on top of an economic crisis in the region.

Another development affecting regionalism in the Americas is the growing Chinese investment, trade, and presence, which challenges both US and EU influence in the region. One consequence is a move by some Latin American countries toward a more nonaligned position, given rising major power rivalry between the United States and China. Since most of the initiatives involve bilateral efforts to improve trade relations with specific countries, there is little to no evidence that China has been promoting regionalism per se.

We look primarily at the hemispheric approach embodied in the OAS and briefly at the approaches associated with Latin American regionalism and subregionalism.

Hemispheric Regionalism and the OAS

Key to inter-American hemispheric regionalism has long been the amount and type of attention given by the United States to Latin America. Historically, periods of US interest have been followed by periods of neglect when the United States put global interests above Latin American concerns. US hegemony was greatest during the 1950s and 1960s, when the United States got the Latin Americans to accept its anticommunist agenda and used the Rio Treaty to legitimate its actions in Guatemala, Cuba, and the Dominican Republic. Because of the Cold War, the United States supported many Latin military regimes in the 1960s and 1970s. In the 1980s, political and economic changes in Latin America and the Caribbean were seen as positive developments by the United States, leading to new hemispheric initiatives in the 1990s, particularly linked to democracy promotion. Since 2000, US attention to Latin America has been diverted, with hemispheric concerns rarely getting high-level attention.

In 1948, twenty-one countries in the Western Hemisphere adopted the Charter of the OAS and simultaneously signed the American Declaration of the Rights and Duties of Man, the first international document devoted to human rights principles. Fourteen other nations later joined, including the Caribbean island states and Canada. Cuba was excluded from participation between 1962 and 2009 for its adherence to Marxist-Leninism and its alignment with the communist bloc, but as of 2022 it had chosen not to rejoin the OAS. No other regional organization in the world includes as strong a North–South dimension as the OAS. The OAS Charter includes provisions for strengthening regional peace and security, addressing transnational criminal threats to security, promoting representative democracy, and economic, social, and cultural cooperation.

The OAS has played a role in numerous regional border disputes, such as the 1995 border war between Ecuador and Peru, a dispute between Belize and Guatemala (2003), and another between Colombia and Ecuador (2008). Because the long armed conflict in Colombia was internal, there was little the OAS could do other than provide humanitarian aid. Ad hoc groups such as the Contadora Group (Mexico, Venezuela, Panama, and Colombia) and the Rio Group (Mexico, Venezuela, Panama, Colombia, Brazil, Argentina, Peru, and Uruguay), which helped secure peace in Central America's conflicts in the 1980s, have often been more effective than the OAS. The OAS has undertaken joint peacekeeping missions with the UN in Haiti, El Salvador, and Nicaragua and been involved in various peacebuilding activities, such as disarmament, demobilization, reintegration, truth and reconciliation, and electoral assistance in Colombia, Guatemala, Haiti, Nicaragua, and Suriname.

The primary organs of the OAS include the General Assembly, the Permanent Council, the General Secretariat, and the Inter-American Council for Integral Development. The OAS is the hub of an inter-American system that includes several autonomous entities, such as the Inter-American Commission on Human Rights, the Inter-American Court of Human Rights, the Pan American Health Organization, and the Inter-American Telecommunication Commission. The Inter-American Commission on Women, established in 1928, was the first IGO in the world to work for women's political and civil rights and support women's participation in governance.

The General Assembly, which meets annually and in special session when requested, is considered the OAS's highest decisionmaking body, with each member state having one vote. Like the UN General Assembly, it may consider any matter relating to relations among American states. Most decisions are made by consensus or when necessary by majority vote, with certain matters such as approval of the budget requiring a two-thirds majority.

The OAS Permanent Council conducts much of the day-to-day business, meeting regularly at headquarters in Washington, DC. Its activities include assisting in peaceful settlement of disputes and undertaking diplomatic initiatives under the Inter-American Democratic Charter (discussed shortly) in the event of an unconstitutional change of government.

Permanent Council decisions require a two-thirds majority, but most decisions are made by consensus.

The OAS General Secretariat supports the work of the organization, including technical assistance projects. The secretary general has traditionally come from one of the Latin American states, with tacit approval by the United States. In 2005, Chilean José Miguel Insulza was the first secretary general not endorsed by the United States. The United States also was skeptical about Uruguayan Luis Almagro, who was elected secretary general in 2015 and reelected in 2020; Almagro later won US support with his outspoken opposition to Venezuela's Nicolás Maduro. The breadth of the OAS's agenda has severely strained its resources, however, with persistent budget shortfalls, staff cuts, and difficulty recruiting and retaining qualified personnel (Meyer 2014: 25).

The United States has historically viewed the OAS as an instrument for advancing its interests in the hemisphere and is the organization's largest financial contributor (more than 56 percent in 2022). During the Cold War, it used the OAS to counter communist subversion and, after 1960, the spread of Cuba's communist revolution. The Cuban government was excluded from participation between 1962 and 2009, and sanctions were imposed. (A 1975 resolution released OAS members from their obligation to enforce the sanctions.) Latin American support for the US anticommunist agenda waned after the mid-1960s when the OAS endorsed the US intervention in the Dominican Republic. In 1979, the United States failed to get OAS support for a peace force in Nicaragua; in 1983, without consulting the OAS, it invaded Grenada, and it invaded Panama in 1989. These unilateral actions, along with US failure to support Argentina in its war with the United Kingdom over the Falkland/Malvinas Islands in 1982, were seen by the Latin Americans as a repudiation of its obligations under Article 5 of the Rio Treaty (Einaudi 2020: 38).

The asymmetry of power between the United States and its neighbors means there will always be some tensions. Whether the US "pulls its weight" and shows interest in the region and the work of the OAS influences the nature and degree of hemispheric cooperation. As Luigi Einaudi, former US ambassador to the OAS and acting secretary general has said, "Many in the hemisphere see the United States as self-interested and unreliable, a Gulliver focused on extending and legitimizing its power. US leaders tend to see their neighbors as Lilliputians using multilateralism as a form of trade unionism of the weak" (Einaudi 2020: 41).

The OAS and the promotion and defense of democracy. Democratic government has been a goal of peoples in the Americas almost since independence. It was endorsed in declarations of inter-American conferences beginning in 1936 and incorporated into the OAS Charter and into the Inter-

American Convention on Human Rights. Nonetheless, the OAS was largely silent during the 1960s and 1970s when right-wing dictatorships became the norm in most countries. The wave of democratizations in the region in the late 1980s and 1990s contributed to member states' efforts to establish "that the standard of unconstitutional change of government prohibited both coups d'etat as well as authoritarian backsliding" and gave the OAS a major role in defending and promoting democracy (Stapel 2022: 199).

The first step toward this new role occurred in 1979 with a resolution condemning the human rights record of the Anastasio Somoza regime in Nicaragua. From the mid-1980s to 2001, the OAS approved a set of legal norms and procedures for defending democracy. Promotion of democracy was declared "an indispensable condition for the stability, peace, and development of the region" in the Protocol of Cartagena de Indias (1985), a revision to the OAS Charter. In 1989, the General Assembly authorized the appointment of OAS election observer missions at the request of member states. The Unit for the Promotion of Democracy (now the Secretariat for Political Affairs) was established in 1990 to help with elections; in 1991 the General Assembly approved Resolution 1080 requiring its organs to take "immediate action" in the event of a "sudden or irregular interruption of the democratic institutional process" of any member state. Such threats to democracy include military coups or leaders' attempts to stay in power past a constitutional term limit, as well as flawed elections and constitutional crises.

That resolution, Sören Stapel (2022: 207) notes, "marked a major turning point in the OAS efforts to promote and protect democracy and rule of law standards in the region . . . [and] paved the way for further developing and changing the design of regional democracy and rule of law institutions." Six years later, the 1997 Protocol of Washington gave the OAS the right to suspend a member whose democratically elected government is overthrown by force (with a two-thirds majority voting in favor). In 2001, the General Assembly adopted the Inter-American Democratic Charter, which proclaimed the people's right to democracy and their governments' obligation to promote and defend it (Article 12); governments failing to uphold this obligation can be suspended from participation in the organs of the OAS. The charter was drafted and approved in a remarkably short period of time (nine months) for an organization noted for its slowness (Cooper 2004: 96–97).

Under the democracy mandate, the OAS has acted against coups and power grabs on a number of occasions, including in Suriname (1990), Haiti (1991–1993, 2004), Peru (1992), Guatemala (1993), Paraguay (1996, 2000), Ecuador (2000), and Venezuela (1992, 2002). It has acted against election failures in the Dominican Republic (1994), Peru (2000), Haiti (2001), and Honduras (2009). These actions have included diplomatic, financial, economic, and military sanctions on Haiti; a mission to Venezuela headed by the OAS secretary general; and suspension of Honduras from membership following the 2009 coup there (lifted in 2011).

Overall, the OAS's record on defending democracy is mixed, however, particularly since 2002. The primary impetus on democracy protection shifted to South American countries who shared a common objective to expand regional autonomy in relationship to the United States and worked through several South American regional groupings to address regional political stabilization (Ramazini, Mariano, and Gonçalves 2021: 309). These groups included UNASUR established in 2008 and Mercosur established in 1991. Both approved democracy clauses that included provisions for suspension of membership and sanctions. One consequence was that the primary discussion of the political crisis in Venezuela between 2012 and 2015 took place in UNASUR with no Latin American countries (except Panama) supporting action through the OAS. Since 2016, there has been a shift back to the OAS as the relevant forum for addressing political crises in part because of increased conflicts and fragmentation in the South American groups (Ramazini, Mariano, and Gonçalves 2021: 312–316). That shift included OAS activation of the Rio Treaty in 2019 with a declaration that the crisis in Venezuela was a threat to peace and security in the hemisphere.

It can be difficult to define situations where democracy is in danger and how to activate a democracy clause in any regional organization (Ramazini, Mariano, and Gonçalves 2021: 316–317). In other words, when should a regional organization act to protect democracy? Unless there are institutional mechanisms that have real coercive power, able to impose political and economic costs that lead to governments changing their behavior, will they be effective?

The OAS and development. Inadequate financial and human resources have always constrained the OAS's role in fostering economic and social development. The Latin American countries have long sought more attention to development needs and preferential treatment in trade and finance, while the United States has preferred that the OAS not be heavily involved in development activities. As a result, the UN's Economic Commission for Latin America and the Caribbean (ECLAC) and other forums have played key roles in regional development (discussed in Chapter 8). Liberalization of most Latin American countries' economic policies in the 1980s led to the creation of the Council for Integral Development and other OAS initiatives to promote new and better cooperation among members to overcome poverty, benefit from the digital revolution, and advance social and economic development. Yet the alternative subregional integration approach has been the dominant one for promoting development and improving countries' competitiveness in a globalized economy. Subregional organizations also have had the advantage of promoting economic integration and political cooperation without the United States and Canada. Nonetheless, the OAS "is still equipped to take on critical issues . . . that newer multilateral mechanisms seem years away from being able to handle adequately" (Shifter 2012: 61).

Subregional Integration

The diversity of the subregions in the Americas, along with the small size and low levels of economic development of many countries, has long driven efforts at subregional integration as an approach to development and to dealing with US dominance. The "integration as road to development" approach emerged from initiatives by the UN-based Economic Commission for Latin America (which became ECLAC after inclusion of the Caribbean countries) and its first executive director, Argentine economist Raúl Prebisch. Both were closely associated with dependency theories of underdevelopment that attributed the lack of development to structural factors in the international system, most notably the dominance of the "center" in production of manufactured goods and unequal exchange of manufactured goods and raw materials. Because many national markets are small and a strategy of industrialization through import substitution had limits, subregional integration was seen as a means to providing larger markets and economies of scale for industrialization. Based on these ideas, there were a number of subregional integration efforts in Central and South America in the 1950s and 1960s. These so-called first-wave schemes varied significantly, from loose trade arrangements (as in the Latin American Free Trade Association) to more interventionist integration systems (the Andean Community), but most were little more than empty shells. The 1973–1974 oil crisis and severe economic difficulties in most Latin American countries, including huge debt burdens, ended much of the effort at regional integration and reinforced inward-looking attitudes from the early 1970s until the 1990s.

Although the first wave of initiatives was largely unsuccessful, with the exception of the Caribbean Community, the second wave, beginning in the 1990s, has been more so as a result of learning, domestic political and economic changes, and changes in the global environment. It included five new subregional integration efforts: NAFTA (comprising the United States, Canada, and Mexico), Mercosur (comprising Argentina, Brazil, Uruguay, and Paraguay), the Andean Community (Venezuela, Ecuador, Peru, Colombia, and Bolivia), the Central American Common Market, and the Caribbean Community. The shared interests exhibited in these communities stemmed from a "common sense of vulnerability" among the many still fragile democracies whose small economies make them susceptible to financial crises, instability, subversion, and drug trafficking (Hurrell 1995: 257).

In 2004, Venezuela and nine other left-leaning countries launched the Bolivarian Alliance for the Peoples of Our America and its Peoples' Trade

Treaty to counter the US-led FTAA. In 2008, under the leadership of Brazil, the South American countries initiated the twelve-member UNASUR and tried to develop a formal organized structure. By 2020, however, virtually all its members had withdrawn. Despite this proliferation of regional integration initiatives, intraregional trade in South and Central America and the Caribbean lags almost every other region of the world in the percentage of trade that happens within the region at just 15 percent in 2018. For Mercosur, the figure is 12 percent—the result of Brazil and Argentina being among the most closed economies in the world, with trade accounting for just 30 percent of GDP. This compares to 55 percent intraregional trade in the EU and 38 percent in North America (O'Neil 2022). Clearly, economic interdependence is still not a major factor in Latin American subregional integration. We look briefly at Mercosur.

South America: Mercosur. Mercosur (Mercado Común del Sur) illustrates what can happen in a region when long-standing interstate rivalries are reduced. Reconciliation between Brazil and Argentina in the 1980s led to a set of bilateral agreements on nuclear issues, energy cooperation, arms control, trade, integration, and development. In 1991, the two countries signed the Treaty of Asunción with Paraguay and Uruguay, creating Mercosur. It was designed to reverse "the dark ages of authoritarianism, intraregional antagonism, economic crisis, and international marginalization" (Hirst 1999: 36). Mercosur was also a response by government leaders to the creation of the EU's single market and NAFTA, which they feared would cost them markets and influence.

Venezuela became a member of Mercosur in 2012 but was suspended indefinitely in 2017. Bolivia's accession has been in process for several years. Meanwhile, it is an associate member, along with Chile, Colombia, Ecuador, Guyana, Peru, and Suriname. Mercosur's various organs operate largely by consensus, and overall, it is considered to be "'light' on institutions," with implementation depending heavily on relations among the members' presidents who are both "decision makers and dispute settlers" (Dominguez 2007: 109).

During the 1990s, trade among members increased five times over and intraregional investment grew, but since 2000, intraregional trade has fallen compared to trade with nonmember states. Notably, Mercosur and the EU have been negotiating wide-ranging agreements to eliminate tariffs on Mercosur's exports to the EU and on more favorable rules on investment and procurement. The EU's insistence on more favorable labor and environmental provisions, however, has slowed those negotiations.

On the democracy front, Paraguay has posed the most problems. After intervening in political crises there in 1996 and 1999, Mercosur adopted a clause similar to that of the OAS in 1997, requiring all members to be constitutional democracies. This provided the basis for suspending Paraguay's membership in 2012 after the ouster of its president and for suspending Venezuela in 2017 for its failure to incorporate key Mercosur rules on trade and human rights into its national law.

Assessments of Mercosur's record overall are decidedly mixed. On the positive side, tariff barriers on goods have been lowered, intrabloc trade has grown, democracy has been defended, and a community of interests has been forged, notably between traditional rivals Brazil and Argentina. On the negative ledger, no agreement on a common external tariff has been forged after more than two decades, and exports to countries outside the community have expanded much more rapidly than internal trade, although the latter rebounded significantly after the 2008 global financial crisis. Mercosur has not achieved its core economic objective of becoming the common market of the South, nor have its members necessarily formed a cohesive bloc in extraregional and international trade negotiations. On other issues, there has been little harmonization of policies and the majority of decisions have not been enforced (Arnold 2016). In addition, Brazil's ambitions to be a global power have tended to undercut the importance of Mercosur.

The European experience teaches us that regional integration is a long-term process "marked by waves and undercurrents. Although scholars of regionalism take notice of the waves . . . often ignored are the undercurrents, the daily actions of the countless smaller actors who keep the project moving forward in response to the waves" (Mace et al. 1999: 36). Such is certainly the case with the undercurrents of both the inter-American hemispheric approach and the various Latin American regional initiatives. There is no question that regionalism in the Americas is undergoing substantial change with the diminished influence of the United States, various shifts in regional alignments and architecture, and China's increasing presence. The challenge with Latin American and Caribbean regional integration, however, is the absence of an overarching regional project. Instead, there has been a proliferation of regional and subregional institutions with overlapping and duplicated roles. It appears that rather than committing to fixing challenges in existing institutions, governments opt to create new ones, and rather than finding the political will to deepen relations, they have opted for limited intergovernmentalism in a widening set of sectors (Murray 2023).

Asia's Regional Organizations

Unlike Europe, the Americas, and Africa, there is no pan-Asian organization (save for the Asian Development Bank), due to what Acharya (2007b: 24) calls the "diversity, ideological polarization, as well as competing national and sub-regional identities." Instead, there are a number of organizations in different parts of Asia with limited overlap, as shown in Figure 5.4.

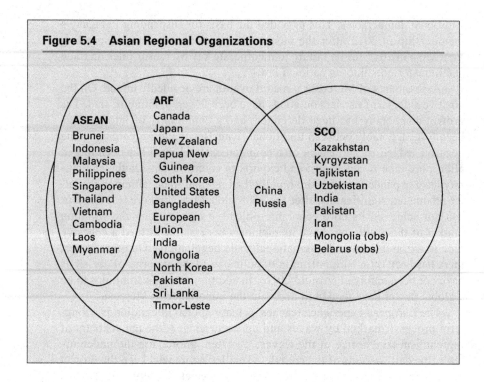

Figure 5.4 Asian Regional Organizations

Thus, for example, Pempel et al. (2005) examine the "construction" of East Asia as a region or what some might term a sub-region. The development of these different parts of Asia is increasingly influenced by China's emergence as a global and regional power and by US bilateral alliance commitments in different parts of the region. Memories of Japanese imperialism in the years leading up to World War II, persistent territorial disputes, distrust, and rivalry between the United States and China and between India and China are among other factors influencing Asian regionalism (Wang and Stevens 2021: 578).

The oldest and most active of the Asian organizations is ASEAN, established by five Southeast Asian nations in 1967. ASEAN has played an important role in establishing a number of other regional forums and dialogue groups, including the East Asian Summits (EAS) and the ASEAN Regional Forum (ARF), which comes closer than any other institution to encompassing most Asian states.

In 2001, the first Central Asian or Eurasian organization, the Shanghai Cooperation Organization (SCO), came into being under Chinese and Russian leadership. As of 2023, it had nine permanent members (including India and Pakistan) and two observers, with Iran becoming a full member.

The SCO is heavily focused on security issues, including terrorism, ethnic separatism, and Islamic fundamentalism, along with trade and economic cooperation (Yuan 2010; Aris 2013). Although not a military alliance, some observers have dubbed it the "anti-NATO."

Asia-Pacific Economic Cooperation (APEC), established in 1989, is unusual in that it spans the Pacific Rim from Asia to the Americas, including seven ASEAN members, several countries of North and South America, plus Australia, New Zealand, China, Russia, Japan, South Korea, Hong Kong, and Taiwan (the inclusion of the latter two explains why APEC members are referred to as "economies" not countries). Created primarily to promote open regionalism and regional trade, APEC also provided a forum for heads of government from all Pacific Rim countries, including the United States and a number of other countries in the Americas until ASEAN initiated the East Asian Summits in 2005. Its importance has diminished in recent years. None of these Asian regional institutions have collective defense or security functions comparable to those of the OAS and NATO.

Defining different parts of the region and building regional identity have been major challenges for Asian states. Over time, choices about whom to include or exclude have shaped these definitions.

Although Asia's regionalism is often compared to that of Europe and particularly the EU, the two could not be more different. One author describes ASEAN, for example, as a "pale imitation" of European regionalism (Beeson 2019: 247). The legalization and bureaucratization of the EU contrast sharply with Asian institutions, which tend to be more informal with few specific rules or binding commitments, small secretariats, consensus decisionmaking, and a strong emphasis on process over substance and outcomes. Informal processes include extensive meetings, consultations, and dialogues; informal outcomes typically refer to agreements on general principles and nonbinding codes of conduct. Where EU members have been willing to cede sovereignty, Asian states have generally been what some call "sovereignty protectionist." Yet as Beeson (2019: 249) notes, despite there being large numbers of meetings in most years and "despite [the region] being the epicenter of some of the world's most pressing and combustible strategic challenges, regional organizations here have had remarkably little direct influence" on strategic, economic, and political issues.

Since most Asian countries gained their independence only after World War II, they have been strongly protective of state sovereignty and suspicious of other forms of dependency or perceived domination. As a result, the norm of nonintervention in states' internal affairs is a strong component of Asian regionalism. Furthermore, the Cold War divided the region. That division persists on the Korean Peninsula, and there are still four communist states in the region (China, Vietnam, Laos, and North Korea). Other factors include the diversity of cultures, levels of development, and distribution of wealth; limited experience with cooperation; and the absence of a clear concept of region. Much like in Latin America, the patterns of interdependence that exist are a consequence of regional initiatives, rather than having been an impetus, as was the case in Europe.

A significant factor affecting East Asian regionalism is the presence of three major powers—the United States, China, and Japan (plus Russia, to the extent it sees itself as an Asian power, and India). The United States, long the dominant economic and military power in the region, continues to play a major role in shaping regional relationships and dynamics. In contrast to its post–World War II encouragement of European regional cooperation through NATO and the EU, the United States never promoted multilateralism in Asia and the Pacific. It preferred a "hub and spokes system" of bilateral relationships with key allies, particularly Japan and South Korea, and never intended the short-lived Southeast Asian Treaty Organization to mirror NATO as a collective defense arrangement in Asia (Hemmer and Katzenstein 2002).

China only became involved in regional activity in the late 1990s, largely as a result of ASEAN initiatives (Johnston 2003; Ba 2006). Now its increasing assertiveness politically, militarily, and economically is creating new tensions and shifts in regional alignments. Japan has consistently given priority to its bilateral ties with the United States and long maintained "an ambivalent attitude to whether it [is] actually part of Asia" (Ravenhill 2007a: 390).

Until the early twenty-first century, the small and middle powers of Southeast Asia provided leadership for regional initiatives based on their shared insecurity and vulnerability. ASEAN began as a coalition of weak states under Indonesian leadership—a factor that helped it build trust with China and other actors. ASEAN prides itself on its "centrality" in promoting East Asian and what is often described as Indo-Pacific regionalism by establishing the ARF and East Asian Summits as well as various free trade agreements (Acharya 2017; Caballero-Anthony 2022). The chief exception is APEC, for which Australia and Japan were leaders in its creation in the 1990s. For the present, ASEAN maintains its position of centrality that results from its structural position as the central node in networks of East Asian regional institutions and its position bridging those networks despite its lack of material power.

Domestic politics has also been a factor influencing the evolution of Asian regionalism. Ruling coalitions have seen ASEAN as a way to sustain themselves and maintain access to export markets and foreign investment (Solingen 1998, 2008). Yet because most states in the region have had authoritarian governments at some point, concern for political legitimacy also explains their reluctance to create strong regional institutions (Narine 2004: 424). The nature of domestic political systems also explains the very limited role of nonstate actors in Asian regionalism—far fewer than has been the case in Europe, for example.

Still, transnational links in the form of networks of business leaders, economists, and security specialists from university centers and think tanks, along with government officials acting in a private capacity, historically have also been drivers of Asian regionalism (Woods 1993; Evans 2005). Except in ASEAN and the SCO, where intergovernmental cooperation came first, these so-called track-two interactions, along with commercial networks (Japanese and US), have played important roles in building confidence among countries with little history of intergovernmental cooperation. They have also provided venues for the formation of epistemic communities, which have been a key source of ideas. Various track-two dialogues have sought to generate agreement on regional solutions for problems such as trade, crime, maritime navigation, health and environmental threats, and security threats, including North Korea's nuclear program. These networks have contributed to the gradual process of regionalization—knitting the countries and elites of East and Southeast Asia in particular into increasingly dense linkages (Katzenstein 2005; Ravenhill 2007b). NGOs and civil society groups such as professional and business associations have been part of this process but have generally been less important than corporate and track-two networks.

Finally, a set of four shocks have had major effects on Asian regionalism: the end of the Cold War; the 1997–1998 Asian financial crisis; the September 11, 2001 terrorist attacks on the United States; and China's rapid rise and assertiveness. The first opened political space for developing regional economic and security ties through ASEAN and APEC. The second demonstrated the vulnerability of East and Southeast Asian economies to globalization and the weakness of both ASEAN and APEC. The third highlighted new types of nontraditional security threats, spurring a broadening of APEC's focus and the creation of the SCO, among other developments. The rise and increasing assertiveness of China and increasing tensions between the United States and China constitute the fourth shock. Uncertainties about US commitment to and defense capabilities in Asia may well provide future shocks for Asian regionalism. We look in more detail at ASEAN and its related institutions.

The Association of Southeast Asian Nations

ASEAN was established in 1967 by Indonesia, Singapore, Malaysia, the Philippines, and Thailand to promote political stability, regime security, and economic growth. Profound historical, cultural, and economic circumstances divided them, but concerns about the US war in Vietnam, the future of the US commitment to regional security, Chinese-supported communist insurgencies, and separatist movements united them. External threats, therefore, were a key impetus since the founding states wanted to minimize the possibility of intervention and domination by the United States and

China and to find "regional solutions to regional problems" (quoted in Acharya 2012: 173).

ASEAN's core norm is nonintervention, derived from the international norm and a series of Asian conferences held between 1947 and the 1955 Asian-African Conference at Bandung, where the ideas of the third world and nonalignment were born. Other important norms are peaceful settlement of disputes, avoidance of military alliances, consultation, and seeking common responses to common problems. ASEAN's norms were meant to guide members' interactions, protect their authoritarian regimes, and keep outside powers from intervening. They have also impeded collective responses to many problems, particularly since the mid-1990s.

The so-called ASEAN Way encompasses these core norms and the process of informal consultation and consensus building derived from Malay culture through which decisions are made. It involves avoiding legalistic procedures and voting, a preference for nonbinding resolutions, and an emphasis on "process over product" (Acharya 2001). If there is no consensus, the members agree to disagree. If there is an intractable dispute, members set it aside and focus on cooperation in other areas. The ASEAN Way has been adopted by other regional groupings, including APEC. Understanding of the ASEAN Way and ASEAN's unique characteristics has largely been the result of constructivists' analyses and their focus on norms and ideas, which has "shed light on processes and security contributions that realist and liberal theorists had considered non-phenomena" (Ba 2014: 297). In contrast, realists have critiqued the ASEAN Way as a mechanism for what Jones and Smith (2007) called "issue avoidance."

One of ASEAN's major tasks has been identity building—defining the region of Southeast Asia—and this task has partly centered on the issue of membership. Between 1967 and 1995, ASEAN admitted only one new member: Brunei (1984). It rejected inclusion of India, Sri Lanka, Australia, and Papua New Guinea, then accepted Vietnam in 1995, Laos and Myanmar (Burma) in 1997, and Cambodia in 1999—completing what was referred to as "the ASEAN ten." This enlargement increased ASEAN's political and economic diversity, but magnified the challenges of consensus decisionmaking. All four newer members were and are less developed than the existing members; two have communist regimes (Laos and Vietnam); one (Cambodia) has been highly unstable and increasingly close to China; Myanmar (then and since 2021 a military dictatorship) was admitted despite protests from the United States, the EU, and human rights NGOs. Because of the difficulties in incorporating new members, there is no assurance that other countries such as Timor-Leste will be allowed to become members.

Structure. ASEAN has been slow to develop the types of organizational structures found in many IGOs. Rather than centralized decisionmaking institutions, the ASEAN Way led to an extremely dense pattern of formal and informal meetings of ministers, heads of government, other senior officials, and diplomats from member governments. These provide regular processes for consultation and searching for accommodation, along with numerous ad hoc and permanent committees.

Initially, only foreign ministers met. The 1975 communist victory in Vietnam and US withdrawal prompted the first summit meeting in 1976. Following the 1997–1998 Asian financial crisis, members' finance ministers began to meet regularly. Similarly, the haze generated by forest fires in Indonesia in the late 1990s prompted environmental ministers to initiate meetings (discussed in Chapter 10). In 1976 a small permanent secretariat was established in Jakarta, Indonesia, to coordinate activities; in 1993 the post of secretary-general was added, but with limited powers and capabilities.

Despite its large number of meetings, forums, strategic plans, and commitments by member states, ASEAN continues to be marked by relatively low levels of institutionalization compared with other regional organizations. As noted by Richard Stubbs (2019: 938), its secretariat remains small and weak (300 as of 2018, compared with 70,000 in the EU) as member states are reluctant to cede too much power to it. Dues payments are very low (geared to the ability to pay of the poorest members) and totaled only $20 million in 2018. (The comparable figure for the EU was $10 billion.) This lack of resources is a major constraint on the organization. ASEAN actually relies heavily on resources provided by external actors, including Japan, South Korea, the United States, Australia, India, and other IGOs, including Asia Development Bank and the EU (Mueller 2021).

Since the mid-1990s, ASEAN has taken several steps that have begun to change its character as a regional organization. The first was the 1992 agreement to create an ASEAN Free Trade Area (AFTA); a second was the ASEAN Surveillance Process, created to monitor capital flows and regional economic developments after the 1997–1998 Asian financial crisis; two others include the 2003 Bali Declaration of ASEAN Concord II and the 2007 ASEAN Charter, which was ratified by all ten members in 2008. The former set in motion a process to create the ASEAN Community based on three "pillars"—the ASEAN Economic Community, the ASEAN Security Community, and the ASEAN Socio-Cultural Community.

Together, these three proposed communities aim to enhance the structures for cooperation if ASEAN's members can move beyond the rhetoric of well-meaning phrases (Narine 2008; Ravenhill 2008). For example, the ASEAN secretariat, although still very small, was given more authority to monitor compliance and settle trade disputes. For the first time, the charter gave ASEAN international legal personality; set out a framework for institutional accountability and a compliance system; included a commitment to promoting democracy, human rights, and human security (but with no definitions of these terms); and called for the creation of a regional human rights body (with no provision for intervening in a members' affairs in the event of gross violations of rights). As a result, the Intergovernmental Commission on Human Rights was established in 2009 (discussed further in Chapter 9). As Jörn Dosch (2008: 542) noted, "for an organization that had strictly avoided any discourse on political order in its 40-year history, even the most reluctant embrace of core democratic norms and values is a major step forward." The charter also renamed and somewhat enhanced the ASEAN Inter-Parliamentary Assembly, whose members are representatives from national parliaments.

ASEAN's goals are ambitious and timetables have continually slipped. Unlike the EU, ASEAN's secretary-general has no authority to negotiate on behalf of the organization or to "drive" processes of institutional development. The four newer members have proven to be a conservative influence, resisting changes in the noninterference principle and lagging in their ability and willingness to commit to new forms of cooperation. China's increasing influence in the region and on Cambodia in particular has proved problematic.

ASEAN's role in maintaining regional peace and security. During its first twenty years, ASEAN's primary focus was regional peace and stability. The 1967 ASEAN Declaration aimed to halt member states' interventions against each other's regimes. In 1971, members created the Zone of Peace and Neutrality to help them resist external Cold War pressures. After the communist victory in Vietnam and US withdrawal in 1975, members concluded the Treaty of Amity and Cooperation (1976). This made political cooperation a formal part of the ASEAN agenda and codified rules of conduct, including the nonuse of force, peaceful settlement (or deferral) of disputes, and common responses to regional problems. The 1978 Vietnamese invasion of Cambodia was seen as a major threat to the ASEAN norm of nonintervention and, for more than a decade, ASEAN was successful in blocking the Vietnamese-backed Cambodian regime from taking Cambodia's UN seat. But the Cambodian issue contributed to ASEAN members' development of greater unity in the 1980s, and they also devised many of the core elements of the 1991 Paris Peace Accords that ended the conflict in that country.

The end of the Cold War, globalization, and other developments of the 1990s created uncertainties for ASEAN members, requiring a redefinition of the group's purpose. The responses included the establishment of the ARF in 1994 to promote multilateral security dialogue, the agreement to create AFTA, admission of the four new members, the initiation of dialogues with outside powers, and the 1995 Bangkok Treaty, which created the Southeast Asian Nuclear Weapon–Free Zone.

There have been numerous territorial disputes in the region and, for the most part, they have highlighted ASEAN's weakness. In the long-running border dispute over the Temple of Preah Vihear between Thailand and Cambodia, ASEAN failed to avert violent clashes in 2011 despite the Treaty of Amity and Cooperation, which commits members to resolve conflicts without armed force; two International Court of Justice rulings; and ample warnings. The effort by Indonesia as ASEAN chair at the time to get agreement to send observers to monitor a cease-fire faltered when Thailand retracted permission, underscoring the organization's weakness in the face of conflicts between members.

With respect to the disputes over demarcation of exclusive economic zones and competing claims to several islands in the South China Sea that involve four ASEAN members and China, the six ASEAN members at the time reached consensus in 1992 on the Declaration on the South China Sea, which called for peaceful resolution of disputes and for developing a code of conduct. In 2002, ASEAN's then ten members and China signed a Declaration on the Conduct of Parties in the South China Sea, but this was nonbinding and included no dispute resolution mechanism, hence it was largely ineffective.

Beginning in 2012, China made clear that it did not feel bound by that agreement and rejected any role for ASEAN in resolving territorial disputes, insisting on bilateral talks. The disputes between China and Vietnam and between China and the Philippines escalated in 2014 when the latter initiated proceedings before the Permanent Court of Arbitration under the UN Convention on the Law of the Sea (discussed in Chapter 3). But ASEAN members have failed to reach agreement on a unified strategy since then in part because only four of its ten members are directly affected and because of China's increasing assertiveness and influence, especially over Cambodia. The nonclaimants are less interested in negotiating with China on this issue, and that has effectively kept ASEAN members from forming a united front.

In 2012, for the very first time in its history, with Cambodia holding the chairship, ASEAN members failed to reach consensus on any mention of the South China Sea disputes in their annual ministerial meeting. In 2014, the communiqué expressed concerns over Chinese activities and called for completing the code of conduct. In 2016, there were reports that China had warned ASEAN against endorsing the Permanent Court's arbitration verdict (Xie 2016). In 2020, the communiqué emphasized the importance of cooperative relations between China and ASEAN and called for continued work on the code.

ASEAN's handling of the South China Sea disputes—not just China's increasingly aggressive assertion of its claims and military buildup of artificially created islands but also the overlapping claims of three of its members (Vietnam, Malaysia, and the Philippines) in the Spratly Islands—illustrates some of its key weaknesses as a regional organization (Koga 2018). These include the reliance on consensus decisionmaking; the unwillingness to delegate to the ASEAN secretariat power to negotiate on members' behalf; and its vulnerability to China's efforts to use a "divide and conquer" approach to dealing with individual members (Jaknanihan 2022). As Beeson (2020) notes, China's territorial claims and aggressive actions in the South China Sea directly threaten the sovereignty of four members.

With regard to nontraditional security threats, particularly threats to human security from epidemics, transnational crime, environmental degradation, and natural disasters, ASEAN's responses have been hampered by its nonintervention norm and by the requirement that all decisions be made by consensus. Members have been unable to put together a collaborative strategy for dealing with the smog and haze from fires caused by logging and land clearing in Indonesia that have blanketed the region almost every year since the late 1990s.

The severe acute respiratory syndrome crisis (SARS) in 2003 revealed how little institutionalized regional cooperation existed in public health policy. Although that crisis and the avian flu pandemic in 2005 led to strengthening of disease-monitoring and -reporting mechanisms and a division of responsibility among ASEAN's original five members for vaccination procedures, emergency preparedness, public awareness, and surveillance systems, this left out the four less developed members of ASEAN, all of which have weak health systems. The Covid-19 pandemic was much more drawn out, and it strained the public health systems of most member countries. ASEAN summit meetings yielded agreements on stockpiling essential medical supplies and equipment, rapid information sharing, and creation of an Recovery Fund and Centre on Public Health Emergencies and Diseases. It proved more difficult to reach agreement on common health and travel protocols (Cabellero-Anthony 2022).

Although not a conventional threat to peace and security, the 2021 coup in Myanmar highlighted the challenges that ASEAN faces in having member states with both autocratic and democratic political systems, including one monarchy (Brunei) and a strong adherence to the nonintervention norm. The brutality of Myanmar's military in cracking down on opposition to the coup and its massive human rights abuses and mismanagement of the economy and health problems have had spillover effects on the region. By mid-2022, fighting between the military, various ethnic armed groups, and what is known as the People's Defence Force had spread to many parts of Myanmar, including urban areas. ASEAN, however, refused to do more than ban the generals from ASEAN meetings, condemn the executions of four activists, and issue "vague threats" to do more (Kurlantzick 2022). In an illustration of how other countries respect ASEAN's desire to handle its regional problems, other major governments refrained from taking action.

ASEAN and economic cooperation. Unlike regional groupings in Latin America, ASEAN member states adopted an outward orientation of integration into the global economy rather than subregional integration as their strategy for growth. They were among the first developing countries to embrace export-led growth and liberalize trade and investment. Four members (Indonesia, Malaysia, Singapore, and Thailand) made great economic and social strides, and ASEAN itself was seen as a successful subregional institution.

Globalization in the 1990s and China's rapidly increasing draw of investment persuaded ASEAN leaders that regional trade integration was the appropriate approach to stimulate economic growth. Still, ASEAN's ability as an organization to promote economic cooperation was inhibited by the outward orientation of most ASEAN economies and the low levels of dependence on trade with other members; members' resistance to meaningful integration, including to mechanisms for monitoring or enforcing agreements; and the disparity between the four newer members and the other six.

The 1997–1998 Asian financial crisis highlighted all these weaknesses and members' vulnerability to global economic trends. Although not set up to deal with financial and monetary relations, ASEAN suffered a loss of confidence as the press and scholarly journals lamented its failure, disarray, and loss of direction. In the aftermath, finance ministers began meeting regularly, the ASEAN Surveillance Process was created, and the ASEAN Plus Three meetings were initiated at various levels with Japan, China, and South Korea.

A number of changes were made after the financial crisis, including rules for trade liberalization, a dispute settlement mechanism (1996), and protocols for notification of changes in commitments agreed earlier (1998 and 2000). Original targets were revised downward, but AFTA was successfully concluded among the six more developed members in late 2002, with the remaining four given longer periods to complete the process.

Although the significance of AFTA remains a matter of debate, the goal of creating the ASEAN Economic Community, with free flow of goods, services, investment, and skilled labor by 2020, aimed to build on AFTA's foundation. Multiple sources concluded that there was no prospect of ASEAN becoming a single market by 2020 or 2025. Although ASEAN was successful in freeing most categories of goods in intraregional trade from tariffs by 2018, nontariff barriers remain a significant problem. The disparities among members—far greater than the inequalities among most members of other regional organizations—are an important variable affecting efforts to foster economic cooperation and integration. Still, ASEAN demonstrated its attachment to its "centrality" with the conclusion in 2020 of the Regional Comprehensive Economic Partnership—a mega–free trade agreement that includes China, Japan, and South Korea (Shimizu 2021).

ASEAN's dialogue partners and regional cooperation mechanisms. In keeping with its emphasis on building and maintaining relationships and its "centrality," one of the notable features of ASEAN is its extensive set of dialogues and consultative institutions with other countries on issues of common concern. This is unique among regional organizations in the Global South (Mueller 2021: 750). The ASEAN Plus Three meetings cover a range of concerns, from economic, trade, and financial cooperation to security, terrorism, environment, human trafficking, piracy, health, and energy. In 2005, the ASEAN Plus Three hosted the first East Asian Summit. These now include Russia and the United States, plus sixteen other countries. In 2022, the United States hosted a US–ASEAN summit with issues ranging from Covid-19 and climate to China's power projection in the Indo-Pacific and the crisis in Myanmar.

The ARF focuses on security issues, including confidence building, preventive diplomacy, the South China Sea islands disputes, denuclearization, maritime security, illegal migration, drug trafficking, and counterterrorism. The ARF has little traction for dealing with crises in the East or South China Seas, however. Still, as Mely Caballero-Anthony (2014: 569–570) notes: "None of the major powers—China, India, Japan, or the United States—would tolerate one of their number, or any other major power, taking the lead in the region. The only viable alternative . . . was and still is ASEAN."

In sum, ASEAN has contributed in many ways to fostering Asian regionalism. The cumulative effect of hundreds of ASEAN-related meetings each year in a region where personal relations are highly valued reinforces ASEAN's importance for regional identity building. Its approach of consensual multilateralism is predominant in all Asian regionalism. As Richard Stubbs (2019: 941–942) has noted, "Overall, proponents' expectations of ASEAN, while often more limited than the skeptics' expectations, tend to be met or exceeded." Taking a long view, he concludes, "ASEAN is generally considered the most successful regional organization in the Global South. . . . Perhaps most importantly it has brought obvious benefits to its members at a surprisingly low cost . . . including peace and stability in a part of the world that used to be characterized by conflict and violence."

Drawing on the Comparative Regional Organizations Project, Anja Jetschke and Patrick Theiner (2020) describe ASEAN as a regional model—different from the model the EU often provides—but similar to other organizations. Still another evaluation calls ASEAN's greatest achievement its continued existence (Beeson 2020)! With its still weak institutions and the divisions between its original and newer members, ASEAN faces a number of problems, however. Among them, according to Mark Beeson (2020: 578), China's emergence is probably "the greatest challenge it has faced since its foundation."

* * *

Overall, the Asian experience with regionalism has had a lot to do with identity construction and community building, processes that are still evolving, with the precise definition of the region uncertain. The future of Asian regionalism will likely turn on the dynamics among existing and rising major powers, particularly China, and on whether ASEAN is able to maintain its centrality.

Africa's Regional Organizations

Identity and community building are not significant issues for regional governance and cooperation efforts on the continent of Africa, where identity construction has not been as problematic and there are no major powers. Many other factors, however, have impeded effective efforts.

Regional unity, self-reliance, economic integration, and cooperation have long been seen by the African countries as means to end the enslavement, imperialism, and colonization by Western European powers from the sixteenth century through the mid-twentieth. At the 1945 meeting of the Pan-African Congress in Manchester, England, for example, participants issued the Declaration to the Colonial Peoples, supporting the right of political freedom and self-government. But Africans disagreed among themselves about what the future might look like. Pan-Africanists advocated for continental unity among independent states while supporters of subregional approaches preferred a minimalist approach, with states agreeing to cooperate but not much more.

In 1964, with thirty-one states having gained independence, those supporting a minimalist approach prevailed and created the Organization of African Unity (OAU).

From the OAU to the African Union (AU)

The OAU was conceived as a loose association based on voluntary cooperation, whose resolutions would carry moral rather than legal obligations. Three overriding principles guided the organization. First, all states were sovereign equals with no greater weight for larger or more powerful states. Second, states agreed not to interfere in the domestic affairs of fellow members. Third, territorial borders were sacrosanct, with no room for alterations in the status quo despite the haphazard way the European colonial powers had drawn those borders in the late nineteenth century. No longer did the newly independent African states want to be dominated by outsiders, risk border changes that would unleash ethnic rivalries and invite outside intervention, or cause the independence leaders to lose their privileged positions. Then and now, they have wanted to find African solutions to African problems (Ayangafac and Cilliers 2011).

Over time, each of the three principles was compromised. Although all states are legally equal, there was implicit recognition that some are able to provide stronger leadership—such as Nigeria, Ghana, Kenya, Algeria, Egypt, or South Africa. The principle of noninterference in domestic affairs was also violated, such as when human rights violations were condemned by other states and when a number of countries intervened in the civil war in the Democratic Republic of Congo in the late 1990s. On a few occasions, the OAU also supported changes in state boundaries, such as when Eritrea gained independence from Ethiopia in 1993.

The OAU enjoyed some notable successes. Members used the Assembly of Heads of State, in particular, as a forum for mediating disputes among states. In 1981, the OAU sponsored an ad hoc, all-African military force to help establish law and order in Chad. At other times, members turned to the UN or subregional organizations such as the Economic Community of West African States (ECOWAS) for dispute resolution or to organize regional military forces, as happened with the civil wars in Liberia and Sierra Leone in the 1990s. The end of white minority rule and apartheid in South Africa was a central OAU goal, achieved in 1994, with the OAU providing consistent support, although the organization was not the determining factor. On economic and development issues, the OAU was largely silent until 1980, however, when members adopted the Lagos Plan of Action for the Economic Development of Africa, 1980–2000 which focused on increasing Africa's self-sufficiency and minimizing links with Western countries.

Since the conditions under which the OAU was founded had changed and the organization's weaknesses had contributed to Africa's marginalization in international politics, the OAU was replaced by the AU in 2002, after two years of negotiations. Unity remained an aspiration, but the AU is primarily designed to meet the challenges of a world characterized by economic globalization and democratization, where African leaders need stronger institutions to respond to African problems (Makinda and Okumu 2008).

The OAU and now the AU have also been complemented by a number of subregional initiatives. Different colonial histories, diverse regional conditions, the weaknesses of the OAU and AU, and changing views about the relationship between regions and subregions all explain this proliferation. Although there is a debate over whether these subregional arrangements are the stepping stones to broader regional integration or detract from continentwide arrangements, there is little question that they have produced "serious inefficiencies, duplication, unintended overlap, and even dissipating efforts" (Makinda and Okumu 2008: 53).

ECOWAS, established in 1975, remains one of the largest and most active of these subregional groupings with fifteen members. Following the end of apartheid in South Africa, the Southern African Development Community (SADC), also with fifteen members, created a free trade area in 2008 but found other initiatives stymied by states' overlapping membership in other subregional groups, including the Southern Africa Customs Union, the Common Market for Eastern and Southern Africa, and the East African

Community. Like ECOWAS, the SADC has been involved with security issues such as the coups in Zimbabwe, Lesotho, and Madagascar and the Democratic Republic of Congo's long conflict. Both have been involved in regional peace operations (discussed further in Chapter 7). We focus here on the AU, however.

The African Union

The AU carried over some of the OAU's overarching principles, including sovereign equality of states and respect for existing territorial borders. Additional principles in the AU Constitutive Act were intended to enable it to respond more effectively to Africa's problems. First, AU members may intervene in the affairs of other states in "grave circumstances, namely war crimes, genocide and crimes against humanity." This is a radical departure from the OAU, although the vague language is open to varying interpretations. Second, to support democratization, AU members pledge support for good governance, democratic principles, and respect for human rights, explicitly rejecting political assassination and unconstitutional changes of governments. Unlike the OAU, the AU can suspend or expel illegitimate governments and has done so on numerous occasions, reinstating them as members when the governments stabilize. Third, resolving disputes peacefully and prohibiting use of force are key principles. The AU charter links peace and security to economic development, noting that the latter depends on the security of states and people. Fourth, achieving balanced social and economic development is a key principle, although the AU's role is only vaguely defined in its charter.

Thus, the principles behind the AU are more supportive of taking definitive actions affecting member state behavior. Leaders pledge to hold free elections and allow opposition parties to campaign freely; failure to support this principle is no longer a shield to hide gross misconduct. As one scholar explains, however, these principles "have been internalized unevenly by the AU's member states," and the move from nonintervention "to what is now commonly referred to as the doctrine of non-indifference" has been slow (Williams 2007: 256). That shift (states care and may act) is most evident in the anti-coup efforts of the AU (discussed below).

Several new organs were established to enable the AU to meet the enhanced objectives. Consistent with the principle of sovereign equality, the annual Assembly of the African Union consists of the heads of state and government. It sets policies, decides what actions to take, considers membership questions, and monitors the implementation of policies and decisions. It is the forum for informal dispute resolution, as under the OAU, but the AU's approach to security is much broader. As defined in the 2004 Common African Defense and Security Policy , security includes human rights, education, health, and rights to protection from poverty. Decisions are generally made by consensus. The Assembly must approve calls for AU intervention and give directives to the Executive Council, which was established to execute the Assembly's decisions regarding the outbreak of violence and other emergency situations.

The AU chairman (not a secretary-general) heads the African Union Commission, the secretariat based in Addis Ababa, Ethiopia, that manages affairs between meetings of the other organs. With a bigger staff and more resources than under the OAU, the AU Commission has authority to take initiatives on behalf of the organization, but unlike the EU Commission, it has no power to enforce treaties or draft regulations. It consists of commissioners responsible for different policy domains. For peace and security issues, for example, the most relevant are the Department of Political Affairs (human rights, democratization, election monitoring) and the larger Peace and Security Directorate. A separate secretariat based in South Africa oversees the NEPAD, the AU's development agency that oversees implementation of Agenda 2063.

The Pan-African Parliament was created in 2004. Its 265 representatives, elected by member state legislatures, focus particularly on the areas of democratization, good governance, and the rule of law. One of its first actions was to send a fact-finding mission to the Darfur region of Sudan, where violence verging on genocide was taking place. The advisory Economic, Social, and Cultural Council was established in 2005 to give voice to members of civil society, including religious and social groups, reflecting the gradual democratization of the continent. The judicial arm of the AU, the Court of Justice, never fully came into existence and was merged in 2004 with the African Court on Human and Peoples' Rights to form the African Court of Justice and Human Rights.

The African Peace and Security Architecture is the umbrella for the AU's peacekeeping and conflict resolution mechanisms. It has a comprehensive agenda, including (1) early warning and conflict prevention; (2) peacemaking, peace support operations, peacebuilding and postconflict reconstruction and development; (3) promotion of democratic practices, good governance, and human rights; and (4) humanitarian action and disaster management. In 2003, the Peace and Security Council (PSC) was established within Peace and Security Architecture as the standing decisionmaking body composed of fifteen members elected by the AU Assembly on a rotating basis, with broad authority to promote collective security and to take action in situations of unconstitutional changes of government. It may institute sanctions against a member state, for example, including suspending membership. The PSC has broad authority to promote collective security. Not only can it use traditional peaceful settlement mechanisms such as mediation and conciliation, it can also undertake peace support operations and humanitarian actions. The PSC's ability to take such actions is limited by political and economic realities, however, notably its limited independent financial and material resources.

The AU's anti-coup initiatives. Of 486 attempted or successful coups carried out around the world between 1950 and 2018, 214 took place in Africa, the most of any region, with 106 of them successful (Schiel, Powell, and Faulkner 2021). Before 1990, coups were a normal occurrence in Africa, but the OAU's noninterference norm meant it did little (if anything) about the problem. That began to change in 2000 with the adoption of the Lomé Declaration. With the goal to consolidate democracy on the African continent by supporting political change through elections and not by other means, the declaration described unconstitutional changes of government (UCGs) as the replacement of an elected government by the military, mercenaries, or rebels, or the refusal of an incumbent to hand over power after free and fair elections (OAU 2000). The declaration was initiated in the post–Cold War, pro-democracy environment that deemed UCGs unacceptable, anachronistic, and undesirable.

The second key instrument is the AU's Constitutive Act of 2001, which declared the AU's zero-tolerance policy on UCGs, enjoins member states "to promote democratic principles and institutions, popular participation and good governance" (Article 3(g)), and prohibits all UCGs (Article 4(p)).

The third instrument is the African Charter on Democracy, Elections and Governance, often referred to as the Addis Charter, which was adopted in 2007 and entered into force in 2012. The charter declares "constitutional amendments to hinder democratic change" as UCGs and thus illegal and was intended to be a comprehensive guideline regarding political transitions in Africa. What is not provided is a clear definition of "what exactly constitutes the successful restoration of constitutional order" (Souaré 2014: 79). There is also no agreement about how to handle situations where authoritarian governments are overthrown by popular uprisings (Ndubuisi 2021).

The AU has worked with subregional organizations such as ECOWAS and international partners like the UN and EU to reduce the occurrence of UCGs, with mixed results. As of late 2021, it had imposed sanctions twenty-two times against fifteen members (Hellquist 2021).

Critics have often accused the AU of being inconsistent and incoherent in its responses, however, and in many cases not being proactive enough in responding to UCGs (Prakathi 2018; Ani 2021). In the case of Burkina Faso in 2015, for example, the AU quickly condemned the coup, whereas in the Zimbabwean case in 2017, the AU did not even declare it a coup. The AU condemned the military's role in overthrowing Sudan's President Omar al-Bashir in 2019, yet some scholars saw the uprising there not as a UCG but as a civilian-led revolution assisted by the military (Tossell 2020; Ani 2021). In 2021, when there were four successful coups, the AU suspended

Mali, Guinea, and Sudan, but not Chad. It suspended Burkina Faso in 2022 after the coup in that country and threatened to impose sanctions following the coup in Niger in 2023. Many saw these inconsistent responses as evidence that the AU "has become little more than a weak and biased dictators' club" (MacLean 2022). Others see the AU's inability to respond effectively as hampered by an overreliance on external support (e.g., from the EU) for sanctions to be effective (Souaré 2014). Clearly the AU is having limited success in deterring the phenomenon.

The AU and threats to peace and security. Many of the anti-coup initiatives that the AU has undertaken have in fact been situations that were viewed as threats to peace and security and prompted peacekeeping, mediation, and other diplomatic initiatives, such as the creation of contact groups to work with the parties to the conflict. Some of these have also involved cooperation between the AU and other regional partners, especially ECOWAS, in what one scholar has described as a division of labor (Suzuki 2020: 184). For example, following a coup in Mali in 2012, the AU and ECOWAS deployed a joint peacekeeping force that was merged in 2013 with the UN-authorized peacekeeping operation of the Multidimensional Integrated Stabilization Mission in Mali, which is discussed further in Chapter 7. Following the 2012 coup in Guinea-Bissau, however, the AU supported an ECOWAS military force and contact group. Because the 2023 coup in Niger followed the coups in Mali, Guinea, and Burkina Faso, it was seen as posing a serious threat across the entire Sahel region, given the weakness and poverty in all four states, the presence of groups linked to al-Qaeda, and Russia's Wagner Group (Walsh 2023).

These types of regional/subregional collaborations reflect Article 16 of the 2002 protocol that established the PSC and the recognition of the AU's "primacy" for addressing regional threats to peace and security, as well as the "subsidiarity" of the regional economic commissions around the continent that also have mandates to intervene in conflicts. Yet as Sanae Suzuki (2020: 174) notes with regard to these partnerships, there are significant issues of coordination, subsidiarity, hierarchy, and overlapping functions, often with no clear division of labor specified during interventions. There have been similar issues, especially with coordination in AU peace operations involving partnerships with the UN and EU. The two largest of these efforts were in Somalia and the Darfur region of the Sudan.

The AU Mission in Somalia (AMISOM), which began in 2008 and ended in 2022, is sometimes viewed as a model of such collaborative efforts involving the AU. It is discussed further in Chapter 7, but the key points to note here are that it began as the AU's fifth peace operation, tasked with supporting dialogue and reconciliation in Somalia, but it morphed into a broad mission of defeating al-Shabaab terrorist forces throughout the country. Beginning with just 1,600 Ugandan soldiers, it became the world's largest peace operation in 2017 with over 22,000 personnel drawn from several African countries. Yet the AU's authority over AMISOM was nominal as the UN Security Council set the mandate and the UN and the EU provided the bulk of the funding. As Paul D. Williams (2018: 98) noted, "In practice, AMISOM's troop-contributing countries exercised a high degree of autonomy and usually conducted unilateral operations within the mission's designated sectors."

AMISOM was also flawed in a number of respects, in part because its partners (the UN, key states, and EU) failed to provide sufficient resources. This meant that its capabilities were not sufficient for its mandated tasks, and there was competition between the partners over priorities and who was really in charge of what. It was also marred by corruption and by the failure of the Somalis to agree on the nature of their own state—a problem that could not be solved militarily (Williams 2018: 104–107). Despite the problems, AMISOM has been something of a model for a number of other AU peace operations, including in Mali, the Democratic Republic of Congo, the Central Africa Republic, South Sudan, and the Lake Chad Basin.

The AU's Agenda 2063 and efforts to boost trade and development. The OAU's 1980 approval of the Lagos Plan of Action sought to promote intra-African trade and reduce reliance on developed countries. In 1991, the Abuja Treaty went further, creating the African Economic Community, forming an African central bank, and establishing a common currency union to promote free trade. The results were limited. Not surprisingly, the Constitutive Act of the AU set some of the same goals for "economic integration of the continent" along with a goal "to coordinate and harmonize the policies between the existing and future regional economic communities."

In 2013, the AU heads of state and government signed a declaration rededicating Africa to attain the pan-African vision of "an integrated, prosperous and peaceful Africa, driven by its own citizens, representing a dynamic force in the international arena." Out of this came Agenda 2063 in 2015—an ambitious framework to guide the continent's development for the second fifty years (AU 2015). The Agenda includes a set of twenty goals and related priorities that are closely tied to the UN's Sustainable Development Goals (SDGs) (also approved in 2015) and discussed further in Chapter 8. Agenda 2063's goals range from aspirations to a high standard of living and well-educated citizenry, environmental sustainability, and healthy, well-nourished citizens to continental financial and monetary institutions, a united Africa, democratic values, a stable and peaceful continent, and Africa as a major partner in global affairs that can finance its own development goals. As with the UN and SDGs, the AU created a system for assessing countries' progress toward the goals along with ten-year implementation plans.

In line with the Agenda 2063 goals, in 2018, the AU Assembly of Heads of State and Government agreed to create the African Continental Free Trade Area (AfCTA) with the goal of enlarging Africa's traditionally small markets. As of late 2022, fifty-four states had signed the agreement (Eritrea being the sole holdout) with forty-four states ratifying it. The UN Economic Commission for Africa and the World Bank lauded the possibilities AfCTA holds for boosting intra-African trade and lifting millions of people out of extreme poverty (World Bank 2022b). The agreement includes a set of protocols that deal with trade in goods, trade in services, dispute settlement, investment policy, and intellectual property rights. A further step was the creation in 2022 of the Pan-African Payments and Settlements System to permit payments among companies operating in different countries to be made in local currencies.

Although consistent with the aspirations stated in the AU's founding documents on the need for economic development, most of these initiatives have led to few achievements. African states still trade more with countries outside the region than with each other, and 70 percent of Africa's exports in 2022 were still primary commodities with just 18 percent of them going to others on the continent. Academic and political figures alike agree that the AU's experience thus far "has failed as a strategy for achieving economic transformation and [as a] development framework" (Aniche 2020: 83). Rwandan president Paul Kagame has referred to this failure as a "crisis of implementation" (quoted in *The Economist* 2022a).

The weaknesses of the AU approach may reflect the presence of many other actors addressing economic development and of overlapping regional and subregional arrangements, many established for economic purposes. The economic goals of the AU have also overlapped with those of the African Development Bank (AfDB) at the continental level. That institution, although aligning with the general goals of the AU, NEPAD, the AfCTA, and Agenda 2063 has emerged as much more capable of harnessing external funding from a variety of multilateral sources and rich donor countries (Nyadera et al. 2022). For one thing, the AfDB has taken a more tailored approach, providing both financing and technical assistance in key sectors, including investment in old and new infrastructure. It is a leader in providing local data and active support for the UN SDGs. It has been a leader in regional integration, providing the institutional home for NEPAD's infrastructure projects and supporting grants to design regional infrastructure projects (Mingst 2015).

The AU and the environment. Environmental issues have never been high on the AU's agenda, but they have not been entirely absent either. Goal 7 of Agenda 2063 calls for "environmentally sustainable and climate resilient economies and communities." Even before it was concluded, the AU had launched the Great Green Wall initiative in 2007 to address the problem of degraded landscapes in the Sahel and developed the African Common Position on Climate Change in 2009. In 2014, the Executive Council decided to target the illicit trade in African wild fauna and flora and develop a strategy to improve collaboration with relevant partners. Ahead of the 2015 Paris Climate Conference, the AU developed a draft strategy on climate change that was updated after the 2021 Glasgow conference with an action plan to guide the continent's response for 2022–2032.

The AU and the future. The AU is not without its relative successes, most notably its attempts at punishing states that overturn elected governments and its wide-ranging efforts to address the conflicts in Darfur and Somalia. These seemingly intractable situations have been approached with conviction by the AU, working with partners, making mistakes, and trying different approaches. In late 2022, the AU was able to secure a cease-fire in the conflict between Tigray Province and Ethiopia. The ongoing dispute over the Grand Ethiopian Renaissance Dam among Ethiopia, Sudan, and Egypt, however, does not provide much cause for optimism about the AU's ability to solve regional disputes. For more than a decade, the parties have been negotiating on water-sharing arrangements. The UN, the EU, the United States, and the AU have been among the parties leading the negotiations. As the water filling the dam rose, the AU-sponsored negotiation ended in April 2021 without a breakthrough. After Egypt's referral of the issue to the UN Security Council, it issued a statement urging the states to reach agreement. Ethiopia proceeded with power generation trials in early 2022, however. In the absence of a negotiated agreement, the dispute threatens regional stability and economic growth in the entire Nile River Basin, as well as the parties' vulnerability to climate change. In one observer's eyes, the AU would benefit from a diplomatic success in the situation (Floyd 2022).

It remains to be seen whether any strengthening of the AU would lead to more success in achieving its ambitious political, security, and economic initiatives. Without that success, it is unlikely that the AU can be effective and exert greater influence in global arenas. Indeed, although the AU has more authority across all issue areas than its predecessor had, the organization faces difficult tasks ahead in a challenging environment.

Regional Organizations in the Middle East

As the first *Arab Human Development Report* (UNDP 2002: 121) suggested, "perhaps no other group of states in the world has been endowed with the same potential for cooperation, even integration, as have the Arab countries." Common language, history, religion, and culture unite the Arab states, but much divides them, as has become increasingly apparent in recent years, and this includes the divide between Sunni and Shia Muslims. Theologically, they differ on who is the legitimate successor to the Prophet Muhammad. Each views the other as heretical. Two factors have politicized these differences. One was the rise of extremist Islamic fundamentalism that was galvanized by the fight between Afghans and their Islamic supporters against the Soviet Union in the 1980s and gained added strength with the more recent emergence of the Islamic State of Syria and Iraq (ISIS). A second factor was the 1979 Shiite revolution in non-Arab Iran and the 2003 US invasion of Iraq, which empowered that country's Shiite majority over its Sunni Arab minority. In more recent years, Iran has emerged as the leader of the Shia, while Saudi Arabia considers itself the leader of the Sunni Muslims, resulting in a regional power rivalry. There are Shia majorities in Bahrain as well as Iran and Iraq, plus a plurality in Lebanon. Sunnis form the majority in Egypt, Jordan, Sudan, and Syria as well as among Palestinians.

In addition to the religious divide, other factors have influenced regional initiatives, among them the mix of different regime types (conservative monarchies, authoritarian regimes, revolutionary regimes, and semi-democracies) with varying political agendas. There are major disparities in wealth between rich oil states with small populations such as Qatar and very poor states with high population densities, such as Yemen; low levels of intraregional trade; and similarity in states' imports and exports, most notably oil, reflecting a lack of complementarity. The region is also notable for the extensive involvement of outside powers, including bilateral alliances and economic and security dependencies (Legrenzi and Calculli 2013: 2–5).

There are two primary regional organizations, but differences have definitely hindered regional cooperation over many years. Twenty-two states in the Middle East and North Africa are members of the Arab League as of 2022, with Syria's membership suspended between 2011 and 2023. Six states make up the Gulf Cooperation Council (GCC), which was established in 1981 as a reaction to the 1979 Iranian revolution and the Iran-Iraq War (1980–1988). Other initiatives over the years include the Organization of Arab Petroleum Exporting Countries and various development funds. The GCC and the Arab League exclude the three non-Arab states in the region: Turkey, Iran, and Israel.

The League of Arab States

The League of Arab States, or Arab League, was formed in March 1945, seven months before the UN, and it has been an important player in the Middle East as much for what it does not do as for what it has accomplished. The Arab League was created as a manifestation of pan-Arabism—the ideological and political project to unite all Arab people into a single Arab nation, to promote political and economic cooperation in a time when several Arab states were gaining independence. The League's charter, however, emphasizes state sovereignty, reflective of the colonial past and concerns about the security of its members' domestic (mostly authoritarian) regimes. Despite the divisions and rivalries within and among Arab states, the organization long promoted Arab unity, particularly in the conflict with Israel over the status of the Palestinians. It has largely failed to achieve much more than ad hoc collaboration among its members, however, in part because the League, for much of its history, has been a tool of Egypt's foreign policy (Maddy-Weitzman 2012: 71).

The Arab League is extensively, though weakly, institutionalized with two core bodies—the Council and the Permanent Secretariat, based in Cairo, and a variety of permanent committees and affiliated agencies such as the Arab League Educational, Cultural and Scientific Organization. The Arab Parliament was created in 2005 with members coming from national parliaments but not representing either their parliaments or governments but the Arab "nation" as a whole. The League's primary decisionmaking body is the Council, which is composed of the foreign ministers of each member state. It meets twice a year, but any two countries can call a special session. All member states have equal voice in the Arab League's bodies, but resolutions can pass with a simple majority. So-called authoritative decisions require unanimity and are binding, but only on states that accept them. This effectively limits the power of the organization over its members. In addition, the practice of convening summit meetings of heads of state, though not mentioned in the Charter, has diminished the role of the Council and other bodies.

Economic, social, and cultural cooperation has been notably more successful than political and security cooperation, despite the League's higher visibility on the latter issues. Its economic initiatives have included steps toward creation of a common market (the Arab Economic Union), the Arab Development Bank, and the Greater Arab Free Trade Area. Intraregional trade remains low, however, as the Arab economies have long been heavily protected and had similar production patterns.

The Arab League's primary focus has historically been its hostility to the state of Israel and its support for the Palestinian cause. Members have spoken with one voice in the UN and enlisted the support of non-Arab states that expressed their solidarity by not recognizing the state of Israel. The League instituted a boycott of Israeli products in 1948 that remains in place today—one of its strongest actions ever. Yet because of internal disputes among members, the League did not coordinate the wars with Israel in 1948, 1967, or 1973. It created the Palestine Liberation Organization in 1964 and pushed its acceptance in 1974 as the legitimate representative of the Palestinian people. It expelled Egypt after the conclusion of the Camp David Accords with Israel in 1979.

The restoration of relations with Egypt in 1989 represented the beginning of weakening the prohibition on diplomatic contact with Israel in the 1990s, as did Jordan's 1994 peace treaty with Israel and contacts between Morocco, Qatar, and Israel. In 2002 the League endorsed Saudi Arabia's proposal to normalize relations with Israel in exchange for full Israeli withdrawal from the Occupied Territories—an initiative it hoped would spur negotiations between Israel and the Palestinians and creation of an independent Palestinian state. The League stayed silent during the conflict between Israel and Hamas in Gaza in 2014, however, and again in 2021 and 2022, despite widespread condemnation of Israel's extensive bombing and the Palestinian civilian casualties. Concern about the spread of Islamist extremism overrode sympathy with the Palestinians.

The normalization of relations between the United Arab Emirates (UAE) and Israel in 2020, as part of the US-initiated Abraham Accords, broke the taboo" against normalization with Israel and signaled the major shifts taking place in the region. The Arab League failed to approve a Palestinian draft resolution condemning the UAE's decision. Since then, Bahrain, Morocco, and Sudan have also normalized relations with Israel. As Gary Gambill (2020) notes, "popular hostility to Israel in the Arab world is still strong enough that, all else being equal, few of its despotic rulers would be inclined to normalize relations with Israel were there not increasingly much to gain." That includes the benefits of cooperation in the face of what is viewed as a growing threat from Iran and US disengagement from the region. This splintering among the Arab League members also accounted for the League's failure to condemn Israeli attacks on Hamas and Gaza in 2021 and 2022, although the Arab Parliament and the secretary-general did condemn the violence and call for international intervention. One writer noted, "By abdicating its common commitment to the core issue of Palestine, the LAS has obviously lost its raison d'être" (Jahshan 2020). In short, as a writer for the *Economist* (2021) noted, the Palestinian cause "no longer binds the Arab world."

The League has had a very mixed record in dealing with other conflicts and security threats in the region. Joint military action was taken in 1961 to prevent Iraq from taking over Kuwait at the time of the latter's independence, and again in 1976 in the Lebanese civil war. The League failed to act in Yemen's civil wars in the 1960s, 1990s, and more recently as well as in the Iran-Iraq War in the 1980s, but it did condemn Iraq's 1990 invasion of Kuwait. League members were divided over how to avert a US war against Iraq in 2003, but did nothing to contribute to ending the conflict in Iraq or reintegrating Iraq into the Arab world. The League supported the government of Sudan in the face of the genocide in the Darfur region of that country in the early 2000s, opposing UN sanctions and International Criminal Court prosecution of Sudanese officials indicted for crimes against humanity.

The Arab League showed limited relevance during the upheavals of the Arab Spring in 2011 and 2012, however, when prodemocracy protests toppled the authoritarian regimes in Tunisia and Egypt and rippled throughout the region. In response to the uprising in Libya, the League condemned the Libyan government's violent crackdown on protesters and suspended it from participating in League meetings—an unprecedented intervention in the domestic affairs of a member state.

Subsequently, the Arab League called for the UN Security Council to impose a no-fly zone to protect Libyan civilians. This provided legitimacy for Security Council action and for US and NATO military intervention, even though Arab state support was not unanimous. Once it became evident that the intervention sought regime change, not just humanitarian protection, the League's secretary-general, Amr Moussa, reversed the earlier decision. Chaos followed the toppling of Libya's leader, Muammar Qaddafi, then political stalemate, with members split over which of two rival claimants to support. As one analyst wrote, "In essence, divisions within the League have been at the heart of its failure to assist a member country such as Libya to accomplish the political stability its people so desperately deserve" (Harb 2020).

In the case of Syria's civil war that began in 2011, the League initially sought to get Syrian president Bashar al-Assad to take steps to defuse the crisis, including accepting a League monitoring mission. When that failed, Syria was suspended from League activities, and the League imposed sanctions, including banning officials from traveling to other Arab countries, freezing Syrian assets in Arab countries, and halting bank transactions. It supported several efforts to mediate an end to the conflict, including the appointment in 2012 of former UN Secretary-General Kofi Annan as the UN–Arab League Special Representative (followed by Lakhdar Brahimi after Annan resigned, and by Staffan de Mistura in 2014).

Ultimately, the Arab League proved to have very little leverage with Syria. It has had virtually no involvement in the civil war in Yemen, where some GCC members are directly involved.

In short, in the Arab League's more than seventy years of existence, member states have seldom demonstrated a desire to support strong regional cooperation except in earlier years on the Israeli/Palestinian issue. In fact, it has declined as an organization "to a mere façade of ineffectual institutions that reflect the prevalent disunity in the Arab world," according to the Washington, DC based Arab Center. It "fell victim to the ideologies of different Arab state elites who pursued their interests and sowed the seeds of discord . . . [which] has limited the League's ability to represent the interests of over 400 million Arabs regionally and internationally" (Al-Qassab et al. 2020). Despite the rhetoric and numerous initiatives concerning social and economic development, the people of the region have seen very little improvement, with the Arab League known primarily for its limited political role. It is a subregional entity—the GCC—that has proved to be a more successful example of regionalism in the Middle East.

The Gulf Cooperation Council

Economically, politically, and culturally, Bahrain, Kuwait, Oman, Qatar, Saudi Arabia, and the United Arab Emirates are among the most homogeneous nations in the world. All are monarchies and oil-producing states. Despite competing visions for cooperation, however, the Cooperation Council for the Arab States of the Gulf or Gulf Cooperation Council (GCC) is seen as one of the more successful initiatives in the Middle East (Fawcett 2013).

The GCC was created in 1981 in response to several threats, including the Iranian Revolution of 1979, whose leaders threatened to sweep away their monarchies; the 1979 Soviet invasion of Afghanistan; and the war between Iran and Iraq (1980–1988). The GCC's charter calls for "coordination, integration, and co-operation among the member states in all fields." Its earliest action was to conclude an agreement to unify the economies of its member states, calling for a uniform system of tariffs, nondiscrimination with regard to capital and labor flows across borders, harmonization of industrial development programs, a common investment policy, and coordination of oil industry policies (Lawson 2012: 6). In 1984, the Peninsula Shield Force, a joint rapid deployment force, was established and, over time, members have shown an ability to coordinate and even unify their responses, especially to internal threats (Valbjorn 2016: 259). Over time, both economic and security concerns have marked GCC activities. Historically, Saudi Arabia has been the dominant power among the six members, but since the Arab Spring in 2011, Qatar has emerged as an activist member in competition with Saudi Arabia.

Institutionally, the primary organ of the GCC is the Supreme Council, which meets annually and is composed of the heads of state of the six member countries. While the Supreme Council finalizes decisions for the body, much of the work of the organization is handled by the Ministerial Council, which includes the foreign ministers, and by the Secretariat, based in Riyadh. Although initially decisions were made on the basis of unanimity, in effect, only Saudi Arabia has a veto given its greater capabilities (Valbjorn 2016: 259).

Although the GCC has outlasted initial predictions of failure, its effectiveness as a regional organization has fluctuated over time. Politically, the GCC was ineffective in responding to the Iran-Iraq War in the 1980s and to Iraq's invasion of Kuwait in 1990, except in formally requesting US help in the latter case. Despite strong anti-American sentiment among citizens and high military spending, GCC members have relied on bilateral agreements with the United States for defense, rather than on joint efforts. Five of the six members provide significant bases for US military forces in the region. Saudi Arabia's base, for example, was used during the 1990–1991 Gulf War, and Kuwait's and Qatar's were used during the 2003 Iraq War. Saudi Arabia requested that the United States give up its air base in that country in 2003. Bahrain and Qatar host US command headquarters, which have become increasingly important in addressing the Iran threat. The GCC countries have faced a number of threats as a result of forces unleashed by the Arab Spring, Syrian civil war, continuing instability in Iraq, terrorism, and Iran's nuclear program as well as its support for militant groups and interference in the internal affairs of Gulf states and across the entire Middle East.

Both the Arab League and the GCC have been increasingly focused on Iran's threat to many member states. In 2020, the League condemned its interference through proxies like Shia militias and political parties in the internal affairs of Arab countries and called for relations to be based on respect for international law, state sovereignty, and refraining from threats or use of force. A 2022 League Council resolution created the Arab Committee to counter the Iranian threat. As the *North African Post* noted (2022), "Iran has had a detrimental role in deepening the inter-Arab divide while undermining the foundations of sovereign Arab states through manipulating armed proxies in Iraq, Syria, Lebanon, [*sic*] Iraq and Yemen." The League expressed its solidarity with Morocco against Iranian threats. There is concern among members of both organizations about Iran's missile and nuclear programs and its opposition to the Israeli-Palestinian peace process. The Gulf states also worry about potential Iranian control of the Strait of Hormuz. Because of the presence of US military bases and US ties with Gulf states, however, Iran has long condemned them as client states of the West.

The issue of nuclear weapons in the region is particularly tricky because it is an open secret that Israel has nuclear weapon capabilities. Iran's continuing development of its potential capabilities since the United States withdrew from the Iran nuclear agreement in 2017 heightens the concern that with or without US support, Israel may act to prevent Iran from achieving weapons capability. It is also possible that Saudi Arabia will seek such capability if Iran is successful—thus launching a potential nuclear arms race in the region. The early 2023 agreement between Iran and Saudi Arabia brokered by China may upend many of the region's and GCC's dynamics.

Economically, the GCC has taken a number of concrete steps to link its members, including duty-free trade among members since 1983, a common market since 2008, and a customs union that came into effect in January 2015. Common citizenship allows citizens among the six states to move freely, but the huge populations of foreign workers are not accorded that privilege. Among the major regional infrastructure projects are a unified pipeline network for natural gas, an integrated regional railway system, and a unified electrical power grid. As Fred Lawson (2012: 17) concludes, "By the second decade of the twenty-first century, the Gulf Cooperation Council had become transformed into a very different type of regionalist project from what it had been either in 1981 . . . or during the mid-1990s."

As the events of the Arab Spring unfolded in 2011, not surprisingly given the vulnerability of the six monarchies, the GCC proved to be more cohesive and active than the Arab League. Their responses focused on pumping billions of dollars into neutralizing potential unrest in their own and other countries. The Peninsula Shield Force (mostly Saudi troops) was deployed in Bahrain in March 2011 to quell the unrest of marginalized Shiite protesters. In Yemen, the GCC undertook prolonged mediation that ended with President Ali Abdullah Saleh stepping down from power in November 2011. In Libya, however, the GCC joined the Arab League in supporting the uprising with the goal of ending Qaddafi's personal rule. In Syria, Saudi Arabia and Qatar supported rival Syrian opposition groups, motivated partly by the desire to end Iranian influence over Syria, but also reflecting their increasing competition (Maddy-Weitzman 2012). With the rise of Islamist groups in the region, the emergence of ISIS in 2014 as a potent force, the ongoing civil wars in Syria and Yemen, and anarchy in Libya, some GCC countries joined a coalition with the United States to mount air strikes against ISIS in Iraq and Syria; some also joined Saudi Arabia in military action in Yemen.

A further split among the Arab states involved Qatar, home to the popular news source *Al Jazeera*, which supported revolution and the Muslim Brotherhood that so many other Arab states opposed, including Saudi Arabia. While both countries had backed the overthrow of President Bashar al-Assad in Syria and fought the Houthis in Yemen, they backed rival groups in Libya. In June 2017, more than six key states, including Saudi Arabia, Egypt, and Jordan, severed diplomatic relations with Qatar and initiated a blockade of its air space, land crossing, and sea routes. Among their demands was that Qatar shut down *Al Jazeera*. In 2021, a GCC summit ended the dispute and blockade, restoring relations among GCC members even though Qatar made no major changes. It was US influence, not GCC action, that was responsible for the outcome, however (Ramani 2021).

One of the most important GCC security-related initiatives has involved improving cross-border intelligence cooperation "as a way of predicting, deterring and responding to transnational terror threats on their own territory" (Miller 2022: 436). According to Rory Miller (2022: 438), a key factor in developing this has again been the role of the United States as a bilateral intelligence partner for the GCC member states along with GCC members' shared fear of Iran, attacks on Saudi targets beginning in 2003 by al-Qaeda networks, and the growth of the Islamic State. The GCC members agreed to create a permanent counterterrorism security committee in 2006, but not something like a joint counterterrorism center that would have responsibility for coordinating intelligence-sharing and common responses to regional threats (Miller 2022: 446).

In Yemen, open warfare broke out in 2015 between government forces supported by a Saudi-UAE joint force and Shiite rebels known as the Houthis, backed by Iran. The Arab League has made no offer of mediation to end the war, which was still ongoing in 2023, however, and has echoed the Saudi view by blaming Iran and the Houthis for the continued conflict that has triggered what the UN calls the worst humanitarian crisis in the world (Chapter 11).

* * *

In sum, Middle East regionalism as exhibited in the Arab League and GCC has a very mixed record of effectiveness despite factors of common culture, language, and identity that might have suggested greater potential success for regional cooperation. Both organizations have faced periods of significant disunity among their members with the greater homogeneity among GCC members and influence of the United States yielding more success on the economic side and to some extent on the security side. The decline in the importance of the Palestinian issue is clearly a significant change for the Arab League in particular.

Regionalism in the Arctic

As with other regions, the precise definition of the Arctic can vary. As Mary Durfee and Rachael Johnstone (2019: 23) note, "There is no single definition of the region; rather, the boundaries depend on what is being studied." The Arctic Council Working Groups use several different lines. One is the Arctic Circle whose latitude (66 degrees North from the Equator) is the farthest south point in the Northern Hemisphere where the sun does not rise in midwinter or set in midsummer. Another is a biogeographical boundary formed by the farthest north point where trees can grow and within which there are unique flora and fauna. Regardless of the boundaries one might draw, the Arctic is rich in natural resources and economic potential. The accelerating melting of sea ice due to climate change is rapidly opening new maritime routes between Asia and Europe with attendant risks of accidents and pollution in remote locations. This is attracting increasing interest from non-Arctic states. Billions of dollars worth of oil and gas and valuable mineral deposits potentially lie in the seabed beneath the ocean. In 2007, Russia's bold action in planting its flag in the seabed beneath the North Pole highlighted the competing claims regarding the delimitation of the continental shelf—a move that Canada likened to a "15th century land grab" (Proffit 2007).

Among the regions examined here, the Arctic is unique in that it encompasses land areas and seas considered to be "global commons." It is also considered to be a "governed space"—that is, some of the land and sea areas are covered by international legal conventions. These include the UN Convention on the Law of the Sea (UNCLOS) and the International Maritime Organization (IMO) International Convention for Ships Operating in Polar Waters (the Polar Code). Other relevant international law includes the International Convention for the Regulation of Whaling and the International Convention for the Prevention of Pollution from Ships and Protocols. The Arctic is also governed by the work of the UN Commission on the Limits of the Continental Shelf—a technical-scientific body that makes recommendations on claims of sovereignty relating to the continental shelf and Arctic seabed. A first step toward addressing Arctic fishing issues came with the 2015 Oslo Declaration Concerning the Prevention of Unregulated High Seas Fishing in the Central Arctic Ocean concluded by the so-called Arctic Five (A5)—Norway, Russia, Canada, Denmark/Greenland, and the United States—the five countries whose territory borders the central Arctic Ocean.

In addition to these elements of governance, the Arctic is governed through the work of the Arctic Council, which was established in 1996 by the five Arctic coastal states (the United States, Russia, Canada, Norway, and Denmark [for Greenland]) and three noncoastal states (Sweden, Iceland, and Finland) as an intergovernmental high-level forum. The Arctic Council is unique in a number of respects but most particularly through the permanent participation of six Indigenous peoples associations that represent the 500,000 Indigenous peoples who live in the Arctic.

The Making of the Arctic as a Region

Before we look more closely at the Arctic Council, it is helpful to understand the "making of the Arctic" as a region. Historically, the areas that form the Arctic were remote, largely neglected territories. Some portions attracted attention during the Cold War as the two major Arctic states—the United States and Russia/Soviet Union—and some of their northern allies established military facilities and presence to take advantage of the proximity to each other's territory for espionage and defense.

In 1989—just as the Cold War was ending—growing concerns about the fragile Arctic environment and the need for joint efforts to address the issue led to the first meeting of the eight Arctic states in Rovaniemi, Finland. Following two years of consultations, the eight produced the Arctic Environmental Protection Strategy in 1991. This focused on cooperation in scientific research, sharing data on effects of pollution, and assessments of the potential environmental impacts of development activities through four specific measures: Arctic Monitoring and Assessment Programme; Protection of the Marine Environment in the Arctic; Emergency Prevention, Preparedness and Response in the Arctic; and Conservation of Arctic Flora and Fauna. An important part of this protection strategy was the inclusion of Indigenous peoples in its work. In 1996, the eight states took the further step of creating the Arctic Council as an intergovernmental high-level forum with the permanent participation of six Indigenous peoples associations.

The making of the Arctic as a region can best be understood through a constructivist lens. The practices of states with clear claims to be part of the region, as well as those outside, and the development of various elements of governance and of identity have contributed to the growing recognition since the late 1980s of the Arctic as a distinct region. Likewise, the inclusion of Indigenous peoples groups has contributed to their development of a sense of Arctic identity. At the same time, regime theory offers an excellent way to understand Arctic governance as an outgrowth of the relevant international legal documents, customary law practices, and the work of the Arctic Council.

The Arctic Council

The Council's membership includes the eight Arctic states plus six Indigenous Peoples Permanent Participants (see Figure 5.5), and six working groups. Eight European states have long been observers; five Asian states were granted observer status in 2013 (China, the Republic of Korea, Japan, Singapore, and India), along with twenty-five IGOs and NGOs in 2022, including the UNDP, the IMO, the World Meteorological Organization, the International Union for the Conservation of Nature, and the World Wildlife Fund. The observers may attend meetings, but only with permission of the chair are they permitted to submit documents or prepared statements. In addition, they were required to recognize the sovereignty and sovereign rights of the Arctic states and the special position of the Permanent Participants (i.e., the Indigenous peoples' groups), and to support the work of the Arctic Council. The working groups are standing bodies that focus on specific issues, including monitoring and assessment, conservation of flora and fauna, emergency prevention, preparedness and response, protection of the marine environment, the Contaminants Action Program, and sustainable development.

The Arctic Council is governed by meetings of senior Arctic officials held twice a year and biennial ministerial meetings. The chair position rotates among the eight Arctic states with each

Figure 5.5
Indigenous Peoples' Permanent Participating Organizations in the Arctic Council

- Aleut International Association
- Arctic Athabaskan Council
- Gwich'in Council International
- Inuit Circumpolar Council
- Russian Arctic Indigenous Peoples of the North
- Saami Council

state holding the position for two years. The Arctic Council Standing Secretariat, based in Tromsø, Norway, provides administrative support to the Council's chair, the permanent participants, and the working groups. There is also an Indigenous Peoples' Secretariat, which has its own board, budget, and work plan but functions within the Arctic Council Secretariat.

From a definitional standpoint, the Arctic Council is an intergovernmental forum, not an IGO. It does not have legal personality as the UN and most IGOs have. It has no "powers" as such, but the discussions in its ministerial meetings and working groups inform actions that the A5 or A8 may take. Among the Council's actions are the Oslo Declaration of 2015 that was an important step toward a regional fisheries management organization for the central Arctic Ocean and the 2018 Agreement to Prevent Unregulated High Seas Fisheries in the Central Arctic Ocean with China, Japan, and Korea as non-Arctic signatories. It has facilitated legally binding agreements on marine oil pollution preparedness, air and marine search and rescue, and scientific cooperation. Not surprisingly, given the fragile environment and active participation of Indigenous peoples groups, the concerns often tend to focus more on human security than national security and are closely linked to the UN's SDGs. Issues concerning delimitation of the continental shelf may be discussed in the Arctic Council but can only be resolved by the UN Commission on the Limits of the Continental Shelf.

There are a growing number of other states with an interest in the Arctic. This has led to references to the "global Arctic" since 2010. In 2013, five Asian states were admitted as observers to the Arctic Council—a step that greatly expanded the focus of the Council and complicated the politics surrounding the increasingly open waters of the Arctic Ocean thanks to climate change. As noted by the Finnish Institute of International Affairs in 2013, "the Arctic is no longer a spatially or administratively confined region, but is instead taking its new form in the midst of contemporary global politics" (Dodds and Woon 2020: 17).

Assessing the Consequences of Regionalism

Regional organizations are key pieces of global governance, and since the 1990s, global regionalization has been a marked trend. Although there is sometimes a tendency to see regionalism in competition with global efforts to address issues and problems, in most areas of governance, regional organizations and activities complement global ones through shared or overlapping responsibilities. To be sure, regional free trade initiatives give rise to a fear of trade blocs and barriers to wider trade patterns. Indeed, the EU eliminated internal barriers to trade among its members and favored partners but raised barriers to trade with others. Its common policies, particularly in agriculture, for example, have provoked fierce trade wars, especially with the United States, and hampered efforts to open agricultural trade on a global basis. Likewise, a regional human rights regime could compromise norms of universal human rights if it were to adopt a more restrictive view, say, of women's rights.

As this chapter has shown, regional organizations vary widely in the nature of their organizational structures, the types of obligations they impose on member states, their resources, and the scope of their activities, from the formality and supranationalism of the EU to the loose, informal political concertization of policies found in ASEAN. Generally, institutions in the developing world tend to be more "sovereignty-preserving than sovereignty-eroding" (Acharya and Johnston 2007: 262). Regardless, developments in the expanding universe of regional organizations are "crucial to understanding the many different directions in which governance is moving, the range of dilemmas being faced, and the different forms that regional politics . . . might take" (Hurrell 2007: 146).

Moving Beyond Regionalism: Transregional Organizations

Many issues and problems require more than regional cooperation, of course. Thus, there are a variety of transregional initiatives, such as the EU-ASEAN dialogue and the Asian summits. Although some of these links may be little more than the rituals of summit diplomacy, they evidence awareness of the value of interactions among groups of nations in different regions and the potential for meaningful collaboration.

Transregional organizations have a long history but have gained increasing urgency to address issues from terrorism, drug trafficking, migration, and certain types of environmental degradation to nontraditional security threats. Some, such as the Commonwealth and Francophonie, are outgrowths of European colonialism, their memberships including the United Kingdom and many former British colonies in the former, and France and many of its former colonies in the latter. Other groups, such as the Alliance of Small Island States (AOSIS), the Non-Aligned Movement, and the Organisation of Islamic Cooperation (OIC) are coalitions of like-minded states.

The OIC brings together fifty-seven states from several regions. When its charter was approved in 1972, one of the key objectives was "to co-ordinate efforts for the safeguarding of the Holy Places and support of the struggle of the people of Palestine, and help them to regain their rights and liberate their land." Other key provisions include respect for self-determination and noninterference in members' domestic affairs. There is no provision for political unity.

Since its inception, the OIC has focused primarily on opposition to Israel, supporting the Palestinian cause, and promoting the unity of Islam.

The US role in the Islamic world (including the 1990–1991 Gulf War and 2003 Iraq invasion) was a particular source of disunity as the OIC includes both member states that view the United States as "the Great Satan" and some that host US troops (Akbarzadeh and Connor 2005: 82–83).

Not only has the OIC failed to further its primary issue, it has also found itself divided on the issue of terrorism. On one hand, it has condemned terrorism, labeling attacks as "un-Islamic"; on the other hand, it has refrained from condemning Palestinian terrorism and suicide attacks. Although the OIC adopted the Convention on Combating Terrorism in 1990, defining terrorism is problematic because such actions are generally viewed as legitimate expressions of the Palestinian struggle for self-determination.

The 2011 Arab Spring caught the OIC by surprise, with many of its members, including Egypt, Yemen, Bahrain, Oman, Jordan, and Syria, confronted by prodemocracy movements and the ouster of autocratic leaders. Instead of addressing these issues, the OIC Executive Committee focused on condemning the Libyan government's violent crackdown on protesters and called for UN Security Council action to impose a no-fly zone to protect Libyan civilians. As Ishtiaq Hossain (2012: 308) concluded, "In terms of politics, security, and defense, the OIC has not succeeded. Although it is difficult the OIC should try to emulate the successes made by the GCC, the ASEAN and the APEC in the areas of economic, political and security."

Thus, the landscape of regional and transregional organizations contains a large number of organizations, some much more important parts of global governance than others. Clearly the processes of regionalization will continue to evolve in response to the dynamics within the regions. Some of these processes have been shaped at least in part by nonstate actors, and we turn to them in Chapter 6.

Suggested Further Reading

Acharya, Amitav. (2021) *ASEAN and Regional Order: Revisiting Security Community in Southeast Asia*. New York: Routledge.

Bach, Daniel C. (2015) *Regionalism in Africa: Genealogies, Institutions and Trans-State Networks*. New York: Routledge.

Börzel, Tanja A., and Thomas Risse, eds. (2016) *The Oxford Handbook on Comparative Regionalism*. New York: Oxford University Press.

Olsen, Jonathan. (2020) *The European Union: Politics and Policies*, 7th ed. New York: Routledge.

Stapel, Sören. (2022) *Regional Organizations and Democracy, Human Rights, and the Rule of Law: The African Union, Organization of American States and the Diffusion of Institutions*. Cham: Palgrave Macmillan.

Valbjorn, Morten. (2016) "North Africa and the Middle East." In *The Oxford Handbook of Comparative Regionalism*, edited by Tanja A. Börzel and Thomas Risse. New York: Oxford University Press, pp. 249–270.

6

The Critical Roles of Nonstate Actors

ALTHOUGH SOVEREIGN NATION-STATES ARE THE MAJOR CONSTITUENTS of the international system, thousands of nonstate actors (NSAs) are also part of global governance. It is important to understand NSAs not only because of their numbers and diversity, but also because of their perceived impact on international affairs. One indicator of their importance is the Nobel Peace Prize, which has been awarded to several types of NSAs: nongovernmental organizations (NGOs such as Amnesty International, Doctors Without Borders, the International Committee of the Red Cross), social movements and transnational advocacy networks (the International Campaign to Abolish Nuclear Weapons, the International Campaign to Ban Landmines), and epistemic communities (the Institute of International Law, the Intergovernmental Panel on Climate Change, International Physicians for the Prevention of Nuclear War).

The Range of Nonstate Actors

Although NGOs are a prominent type of NSA, as shown in Figure 6.1, "nonstate actors" is a broad category that also includes social movements and transnational advocacy networks, epistemic communities, foundations, multinational corporations, the media, and even transnational terrorists and criminals. Something that unites these NSAs is that they operate within the state-centric system—even though they are not sovereign, do not have the same kind of power, and generally do not control territory.

Nongovernmental Organizations

NGOs are perhaps the most conspicuous NSAs, often garnering even more attention when they work together. Unlike political parties, NGOs neither have a mandate from government nor seek to share government power. As

---

Figure 6.1 Types of Nonstate Actors

Nongovernmental Organizations (NGOs)
- Voluntary organizations formed by private individuals operating at the local, national, or international level, pursuing common purposes and policy positions
- Examples: Nature Conservancy; Transparency International; Doctors Without Borders

Social Movements and Transnational Advocacy Networks (TANs)
- Linked civil society groups working on behalf of a particular issue or cause
- Examples: Black Lives Matter; International Campaign to Ban Landmines; Cluster Munition Coalition

Epistemic Communities and Think Tanks
- Experts drawn from variety of governmental or nongovernmental bodies, with a dedication to policy-relevant knowledge, research, or advice
- Examples: Intergovernmental Panel on Climate Change; International Institute for Sustainable Development; Chatham House

Foundations
- Not-for-profit organizations funded by individuals, families, or corporations for charitable or community purposes
- Examples: Ford Foundation; Bill and Melinda Gates Foundation; Rockefeller Foundation

Multinational Corporations (MNCs) and Business Associations
- Private firms engaged in for-profit business transactions and operations across national borders
- Examples: Monsanto, Shell, International Chamber of Commerce

Traditional Media and Social Media
- News sources using print, radio, television, internet, etc.
- Examples: New York Times; BBC; Facebook

"Bad" Nonstate Actors
- Examples: terrorist cells, drug dealers, pirate groups

---

defined in Chapter 1, NGOs are voluntary organizations formed by people to achieve a common purpose. However, it is unclear whether that common purpose must be altruistically oriented toward the "public good." UN guidelines suggest that such an orientation is part of the definition of an NGO, but other contexts treat any common purpose as sufficient. The reality is that not every NGO is altruistic or beneficial to the public interest.

NGOs vary in many ways. They may address a broad issue (e.g., the Nature Conservancy's protection of many aspects of the environment) or work on a narrower topic (e.g., the Audubon Society's protection of birds). They may focus on providing information (e.g., Transparency International), delivering services (e.g., Grameen Bank), or advocating for particular causes (e.g., Human Rights Watch). They may be small and local like Tostan, an African NGO that addresses community-level issues related to women and children; or they may be big and global like Oxfam, an international NGO that addresses poverty around the world. Many major NGOs are headquartered in Northern and Western developed countries, funneling vast funds from private donors, governments, and intergovernmental organizations (IGOs) to groups and causes in the Global South.

Whether well-resourced or not, NGOs share an important commonality: unlike states and IGOs, they have no independent international legal personality under traditional international law. They sometimes have been allowed to bring cases in particular adjudicatory settings or enforce international rules. Nevertheless, NGOs remain subject to the laws and rules of the states in which they operate. While states such as Bangladesh and Haiti have a long history of vibrant and largely unrestricted NGO communities, states such as Japan have gradually eased their legal and financial constraints on NGOs over time. Other states, such as China, Egypt, and Russia, continue to regulate NGOs strictly. In fact, NGOs' differing relationships with governments and varying sources of funds sometimes result in organizations that have been initiated by governments or businesses, further blurring the definition of an NGO.

NGOs can work on their own in a single country, but there are multiple ways to link with counterparts across national borders. One is through federations, used by the World Wide Fund for Nature (WWF), Save the Children, and others. With a federation, there are individual country chapters and a main "international" office. The international offices usually disseminate shared goals but vary in how much they try to control or coordinate the chapters; sometimes the chapters become influential in their own right, particularly if they are in powerful countries and do their own lobbying or fundraising (Wong 2012). Oxfam International is an example of an entity that was once a UK NGO but is now a transnational federation with chapters in Belgium, Canada, New Zealand, Spain, the United States, and elsewhere.

Another way for NGOs to link across borders is through coalitions. Coalitions tend to be less hierarchical than federations because they connect organizations beyond an immediate "family." For instance, large and small NGOs work together to deliver short-term emergency relief and long-term development assistance.

Coalitions vary in their level of formality, as demonstrated by two that formed in the 1980s and 1990s around the issue of protecting elephants and banning trade in ivory (Princen 1995). One, loosely composed of animal-rights NGOs such as the Humane Society and Friends of Animals, focused on influencing governmental decisions by raising public awareness through media campaigns. Funding came exclusively from members, and there was no organizational structure dedicated to implementing long-term solutions. This contrasts with a second and much more formalized coalition (further discussed in Chapter 10). Composed of major environmental organizations such as WWF International and the International Union for the Conservation of Nature (IUCN), the second coalition was concerned with not just changing government policies but also enforcing those policies over time through the Trade Records Analysis of Flora and Fauna in Commerce (TRAFFIC) initiative. With many members based in developed countries, this integrated coalition conducted research, worked on the ground in several African countries, educated governments, raised funds from outside the membership, and partnered with the UN Environment Program (UNEP) and the secretariat of the Convention on International Trade in Endangered Species of Wild Fauna and Flora (CITES).

In a few unusual cases, NGOs have taken the place of governments, either by providing services neglected by an inept or corrupt state or by stepping up in a failed state. For instance, Haiti has been dubbed "the republic of NGOs" because with thousands on the ground, it has more NGOs per capita than any other country, and these NGOs are the country's largest provider of basic services such as healthcare and sanitation (Kristoff and Panarelli 2010). For many years, Bangladesh had hosted the largest NGO sector in the world (more than 20,000 by one count), with NGOs assuming traditional governmental functions in agriculture, education, finance, and health. Bangladesh's poverty rate has dropped dramatically since the 1970s, and the government has improved its capacity to resume some of the functions performed by NGOs.

Social Movements and Transnational Advocacy Networks

Compared to NGOs, social movements represent a looser, mass-based association of individuals and groups dedicated to defending or changing the status quo. Social movements can be conservative or progressive, and they may oppose particular issues (e.g., family planning, nuclear weapons, racial discrimination) or promote particular issues (e.g., environmental protection, immigration, women's rights). They may form around major societal cleavages such as class, gender, religion, language, or ethnicity. As constructivists assert, social movements even may help forge new identities or communities among Indigenous peoples, the poor, and others.

The world witnessed the power of social movements in 2020 when millions of people took to the streets as part of the Black Lives Matter movement. This movement had existed for several years on social media and had drawn attention to discrimination, racially motivated violence, and police brutality experienced by people of color. It became even more widely known after a white Minneapolis police officer killed an African American man named George Floyd during an arrest for a minor offense, spurring summer protests in hundreds of cities in the United States and other countries.

Social movements vary enormously in their durability, effectiveness, and the types of formal or informal structures they use to mobilize support

(Tilly 2004). Sometimes social movements are aided by NGOs, which frame issues for the public or help leverage institutions and resources (Smith and Wiest 2012: chap. 5). However, because NGOs are sometimes implicated in helping states or IGOs "tame" social movements by linking them to government-dominated institutions, some actors in social movements are reluctant to work with formal NGOs.

Social movements are related to what are called "transnational advocacy networks" (TANs). TANs are voluntary, reciprocal, horizontal networks of groups that operate across national borders to defend a particular cause or proposition (Keck and Sikkink 1998: 8). NGOs can be prominent operators in TANs, but, as with social movements, TANs do not distill to NGOs alone (Ohanyan 2012: 377–378). Sometimes transnational networks of nonstate actors link with transgovernmental networks of substate actors (e.g., mayors, regional officials, judges, police), with the result that policy coordination sometimes occurs without the direct engagement or even knowledge of the national government (Slaughter 2004).

Formal and informal connections among participating groups are pivotal for TANs, and such networking has been greatly facilitated by advances in communication. The communications revolution—especially the growth of the internet and social media—has connected NSAs to states and to one another. Over time, TANs have forged multilevel links among many different groups. For example, a small local group may provide first-hand details about specific human rights violations or environmental disasters, including stories from people who have been harmed. In response, a large global group may publicize those stories, offer resources or know-how, and push for changes in national or international policies. Such links enhance power, information-sharing, and reach while allowing the linked groups to retain their own character and memberships.

In addition to bringing new information or ideas to policy debates, TANs offer new ways of framing issues to make them more comprehensible and motivating. For example, the International Campaign to Ban Landmines (ICBL) was once a loose transnational network without an address, formal organizational identity, or bank account. Over time, it reframed landmines as less of a disarmament issue and more a humanitarian one, since mines left from past conflicts often maimed civilians and children. By the late 1990s, the ICBL had built support for an international legal convention banning antipersonnel landmines (Thakur and Maley 1999). However, the ICBL's achievement does not mean that TANs always attain their goals or manage to mobilize. Although some issues do take off, others—such as banning killer robots or male infant circumcision—remain latent "lost causes" (Carpenter 2014).

Through the exchange of information, funds, and personnel, TANs can learn from each other. For instance, to conclude the 2008 convention banning cluster munitions, the Cluster Munition Coalition adopted many of the strategies previously used by the ICBL. Learning occurs across issue areas, too. For example, close relationships between groups working on human rights and women's rights led to the mainstreaming of women's rights into the human rights movement. In seeking protection for public spaces, environmentalists also have adopted the language of human rights.

Epistemic Communities and Think Tanks

Experts are another important type of NSA in global governance. Drawn from government agencies, research institutes, private industry, universities, and elsewhere, experts often form so-called epistemic communities: networks of people whose knowledge is critical to understanding, framing, and solving particular problems. These knowledge-based communities have an authoritative claim to policy-relevant knowledge within their domains of expertise. Although they may come from a variety of research disciplines and institutions, they share a set of causal beliefs, normative views, criteria for weighing conflicting evidence, and a commitment to seeking policy solutions (Haas 1992: 3).

Epistemic communities can be found wherever shared knowledge is valuable. Thus, they have been influential in many issues, from intellectual property to pandemic responses to nuclear nonproliferation. Several epistemic communities are discussed in later chapters.

They are particularly common in environmental issues. One long-standing example is the Intergovernmental Panel on Climate Change (IPCC), which periodically produces highly publicized reports synthesizing the latest climate science. Another example involves regional seas. In the 1980s, amid growing concern that the Mediterranean Sea was dying, all eighteen governments in the region worked under UNEP's auspices to negotiate the "Med Plan." A network of ecologists—in UNEP, the Food and Agriculture Organization (FAO), and several states—was crucial for getting governments to meet and agree on how to address the problem. The strongest measures for pollution control were taken in countries where members of this epistemic community wielded the most influence over government agencies (Haas 1990). The Med Plan became a model for arrangements concerning several other regional seas.

Think tanks are cousins of epistemic communities. Similarly dedicated to policy-relevant knowledge, these institutions produce research on domestic and international policy matters. A few go beyond research. The International Peace Institute, for example, has trained military and civilian personnel for peacekeeping roles and produces analyses of peacekeeping-related issues.

Like other NSAs, think tanks come in different forms. They vary in their partisan orientation, some leaning conservative and others more progressive. They also vary in their scope. Some (e.g., the International Institute for Sustainable Development or the Peterson Institute for International Economics) advise on specific issues, and others (e.g., Chatham House or the Brookings Institution) advise on an array of issues. Some think tanks—such as the Carnegie Endowment for International Peace—no longer focus on a single country but have staff in various locations and offer recommendations to multiple governments and IGOs. As with NGOs, many of the best-known think tanks are headquartered in the Global North, even if they work on issues in the Global South.

Foundations

Private foundations are another type of nonstate actor. These are not-for-profit organizations that serve charitable or community purposes and are funded by (and often named for) particular individuals, families, or corporations. In most developed countries, foundations are legal entities that must abide by specific rules to retain their status and privileges.

With a philanthropic tradition and favorable tax provisions, the United States has a long history with foundations. Many stem from influential entrepreneurs and economic sectors, such as Ford (automobiles), Rockefeller (oil), Johnson (pharmaceuticals), Gates (computers), and Bloomberg (media). Chapter 11 discusses the Bill and Melinda Gates Foundation, which has played a crucial role in funding and mobilizing multistakeholder health initiatives.

Some foundations link their charitable activities to the economic sector in which their donors conducted business, but many do not. For example, the Rockefeller Foundation was created by oil profits but has long funded medical and agricultural programs. However, even if the work is not closely related to donors' sources of wealth, questions remain about the wisdom of allowing international policy issues to be shaped by private foundations associated with particular businesses or businesspeople.

Multinational Corporations and Business Associations

Another type of NSAs is multinational corporations (MNCs), which engage in for-profit business transactions and operations across national borders. MNCs exist in various forms. Some (e.g., Monsanto) are privately held; others (e.g., China National Petroleum Corporation) are at least partly under government ownership and control. Government involvement is especially common in politically sensitive sectors, such as energy or defense. Regardless of whether governments are involved, MNCs are an important part of the global economy (discussed in Chapter 8).

Like other NSAs, MNCs sometimes try to amplify their activities through coalitions. Business associations are coalitions that link MNCs, thereby facilitating information sharing, standard setting, and policy influence.

Some business associations focus on a particular theme—membership in the World Business Council for Sustainable Development, for example, is restricted to large companies that commit to sustainable development. Other business associations are much broader. For example, the International Chamber of Commerce has 45 million members in 100 countries, spanning nearly every imaginable sector of the global economy.

MNCs and business associations have long attracted pushback. Accused of corruption, environmental harm, or human rights abuses, MNCs such as Apple, McDonald's, Nike, Shell, Starbucks, Walmart, and others have been pressured to change their practices—sometimes successfully, especially if consumers boycott particular products. In 2010, for instance, Greenpeace publicly shamed the Nestlé Corporation into promising to source palm oil only from suppliers that did not engage in deforestation.

Sometimes MNCs and business associations are viewed more collaboratively. For example, some NGOs have teamed with businesses to devise voluntary codes of conduct, monitoring mechanisms, or certifications for standards such as safe labor practices or sustainable timber harvesting. As noted in Chapter 8, the UN also has pivoted since the late 1990s to viewing MNCs and business associations as potential partners (Gregoratti 2014: 310). First with the 1999 Global Compact, and later with the 2011 Guiding Principles on Business and Human Rights and the 2015 Sustainable Development Goals, the UN has acknowledged that MNCs and business associations can be valuable for carrying out or financing international policies. MNCs have had an especially large influence on how to think about and deliver development. Under the rubric of "corporate social responsibility," corporations have made concessions that would have been inconceivable just a few decades ago.

The Traditional Media and Social Media

The media is also a nonstate actor, albeit one that comes in multiple forms. Besides being publicized through traditional media outlets such as newspapers, magazines, radio, or television, current events can be publicized through newer social media outlets such as websites, blogs, podcasts, smartphone applications, or text messaging. The Arab Spring—the series of antigovernment protests that spread in the Middle East and North Africa between 2010 and 2012—is often mentioned as a turning point. It demonstrated how Facebook, YouTube, Twitter, and other social media platforms could foment revolution and expose governments' vulnerability to people's discontent.

The media's power is not new. Various types of media have long been central in educating citizens, monitoring governments, and solidifying a public sphere (McNair 2005). The media is a two-way conveyor belt that carries transmissions from policy elites to the public and transports public opinion to elites (Baum and Potter 2008). The media is also influential because it shapes which information is worth disseminating, how stories are framed, and the degree to which the public trusts various news sources.

With the advent of social media, the media has undergone massive changes. Political leaders in many countries can easily broadcast their thoughts on social media without going through traditional media outlets or conventional diplomatic vetting. With Facebook and other social media platforms offering stories about current events, ordinary people can more easily find news sources that align with their individual views and identities. Hearing from a variety of voices may protect against unreflective groupthink, but it also may prevent a society from agreeing on even the most basic facts. The ubiquity of the internet, the demise or consolidation of traditional media, and the surge of "citizen journalism" undercuts the standards and credentialization that had been cultivated by professional journalists.

Such a transformation might be beneficial, making the media more egalitarian (Kreps 2020). But it could be harmful, too: rather than being delivered by professionals who strive to triple-check their sources and keep themselves at arm's length from their material, current events are reported and framed by amateurs with a personal stake in the outcome (Adler-Nissen and Eggeling 2022). An international public opinion survey found that many respondents praised social media for giving ordinary people more say in the political process and helping advocacy groups promote their causes, but many also noted that social media could permit manipulation by domestic leaders or election interference by foreign powers (Smith et al. 2019).

The risks are real. As discussed in Chapter 9, there is evidence that military personnel in Myanmar used Facebook to stoke domestic hostility toward the minority Rohingya group, inciting forced migration and assaults (Mozur 2018). Likewise, some sponsored news feeds and ads on Facebook have been traced to Russia-linked groups that used geographic and demographic microtargeting to interfere with the 2016 US presidential election (Kim et al. 2018) and the 2019 EU parliamentary elections (Santariano 2019). Social media outlets have been exploring ways to reduce fake news, misinformation, hate speech, and problematic users, but they remain wary about moderating content or being held legally liable for information that is spread through their platforms.

"Bad" Nonstate Actors

NSAs also include terrorist cells, hacker networks, crime syndicates, drug dealers, pirate groups, human trafficking rings, Dark Web users, paramilitaries, and more. Similar to social movements, some of these NSAs operate in networks, leveraging ties based on family, neighborhood, ethnicity, language, religion, or other factors (Madsen 2014: 401). For instance, the terrorist group al-Qaeda has branches and affiliates in various Muslim countries, from al-Qaeda in Iraq and the Arabian Peninsula to al-Shabaab in

Somalia, Jemaah Islamiyah in Indonesia, Boko Haram in Nigeria, and the Islamic State spinoff.

Similar to MNCs, some "bad" NSAs utilize supply chains, taking advantage of links that are organized, resilient, and replaceable. For example, crime syndicates use joint ventures and subcontracting to produce illicit goods in low-risk areas and sell them in high-income areas. What is trafficked can be shifted: from drugs to humans, from weapons to ivory, and so on.

As communication and transportation have become cheaper and more accessible, "bad" NSAs can more easily distribute their messages and people. After all, some of the Saudi perpetrators of the September 11, 2001 terrorist attacks on the United States were able to obtain visas at the US consulate in Riyadh by posing as tourists, and many human traffickers have found it simpler to enter Western Europe since the 1995 Schengen Agreement largely eliminated border checks among European member-states. States and IGOs struggle to stamp out such decentralized and flexible NSAs, in part because states and IGOs tend to be more hierarchical and rigid.

Multistakeholder Arrangements and "Global Civil Society"

Because the range of NSAs is wide, there is broad recognition that these actors, whatever their particular form, have a stake in international policy-making (Reincke 1999–2000: 47). This recognition plays out in multistakeholder arrangements such as the UN's Sustainable Development Goals (SDGs), discussed in further detail in Chapter 8. In contrast to the earlier Millennium Development Goals, which were largely a creation of people working in the UN Secretariat, the process for developing the SDGs included states, IGOs, and NSAs from the beginning. Multiple stakeholders participated in the negotiations that finalized the seventeen SDGs in 2015 and will continue to participate in implementing and measuring the goals until their conclusion in 2030.

The SDGs and other multistakeholder arrangements point to the importance of civil society: associations and organizations that exist outside of "the state" and "the market." In addition to entities (e.g., labor unions) with a clear interest in public policy, civil society encompasses entities (e.g., sporting associations) whose interest in public policy is less obvious. Civil society links individual citizens (Wapner 1995: 5).

Have individuals and groups connected across borders to a sufficient extent to suggest that civil society is now global? Do people have an associational life beyond their nation-state? Are personal norms and values shared transnationally?

Some observers say yes, arguing that as global governance has become more transparent and inclusive, democratic values have been embraced all around the world, and there is an expanding civil sphere that is separate from the Westphalian state system. Other observers say no, arguing that global governance remains unrepresentative of the world's full population, democratic values are hardly universal, and many nonstate actors amplify rather than challenge state power. Regardless of whether a global civil society actually exists, most observers agree that the numbers of NSAs and their importance have grown tremendously.

The Growth of NSAs

NSAs developed and proliferated during the 1700s and 1800s; since then, they have played important roles in global governance (Johnson forthcoming). According to Tallberg et al. (2013), the explosion in the quantity and activities of nonstate actors is "one of the most profound changes in global governance." It is also the result of increased demand (greater needs of governments and IGOs) and increased supply (greater availability of NSAs).

NSAs in the 1700s and 1800s

The antislavery campaign was an early NSA-initiated effort that organized transnationally to ban a morally unacceptable social and economic practice. Its genesis lay in 1787 and 1788, when societies dedicated to abolition were established in Pennsylvania, England, and France. The history of this campaign, spanning much of the nineteenth century, is examined in Chapter 9. In Europe and the United States, the nineteenth century also witnessed the emergence of peace societies. A group of peace societies convened their first congress in 1849 and developed a plan for what later became the Permanent Court of Arbitration (discussed in Chapter 3). Peace societies collectively supported many of the ideas that emerged from the Hague Conferences, including the commitment to finding noncoercive means for dispute resolution. By the end of the 1800s, there were 425 peace societies in the world (Charnovitz 1997).

In addition, the nineteenth century saw the establishment of transnational labor unions, associations promoting free trade, and groups dedicated to international law. In 1910, NSAs convened the World Congress of International Associations, with 132 groups participating. From this emerged the Union of International Associations (UIA), which has tracked international institutions' demographics and activities ever since, becoming a key source of information about intergovernmental and nongovernmental organizations (UIA 2023). NSAs were also heavily involved in promoting intergovernmental cooperation and regime creation in functional areas such as transportation, workers' rights, species conservation, and sanitation during the latter part of the nineteenth century.

Within the broad set of NSAs, NGOs were beginning to take shape. Among those founded in the nineteenth century was the highly influential International Committee of the Red Cross (ICRC), established in the 1860s by Swiss national Henry Dunant and other individuals concerned with protecting people during war. Dunant engaged in several conferences that explored principles governing care of the wounded, rights of prisoners of war, and neutrality of medical personnel. The 1864 Geneva Convention for the Amelioration of the Condition of the Wounded in Armies in the Field laid the foundation for international humanitarian law, and the ICRC and its national affiliates became neutral intermediaries in war. The ICRC's special and long-standing access to IGOs is discussed later in this chapter.

NSAs in the League of Nations

In the early twentieth century, peace groups such as the League of Nations Society of London and the League to Enforce Peace developed ideas that shaped major IGOs: first the League of Nations and then its successor, the United Nations. The League began operating in 1920, and Article 25 of its Covenant called on member states to encourage the creation of national Red Cross organizations and additional nonstate actors. The League of Nations invited NSAs to participate in meetings such as the 1920 Financial Conference in Brussels, the 1927 World Economic Conference, and the 1932 Disarmament Conference. NSAs were represented on League of Nations committees, such as those dedicated to child welfare or the trafficking of women and children, and their representatives were generally considered full members of League committees, except that only states' representatives could vote.

Despite lacking the right to vote, NSAs often managed to get their proposals incorporated into draft treaties. Many NSAs established offices in Geneva to facilitate contacts with the League (and have remained there, since Geneva is the European headquarters of the UN). In the League's work on minority rights, NSAs were very active, particularly in submitting petitions. In 1920, a cofounder of the UK NGO Save the Children drafted what became the Declaration of the Rights of the Child, which was approved by the League Assembly in 1924.

NSAs' influence diminished between 1930 and 1945 as governments became preoccupied with economic and security crises, and the League itself declined. However, NSAs again became influential in the early 1940s, as the United States and its allies planned for the post–World War II order. Ideas from NSAs shaped the UN Charter, including its opening phrase "We the *peoples* of the United Nations," and representatives from 1,200 voluntary organizations attended the 1945 San Francisco Conference that established the UN.

NSAs in the United Nations

Although the UN's members are states, the organization has long recognized the importance of NSAs—particularly NGOs. Article 71 of the Charter authorized the UN's Economic and Social Council (ECOSOC) to accredit and grant consultative status to international NGOs. Domestic NGOs whose activities touched on international issues could also be accredited by ECOSOC, but the UN member state where the domestic NGO was based had to be consulted first.

By 1948, ECOSOC had accredited more than forty organizations. Many NGOs set up liaison offices not only near the UN's main facilities in New York and Geneva but also near the headquarters of UN specialized agencies, funds, and programs. Such offices enabled informal interactions among NGOs, government officials, and UN staff to share information, promote particular issues or activities, and monitor programs.

Alongside these informal interactions, over the years the UN has altered its rules concerning NGOs. Initially, NGOs were channeled through ECOSOC and its subsidiary bodies, such as the commissions on human rights, the status of women, or population. By the 1960s, a larger number and variety of NGOs were seeking consultative status, and in 1968 ECOSOC adopted Resolution 1296, formalizing several parts of the accreditation process and standards. Beginning in the late 1980s, NGOs gained access to General Assembly committees such as the Second Committee (Economic and Financial) and the Third Committee (Humanitarian and Cultural).

Then in 1996, ECOSOC adopted Resolution 31, which made accreditation easier for domestic NGOs and renamed the types of consultative status. NGOs with "roster" status were the most constrained; when invited by ECOSOC or its subsidiary bodies, they could attend meetings and submit statements related to their area of expertise. NGOs with "special" status were given more access: the right to attend meetings, submit statements, consult with UN staff, and make oral presentations when permitted. NGOs with "general" status were granted the broadest access: besides all of the rights as those with special status, they were allowed to place items on agendas in ECOSOC and related bodies.

The number of NGOs with UN consultative status has skyrocketed. The highest-tier classification remains relatively rare; most of the growth is in the other two tiers. By 2022, more than 6,000 NGOs had been granted roster, special, or general consultative status in the UN.

Beyond ECOSOC, some NGOs have interacted with the UN Security Council and the UN General Assembly. Amnesty International, the Global Policy Forum, EarthAction, the World Council of Churches, and others organized the NGO Working Group on the Security Council to offer private, off-the-record policy input to UN officials and member states (Alger 2002: 100–103). Since 1997, the Security Council has initiated selective consultations with NGOs under the Arria formula (discussed in Chapter 4). NGOs, especially those with expertise on humanitarian crises, have participated in Security Council discussions about the security dimensions of issues such as pandemics or climate change. As of early 2023, six

NGOs—the ICRC, the International Federation of the Red Cross and Red Crescent Societies (IFRC), the Sovereign Military Order of Malta, the Inter-Parliamentary Union, the International Olympic Committee, and the International Chamber of Commerce—had gained special privileges as observers in General Assembly sessions.

Since the 1990s, NGOs also have become central in UN activities related to humanitarian relief and economic development. Besides operating on the ground in crisis-stricken places, they take on planning and policymaking roles as members of the UN's Inter-Agency Standing Committee. Meeting regularly in New York and Geneva, this committee brings together the executive heads of several UN agencies, including the UN Office for the Coordination of Humanitarian Affairs, the FAO, the International Organization for Migration, and the World Health Organization (WHO) with key NGOs (e.g., the ICRC, the IFRC, Save the Children, and World Vision International), plus several NGO coalitions (e.g., InterAction and the International Council of Voluntary Agencies). The committee's task is high-level humanitarian coordination, including setting priorities and allocating resources.

Although much of the UN's early attention focused on NGOs, the system incrementally opened itself to other nonstate actors. The 2004 Cardoso Report, commissioned by UN Secretary-General Kofi Annan, strongly endorsed wider participation by civil society in all aspects of the UN's work, both at headquarters and the country level (Willetts 2006). Through the Conference of Nongovernmental Organizations in Consultative Status with the UN Economic and Social Council, NGOs have continued to lobby for greater participation rights. Some of this lobbying has benefited NSAs more generally by allowing them to participate throughout the policymaking process.

NSAs and UN-Sponsored Conferences

Since the 1970s, UN-sponsored ad hoc and global conferences also have included NSAs, as discussed in Chapter 4. The UN Conference on the Human Environment, held in Stockholm in 1972, set a precedent: nearly 250 NGOs participated in a parallel forum. As shown in Figure 6.2, this model was repeated at subsequent conferences.

These UN-sponsored conferences—on environmental protection, children, development, human rights, women, and other topics—have been catalysts in several respects. They have been forums where states and NSAs discuss issues that governments cannot solve alone. Furthermore, they have allowed NSAs to engage in policy discussions. In addition, through the parallel forums for nonstate actors, the conferences have spurred networking among NSAs.

Each UN conference has adopted its own rules for NSA participation. Whereas the NSAs present in Stockholm in 1972 were permitted to make formal statements without limits, the 1980 Second World Conference on

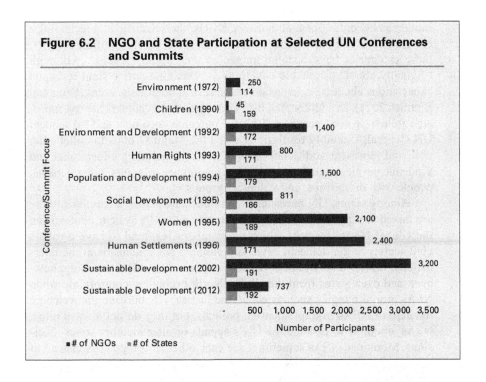

Figure 6.2 NGO and State Participation at Selected UN Conferences and Summits

Women granted only fifteen minutes of total speaking time for NSAs/NGOs. The human rights conference in 1993 excluded NSAs from the official process, largely at the behest of Asian and Arab states. However, for the 1994 Cairo Conference on Population and Development, governments were urged to include NSAs in their delegations; at the Habitat II conference in 1996, representatives of NSAs were allowed to sit with governments and propose amendments to texts. Thus, NSA participation has varied dramatically across conferences.

It is an open question whether NSAs' participation in UN-sponsored conferences eventually translates into greater access to the UN system and beyond. One study, which examined fifty IGOs between 1950–2010, found no clear causal link between conference participation and access to IGOs (Tallberg et al. 2013: 241). With states' more recent pushback against enormous UN conferences (discussed in Chapter 4), the opportunities to participate in conferences are rarer and sometimes more restrictive, possibly undermining greater NSA access to IGOs.

An innovation from the 1992 UN Conference on Environment and Development has persisted. Agenda 21, one of the conference's outcome documents, formally stated that international policymaking ought to include nine parts of society: business and industry, children and youth, farmers,

Indigenous peoples, local authorities, NGOs, the scientific and technological community, women, and workers and trade unions. Within the UN, these categories have become known as the "Major Groups." Although originally about sustainable development, this nine-part system reshaped expectations about NSA inclusion and access in other issue areas (Sénit and Bierman 2021). In addition, the list of recognized stakeholders has expanded. At a follow-up conference in 2012, the outcome document and subsequent UN General Assembly resolutions urged the Major Groups to collaborate with and represent additional parts of society, including educational and academic entities, foundations, local communities, migrants, older persons, people with disabilities, and volunteer groups.

Among states, UN bureaucrats, and nonstate actors themselves, there are mixed feelings about NSA involvement in the UN system. States from the Global North, most of which are democracies, tend to have a robust civil society at the domestic level and promote NSA inclusion at the international level. States from the Global South can find this threatening, however, and even states from the Global North become uncomfortable when NSAs promote topics such as economic justice. UN bureaucrats welcome the help of NSAs in implementing policies, but they do not always relish NSAs' attempts to reshape the UN's agenda or alter member states' decisions. Moreover, NSAs sometimes see each other as competitors instead of allies, especially as the UN continues to open to NSAs that are more geographically and ideologically diverse (McKeon 2009).

Why NSAs Are in Greater Supply and Greater Demand

Growth in NSAs has been especially high in some time periods, such as the end of World War II in the 1940s and the end of the Cold War in the 1990s. Growth has been especially high in particular issue areas, such as human rights and the environment. The increased number and diversity of NSAs is driven not only by supply-side factors that aid the creation or operation of NSAs, but also by demand-side factors that make the nature or activities of NSAs more attractive.

One supply-side factor is the revolution in communication and transportation. From telegraphs to phones to the internet, enhanced communication helps NSAs form connections not bound to location. This makes it easier to attract staff, donors, and partners; improve services for members; disseminate information to the outside world; shape public perceptions; and increase political engagement. At the same time, revolutions in transportation—not just physical infrastructure such as highways or airports but also logistical considerations such as waiving visa requirements for some short-term stays—have enabled face-to-face gatherings with allies, funders, and policymakers from around the world. Cheaper, faster, more reliable, and more accessible transportation also facilitates the creation and operation of NSAs.

On the demand side, an important factor is some states' withdrawal from providing schools, clinics, and other services. Such withdrawal happens for several reasons. Governments suffering from low capacity or corruption may neglect some services. Even high-capacity states occasionally reduce their domestic or international activities, perhaps because of changes in leadership, ideology, priorities, or even "hegemonic fatigue." The result is greater demand for NSAs. With their ability to represent various interests, collect on-the-ground information, and target resources, NSAs can fill gaps left by states.

Some forces affect both demand and supply. One example is European integration. The organs charged with various aspects of European integration value the assistance and legitimation that come from NSAs, and they have facilitated the creation and operation of NSAs. Already in the 1950s, the European Community's Economic and Social Committee sought input from businesses, workers, and other NSAs. Over time, the European Commission and Parliament also encouraged NSA expertise, buy-in, and the legitimacy their participation provides. In addition to affording various formal and informal routes for NSAs to participate in the policymaking process, the EU offers grants and other resources to NSAs.

The end of the Cold War in 1991 had an enormous effect on supply and demand for NSAs. The spread of democratic political systems and norms in the 1990s empowered individuals to be more socially and politically active (Heins 2008: 44–45). At the same time, the dismantling of barriers between East and West led to newly independent states and the creation of additional IGOs (Reimann 2006: 48). These changes made NSAs more in demand and easier to supply. In addition, globalization has intensified states' interdependence, further limiting their ability to pursue policymaking without NSAs.

NSAs and Policymaking

The numerous activities in which NSAs engage can be sorted by three major stages in the policymaking process: agenda-setting, decisionmaking, and implementation. Agenda-setting establishes which issues will be discussed and how they are framed. Decisionmaking determines whether and how concrete actions will be taken. Implementation puts decisions into practice and evaluates whether things work as intended. As depicted in Figure 6.3, the three stages are linear but also cyclical. Actors proceed from agenda-setting to decisionmaking to implementation, and implementation then feeds back into agenda-setting for future policymaking.

Agenda-Setting, Decisionmaking, and Implementation

To see the roles NSAs can play at each stage, consider efforts to control tobacco use. By the 1990s, the tobacco market had shifted: increased

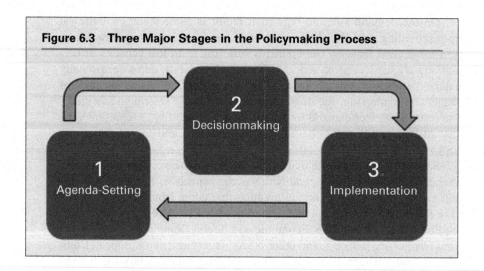

Figure 6.3 Three Major Stages in the Policymaking Process

government regulations and legal battles in developed countries had depressed sales and pushed tobacco companies to consolidate and refocus their marketing on developing countries, where regulations were looser. Just four tobacco companies accounted for 70 percent of cigarettes sold around the world, and the number of smokers in developing countries came to surpass the number in developed countries.

This set off a battle for agenda-setting, with different NSAs taking different sides. Antitobacco researchers, NGOs, and others urged national governments and the WHO to regulate tobacco through a binding international treaty (Roemer, Taylor, and Lariviere 2005). Tobacco companies pushed back, arguing that a treaty would defy World Trade Organization (WTO) rules and the Global South should not have to abide by regulations from the Global North. Despite the pushback, the agenda was set when the new WHO director-general—Dr. Gro Harlem Brundtland—announced in 1998 that tobacco regulation was a priority of the WHO.

The next stage was decisionmaking, in which NSAs representing various societal groups (e.g., researchers, farmers) lobbied the member states that would vote in WHO meetings. Protreaty NSAs emphasized tobacco's addictiveness and links to various health problems; antitreaty NSAs emphasized tobacco's importance for jobs, free trade, and consumer choice. After several years of deliberation, in 2003 WHO member states approved the Framework Convention on Tobacco Control, a binding treaty.

Then came the implementation stage. Almost two years passed before enough governments had ratified the treaty to bring it into force. Even then, there were holdouts, such as the United States, with its concentration of tobacco farmers and companies opposing international regulations. Numerous states that ratified the treaty did not comply with it, according to NGOs and other NSAs who monitored implementation.

The treaty's partial implementation fed into a new round of agenda-setting, decisionmaking, and implementation. In 2002, an amendment to the WHO's constitution formalized NSAs' rights and responsibilities within the organization. NSAs supporting stricter regulations helped craft a supplementary Protocol to Eliminate Illicit Trade in Tobacco Products, which entered into force in 2018.

In addition to illustrating how the policymaking process can be simultaneously linear and cyclical, the tobacco example emphasizes that nonstate actors play less central roles in IGO decisionmaking than in agenda-setting or implementation (Steffek 2013) since voting is generally reserved for states (Tallberg et al. 2013).

NSAs' Different Goals and Approaches

Whether, where, and how NSAs engage in the policymaking process can depend on their goals and approaches. A traditional way to categorize NSA aims is by distinguishing between those that focus on service (e.g., emergency food, mobile health clinics, patrollers to prevent poaching) and advocacy (e.g., high-yield agriculture, vaccination of children, restrictions on trade in endangered species). Service NSAs are particularly active at the stage of implementation. Advocacy NSAs, which aim to alleviate problems that are systemic, are more active in the earlier stage of agenda-setting.

Different goals also call for different kinds of resources. Service NSAs benefit from resources such as strong donor bases, the flexibility to shift staff rapidly among crisis locations, or grassroots links that enable operations in remote regions. Meanwhile, advocacy NSAs benefit from resources such as credible data, funds to maintain a presence in national capitals or other key spots, or publicists that can reach laypeople and elites.

Over time, the service/advocacy distinction has broken down, however. Service groups recognized that many of the immediate problems they worked to alleviate would recur unless systemic problems were also addressed. And, as service groups operated "on the ground," they gained valuable insights into broader or deeper problems that fed into advocacy. Today, many relief organizations—including CARE, Catholic Relief Services, Doctors Without Borders, Oxfam, Save the Children, and World Vision—blend service and advocacy activities.

As the advocacy aim has grown, NSAs have adopted pressure group tactics that can be broadly sorted into "insider" or "outsider" approaches (Dellmuth and Bloodgood 2019). An insider approach aspires to participate in all three policymaking stages; an outsider approach tries to redirect or even derail a policymaking process that is perceived to be so wrongheaded or illegitimate that it would corrupt NSAs if they worked within any of its stages (Smith et al. 2018). An insider approach facilitates the process by offering resources such as information or personnel, whereas an outsider approach hinders the process by mounting disruptive activities such as street protests or media campaigns.

Tensions between the approaches make it difficult for a single NSA to employ both. An NSA that objects to the policymaking process is unlikely to operate smoothly within it. Conversely, an NSA that has cultivated access to the policymaking process is unlikely to call for its overhaul (Stroup and Wong 2017).

Variations in NSA Access to IGOs

Since the mid-1980s, many NSAs and some states have pressured IGOs to grant greater access to nonstate actors, arguing that NSAs could carry out tasks for IGOs, mitigate public opposition that threatens IGOs' authority or legitimacy, and embody the norm of participatory democracy (Tallberg et al. 2013: 22, 139). Some IGOs have established practices of consultation or participation, but others have done relatively little to involve NSAs. Why does this checkered pattern exist? The pattern has been particularly mixed across the various UN specialized agencies.

Policy areas are one explanation. NSA access tends to be greater in IGOs dealing with human rights or the environment, compared with IGOs dealing with finance or security (Tallberg et al. 2013). Access has been particularly forthcoming in humanitarian IGOs thanks to the unique role of the International Committee of the Red Cross. Through the 1949 Geneva Conventions and related agreements, states made the ICRC a "controlling authority" with a mandate to protect refugees, wounded soldiers, prisoners, and other victims of armed conflict. The ICRC is known for neutrality, independence, and aiding people on all sides. For example, after Russian troops entered Ukraine in 2022, the ICRC intensified its presence there; sent teams to neighboring countries such as Moldova, Poland, and Russia; engaged in confidential dialogue with all sides of the conflict; and provided water, medicine, and other assistance to displaced people. As discussed in Chapter 4, the ICRC's long-standing reputation has justified its observer status with the UN General Assembly and its informal consultations with Security Council members. Beyond the ICRC, many other NSAs operate alongside IGOs to address humanitarian issues (Barnett 2011).

Access varies not only across but also within policy areas, as IGOs in similar policy areas react differently to NSAs. Consider the Bretton Woods institutions, discussed in Chapters 3 and 8. All three of the original institutions—the International Monetary Fund (IMF), the General Agreement on Tariffs and Trade (GATT), and the World Bank—work on economic policy. Initially there were no formal provisions for NSA access to any of these institutions. Over time, the three have diverged.

The IMF has been particularly slow to provide formal access for many NSAs. Starting in the 1990s, under intense pressure during debt crises, the IMF adopted the practice of inviting civil society groups to semi-annual forums at its Washington, DC, headquarters. Nevertheless, the IMF is widely considered a laggard in NSA access, partly because its work involves expertise that relatively few NSAs have, and states are wary about monetary policies impinging on sovereignty.

A second Bretton Woods institution, the GATT, spent decades mired in a "culture of secrecy" surrounding states' trade negotiations. However, the 1994 agreement that merged the GATT into the new World Trade Organization allowed dispute settlement panels to speak with experts and also empowered the WTO General Council to engage with other NSAs concerned with trade policy. The WTO Secretariat, which has primary responsibility for relations with NSAs, holds regular briefings and circulates most documents without restrictions. Governments and Secretariat staff continue to be ambivalent about guaranteeing a greater role for NSAs, however, and the WTO has not granted NSAs any form of consultative status. The lawlessness surrounding the WTO meeting in Seattle in 1999—when labor unions, environmental groups, and other NSAs physically blocked and confronted government officials trying to reach the meeting venue—has not been forgotten. Moreover, because some of the most vocal NSAs question liberal economic theory, greater access could fuel antiglobalization forces and amplify demands for radical changes in institutional structures, policies, and programs (Murphy 2010).

The third Bretton Woods institution, the World Bank, has become much more open than the WTO or the IMF to NSA participation, partly because development policy is not generally as technical or secretive as finance or trade. In response to NSAs' demands for a women-in-development agenda and a procedure for assessing the environmental impact of prospective projects, the World Bank established an advisory post on women in 1977 and an environment department in 1987. NSAs' desire for more information and inroads was further helped when the organization agreed to increase public access to its documents through a Bank Information Center created by NGOs. Like the UN Development Programme and other IGOs working on development policy, the World Bank has increasingly embraced the importance of local knowledge and participatory democracy, seeing NSAs as entities that enhance on-the-ground effectiveness and organizational legitimacy. Regional development banks have tended to follow the World Bank's lead.

Proponents of NSA access emphasize how NSAs and IGOs can help one another (Lall 2023). For example, researchers draw attention to "orchestration," a process in which IGO staff mobilize and partner with NSAs to achieve IGOs' international regulatory goals (Abbott et al. 2015; Andonova 2017). Similarly, researchers highlight human rights "boomerangs," whereby NSAs bypass the national government in a rights-violating state in which they operate and link to IGOs that can pressure that state to change its ways (Keck and Sikkink 1998).

NSA access can be a double-edged sword, however, since NSA–IGO relationships are not guaranteed to be cooperative. Cooperative relationships occur when NSAs and IGOs with shared values and different resource pools engage in a common effort toward a broad goal (Johnson 2014). But relationships also can be marked by co-optation (in which one actor overwhelms the other), competition (in which the actors rival each other), or conflict (in which the actors oppose one another) (Johnson 2016). For example, the Food and Agriculture Organization opened to many NSAs in the 1960s, when charitable foundations and MNCs were eager to help it convince hunger-plagued developing countries to adopt chemical pesticides, high-yield seeds, and other agricultural technologies. But the FAO came to regret its openness to NSAs in later decades, as environmental NGOs and scientific experts pushed the organization to stop promoting agriculture at the expense of nature.

Observing how some IGOs have struggled since opening to NSAs, member states and IGO staff have become wary about exposing their organizations to such difficulties. Thus, NSA access in IGOs continues to vary. Calls for greater access have not stopped, however, as NGOs and other NSAs continue to claim they are uniquely equipped to represent the public interest.

Issues with NSAs

NSAs' access in global governance raises several issues. Compared with states or IGOs, are NSAs better suited to pursue the interests of the public? Do NSAs actually "democratize" global governance? How can the impact of NSAs be distinguished from the effect of other factors? Are NSAs tools of powerful states or threats to them?

Serving the Public Interest, Playing Politics, or Doing Harm?

Some early researchers of NSAs, focusing on NGOs in particular, highlighted NGO activities like defending human rights, fighting disease, delivering humanitarian relief, or protecting the environment. Unlike states, many NGOs do not favor any particular ethnic group, socioeconomic class, or nationality. Unlike IGOs, many NGOs are willing to work in nearly any country, even those that influential states have deemed a "pariah" or placed under punitive sanctions. Moreover, many NGO personnel are volunteers or accept below-market pay. Thus, early research depicted NGOs and other NSAs as generally altruistic and concerned with the public interest (Keck and Sikkink 1998: 1; Clark 2001; Forsythe 2005).

Subsequent research has disputed this optimistic view, arguing that NGOs and other NSAs behave much like any political actor. They come in many forms but can be self-appointed, hierarchical, concerned with their own survival or reputation, and focused on advancing their own agendas (Heins 2008: 41). MNCs and the media are relatively easy to see as conventional political players, but even NGOs fit this description. Service NGOs seek subcontracting positions in humanitarian or development projects—a major source of their financial support—and in scrambling to win short-term contracts they may cut corners or exaggerate their accomplishments, thereby jeopardizing long-term project viability and normative goals (Cooley and Ron 2002). Advocacy NGOs seek attention for their particular policy area even at the expense of other worthwhile policy areas (Bob 2005). To attract and satisfy donors, NGOs market themselves aggressively and choose their activities carefully. In short, all types of nonstate actors play politics.

Sometimes NSAs also do harm, as MNCs pursue quarterly profits, private foundations cater to their billionaire benefactors, media outlets look for sensational headlines, epistemic communities fall prey to groupthink, and social movements fixate on one problem among many. A particularly tragic example comes from Rwanda, where Doctors Without Borders and other NGOs ran UN refugee camps that became incubators for mass killings after perpetrators of the 1994 Rwandan genocide used the camps as havens (Uvin 1998) and even diverted some camp resources to finance further bloodshed (Terry 2002: 2). The International Rescue Committee and the French chapter of Doctors Without Borders withdrew their aid, cutting off resources for perpetrators and ordinary refugees alike. Other NGOs, including other chapters of Doctors Without Borders, continued serving the camps and accepted the risk that they would help both the guilty and the innocent. Neither response avoided harm.

Some NSAs may cause harm intentionally. After all, NSAs include terrorist cells, hacker networks, crime syndicates, drug dealers, pirate groups, human trafficking rings, Dark Web users, paramilitaries, and more. Instead of assuming that all NSAs serve the public interest, it is best to acknowledge that actors in this broad category sometimes do so, but they also may play politics or even do harm.

Democratizing Global Governance?

Proponents have argued that NSAs "democratize" global governance by increasing transparency, representativeness, and accountability. Transparency means open information and communication; representativeness means standing in for groups of people who do not participate in global governance directly; accountability means being known by and answerable to the people for whom they speak. For all three, the record for NSAs is mixed.

Many nonstate actors—particularly transnational advocacy networks, epistemic communities, and the media—demand transparency, publicizing information that states and IGOs would be inclined to keep to themselves. Not all NSAs are inclined or forced to reveal much about their own internal workings, however, and not all have the resources to devote to such transparency. For many NSAs, relatively little is known about their personnel, operations, funding, expenditures, or relationships.

Besides transparency, another dimension of democratization is representativeness. For elected national governments in democratic states, being representative of citizens is a key part of their claim to legitimacy. Yet there are no analogous elections for NGOs, social movements and TANs, epistemic communities, foundations, MNCs, the media, or transnational terrorists or criminals (Gourevitch and Lake 2012). An alternative path to representativeness is not to have any single group speak for everyone, but to keep barriers low so that many different groups can participate and speak for various stakeholders. Yet often, the barriers to participating in global governance are not low, so voices that are marginalized in society overall are also likely to be marginalized in global governance.

Historically, NSAs from the Global North have been disproportionately active in global governance, either crowding out voices from the Global South or claiming to speak for them. This has subsided as NSAs proliferated in developing countries, northern NSAs learned to treat them more like equals, and IGOs dedicated more space for traditionally marginalized people. Nevertheless, the imbalance has not vanished. For instance, a study of the UN's Major Groups system in the SDGs deliberations found continued marginalization of the world's most impoverished people. Few of the nine officially recognized groups had genuine connections to this "bottom billion" through procedures, discourse, or geographic origins (Sénit and Bierman 2021). The most marginalized people can be hard to reach and represent because they often live in remote areas, lack transportation or communication links, and do not speak one of the UN's official languages.

Transparency and representativeness feed into NSAs' accountability. Without the legitimacy that accompanies accountability, NSAs do little to mitigate global governance's democratic deficit. They often serve narrow mandates and constituencies, and their leaders generally enjoy substantial discretion in deciding which policies to pursue and how. They do not usually face trade-offs among issues in the same ways that states do, and this is what gives them freedom to campaign against landmines, publicize the latest climate science, emphasize vaccines for children, or operate supply chains in volatile areas.

For several years, the organization One World Trust published annual reports comparing accountability in IGOs, NGOs, and MNCs. Generally, these reports found IGOs to be more accountable and transparent than

NGOs, while NGOs were more representative than MNCs and IGOs. Specific entities sometimes defied the dominant trends. However, if nonstate actors must be transparent, representative, and accountable to erase the democratic deficit, then global governance does not seem to have overcome this problem yet. Thus far, little ensures NSAs' transparency, representativeness, or accountability except their own integrity or the knowledge that missteps could be costly.

Impact on Global Governance?

Nonstate actors lack the power typically associated with states. They have neither the spending power nor the coercive power of governments, which can print money and raise armies. Instead, NSAs must rely on soft power and the willingness of governments and international bureaucracies to let them operate. Given these limitations, it is natural to wonder which NSAs have the biggest impact on global governance—and how.

This is difficult to gauge for at least five reasons. First, nonstate actors are numerous and diverse; even within subtypes, NSAs are far from identical. A second difficulty is evaluating NSA impact in a way that is feasible and generalizable. Reducing the scope of inquiry makes it easier to trace and measure NSA impact but harder to say whether the findings would hold in other situations. For example, one analytical framework focuses on treaty negotiations spearheaded by the UN Environment Programme and looks for evidence that NGOs altered the items on the agenda, persuaded governments to change their votes, or drafted passages in the final text (Betsill and Corell 2008). Such a targeted study sheds light on the influence of a particular kind of NSA in a particular type of situation, but it does not say much about the impact of NSAs more generally.

A third difficulty arises in discerning whether influence at one point in time resulted in meaningful change in the long run. If NSAs shaped a treaty, but the treaty did not change states' behavior, then perhaps NSAs did not really have much impact. This is tricky to untangle because researchers must compare the long-term result to the counterfactual question: what would the situation have looked like if the NSAs had not been involved? To substantiate a beneficial effect, researchers would need to spot outcomes that would have happened anyway but would have been "more bad" or "less good." Even more difficult, they would need to spot tragedies that would have happened but ultimately did not.

The importance of counterfactuals points to a fourth difficulty: acknowledging that NSAs can have negative or opposing effects. If NSAs had not intervened, perhaps the outcome would have been better. For instance, humanitarian NGOs have sometimes been accused of paternalistic behavior that disregards local culture, ignores public opinion, and cultivates dependency instead of self-sufficiency (Barnett 2011). Alternatively, perhaps NSAs were on both sides of a particular issue, countering each other and producing a less ambitious outcome—a phenomenon that in US domestic politics is referred to as countervailing pressures. The example of fossil fuels such as oil and coal, whose carbon emissions are implicated in climate change, is illustrative. Climate scientists argue that climate change mitigation hinges on a massive shift away from fossil fuels, but businesses that are reliant on oil and coal have resisted this shift. With NSAs on both sides of this issue, movement away from fossil fuels has been slow. Even if NSAs work on the same side to bring about a particular policy, they may follow a problematic process that reflects and reinforces existing inequalities and power disparities (Dany 2014: 425, 433).

A final difficulty is that the impact of NSAs is affected by contextual factors, such as outside events or the behavior of other actors. For instance, states have tended to sideline NSAs during inter-state conflicts but give them more leeway in times of peace. This hints at the cyclical and time-dependent nature of demand (the needs of governments and IGOs) and supply (the availability and capabilities of NSAs) (Charnovitz 1997: 268–270). Thus, the full impact of NSAs cannot be understood without data and analysis at three levels: the internal traits of an NSA, the interactions between an NSA and other actors, and the overall institutional environment that defines the boundaries of NSA action (Heiss and Johnson 2016). NSAs might have an impact only at particular times or under specific conditions, and changes in policy or behavior may be explained by factors other than NSAs.

All five difficulties—the number and diversity of NSAs, the trade-off between feasible and generalizable studies, the differences in time horizons, the possibility of negative or opposing effects, and the interference of other factors—make it difficult to assess NSAs' impact. It is challenging to pinpoint the effect of even one NSA, let alone generalize about the entire category. Nonstate actors do wield some power and authority in global governance, but states continue to guard their sovereignty and remain pivotal.

Threats to State Sovereignty?

States and NSAs have different roles and strengths in global governance, but only states can claim sovereignty—that is, ultimate authority over territory, people, and decisionmaking. International relations theorists disagree about whether NSAs are merely tools of states or actual threats to state sovereignty.

To many realists, NSAs are epiphenomenal: they exist because powerful states find them useful (or at least harmless), and hence they are no threat to sovereignty and actually may make it more resilient (Heins 2008: 102–104). In contrast, scholars from both the constructivist and liberal camps have suggested that state sovereignty is contested, compromised, or even usurped by the growth of global civil society. NSAs are important sources and transmitters of norms and ideas that can shape or redefine states' interests and abilities (Keck and Sikkink 1998: 212). In this view, the erosion of sovereignty is not yet widespread, but the line between what is international and domestic has blurred.

Realists, liberals, and constructivists all acknowledge that NSAs face constraints. The more that they operate through full-fledged organizations, the more they encounter well-known organizational limitations. Many NGOs start as loose structures run by volunteers, but over time they may morph into more bureaucratized entities with standardized procedures, annual reports, budgets, and highly specialized staff. This bureaucratization can address demands from donors or the public for predictability and professionalism, but it can also undermine flexibility and responsiveness, impede risk-taking, prompt NGO personnel to conceal failures, and encourage rent-seeking.

Another constraint involves funding. Unlike states, NSAs have no ability to fund their activities by collecting taxes. They may be able to raise funds through donations, membership dues, or fees for services, but the people who contribute are unlikely to be a very large or representative sample of the public. Therefore, NSAs may become reliant on a few major private funders whose resources come with strings attached. Alternatively, NSAs may end up being funded in various ways by states. In some cases, states offer favorable tax treatment that incentivizes private donations and reduces the taxes owed by NSAs on the money they raise. In other cases, states fund NSAs more directly, such as by contracting for services. Whether funding comes from private or public sources, the danger is the same: NSAs risk compromising their identities, their independence, and their ability to "bite the hands that feed them" (Spiro 1996: 966).

Even if NSAs avoid financial reliance on states, all are somewhat logistically reliant on states. Governments can make it very difficult for NSAs to operate within their borders or internationally. Egypt and Russia have used stringent domestic registration and reporting requirements to drive out foreign NGOs, foundations, and media (Heiss and Kelley 2017). States have also resisted greater NSA participation in international forums such as the UN—with China, South Africa, India, Cuba, and Russia proving particularly adept at stalling NGO applications for consultative status with ECOSOC (Inboden 2021). Some governments see nonstate actors as both a challenge to their authority and a form of neocolonialism (Bush 2016).

Wariness about NSAs is not unique to authoritarian governments or the Global South. Many states block foreign corporations from investing in sensitive industries, such as energy, telecommunications, or biotechnology. Because NSAs operate in multilevel games in which they need to consider individual countries and the wider international context, their operations can come to a standstill if governments oppose them actively or even passively (e.g., by failing to ensure their physical safety). In short, NSAs depend on states' help or at least acquiescence to get access to domestic and international arenas.

A final constraint comes from the number and diversity of NSAs. Their variety means they have no single agenda. They may prioritize different issues. Alternatively, they may prioritize the same issue but demand different solutions and compete for influence, instead of working cohesively.

In short, NSAs do not always pose a significant and concerted threat to state sovereignty (Friedman, Hochstetler, and Clark 2005: 130). Nonetheless, they are important players in global governance. Next we turn to governance of peace and security—an issue area where states retain primary authority, but nonstate actors have long been active working on behalf of peace while also posing threats to peace and security (as in the case of NSAs such as terrorist groups).

Suggested Further Reading

Abbott, Kenneth, Philipp Genschel, Duncan Snidal, and Bernhard Zangl. (2015) *International Organizations as Orchestrators*. New York: Cambridge University Press.

Andonova, Liliana. (2017) *Governance Entrepreneurs: International Organizations and the Rise of Global Public-Private Partnerships*. London: Cambridge University Press.

Johnson, Tana. (2016) "Cooperation, Co-optation, Competition, Conflict: International Bureaucracies and Non-Governmental Organizations in an Interdependent World." *Review of International Political Economy* 23(5): 737–767.

Keck, Margaret E., and Kathryn Sikkink. (1998) *Activists beyond Borders: Advocacy Networks in International Politics*. Ithaca, NY: Cornell University Press.

Stroup, Sarah, and Wendy Wong. (2017) *The Authority Trap: Strategic Choices of International NGOs*. Ithaca, NY: Cornell University Press.

Tallberg, Jonas, Thomas Sommerer, Theresa Squatrito, and Christer Jönsson. (2013) *The Opening Up of International Organizations: Transnational Access in Global Governance*. London: Cambridge University Press.

7

Seeking Peace and Security

Case Study: Somalia, the Continuing Challenge

At the beginning of the 1990s as the Cold War ended and today, more than thirty years later, Somalia—a key country in the Horn of Africa—has been emblematic of some of the major challenges in international peace and security governance. In 1991 and 1992, civil order in Somalia collapsed as warring clans seized control of different parts of the country. Widespread famine and chaos accompanied the fighting, forcing hundreds of thousands of civilians to the brink of starvation. Food was a vital political resource for the Somali warlords and a currency for paying the mercenary gangs who formed their militias. In November 1992, with as many as a thousand Somalis dying every day and three-fourths of the country's children under the age of five already dead, UN Secretary-General Boutros Boutros-Ghali informed the Security Council that the situation "had deteriorated beyond the point at which it is susceptible to the peacekeeping treatment. . . . The Security Council now has no alternative but to decide to adopt more forceful measures" (UN 1992: 2).

Although Somalia has finally made some gains in establishing a national government and functioning economy, an African Union (AU) peacekeeping force from six African countries is still deployed there; conflict and drought-induced famine remain a threat; more than a million Somalis are displaced within the country and almost a million are refugees in neighboring Uganda and Kenya. In addition, the al-Qaeda–linked Islamist group al-Shabaab is active in the country. As of early 2023, it controlled large sections of territory in central and southern

(continued)

Somalia; has carried out bombings and raids in neighboring Uganda and Kenya and mounted an incursion into Ethiopia in 2022; and is considered a threat to the United States because of its success in recruiting Somali Americans and its potential for turning Somalia into a refuge for terrorist groups. Somalia therefore offers an excellent case study of contemporary threats to international peace and security and the governance dilemmas posed by the changing nature of armed conflicts, state failure, complex humanitarian crises, internationally linked terrorist groups, and the links between nonstate actors and criminal activities.

When order collapsed in Somalia in 1992 and famine became widespread, the United Nations was initially slow to react because the Security Council assumed that it needed the consent of the Somali warlords to provide humanitarian assistance, as for traditional UN peacekeeping operations. A contingent of 500 lightly armed Pakistani peacekeeping troops, deployed in August 1992 as the UN Operation in Somalia (UNOSOM I) with a mandate to protect relief workers, proved totally inadequate for the task at hand.

In December 1992, the Security Council (Resolution 794) authorized a large US-led military and humanitarian intervention—the Unified Task Force on Somalia (UNITAF), known to the US public as Operation Restore Hope. Its goal was to secure ports and airfields, protect relief shipments and workers, and assist humanitarian relief efforts. There were disagreements with UN officials over objectives, however, which complicated relations between the US and UN contingents in Somalia.

Although the US-led effort largely achieved its humanitarian objectives of supplying food to those in need and imposing a de facto cease-fire in areas of its deployment, the larger tasks of peacemaking in Somalia remained unfulfilled. In 1993, UNITAF was replaced by a smaller UN force (UNOSOM II), which gave up any pretense of impartiality in dealing with the Somali clans. As a result, the UN's role shifted from neutral peacekeeper to active belligerent, and remaining US troops were targeted as well, leading to public outcry after the body of one soldier was dragged through the streets of Mogadishu. President Bill Clinton announced that the US contingent would be strengthened temporarily, then withdrawn by March 1994.

After the United States withdrew its troops, it was only a matter of time before all UN forces were withdrawn. UN operations in Somalia succeeded in ending the famine but not in helping the Somalis reestablish a national government or end their internal strife.

In the late 1990s, there were several largely unsuccessful regional efforts to help the Somali warlords and clans negotiate an end to fighting and set up a transitional government.

(continued)

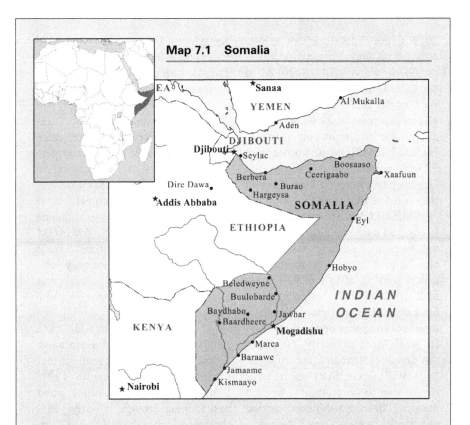

Map 7.1   Somalia

Within Somalia, however, northern clans declared independence as the Republic of Somaliland, and leaders in the northeast formed the self-governing Puntland State (neither has been internationally recognized). The Islamic Courts Union became increasingly active, seeking to establish an Islamic state in Somalia and, after the September 11, 2001, attacks on the United States, Somalia seemed like a possible haven for international terrorists. In 2006, heavy fighting between the Islamic Courts Union and clan militias supporting the transitional government broke out and triggered new humanitarian and security crises, including large-scale famine and more than a million people displaced.

In 2007, the UN Security Council authorized an AU peacekeeping operation (the AU Mission in Somalia, AMISOM) to protect the transitional government, plus logistical support, a UN support office, and an EU training mission to rebuild a Somali national army. The AMISOM forces, along with newly trained Somali forces, were able to greatly expand control of much of the country by

(continued)

2012; a new federal parliament was established, and elections for a new president were held in 2012. In early 2013, the UN political mission for Somalia relocated to Mogadishu after seventeen years in Nairobi—a measure of improved security. By 2017, AMISOM had more than 22,000 personnel, making it the largest peacekeeping operation in the world at that time.

AMISOM has had mixed results. It enjoyed early success in protecting Somalia's nascent government and helping expand humanitarian access and relief to many Somalis in 2010–2011. But those successes have been "limited by serious structural, political, and operational challenges." Most critically, "it could not defeat al-Shabab," according to Paul Williams (2018) as it "was rarely able to function as a unified mission." Indeed, al-Shabaab carried out attacks in Kenya and Ethiopia in 2013, 2014, 2015, and 2022 and was believed to be responsible for truck bombings in Mogadishu in 2017, 2019, and 2022.

Thus, AMISOM has faced problems similar to those of other contemporary peace enforcement missions, particularly in Africa. These included the absence of a functional central government and a peace process; a gap between capabilities, resources, and mandated tasks; and the challenges of partnering with multiple IGOs and states some of whom were training a Somali national army (e.g., United States, United Kingdom, EU, Turkey). It also was combating transnational armed groups with ties to the local population (Williams 2018, 2019).

AMISOM ended officially in 2022, transitioning to the AU Transition Mission in Somalia with much the same mandate but reduced personnel. For the AU, according to Williams (2019: 1), AMISOM has been its "longest, largest, most expensive, and deadliest peace operation. For the UN, AMISOM remains the organization's most profound experiment not only with providing logistical support in a war zone but also in partnering on the political front."

At the end of 2022, in addition to persistent insecurity and violence, Somalia faced the same threat that characterized the crisis in 1991: famine. A combination of the worst and longest drought in forty years threatened what the UN called "catastrophic" levels of food insecurity affecting 7.8 million people—almost half the population (UN News 2022). Climate change is a major factor affecting Somalia and much of the Horn of Africa, along with the decades of conflict, weak government, and their combined effects on food production. Some 1.5 million Somalis were internally displaced, and the population of one of the largest refugee camps in the world—Dadaab across the border in Kenya—was growing by about 3,000 people a week, most of them Soma-

(continued)

lis. Complicating the humanitarian situation is al-Shabaab's control of parts of Somalia, which limits the access of humanitarian organizations. Attacks by al-Shabaab on the Kenyan side of the border force humanitarian aid workers to be escorted by armed police.

For students of international organizations and global governance, Somalia illustrates many of the challenges to international peace and security governance since the end of the Cold War in 1991—some of which have changed and some of which have not. The UN's experience in Somalia in the 1990s remains a symbol of a failed post–Cold War effort that offered a set of lessons, rightly or wrongly, for peacekeeping in situations of state failure, civil war, and complex humanitarian disaster. The AU's experience illuminates the potential contributions regional organizations can make to international peace and security and the challenges they may encounter in difficult environments.

Wars as the Genesis for Security Governance

War historically has been *the* fundamental problem in international politics; it has also been a primary factor motivating the creation of IGOs, from the Concert of Europe in the nineteenth century to the League of Nations and the UN in the twentieth century. Underlying functionalist theory is the premise that getting states to work together in solving practical problems of international relations will build the conditions for enduring peace. International law was traditionally seen as providing the rules that would help create order in the relations among states, and international courts or arbitration procedures would provide the means to settle legal disputes peacefully. Despite being the most destructive century in human history, the twentieth century was also the time of developing various governance approaches for preventing war.

Many of those approaches developed out of international relations theories. Liberals have traditionally supported international law and organizations as approaches to peace. IGOs and NGOs, as well as individual states and ad hoc groups, can play roles as third parties to settle disputes and secure a negotiated peace. So, too, have "soft" realists, who consider diplomacy and mediation as valuable for dealing with conflicts and use of force.

Governance approaches to peace and security have not changed dramatically over time, but the nature of wars and conflicts and the concepts of security have changed in significant ways. Since the 1950s, the incidence of interstate war (wars between two or more states) has decreased sharply, but other types of conflict have increased. Russia's invasion of Ukraine in

2022 marked a revival of major power aggression against a neighbor and a potential for a widened war with NATO's support of Ukraine. Up to then, studies of armed conflicts had shown a significant increase in the number of active conflicts and wars to fifty-six in 2020—a record high since 1946 (Strand and Hegre 2021). Of these, the Islamic State was involved in sixteen, illustrating the complexity of many conflicts. Since 1980, interstate conflicts have included the Iran-Iraq War (1980–1988), the Ethiopia-Eritrea War (1999–2000), and the Russo-Georgia War (2008). China's rise and tensions between the United States and China along with Russia's invasion of Ukraine have revived the potential for great power interstate conflict. In contrast, the number of intrastate (internal) armed conflicts rose dramatically from the mid-1950s to the mid-1990s and then declined (see Figure 7.1). This trend resulted from struggles for self-determination, such as those of the Tamils in Sri Lanka and Bengalis in East Pakistan; the problem of weak states, as in Somalia; ethnic conflicts, as in the former Yugoslavia and Rwanda; and civil wars between governments and opposition groups, such as the north–south civil war in Sudan (1983–2005). Some civil wars, such as in Democratic Republic of Congo (since 1996), Libya (since 2011), and Yemen (since 2015) have been internationalized with intervention by other states in support of either the government or opposition groups. All three of these have Islamic State and other jihadist groups actively involved along with criminal groups in the Democratic Republic of Congo.

In the 1990s and early 2000s, there was a surge in terminations of active conflicts, which led researchers to conclude that conflict resolution efforts had become more effective (Hewitt 2008: 24). Particularly troublesome is the evidence of recurrences—that is, conflicts and especially major civil wars that are ended or become inactive for a period of time, only to reignite, a problem that researchers at the UN University Centre for Policy Research have found to be greater than in the past and less conducive to political settlements (von Einsiedel 2017). In addition, violence against civilian populations has increased and numbers of displaced people have surged. The World Bank's 2022 list of high-intensity conflict situations listed Afghanistan, Syria, Yemen, Somalia, Armenia, and Azerbaijan with a longer list of sixteen countries as medium-intensity situations, all but three of which (Myanmar, Haiti, Iraq) were in Africa (World Bank 2022a).

Many post–Cold War intrastate conflicts have been accompanied by humanitarian disasters resulting from the fighting. Traditionally, security in the Westphalian system meant state security—security of borders, control over population, and freedom from interference in a state's internal affairs. With the body of internationally recognized human rights norms steadily expanding after World War II, the balance between the rights of sovereign states and the rights of people has shifted. Increasingly, it has been argued that human security should take precedence over security of governments

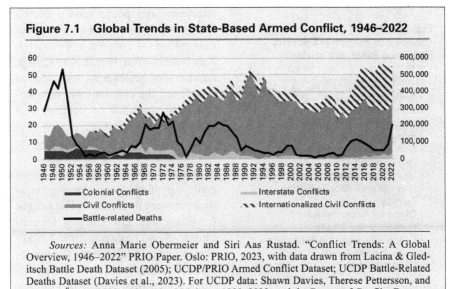

Figure 7.1 Global Trends in State-Based Armed Conflict, 1946–2022

Colonial Conflicts
Civil Conflicts
Battle-related Deaths
Interstate Conflicts
Internationalized Civil Conflicts

Sources: Anna Marie Obermeier and Siri Aas Rustad. "Conflict Trends: A Global Overview, 1946–2022" PRIO Paper. Oslo: PRIO, 2023, with data drawn from Lacina & Gleditsch Battle Death Dataset (2005); UCDP/PRIO Armed Conflict Dataset; UCDP Battle-Related Deaths Dataset (Davies et al., 2023). For UCDP data: Shawn Davies, Therese Pettersson, and Magnus Öberg (2023). "Organized Violence 1989–2022, and the Return of Conflict Between States." *Journal of Peace Research,* 60(4): 691–708.

or states. This shift has provided support for the concept of a responsibility to protect (R2P) and armed intervention to protect human beings against the violence of governments, paramilitary forces, militias, and police. This shift is most clearly evidenced in the increased numbers of UN Security Council meetings devoted to human security issues, discussed in a later chapter.

The changing nature of conflicts and complex humanitarian disasters are two major challenges to peace in the twenty-first century. Others include weapons of mass destruction (chemical, biological, and nuclear), the threat of cyberwarfare, and the presence of terrorist groups and use of terrorist tactics in asymmetric conflicts. With the Russian Wagner Group's presence in the Ukraine and Mali conflicts, there has also been a renewed presence of nonstate mercenaries.

The UN provides the global structures for dealing with security issues, and the five major geographic regions each have at least one IGO dealing with security issues (see Figure 7.2). In addition, many international NGOs have long been active in trying to promote peaceful settlement of conflicts, disarmament, and humanitarian relief (see Figure 7.3).

IGOs and Security

The idea of a global organization to promote security among states was born in the early years of the twentieth century and promoted by prominent

Figure 7.2
Global and Regional Security IGOs and Related Entities
United Nations
• Security Council
• General Assembly
• Office of the Secretary-General
• International Court of Justice
• Comprehensive Test Ban Treaty Organization
• High Commissioner for Refugees
• International Atomic Energy Agency
• Office for Coordination of Humanitarian Affairs
• Organization for the Prohibition of Chemical Weapons
• Department of Peace Operations
• Department of Field Support
• Peacebuilding Commission
• Permanent Court of Arbitration
Regional IGO Venues for Security
• Africa: African Union, Economic Community of West African States, Southern African Development Community
• Asia: ASEAN Regional Forum, Association of Southeast Asian Nations, Shanghai Cooperation Organization
• Europe: EU, NATO, Organization for Security and Co-operation in Europe
• Latin America: Rio Pact
• Middle East: Arab League, Gulf Cooperation Council

statesmen and peace groups during World Wars I and II. The history of these efforts is covered in Chapter 3. Particularly after World War I, large numbers of statesmen and citizens repudiated the conventional balance-of-power approach to dealing with international conflict.

The League of Nations and the UN both reflected convictions that a permanent international organization made up of all peace-loving states could prevent future wars. The League Covenant and UN Charter focused extensively on basic principles for preventing war, mechanisms for peaceful settlement of disputes, and provisions for enforcement actions. Both recognized the special prerogatives of major powers with respect to peace and security and the necessity of a small decisionmaking body with authority to take action on behalf of all members. A key difference was the League's requirement for unanimity among Council members, in contrast to the UN Security Council's requirement for a majority of the nonpermanent members, coupled with no opposition from any permanent member (the veto power).

Both the UN and the League were also based on the concept of collective security, articulated by US President Woodrow Wilson, as an alternative to the traditional balance-of-power politics that had frequently led to wars. Regional security arrangements established during the Cold War were either traditional alliances—formal or informal commitments for mutual aid in case of attack, such as the Inter-American Treaty of Reciprocal Assistance or Rio Pact—or collective defense organizations, such as NATO, that involved more institutional development and commitments on the part of members. The EU's rapid reaction force has been deployed in several conflict areas since 2003. The Economic Community of West African States (ECOWAS) and the Southern

African Development Community (SADC) have taken on security obligations when the UN and OAU or AU have been unable to act. The Association of Southeast Asian Nations (ASEAN) Regional Forum (ARF), created in 1994, is a forum for general Asian security-related dialogue among its twenty-seven participating states and security experts. The Shanghai Cooperation Organization (SCO) has focused more specifically on Central Asia and the threat of terrorism since its founding in 2000.

The UN Charter is clear that the Security Council has sole authority to authorize the use of force and obligate member states to undertake sanctions, except in situations where states may exercise their right of individual or collective self-defense (Article 51). Although this opens the door for regional organizations to use force for collective defense and for the UN to use regional security agencies for enforcement action, Article 53 clearly states that "no enforcement action shall be taken under regional arrangements or by regional agencies without the authorization of the Security Council." Regional organizations are to inform the Security Council of any activities, planned or undertaken, to maintain international peace and security (Article 54). The NATO bombing of the former Yugoslavia and Kosovo in 1999 was not authorized by the Security Council, which contributed to the intense controversy over the legitimacy of those actions. Its 2011 involvement in Libya (discussed later) was indirectly authorized by the Security Council.

Although the UN Charter's provisions implied shared responsibility between the UN and regional organizations, there was no clear division of labor. This became important after the Cold War's end, when the UN undertook more peace operations than ever before and regional organizations took a number of initiatives to address the surge in violent conflicts. Since 1992, there have been numerous cases of peacekeeping and enforcement activity by regional and subregional organizations, sometimes delegated under Security Council authorization (discussed later in the chapter), sometimes

---

**Figure 7.3
Security-Related INGOs**

Peace Groups
- International Crisis Group
- International Peace Institute
- Stockholm International Peace Research Institute
- Women's International League for Peace and Freedom

Disarmament Groups
- Cluster Munition Coalition
- Greenpeace International
- International Campaign to Ban Landmines
- International Physicians for the Prevention of Nuclear War

Humanitarian Relief Groups
- CARE
- Catholic Relief Services
- Doctors Without Borders
- International Committee of the Red Cross
- Lutheran World Federation
- Oxfam
- Save the Children Federation
- World Vision

with retroactive approval, sometimes in collaboration or partnership, and sometimes transitioning to a UN operation.

The UN and regional IGOs use various governance approaches to peace and security problems. UN efforts have included different types of peaceful settlement approaches, such as mediation and good offices; it invented the ideas of peacekeeping operations and postconflict peacebuilding. It has applied sanctions extensively since 1990. The UN also a long record on disarmament issues and has been involved in efforts to address terrorism, primarily by creating international law and imposing sanctions. ASEAN, the OAU/AU, and the Organization of American States (OAS) have frequently used preventive diplomacy and mediation. The Arab League, ECOWAS, the OAS, and the EU have all employed sanctions, while NATO, the AU, ECOWAS, SADC, and the EU have undertaken peace operations.

NGOs and Security

Security-related international NGOs vary considerably. Some are think tanks whose research aids other groups. For example, the Stockholm International Peace Research Institute (SIPRI) conducts research on conflict, arms transfers, and military budgets to inform understanding about conditions for a stable peace, while the International Peace Institute (IPI), in New York, specifically provides policy research and expert advice to the UN. The International Crisis Group (ICG), founded in 1995, has become a leading independent source of analysis and advice on conflict prevention and resolution to governments and IGOs, including the UN and EU. Unlike SIPRI and the IPI, the ICG also seeks to mobilize effective international action at the highest levels of governments and IGOs, using prominent former government officials to press the initiatives. With field staff covering situations of potential or actual conflict around the world, the ICG is particularly noted for its "crisis alerts," advising peace negotiations, detailed analysis, and high-level advocacy with policymakers on preventing, managing, and resolving conflicts.

Some INGOs focus on arms control and disarmament issues. For example, Greenpeace has long been active in efforts to block nuclear testing and advocating the elimination of all nuclear weapons. The International Campaign to Ban Landmines and the Cluster Munition Coalition illustrate NGO advocacy coalitions that secured international arms control treaties, as discussed later in the chapter.

Other security-related INGOs are involved in humanitarian relief operations. The relief organizations listed in Figure 7.3 represent but a small proportion of the relief-oriented NGOs. Among them, the International Committee of the Red Cross has a unique status because of its special responsibilities under the Geneva Conventions for holding states accountable for violations of humanitarian law and for protecting and assisting military and civilian victims of conflict. It has observer status in the UN General Assembly because of this unique role. Partnerships among state, intergovernmental, and nongovernmental actors have become common.

Norms Related to the Use of Force

From the dawn of history, leaders of tribes and nations have claimed the right and even duty to engage in large-scale organized violence. Warfare was considered acceptable and even noble. This idea began to change in the early twentieth century as new norms developed that served to limit the use of force. International theorists in the constructivist tradition have contributed to understanding this evolution and role of norms as well as reconceptualizing security.

Outlawing war. The Covenant of the League of Nations required member states to respect and preserve the territorial integrity and political independence of states and try different methods of dispute settlement, but it contained no explicit prohibition on the use of force to settle disputes. In 1928, most states signed the Kellogg-Briand Pact "to condemn recourse to war for the solution of international controversies, and renounce it as an instrument of national policy." This was the basis for Article 2 (sections 3 and 4) of the UN Charter, which obliges all members to settle disputes by peaceful means and "refrain in their international relations from the threat or use of force against the territorial integrity or political independence of any state."

The reality is more complicated. The use of force for territorial annexation is now widely accepted as illegitimate: witness the broad condemnation of Iraq's invasion of Kuwait in 1990 and the many countries that contributed to the US-led multilateral effort to reverse that occupation. The same held for the international condemnation of Russia's annexation of Crimea in 2014 and its invasion of Ukraine in 2022, which is widely considered to be a fundamental violation of the UN Charter and an act of aggression.

The use of force in self-defense against armed attack is accepted and was the basis for the Security Council's authorization of US military action in Afghanistan after the September 2001 terrorist attacks. International norms prescribe that the response must be proportional to the provocation, however. This is the basis for widespread condemnation of Israel's large-scale military responses in 2006, 2009, and 2014 to rockets fired by Hezbollah and Hamas from Lebanon and Gaza, respectively.

A large majority of states accept the legitimacy of using force to promote self-determination, replace illegitimate regimes, and correct past injustices. In 2003, the UN Security Council refused to authorize the US use of force against Iraq to remove Saddam Hussein from power and to destroy the weapons of mass destruction that the United States claimed Iraq possessed. The lack of agreement on a definition of terrorism has complicated international efforts to create a norm outlawing terrorism. For many years, agreement on a clear definition of aggression proved elusive, but was approved by the UN General Assembly in 1974 (Resolution 3314). Then, in 2010, an amendment to the Rome Statute of the International Criminal Court (ICC) defined the crime of aggression (see Figure 7.4).

Promoting human security and humanitarianism. There are a number of other important norms relating to the use of force that have emerged out of a century and a half of concern for the effects of war on people, particularly civilians, wounded soldiers, prisoners of war, and refugees. These include the humanitarian norms described in the four 1949 Geneva Conventions, which have been ratified by 196 states, and their three additional protocols; international refugee law, particularly the 1951 UN Convention Relating to the Status of Refugees and its 1967 protocol; the taboos on the use of chemical and nuclear weapons plus the 2017 Treaty on the Prohibition of Nuclear Weapons; and conventions on antipersonnel landmines and cluster munitions, discussed later in the chapter.

The Geneva Conventions form the core of international humanitarian law—designed to protect civilians, prisoners of war, and wounded soldiers and to ban particular methods of war (e.g., bombing hospitals). They also form the legal basis for war crimes and crimes against humanity. War crimes and crimes against humanity (see Figure 7.5) are also spelled out in Articles 7 and 8 of the Rome Statute, along with genocide. All are discussed further in Chapter 9. Most of the norms regarding armed conflict apply only to interstate wars and to states, not to nonstate actors; only the second protocol to the Geneva Conventions approved in 1977 applies specifically to victims of noninternational armed conflicts.

What constitutes war crimes, crimes against humanity, or acts of genocide has gradually expanded to include sexual violence and rape and targeting civilians more generally as tactics of war. In milestone actions in 2000 and 2008, the Security Council mandated gender training in peacekeeping operations, protection of women and girls, and gender mainstreaming in the UN reporting and implementation systems relating to peace and security (Resolution 1325). The Council also condemned sexual

Figure 7.4
The Crime of Aggression Defined

The crime of aggression is defined as "the planning, preparation, initiation or execution, by a person in a position effectively to exercise control over or to direct the political or military action of a State, of an act of aggression which, by its character, gravity and scale, constitutes a manifest violation of the Charter of the United Nations." Aggression is characterized as "the use of armed force by a State against the sovereignty, territorial integrity or political independence of another State, or in any other manner inconsistent with the Charter of the United Nations."

Amendment to the Rome Statute of the International Criminal Court approved on June 11, 2010 and entered into force on September 26, 2012.

violence when used to deliberately target civilians in wartime (Resolution 1820). To promote these newer norms, peacekeeping operations now routinely include language on protection of civilians (POC) and on women and gender, designating gender advisers and gender-sensitive training programs.

The expansion of human rights and humanitarian norms has placed new demands on the UN, other IGOs, and international actors to curb abuses in the face of publicity by the media and global networks of NGOs of situations involving mass starvation, ethnic cleansing, genocide, gender-based violence, use of chemical weapons, and other atrocities. This has led to debate over humanitarian intervention, invoking differing views of state

**Figure 7.5
Crimes Against Humanity**

Attack against or any effort to exterminate a civilian population

- Enslavement
- Deportation or forcible transfer of population
- Imprisonment or other severe deprivation of physical liberty
- Torture
- Rape, sexual slavery, forced prostitution, pregnancy, or sterilization
- Persecution of any group or collectivity based upon political, racial, national, ethnic, cultural, religious, or gender grounds
- Enforced disappearance of persons

sovereignty and concerns about just cause and authority derived from the "just war" tradition. The Genocide Convention (1948) provides for the possibility of UN action under the Charter to prevent or suppress crimes against humanity. The International Criminal Court provides the means to prosecute those accused of crimes (discussed in Chapter 9).

Military intervention to enforce compliance is a different story. Although the Universal Declaration of Human Rights (1948) warns that people whose rights are violated may "be compelled to have recourse, as a last resort, to rebellion against tyranny and oppression," does large-scale human suffering justify the use of armed force to rescue others even in situations where governments may be the primary perpetrators?

Since the late 1990s, NGOs, civil society activists, prominent individuals, and an independent international commission have pushed for acceptance of national and international accountability, for using human rights norms to judge state conduct, and for new interpretations of sovereignty. With the failure of the UN and international community to halt the 1994 genocide in Rwanda and the controversy over NATO's 1999 intervention in Kosovo to halt large-scale ethnic cleansing by Serbian forces, UN Secretary-General Kofi Annan articulated how state sovereignty was being redefined in a 1999 report and subsequently called for an effort to forge consensus on when intervention should occur, under whose authority, and how.

In response, the Canadian government established the independent International Commission on Intervention and State Sovereignty (ICISS).

Led by former Australian foreign minister Gareth Evans and Mohamed Sah-noun of Algeria, the ICISS proposed six criteria for military intervention for human protection: right authority, just cause, right intention, last resort, proportional means, and reasonable prospects. The "threshold" criteria include "large scale loss of life, actual or apprehended, with genocidal intent or not, which is the product either of deliberate state action, or state neglect or inability to act, or a failed state situation; or large scale 'ethnic cleansing,' actual or apprehended, whether carried out by killing, forced expulsion, acts of terror or rape" (ICISS 2001: 32). The commission's report articulated the responsibility to protect (R2P) as an obligation of states and the international community and endorsed the UN Security Council as the only body with the authority to deal with intervention issues.

International law requires multiple cases to demonstrate the existence of a new customary practice. When new norms are emerging, there is often a period of conflict between advocates of the new and supporters of the old (Finnemore and Sikkink 1998; Sandholtz and Stiles 2009). If a large enough group of states is prepared to adopt the new, it will replace the old. Those violating the old norm can set in motion "norm cascades" that result in new norms replacing the old. But new norms usually do not replace the old without considerable debate, as constructivists remind us. The debate over whether there is a norm of humanitarian intervention, therefore, is ongoing. Although the 2005 UN World Summit endorsed R2P, Security Council members never translated that into authorization for sufficient force to halt the genocide in Darfur, for example (see Chapter 9). They did authorize action in Libya in 2011, but not in Syria, as discussed later in this chapter. Some analysts are skeptical that the UN Security Council will authorize any humanitarian interventions in the future.

As controversial as R2P may be, norms matter. Norms have led to the view that nuclear weapons are "disproportionately lethal" (Price and Tannenwald 1996: 138) and their use is unacceptable (Thakur 2006: 162). A similar norm against use of chemical weapons posited that such weapons are contrary to "standards of civilized conduct" (Price and Tannenwald 1996: 131). More recently, norms have also been established to ban the manufacture, stockpiling, and use of biological weapons, antipersonnel landmines, and cluster munitions.

Norms on the use of force, humanitarian intervention, and certain weapons are strongly influenced by constructivist thought. Meanwhile, much of the conflict resolution literature rests on liberal principles. However, no definitive theory stipulates clear conditions under which wars will occur or peace will be secured and by whom. The contextual factors shaping human choices—for war or peaceful dispute settlement—defy tidy theorizing. We know a lot about both, but not enough to lay out a single theory to guide the maintenance of international peace and security.

Mechanisms for the Peaceful Settlement of Disputes

The broadest category of security governance approaches is also the oldest. As early as the Greek city-states, there was agreement about the desirability of settling disputes peacefully. The 1899 and 1908 Hague Conferences produced the Conventions for the Pacific Settlement of International Disputes, laying the foundations for mechanisms still in use today (discussed in Chapter 3). These assume that war is a deliberate choice for settling a dispute and that it is possible to create mechanisms to influence actors' choices. For example, one assumption is that war can result from ignorance and that providing information through an independent commission of inquiry can change the choice. Another assumption is that states often get themselves into "dead-end streets," from which a third-party mediator can help them escape. The Hague Conventions established the international community's stake in preventing war. They created mechanisms for third-party roles, variously labeled good offices, inquiry, mediation, conciliation, adjudication, and arbitration, which were incorporated into the League of Nations Covenant and Chapter VI of the UN Charter. The latter specifies a sequence of ways the Security Council can promote peaceful settlement of disputes, from inquiry to mediation.

The involvement of the UN, regional IGOs, NGOs, individuals, states or coalitions of states, or ad hoc groups in efforts to find a peaceful settlement for a conflict is considered a third-party intervention. UN Secretaries-General have often offered their "good offices" for peacemaking initiatives, with or without a Security Council mandate. Such efforts can range from simply getting the parties together to actual mediation by the Secretary-General or a designated special representative. Similar roles have been undertaken on occasion by officials of the EU, OAS, and OAU/AU. Some high-profile situations, such as the Arab-Israeli-Palestinian conflict and the civil war in Syria, generate multiple third-party efforts over time. Sometimes those efforts occur sequentially; sometimes they are simultaneous; but they are often messy and rife with questions of who does what, when, and where.

The use of peaceful settlement mechanisms, however, does not necessarily mean no use of armed force. Force can be critical to securing a peaceful outcome in some situations, helping change the perceptions of the parties regarding the costs and benefits of continued fighting. Cutting off the supply of money and arms or engineering a change of leadership particularly in a civil war may also lead to a peaceful settlement as the costs and benefits are recalculated. Every situation is unique.

Determining who can most effectively intervene, what means are required, and what political goals should be set are key issues. What constitutes success? Is it a permanent end to a conflict (Liberia's civil war), a freeze on active fighting (stalemate in Cyprus; potential cease-fire in Ukraine), a short- to medium-term end to violence (independence for South

Sudan), getting parties who previously would not speak to each other to meet face to face (Israeli-Palestinian Oslo peace process), or building the foundations for long-term peace (Bosnia and Timor-Leste)? Many answers to the who, what, and when questions depend on the stage of the conflict at which intervention occurs. Some conflicts, such as that between the Tamil Tigers and the government of Sri Lanka, are neglected or forgotten by the international community (Crocker, Hampson, and Aall 2004).

Mediation

Mediation is a key tool for peaceful dispute settlement: "a mode of negotiation in which a third party helps the parties find a solution which they cannot find by themselves" (Zartman and Touval 1996: 446). It may involve persuading the parties to accept mediation in the first place or include multiple mediators over time, for different phases of a conflict, and a search for settlement. For mediation to have a chance, a conflict must be at what is called a "hurting stalemate" or "ripeness" stage, when parties see the costs of continuing the conflict as greater than the benefits of doing so, and thus are more willing to consider some form of settlement.

Among the peaceful settlement approaches, the UN has employed good offices and mediation led by the Secretary-General, a Special Representative of the Secretary-General (SRSG), "contact groups" or "Friends of the Secretary-General." Secretary-General Javier Pérez de Cuéllar secured agreement on the Soviet Union's withdrawal from Afghanistan in 1989, for example, and Álvaro de Soto, his SRSG, mediated an end to the conflicts in Central America in the late 1980s. The Community of Sant'Egidio, an Italian Catholic NGO, played an active role in peacemaking and peacebuilding in Mozambique, illustrating the mediating roles NGOs can play. Pope Francis was instrumental in negotiations between the United States and Cuba in 2014, and a number of ad hoc groups have formed to aid peacemaking efforts. The first such ad hoc group was the Western Contact Group, formed in 1978 by the United States, Canada, the United Kingdom, France, and Germany—all members of the UN Security Council at the time. It was able to negotiate an agreement for Namibia's independence from South Africa in part because of the relationships the countries had with the different parties, including the South West Africa People's Organisation (SWAPO) (Karns 1987). In addition, numerous "friends" groups have formed to aid the UN Secretary-General in addressing conflicts in Haiti, Angola, Iraq, and elsewhere (Whitfield 2007). Since 2002, the Middle East Quartet, made up of senior UN, EU, US, and Russian officials, has endeavored to support the Israeli-Palestinian peace process.

A mediator may play a variety of roles: organizer, educator, visionary, interpreter, conciliator, provocateur, risk-taker, catalyst for change, and policymaker (Crocker, Hampson, and Aall 1999: 686). Even without political power or economic resources, a nonofficial mediator such as former US

President Jimmy Carter or the nongovernmental Centre for Humanitarian Dialogue in Geneva can be helpful in the prenegotiation phases of a peace process in bringing parties together, especially if there is a nonstate armed actor involved (Whitfield 2007: 42). Some situations, however, call for "mediation with muscle"—a role the United States has sometimes played— to provide incentives and assurances for formal settlements.

Mediation does not work in all situations, even if the mediator is a good fit and skillful and even if the situation is thought to be "ripe." The global landscape is littered with failed attempts. Although it has been one of a number of tools employed in recent years in efforts to prevent violent conflicts, postcolonial theorists warn us of potential shortcomings. Mediators may be but tools of hegemonic powers, justifying agreements in weak states on the grounds of putting things right—that is, in their own national interest (Richmond 2001).

Preventive Diplomacy
The idea of preventive diplomacy as an innovative approach to peaceful settlement was introduced by UN Secretary-General Dag Hammarskjöld in the late 1950s. His successor, Boutros Boutros-Ghali (1992), later defined it as "action to prevent disputes from arising between parties, to prevent existing disputes from escalating into conflicts and to limit the spread of the latter when they occur." Most often, this takes the form of diplomatic efforts, sometimes coupled with sanctions of some sort. Preventive deployment of peacekeeping troops is intended to change the calculus of parties regarding the purposes of using force and prevent the spread of conflict, as when the UN sent troops to Macedonia in 1995 to prevent the spread of war from other regions of the former Yugoslavia.

The actors involved in preventive activities now include the Organization for Security and Co-operation in Europe (OSCE), EU, OAS, ASEAN, AU, ECOWAS, Gulf Cooperation Council (GCC), and other organizations that have established regional prevention initiatives. These are largely civilian international officials and experts with a mandate to find sustainable solutions. The UN itself has created regional offices for preventive diplomacy in Central Asia, West Africa, and Central Africa and, in 2022, had twenty-four political missions in the field whose mandates included conflict prevention. NGOs have created the Global Partnership for the Prevention of Armed Conflict, and a variety of private and local groups are active in preventive activities, including the International Crisis Group, which has emerged as a key actor. The UN High Commissioner for Refugees has also been involved in preventive diplomacy, along with the Secretary-General and special representatives of the Secretary-General (UNHCR 2011).

The tools for prevention include early warning, fact-finding missions, political missions, special envoys, early response systems, good offices, mediation, conciliation, and locally based approaches. Some staff in UN political missions may focus on human rights or legal issues; others may be constitutional experts, and still others provide technical support for managing elections. The missions often provide support to those seeking to prevent conflict. In addition to political missions, the UN established the Standby Team of Mediation Experts in 2008, consisting of individuals experienced in mediation and peacebuilding who bring specialized skills, such as expertise in process design, transitional justice, security arrangements, gender inclusion, and constitution-making. That approach was expanded in 2017 with the addition of women, consistent with the feminist belief that with women engaged as mediators, the needs and perspectives of women and other marginalized communities will be addressed.

The exact nature of preventive diplomacy tends to vary with phases of the conflict cycle. In situations of latent tension, such as in Eastern Europe and Central Asia after the end of the Cold War, the OSCE was active in helping address issues of minority rights, particularly among ethnic Russians in newly independent former Soviet republics. The OSCE also played a role in eastern Ukraine in monitoring violence between pro-Russian separatists and the government between 2014 and 2022. When all-out conflict threatens, as it did in Kenya following presidential elections in 2007, intense, well-supported diplomatic efforts can still "save the day," as happened under the AU-mandated leadership of former UN Secretary-General Kofi Annan, whose mediation was supported by UN staff and advisers from the NGO Center for Humanitarian Dialogue (Gowan 2011).

Successful preventive diplomacy depends on timeliness, which has provoked debate within the UN about early warning systems—a role the International Crisis Group strives to fulfill. In 2022, outside the UN or any IGO, a group of former diplomats and experts from thirteen countries created a new organization called Diplomats Without Borders designed to marshal members' expertise with the goal of finding solutions to conflicts where traditional diplomacy is not working (Rade 2022). Preventing conflicts and finding innovative solutions, however, is rarely easy, and opportunities are frequently missed.

Adjudication and Arbitration

Two other tools for peaceful settlement—adjudication and arbitration—are legal in character and involve referring a dispute to an impartial third-party tribunal for a binding decision. They emphasize finding a basis for settlement in international law (rather than in a political or diplomatic processes or formulas) and can be used only when states consent to submit a dispute and be bound by the outcome. The tools differ in the permanence of the tribunals, the scope of their jurisdiction, and the extent to which parties can control the selection of arbitrators or judges.

Arbitration involves the settlement of disputes on the basis of legal criteria by individuals who are assigned to the task on an ad hoc basis, usually by the disputants. Once the problem is resolved, the arbitrators are relieved of their duties. Arbitration dates back at least to the early Greek city-states. As discussed in Chapter 3, the Hague Peace Conference of 1899 established the Permanent Court of Arbitration (PCA). The PCA is an IGO with 122 parties whose secretariat is based in The Hague, but whose "court" is a list of potential international arbitrators—lawyers, judges, diplomats, academics, and former government officials. Arbitration panels can be composed of a single neutral individual, such as the UN Secretary-General, or a panel of three individuals (two of whom have been chosen by the parties, plus a neutral third member selected by agreement), or an impartial third party such as the president of the International Court of Justice (ICJ). Tribunals can have up to nine members, as in the case of the Iran-US Claims Tribunal, which worked for many years to arbitrate several thousand claims arising out of the seizure of US hostages by Iran in 1979. The agreement between parties to resort to arbitration defines the issues to be decided, the method for selecting arbitrators, the machinery and procedures to be used, and how expenses will be paid.

The PCA has handled many cases over the years, including interstate cases involving boundary issues and cases involving a state party and a private corporation. Examples include the border dispute between Ethiopia and Eritrea (2009), the Abyei disputed border region between Northern and Southern Sudan (2009), Chevron and Texaco versus Ecuador (2011), the dispute over coastal state rights in the Black Sea (Ukraine v. Russia 2017), and the dispute between Pakistan and India over the Indus Waters Treaty initiated in 2010, but ongoing still in 2023.

One highly publicized case was brought by the Philippines against China under the UN Convention on the Law of the Sea. It concerned the status of various maritime features in the South China Sea and lawfulness of certain actions by China; the case concluded in 2016. China appointed no agent and noted throughout the three years of proceedings that it did not accept the arbitration. The judgment affirmed the legality of the Philippines' claims, but left the conflict over China's expansive claims and aggressive actions unresolved. This showed how arbitration can settle legal questions but not necessarily end conflicts, especially when one party has not accepted the PCA's jurisdiction, even if it is a member.

The ICJ and other international courts have one primary advantage over arbitral tribunals: they already exist and the international community pays the expenses of the proceedings. Distinguishing between legal or justiciable disputes and political or nonjusticiable disputes is a difficult task, however, and countries that want to avoid adjudication will frequently protest that certain disputes are inherently inappropriate for adjudication. Iran made this argument concerning US diplomatic and consular staff in the Tehran hostages case (ICJ Contentious Case 1980), as did the United States in the Nicaragua case (ICJ Contentious Cases 1984b, 1986), although neither claim was persuasive and the cases moved forward. There can also be significant questions regarding the ICJ's jurisdiction to hear a case especially since the ICJ has noncompulsory jurisdiction (see Chapter 4). Sometimes, unwilling respondent states will refuse to appear before the court at all—as did France in a case brought against its nuclear testing by Australia and New Zealand (ICJ Contentious Case 1974), Iran, and the United States, respectively, in the two cases mentioned above.

The Nicaragua case illuminates the limitations on adjudication for dealing with peace and security issues. It arose out of the 1979 victory of the left-wing Sandinistas over longtime Nicaraguan dictator General Anastasio Somoza, and US concerns about their ties to Cuba and the Soviet Union. In 1984, Nicaragua brought suit in the ICJ, charging that the United States was illegally using military force against it and intervening in its internal affairs. Because it involved one of the two superpowers, the case was closely watched by many developing countries. The United States argued that the ICJ had no jurisdiction over the case and refused to participate when the court determined that it did have jurisdiction. It took the added step of withdrawing its acceptance of the court's jurisdiction for any Central American case, and terminated its acceptance of the court's compulsory jurisdiction whereby states commit to participating in ICJ cases in advance.

The ICJ's 1986 ruling represented a stunning defeat for the United States and a moral victory for Nicaragua. The court found that the mining of Nicaragua's harbors, attacks on port installations, and support for the Contras infringed on the prohibition against use of force. The justices rejected the US claim of collective self-defense on behalf of El Salvador. The court found no basis in international law for a general right of intervention in support of an opposition to the government of another state, however just its cause might appear.

The case had little effect on the conflicts in Central America, but did lead to a significant increase in the ICJ's stock among developing countries. Thereafter, many accepted the ICJ's jurisdiction, withdrew previous reservations to ICJ jurisdiction, and brought cases before the court. The case reinforced suspicions in the United States about international institutions, but the United States subsequently brought new cases to the court and participated in others.

States have used both adjudication and arbitration to resolve territorial and maritime boundary disputes, questions of river usage, and fishing zones—all potential sources of armed conflict. As discussed in Chapter 4, the ICJ has been used to rule on a number of other peace and security-related issues, including nuclear tests, genocide in the former Yugoslavia, and, through advisory opinions, Israel's construction of a barrier wall in the Occupied Palestinian Territories and the legal status of Kosovo's 2008 unilateral declaration of independence.

Beth Simmons (2002), among others, has explored the question of what leads states to use arbitration or adjudication in relation to territorial disputes, noting that realist theory sees territory as a zero-sum issue. She argues there are joint gains to be reaped from settling territorial disputes, such as greater stability for private investment and greater opportunities for trade, as well as reduced need for military expenditures. For example, the United States and Canada accepted a maritime boundary delimitation by the ICJ even though both objected to the court's reasoning. Resolving the dispute took precedence over winning or losing. Domestic groups may more readily accept an arbitration or ICJ judgment than a negotiated one. In some cases, bilateral treaties specify arbitration or adjudication to resolve disputes. Despite agreeing to be bound by the outcome, one or another party may decide not to implement a settlement, giving rise to compliance and enforcement issues. They may seek Security Council help in enforcing a judgment, as Nicaragua did, or use other "self-help" measures to secure compliance of the recalcitrant party. One party may also reject the decision and war may ensue, as in the case of Ethiopia, Eritrea, and the PCA's ruling, requiring other types of actions to end the conflict.

Collective Security, Enforcement, and Sanctions

Collective security is based on the conviction that peace is indivisible and all states have a collective interest in countering aggression whenever and wherever it may appear. States commit to defending any member of the collective security arrangement against attack by any other state, including other members of the arrangement. It assumes that potential aggressors will be deterred by the united threat of counterforce mobilized through an IGO like the League of Nations or the UN. If enforcement is required, then a wide range of economic and diplomatic sanctions as well as armed force may be used.

The League of Nations failed to respond to Japan's invasion of Manchuria in 1931 and responded belatedly with voluntary sanctions when Italy invaded Ethiopia in 1935. Chapter VII of the UN Charter (refer to Figure 4.1) provides the legal foundation for the UN's collective security role and for enforcement decisions that bind all UN members, specifying actions the UN can take with respect to threats to the peace, breaches of the peace, and acts of aggression. Because of the veto power of the five permanent Security Council members (P-5), the UN is a limited collective security organization. The Cold War made concurrence among the Security Council's members almost impossible to achieve, and Chapter VII was invoked on only two occasions. As a result, the UN dealt primarily with regional conflicts, using various forms of peacekeeping and mechanisms for peaceful settlement of disputes. The situation changed dramatically with the Cold War's end, unprecedented cooperation among the P-5, and the success of the 1990 Gulf War.

Since 1989, the Security Council has invoked Chapter VII on many occasions to authorize the use of force and various types of sanctions by the UN alone, by a regional organization such as NATO (Bosnia and Afghanistan), or by a "coalition of the willing" led by a country willing to commit military forces to the effort, such as the United States (Haiti), Australia (Timor-Leste), France (Rwanda, Côte d'Ivoire, Mali), and the United Kingdom (Sierra Leone). It has become common in recent years for most peacekeeping operations to have a mandate under Chapter VII, which has contributed to the sharp increase in the number of resolutions invoking Chapter VII, as shown in Figure 7.6. This, in turn, has blurred the line between enforcement and peacekeeping, as discussed further later in the chapter.

With the UN and international community engaged in managing a wide array of threats to human security, the concept of collective security and Chapter VII enforcement has expanded. The 2004 report of the UN-appointed High-Level Panel on Threats, Challenges and Change captured this reconceptualization of shared vulnerability to a wide variety of threats as the new basis for UN-led collective security (UN 2004) and the 2005 World Summit advocated stronger relations between the UN and regional and subregional organizations to meet the new challenges.

Collective Security Efforts Involving Armed Force

Korea. The sanctioning of US-led UN forces to counter North Korea's invasion of South Korea in 1950 was made possible by the temporary absence of the Soviet Union from the Security Council in protest against the UN's refusal to seat the newly established communist government of the People's Republic of China. The "Uniting for Peace" resolution was used by the General Assembly to authorize continuance of those forces once the Soviet Union returned to the Security Council and exercised its veto. Thus, the UN provided the framework for legitimating US efforts to defend the Republic of Korea and mobilizing other states' assistance. A US general was designated as the UN commander, but he took orders directly from Washington. Some fifteen countries contributed troops during the three-year war. Since the 1953 cease-fire, the United States has maintained a strong military presence in South Korea; the UN has maintained a token presence.

The Gulf War. The Cold War's end led many to speculate that the UN Security Council could finally function as a collective security body. The first test of that belief came with Iraq's invasion of Kuwait in the summer of 1990, which triggered unprecedented actions in response to an act of

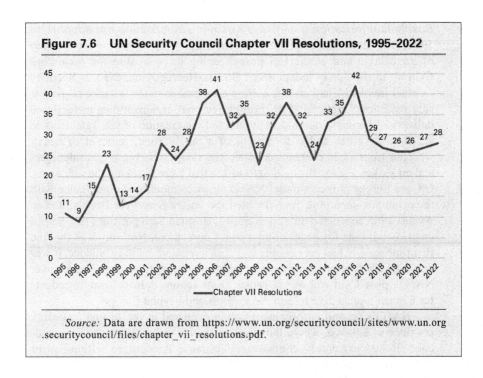

Figure 7.6   UN Security Council Chapter VII Resolutions, 1995–2022

Source: Data are drawn from https://www.un.org/securitycouncil/sites/www.un.org.securitycouncil/files/chapter_vii_resolutions.pdf.

aggression against a UN member state. Unity among the P-5 (including the Soviet Union, despite its long-standing relationship with Iraq) facilitated the passage of twelve resolutions over a four-month period, activating Chapter VII of the Charter. These included, most importantly, Resolution 678 of November 1990, which authorized member states "to use all necessary means" to reverse the occupation of Kuwait and "restore peace and security in the region."

The military operation launched was a US-led multinational effort resembling a subcontract on behalf of the UN. US commanders did not regularly report to the UN Secretary-General, nor did senior UN personnel participate in military decisionmaking. Coalition forces did not use the UN flag and insignia. After the fighting stopped in February 1991, a traditional, lightly armed peacekeeping force was organized to monitor the demilitarized zone between Iraq and Kuwait.

The US-led military action in the Gulf was widely regarded as exemplifying a stronger post–Cold War UN. Many developing countries, although supporting the action, were troubled by the autonomy of the US-led operation. The Gulf War marked only the beginning of efforts to deal with Iraq's threats to regional peace, however.

Bosnia (authorization given) and Kosovo (authorization not sought). In 1992, after the failure of various peacemaking efforts following the breakup of Yugoslavia and of the UN peacekeeping force to stop the escalating fighting in the newly independent Bosnia-Herzegovina, the UN Security Council invoked Chapter VII, calling on member states to "take all necessary measures," nationally or through regional organizations, to facilitate delivery of humanitarian aid. It authorized the creation of UN safe areas in six Bosnian cities and enforcement of a no-fly zone, removal of heavy weapons from urban centers, economic sanctions on Serbia and Montenegro, and air strikes against Bosnian Serb forces that were attacking the safe areas. US and European forces under NATO auspices monitored compliance with the economic sanctions, implemented the no-fly zone over Bosnia, and in August 1995 conducted air strikes against Bosnian Serb positions that helped create conditions for negotiating a peace agreement. Not only was this the first time the UN had ever cooperated with a regional military alliance, it was also NATO's first ever enforcement action. In the context of the debate over NATO's post–Cold War role (Chapter 5), its actions in Bosnia set precedents for a much more active role in the Balkans and beyond Europe.

NATO's second enforcement action occurred in the former Yugoslav province of Kosovo, where the ethnic Albanian majority sought independence. It was extremely controversial because it occurred without prior authorization from the UN Security Council due to opposition from Russia and China. In March 1999, NATO began more than two months of aerial bombing in Kosovo and parts of the former Yugoslavia after Yugoslav (Serbian) rejection of a negotiated settlement for Kosovo and growing evidence of ethnic cleansing. UN Secretary-General Kofi Annan captured the dilemma when he stated: "there are times when the use of force may be legitimate in the pursuit of peace. . . . [But] the Council should be involved in any decision to resort to the use of force" (UN 1999c). Russia, China, and other countries loudly protested the illegality of NATO intervention, but the United Kingdom argued that "force can also be justified on the grounds of overwhelming humanitarian necessity without a [Security Council resolution]" (Roberts 1999: 106) and Russia's draft resolution condemning the NATO action was decisively defeated. Still, others noted that NATO's military action actually worsened the humanitarian crisis by prompting a huge refugee outflow, civilian casualties of bombing, and destruction of infrastructure such as power plants and bridges on the Danube River.

The NATO-led action in Kosovo highlighted a primary issue relating to the UN's collective security and enforcement role, namely, whether and when a regional organization or individual member states, including major powers such as the United States, must obtain authorization from the Security Council to use force. The issue was sharply debated again in 2002–2003 when the United States pushed for Security Council endorsement of enforcement actions against Iraq for its failure to implement earlier Security Council resolutions, ouster of UN weapons inspectors, and development of weapons of mass destruction.

Iraq: Authorization denied. Concerns about Iraq persisted through the 1990s after the Gulf War. The strict comprehensive sanctions and disarmament regime imposed on it became increasingly controversial from a humanitarian standpoint, but there were also worries about whether it was covertly seeking to develop nuclear weapons, particularly after it blocked UN weapons inspections.

As a result of those concerns, during the fall and winter of 2002–2003, the United States expended a great deal of diplomatic effort in trying to muster Security Council support for a Chapter VII operation unless Iraq agreed to be peacefully disarmed of all weapons of mass destruction and accept the return of UN weapons inspectors. In November, the Security Council unanimously passed Resolution 1441 reinforcing the inspections regime and giving Iraq a final opportunity to provide full information on its weapons and missile programs. Despite UN and International Atomic Energy Agency (IAEA) reports showing that Iraq was cooperating with the inspections regime, the United States and the United Kingdom sought Security Council authorization in early 2003 for military action to disarm Iraq and were unsuccessful.

By deciding to go to war in Iraq in 2003 in defiance of the majority of the Security Council members, the United States, United Kingdom, and their coalition allies posed a serious challenge to the Security Council's authority to authorize the use of force, however. Because a major argument for military action involved "anticipatory self-defense," there were questions of principle and practice, including the fundamental question of the UN's relevance. Did the Security Council's failure to support the US action in Iraq illustrate the UN's ineffectiveness and waning legitimacy in the face of a superpower with overwhelming military power, as some argued? Or did the Security Council work as its founders envisioned, not supporting UN involvement unless the P-5 and a majority of nonpermanent members concurred? The debate was intense (Glennon 2003). Despite the controversy, the UN later initiated peacebuilding activities under the United Nations Assistance Mission for Iraq.

Libya and humanitarian intervention. The story of Security Council authorization for the use of "all necessary measures" in Libya in 2011 illustrates how attitudes can change when the consequences of enforcement action become evident. In Libya, the mass demonstrations that marked the 2011 Arab Spring turned into civil war, as the eastern half of the state declared autonomy and factions in the military and government defected from the government ruled by Muammar Qaddafi for more than forty years. Qaddafi publicly predicted "rivers of blood" and "hundreds of thousands of dead"; he threatened to use all weapons available "to cleanse Libya house by house"; and he referred to the protesters as "cockroaches," the same word used by Hutus to dehumanize the Tutsis during the 1994 Rwandan genocide. The international community feared a humanitarian crisis and the threat this posed to Libya's people and the large number of foreign nationals in the country.

The Security Council initially imposed targeted sanctions on Libya, freezing assets, imposing an arms embargo, and referring the matter to the International Criminal Court. Citing "widespread and systematic attacks," the Council stated that government actions "may amount to crimes against humanity" and that Libyan authorities had a responsibility to protect the population. With violence mounting, the Security Council passed Resolution 1973, authorizing UN members to "to take all necessary measures" to protect civilians, establish a no-fly zone, enforce the arms embargo, and undertake air strikes and military action short of landing troops—the first effort to enforce R2P. The resolution received ten affirmative votes and five abstentions (Russia, China, India, Germany, and Brazil), thanks in no small part to the support of the Organisation of Islamic Cooperation (OIC), the GCC, and the Arab League and the fact that Qaddafi had few friends.

Like other UN-authorized operations requiring strong military assets, enforcement began with air strikes by the United States, France, Italy, Canada, and the United Kingdom designed to protect civilian supporters of the secessionists and establish a no-fly zone. NATO subsequently took over the bulk of military operations, aided by Qatar, Jordan, the United Arab Emirates, and Sweden. As the intervention dragged on in 2011, concerns even among R2P advocates grew that it had become a justification for war. As discussed later in the chapter, Libya did not set a precedent for UN-authorized enforcement in the subsequent humanitarian crisis in Syria. After the intervention, Libya descended into civil war with foreign fighters joining sides and contributing to a political and humanitarian crisis. As of early 2023, Libya remained without an internationally accepted government.

Enforcement and Sanction

Sanctions have long been a favorite tool in states' efforts to get others to do what they want them to do. Unilaterally imposed sanctions are problematic, however, because they do not close off alternative markets and sources of supply for the targeted states. Yet organizing multilateral sanctions without a multilateral forum or organization through which to reduce the diplomatic transaction costs of securing other states' cooperation is a difficult undertaking. Beginning with the League of Nations, the potential for using sanctions as an instrument of security governance was significantly enhanced.

Multilateral sanctions were rarely used, however, until the 1990s. The League applied voluntary sanctions once (on Italy). Before 1990, the UN imposed mandatory sanctions under Chapter VII only twice (on the white minority regime in Southern Rhodesia, now Zimbabwe, and on South Africa). The Arab League imposed sanctions on Israel in 1948 and the OAS imposed them on Cuba between 1964 and 1975.

Sanctions are now a key enforcement instrument, particularly for the UN, serving one or more purposes: to coerce a change of behavior, constrain access to critical goods and funds and thereby raise costs and force changes in a target's behavior, or signal and stigmatize targets in support of international norms (Biersteker et al. 2016). Beginning with the comprehensive sanctions imposed on Iraq in 1990, the Security Council used different forms of sanctions in fourteen situations over the next eleven years, leading one study to dub the 1990s the "sanctions decade" (Cortright and Lopez 2000). Over the twenty-year period from 1992 to 2012, the Security Council imposed sanctions in twenty-two situations. Fourteen cases involved peace enforcement, all but one in intrastate conflicts; four were related to terrorism; three were related to proliferation of weapons of mass destruction, specifically nuclear weapons (Iraq, Iran, North Korea); four were related to upholding democratically elected governments (Haiti, Guinea-Bissau, Côte d'Ivoire); and one was related to protecting civilians under R2P (Libya). As the authors of a major project on targeted sanctions note, "Because the affirmation of an international norm is embedded in the *signaling* aspect of every episode, sanctions function as a central mechanism for the strengthening and/or negotiation of international norms" (Biersteker et al. 2013). Clearly, the purposes for which sanctions have been employed have broadened.

As of early 2023, there were fifteen active Security Council sanctions committees overseeing the implementation of and compliance with Council-approved sanctions. Work on these committees takes a large portion of council members' time, and briefings on sanctions are on the council agenda almost monthly.

Regional IGOs and sanctions. Regional organizations have applied sanctions in many of the same situations as the UN and, in a few cases, ahead of the UN, as when ECOWAS first imposed sanctions on Sierra Leone in 1997 and the EU imposed an arms embargo on Yugoslavia in 1990. The EU and United States imposed counterterrorism sanctions against Libya and Syria in the 1980s, well ahead of the UN.

The OAS and AU have used suspensions of membership in more recent years to promote the norm of democratic rule and punish unconstitutional changes in government, such as military coups. ECOWAS and SADC have also imposed subregional sanctions on specific states for unconstitutional changes, including Côte d'Ivoire, Guinea, Mali, Sierra

Leone, and Madagascar. Where human rights violations and unconstitutional changes of government or refusal to recognize election results are involved, the EU, ECOWAS, and the AU have used sanctions, but the UN Security Council generally has not. For this reason, Andrea Charron and Clara Portela (2016: 116) regard regional IGOs as "'pioneers' of democracy support and human rights sanctions."

There is no clear division of labor between regional IGOs and the UN. In some situations, the EU has chosen to go beyond what the Security Council authorized, often following the lead of the United States. Where the African organizations use sanctions against their own members to resolve regional security concerns, the EU imposes sanctions more commonly on nonmembers as part of its Common Foreign Policy, which includes support of democracy, rule of law, and human rights. In 2014, the United States, EU, and a number of other countries imposed sanctions on Russia after its annexation of Crimea and in support for separatists in Ukraine. These were expanded after Russia's 2022 invasion of Ukraine. In neither case was it possible for the UN Security Council to act because of Russia's veto and likely support from China.

Sanctions are typically viewed as a cheaper and easier tool for coercion and punishment than the use of armed force. Comprehensive trade sanctions are expected to have a political effect by imposing the costs of economic and other forms of deprivation on the offending state's government and people. By implication, the pain of sanctions will be lifted once there is a change in behavior, which may also mean a change of government. An alternative approach to sanctions is a bargaining model (carrot-and-stick approach) in which the target state is offered rewards for taking successive steps in the desired direction, rather than having to do everything that was expected to see any lifting of sanctions. The range of sanctions has included comprehensive economic and trade restrictions, but also more targeted measures, such as arms embargoes, travel restrictions on specific people, and bans on exports or imports of specific commodities. We use four case studies to illustrate the UN's and EU's use of sanctions. Table 7.1 provides an overview of the UN's use of different types of sanctions since 1990.

Iraq and the problems with comprehensive sanctions. When Iraq invaded Kuwait in August 1990, the Security Council immediately invoked Chapter VII to condemn the invasion and demand withdrawal. Subsequent resolutions imposed mandatory economic and transport sanctions against Iraq and established a sanctions committee to monitor implementation. Following the Gulf War's end in April 1991, Resolution 687 enumerated terms of the cease-fire agreement and a far-reaching plan for the destruction, under international supervision, of Iraq's chemical and biological weapons and ballistic missiles, the renunciation of nuclear weapons, and the placement of all nuclear-usable material (such as for power plants) under international control. The comprehensive sanctions were to continue until all the provisions were carried out to the Security Council's satisfaction. The only exception was oil sales authorized under the 1995 Oil-for-Food Programme to pay for food and medical supplies.

The Iraq sanctions became highly controversial as they produced a mounting humanitarian crisis among ordinary Iraqis, aggravated by the

Table 7.1 Selected Types of UN Sanctions, 1990–2022

Type of Sanction	Target Country or Entity	Years
Comprehensive sanctions	Iraq	1990–2003
	Yugoslavia	1992–1995
	Haiti	1993–1994
Arms embargo	Angola and UNITA	1993–2002
	Libya	1992–2003, 2011–
	Somalia	1992–
	Afghanistan	1990–2000
	Sierra Leone (RUF only)	1998–
	al-Qaeda and Taliban	1999–
	Liberia (militias)	2003–
	DRC (militias)	2003–2008, 2008–
	Côte d'Ivoire	2004–
	Sudan (militias)	2004–
	Iran	2006–
	North Korea	2006–
	Al-Shabaab	2010
	ISIS and Al Nusra Front	2014–
	Central African Republic	2018
	Yemen (targeted)	2020–
	ISIL-Tunisia	2021–
Export or import limits	Cambodia (logs, oil)	1992–1994
(ban exports of selected	Angola (diamonds)	1993, 1998–2002
technologies, diamonds,	Sierra Leone (oil, diamonds)	1997–1998, 2000–2003
timber, etc., or place	Liberia (diamonds, timber)	2001–2007
embargo on imports of	Côte d'Ivoire (diamonds)	2004–
oil, etc.)	Somalia (charcoal)	2012–
	North Korea (coal, iron ore, textiles)	2017–
Asset freeze	Libya	1993–1999
	Angola (UNITA only)	1998–2002
	al-Qaeda and Taliban (targeted)	2000–
	DRC (militias) (targeted)	2003–
	Côte d'Ivoire (targeted)	2004–
	Sudan (targeted)	2004–

(continues)

Table 7.1 continued

Type of Sanction	Target Country or Entity	Years
Asset freeze	Iran (targeted)	2006–
	North Korea (targeted)	2006–
	ISIS and Al Nusra Front	2014–
	Central African Republic	2014–
	South Sudan	2015–
	Mali (targeted)	2017–2020
Denial of visas (travel bans)	Libya	1992–1999
	Angola (UNITA only)	1997–2002
	Sudan (targeted)	2004–
	al-Qaeda and Taliban (targeted)	1999–
	DRC (militias) (targeted)	2005–
	Côte d'Ivoire (targeted)	2003–
	Iran (targeted)	2004–
	North Korea (targeted)	2006–
	Al-Shabaab	2010–
	ISIS and Al Nusra Front	2014–
	South Sudan (targeted)	2015–
	Mali (targeted)	2017–
	Houthis, Yemen	2022–
Cancellation of air links	Libya	1992–1999
	Afghanistan	1999–2001

Notes: "Targeted" indicates that the relevant UN sanctions committee maintains a list of specific individuals and entities that are targeted by the sanction. DRC: Democratic Republic of Congo; ISIL: Islamic State of Iraq and the Levant; ISIS: Islamic State of Iraq and Syria; RUF: Revolutionary United Front (Sierra Leone); UNITA: National Union for the Total Independence of Angola.

government's diversion of funds from the Oil-for-Food Programme. Evidence of malnutrition, contaminated water supplies, increased infectious disease, and higher infant and child mortality rates generated widespread sympathy and calls for ending sanctions. The Iraqi government exacerbated the crisis for political purposes and rejected proposals to alleviate it. Sanctions fatigue among countries that relied on trade with Iraq grew, and compliance eroded as unauthorized trade and transport links multiplied. The United States and United Kingdom, however, insisted on complete compliance before lifting sanctions and rejected proposals to reward Iraq's cooperation and encourage further progress by partially lifting them. The result was a stalemate, since Saddam Hussein had little incentive to cooperate (Thakur 2006: 145).

The sanctions were finally lifted in 2003 after the US invasion of Iraq. In retrospect, former Canadian UN ambassador David Malone (2006: 135) concluded: "On many levels, the Program [i.e., sanctions] worked: it saved many lives, it drove the disarmament process, and it prevented rearmament by keeping the lion's share of Iraq's oil wealth and imports—which could be used to produce [weapons of mass destruction]—out of the hands of Saddam Hussein." Still, the sanctions created broad resentment of the United States and its allies, which were seen as the key supporters of sanctions and thus may have had the unintended consequence of fueling militant Islam and anti-Westernism in Iraq and the region.

Angola: Learning from experience. More lessons came from the experience with sanctions on Angola that were initiated in 1993 in an effort to end a bitter civil war. Until 1999, there had been almost no monitoring to ensure compliance. In 2001, after the Security Council created an independent monitoring group, arms deliveries were greatly reduced; countries were no longer providing safe havens to leaders of the rebel National Union for the Total Independence of Angola(UNITA); and diamond export revenues that had been targeted by sanctions had dropped. As a result, Angola became what David Cortright and George Lopez (2002: 71) called "one of the most important developments in sanctions policy in recent years."

The Security Council drew four important lessons from the experience with sanctions on Iraq and Angola. The first involved the large-scale negative humanitarian effects, especially of general trade sanctions, which had changed many people's perception of the pain/gain trade-offs in sanctions. The second lesson was that strangling a target state's economy did not necessarily impose any economic pain on government leaders and their personal wealth. Prospects for compliance were low unless sanctions affected them specifically. Third, in intrastate conflicts and failed states, generalized sanctions were largely ineffective in an environment without normal governmental controls over taxation and documentation of cross-border trade. Fourth, the ability to monitor sanctions imposed is vital to ensuring compliance.

In short, a major lesson was that sanctions must be tailored to the specific situation if they are to be effective. Since 1994, no comprehensive sanctions have been initiated by either the Security Council or regional organizations. Instead, sanctions target not just "what" but "who." Targets have included entire governments, government leaders, rebel factions, terrorist groups, leaders' family members, and specific individuals. Humanitarian impact assessments are standard practice now, though they are often difficult to conduct.

Since the early 2000s, then, the Security Council has strengthened the UN's capacity to administer various types of sanctions, including by creating sanctions committees. These include independent experts who gather and analyze data on sanctions violators, supply routes, networks, and transactions. In addition, the Council has set time limits (generally twelve months) for sanctions, thereby forcing itself to review the sanctions and decide whether they should be renewed or changed.

Many other actors are involved in monitoring and enforcing sanctions, including government finance and trade ministries, border control agencies, the US Treasury Department, and nuclear regulatory agencies. For example, the Financial Action Task Force (FATF), created by the G-7 in 1989, enforces anti–money laundering measures, and the Offshore Group of Banking Supervisors monitors offshore banking. NGOs now also play significant roles in the implementation, monitoring, and evaluation of sanctions, such as in monitoring and documenting illegal trade in conflict diamonds.

Despite these difficulties, targeted sanctions with more careful monitoring of compliance have become the norm, even though their effectiveness as a global governance tool remains at issue. The UN Targeted Sanctions Project found that they have primarily been used to coerce and constrain, but signaling was also important, "often accomplished by the *very act* of the Security Council" (Giumelli 2016: 52; emphasis in original). Because sanctions are used in coordination with other policy instruments, it can be difficult to determine to which specific instrument(s) to attribute outcomes.

The impact of lessons learned in the 1990s about how to target and monitor sanctions can be seen in UN efforts to counter terrorism and halt Iran's nuclear weapons program.

Using sanctions to counter international terrorism. Starting in the early 1990s, the UN and EU imposed various types of sanctions, including diplomatic and aviation bans, on Libya, Sudan, and Afghanistan's Taliban regime for their roles in supporting terrorism. Generally, military force is not an option for addressing terrorism, including state-sponsored terrorism.

Sanctions targeting sources of funds for terrorists are crucial and depend particularly on the US Treasury Department, bank regulatory agencies, and private financial institutions for implementation, along with the cooperation of offshore financial havens in the Caribbean and Pacific island nations, such as Barbados, Antigua, Nauru, and Vanuatu. They require countries and private institutions to develop the legal and technical capabilities to monitor financial transactions (and be willing to do so), freeze assets of particular individuals, and act quickly to deny terrorists (and states sponsoring terrorists) time to move funds. UN sanctions imposed in 1999 on Taliban-controlled Afghanistan for its support of al-Qaeda (Resolution 1267) included a freeze of all financial assets along with an arms embargo and travel ban. These were later extended to target more than 500 people and groups associated with the Taliban and al-Qaeda, but not Afghanistan itself after 2001 (Boucher and Clemont 2016: 125). The Security Council's 1267 Committee monitored compliance, assisted by experts in international financial transactions, border enforcement, drug trafficking, arms embargoes, and counterterrorism legislation.

The most extensive set of measures was taken after the September 2001 terrorist attacks when the Security Council adopted Resolution 1373, requiring all states to block funding and recruitment for terrorist groups, freeze their assets, and deny them safe haven. It also established the Counter-Terrorism Committee (CTC) to monitor states' actions, and a group of independent experts to assist the committee with implementation.

As Table 7.1 shows, targeted sanctions have been a primary means of countering terrorism, including state-sponsored terrorism. Many of these sanctions have been in place for more than twenty years with no sign of ending, but with shifts in their intent and specific targets. The use of targeted sanctions against individuals, especially of those associated with al-Qaeda, has raised serious concerns about the open-ended denial of individual rights. This has led to legal challenges, particularly cases brought to the European Court of Justice, some of which have been successful. Also, as Biersteker et al. (2016: 273) note, "The scope of the problem and the geographical reach of designations have expanded to include listings associated with Boko Haram in Nigeria, al Shabaab in Somalia and Kenya, and the Islamic State of Iraq and the Levant (ISIL) operating in Iraq and Syria" (and now well beyond). The indefinite length problem also is the case for efforts to deal with nuclear weapons proliferation. In short, too little thought is given to how and when to end sanctions.

Using sanctions to halt Iran's nuclear weapons program. Since 2006, UN sanctions supplemented by EU and US measures have been used to try to prevent Iran from developing nuclear weapons. The Security Council's first sanctions resolution (1737), in 2006, called for Iran to cooperate fully with the IAEA and suspend all enrichment and reprocessing activities. It also called for states to block the direct or indirect supply, sale, or transfer of any items, materials, goods, and technology that could contribute to Iran's enrichment-related and reprocessing activities and ballistic missile programs "from their territories, or by their nationals or using their flag vessels or aircraft." It imposed financial sanctions and created a monitoring body, the 1737 Committee. The Security Council spelled out humanitarian exemptions and the actions Iran had to take for the sanctions to be suspended or terminated. In 2007, a second resolution authorized inspections of sea and air cargo to and from Iran, tightened monitoring of Iranian financial institutions, extended travel bans and asset freezes, and enlarged the list of targeted individuals and companies.

Resolutions in 2008 and 2010 extended the sanctions, targeting Islamic Revolutionary Guard Corps–owned businesses, the shipping industry, and the commercial and financial sector. The EU added a ban on oil purchases from Iran in 2012. The UN, EU, and extensive US sanctions isolated Iran from the international banking system, banned investment and aid to Iran's energy sector, blocked US and European firms from doing business in the country, and progressively added groups targeted for asset freezes.

In 2012, the P-5 plus Germany and senior EU officials began negotiations to address the possibility of lifting some or all of the UN, EU, and US sanctions as a big "carrot" to motivate Iran. That effort coincided with Iran's 2012 election, which brought President Hassan Rouhani to office vowing to try to get the sanctions lifted and improve the devastated economy. After agreement was reached in 2015 and endorsed by the UN Security Council, all UN sanctions on Iran (except the arms embargo) were terminated as of January 2016. When it was clear that Iran was violating the agreement, the Security Council rejected a US proposal to extend the arms embargo, which expired in 2020, under the terms of the 2015 agreement (Hansler and Roth 2020). The United States reimposed unilateral sanctions in 2018 and extended them in 2019 and 2020; the EU reimposed sanctions in 2022.

The various lessons about sanctions have been brought to bear in a number of ways to respond to Russia's 2022 invasion of Ukraine even though the UN itself has not been directly involved.

Russia's invasion of Ukraine and the use of sanctions. Russia's invasion of Ukraine in 2022, even more than its seizure of Crimea and claims over other parts of Ukraine in 2014, posed one of the most serious challenges to global peace and security governance since the end of World War II. The invasion challenges fundamental norms regarding the use of force to annex territory, the right of nations to self-determination, and the pledge to settle disputes by peaceful means. Although there have been numerous occasions over the years when one of the P-5 was directly or indirectly involved in a situation and blocked action by the UN Security Council, the palpable frustration and anger this time was different. Russia's isolation was evident in three General Assembly Emergency Special Sessions on Ukraine with over 140 of the UN's 193 member states voting to condemn its invasion in March 2022, condemn its illegal annexation of four regions of Ukraine in October 2022, and demand that Russia recall its troops in February 2023. As the EU's ambassador to the UN stated, "Some of the most passionate and important statements today were made by small countries, far away from Ukraine, expressing the concerns of every continent and country . . . about what Russia is doing" (Banjo 2022).

Clearly, it was impossible for the Security Council to approve any sanctions on Russia. The EU, United States, and many other countries around the world imposed sanctions and extended them as the war ground on. As Nicholas Mulder (2022) noted, "Not since the 1930s has an economy the size of Russia's been placed under such a wide array of commercial restrictions as those imposed in response to its invasion." Unlike the situation with Italy and Japan in the 1930s, "Russia today is a major exporter of oil, grain, and other key commodities, [a structurally significant position] and the global economy is far more integrated." The result is far wider effects, including on human security issues like global food supply and migration and refugees.

Given Ukraine's geographic position and Eastern Europe's experience with Russian aggression in the past, the EU responded by providing arms to Ukraine and implementing an unprecedented range of sanctions, including a ban on importation of Russian coal and oil. The sanctions included lists of individuals targeted with travel bans and asset freezes, including President Valdimir Putin and Foreign Minister Sergey Lavrov; restrictions on financial transactions with Russian banks; a halt to air travel; embargoes on Russian technology and luxury goods; a ban on many EU exports to Russia; and suspension of an agreement that facilitated visa approvals (Lefebvre 2023: 2). Only Hungary contested the sanctions, but it did not block the decisions. There were goods and sectors exempted in part to maintain unanimity on the sanctions. These included trade in Russian diamonds, Greek ships carrying Russian oil, and imports of Russian uranium for nuclear power generation (Stevis-Gridneff 2022: A7). Imports of Russian gas became moot after the closure of the Nord Stream pipeline, first by Russia itself, then by an unexplained explosion.

The EU's sanctions mirrored many of the extensive sanctions imposed by the United States and its partners and allies, including NATO members, members of the G-7, and others. Altogether, these targeted a wide range of individuals and entities tied to energy, defense, raw materials, services, transport, banking, and investment. They cut Russian financial institutions' access to the Society Worldwide Interbank Financial Telecommunication (SWIFT) system. Belarus was also targeted for its involvement in Russia's invasion, as was Iran for providing drones used in Russia's military actions in Ukraine. The clear intent was to weaken Russia's economic base and its ability to wage war and punish it for its act of aggression (Welt et al. 2022). Few observers were optimistic, however, and this reinforces other analyses that show the limits of sanctions in coercing or compelling states—in this case, a major power—to change their behavior. Unquestionably, the extent and nature of the sanctions were a clear signal of many countries' strong disapproval of Russia's aggression.

Clearly, sanctions have become a major tool for the UN, some regional organizations, and major states to address threats to international peace and security. Yet these cases illustrate that their effectiveness, beyond imposing costs on an offending state, can be questionable and indeterminate. They "are not a magic bullet for achieving foreign policy goals" (Hufbauer et al. 2007: 141).

This leads us to look next at various types of peace operations that have been used extensively by the UN and some regional organizations.

Peace Operations

The UN's very first peace operation was created in the late 1940s to provide observer groups for cease-fires in Kashmir and Palestine, and those observers are still there (see Table 7.2)! At the height of the Suez crisis in 1956, the idea of what became known as "peacekeeping" was formally proposed by Lester B. Pearson, Canada's Secretary of State for External Affairs, as a means of securing the withdrawal of British, French, and Israeli forces from Egypt, pending a political settlement. Its subsequent development enabled the UN to play a positive role in dealing with regional conflicts at a time when hostility between East and West prevented the use of the Chapter VII provisions for sanctions and collective security.

The UN and some regional IGOs have deployed various types of peace operations to help maintain cease-fire agreements, stabilize conflict situations, create an environment conducive to peaceful settlement, implement peace agreements, protect civilian populations at risk in humanitarian crises, and assist in laying the foundations for durable peace. There have been more than seventy operations since 1948, the majority of them initiated since 1990. The twelve operations in the field at the end of 2022 had more than 150,000 personnel (military and civilian), and, in the case of the UN, a 2023 budget of more than $7 billion. In short, peacekeeping in various forms is "one of the most visible symbols of the UN role in international peace and security" (Thakur 2006: 37). It has also become a major activity for several regional organizations, most notably the AU, ECOWAS, and EU. The majority of contemporary peace operations are in Africa, and many of these involve multiple organizations (e.g., the UN with ECOWAS and/or the AU) carrying out different parts of mandates from the UN Security Council. This has made Africa a "giant laboratory for global peacekeeping" (Adebajo 2014: 183). But "no two peace operations are the same, and hence they all face a unique set of challenges." (Williams 2011: 192)

Distinguishing Between Enforcement and Peacekeeping

The UN has long defined peacekeeping as "an operation involving military personnel, but without enforcement powers, undertaken by the United Nations to help maintain or restore international peace and security in areas of conflict" (UN 1996: 4). Without a Charter provision, peacekeeping lies in a gray area between the peaceful settlement provisions of Chapter VI and the military enforcement provisions of Chapter VII and is sometimes referred to as "Chapter VI and a half." Some operations have crossed that gray area, though, and more closely resembled enforcement, creating controversy and operational problems.

Table 7.2 Traditional UN Peacekeeping Operations (representative cases)

Operation	Title	Location	Duration	Maximum Strength
UNEF I	First UN Emergency Force	Suez Canal, Sinai Peninsula	November 1956–June 1967	3,378 troops
UNFICYP	UN Peace-keeping Force in Cyprus	Cyprus	March 1964–present	6,411 military observers
UNIFIL	UN Interim Force in Lebanon	Southern Lebanon	March 1978–present	11,790 troops, 1,004 civilians
UNIIMOG	UN Iran-Iraq Military Observer Group	Iran–Iraq border	August 1988–February 1991	400 military observers
UNMEE	UN Mission in Ethiopia and Eritrea	Ethiopia–Eritrea border	September 2000–July 2008	3,940 troops, 214 police

Since the end of the Cold War, "peacekeeping has evolved from a primarily military model of observing cease-fires and the separation of forces after inter-state wars, to incorporate a complex model of many elements—military, police and civilian—working together to help lay the foundations for sustainable peace" (UN 2008: 18). It has become common to distinguish between traditional peacekeeping and complex, multidimensional peacekeeping and peacebuilding operations. Thus, peacekeepers' tasks have varied significantly over time and with Security Council mandates for different types of peace operations, as outlined in Figure 7.7.

Peacekeeping may be easier than enforcement because no aggressor need be identified, so no one party to the conflict is singled out for blame—making it easier to get approval for an operation. This is also why it is important for UN peacekeepers to maintain credibility as an impartial force; otherwise, they can become a target, as has happened in Somalia, Mali, and the Central African Republic. Another advantage of peacekeeping over enforcement is that most operations require relatively small numbers of troops or police from contributing states, a critical factor because the UN relies on ad hoc military units or subcontracts operations to a coalition of states or regional IGO. The size of UN peacekeeping forces has varied from small monitoring missions numbering fewer than 100 to major operations requiring 20,000 or more troops.

Figure 7.7   Types of Peace Operations Tasks

Traditional Operations

Observation, monitoring, and reporting
- cease-fires and withdrawal of forces
- investigating complaints of violations

Separation of combatant forces
- establish buffer zones
- use of force only for self-defence

Complex, Multidimensional Operations

The above tasks, plus many of the following:

Observation and monitoring
- democratic elections
- human rights
- arms control

Limited use of force
- maintain or restore civil law and order
- disarm combatants
- demining

Humanitarian assistance and intervention
- open food and medical supply lines; guard supplies
- protect aid workers
- protect refugees
- create safe havens

Peacebuilding
- rebuild and train police and judiciary
- organize elections and promote civil society
- repatriate refugees

Statebuilding
- security sector reform (military and police)
- strengthen rule of law, rebuild judiciary
- reform bureaucracy, reduce corruption
- promote market-led development
- provide interim civil administration

Theoretically, three core principles give peacekeeping additional advantages over enforcement. The first is consent of the parties in a conflict, which means the UN must be invited. The second is that UN operations endeavor to maintain strict impartiality. Under the third principle, UN forces are lightly armed and prohibited from using armed force except in self-defense or in defense of their mandate.

All three of peacekeeping's core principles have become problematic with different types of operations. Obtaining consent is difficult in conflicts involving armed rebel, paramilitary, and militia groups, as in the Democratic Republic of Congo, or terrorist groups, like in Mali and Somalia. Even having given consent to UN presence, states may prohibit certain actions, as Eritrea did by denying UN peacekeepers permission to use helicopters and land patrols to monitor the cease-fire with Ethiopia. Governments may call for premature withdrawal of a mission (that is, before the mandate has been fulfilled), as Egypt did in 1967. In short, "Peacekeeping operations are increasingly being tested by deteriorating consent. . . . [Yet] consent should not be understood to require absolute deference to the wishes of the host government" (Johnstone 2011: 172).

In more "muscular" operations, troops are more heavily equipped than traditional peacekeepers, and their Security Council mandate likely invokes

Chapter VII of the Charter and permits the use of force other than in self-defense. This blurs the line between peacekeeping and enforcement. Some recent UN operations are "stabilization efforts" and include elements of counterinsurgency and counterterrorism (e.g., Mali, Democratic Republic of Congo, and South Sudan). In these situations, often there is no peace to keep, no cease-fire to monitor, and no consent for the mission from the local parties, who are not states or include a failed state.

UN peacekeeping today reflects many adaptations in the field and at UN headquarters. Other than the long-standing traditional operations discussed below, most peace operations more closely resemble war operations, and a number of them involve regional organizations. First, we look at traditional peacekeeping (Karlsrud 2015).

Traditional Peacekeeping

When peacekeeping was first used in Palestine and Kashmir in 1948, a few military observers were deployed to monitor armistice agreements that halted fighting between Israel and the Arab states and between India and Pakistan. Beginning in 1956, it became a valuable tool for the UN in dealing with conflicts in the Middle East (four traditional peacekeeping operations in the Arab-Israeli conflict alone) and other areas where the superpowers' interests were not directly at stake but Cold War tensions made it impossible to use collective security or enforcement measures.

As illustrated in Table 7.2, traditional peacekeeping is still important in the Middle East. In the late 1980s, it was used to facilitate the withdrawal of Soviet troops from Afghanistan and supervise the cease-fire agreement between Iran and Iraq. It was used again to monitor the cease-fires between Iraq and Kuwait after the Gulf War in 1991 and between Ethiopia and Eritrea in 2001. These conflicts were all interstate conflicts. The peacekeepers' mission was to contain fighting or monitor the cease-fire until negotiations produced a lasting peace agreement. The peacekeepers were unarmed or lightly armed, often stationed between the hostile forces to monitor truces and troop withdrawals, and provide a buffer zone, report violations; they were authorized to use force only in self-defense. Traditional peacekeeping forces, limited in size and capacity, cannot stop a party that is determined to mount an offensive, as Israel has repeatedly shown in attacking Lebanon despite the presence of the UN Interim Force in Lebanon (UNIFIL). Host-state consent for a peacekeeping force can be withdrawn, forcing the withdrawal of UN troops, as happened in the Sinai when Egypt withdrew its permission for the UN Emergency Force (UNEF I) immediately before the onset of the 1967 Arab-Israeli War.

During the Cold War, many important peace and security issues, including the Vietnam War, never made it onto the UN agenda. But the innovation of UN peacekeeping provided a valuable way of limiting superpower involvement in regional conflicts and coping with threats to peace posed by the emergence of new states, border conflicts among those states, and intractable conflicts in Kashmir, the Middle East, and Cyprus. In the process, the UN and the international community developed a body of experience and practice in peacekeeping that proved even more valuable in the late 1980s and the 1990s, when the Cold War's end created political conditions conducive to expanding the tasks given to peacekeepers (and new types of threats demanding creative responses). The success of its peacekeeping activities in the late 1980s earned the UN the Nobel Peace Prize in 1988 and led to many new missions.

The principles that guided traditional peacekeeping have become more problematic with different types of operations since 1990, particularly those in intrastate conflicts that have required a more "muscular" and multidimensional approach.

Complex, Multidimensional Peacekeeping

The UN defines multidimensional peacekeeping operations as "operations comprising a mix of military, police and civilian components working together to lay the foundations of a sustainable peace" (UN 2008: 97). Such operations involve more troops, often more heavily equipped than traditional peacekeepers, and with mandates that permit the use of force other than in self-defense, blurring the line with enforcement. While troop contingents in such operations may engage in observation activities characteristic of traditional operations, they are more likely to be monitoring the cantonment, disarmament, and demobilization of military forces and clearing landmines. Other military personnel, civilians, and police, along with NGOs and UN agencies such as UHCR, UNICEF, and UNDP are involved in restoring law and order; repatriating and resettling refugees; organizing and supervising democratic elections; monitoring and promoting human rights; and rebuilding the police and judiciary—tasks that are variously characterized as postconflict peacebuilding or statebuilding. With the variety of actors, coordinating the military and civilian components is a significant challenge. In four post–Cold War situations (Namibia, Cambodia, Kosovo, and Timor-Leste), the UN also provided interim or transitional civil administration. Often, in such cases, there has been no peace to keep, no cease-fire to monitor, and no consent for the mission from local parties that are not states or perhaps failed states, such as in Somalia and the Democratic Republic of Congo. As discussed already, the resolutions for most peace operations now invoke Chapter VII to provide the legal basis for a range of actions, show the Security Council's political resolve, and remind member states of their obligations to give effect to Council decisions. Table 7.3 shows selected complex UN peacekeeping operations, including the variety of tasks undertaken.

UN Secretaries-General since 1990 have contributed ideas and initiatives to peacekeeping. In addition, there have been major reviews that have

Table 7.3 Complex UN Peacekeeping Operations (representative cases)

Country	Somalia	Cambodia	E. Timor	Bosnia/Croatia	DR Congo	Sudan-Darfur	DR Congo	Mali
Mission	UNOSOM II	UNTAC	UNTAET	UNPROFOR	MONUC	UNAMID	MONUSCO	MINUSMA
Dates	5/93–5/95	7/91–4/95	10/99–5/02	2/92–12/95	11/99–7/10	7/07–12/20	5/10–	4/13–12/23
Maximum strength								
Troops	28,000	15,900	6,281	38,599	19,815	17,711	19,815	11,726
Police		3,600	1,288	803	1,229	5,109	1,665	1,744
Observers			118	684	760	235	760	
Civilians	2,800	2,400	2,482	4,632	3,756	3,876	3,769	3,384
Chapter VII authority								
Military tasks	✓	✓	✓	✓	✓	✓	✓	✓
Monitor cease-fire	✓	✓	✓	✓	✓	✓	✓	✓
Peace enforcement	✓	✓	✓	✓	✓	✓		✓
Disarmament	✓	✓			✓			
Demining	✓				✓			
Refugee and humanitarian aid								
Refugee return	✓	✓	✓	✓	✓	✓	✓	✓
Assist civilians	✓	✓	✓	✓	✓	✓	✓	✓
Protect intl. workers			✓		✓			✓
Civil policing		✓	✓		✓			
Police retraining			✓		✓			
Electoral assistance								
Monitor elections		✓	✓		✓		✓	✓
Legal affairs								
Constitution/judicial reform	✓	✓	✓		✓		✓	✓
Human rights oversight		✓			✓			✓
Administrative authority		✓	✓		✓			✓

contributed to strengthening the management and planning for peace operations. These include the 2000 report on UN peacekeeping reform by the Panel on United Nations Peace Operations, known as the Brahimi Report, and the 2014–2015 review by the High-level Panel on Peace Operations, known as the HIPPO Report. The latter called for "an awakening" at UN headquarters to the "distinct and important needs of field missions" and to "sequenced and prioritized mandates" with "strengthened global and regional partnerships" (UN General Assembly 2015).

Case studies of the former Yugoslavia, Democratic Republic of Congo, and Mali where there have been large humanitarian crises but no peace to be kept, illustrate the challenges faced by and the evolution of complex missions over time.

Former Yugoslavia and Bosnia-Herzegovina. Yugoslavia's disintegration into five separate states in the early 1990s unleashed the fiercest fighting in Bosnia-Herzegovina where Croats, Serbs, and Bosnian Muslims were intermingled. Nationalist leaders of each group fueled ancient suspicions and hostilities; each group's military and paramilitary tried to enlarge and ethnically cleanse its territorial holdings. The resulting war killed more than 200,000 people, produced millions of refugees, and subjected thousands to concentration camps, rape, torture, and genocide.

Between 1991 and 1996, the Security Council devoted a record number of meetings to debate whether to intervene, to what end, and with what means. The UN Protection Force for Yugoslavia (UNPROFOR) was authorized in February 1992, and its mandate gradually broadened from maintaining a cease-fire in the heavily Serbian areas of Croatia, disbanding and demilitarizing regular and paramilitary forces, and delivering humanitarian assistance, to creating safe areas for refugees in Bosnia, relieving the besieged city of Sarajevo, protecting basic human rights, and using NATO to enforce sanctions, a no-fly zone, and safe areas and conduct air strikes on Serbian forces. In short, what began as a traditional peacekeeping mission was transformed into a much more complex one involving use of force bordering on enforcement. The lightly armed UN peacekeepers encountered massive violations of human rights, a situation demanding more vigorous military action, and very little interest by the parties in making peace.

By late 1992, with no cease-fire in place, the Security Council invoked Chapter VII, calling for member states to "take all necessary measures." This turned UNPROFOR into more of an enforcement operation. The Security Council met almost continuously and passed resolution after resolution, progressively enlarging UNPROFOR's mandate, but resolutions did not produce the manpower or the logistical, financial, and military resources needed to fulfill the enlarged mandate. UN personnel were reluctant to use the authority given them to call for NATO air strikes. All sides interfered with relief efforts and targeted UN peacekeepers and international aid personnel. The UN-declared safe areas were anything but safe for the civilians who had taken refuge in them. Srebrenica, in particular, became a humiliating defeat when UN peacekeepers failed to prevent the massacre of more than 7,000 Bosnian Muslim men and boys by Bosnian Serbs in July 1995 (UN 1999a).

The UN's peacekeeping role in Bosnia ended with the US-brokered Dayton Peace Accords of November 1995. UNPROFOR was replaced by NATO's Implementation Force (IFOR) of 60,000 combat-ready troops, including units from almost twenty non-NATO countries (including Russia)—NATO's first effort at peacekeeping. Many IGOs and NGOs were involved in implementing parts of the Dayton Accords. The UN was charged with monitoring and reforming Bosnia's police forces. The OSCE was responsible for overseeing elections and, along with NGOs, promoting human rights and civil society groups. The UNHCR oversaw the return, resettlement, and rehabilitation of refugees and internally displaced persons. The World Bank, European Bank for Reconstruction and Development, and NGOs promoted economic development.

In late 1996, IFOR was replaced by the smaller NATO Stabilization Force; the EU took over from NATO in 2004 and continues to operate a small force under Security Council authorization, with troops from twenty-one countries as of 2023. The primary purpose is to maintain a safe and secure environment and provide training for Bosnian forces.

More than twenty-five years after the Dayton Accords, Bosnia remains a kind of international protectorate under the quasi-colonial authority of a "high representative." The country is still dependent on aid; its economy remains highly criminalized and lags behind comparable economies in Eastern Europe. The country remains effectively partitioned among its constituent Bosniak, Croat, and Serb territories, and nationalist parties still dominate the government.

The international community's experience in Bosnia demonstrates the difficulties of complex, multidimensional peace operations. The resources expended—60,000 troops and more than $5 billion in aid for a country of four million people—yielded what one study published a decade after the Dayton Accords called "a vastly improved but still frankly disappointing outcome" (Cousens and Harland 2006: 121). This level of international engagement, the study's authors added, was "unlikely to be replicated in many other contexts, particularly where the strategic interests of key states and organizations are not seen to be heavily at stake."

Democratic Republic of Congo: The "infinite crisis." The situation in the Democratic Republic of Congo (DRC) provides a useful comparison with that in Bosnia. It has ten times more people and fifty times more territory than Bosnia, and a conflict far more violent and complex. Only after more

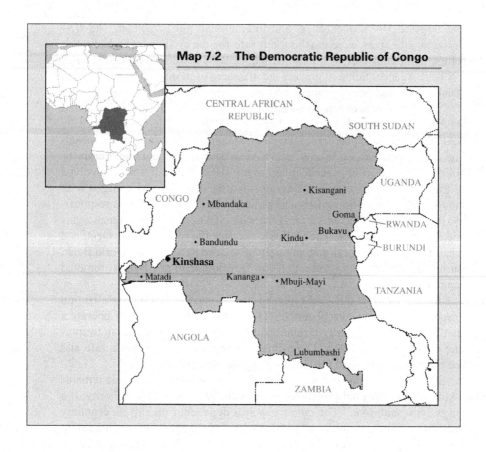

Map 7.2   The Democratic Republic of Congo

than five years of fighting (and a peace agreement) did the peacekeeping force reach one-sixth the size of IFOR and receive Chapter VII authority. More than twenty-five years later, the DRC case exemplifies a multidimensional peace mission operating in a situation of internationalized civil war with multiple belligerents, large-scale humanitarian crisis, lootable resources, and a failing state. With more than 5.4 million people killed, 5 million displaced, and more than 20 million food insecure, it is one of the world's deadliest conflicts.

Crises in the Congo have threatened international peace and security in three different periods. The first occurred when the country gained independence from Belgium in 1960 and civil order collapsed, leading to a four-year UN peace operation that failed to create much stability. The second followed the genocide in Rwanda in 1994, when Hutu extremists responsible for the genocide fled to UN-operated refugee camps in eastern Zaire, as it was then called, and no peacekeeping force was established to disarm or prevent them from regrouping and carrying out attacks in Rwanda. The third began with a 1996 rebellion against longtime Zairean dictator Joseph Mobutu, backed by Uganda and Rwanda. These two along with six other African countries intervened in what was dubbed "Africa's first world war," which lasted from 1998 to 2002 and was disastrous for civilians.

Despite the signing of a peace agreement in late 2002, violence persisted, as did the massive humanitarian crisis, large population displacements, violent systematic rapes, and collapse of the health and food systems. The economic interests of neighboring states and various militias in the DRC's rich and lootable resources have impeded peacemaking efforts. The UN force has been tarnished by failure to protect civilians adequately and by widespread sexual exploitation and abuse by peacekeepers.

Initial efforts to halt fighting in the DRC were led by SADC countries as well as the OAU and the Francophonie (the organization of former French-speaking colonies). The 1999 Lusaka Agreement, mediated by SADC, was the basis for the UN's initial deployment of a relatively small number of peacekeepers of 4,900 in the UN Organization Mission in the Democratic Republic of the Congo (MONUC). But that force was not allowed to deploy outside of the capital, and there were numerous cease-fire violations. In 2003, an upsurge of ethnic violence in the east led the Security Council to authorize deployment under Chapter VII of an interim emergency multinational force. The French-led EU operation, Operation Artemis, was the EU's first military operation. Mandated to reinforce MONUC and halt the rapidly deteriorating humanitarian situation in the city of Bunia, troops from five EU countries were on the ground within a week, but the operation was limited in duration (three months) and scope. In 2004, the Security Council authorized an enlarged MONUC to use force to protect civilians, assist the transitional government, fill the security vacuum, and disarm and repatriate former armed militias, including the Rwandan Hutu *genocidaires*. Not only was MONUC understaffed for its mission, but with its more aggressive tactics the UN peacekeepers also became targets themselves—just as in Somalia.

In 2006, MONUC's mission was again enlarged and with support of an EU rapid reaction force and EU funding, the DRC held its first multiparty presidential and parliamentary elections in forty years. Remarkably, the elections were considered reasonably free and fair. To many, this appeared to signal the success of UN-led peace operations. Living conditions for the majority of Congolese improved, violence against civilians diminished, displaced persons returned to their villages, and humanitarian organizations gained access to much of the country (Autesserre 2010).

Despite these signs of progress, violence persisted and, after 2008, worsened in the DRC's eastern provinces, and the country remained unstable. The Hutu militias were still active, along with various Congolese militias, the

Rwandan and Ugandan government troops, and the Ugandan-based Lord's Resistance Army. Looting of the DRC's rich natural resources continued, as did the humanitarian crises and the worst cases of sexual violence in the world committed by militias and Congolese government troops alike. The Security Council successively increased the size and mandate of the UN force over the next three years in an effort to address the persistent violence and continue various peacebuilding activities, but in 2009, tensions with the government led to a request that the UN withdraw all peacekeeping forces by mid-2011.

Subsequently, the UN and the DRC government reached an agreement to reconfigure the UN operation as a smaller stabilization mission (the UN Organization Stabilization Mission in the Democratic Republic of Congo, or MONUSCO after its French name). The mandate concentrated on civilian protection and military operations in eastern DRC.

In 2012 a new rebel group, M23, backed by Rwanda and Uganda, emerged to pose serious security problems, including the fall of one key city to M23 forces as Congolese troops fled and MONUSCO forces provided little resistance (or protection for civilians). This galvanized several important steps, including a Security Council–imposed arms embargo on M23; targeted sanctions on its leadership; and a framework agreement signed by the UN, the AU, SADC, the International Conference on the Great Lakes Region, and eleven neighboring countries, with Rwanda and Uganda pledging not to interfere in the Congo's internal affairs. The Security Council also authorized an ad hoc intervention force and use of surveillance drones to monitor the DRC's borders.

The Force Intervention Brigade, composed of 3,000 South African, Tanzanian, and Malawian troops with tanks and helicopter gunships, was initially deployed in mid-2013 under MONUSCO and alongside the Congolese army to neutralize and disarm warring militias. The use of the brigade raised concerns among aid organizations about the risks to the officials on the ground, as well as for future peacekeeping operations and the willingness of troop-contributing countries to put their soldiers at greater risk. Although the Security Council was careful to make clear that the force set no precedents for "the agreed principles of peacekeeping," others saw a "stronger approach that can give peacekeeping operations more strength in the future and help resolve knotty problems" (Kulish and Sengupta 2013: A10). An assessment of the legal issues raised by the brigade's mandate concluded that it effectively made MONUSCO a party to the armed conflict and could thus affect other UN operations, especially those in "high-threat environments" where their mandates make it likely they might be seen as "taking sides" (Sheeran and Case 2014: 19).

Waves of violence, including gender-based violence, have continued in the DRC, which remains a weak state teetering on the brink of failure. In early 2021, the Security Council noted the high levels of militia group violence included a group linked to the Islamic State. In many ways, the problems in the DRC defy categorization or comprehension and the UN peacekeepers have exacerbated them, failing to protect civilians from rape and abuse and engaging in corrupt practices themselves. A culture of impunity has pervaded MONUSCO. In short, the conflict is far more complex than the situations in Somalia or Yugoslavia.

The Congo's huge size and its geographical position in the heart of Africa have presented enormous logistical and operational difficulties that have magnified the cost of peace operations since roads and railroads are virtually unusable. Neither the SADC nor the AU have had the resources for significant enforcement action. And while the UN and other international actors have largely focused on national and regional causes of the violence, there are long-standing local conflicts over land, the DRC's rich resources, and political power that need to be addressed.

The Congo case underscores the UN Security Council's difficulty in crafting an overall strategy for dealing with complex conflicts. It also raises the difficult question of whether it is better to undertake a weak operation or none at all when there is no will for a robust one. A weak operation raises expectations that civilians will be protected and peace kept, yet hundreds of thousands have died and suffered human rights abuses, despite and even because of the presence of UN peacekeepers. But according to the Effectiveness of Peace Operations Network (2019), MONUSCO has prevented the recurrence of widespread conflict, reunified the country, stimulated the local economy, and helped create a more robust civil society. The UN has developed strategies for protection of civilians that are now used throughout UN operations.

Mali: When peacekeepers meet terrorists. Our third case study of complex, multidimensional peacekeeping deals with Mali, where the actors once again include African regional groups and, similar to Somalia in recent years, a terrorist group, al-Qaeda in the Islamic Mahgreb (AQIM). Mali exemplifies an operational environment where UN peacekeepers have had to coordinate with regional organizations and engage in activities that come close to enforcement operations.

Since the former French colony gained independence in 1960, Mali has witnessed repeated conflicts as the Tuaregs, an ethnic group from the northern region, have campaigned for self-determination. In early 2012 this group joined forces with AQIM and seized control of northern Mali. They had links to transnational organized crime, and kidnappings for ransom were a major problem. In late 2012, the Security Council authorized an ECOWAS/AU plan for an African-led International Support Mission to Mali. Shortly thereafter, France intervened to prevent the rebels from seizing parts of southern Mali, including the capital. In April 2013, the Security Council authorized the UN

Multidimensional Integrated Stabilization Mission in Mali (MINUSMA) in response to attacks on civilians, use of child soldiers, disappearances, rape, forced marriages, and displacement of 500,000 people.

Although concerned about involving the UN in offensive operations against the rebels or Islamist groups, the Council gave MINUSMA a robust Chapter VII mandate to support the establishment of government authority throughout the country, protect civilians, and pave the way for humanitarian aid. It did not explicitly authorize offensive operations against AQIM, but it did authorize French troops to "use all necessary means" to support MINUSMA when taking over from the AU/ECOWAS operation. Coordinating these different elements has been a major challenge. In 2014, the African countries formed a rapid intervention force similar to that in the DRC to fight terrorists and criminal groups and strengthen MINUSMA's ability to stabilize Mali, even deploying an intelligence unit made up of Swedish and Dutch personnel.

Other Islamist groups besides AQIM have been active in the country, along with criminal networks and violence has spread across the Sahel region. Mali's military seized power in 2020, the second coup in eight years, and expelled the French ambassador. The French pulled out entirely in 2022, and the UN was asked to leave in 2023. The Russian mercenary Wagner Group remained to help fight the jihadists.

Like the DRC, Mali raises questions about the nature of such multidimensional UN operations. With the combined AU, ECOWAS, Malian, and French special forces effectively conducting war against AQIM and other groups, MINUSMA has amounted to something much closer to enforcement. Even though it was the second largest UN operation after MONUSCO, it was unable to quell terrorist attacks, prevent hostage taking, or keep security even in Mali's capital. One analyst described MINUSMA even in its early days as a "flawed peace operation" and accused the Security Council of creating a peacekeeping operation with no peace to keep (Gowan 2013). Ten years later, the situation had hardly improved.

The cases of the DRC and Mali raise significant concerns about the line between peacekeeping and peace enforcement and whether the UN is actually at war (Karlsrud 2015). The authorization to use force other than to protect civilians for a limited period of time looks more like war than keeping peace and jeopardizes the safety of peacekeepers as well as civilian and humanitarian UN workers. It is unclear whether this signifies "a need to update principles, or whether this is a function of practice leaving still valid principles behind" (Karlsrud 2015: 50).

The contrasts between these more recent and older multidimensional UN missions are particularly evident in operations involving peacebuilding and statebuilding mandates. We look at three cases here—two involving postconflict peacebuilding from the early 1990s and one involving statebuilding in the world's newest state, South Sudan.

Postconflict Peacebuilding and Statebuilding

In various forms and degrees, postconflict peacebuilding activities are an integral part of most complex, multidimensional UN peace operations today, involving a variety of UN agencies and other IGOs and NGOs. The concept was first put forward by former Secretary-General Boutros Boutros-Ghali in *An Agenda for Peace* (1992), but its roots lie in the UN's role in the process of decolonization and its responses to the Namibia, Cambodia, and Central America conflicts in the late 1980s and early 1990s (Karns 2012). Precursor notions can actually be traced to liberal theory in the belief that armed conflict will be reduced and long-term stability assured as economic development occurs, democracy spreads, and human rights respected. This so-called liberal democratic peace is essentially the foundation for contemporary postconflict peacebuilding (Paris 2004).

When the UN first undertook these wide-ranging goals, there were serious questions regarding its authority for doing so, given Article 2(7) of the UN Charter—long seen as marking the line between states' sovereignty and UN authority. At the beginning of the 1990s, the Security Council authorized several missions that crossed the line, and the Security Council's endorsement of *An Agenda for Peace* marked their acceptance.

At the heart of peacebuilding is the recognition that "prevention and rebuilding are inextricably linked . . . [and] a formal agreement ending a civil [war] is meaningless unless coupled with long-term programs to heal the wounded society" (Weinberger 2002: 248). Peacebuilding operations, therefore, are multifaceted, often including long lists of military and civilian tasks associated with such operations (see Figure 7.6). Barnett and colleagues (2007: 44) found significant agreement "that peacebuilding is more than stability promotion; it is designed to create a positive peace, to eliminate root causes of conflict, to allow states and societies to develop stable expectations of peaceful change." Some analysts suggest that the breadth of the concept is problematic, given the lack of an agreed definition. And, because often there is no clear end to violence and beginning to postconflict activities, many peacebuilding activities take place simultaneously with efforts to end violence, as the DRC case illustrates. In some cases, such as Kosovo, Timor-Leste, and South Sudan, the UN has gone beyond peacebuilding to activities associated with actual statebuilding—that is, working with local actors to create the foundations and institutions of a government. To examine peacebuilding and statebuilding operations, missions in Namibia, Cambodia, and South Sudan are instructive.

Namibia: The first experiment in peace- and statebuilding. A former German colony (South West Africa) that was administered by South Africa as a League of Nations mandate after World War I, Namibia became the object of intense international efforts through the UN over many years to secure its independence. In the late 1970s, the Security Council approved a plan setting the terms for this with the approval of South Africa and the main Namibian liberation group (Karns 1987). Implementation stalled for a decade, however, until there was agreement on the withdrawal of both Cuban and South African troops from neighboring Angola.

The UN Transition Assistance Group in Namibia (UNTAG), deployed in April 1989, had the most ambitious and diverse mandate of any UN mission to that point. It included supervision of the cease-fire between South African and South West Africa People's Organizationn(SWAPO) forces, monitoring the withdrawal of South African forces and the confinement of SWAPO forces to bases, supervising the civil police force, securing repeal of discriminatory legislation, arranging for the release of political prisoners and return of exiles, assisting in drafting a new constitution, and creating conditions for free and fair elections. With military and civilian personnel from 109 countries, UNTAG managed the process by which Namibia moved step by step from South African rule to a cease-fire, full independence, and political stability (Howard 2008).

UNTAC is widely regarded as one of the UN's greatest peacekeeping success stories. That success owed much to factors that have not been present in other situations, however, including South Africa's competent administration and security forces, agreement on how to reach the goal of Namibian independence, and a strong sense of responsibility for providing the necessary resources (Dobbins et al. 2005: 42). The experience in Namibia led the UN to undertake other complex missions, not all of which enjoyed the same success. One of those was the Cambodian peace operation.

Cambodia: Experimenting with interim administration. In 1991, following the twenty-year civil war in Cambodia, the Agreements on a Comprehensive Political Settlement of the Cambodia Conflict were signed in Paris with US, Soviet, Chinese, and Vietnamese support. ASEAN also played a key role in the diplomatic settlement. The agreements "charged the UN—for the first time in its history—with the political and economic restructuring of a member state as part of the building of peace under which the parties were to institutionalize their reconciliation" (Doyle 1995: 26).

A small advance mission helped the four Cambodian parties implement the cease-fire. In 1992, the UN Transitional Authority in Cambodia (UNTAC) was deployed under a mandate that called for up to 22,000 military and civilian personnel. UNTAC's military component was charged with supervising the cease-fire and disarming and demobilizing forces; the civilian personnel had responsibility for Cambodia's foreign affairs, defense, finance, and public security. UN personnel monitored the police, promoted respect for human rights, assisted in the return of 370,000 Cambodian refugees from camps in Thailand, organized the 1993 elections that returned civil authority to Cambodians, and rehabilitated basic infrastructure and public utilities. As

Secretary-General Boutros Boutros-Ghali observed, "Nothing the UN has ever done can match this operation" (UN 1993: 26).

UNTAC's presence helped end Cambodia's civil war and bring a peace of sorts to most of the country. UNTAC was unable to achieve a full cease-fire and demobilization of forces or complete its civil mission. General John Sanderson (2001: 159), the Australian commander of UNTAC from 1992 to 1993, observed: "UNTAC was a peacekeeping mission which achieved its objectives but failed to leave the country in the progressive democratic state intended by those who set up the peace process." He cited insufficient attention to building an effective rule-of-law and justice system and the UN's limited role in the constitutional process. In this respect, the UN's mandate was not ambitious enough. UNTAC was abruptly ended in 1993 after Cambodia's successful elections that year, but a military coup in 1997 erased many of its gains. Cambodia, therefore, illustrates the difficulty of carrying out all aspects of a complex peacekeeping, peacebuilding, and statebuilding mission.

South Sudan: The challenges of state-making. The UN built on its experience in Namibia and Cambodia to address the situation in South Sudan starting in 2011, undertaking multidimensional operations with even more extensive peace and statebuilding responsibilities. South Sudan gained independence after the 2005 Comprehensive Peace Agreement ending Sudan's long-running civil war and a 2011 referendum in the south. The UN Mission in South Sudan (UNMISS) was authorized to support the development of state institutions and has had a Chapter VII mandate to use force to protect civilians. A separate UN Interim Security Force was authorized for Abyei, the disputed territory. In South Sudan, as in Namibia, the outcome was independent statehood, but there were unresolved border disputes with Sudan and over division of oil. Similar to the situation in Cambodia, UNMISS personnel have been embedded within the country's government. The UN, however, had great difficulty securing commitments for troops and equipment. Other key actors are the EU, the AU, the Intergovernmental Authority for Development, the United States (which played a major role in the peace negotiations), and China, which has a strong interest in South Sudan's large oil reserves.

Little more than two years after independence, the new country descended into open civil war as a result of rivalry between the former guerrilla leader turned president, Salva Kiir, and his vice president, Riek Machar. By early 2014, more than a million people had been displaced and more than 10,000 killed; ethnic cleansing bordering on genocide between Dinka and Nuer elements accompanied great brutality in killing; sexual violence was widespread; tens of thousands of people had taken refuge within UN bases, but the bases and UN peacekeepers were also attacked by heavily armed militias. In 2015, the Security Council imposed targeted sanctions against senior South Sudanese officials, as shown in Table 7.1. Yet despite four peace agreements and 17,000 peacekeepers at its peak in 2016, South Sudan remains in turmoil. For several years, sectors of the government blocked UNMISS efforts to protect civilians and deescalate the violence. In many respects, the situation in South Sudan resembles the DRC far more than the situations in Namibia or Cambodia, at least partly because there was no desire to create a transitional administration or international authority.

The effectiveness of UNMISS is clearly debatable. A 2019 study concluded "without UNMISS there would have been a genocide here" (Day 2019). Because UNMISS has been just one of the regional and international actors involved in efforts to stabilize the country, we cannot assess the effectiveness of the UN mission independently.

The Challenges of Organizing for Peace Operations

Given the evolution from traditional peacekeeping to complex multidimensional peacekeeping, peacebuilding, and statebuilding, organizing these various peace operations has become more complex. When a new UN mission is approved or a mission mandate expanded by the Security Council, the UN's Departments of Peacekeeping Operations and Field Support are responsible for determining the exact requirements, seeking the necessary military and civilian contingents and logistical support, and servicing the operation. The UNSG appoints a force commander from the top officer corps of a member country and, for major operations, also appoints a special representative of the secretary-general to oversee the mission. When a peace operation mandate includes peacebuilding elements, the UN Department of Political and Peacebuilding Affairs is involved.

Matching mandates and capacities. Since the early 1990s, the UN has undertaken a number of major reforms to improve its capacities to support peace operations and better match mandates to those capacities. Where mandates for older traditional missions like the UN peacekeeping force in Cyprus were laid out in a single paragraph, the mandate for the operation in the Central African Republic initiated in 2014 ran to fourteen pages. Often, the same general mandate is used for multiple operations, rather than being targeted to specific situational needs (Campbell 2018: 150). Operational reforms have included larger staffs, including military personnel and experts in demining, training, and civilian police. Structural reforms include the creation of the Peacebuilding Commission in 2006, the Department of Field Support in 2007, and the merger of several entities into the Department of Political and Peacebuilding Affairs in 2014–2015.

Recruiting personnel. It is not uncommon for the number of troops and police to be significantly smaller than the number authorized by the Security Council, as UN member states often do not provide the personnel. Civilian police units have proven particularly hard to recruit as few states have police officers readily available or trained for international duties and situations are likely to be very different from what they are accustomed to. In addition, some countries' units have proven more effective than others, making them more desirable.

Since the permanent UN military forces envisioned by the Charter (Articles 43–45) were never created, the UN relies on ad hoc military, civilian, or police units volunteered by member states to create multinational operations. During the Cold War, these were drawn almost exclusively from the armed forces of states other than the P-5 (often middle powers and nonaligned members, such as Canada, India, Sweden, Ghana, and Nepal) to keep the two superpowers out of regional conflicts or, in the case of postcolonial problems, to keep former colonial powers from returning.

Major powers, including the United States, the United Kingdom, France, and Russia, have also contributed forces since the end of the Cold War, especially with some larger peace operations—a departure from the original principle that UN forces did not include troops from the P-5. Top troop and police contributors to UN missions in 2022 were Pakistan, Bangladesh, India, Rwanda, and Nepal. China first provided personnel (civilian police) for the UN mission in Haiti in 2004; in 2022, it had about 2,128 military and police deployed in UN operations.

The sexual misconduct by some peacekeepers has created thorny issues for Departments of Peacekeeping Operations and Field Support and for contributing states. The problem has existed at least since the 1990s but became significantly worse with operations in the DRC and, more recently, the Central African Republic. The UN's zero-tolerance policy and enhanced training and enforcement has been hampered by the fact that only troop-contributing member states can discipline their personnel. In 2016, the Security Council authorized the Secretary-General to repatriate military or police units where there is credible evidence of widespread or systematic sexual exploitation; replace units from contributing countries that fail to address allegations; and take steps to strengthen complaint procedures and assist victims.

An important innovation in personnel occurred in 2000 with the passage of a Security Council resolution calling for greater participation of women in peace and security governance. In 2021, there were more than 4,000 women in UN peace operations—a quadrupling of female military and police personnel since the first statistics were published in 2005, but still just a little over 6 percent of personnel. The impetus for adding women came from NGOs' advocacy of the importance of greater representation of women in operations and from the sexual violence accompanying many conflicts.

In keeping with Security Council Resolution 1325 and the Women, Peace, and Security (WPS) Agenda, the UN aims to increase the number of women in peacekeeping substantially by 2028. Female peacekeepers serve as role models to local women, address needs of women ex-combatants, and help make the peacekeeping force more approachable to local women—all key concerns voiced by feminist theorists. Although three women held senior leadership positions in peace operations in 2022, few states have significant numbers of women military or police to offer, making it difficult to meet the UN's goals.

For many countries, there are important benefits to be served by peacekeeping participation. The difference between poorer countries' military salary levels and those paid by the UN makes troop contributions economically attractive. Small states like Fiji and Nepal gain prestige, valuable training, and field experience. Canada and the Nordic countries long saw peacekeeping contributions as a way to underscore their commitment to multilateralism in addressing world problems. Brazil, Japan, and Germany's contributions reflected their desire to secure permanent seats on the Security Council. China's participation reflects its shifting interests and growing role as a major power in global governance. The heavy UN reliance on personnel from African and South Asian countries, however, may undermine future UN peacekeeping if developing countries perceive that they shoulder an unfair and disproportionate burden, especially if the number of casualties among peacekeepers in UN operations continues to grow. But the steady decline in peacekeepers from large Western countries does undermine the critique reiterated by postcolonial scholars that the UN and its peace and security activities are tools of great powers seeking to maintain their hegemony (Ayoob 2020: 251–261).

Regional and subregional organizations and peace operations. Although peacekeeping was a UN invention, regional and subregional organizations have often been part of some UN operations and have undertaken various types of peace operations on their own (Karns 2009). In the early 1990s, the sheer number of new operations that the UN undertook taxed its capacity to organize and supervise missions, leading to a call for regional organizations to share more equally in the burden. Initially, two African organizations, ECOWAS and SADC, took up the challenge. ECOWAS undertook peace operations in Liberia and Sierra Leone and later in Guinea-Bissau, Côte d'Ivoire, and Mali; SADC sent peacekeeping troops into the DRC and Lesotho in 1998. Since its creation in 2002, the AU has undertaken or participated in many operations, including the joint UN-AU operation in Darfur and the UN-authorized AMISOM in Somalia initiated in 2007 and discussed in the chapter's opening case.

As shown in Table 7.4, several other regional organizations have undertaken peace operations of various types. Many have been small observer missions; many involve partnerships, sometimes with the UN or other regional groups or ad hoc coalitions of states. In its 2021 study of multilateral peace operations, SIPRI found that regional organizations and alliances were responsible for thirty-seven out of sixty-three multilateral peace operations in 2021, twenty-two of which were in sub-Saharan Africa

Table 7.4 Regional Organizations and Peace Operations (selected cases)

Regional IGO	Conflict	Partnership with UN	Duration
ASEAN	Indonesia/Aceh	No	2005–2006
AU	DR Congo	Yes	1999–
	Burundi	No	2001–2004
			2006–2009
	Sudan/Darfur	Yes	2004–2020
	South Sudan	Yes	2005–2011
	Central African Rep.	No	2014
	Somalia	No	2008–
	Mali	Yes	2012–13
ECOWAS	Liberia	No	1990–1997
	Guinea-Bissau	No	1998–1999
		Yes	2012–2020
	Sierra Leone	No	1998–1999
	Côte d'Ivoire	No	2003–2004
	Mali	Yes	2012–
EU	Bosnia	Yes	2003–
	DR Congo	Yes	2003, 2006, 2007–
	Kosovo	Yes	2008–
	South Sudan	N/A	2012–
	Central African Rep.	No	2014–
	Mali	N/A	2013–
	Indonesia/Aceh	No	2005–2006
	Somalia	No	2008–
NATO	Bosnia	Yes	1995–2003
	Kosovo	Yes	1999–2008
	Iraq	No	2018–
OAS	Haiti	Yes	1993
OSCE	Bosnia	Yes	1995–
	Kosovo	Yes	1999–
SADC	DR Congo	Yes	1998–2002
	Mozambique	No	2021–

(SIPRI 2021). As the case study of the DRC showed, countries with large deployments of UN peacekeepers may also host other operations. The Central African Republic had five operations in late 2021; Mali had four; South Sudan had two; Kosovo had four (SIPRI 2021).

The increased involvement of regional IGOs in peace operations has raised issues of authority and legitimacy. In some cases, such as AMISOM in Somalia, the UN Security Council has delegated responsibility to a regional IGO like the AU or given its approval retroactively. In other cases, regional operations have been undertaken in collaboration or partnership with the UN (as in Darfur) and sometimes have subsequently transitioned to a UN operation, as happened with the ECOWAS missions in Sierra Leone and Liberia. In such cases, soldiers have simply changed their hats to don the UN's blue berets and the Secretary-General names a new commander. There have been major steps by various regional organizations since 2010 to address problems of poor performance and lack of accountability, but considerable challenges remain. It is particularly difficult, however, to ensure individual and collective accountability for misconduct, smuggling, and sexual exploitation and for situations such as that in Haiti when UN peacekeepers from Nepal brought cholera into the country in 2010.

Regional and subregional IGOs vary widely in their organizational capacities. Resource constraints particularly afflict all of the African organizations. AMISOM's difficulties in Somalia illustrate these shortcomings. As a result, the UN, EU, and the United States often provide most of the funding for AU peace operations. Private contractors are also important for everything from training and transportation to logistics and communications. Limited capabilities are one reason for many partnership operations.

Support for peacebuilding. As noted already, peacebuilding activities are also now part of the activities of many UN agencies and other organizations. Particularly with non-UN actors involved, there has been a continuing call for better coordination. The establishment of the UN Peacebuilding Commission (PBC) in 2006 was designed to meet that call by bringing together all the relevant actors to develop integrated strategies and sustained attention for postconflict peacebuilding and recovery.

The PBC is composed of thirty-one UN member states, including the P-5 and forms what are known as "country-specific configurations" for each country in which it is involved. These include the PBC members; representatives from the World Bank, the International Monetary Fund, and regional banks; top providers of financial aid, military personnel, and civilian police in the country; relevant regional and subregional organizations; the senior UN representative in the field; and other relevant UN staff. In short, the PBC serves as an advisory body to marshal resources and advise on strategies, with a permanent representative of a member state serving as an advocate for the country. The UN General Assembly also created the Peacebuilding Fund for postconflict reconstruction, to be financed by voluntary contributions.

In 2015, the PBC underwent a review that found that peacebuilding continues to be conceived of as a postconflict activity, rather than as a set of activities that can take place during any phase of the conflict cycle. Still needed are better financing, longer-term commitments to conflict situations, and a more integrated approach in the UN and with other actors.

Humanitarian Intervention: Debates over R2P and Protection of Civilians

Many UN peace operations since 1990 have involved major humanitarian crises. Despite the long-standing norm of noninterference in states' domestic affairs, these humanitarian crises triggered debate in the early 2000s about an emerging norm of humanitarian intervention and new concepts of R2P, protection of civilians (POC), and human security. We examine how the UN has handled these threats.

Horrific as earlier twentieth-century conflicts were, many post-1990 conflicts have been marked by major humanitarian crises, including genocide, crimes against humanity, widespread human rights abuses, huge numbers of refugees and IDPs, and deliberate targeting of civilians (see Table 7.5). It is important to note that these are not the types of humanitarian crises associated with natural disasters. UN peace operations and the UNHCR, the UN Office for the Coordination of Humanitarian Affairs (UNOCHA), and humanitarian NGOs have been challenged as never before to treat these humanitarian crises as threats to international peace and security under Security Council Chapter VII.

International community responses to these humanitarian crises have been inconsistent and selective. The creation of safe havens and no-fly zones in northern and southern Iraq in April 1991 by the United States, United Kingdom, and France after the Gulf War protected Iraqi Kurds and Shiites, but without the consent of Iraq's government or the UN. Similarly, NATO intervened in Kosovo in 1999 to protect Kosovar Albanians without UN authorization. Humanitarian crises also prompted the UN authorized operations in Bosnia, Rwanda, and Darfur, albeit belatedly. In 2011, the UN authorized intervention in Libya, but not in Syria's much more devastating civil war. Varying great power interests and political will in the Security Council, along with selective media and NGO attention, play roles in determining which situations get action.

Two major consequences of the humanitarian crises in the 1990s have been the debate over the emerging norm (or principle, some would argue) of R2P and the POC mandate now included in many peace operations. Although R2P and POC are related—"sisters but not twins" as one scholar puts it, R2P applies to situations of mass atrocities and involves all types of war crimes—

Table 7.5   Selected Post–Cold War Humanitarian Crises

Crisis Period	Country	People at Risk
1991–1995	Bosnia	250,000 deaths 1.4 million refugees 2.7 million IDPs
1992–1993	Somalia	300,000 deaths 1 million refugees 95 percent of population malnourished
1994	Rwanda	850,000 deaths 2 million refugees 1.5 million IDPs

1998–	Democratic Republic
	  of Congo
		5.4 million deaths
		  (est. as of 2008)
		1 million refugees (2022)
		5.6 million IDPs (2022)

2003–2005	Sudan/Darfur	300,000 deaths (est. 2014) 370,000 refugees (est. 2014) 2 million IDPs (est. 2014)
2011–	Syria	306,887 deaths (2022) 6.6 million refugees (2022) 6.7 million IDPs (2022)
2011–2012	Libya	1,000–30,000 deaths (est.) 630,000 refugees (2022) 435,000 IDPs (2022)

Note: IDPs: internally displaced persons.

a narrower scope than POC, which applies to the effects of armed conflicts on civilians and only those war crimes that involve civilians (Popovski 2011). Whereas POC applies to all parties in a conflict (states and nonstate actors), R2P applies only to states. Altogether, between 2006 and late 2022, the Security Council approved eighty-eight resolutions and fourteen presidential statements referring to R2P and/or POC. The language of those referring to R2P, it is important to note, refers to this as the responsibility of "authorities," meaning state governments.

What has particularly been missed in many debates over R2P is that this emergent norm is not just or primarily about military intervention. "R2P is about a whole continuum of reaction from diplomatic persuasion to pressure, to non-military measures like sanctions and International Criminal Court process, and only in extreme, exceptional and last resort cases military action," as one of its earliest proponents has put it (Evans 2012). Primary responsibility lies with states to protect their own people, secondarily with the international community; when prevention fails and a state is not protecting its own people, then R2P's advocates argue that the UN has responsibility for acting under the Charter. What is needed is more thinking about whether and how these responsibilities should be carried out.

In short, as Jennifer Welsh (2014: 123) notes, there is "continued substantive contestation" about when R2P action should be taken, in what situations and what actions. She calls it a "complex norm" because it "contains more than one set of prescriptions" where the key is "a responsibility to *consider*" and what happens depends on a variety of factors including agreement on the facts of the situation and with regard to military action whether it is likely to have a positive effect (Welsh 2014: 126; emphasis in original).

Why Libya and Not Syria? Since the 2011 intervention in Libya, there has been vigorous debate in scholarly and policy circles about "why Libya and not Syria" and whether the UN and international community's failure to intervene in Syria marked the death of R2P. There is consensus, however, that the situations were not directly comparable. The UN-sanctioned intervention in Libya had strong endorsements from four regional organizations— the Arab League, GCC, OIC, and AU—and Qaddafi had few friends. In addition, the United States, United Kingdom, and France were willing to act and believed that they could foil Qaddafi's threats of mass atrocities relatively quickly and easily. Although there were no explicit references to R2P in Security Council debates, analysts have concluded that "states were surely moved to intervene, or not to block intervention [in Libya], in large part because of the power of ideas and norms of human protection related to R2P" (Glanville 2014).

Because the NATO intervention evolved to include regime change, the doubts of Russia, China, Brazil, India, and others quickly turned to opposition, however, creating a "shadow of Libya" effect over Security Council discussions of possible action in Syria. To be sure, more than ten years after the war began, the humanitarian crisis in Syria continues to be far greater than any imagined in Libya, as the data in Table 7.5 show. The problems are attributable not only to the Assad government but also to various rebel groups, the presence of the Islamic State of Iraq and Syria, Kurdish militias, and Turkish and Russian involvement. There has never been a call from the Arab League, GCC, or OIC for intervention; the Arab states are divided. President Bashar al-Assad has Russia and China exercising their veto power in the Security Council, and the United States has been unwilling to act. Since 2014, annual Security Council resolutions have affirmed the primary responsibility of the Syrian authorities to protect the population and called for parties to the conflict to "take all feasible steps to protect civilians." This demonstrates why R2P has not been fully accepted as a norm, but not fully forgotten.

There is little doubt that the Security Council's inability to act in the Syrian crisis—even to condemn the use of force against civilians by the Syrian government and the humanitarian crisis—has been shameful. Since 2012, various UN organs and agencies have deplored the Security Council's failure to respond to the crisis and condemned the violations of human rights. Beginning in 2019, Russia used its Security Council veto to limit the number of Syrian border crossings for UN humanitarian aid, exacerbating the humanitarian crisis.

Clearly, an important lesson of these two cases is that many states remain wary of approving an outside intervention in an intrastate conflict without that state's consent and when the interests of several great powers oppose intervention. Just as clearly, the support of regional organizations, the general opposition of many in the international community to Libya's leader, and the willingness of some major powers to step up with military action were key in the Libyan case and absent in Syria.

The debate about R2P and humanitarian intervention is likely to persist. By their very nature, norms are "open to contestation and evolution in meaning *as they are used*. R2P . . . is particularly susceptible to these processes" (Welsh 2014: 135; emphasis in original). If R2P as a norm of humanitarian intervention is ultimately confirmed, there is all the more need for early warning, preventive actions, and peacebuilding once interventions have taken place, as the chaos that continues to engulf Libya has demonstrated. POC is in fact considered key to the success and legitimacy of peacekeepers (Gilder 2023), although that requires greater consistency and clarity in POC mandates. In the future, partnerships involving the UN and regional IGOs, perhaps bolstered by a coalition of powerful states, are likely to mark international humanitarian interventions.

Evaluating Success and Failure in Peace Operations

Given all the difficulties evident in contemporary peace operations, it is not surprising that the scholarly literature on success and failure is voluminous and rich with both quantitative and qualitative work. What defines success in peace operations? The absence of armed conflict? The end of a humanitarian crisis? A political solution in the form of a peace agreement? A "positive peace" that addresses the root causes of a conflict? Establishment of a stable, liberal, democratic state? A period of years (two, five, ten) without renewed fighting? The successful holding of free elections? The completion of a mandate? Success in protecting civilians?

Because the mandates of different types of peace operations differ significantly, it is important to link the answer to the mandates of those different missions (Diehl and Druckman 2010). Also, the various stakeholders in peace operations may well have different standards for judging success (Diehl 2008: 119; Autesserre 2014: chap. 1). The local population may define success in terms of returning to their homes; troop-contributing countries may see success in terms of mission termination and troops returning home; the UN Secretariat may link it to mandate completion (e.g., the successful holding of UN-organized elections); the Security Council may define it in terms of long-term stability.

In assessing success and failure, we need to remember where peace-keepers go. Peacekeepers tend to go where peace will be most difficult to keep: "where neither side has been able to win outright, where refugee flows cause conflicts to spill over borders, threatening regional peace, and where the level of mistrust between belligerents is particularly high" (Fortna 2008: 75). Since peacekeepers seem to be deployed to the "hard" cases, "it might be too much to expect those [missions in the most difficult conflicts] to make a significant difference in the behavior of implacable enemies" (Diehl and Balas 2014: 154).

Since the late 1990s, there have been a number of empirical studies of peace operations using different categories of operations, types of conflicts, and time periods. There are significant methodological issues and variations in data sets that make comparisons difficult. But there is considerable consensus emerging from these studies and some important divergence. More than fourteen studies as of 2020 showed that UN peacekeeping missions save civilian lives, prevent the recurrence of civil war, reduce the spread of conflict across borders, increase civil society activity, and help build institutions (Howard 2020).

With respect to interstate wars, there is strong evidence that observer or traditional peacekeeping missions reduce the risk of resumed fighting (Diehl 2000). The Cyprus mission, for example, has prevented overt hostilities between Greek and Turkish Cypriots on the island for close to sixty years. Hostilities between India and Pakistan in Kashmir have been limited to intermittent clashes for more than seventy-five years. Having UN monitors for a truce may keep warring parties apart and curb armed clashes, but it does not resolve the underlying conflicts.

In civil wars, the number and coherence of belligerents, the deadliness of the conflict, the roles of neighboring states, the presence of spoilers, a coerced peace, and the availability of lootable natural resources can affect the outcomes of peace operations (Stedman, Rothchild, and Cousens 2002). Most of these elements were present in Sierra Leone and Liberia in the 1990s and early 2000s, but neither has relapsed into conflict more than twenty years later. To be sure, this success is not entirely attributable to the UN operations, but the role of those operations, including in disarming, demobilizing, and reintegrating armed groups, was an important factor (Doss 2023).

In complex, multidimensional operations, some goals may be achieved and some may not be, and mandates often change over the course of the operation, complicating assessment. According to Cedric de Coning (2019), in the DRC and Mali missions, large-scale violent conflict was prevented with UN peacekeepers seemingly having a deterrent effect. In both cases, conflict has not ended, and no political project was aimed at resolving the conflicts. UNMISS has been plagued with many of the same problems, but there have been significant diplomatic efforts to end the conflict. None of these missions has been able to protect civilians or prevent widespread sexual abuse and exploitation.

In addition to particularities of the conflict environment, a number of factors correlate with success (or failure). Some may seem obvious, such as the desire of combatants for peace, a negotiated peace settlement, and the consent and cooperation of the parties. The difficulty of a peace operation's mission and its mandate are important variables, as are the degree of international support (particularly of the P-5), consistent funding, and the leadership, command structure, and quality of mission personnel, who must turn vague Security Council mandates into concrete tasks to implement. Studies have shown that learning and adaptation by UN personnel in both the field and at UN headquarters in New York make a major difference (Dobbins et al. 2005; Howard 2008).

The timing of deployment and withdrawal is also critical. Delays in deployment of UNTAC in Cambodia and UNMISS in South Sudan contributed to the parties losing confidence in the peace process. The Brahimi Report (UN 2000) on UN peace operations concluded that the first twelve weeks after a cease-fire or agreement were key. A study of four regional organizations involved in peace operations shows that the EU's response time has been the longest (six months), with the OSCE, OAS, and AU averaging just over or under four months. The variations are explained by differences in organizational decisionmaking processes and levels of informal interaction (Hardt 2013: 379).

In multidimensional operations, other factors that may contribute to success include the demobilization, disarmament, and demilitarization of combatants; the widespread deployment of police monitors along with police and judicial reform; the training of election monitors; appointment of women protection advisers in missions where sexual violence has been a feature of the conflict; and, most critical, continuous political support, patience, and adequate resources.

Complicating factors for multidimensional operations, especially those involving peacebuilding, include lack of knowledge of local populations and circumstances among UN agency and NGO staff in the field (Autesserre 2014: 23; Campbell 2018). Local engagement and perspectives clearly matter in such missions where local communities often want more ownership of the process. Postcolonial theorists are especially critical of peace operations that subordinate local cultures and embody deeply rooted assumptions of racial inequality.

Multidimensional operations involving arms control verification, human rights monitoring, and election supervision tend to be successful, because they are most similar to traditional peacekeeping. They are also generally linked to a peace agreement and thus involve consent of the parties. UN peacekeepers have compiled an excellent record in facilitating elections in Namibia, Cambodia, Mozambique, Eastern Slavonia, Timor-Leste, and even the DRC. Yet as Page Fortna (2004b: 193) has noted, "peacekeeping is clearly not a magic bullet" for containing conflicts, preventing their recurrence, or creating conditions for durable peace.

With regard to operations involving peacebuilding efforts, judging relative success depends on the standard applied (legitimate political institutions meeting minimal societal needs, redressing root causes, or no renewed large-scale violence plus improved governance) as well as on the time frame (Dobbins et al. 2005; Doyle and Sambanis 2006; Coll 2008). McCandless (2013: 228) concluded that there is "insufficient consensus on concepts, tools, and processes to measure peacebuilding and statebuilding." Others have tried to do so, and the results show the rate of success for peacebuilding varies from 31 percent to 85 percent, with divergent views making clear conclusions difficult (cited in Autesserre 2014: 22). Success in one dimension is not necessarily followed by success in another.

Should peacebuilding and statebuilding be assessed against the Western blueprint for a liberal peace and a liberal concept of governance involving representative democracy, the rule of law, and a market economy? That has certainly been a widely shared assumption since the late 1990s, and blueprints and checklists marked many of the early peacebuilding efforts. Yet Barnett, Fang, and Zürcher (2014: 608) note that "the weight of the evidence is increasingly pointing to the conclusion that, if democracy is the measure of a successful outcome, peacebuilding has a poor track record." Their conclusions show that local conditions determine whether peacebuilding is likely to have an effect on the prospect of a liberal peace, some being unfavorable (Cambodia) and some being favorable (Namibia). In cases that they label "compromised peacebuilding," there may be a mixture of liberal and illiberal outcomes, including the symbols of liberal democracy ("ceremonial democracy") that may improve the chances of a liberal peace in the long term (Barnett, Fang, and Zürcher 2014: 617).

With regard to statebuilding, the dominant assumption has been that nation-states can be rebuilt in a relatively short time span despite the fact that nation-building historically has been a bloody and rarely (if ever) democratic process (von der Schulenburg 2014: 7; Tansey 2014). The various international agencies involved in supporting statebuilding efforts, such as the OECD, World Bank, and UNDP, all have different approaches, assumptions, and definitions "driven as much by ideology and institutional mandates [as by] evidence" (McCandless 2013: 235). The reality is that peacebuilding and statebuilding are expensive and long-term and involve many actors, making it difficult to establish metrics to assess success and failure. In short, Barbara Walter, Lise Morjé Howard, and V. Page Fortna (2020), after surveying numerous empirical studies that used different data sets and measured peacekeeping in different ways, concluded that "dozens of researchers . . . have all found that peacekeeping has a large, positive and statistically significant effect on reducing violence of all sorts. Despite the very real problems associated with UN peacekeeping, it is remarkably effective at bringing peace."

* * *

Arms control and disarmament have often been incorporated into different types of peace operations and remain a long-standing approach to reducing conflict. We turn to look at the roles of international organizations in using these two approaches to governing international peace and security.

Arms Control and Disarmament

The concept of disarmament, which includes limiting, controlling, and reducing the weapons for waging war, has long had a prominent place in proposals to promote peace. Thucydides reported that Sparta sought to get Athens to abstain from building fortifications. Immanuel Kant called for eliminating standing armies in "Preliminary Articles of Perpetual Peace Between States," and Jeremy Bentham published a set of arms control proposals as a prelude to peace. Numerous proposals were put forward in the nineteenth century by heads of state and newly formed peace groups, but only in the twentieth century did they begin to bear fruit.

Advocates believe that disarmament and arms control reduce the levels of violence in war, diminish the urge to engage in an arms race, redirect funds to more socially beneficial activities, and reduce the chances of accidental war. They may also lead to habits of cooperation and trust that will defuse conflict and promote peace.

The history of disarmament and arms control efforts, in fact, is mixed. The movement has been highly successful in getting the subject established permanently on IGO agendas. Yet as Inis Claude (1964: 267) noted, "it is important to avoid confusing long hours of international debate, vast piles of printed documents, and elaborate charts of institutional structure with meaningful accomplishment." Still, there have been some notable achievements since the early 1960s, particularly with regard to controlling chemical, biological, and nuclear weapons of mass destruction as well as landmines, cluster munitions, and small arms.

Putting Arms Control on the Agenda

The effort to create international rules and agreements limiting armaments began at the first Hague Conference in 1899 with a resolution urging states to reduce their military budgets and a declaration banning the use of asphyxiating artillery shells. The latter was the first key step in creating the taboo on chemical weapons. Peace groups pioneered a number of strategies used by NGOs much later in the twentieth century, such as petitions, lobbying of delegates, and publishing a daily chronicle. At the Paris Peace Conference in 1919, groups such as the Women's International League for Peace and Freedom pushed for arms control. Article 8 of the League of Nations Covenant charged the League Council with responsibility for drafting disarmament agreements. The League confronted sharp national differences over the relationship of disarmament to security guarantees and relative power positions, however. As a result, the major arms control agreements of the interwar period were largely negotiated outside the League. These included the 1922 Washington Naval Conference, in which the United States, United Kingdom, Japan, France, and Italy agreed to limit the number of battleships and not build any new ones for ten years. The London Naval Treaty of 1930 extended the moratorium and set limits on the size of destroyers and submarines. The most enduring arms control agreement is the 1925 Geneva Protocol for the Prohibition of the Use in War of Asphyxiating, Poisonous, or Other Gases, and of Bacteriological Methods of Warfare, which entered into force in 1928 and remains in effect today.

Those negotiating the UN Charter did not envision a major role for the UN with respect to arms control and disarmament, although Article 26 gave the Security Council responsibility for formulating plans for regulating armaments. Disarmament as an approach to peace had been discredited during the interwar era because it had failed to avert World War II. The use of two atomic bombs on Japan on August 6 and 10, 1945, initiated a scientific and technological revolution in warfare, however, and immediately put disarmament and arms control on the UN agenda. The General Assembly's very first resolution called for the creation of the Atomic Energy Commission to propose how to ensure that atomic energy was only used for peaceful purposes. Hence, the nuclear threat made the UN a key place for pursuing disarmament and arms control agreements. As with all international treaties, the UN is the depository for such agreements.

Arms control and disarmament efforts have been directed at concluding international conventions limiting or banning various categories of weapons; reducing arms expenditures, transfers, and sales; establishing mechanisms for monitoring and enforcing states' compliance; and limiting nonstate actors' access to arms, particularly weapons of mass destruction (WMDs). The UN General Assembly has played a key role in developing norms and international law, including the 1967 Treaty on Nuclear Non-Proliferation (NPT), the 1996 Comprehensive Test Ban Treaty (CTBT), the 2014 Arms Trade Treaty, and the 2017 Treaty on the Prohibition of Nuclear Weapons (TPNW).

The General Assembly also created the Disarmament Commission in 1952, replacing the Atomic Energy Commission and the Commission for Conventional Armaments, and established the Conference on Disarmament in 1979 as the primary negotiating forum following a Special Session on Disarmament in 1978. Over time, there have been reorganizations with accompanying name changes that often reflected debates about which countries should participate in disarmament negotiations. In reality, the most fruitful negotiations on nuclear issues have often taken place outside the UN among the relevant major powers, however, and produced the Strategic Arms Limitation Talks agreements (SALT I and II) in the 1970s and the Strategic Arms Reduction Treaty (START) in the 1990s, among other agreements. The cases of landmines, cluster munitions, and the TPNW have demonstrated the ability of middle powers and coalitions of NGOs to provide leadership for arms control initiatives without major power participation, in view of what Ramesh Thakur (2017: 181) calls "a widespread sense today that the UN has become dysfunctional and moribund as a forum for negotiating arms control and disarmament treaties." Regional IGOs have addressed arms control issues largely through efforts to create regional nuclear weapon–free zones.

Limiting Proliferation of Nuclear Weapon Capability

Efforts to contain the spread of nuclear weapons have rested on three pillars: norms, treaties, and coercion (Thakur 2006: 161). Preliminary agreements between the United States and Soviet Union were crucial in creating an international regime for nuclear nonproliferation. Following President Dwight Eisenhower's "Atoms for Peace" proposal in 1954, the two superpowers (surprisingly) collaborated in creating the International Atomic Energy Agency (IAEA) in 1957 to spread information about peaceful uses of atomic energy and provide a system of safeguards to prevent diversion of fissionable material. General Assembly resolutions from 1959 on called for a nonproliferation treaty and in 1965 outlined five principles of nonproliferation submitted by nonaligned countries. In 1967, the Soviet Union, United States, and United Kingdom signed the NPT, which was then opened to other nations to sign and entered into force in 1970. One hundred ninety-one states are now parties to the NPT.

The NPT is a bargain between the declared nuclear weapon states and the non–nuclear weapon states, with the latter pledging not to develop nuclear weapons, and the former promising to give up their own nuclear weapons at some future time and help the latter in gaining access to peaceful nuclear technologies. It effectively creates a two-class system, with five declared nuclear weapon states (the United States, the Soviet Union/Russia, the United Kingdom, France, and China) and all others being non–nuclear weapon states. This two-class system has always been offensive to some countries, most notably India, which conducted a peaceful nuclear test in 1974 and five weapon tests in 1998. India, Pakistan, Cuba, North Korea, and Israel are the only states that are not parties to the NPT, and all but Cuba have nuclear weapons. Three states that previously had nuclear weapon programs (South Africa, Brazil, and Argentina) but abandoned them became parties to the treaty in the 1990s, along with three new states— Belarus, Kazakhstan, and Ukraine, which gave up nuclear weapons left on their territory after the dissolution of the Soviet Union.

The 1995 UN-sponsored NPT review conference agreed to an indefinite extension of the treaty, conditioned on renewed efforts toward disarmament, a pledge by the nuclear weapon states to conclude the CTBT, and five-year reviews. The 2010 review conference concluded with an affirmation of parties' commitment to nuclear disarmament. Although the global nuclear stockpile has fallen dramatically from its Cold War peak, none of the five declared nuclear weapon states has a serious plan for disarmament, and most are engaged in modernizing their weapons systems. China, in particular, is currently increasing its stock of nuclear weapons.

The IAEA—a related organization in the UN system—is a critical part of the nuclear nonproliferation regime, especially its safeguard system of inspections, which provides transparency about the security of non–nuclear weapon states' nuclear power plants—that nuclear fuel is not being diverted from peaceful to weapon purposes. The IAEA system is supplemented by export control agreements of the forty-four-member Nuclear Suppliers Group.

Although the IAEA system appeared reliable for many years, the discovery of a secret Iraqi nuclear weapons program in 1991—in direct violation of Iraq's IAEA safeguard agreements and its obligations under the NPT— brought it under scrutiny. It also drew the UN Security Council into discussion of arms control issues for the first time. The Gulf War cease-fire resolution (Security Council Resolution 687) created the Iraq disarmament regime, the most intrusive international inspections regime ever established. To oversee the destruction of Iraq's chemical and biological weapons and missiles as well as production and storage facilities, and to monitor its long-term compliance, the Security Council created the UN Special Commission for the Disarmament of Iraq (UNSCOM) (Resolution 699). The IAEA was responsible for inspecting and destroying Iraq's nuclear weapons. The focus on WMDs and ballistic missiles was the result of Iraq's use of chemical weapons against Iran and its Kurdish population and ballistic missiles against Iran, the United States, and Israel, plus the potential threat posed to neighboring countries (including Israel), and concerns about proliferation.

Between 1991 and 1998, UNSCOM and IAEA inspectors moved throughout Iraq, carrying out surprise inspections of suspected storage and production facilities, destroying stocks of materials, and checking documents. Iraq continually thwarted the inspectors, removing or destroying equipment, and arguing that some sites were off-limits. It severed all cooperation in 1998. In 2002, UNSCOM's successor, the UN Monitoring, Verification, and Inspection Commission, began inspections anew and, with the IAEA, verified that Iraq had not rebuilt its program. Its work ended with the US invasion in 2003.

The problems that the IAEA and UNSCOM encountered in Iraq mirror the broader problems with international enforcement and with North Korea and Iran. After the revelations about Iraq's nuclear program in 1991, the IAEA Board of Governors strengthened nuclear safeguards through increased access to information, facilities, and sites. The IAEA and the UN Security Council are involved in efforts to enforce North Korea's and Iran's compliance with the NPT, while ad hoc groups of states have undertaken diplomatic initiatives in both cases.

North Korea and Iran. In 1993, North Korea refused to admit IAEA inspectors to suspected sites and threatened to withdraw from the NPT. In 2002, it abrogated the 1994 agreement that renewed inspections and froze its nuclear program in return for two proliferation-resistant nuclear reactors and fuel oil. Starting in 2003, North Korea withdrew from the NPT, began producing additional plutonium for bombs, tested its first device in 2006, declared itself a nuclear weapon state, and refined its missile technology. In response, the Security Council approved targeted sanctions on North Korea (see Table 7.1). Between 2006 and 2009, however, North Korea also participated in the so-called six-party talks (the United States, China, South Korea, North Korea, Russia, and Japan) until they were suspended after its second nuclear test in 2009. Thereafter, the Security Council enhanced the sanctions to allow UN members to inspect cargo vessels and planes suspected of carrying military material in or out of the country. They were further tightened in 2012 and 2013 in response to additional nuclear tests, a long-range missile launch, and the North Korean threat of a preemptive nuclear strike on the United States and South Korea. In 2017, sanctions targeting coal, iron ore, textiles, fisheries, and all other major North Korean exports were added.

In addition to weapons development, North Korea has steadily increased its missile systems, including intercontinental ballistic missiles, which it claims are capable of delivering nuclear weapons to North America. Despite attempts at personal diplomacy by US President Donald Trump in 2018, there has been no progress toward persuading North Korea to halt its nuclear weapons program as of 2023, but also no further weapons tests. China and

Russia are considered key for enforcing sanctions, but neither country's influence with North Korea has proven decisive, and both are suspected of helping North Korea evade the sanctions. North Korea's isolation from the world and the fact that the regime sees its weapons program as key to its own survival provides little incentive to reach an agreement that would require dismantling that program. This makes it likely that there is little more to be done in the foreseeable future other than keeping the sanctions in place and continuing to watch for an opening for diplomacy.

Iran remains a major concern despite its announced intention to develop nuclear capacity only for peaceful purposes. As of mid-2023, the IAEA estimated that Iran had enriched uranium close to the point required for creating a nuclear weapon. Before 2003, the extent of Iran's nuclear program had eluded IAEA inspectors, and although many of its activities have been permissible under the NPT, because they have been carried out surreptitiously, there is concern that Iran seeks to develop the capacity to build and deliver nuclear weapons. In 2004–2005, the EU (particularly Germany, the United Kingdom, and France) took the lead to get Iran to stop its nuclear enrichment program in return for aid in building a light water nuclear reactor and guaranteed supplies of enriched fuel. In 2005, however, the IAEA's board voted to report Iran's failures and breaches of its NPT obligations to the UN Security Council. Despite Iran's threat to withdraw from the NPT if sanctions were imposed, in 2006 the Council approved and has periodically extended sanctions (see Table 7.1). The 2008 resolution (1747), for example, authorized inspections of sea and air cargo to and from Iran, tightened monitoring of Iranian financial institutions, extended travel bans and asset freezes, and enlarged the list of targeted individuals and companies. It also welcomed a proposal of the P-5 plus Germany (P-5+1) to offer economic incentives and technology transfer in the civilian nuclear field if Iran permanently gave up its uranium enrichment program.

Outside the UN, intense and largely secret negotiations took place between Iranian, EU, and P-5+1 negotiators in Geneva, New York, Vienna, and Oman between 2012 and 2015. During this time, Iran remained a party to the NPT and permitted IAEA inspections, although keeping some sites off limits. It also signaled its interest in a deal that would end sanctions. The negotiations sought to resolve what capabilities Iran would be allowed to keep, the length of time an agreement would be in effect, and the speed and conditions for lifting UN and other sanctions. In July 2015, the Joint Comprehensive Plan of Action (JCPOA) agreement was reached and endorsed unanimously by the Security Council (Resolution 2231). The plan linked the end of all UN sanctions to a verification process where the IAEA would establish that "all nuclear material in Iran remains in peaceful activities." In 2016, the IAEA certified Iran's compliance with the agreement, which triggered the lifting of many (but not all) of the UN sanctions.

After the Trump administration withdrew the United States from the JCPOA in 2018, Iran initially continued to abide by the agreement and only gradually began to violate some of its provisions in 2019 as the United States reimposed harsh unilateral sanctions. With the change of presidential administrations in 2021, the United States announced its desire to rejoin the agreement, but this became increasingly unlikely as evidence of Iran's continuing activities grew and the IAEA was denied access for inspections. The UN has had no direct role in the process except to exhort the parties to reach agreement. In early 2023, Iran admitted the IAEA again and agreed to restore cameras and monitoring equipment removed from nuclear sites in 2022, but whether it would allow monitoring was still uncertain. At this point, the IAEA estimated that it would take Iran just twelve days to build a nuclear weapon, in contrast to the twelve months it had estimated in 2015 when the JCPOA was signed. There appeared to be little chance that the agreement would be renewed, however, as Russia's war in Ukraine and increasing reliance on Iranian drones made Russian and Chinese support for new negotiations unlikely.

The danger of failing to halt North Korea's and Iran's nuclear programs is threefold: first, the greater risk of weapons being used; second, the risk that other countries in both regions will feel pressured to reconsider their nonnuclear status (e.g., South Korea and Japan in Northeast Asia and Saudi Arabia and Egypt in the Middle East); and third, that these countries will supply nuclear weapons to ISIS or some other nonstate group. There is also fear that North Korea could help Iran by supplying components for nuclear weapons. These risks clearly threaten the entire NPT regime.

Following the discovery in early 2004 that Pakistan's chief nuclear scientist, Dr. A. Q. Khan, ran a secret global network of nuclear suppliers, it became clear that other strategies were needed to prevent proliferation and to prevent nonstate groups from gaining access to nuclear materials. As a result, the Security Council approved Resolution 1540, which invokes Chapter VII, affirms WMD proliferation as a threat to international peace, and directs all states to take and enforce effective measures to protect nuclear materials and block illicit trafficking in WMD material. It is supplemented by the 1980 Convention on the Physical Protection of Nuclear Materials and the 2005 International Convention for the Suppression of Acts of Nuclear Terrorism. In 2010, US President Barack Obama convened the first Nuclear Security Summit with the aim of establishing controls over nuclear materials. Two more summits reviewed countries' work to improve their nuclear security. A fourth summit was canceled when Russia annexed Crimea in 2014.

Banning nuclear testing. The NPT regime also includes a ban on testing. After the Cuban missile crisis in 1962, the United States, Soviet Union, and United Kingdom took the first step with the Partial Test Ban Treaty. In the

1990s, France and China, under pressure from Asia-Pacific countries and a legal challenge from New Zealand in the ICJ, agreed to stop testing, and in 1996 the (CTBT) was concluded under UN auspices. India's and Pakistan's 1998 tests set back efforts to bring the CTBT into force, but the most important blow was the US Senate's failure to ratify the treaty in 1999.

The CTBT is intended to serve two key roles: prevent the declared nuclear weapon states and other parties to the treaty from developing new weapon designs, and to reconfirm the norm against nuclear proliferation. It strengthens the NPT regime with an international monitoring system, authority to conduct challenge inspections in cases of suspected cheating, and establishment of the Comprehensive Test Ban Treaty Organization (CTBTO) to implement the verification procedures. Although ratified by 177 states as of 2023, the CTBT can only enter into force after ratification by the group of 44 nations that as of 1996 had nuclear research programs or nuclear power reactors. This group includes all the states known or suspected to have nuclear weapons, as well as Iran. In addition to the United States, China and Israel have signed but not ratified the treaty; three states in the group (India, Pakistan, and North Korea) have yet to sign the treaty. A global moratorium on testing, however, has been in effect since 1998 (except for North Korea) and the CTBTO Preparatory Commission functions in lieu of the CTBTO itself. This includes overseeing the treaty's verification system, which includes an extensive global monitoring system with seismic, acoustic, and other sensors in 337 locations around the world to detect signs of nuclear explosions.

Regional nuclear weapon–free zones. The final piece of the nonproliferation regime comprises the treaty-based regional nuclear weapon–free zones. Five zones now exist: in Latin America, Southeast Asia, the South Pacific, Africa, and Central Asia (see Figure 7.8). They preclude nuclear weapon states from placing nuclear weapons on the territory of states within the zone, and prohibit the acquisition, testing, manufacture, or use of such weapons. Protocols attached to each of the treaties and signed by the nuclear weapon states bind the latter to respect de-nuclearization and not to use or threaten to use nuclear force against any of the parties. These zones indicate the widespread support for nuclear disarmament outside the relatively small group of states that already have or seek to acquire nuclear weapons. In addition, there are treaties banning the placement of nuclear weapons in the seabed, Antarctica, and outer space and Mongolia's declaration of a nuclear weapon-free zone was endorsed by the UN General Assembly in 1992.

The nuclear ban treaty. The newest initiative in efforts to address the problem of nuclear weapons is the successful campaign to secure UN General Assembly approval in 2017 of the Treaty on the Prohibition of Nuclear

---

Figure 7.8 Arms Control Treaties for Weapons of Mass Destruction

1925	Geneva Protocol on Chemical and Biological Weapons (1928)
1959	Antarctic Treaty (1961)
1963	Partial Test Ban Treaty
1967	Outer Space Treaty (1967)
1967	Treaty of Tlatelolco (Latin American Treaty for the Prohibition of Nuclear Weapons) (1968)
1968	Nuclear Non-Proliferation Treaty (1970)
1971	Seabed Treaty (1972)
1972	Biological Weapons Convention (1974)
1979	Strategic Arms Limitation Talks (SALT) Treaty (United States, Soviet Union)
1980	Convention on the Physical Protection of Nuclear Materials (1987)
1985	Treaty of Rarotonga (nuclear-free zone in South Pacific) (1986)
1991	START I Treaty (United States, Russia)
1992	Mongolia Nuclear Weapon-Free Zone
1993	Chemical Weapons Convention (1997)
1993	START II Treaty (United States, Russia, three former Soviet republics) (2000)
1995	Bangkok Treaty (nuclear weapon–free zone in Southeast Asia) (2002)
1996	Comprehensive Test Ban Treaty; Preparatory Commission for the Comprehensive Test Ban Treaty Organization
1996	Indefinite Extension of Nuclear Non-Proliferation Treaty
1996	Pelindaba Treaty (nuclear weapon–free zone in Africa) (2009)
2006	Treaty on a Nuclear Weapon–Free Zone in Central Asia (2009)
2017	Treaty on the Prohibition of Nuclear Weapons (2021)

Note: Parenthetical dates indicate years of entry into force as determined by the minimum number of ratifications needed.

---

weapons or TPNW. With 122 votes in favor, approval clearly signaled that the majority of states regard nuclear weapons as unacceptable. With fifty-one state ratifications as of early 2021, the TPNW came into force. Three things stand out about this development. First, the treaty was the result of a civil society–led coalition movement, the International Campaign to Abolish Nuclear Weapons (ICAN), founded in 2007 and led by a young Swedish woman, Beatrice Fihn, who saw the treaty as a way to "dislodging the old order . . . built on the idea that nuclear weapons are the preserve of 'superpowers,' who see the world as their 'playing field'" (Banjo 2023). Together with like-minded states, the campaign forged a global coalition to push for the treaty. Second, the advocates framed the issue of nuclear weapons as a humanitarian concern, that is, nuclear weapons are inherently indiscriminate, inhumane, and unacceptable. This reframing followed precedents set in the treaties that banned antipersonnel landmines and cluster munitions as discussed below. For its role in bringing the treaty into existence, ICAN was awarded the 2017 Nobel Peace Prize. Third, the ban treaty's entry into force marks a new nuclear order—a "new normative settling point on the ethics, legality and legitimacy of the bomb," according to Ramesh Thakur (2022). "A legal game-changer" is how another supporter put it (Pretorius 2020).

A major impetus for the treaty also came from the indefinite extension of the NPT in 1995, which removed pressure on the nuclear weapon states to disarm. As one TPNW proponent put it, "as long as some states get to have nuclear weapons [under the NPT], others may come to feel they need them too . . . because of that the NPT has become a weak and dangerous instrument for nonproliferation" (Pretorius 2020).

Nuclear proliferation and arms control will remain high-priority issues for the foreseeable future, given the lack of evidence that the nuclear weapon states take seriously the NPT pledge to disarm themselves, the threat that Iran and North Korea pose to the regime, and concerns about terrorist groups and other states obtaining nuclear weapons.

After Russia's 2022 invasion of Ukraine, its threat to use battlefield nuclear weapons and the risks or either accidental or deliberate strikes on nuclear power plants triggered global alarms about the possibilities of catastrophic damage and deadly radioactive fallout. They also threatened a breach in the taboo on the use of nuclear weapons that had developed during the Cold War years. As Nina Tannenwald (2022: 37–38) put it, "The Russia-Ukraine war serves as a harsh reminder of some old truths about nuclear weapons. There are limits to the protection nuclear deterrence provides. . . . There is always the chance that it could fail." She added, "We have no idea what would happen if a nuclear weapon were actually used. . . . The war also reminds us that norms are ultimately breakable."

In short, in 2023, many people felt that the world had become a much more dangerous place and that the "global nuclear order [was] in shambles" (Diaz-Maurin 2022). UN Secretary-General António Guterres warned that the world was just "one miscalculation away from nuclear annihilation" (Lederer 2022). The *Bulletin of Atomic Scientists* put its "doomsday" clock at ninety seconds to midnight—the closest it has ever been. Russian President Vladimir Putin didn't help the pessimistic mood when he announced in February 2023 that Russia was suspending participation in the New START Treaty signed in 2010—the last surviving arms control agreement between the United States and Russia and one with important reciprocal inspections provisions.

Nuclear weapons are not the only types of arms to be the subject of global arms control and disarmament efforts, however. Concerns about two other types of WMDs—chemical and biological weapons—also persist.

Chemical and Biological Weapon Prohibition

When the Hague Conference of 1899 issued its declaration banning asphyxiating shells, such weapons did not exist. Later prohibitions on chemical weapons, including the 1925 Geneva Protocol that banned chemical and bacteriological weapons, reaffirmed the Hague norm based on reactions to the use of chemical weapons in World War I. A campaign against gas warfare and the chemical industry successfully defined use of chemical weapons as "a practice beyond the pale of civilized nations" on the grounds that these were "an especially inhumane method of warfare" (Price and Tannenwald 1996: 129). There is, in fact, a rather remarkable history of nonuse of chemical weapons since the 1920s, with only a few exceptions, including ones by Iraq in the 1980s, Aum Shinrikyo in the Tokyo subway in 1995, and Syria in 2013.

Beginning in 1969, the issue of chemical and biological weapons appeared regularly on the agenda of the UN General Assembly, but Cold War politics—notably US opposition—blocked action. Pressures for controls on these weapons stemmed from the fact that large stockpiles of them were known to exist in several countries. Although the destructive power of nuclear weapons is well known, that of chemical and biological weapons is less so. Chemical weapons, if effectively used, have the potential to kill tens of thousands of people; the potential toll from biological weapons could number in the hundreds of thousands. It is hardly surprising, therefore, that major efforts for more than a century have been directed at suppressing chemical and biological weapons as instruments of warfare. These efforts have been given added impetus with the threat that terrorist groups, who cannot be bound by international treaties, could acquire and use such weapons.

Following unilateral renunciation by the United States of the use or production of biological weapons in 1969, the Convention on the Prohibition of the Development, Production and Stockpiling of Bacteriological (Biological) and Toxin Weapons and on Their Destruction (the Biological Weapons Convention [BWC]) was concluded in 1972. It came into force in 1975 and had 183 parties in 2023. The BWC is a true disarmament treaty that calls for destruction of existing stocks and restriction of materials to research purposes. Its major weakness is the absence of verification or inspection mechanisms. Several states, most notably Iran, North Korea, and Russia, are still thought to possess such weapons even though they are parties to the BWC; Syria is not a party and has used chemical weapons in its civil war as discussed below. In 1994, a group of experts was authorized to draft proposals for a protocol to strengthen the BWC, but the United States rejected the draft text in 2001 in view of the absence of verification measures and concerns that the draft protocol would compromise US biodefense security and confidential business information of the biotech industry. This effectively ended negotiations on a BWC protocol. The ongoing biotechnology revolution creates a future proliferation risk.

The September 2001 terrorist attacks on the United States and the later anthrax scare led the United States to push a different approach, including an initiative by the G-8 in 2002 to create a Global Partnership Against the Spread of Weapons and Materials of Mass Destruction. In other steps, the WHO strengthened its surveillance system in the event of biological weapon attacks. The Australia Group, established in 1985 by thirty-three states to coordinate national controls on chemical and biological weapons technology and exports, tightened export control measures in 2002 to keep chemical and biological weapons out of the hands of terrorist groups. The group now includes forty-two states and the EU. Still, many European and developing countries were deeply troubled by the US rejection of the BWC revision process and, more than two decades later, there is as yet no further strengthening of the BWC.

A taboo on the use of chemical weapons has existed for more than a century. The Hague Conference of 1899 first articulated the norm banning asphyxiating shells. Following the use of chemical weapons in World War I, the 1925 Geneva Protocol reaffirmed the ban and a follow-up campaign successfully defined their use as "a practice beyond the pale of civilized nations" and "an especially inhuman method of warfare" (Price and Tannenwald 1996: 129). Efforts to negotiate a convention stalled during the Cold War, but the Chemical Weapons Convention (CWC) was finally signed in 1993, banning the production, acquisition, stockpiling, retention, or usage of such weapons. Like the BWC, it calls for the complete destruction of all weapons and production facilities in a phased process that was originally to end in 2012, but the United States and a few other countries were given until the end of 2023 to complete the process. Unlike the BWC, the CWC includes on-site verification provisions and the threat of sanctions against violators, including those that have not signed the treaty. It came into effect in 1997 and had 193 parties as of early 2023. Israel has signed but not ratified; North Korea, Egypt, and South Sudan have neither signed nor ratified.

The Organization for the Prohibition of Chemical Weapons (OPCW) began operations in early 1997 and has since conducted hundreds of inspections at military and industrial facilities. By the beginning of 2023, OPCW reported that only the United States and Syria had not destroyed all their facilities and stockpiles, and the United States was scheduled to do so before the end of the year. This is no small accomplishment for disarmament. A complicating issue is that many of the ingredients in chemical weapons (unlike nuclear weapons) are used in ordinary industrial and agricultural production. Hence, it is impractical to eliminate their manufacture. Thus, the focus is on eliminating stockpiles of chemical weapons and declarations regarding production facilities, laboratories, and transfers or receipts of chemical weapons or weapons-production equipment.

The key difference between the chemical and biological weapons conventions and the NPT is the acceptance by all parties of a total ban on possession, development, and use of these WMDs. There is no two-class system; total disarmament and the taboo on use are the core regime norms. The chemical and biological weapons treaties require parties to enact domestic legislation to permit criminal prosecution of individuals and companies that violate treaty provisions. The three treaties have in common an initial agreement between the United States and the Soviet Union/Russia. For the CTBT, commitments from France and China were key. Only by having these major powers on board could the UN proceed with drafting the treaties. The experiences of the CTBT and BWC also demonstrate the damage done when US support for multilateral arms control treaties is lost. The experience with the intrusive WMD disarmament program in Iraq in the 1990s demonstrated the possibilities of international monitoring as a tool of disarmament and the difficulties of enforcing compliance with international norms on chemical and biological weapons. Although the IAEA succeeded in destroying Iraq's existing nuclear weapon materials and production facilities, UNSCOM was unable to certify that it knew the full extent of Iraq's chemical and biological weapon–production facilities, since materials are easily concealed. Even so, that process was completed in 2007.

The case of Syria and chemical weapons use in 2013–2014 clearly reinforced the taboo on the use of such weapons and the chemical weapons regime. In July 2012, Syria confirmed that it had chemical weapons but said they would only be used against an outside aggressor. Yet in a six-month period, there were at least six reports that Syrian government forces had used various types of chemical weapons, leading UN Secretary-General Ban Ki-moon to announce that the UN, along with the WHO and OPCW, would conduct an investigation.

In summer 2013, the Syrian government allowed a UN inspection team to investigate three possible uses but not establish who used the weapons. Days later, there were reports of a large-scale chemical weapons attack in the Damascus suburbs with thousands of noncombatant victims. This triggered emergency meetings of the Security Council and the threat of US military strikes. A French government report found that the Assad regime had used sarin gas in those attacks, a clear violation of the 1925 Geneva Protocol. Instead of military intervention, a remarkable diplomatic initiative led to an agreement between the United States and Russia with Syria acceding to the CWC and to a plan to account for, inspect, control, and destroy its chemical weapons stockpile and production facilities within a year. The agreement was unanimously endorsed by the Security Council, and the OPCW established the necessary procedures to carry it out. In short order, Syria submitted a declaration of its stockpiles, the OPCW and UN began destruction, and by January 2014, the first shipment of weapons was loaded on a Danish ship; six months later the last 8 percent were shipped out. Destruction of the weapons was carried out at sites in several countries, and

Syria's facilities were destroyed or permanently sealed. For its work, the OPCW received the 2013 Nobel Peace Prize.

Concerns persisted about whether Syria had declared its entire stockpile, however, and in 2015 there were reports of the use of chlorine and mustard gas by both the government and the Islamic State. In 2017 and 2018, there were more attacks and a 2020 OPCW report declared that there was incontrovertible evidence that chlorine and sarin gas had been used on civilians in those attacks (Barber 2019). Despite council efforts to place new punitive measures on Syria, Russia vetoed four resolutions on Syria in 2017, including one extending the OPCW mandate. As of 2023, the OPCW noted that Syria still had undeclared chemicals and had given no projected timeline for their destruction.

Overall, the BWC and CWC are considered relative success stories in arms control and disarmament. To be sure, there are continuing challenges with all WMDs and emerging issues related to technological innovations such as autonomous weapons, which have been used extensively in the Russia-Ukraine war, hypersonic weapons, and the potential use of arms in space. We turn to look briefly at two successful NGO-led disarmament initiatives that provided the example for the ICAN and nuclear ban treaty discussed earlier.

Banning Landmines and Cluster Munitions: The Role of NGOs

A very different path to arms control was followed in an initiative involving a very conventional but widely used and deadly weapon—landmines—and then with cluster munitions. Like the nuclear treaty ban, both reflected humanitarian concerns far more than the security threats posed by WMDs. Just as nuclear arms were a symbol of the Cold War, antipersonnel landmines have been a symbol of conflicts in the post–Cold War era. These weapons have been widely used by regular and irregular military forces in conflicts from Angola, Afghanistan, Cambodia, and Bosnia to Sri Lanka, the DRC, Kashmir, and Ukraine. They are indiscriminate and long-lasting and cause extensive civilian casualties when unsuspecting people go into mined areas. Although landmines cost as little as $3 each, demining can cost $300 to $500 per mine. The issue captured the attention of NGOs in a way not seen in most other arms control issues, in part because they are a human security issue.

The International Campaign to Ban Landmines (ICBL), a network of more than a thousand organizations in sixty countries, was formed in 1993 to campaign for a ban on the use, production, stockpiling, sale, transfer, and export of antipersonnel landmines. Its primary goal was to conclude, implement, and monitor a landmine treaty and provide resources for demining, mine awareness programs, and victim rehabilitation and assistance. In a record time of fourteen months between October 1996 and December 1997, under the leadership of Canadian foreign minister Lloyd Axworthy, countries that supported a treaty banning landmines participated in the ad hoc Ottawa negotiating process, bypassing the UN Conference on Disarmament. Over a hundred countries signed the Convention on the Prohibition of the Use, Stockpiling, Production and Transfer of Anti-Personnel Mines and on Their Destruction, and in 1999 the treaty came into force. In acknowledgment of the ICBL's success, the organization and its coordinator, Jody Williams, were awarded the Nobel Peace Prize in 1997.

Among the convention's unusual features is the detailed role outlined for NGOs, particularly the International Committee of the Red Cross (ICRC), in assessing the scope of the problem and providing financial and technical resources for implementation. NGO monitors report through the UN Secretary-General to meetings of state parties that are attended by relevant governmental and nongovernmental groups. The UN had "mine action" programs in nineteen countries and territories in 2023, with NGOs doing much of the demining and mine-risk education.

The ICBL continues its work to universalize the treaty and promote mine clearance, survivor assistance, and stockpile destruction. As of 2022, 164 countries or territories, including Palestine, had ratified the treaty; mine use has ceased in several countries where it was prevalent; there have been large reductions in mine stockpiles; and casualties from landmines have declined significantly. There are still twelve countries that produce landmines, including Myanmar, China, India, North and South Korea, Pakistan, Russia, and Iran. Russia and Myanmar used landmines in 2022, as did nonstate actors in many conflicts, including those in the DRC, Central African Republic, Myanmar, Colombia, Mali, and Niger. The United States announced in 2014 that it would abide by the treaty except for landmines used in Korea and would work toward accession to the treaty—a policy that was reversed under the Trump administration, then reaffirmed in 2022.

With support from the ICBL, the same approach to banning the use of cluster bombs was taken by the Cluster Munition Coalition, formed in 2003 and comprising some 300 NGOs in more than eighty countries. Norway took the lead for the Oslo Process, through which a core group of states, together with the Cluster Munition Coalition, the ICRC, and the UN, pushed the negotiation of a treaty banning these weapons. The Convention on Cluster Munitions, signed by ninety-four states in December 2008, like the landmine treaty, was concluded in a short period: just eighteen months. As of 2023, it had been ratified by 110 states. This arms control effort was largely successful because of the campaign's emphasis on the humanitarian problem these weapons pose. As with landmines, the majority of victims are civilians, and the treaty calls for a ban on cluster munitions and for clearance efforts, stockpile destruction, and victim assistance, with extensive global civil society involvement. In 2011, the ICBL and Cluster Munition Coalition merged into one structure to realize organizational efficiencies while continuing their respective campaigns.

Countering Terrorism as a
Threat to Global Peace and Security

Terrorism is an old threat to individual, state, and regional security that is now universally recognized as a threat to global peace and security and for multilateral institutions. Historically, terrorist acts were often individual acts of violence against a ruler or tools of separatist and other groups seeking a homeland or regime change. Organized state terrorism reached its zenith in Nazi Germany and in the Soviet Union under Joseph Stalin.

Since the 1970s, much of the terrorist activity has originated in the Middle East, from the Palestinians' quest for self-determination, rivalries among various Islamic groups, and the rise of Islamic fundamentalism. Since 1980, religious-based groups (Islamic and others, such as Hindu nationalists) have increased significantly. Many were trained in Afghanistan during the mujahidin's war against the Soviet Union in the 1980s and went on to commit terrorist acts in the 1990s. Of particular importance has been the development of al-Qaeda—a shadowy network of Islamic fundamentalist groups in many countries. In Latin America and elsewhere, terrorist groups have increasingly been linked with organized criminal groups to tap profits from drug, weapons, antiquities, organ trafficking, and kidnapping. The increased ease of international travel and telecommunications have made transnational terrorism less confined to a particular geographic locale and enabled terrorist groups to form global networks and move money, weapons, and peoples from one area to another. Weak, failed, or conflict-ridden states such as Somalia, Libya, Afghanistan, and Syria create gaps in efforts to control borders and flows of people, money, and arms and deny terrorists sanctuaries for training camps and operations.

The tactics of terrorists and whether the actions were local or global have tended to drive international responses. From the late 1960s through the 1970s, airline hijackings were a popular terrorist method. Hostage-taking has been another tactic. The most common terrorist incidents involve the use of bombs on airplanes, trucks, cars, and ships or in suicide attacks. Prominent examples include Pan American Flight 103, which blew up over Lockerbie, Scotland, in 1988; the 1998 attacks on the US embassies in Kenya and Tanzania; and the boat-delivered bombing of the USS *Cole* in 2000 in Yemen. Although the four planes involved in the September 11, 2001, attacks were initially hijacked, they were turned into lethal WMDs in a new twist on the old car-bomb strategy. Suicide bombings were pioneered by young members of the Tamil Tigers in Sri Lanka and then adopted by

Palestinians during the Second Intifada, the 9/11 hijackers, Sunni insurgents and al-Qaeda in Iraq, and Islamic militants in Afghanistan, Pakistan, and elsewhere. Concerns about terrorist groups gaining control of WMDs or the materials to produce them magnify the importance of controlling these weapons, particularly nuclear materials, as previously discussed.

The rapid emergence of the Islamic State in 2014 introduced a new dimension to terrorism: the seizure of territory and declaration of a caliphate—a single, transnational Islamic state based on sharia law. Its brutality toward non-Muslim and non-Arab minorities, Shiites, and all who opposed it included beheadings, mass slaughter, and enslavement, particularly of women and children. With its control and administration of territory and cities in Iraq and Syria, including tax collection and public services, ISIS was clearly different from other terrorist groups. It drew declarations of allegiance from other jihadist groups in Afghanistan, Egypt, Libya, Nigeria, Yemen, and elsewhere and declared its ambition to create an Islamic state throughout the Middle East and Africa.

Speaking at a special Security Council session in 2014, UN Secretary-General Ban Ki-moon said that "the world is witnessing a dramatic evolution in the nature of the terrorist threat" (UN 2014). Part of that evolution included a major increase in the number of terrorist attacks and the number of people killed between 2011 and 2014. Since then, the Global Terrorism Index has reported significant declines in deaths and numbers of attacks between 2015 and 2022 (Institute for Economics and Peace 2023). There has also been a significant shift in where terrorist attacks are taking place. They are now more concentrated in regions and countries with high political instability and conflict, such as the Sahel, Afghanistan, Somalia, the DRC, Mozambique, and Iraq. Among the active groups, the Islamic State West Africa and Jama'at Nasr al-Islam wal Muslimin were responsible for the greatest number of attacks and deaths in 2021. Although the index reported that the Islamic State was still the deadliest terror group globally, it appeared to be in decline, and more terrorist attacks were politically than religiously motivated. Surprisingly, attacks in the Middle East and North Africa had declined, but they increased in South Asia, especially Pakistan. The index linked sharp declines in Europe and other parts of the West to pandemic-related restrictions still in effect in 2021. A further finding involves the use of new technologies such as cell phone–guided drones and missiles.

Another change in the nature of the terrorist threat in recent years is the increased targeting of UN personnel in Iraq, Mali, Nigeria, and Somalia by al-Qaeda and other groups. In January 2019, for example, a terrorist attack killed ten UN peacekeepers in Mali.

International efforts to address terrorism have long been hobbled by the inability to agree on a definition. The problem is "how to formulate the term without criminalizing all armed resistance to oppressive regimes[,] . . . how to distinguish legitimate armed struggle from terrorism and how much emphasis to place on identifying root causes of grievances that lead individuals and groups to adopt terrorist methods" (Peterson 2004: 178). This is often cast as the problem of distinguishing "freedom fighters" from terrorists.

International Responses to Terrorism

The UN system has long been the hub for many counterterrorism efforts (including efforts to define terrorism) because of its global reach, legitimacy, and the legal authority of the Security Council and General Assembly. The UN's limited resources and operational capacity, however, mean that a number of counterterrorism activities take place elsewhere. As of 2021, thirty-eight bodies in the UN system were engaged in counterterrorism efforts. They collaborate in different ways with many other international groups, including the international police agency Interpol, several bodies within the EU, counterterrorism entities in the G-8, APEC, OAS, ECOWAS, AU, and SCO, and a number of functional IGOs outside the UN system. States also play an active role, though they differ in their approaches to dealing with terrorism. For example, the United States has often taken a military approach first (e.g., using drones against al-Qaeda in Yemen and al-Shabaab in Somalia, and air strikes against ISIS in Syria and Iraq) and a law enforcement and transnational cooperation approach second. A number of regions, including Europe, have emphasized law enforcement, regional cooperation, and crime-fighting measures.

The international governance responses to terrorism by IGOs and states have included developing a global legal regime to outlaw various types of terrorist actions; applying sanctions and various means of enforcement, including cutting off terrorist groups' access to financing, financial transactions, and money laundering; and enhancing the capacities of states and international police agencies to track, gather intelligence on, and arrest suspected terrorists and to enhance border controls. In addition, the responses include controls on WMDs (discussed earlier) to prevent terrorists from gaining possession of weapons or their materials.

Developing the global legal regime. Between 1963 and 2020, the UN General Assembly and the International Civil Aviation Organization (ICAO) fostered the conclusion of nineteen international conventions and four supplementary protocols that form the heart of the global legal regime against terrorism. They outlaw terrorist acts against civil aviation, airports, shipping, diplomats, and nuclear materials (see Figure 7.9). They also address the problems of bombings, terrorist financing, and nuclear terrorism. Since the September 2001 attacks, there has been a concerted effort to secure

---

**Figure 7.9   The Global Counterterrorism Legal Regime
(selected conventions and protocols)**

Conventions Relating to Terrorism in Transportation

1969   Convention on Offences and Certain Acts Committed on Board
            Aircraft
1971   Convention for the Suppression of Unlawful Seizure of Aircraft
1989   Protocol on the Suppression of Unlawful Acts of Violence at Airports
            Serving International Civil Aviation
1992   Convention for the Suppression of Unlawful Acts Against the Safety
            of Maritime Navigation
2010   Convention for the Suppression of Unlawful Acts Relating to
            Civil Aviation

Conventions Relating to Weapon Controls

1987   Convention on the Physical Protection of Nuclear Material
1998   Convention on the Marking of Plastic Explosives for the Purposes
            of Detection
2007   International Convention for the Suppression of Acts of Nuclear
            Terrorism

General Conventions

1977   Convention on the Prevention and Punishment of Crimes Against
            Internationally Protected Persons, Including Diplomatic Agents
1983   International Convention Against the Taking of Hostages
2001   International Convention for the Suppression of Terrorist Bombings
2002   International Convention for the Suppression of the Financing of
            Terrorism

Note: Dates indicate the years of entry into force as determined by the minimum number of ratifications needed.

---

universal ratification, with technical assistance provided to countries whose legal systems are weak.

There is still no comprehensive convention against terrorism because of the long-standing difficulty in getting agreement on a definition. Because terrorism is inherently political, it triggers different reactions depending on perceptions about the aims of the terrorists and whether they are justified. Two issues have dominated the discussion: whether official acts of a state's armed forces should or should not be included in the definition of terrorism, and whether violent acts conducted in a struggle against foreign occupation should be considered terrorism. A major step toward a consensus definition of terrorism and a comprehensive convention occurred with the 2005 UN World Summit Outcome, which condemned terrorism "in all its forms and manifestations, committed by whomever, wherever and for whatever purposes, as it constitutes one of the most serious threats to international peace and security" (UN 2005). This was still not sufficient to allow conclusion of the comprehensive convention. In practice, therefore, states continue to act on the basis of competing definitions.

The global legal regime to counter terrorism also includes several UN Security Council resolutions adopted under Chapter VII authority that impose legal obligations on member states. The first and most important is Resolution 1373 (2001), adopted after the September 2001 attacks. It was unprecedented in obliging all states to block the financing and weapons supply of terrorist groups, freeze their assets, prevent recruitment, deny them safe haven, and cooperate in information-sharing and criminal prosecution. Resolution 1373 also established the Counter-Terrorism Committee (CTC), a committee of the whole Security Council discussed in Chapter 4, that monitors states' capability to deny funding and haven to terrorists under threat of sanctions for noncompliance. In 2004, the Security Council established the Counter-Terrorism Executive Directorate (CTED) to provide more permanent and expert staff.

A key aspect of Resolution 1373 is its reporting requirements. The CTED assists committee members in reviewing and analyzing reports from member states concerning their counterterrorism actions. In an extraordinary show of compliance, every UN member state submitted a report for the first round; response has been more variable since then, suggesting reporting fatigue. The threat of sanctions has also been dropped in favor of a more facilitative role for the CTED. Although the reports provide a large body of information on the counterterrorism capabilities of most UN members, they pose a significant burden for processing. Between 2005 and 2022, CTED members also carried out 182 site visits to 112 UN member states to assess states' counterterrorism efforts and technical assistance needs. More than twenty additional Security Council resolutions have extended the measures that states are expected to take in light of the evolution of threat of terrorism and the mandates of the CTC and CTED.

Although there originally were questions raised about whether the Security Council exceeded its Charter mandate with Resolution 1373 and the Council's shift to what former Canadian UN ambassador David Malone (2006: 265) called a "global legal-regulatory architecture [where it] . . . legislates for all states on critical new security threats such as terrorism and WMD," the passage of time has largely laid those concerns to rest.

In 2004, the Security Council took a similar approach when it approved Resolution 1540, requiring all UN member states to take legislative and other steps to prevent nonstate actors (including terrorist groups) from gaining access to WMDs and WMD materials and to report regularly on their efforts. Thus, as Huma Rehman and Afsah Qazi (2019: 53) note, the resolution is "a connecting dot in the webs of UNSCR, bridging those dealing with counterterrorism and nonproliferation." It is also important particularly for efforts to prevent proliferation of bioweapons, they add, as the BWC has no

IO for ensuring implementation and verification (54). The Security Council created the 1540 Committee to monitor states' compliance. A group of eight experts supports the committee's work and helps countries in devising measures to keep WMDs out of the hands of terrorists. That 129 states submitted reports by April 2006 was seen by experts as one measure of the resolution's initial success (Bosch and van Ham 2007: 212), but as with Resolution 1373, these reports tend to highlight states/ compliance and hide their noncompliance. The requirement also ignores the wide variations in states' human and financial resources for reporting and implementation. In 2022, the Security Council extended the mandate of the 1540 Committee to 2032 (Resolution 2663), but it has not been updated to take into account the evolving nature of proliferation threats (Rehman and Qazi 2019: 58–63).

In 2014, in response to growing concerns about the Islamic State, al-Qaeda–related groups, and foreign terrorist fighters joining them from different parts of the world, the Security Council, acting under Chapter VII, unanimously passed two resolutions. The first, Resolution 2070, condemned the Islamic State of Iraq and the Levant and related groups, violent extremist ideology, gross and systemic violations of international humanitarian law, and the recruitment of foreign fighters. It also called on states to take steps to suppress the flow of money, reaffirming the applicability of Resolution 1373 to funds for financing foreign fighters. Resolution 2178 defined the term "foreign terrorist fighter"; called for countries to prevent the recruitment, entry, or transit of individuals believed to be traveling for terrorism-related purposes; and extended the CTED mandate. The resolution also required countries to prevent financing of foreign fighters and to have laws that permit prosecution of their nationals and others who attempt to travel for such purposes.

This global legal regime is complemented by conventions concluded by eight regional and multiregional organizations: the Arab League, OIC, Council of Europe, OAS, South Asian Association of Regional Cooperation, Commonwealth, OAU/AU, and SCO. There are other specialized legal regimes, such as under the International Maritime Organization regarding ship and port security; under the ICAO on travel document security; and the Financial Action Task Force (FATF) on money-laundering, as discussed below.

Enforcement. The use of sanctions to deal with state sponsors of terrorism and al-Qaeda was discussed earlier, as was the US military action against Afghanistan's Taliban regime and al-Qaeda after the September 11, 2001, attacks. In 2011, the Security Council split the sanctions regime targeting al-Qaeda and the Taliban, creating a separate sanctions list of individuals, groups, and undertakings associated with al-Qaeda. In response to the changing al-Qaeda threat and emergence of the Islamic State, the Security Council further strengthened the sanctions regime in 2014 (Resolution

2161) to address the splintering of both entities and the problem of foreign fighters by targeting ISIS and the Al Nusra Front, as shown in Table 7.1.

To date, UN sanctions on state sponsors of terrorism have been more effective than those on al-Qaeda and other nonstate groups. In this regard, the Libyan case is particularly instructive because of the success in getting that country to end its sponsorship and support of terrorist groups and its nuclear program. The effort took almost thirty years, however, and a combination of multilateral and unilateral sanctions, beginning with a US ban on military equipment sales to Libya in 1978, listing Libya on the US State Department's list of state sponsors of terrorism in 1979, diplomatic and economic sanctions against Libya for its support of international terrorism in 1981, and freezing Libya's assets and imposing comprehensive trade and financial sanctions in 1986. Only after conclusive evidence linked Libya to the bombings of Pan Am Flight 103 and UTA Flight 772 did the United States, France, and the United Kingdom initiate multilateral efforts by taking the issue to the Security Council. Resolution 731 (1992) was the first Chapter VII resolution to condemn terrorist acts and Libya's role in the airline bombings. Subsequent resolutions imposed the first targeted sanctions on civil aviation, arms sales, and diplomatic links, leading to Libya's isolation from the rest of the world. Support for the UN sanctions was slipping, however; diplomatic initiatives and a 1998 ICJ ruling opened the way to an agreement to turn over the suspects in the bombings for trial in the Netherlands and for Libya to pay compensation to the families of those killed on the flights. The UN sanctions were lifted in 2003; it took until 2006 for the United States to lift its sanctions and to remove Libya from the list of states sponsoring terrorism.

The Shanghai Cooperation Organization is unique among regional organizations in having prepared itself for military enforcement action against terrorism through periodic joint military exercises. NATO's operation in Afghanistan that began in 2001 was directed against Islamic militants and the Taliban, in addition to its efforts to strengthen Afghanistan's government and armed forces. Further examples of regional organization enforcement efforts relating to terrorism include the AU's role through AMISOM in combating al-Shabaab in Somalia and its collaboration with ECOWAS, the UN, and French forces against AQIM and other extremist groups in Mali beginning in 2012. In 2015, the AU and ECOWAS authorized Cameroon, Chad, and Niger to aid Nigerian forces in combating Boko Haram.

Building state capacities to combat and prevent terrorism. Building the capacity of states to control their borders, improve their laws and banking systems, and enhance their ability to take other steps to combat terrorism is critical to global governance efforts. Likewise, countering or preventing violent extremism has become "among the most important developments in counterterrorism per se . . .[and] represents a conscious departure from the tactile, coercive counterterrorism tools favored both domestically and multilaterally after 9/11" (Romaniuk 2018: 505).

Technical assistance is provided by a variety of IOs, with the CTED playing a key role. The directorate has assisted states in drafting legislation and adapting money-laundering laws and controls on informal banking systems and has provided training in counterterrorism standards. The need has been greater than the supply of its services. The UN Office on Drugs and Crime's Terrorism Prevention Branch helps states in ratifying and implementing the conventions, strengthening national criminal justice systems, and drafting legislation. The IMF provides technical assistance with legislation to counter financing for terrorism more generally. In the early 2000s, the EU used a unique "twinning program" that paired older EU members with candidate countries to share counterterrorism expertise and provide assistance in conforming to EU standards on border controls and legislative, judicial, and administrative procedures. In 2015, the UN Secretary-General released a Plan of Action to Prevent Violent Extremism and encouraged member states to develop national plans. This was followed in 2017 by Security Council Resolution 2354, which included a comprehensive framework for countering terrorist narratives, guidelines for states, and mandates for the CTED.

Cutting off terrorists' financing. Key to counterterrorism efforts is cutting off the sources of funds for terrorist activities and related money-laundering and financial crimes. Most countries have inadequate money-laundering legislation and ability to monitor financial transactions or the informal banking networks that are widely used by many terrorist organizations. Terrorist groups have used a variety of illegal activities, including trafficking in weapons and drugs, kidnapping, and exploiting natural resources. The Islamic State has sold oil and gas from wells it controls and taxed residents of areas it controlled; the Taliban relies on heroin sales; and al-Shabaab benefits from the sale of charcoal.

Targeted sanctions are one means of addressing the problem of terrorist financing, but there are some significant governance challenges to making such sanctions effective, such as ending bank secrecy (including for Swiss banks) and regulating offshore financial havens in Caribbean and Pacific island nations. Countries have to develop the legal and technical capabilities to monitor financial transactions, interdict accounts of particular individuals, and act quickly to deny terrorists time to move funds.

The International Convention for the Suppression of Financing for Terrorism, which came into force in 2002, provides the normative and legal basis for these activities. Key actors include the US Treasury Department, finance ministries, major banks, the IMF, the FATF, the Asia/Pacific Group on Money Laundering, the Middle East and North Africa Financial Action Task Force, and the Caribbean Financial Action Task Force. There is no central international organization, however, with the mandate and expertise to coordinate global efforts to deal with the problem of terrorist financing.

Without such an organization, the FATF develops and promotes policies at the state and international levels to combat money laundering and terrorist financing. As noted, it is crucial for enforcing financial sanctions because of its role in combating money laundering for drug trafficking and other transnational crimes. It has periodically revised its counterterrorist financing standards as the threat has evolved. The FATF evaluates states' ability to prevent, detect, and prosecute terrorist financing and aids states in implementing the financing sections of Security Council resolutions. It also sets global standards and monitors members' progress and trends. As of 2023, thirty-six states are members (Russia was suspended in 2023); ten entities, including regional financial action task forces, are part of the FATF Global Network. Membership requires adoption of money-laundering legislation and a FATF evaluation.

One of the FATF's major challenges is that terrorist financing is a moving target, given the continual evolution of money laundering and the use of noncash types of transactions through charities, informal banking systems, and commodities such as diamonds, heroin, charcoal, gas, oil, and metals, which are hard to track. Furthermore, the amounts of money required for most terrorist activities are small compared with those for other criminal activities. The FATF uses a peer review process of monitoring and assessment along with self-reporting to identify areas in which technical assistance and aid should be targeted (Gardner 2007).

Criminal justice approaches. Beyond creating a framework of international rules dealing with terrorism, interrupting the flow of money to terrorist groups and enhancing state capacities are state and multilateral efforts to increase security, tighten border controls, step up counterintelligence activities, and improve cooperation among law enforcement agencies. The two international police agencies—Interpol and Europol—are particularly important in tracking and apprehending terrorists.

The EU has been very active with respect to criminal justice approaches to counterterrorism under the rubric of justice and home affairs. Among the key developments have been a European arrest warrant, enhanced enforcement and intelligence cooperation through Europol, judicial cooperation through the European Judicial Cooperation Unit, and identification of presumed terrorist groups. The 2004 Madrid train bombings provided impetus for these steps, serving a "a grim reminder to EU member states of the costs of moving too slowly to implement counter-terrorism measures" (Bures and Ahern 2007: 216). Starting in 2014, the concerns about returning foreign fighters prompted a new look at border security, specifically monitoring those who traveled to areas such as Iraq, Somalia, Syria, and Yemen, where Islamic extremist groups were then active. In 2015, the European Council issued a statement calling for specific measures to ensure citizens' security, prevent radicalization, safeguard values, and enhance cooperation with international partners. Terrorist attacks in France, Germany, and Austria in 2020 led to further initiatives to combat radicalization, terrorism, and violent extremism. A 2021 EU Council regulation addressed the problem of terrorist online content.

Coordinating strategy and action. A variety of steps have been taken since the early 2000s by the UN, regional IGOs, and new multilateral entities to improve coordination of and cooperation of counterterrorism efforts. In 2006, the UN General Assembly adopted the UN Global Counter-Terrorism Strategy (A/RES/60/288)—the first attempt to provide a comprehensive global framework for addressing terrorism. That strategy is built on four pillars—addressing conditions conducive to the spread of terrorism, preventing and combating terrorism, building state capacity, and defending human rights while combating terrorism. A Counterterrorism Implementation Task Force, composed of representatives from various specialized agencies, the Department of Peace Operations, CTED, 1540 Committee, many other UN offices, and Interpol, works to ensure overall coordination of activities throughout the UN system.

In addition to its action plan, the EU created the position of a counterterrorism coordinator. ECOWAS and ASEAN created counterterrorism task forces. The AU has the African Centre for the Study and Research on Terrorism and the post of Special Representative for Counter-terrorism Cooperation created in 2010. The OAS not only created the Inter-American Committee Against Terrorism but also established a separate secretariat to support its work. The SCO's Regional Anti-Terrorism Structure, established in 2002, represents a significant part of that organization's activities. Still, other than the EU, most of these institutions lack capacity, funding, and political will to pursue counterterrorism effectively, let alone in coordination with UN and other regional programs.

Additional efforts to improve cooperation include the Global Counterterrorism Forum—an informal entity—created in 2011 and comprising thirty member countries and a number of other partner organizations, including the UN, Council of Europe, ASEAN, AU Centre, OSCE, and Interpol, plus research institutions. As a platform for experts to share strategies and best practices, it focuses on reducing terrorist recruitment, increasing civilian capabilities for dealing with terrorist threats, and implementing the UN Global Counterterrorism Strategy. Another entity is the eighty-five-member Global Coalition Against Daesh formed in 2014 to dismantle the Islamic State's networks and ensure its defeat.

Many traditional security governance approaches—such as preventive diplomacy, adjudication, mediation, peacekeeping, and arms control—are irrelevant when dealing with terrorism. Meanwhile, the continuing evolution of the threat poses serious challenges to peace and security in many parts of the world. This makes efforts to address the threat and its root causes even more urgent. It requires delegitimating the appeal of suicide bombings among young people in groups such as Hamas, Islamic Jihad, and Boko Haram. In cases where grievances are known, such as the long-standing Palestinian cause, renewed efforts to find peaceful and just solutions are needed. In cases such as the branches of al-Qaeda and the Islamic State, where there are no specific political objectives but broad anti-Western sentiments, fundamentalist Islamic or other religious concerns, and deep alienation from static societies such as Saudi Arabia and Egypt, identifying appropriate governance responses is a far more elusive task.

The Challenges of Human Security

This chapter began with a case study of the conflict in Somalia and the humanitarian crisis of famine, which are emblematic of post–Cold War security problems of the 1990s and the contemporary problems of weak states, terrorism, and large-scale humanitarian crises. We end with the security threats that terrorism poses to people, states, and regions and the various governance approaches to countering those threats. Presently there are an extraordinary variety of threats to international peace and security. A corresponding variety of new governance initiatives have been taken while not negating the value of older approaches.

Traditionally, international peace and security have meant states' security and the defense of states' territorial integrity from external threats or attack. But as the R2P and POC norms suggest, the concept of human security—the security of humans in the face of many different kinds of threats—has gained increasing attention. The growing concerns for human security are reflected in discussions in successive chapters about the need to eradicate poverty and reduce the inequalities exacerbated by globalization; to promote environmentally sustainable development and greater respect for human rights, particularly the rights of women and children; to prosecute war crimes and crimes against humanity more aggressively; and to address the security threats posed by climate change. This edition of the book adds a dedicated chapter on human security (Chapter 11) to examine the roles of various IOs and global governance in addressing human security issues relating to health, food, refugees, migration, and human trafficking.

Suggested Further Reading

Biersteker, Thomas, Sue Eckert, and Marcos Tourinho, eds. (2016) *Targeting Sanctions: The Impacts and Effectiveness of UN Action*. New York: Cambridge University Press.

Campbell, Susanna P. (2018) *Global Governance and Local Peace: Accountability and Performance in International Peacebuilding.* New York: Cambridge University Press.

Fortna, Virginia Page. (2008) *Does Peacekeeping Work: Shaping Belligerents' Choices after Civil War.* Princeton, NJ: Princeton University Press.

Howard, Lise Morjé. (2019) *Power in Peacekeeping.* New York: Cambridge University Press.

Koops, Joachim A., Norrie MacQueen, Thierry Tardy, and Paul D. Williams, eds. (2015) *The Oxford Handbook of UN Peacekeeping Operations.* New York: Oxford University Press.

Thakur, Ramesh. (2018) *The United Nations, Peace and Security: From Collective Security to the Responsibility to Protect*, 2nd ed. New York: Cambridge University Press.

8

Pursuing Economic Well-Being

The news was astonishing. In May 2020, in the early months of the Covid-19 pandemic, Brazilian diplomat Roberto Azevêdo announced his resignation as director-general of the World Trade Organization (WTO). The WTO—which was established in 1995 to continue the trade promotion and regulation work of its predecessor the 1947 General Agreement on Tariffs and Trade (GATT)—was once heralded for its effective economic governance, particularly in adjudicating countries' trade disputes. However, by the time of Azevêdo's surprise resignation, the organization had become hamstrung by competition between China and the United States and broader divisions between the Global South and the Global North. Its dispute settlement body was short-staffed, unable to resolve controversial issues such as intellec-

tual property or agricultural subsidies. The WTO director-general had watched helplessly as governments restricted trade in ventilators, personal protective equipment, and other pandemic-fighting gear.

Replacing Azevêdo was complicated. At the time, the organization had 164 member governments. As with many WTO activities, the process of appointing a new director-general required consensus and could be stymied by even a single member. Eight countries (Egypt, Kenya, Mexico, Moldova, Nigeria, Saudi Arabia, South Korea, and the United Kingdom) wanted the next director-general to be one of their own citizens. It took nine months, three decision rounds, and substantial in-fighting to narrow the field. The African countries fielded three

(continued)

contenders. China opposed candidates that appeared to be aligned with the United States, and the United States acted similarly. Complaining that there had been only two GATT/WTO directors-general from the Global South, developing countries insisted that the new leader must come from among their ranks.

Beyond the WTO's member governments, trade has stakeholders such as nongovernmental organizations, labor unions, and business associations. These nonstate actors (NSAs) also weighed in. For example, a group of nineteen civil society groups helped eliminate the Saudi Arabian candidate when they publicized his complicity in human rights abuses.

By October 2020, only two candidates remained, and both were women: Yoo Myung-hee of South Korea and Ngozi Okonjo-Iweala of Nigeria. This alone was momentous, ensuring the first female director-general in the history of the GATT and the WTO. These women also embodied an enduring debate about whether the WTO is primarily about trade policy or development policy (Johnson and Urpelainen 2020). Yoo had a long career in government and was then serving as South Korea's trade minister. In contrast, Okonjo-Iweala had worked in the World Bank for twenty-five years and chaired the Global Alliance for Vaccines and Immunizations (GAVI), a public–private partnership that distributes vaccines in developing countries. The United States fought

Okonjo-Iweala's candidacy, with the US Trade Representative dismissing her as "somebody from the World Bank who does development," with "no experience in trade" (Campbell 2021).

Since the director-general post already had been vacated and an individual WTO member can block decisions indefinitely, things were at an impasse. Instead of the "nuclear option" of voting by simple majority, the WTO's selection committee agreed to take stock again after the 2020 US presidential election. When Joseph Biden became the new US president, he endorsed Okonjo-Iweala, who then became the first woman and first African to lead the WTO. Her selection added to the growing number of major international economic institutions—including the European Central Bank, the International Monetary Fund, the International Trade Center, and the UN Conference for Trade and Development—that have been led by women.

Okonjo-Iweala's path to becoming WTO director-general illustrates core themes of global economic governance: North/South tensions, development policy's inextricable links with other areas of economic policy, and the interaction of states and nonstate actors. First, the worry of the Donald Trump administration that Okonjo-Iweala was more devoted to development than to trade, and developing countries' insistence that

(continued)

it was "their turn" for the director-general spot, show how tensions between developed and developing countries can play out in global economic governance. As a US-trained economist with dual Nigerian and US citizenship, Okonjo-Iweala is particularly well equipped to bridge North/South tensions. Second, governing international trade or finance requires thinking about development and vice versa. The WTO's founding document makes this link explicit, declaring in its opening paragraph that one of trade's core purposes is to facilitate development through improvements such as "ensuring full employment" and "raising standards of living." Third, stakeholders in global economic governance include not only states but also nonstate actors. In the selection process for the WTO director-general, NGOs and other NSAs certainly made their preferences known. Perhaps it helped that Okonjo-Iweala had chaired GAVI, a prominent public–private partnership that blurs the distinction between the public and private spheres. Regardless of whether her term is renewed in 2025, her path to WTO leadership showcases core themes of global economic governance and is a notable first for women and for Africa.

Global Economic Governance: Key Ideas and Events

This chapter addresses the governance of trade, finance, and development. Before moving into detailed discussions of each, it is important to highlight some of the main ideas and events that have shaped the evolution of global economic governance. International economic relations are vastly different in the second decade of the twenty-first century than at the end of World War II (when the Bretton Woods system was established), let alone in earlier times.

Key Ideas: Mercantilism, Liberalism, Socialism

In the late 1700s, the system of nation-states that we know today was in its infancy. Europe was the home of some states that competed or cooperated with each other, and several sought to boost their economic power by colonizing wide swaths of Africa, the Americas, Asia, and Oceania. The thirteen English colonies in North America were in the midst of winning their independence and establishing a new country called the United States.

At this time, Britain and other colonial powers tended to follow early versions of mercantilism, which emphasizes the role of the state and the subordination of economic activities to the goal of state-building. Through colonization, competing states tried to improve their own economic potential by controlling natural resources, workers, territory, and particular industries. The colonial powers often relied on hybrid public–private entities, such as the Hudson Bay Company or the Dutch East India Company, to achieve these aims.

Mercantilism faced a challenge from economic liberalism, however. The year 1776 was not only when the American colonies declared their independence but also when Scottish economist Adam Smith debuted his famous book *The Wealth of Nations*. Smith and his successors envisioned a different relationship between states and the economy. According to liberalism, humans act in rational and self-interested ways. As a result, markets develop to produce, distribute, and consume goods. Markets stimulate individual and collective economic growth through specialization, competition, a division of labor, and efficient allocation of resources. Government institutions perform critical functions of providing order, infrastructure, and stability so that markets can operate. Put starkly, whereas mercantilism is about markets serving states, liberalism is about states serving markets. The first is about using economic means for political ends, and the second is about using political means for economic ends. Ideally, if national governments and international institutions allow markets to allocate resources efficiently, then the increased interdependence among economies will lead to greater economic development for all countries involved.

Eventually, mercantilism and liberalism faced challenges from a third set of ideas: socialism. In the mid-1800s and early 1900s, writers such as Karl Marx and political leaders such as Vladimir Lenin opposed private ownership of land, factories, and other means of production. They believed ownership should be socialized—either collectively held by workers or entrusted to the state. Socialists accused liberals and mercantilists of exploiting their colonies abroad and laborers at home.

Various powerful states have been champions of socialism, economic liberalism, or mercantilism. Among the combatants of World War II, all three ideas were represented. While the United Kingdom, the United States, and many other Allied nations were associated with liberalism, the Soviet Union espoused socialism. Japan and Germany adopted mercantilism for state-building, economic catch-up, and greater military might. After World War II, the Cold War between the United States and the Soviet Union amplified the contestation between liberal and socialist economic systems. And, even though Japan and Germany had been defeated, their earlier successes with mercantilism became models for other late industrializing countries, particularly in Asia.

The 1940s: Making the US-Led Liberal Economic Order

Liberal, socialist, and mercantilist ideas continued to shape the twentieth century, but World War II was a turning point for colonialism. War-torn

France, the United Kingdom, and other colonial powers had to focus on reconstruction, and over time they lost the will or ability to control distant peoples and lands. In the process of decolonization over the next twenty years, most European colonies became independent states whose governments then chose whether their own economic approach would be mercantilist, liberal, or socialist.

Hybrids of these economic models were also possible. Prominent British economist John Maynard Keynes combined liberalism's emphasis on markets, mercantilism's emphasis on state interventions, and socialism's emphasis on providing social safety nets. His mixed approach, known as Keynesianism, was adopted by individual countries and by new international economic IGOs.

Keynes attended and strongly influenced the outcomes of the 1944 Bretton Woods conference that proposed three new institutions: the International Monetary Fund (IMF), the International Bank for Reconstruction and Development (IBRD or World Bank), and the International Trade Organization (ITO). As discussed in Chapter 3, the IMF was to provide short-term aid to compensate for balance-of-payments shortfalls and ensure a stable financial system, the World Bank was to rehabilitate war-damaged economies and provide capital for development, and the ITO was to facilitate economic growth through reduced barriers to international trade. The IMF and the World Bank began operating shortly after the conference, but the ITO did not come to fruition; instead, its aims were partially accommodated by the 1947 General Agreement on Tariffs and Trade (GATT).

The World Bank's initial task was to facilitate reconstruction in post–World War II Europe. The United States, however, channeled the bulk of its contributions through the Marshall Plan that it set up in 1948 to strengthen the political and economic systems of European countries in the face of the growing threat from communist parties in Europe and the Soviet Union. The United States and Canada also set up the Organisation for European Economic Cooperation (OEEC) to funnel aid to Western Europe and push the European governments to work together in planning their recovery.

The Bretton Woods institutions and the OEEC were integral to what became known as the US-led postwar "liberal order" (Ikenberry 2001). Still, they were not built on liberalism alone. The institutions also reflected a Keynesian approach that saw a strong role for governments in promoting trade and investment, as well as stimulating growth during periods of economic contraction. The goal was an ever-expanding global market and the assurance that states would provide assistance to mitigate the dangers of international forces. Full employment, equalization of incomes, and a strong safety net were key parts of this social contract, which was supported by US hegemony and has been called "embedded liberalism" (Ruggie 1982).

The 1950s to 1980s: Changes and
Challenges in the Liberal Economic Order

By the 1950s, Cold War hostility had solidified. The United States led the "first world," a bloc of mostly Western European or North American countries; the Soviet Union led the "second world," a bloc of mostly Eastern European countries. Developing countries, many of whom were newly independent and hesitant to antagonize one superpower by working too closely with the other, became known as the "third world."

These divisions permeated global economic governance. The Soviet Union was very active in the United Nations but refused to join the three Bretton Woods institutions and pressured its allies to do likewise. Unlike in security policy, where the Soviet-led Warsaw Pact mirrored the American-led North Atlantic Treaty Organization, the Soviet Union never created complete economic counterparts for the World Bank, IMF, and GATT. Some developing countries joined the Bretton Woods institutions (discussed below), but most viewed these institutions as tools of the developed countries.

Between the 1950s and the 1970s, three major changes reshaped the world economy. One was the process of European economic integration discussed in Chapter 5. That began in 1951, with six states—France, West Germany, Italy, Belgium, the Netherlands, and Luxembourg—establishing the European Coal and Steel Community, then the European Economic Community (EEC). Incrementally, these states eliminated various barriers to internal trade, standardized an external tariff, and agreed on a Common Agricultural Policy. Through the 1970s, European integration did not deepen much, but the EEC did broaden its membership to include Denmark, Ireland, and the United Kingdom.

A second change was the explosive growth of multinational corporations (MNCs). According to economic liberalism, MNCs use economies of scale to deliver economic growth and prosperity. They invest capital around the world, introduce new technologies, open markets, provide jobs, and finance industrial and agricultural improvements. By providing foreign direct investment (FDI), MNCs serve as conduits for capital, ideas, and economic growth. The existence of MNCs is not novel—after all, early forerunners include colonial-era entities like the Hudson Bay Company. But their prevalence is new. Partly facilitated by European economic integration, the population of MNCs grew dramatically. Companies such as Shell, General Motors, and Hitachi became global forces and household names.

A third change was the increased tension between developed and developing countries. In 1960, the OEEC was refashioned into the Organisation for Economic Co-operation and Development (OECD). With Europe's postwar recovery complete, the new organization pivoted away from administering Marshall Plan aid and expanded into almost everything except military matters. Operating through consensus-based meetings of high-level officials, the OECD became a channel for developed countries to coordinate macroeconomic policies and financial aid to developing countries. With membership extended to a few non-European countries such as Australia and Japan, it soon became known as a club for rich states. Using the OECD and other economic forums, developed countries promoted the idea of "trade, not aid." The thinking was that economic growth would be more robust if poorer countries opened up to international markets, rather than relying on mercantilist industrial policies and development assistance.

Developing countries had very different views, however, and those views became increasingly influential as the number of newly independent states grew. Already in the 1950s, economists in the UN Economic Commission for Latin America (ECLA) began challenging US-backed economic liberalism. ECLA aligned with the dependency school which (as discussed in Chapter 2) argued that the developing world was permanently mired in poverty and unable to grow. To break the cycle of dependency, ECLA encouraged import-substitution industrialization: governments would pinpoint strategic or high-value sectors (e.g., cars) that were dominated by imports, then use a combination of internal incentives and external trade barriers to nurture domestic substitutes. The hope was that with enough time and resources, this approach would enable developing countries to enhance their know-how, grow richer, and gain more influence in international economic affairs.

In 1964, developing countries who had created the Group of 77 (G-77) at the UN used their majority of votes to establish the UN Conference on Trade and Development (UNCTAD) with the support of ECLA. Despite the term "conference" in its name, UNCTAD is a permanent intergovernmental body in the UN system. Because of the limited expertise of many newly independent governments, UNCTAD's secretariat became very important in providing technical assistance and challenging predominant liberal thinking about development. In 1974, again using its numerical voting majority in the UN General Assembly, the G-77 secured adoption of the Declaration on the Establishment of a New International Economic Order and the Charter of Economic Rights and Duties of States. Through these, the G-77 sought changes in five major areas: commodity pricing, regulation of MNCs, technology transfer, foreign aid, and trade. The result was a period of sharp confrontation between North and South, a divide that affected every UN body for several years (see Chapter 4). On most issues, the North refused to negotiate. But the G-77 did win some concessions in trade, such as GATT's recognition of the principle of preferential treatment for developing countries' exports.

In the 1960s and 1970s, many developing countries also began cooperating through narrower arrangements, such as commodity cartels. The most well-known is the Organization of the Petroleum Exporting Countries (OPEC), founded in 1960 by Iran, Iraq, Kuwait, Saudi Arabia, and Venezuela to counter the international oil companies that controlled the production and sale of most of the world's traded oil in return for fixed royalties to the host governments. In addition to being an economic actor that aims to secure higher prices and influence for oil-producing countries, OPEC is a political actor. During the 1973 Yom Kippur War between Israel and a coalition of Arab states, a subset of OPEC's membership—calling themselves the Organization of Arab Petroleum Exporting Countries—initiated an oil embargo against the United States, the Netherlands, and other countries that had sided with Israel. Although the embargo officially ended after a few months, the oil-producing countries had memorably demonstrated their power. The targeted countries did not soon forget their feeling of vulnerability, and other developing countries were inspired to form cartels for tin, coffee, and other commodities. Not every cartel thrived: whereas oil is an essential commodity with no close substitutes and a relatively small set of producing countries, many other commodities are price-elastic and have a multitude of suppliers who are eager to undercut one another. Nevertheless, commodity cartels became another means for developing countries to assert themselves vis-à-vis developed countries.

These three changes—Europe's economic integration, MNCs' explosive growth, and increased tensions between developed and developing countries—meant the world economy of the 1970s was quite different from that of 1945. Even the United States, the primary backer of the post-World War II liberal economic order, sought to change the system. In 1971, the US government abandoned a key arrangement from the 1944 Bretton Woods conference: it "closed the gold window" so foreign governments could no longer convert US dollars into a fixed amount of gold. Although the gold-backed US dollar had provided international stability and endowed the United States with the world's preferred reserve currency, domestic inflation and foreign competition had made the arrangement harmful to the United States. By 1973, the fixed exchange rate had given way to a quasi-floating exchange rate system in which currency values could fluctuate within an agreed range. With a large part of its original purpose demolished, over the next decade the IMF pivoted to providing financial assistance for developing countries experiencing long-term structural economic problems, including high debt and balance-of-payments disequilibrium.

As the United States scaled back its leadership role with the end of the gold standard, there was a greater need for economic policy coordination among economically advanced countries. The OECD became more important in this connection, and in the mid-1970s seven of the developed countries (Canada, France, Germany, Italy, Japan, the United Kingdom, and the United States) initiated annual meetings of finance ministers and heads of government, forming the Group of Seven (G-7). The G-7 has never become a formal IGO; rather, member-states take turns holding the presidency, setting the year's policy agenda, and hosting the annual summit. The G-7 has proven valuable for establishing personal relationships among leaders and learning from each other's experiences.

Another innovation in the 1970s was the World Economic Forum (WEF), also an elite forum, but with roots in the private sector. Originally called the European Management Forum, the first meeting in 1971 consisted of hundreds of European executives who were invited to Davos, Switzerland, by business professor Klaus Schwab. Within a few years, the annual meetings included government officials and other "influentials" for broad discussions on global issues. The WEF's influence on economic and other policymaking is the subject of debate, but its annual gatherings in Davos continue to attract a range of potentially influential people.

By the 1980s, the liberal economic order was being challenged from two different directions. First was Asia, where Japan and then South Korea, Hong Kong, Singapore, and Taiwan developed rapidly as major exporters in strategic sectors such as electronics, plastics, and steel. State involvement was key, with all of these Asian governments investing in public education and infrastructure, and some even attempting to manipulate currency values or deliver preferential funding to particular companies. Unlike Latin America, with its socialism-inspired practice of import-substitution industrialization, East Asia opted for export-led growth, which exploited the liberal international system to pursue mercantilist aims. The second set of challenges came from the developing world and the growing problem of debt, which, as noted already, led the IMF to focus much of its attention on structural adjustment policies and debt relief.

The 1990s: Emergent Globalization after the "Victory" of the Liberal Economic Order

The sudden end of the Cold War in the early 1990s was a turning point for economic governance. European integration received an enormous boost when market-oriented West Germany and socialist East Germany became a single state. Buoyed by a unified Germany, in 1992 the twelve states of the EEC agreed on the Maastricht Treaty, binding themselves together in the European Union (EU) to further integrate their economies and ultimately create a full-fledged monetary union based on a shared new currency called the euro.

The end of the Cold War also transformed economic governance at the global level. From the 1950s to the 1980s, the liberal economic order had weathered challenges from the Soviet-led Eastern bloc, the Global South, the mercantilist industrializers of East Asia—and even from the United States. By the early 1990s, economic liberalism seemed to have triumphed. As the Soviet Union rapidly disintegrated, many socialist countries transitioned to market economies. Brazil, India, and other pivotal parts of the Global South also cooled on socialism, opting for greater economic liberalization. Richer and increasingly integrated into international markets, Japan and the four "Asian Tigers" (Hong Kong, Singapore, South Korea, and Taiwan) began moving away from statist mercantilism. The United States, the sole remaining superpower and the leader of a liberal economic order covering many more countries, promoted greater opening of economies and markets through globalization.

US-backed economic policy prescriptions coalesced in the 1990s into a neoliberal ideology known as the Washington Consensus. This held that states could achieve economic development only by following the "correct" economic policies—that is, those espoused by the Bretton Woods institutions and the US government. Elements of the Washington Consensus included deregulation of economic activities, privatization of state-owned enterprises, governmental budget austerity, greater competition in trade and investment markets, and tax reform. This became the dominant approach undergirding the World Bank's development funding and the IMF's emergency assistance. Through "conditionality," these organizations stipulated that money would be available only to states that committed to these liberal economic reforms—even if the reforms sometimes resulted in social unrest, less social spending, more income inequality, or increased poverty.

These moves by the Bretton Woods institutions were part of a broader phenomenon of opening and linking markets. The result was greater globalization: a shift in the scale of human organization that links distant communities and expands the reach of power relations across the world (Held 2004: 1). Spanning economic, political, and social spheres, globalization entails disruptions and interdependencies that are unsettling for many people.

By the late 1990s, opponents of globalization had formed a broad movement of workers, environmentalists, farmers, religious activists, women, human rights advocates, and other groups seeking economic and social justice. These groups had different agendas but united in denouncing globalization and seeking a return to governance at the local or national level. To many, the neoliberal goals of economic efficiency and being able to buy the cheapest goods should be replaced by support for local employment, fair working conditions, and environmentally sustainable practices. Many activists found common cause in the streets, staging mass protests in conjunction with meetings of international economic institutions such as the WTO and IMF. Antiglobalization efforts also arose in the marketplace as consumers strove to support local agriculture, buy fair-trade products, or pressure MNCs to reform their labor practices.

When a financial crisis struck Asia in 1997–1998, the dangers of globalization and the Washington Consensus went on full display. The crisis began in Thailand, then spread to other Southeast Asian countries as well as South Korea and even Russia. Exchange rates plummeted, stock markets fell, real income dropped, and millions of people were forced into poverty.

The crisis revealed weaknesses in many countries' banking systems: heavy levels of short-term debt and current-account deficits, along with corrupt "crony capitalism" in business–government relations. The huge inflows of private investment capital that had fueled rapid development stopped, reflecting a crisis of confidence not only in Asian countries but in emerging markets more generally.

The IMF responded to the social and political upheaval with large, controversial bailout packages to Thailand, Indonesia, and South Korea, which faced stringent conditions and compliance monitoring. Governments had to agree to carry out extensive structural reforms that would transform their economies from semi-mercantilist to more market-oriented. In South Korea, for example, the government restructured financial institutions, lifted restrictions on capital movements and foreign ownership, and allowed companies to lay off workers. These reforms led to public outcries, boycotts of foreign products, and exposés of how foreigners benefited at the expense of Koreans (Moon and Mo 2000).

Many of the IMF's actions were copied from its approach to previous crises in Latin America. Yet the Asian financial crisis was different. Having misdiagnosed some of the underlying problems, the IMF soon found that not all of its prescribed solutions were appropriate. High interest rates pushed indebted companies into bankruptcy. Budget cuts eliminated social services and put more families below the poverty line, leading to backlash against governments and the IMF. Gradually, the policy prescriptions of the Washington Consensus lost influence as the Bretton Woods institutions and major donor states concluded that a cookie-cutter approach was inferior to locally tailored solutions.

In addition to revealing limitations of the IMF, the Asian financial crisis highlighted shortcomings of the G-7. The G-7 could not address the crisis alone; its members needed the participation of developing countries, other industrialized countries, and the European Union. Thus, the Group of 20 (G-20) was created at a December 1999 meeting of finance ministers from the G-7 countries plus Argentina, Australia, Brazil, China, India, Indonesia, Mexico, Russia, Saudi Arabia, South Africa, South Korea, Turkey, and the EU. The finance ministers began meeting annually, and the G-20 mirrored the G-7's informality, with rotating leadership rather than a founding charter or permanent secretariat.

The Asian financial crisis drew attention to the uncertainty and volatility of foreign direct investment (FDI)—not only for investors but also for recipient countries. Yet instead of governing investment through an overarching multilateral structure, the world witnessed a surge in bilateral investment treaties (BITs). BITs are legal agreements between two countries, stipulating the rights and responsibilities held by private investors from one country when they invest in the other country. These treaties tend to be pro-investor, with language guaranteeing that the host government will treat the foreign investors fairly and equitably, provide adequate compensation for any nationalized assets, and not channel disputes through its domestic courts. Some BITs also prohibit host governments from requiring technology transfers, worker training, or local procurement.

When BITs are between two rich countries, each is likely to have investors who benefit. But when BITs are between countries at very different development levels, the situation becomes lopsided: since the richer country tends to have many more investors, a pro-investor slant would privilege the richer country while tying the hands of the poorer country. The United States, Canada, and other states with heavy outflows of investment have become known for their "model BITs," in which the other signatory may differ but much of the treaty text does not. Developing countries continue signing such agreements in the hopes of attracting FDI.

2000 to the Present:
Globalization and Backlash to Globalization
Through FDI and other economic means, many developing countries have established international economic links, propelling globalization even more. Some parts of the Global South, such as China, India, Mexico, and Nigeria, have developed more rapidly than others. These emerging powers have not all adopted liberal economic reforms to the same degree or in the same way, however. China, for example, incrementally shifted from a socialist system to a more market-oriented one, even joining the WTO—but state-owned companies and banks continue to control a significant portion of the economy. This divergence from the prescriptions of the Washington Consensus came to be known as the Beijing Consensus. By adopting some elements of liberal economic ideology but rejecting others, dynamic developing countries challenged and altered key parts of the international economic order. They also did something that previous rapid-developers like Japan and South Korea had not: instead of eagerly joining the ranks of the Global North, they continued to identify with poorer parts of the Global South. They also began positioning themselves as leaders and representatives of developing countries as a whole (Johnson and Urpelainen 2020).

This leadership solidified after the global financial system came close to imploding in 2008–2009. Global stock markets plummeted. One of the world's largest banks, Lehman Brothers, collapsed. Industrial output and world trade levels dropped precipitously. Global FDI and migrant workers' remittances plunged. Unemployment skyrocketed all over the world. The crisis had many causes: irresponsible lending in the United States and Europe; overconfidence from many years of low inflation and stable growth; a glut of savings in Asia that reduced global interest rates; and central bankers and other regulators who tolerated risky practices.

Economic interdependence enabled the crisis to spread globally, but the pain was not distributed evenly. The United States and Europe were most severely affected, but in many developing countries, the repercussions were milder. Thus, initial responses to the financial crisis were mostly at the national level, with the United States and various EU member governments taking unprecedented steps in bailing out banks and insurance companies to stimulate credit markets and investor confidence. Later, central banks such as the US Federal Reserve, the Bank of England, and the European Central Bank undertook coordinated action.

None of these institutions, however, was up to the task of overseeing all the short-term and long-term responses that were needed (Cooper and Thakur 2013). As with the crisis in Asia a decade earlier, the G-7 countries could not resolve this global financial crisis on their own. As a result, in November 2008, US President George W. Bush convened the G-20, but instead of finance ministers, he invited heads of government for the first time. Over the course of ten months, the G-20 met three times, establishing the group's reputation as a first responder in crises. It produced a number of major initiatives, including support for large domestic stimulus packages and new resources for the IMF and World Bank. Bolstered by their inclusion in the G-20, major developing countries were becoming world leaders.

China's rise has been especially dramatic. In 2004 its gross domestic product ranked fifth in the world, and by 2010 it had overtaken Japan to rank second. By 2021, the IMF reported that the United States had the world's largest economy in terms of nominal gross domestic product (GDP, the market value of all goods and services produced within a country in a year), but China had the world's largest economy if GDP was adjusted to account for the lower cost of living in China. Despite slowdowns, China's GDP growth rate has regularly exceeded that of developed countries; with a population of over 1.4 billion people, however, its per capita income still lags behind.

China's economic strategy, with an emphasis on state-guided exports, has presented a direct challenge to Bretton Woods models. By exporting much more than it imported, China amassed a large trade surplus, enabling it to provide credit to the rest of the world. In fact, China alone came to account for over 15 percent of the US government debt held by foreigners as of 2022, although Japan was still the largest foreign holder. If China sold its US Treasury bills, notes, and bonds in large quantities, the United States would have to dramatically increase taxes and reduce spending.

Since 2013, when Xi Jinping became president of China, the government has pursued an increasingly assertive foreign policy, raising tensions over political and security issues. Notably, under President Xi, China launched projects such as the Belt and Road Initiative (BRI), aiming to build sea and land routes connecting China to Central Asia, Europe, Africa and beyond. In recent years, China has become a major source of emergency loans to

Argentina, Sri Lanka, Turkey, and other countries. Although its lending is not yet equal to that of the IMF, China gave $40.5 billion in emergency loans in 2021, up from none in 2010 and $10 billion in 2014 (Bradsher 2023). In addition to charging higher interest rates than the IMF and the United States, China makes its loans in renminbi rather than other currencies. China has also accepted repayments in commodities. In 2020, an attempt by the G-20 to bring China "into the fold" of a common framework was unsuccessful. Preferring to work alone and avoid sharing information with other lenders, by 2023 China had restructured the finances of 71 countries (*The Economist* 2023).

China's increased importance in the international economy has led to pressures to change voting structures in the Bretton Woods institutions—or failing that, to challenge those institutions with organizations that reflected changing distributions of power. In 2014, China helped create two new financial institutions. One was the Asian Infrastructure Investment Bank (AIIB), which has leveraged Chinese know-how in building roads, dams, railways, and other infrastructure and has offered developing countries loans that do not come with the same conditions as World Bank loans. Along with its fellow BRICS countries of Brazil, Russia, India, and South Africa, China also launched the New Development Bank (NDB), which has supplemented traditional North-to-South lending with funds from more donors in the Global South. Both institutions are based in China, fueling perceptions that the AIIB and the NDB are China-led rivals to the US-led World Bank and to its regional counterpart, the Japan-led Asian Development Bank. Figure 8.1 depicts how these leading economic groups—the OECD, G-7, G-20, and the BRICS—relate to one another and have overlapping memberships.

Paradoxically, ostensible victories for the liberal economic order also threaten its future (Johnson and Heiss 2022). Western Europe rapidly recovered from World War II, then embarked on unprecedented economic and political integration. Scores of developing states and formerly socialist countries became linked to international markets and economic institutions, but rejected the underlying ideology and US dominance. China and other emerging powers selectively engaged with liberalized markets, becoming economic powerhouses capable of challenging traditional ideas and leaders.

A further unsettling of global economic governance came with Brexit (the United Kingdom's 2016 decision to withdraw from the EU, discussed in Chapter 5), increased superpower rivalry, and the Covid-19 pandemic. In the United States, for example, a growing number of Americans complained that "regular people" had been harmed by globalization and the burdens of hegemonic leadership (Copelovitch and Pevehouse 2019). Some have called for a more protectionist or strategic economic approach, akin to mercantilism; others have demanded redistribution and social safety nets, akin to socialism. Despite their very different prescriptions, however, both sides agreed that continued globalization posed grave dangers.

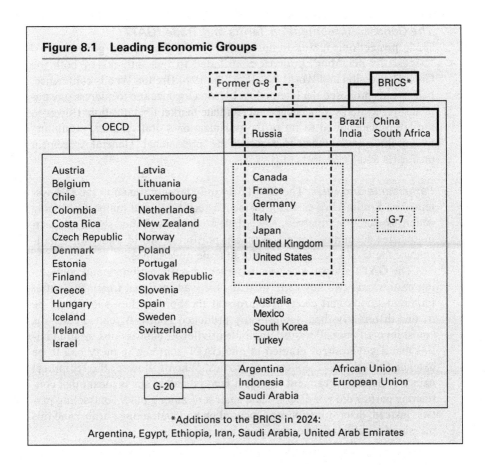

Figure 8.1 Leading Economic Groups

*Additions to the BRICS in 2024:
Argentina, Egypt, Ethiopia, Iran, Saudi Arabia, United Arab Emirates

Thus, key economic ideas (mercantilism, liberalism, and socialism) and events (World War II, the Cold War, decolonization, the rise of Asia, globalization and the backlash against globalization) have shaped the world economy. This underlying history is helpful for understanding the governance of three aspects of the world economy: trade, finance, and development. We look first at the governance of trade.

Governance of Trade

Trade, as one of the oldest forms of economic interaction, is a prominent area within economic governance. Although liberal economic thinkers debate whether trade necessarily results in economic development, they tend to agree that opening markets in line with comparative advantage is a prerequisite for economic growth (Rodrik 2007). Trade expanded greatly in the latter half of the twentieth century, partly because of the institutions, rules, norms, and other components of trade governance.

The General Agreement on Tariffs and Trade (GATT)

Trade protectionism was rampant after World War I, and governments' "beggar-thy-neighbor" policies contributed to the outbreak of both the Great Depression and World War II. At the 1944 Bretton Woods conference, participants proposed the International Trade Organization to address governments' protectionist tendencies and facilitate market liberalization. However, the US Senate failed to ratify the organization's draft charter, prompting twenty-three governments to negotiate the "provisional" General Agreement on Tariffs and Trade instead.

Participants and rules. The GATT was only loosely linked to the UN system. The Soviet Union, much of the Eastern bloc, and many developing countries were not involved. Nevertheless, since its limited set of contracting parties accounted for a substantial portion of world trade, for a half-century the GATT was a focal point in trade governance.

The GATT's broad aim was to prevent discrimination among contracting parties, and two key rules helped. One was "national treatment": after imported goods had cleared controls at the border, they should not be treated differently than domestically produced goods. A second rule was "most favored nation" status: any trade privileges, concessions, or immunities that a government granted to one GATT contracting party had to be extended to all GATT contracting parties. When followed, the reciprocal nature of national treatment and most favored nation status meant that contracting parties did not discriminate against or among other contracting parties. Instead, discrimination was focused on noncontracting parties, and this pressured additional governments to join the group.

As a set of rules negotiated by governments, the 1947 version of the GATT was very sensitive to its contracting parties' domestic political concerns. It championed trade liberalization but also recognized several reasons (e.g., health, national security, public morals, or environmental protection) for which governments would be justified in maintaining trade barriers. The GATT also preserved governmental sovereignty by establishing little enforcement power or infrastructure beyond the contracting governments. Although a director-general and a few hundred staff in Geneva served as the secretariat, they concentrated on serving governments, not monitoring them. The GATT included a mechanism for adjudicating trade disputes, but it relied on contracting governments for enforcement. Governments made decisions by consensus, effectively giving each member a veto. Consensus decisionmaking was sometimes problematic—for example, because rulings in trade disputes were not binding until accepted by all contracting parties, governments that "lost" disputes simply refused to accept the rulings.

Negotiating rounds. The heart of the GATT-based trading system was an eight-round series of negotiations that incrementally reduced trade barriers.

After the first round in 1947, there was a quick succession of four more rounds (1949, 1951, 1956, and 1960–1961) focusing on tariff reductions and involving only a few dozen governments. Since the GATT was not a full-fledged organization, these rounds usually did not feature formal voting. Instead, many rules were first negotiated among the biggest trading countries, then presented to the rest of the contracting parties for adoption.

By the sixth round in the mid-1960s, the contracting parties were more numerous and less like-minded about liberal economic principles. More than sixty governments participated in the negotiations, and many of the newcomers were developing countries whose trade policies had been shaped by their experiences with colonialism, mercantilism, and socialism. In addition, the European Economic Community had become one of the biggest actors in global trade, but it was a novel entity, not a traditional state.

By the seventh round in the 1970s, the context was even more complicated. The EEC had implemented its Common Agricultural Policy and become a single negotiating entity in world trade negotiations. The GATT negotiations took aim for the first time at nontariff barriers such as subsidies, technical standards, or rules about government procurement. The number of contracting parties surpassed 100, with developing countries in the majority. The round resulted in promises of preferential market access for the world's least developed countries, plus a set of "codes" to reduce various nontariff barriers. In an unprecedented move away from a common set of rules for all GATT contracting parties, the codes were voluntary and governments could choose to be bound by only some or none. Some wealthy countries adopted all the codes, whereas many poorer countries opted out, and the result was a two-tiered system within the GATT.

An eighth round, the Uruguay Round of 1986–1994, was even more consequential. With more than 120 governments negotiating, it produced a 400-page trade agreement, the most comprehensive ever. The round covered new items such as services (insurance, tourism, banking) and intellectual property rights (copyrights, patents, trademarks). It even touched on the long-standing issues of agriculture and textiles, which had been too politically sensitive for Europe and the United States in earlier rounds. The most important outcome was an agreement to create a full-fledged international organization to govern trade. Finally fulfilling the 1940s vision, the new WTO was to be a near-global body, providing a more robust dispute settlement system and overseeing trade arrangements constructed inside and outside of the GATT system.

The World Trade Organization (WTO)

The WTO's founding document is the 1994 Marrakesh Agreement, with 123 initial signatories. The new organization retained the GATT's government-only membership policy, consensus-based decisionmaking, and director-general role. As summarized in Figure 8.2, the WTO also retained central GATT principles such as national treatment and most favored nation status.

**Figure 8.2
Central Principles of the
World Trade Organization**

Nondiscrimination
  a. Most favored nation treatment:
     products made in one member
     must be treated as favorably as
     like products originating in
     another member
  b. National treatment: foreign-
     made products must be treated
     as favorably as like products
     made domestically

Reciprocity: members try to make
equivalent changes in policies;
protection occurs through tariffs
only; members cannot use quotas

Transparency: members must
publish their trade regulations and
have procedures for review of
administrative regulations

*Safety valves for members to attain
noneconomic objectives*
  a. Protect public health and
     national security
  b. Protect domestic industries from
     serious injury

Enforcement of obligations:
mechanism for members to bring
cases before the WTO for dispute
settlement

Governance innovations. The WTO differs from the GATT in several ways. For one thing, governing procedures are different. Member governments are served by a secretariat based in Geneva, Switzerland. Numbering around 600 employees, the secretariat is small compared with that of economic institutions such as the IMF, but it is larger than during the GATT era. The WTO director-general has limited formal powers but has opportunities to set agendas and broker deals, and is also an important symbol (as indicated in this chapter's case study of Okonjo-Iweala becoming the first woman and the first African to head the WTO). Member governments meet several times per year in the General Council and at least every two years in the WTO's top decisionmaking body, the Ministerial Council. Regular meetings of high-level officials give the WTO a political prominence that the GATT lacked.

The WTO's scope is also wider. About sixty agreements, decisions, annexes, and understandings are among its core documents. The WTO subsumed a 1994 update to the GATT and encompasses several other agreements (on issues such as services, intellectual property, technical guidelines, and agriculture) that have been accepted by all members. Among these, the Agreement on Trade-Related Aspects of Intellectual Property Rights is particularly notable because it formally injects intellectual property rules into the trade system and frequently is viewed as an impediment to developing countries that are trying to access medicines, clean energy, modified seeds, and other inventions. In addition to agreements that are legally binding on the entire membership, the WTO includes a few "plurilateral" agreements (on issues such as civil aircraft and government procurement) that apply to a subset of the membership. This two-tiered system, in which some rules are obligatory and universal while others are voluntary and à la carte, intensifies North/South tensions that were already present in the GATT system.

Another difference is that the WTO's membership has become nearly universal, with governments that had not been part of the GATT joining the WTO. For example, China became a member in 2002, Saudi Arabia in 2005, Vietnam in 2007, and Russia in 2012. The process of accession is complicated because new members must accept all GATT/WTO rules and satisfy additional demands from existing WTO members, any of which can unilaterally block the accession process. The negotiations surrounding China's accession took fifteen years. The negotiations for Russia took even longer because the US Congress decried Russian human rights violations; Russian businesses and ministries were concerned about increasing economic competition; and Georgia withheld approval to retaliate for Russia's support of Georgian secessionist movements. Nevertheless, by 2023 the WTO had grown to 164 member governments, with an additional 25 governments holding observer status and working toward membership.

Perhaps the biggest difference between the WTO and the earlier GATT system is how member governments have opened themselves to new forms of scrutiny. Each member is examined through the Trade Policy Review Mechanism, with reviews occurring most frequently for those that account for the largest shares of world trade. Secretariat staff prepare a report describing the member's trade policies, practices, objectives, institutions, and macroeconomic context. Then the WTO General Council, comprising all member-governments and operating under special guidelines, holds the review meeting where the scrutinized member responds to questions and comments from peers.

An even more prominent form of scrutiny occurs through the WTO's dispute settlement process. It uses two distinct mechanisms: the Dispute Settlement Body (DSB) and the Appellate Body (AB). The DSB is a special convening of the full membership via the General Council, which attempts to find diplomatic means for resolving trade disputes between complainants and respondents. If that does not work, the DSB establishes an ad hoc panel composed of three experts, whose report is generally due to the parties in six months. In contrast to the earlier GATT system, panel reports are bolstered by "reverse consensus": instead of needing all WTO members to agree for a report to be adopted, all WTO members would have to agree for a report to be rejected. A complainant or respondent that is dissatisfied with the panel report can call for the dispute to be considered by the AB. The seven people on the AB are experts who hold four-year (once-renewable) terms and are unaffiliated with any specific government. Even when a dispute goes to appeal, the process often takes less than eighteen months. Then the parties are directed to implement what the experts have recommended;

compliance panels monitor the parties' progress and eventually may authorize retaliatory trade measures if implementation is unsatisfactory. By virtue of WTO membership, governments acknowledge this process as compulsory (they cannot opt out of its jurisdiction) and exclusive (they cannot take disputes under WTO trade rules to a non-WTO venue).

From 1995 to 2022, the WTO's system managed more than 600 requests for consultations and issued more than 350 panel rulings, with the remaining disputes withdrawn or settled "out of court." Although many disputes involve the United States, China, the EU, and other large economies, more than 110 of the WTO's member governments have participated in disputes as complainants, respondents, or third parties. Historically, about 60 percent of panel rulings are appealed (Hopewell 2021). The dispute settlement process puts governments under a great deal of scrutiny, but it also reduces uncertainty and helps trade continue.

Challenges. The differences noted above—political prominence, a wide scope, nearly universal membership, and the authority to scrutinize governments' trade activities—make the WTO appear much more powerful than the GATT. Particularly in the late 1990s and early 2000s, the WTO gained a reputation as a body that forced economic globalization on unwilling countries despite valid worries about labor rights, environmental protection, or health (Johnson 2015). For example, numerous governments and interest groups decried WTO prohibitions against banning products based on the process by which they were produced. This "product versus process" issue was at the heart of several controversies, including the WTO's rulings against the EU for its ban on hormone-treated beef and against the United States for its ban on shrimp caught without turtle-excluding devices. These rulings pressured governments to change their policies or face economic punishments authorized by the WTO. Over time, however, dissatisfaction with the WTO has mutated: instead of being seen as too forceful, in recent years the organization is often seen as too feeble.

One reason for this perception is the failure to complete further large trade negotiations. The Doha Development Round, begun in 2001 as the first round under WTO auspices, was pitched as serving the interests of developing countries. However, a key sticking point has been agricultural subsidies, an issue that pits developed countries against developing ones and against each other. Since foodstuffs are vital for national security, governments are wary of dependence on foreign markets. The EU, through its Common Agricultural Policy, maintains a complex and expensive system in which the EU purchases surplus products from farms at a guaranteed price and then stores, donates, or absorbs a loss from those products. The EU is deeply attached to the Common Agricultural Policy and has adopted very strict regulations on food imports—including a ban on genetically modified foods, many of which come from the United States. At talks in Bali in 2013, the United States (as part of the Global North) and India (as part of the Global South) agreed to a temporary solution on food security, stockpiles, and safeguards for farmers in poor countries. However, the Bali Package was not fully implemented. WTO members have had some achievements, such as a 2015 enlargement of the Information Technology Agreement and a 2022 deal on fishing subsidies. But the ambitious agenda of the Doha Development Round is widely considered dead, even though it has not been formally ended.

Since 2011, the WTO has experienced a new weakness: an impeded Appellate Body (AB). The US government has complained about the dispute settlement system since the early 2000s, particularly as China joined the WTO and quickly became a frequent complainant and respondent. US grievances center on China's noncompliance with WTO rulings, self-designation as a developing country that can maintain higher tariffs, incomplete adoption of intellectual property rights and other elements of the rule of law, and heavy governmental role in the economy (US Trade Representative 2013). To register dissatisfaction with the perceived "judicial overreach" of particular AB experts, US President Barack Obama began blocking reappointments to the AB. His administration first blocked an American expert in 2011, then a South Korean expert in 2016. The next US president, Donald Trump, continued the tactic. By December 2019, the AB could no longer muster three judges to hear appeals; in November 2020, the final expert's term expired, leaving the AB completely vacant. As a temporary way to deal with the backlog of appeals, the EU spearheaded an interim arbitration arrangement that is open to any WTO member government, follows WTO guidelines about arbitration procedures, and mimics many of the AB's practices. This stopgap measure was necessary because the WTO has faltered in providing an efficient adjudicatory mechanism with powers of enforcement.

The Covid-19 pandemic presented another hurdle as the WTO did not prevent member governments from restricting exports of vaccines and personal protective equipment (Johnson 2020). The crisis hit some developing countries particularly hard, unraveling hard-won gains in poverty alleviation and exacerbating North/South tensions. Numerous WTO mechanisms—such as the Generalized System of Preferences that puts lower tariffs on products from poor countries, or the collaboration with UNCTAD to provide training for developing country officials through the International Trade Center, and the Aid for Trade initiative that mobilizes donors to relieve structural constraints—are designed to allay concerns that the international trade regime is stacked against the Global South. But the chaos of the Covid-19 pandemic, coupled with the collapse of the Doha Development Round, reinforced a negative impression that the WTO's talk of development may warm hearts but does not fill bellies (Christy 2008: 24).

Since its creation, the WTO has been a lightning rod for people who believe it is a usurper of state sovereignty, a violator of domestic interests, and a culprit in globalization's negative consequences. The Global South has accused it of being captured by the Global North; the Global North has criticized it for deferring to the Global South. In the past, such accusations could be counterbalanced by what the WTO accomplished for its member governments. However, such counterbalancing is tougher if the organization does not produce new agreements, settle disputes, or alleviate crises.

Preferential Trade Agreements (PTAs), Monetary Unions, and Regionalism

Although the WTO was expected to bring order to trade and fold regional economic governance into a global organization, an array of other trade arrangements and regional initiatives persist. As illustrated in Figure 8.3, trade arrangements vary in their level of integration and the extent to which they require states to make policy changes. Relatively shallow arrangements include preferential trade agreements and free trade areas. A PTA gives special privileges to particular trading partners; a free trade area goes further by maintaining each country's trade barriers for nonmembers but removing trade barriers among members.

A somewhat deeper arrangement is a customs union, in which member states impose identical trade barriers vis-à-vis outsiders while permitting free trade among themselves. Even deeper economic arrangements include common markets (a customs union plus free movement of capital and labor) and monetary unions (a common market plus additional policy har-

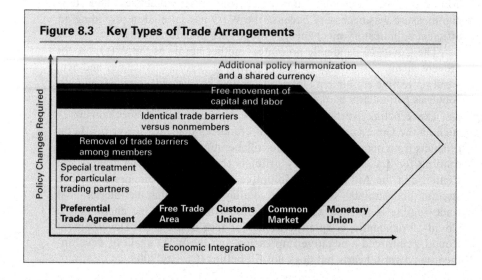

Figure 8.3   Key Types of Trade Arrangements

monization and a shared currency). The deeper the integration, the more it impinges on states' sovereignty in national policymaking. Therefore, monetary unions have been much rarer than PTAs.

Debates about PTAs. PTAs may be bilateral; they may unite a handful of countries sharing geographic proximity or some other attribute; or they may span a large number of heterogeneous countries around the world. PTAs—especially the subset called regional trade agreements and based on geographic proximity—have been particularly popular since the end of the Cold War. For instance, the number of regional agreements rose from about 50 in 1990 to about 350 in 2022.

PTAs may challenge the WTO by tackling issues the WTO has not yet covered or subdividing the WTO membership. For example, the Comprehensive and Progressive Agreement for Trans-Pacific Partnership—negotiated by eleven Pacific Rim countries (Australia, Brunei, Canada, Chile, Japan, Malaysia, Mexico, New Zealand, Peru, Singapore, Vietnam) after the United States abandoned an earlier draft agreement—started operating in 2018 and is breaking new ground on intellectual property rights. The US-Mexico-Canada Agreement (USMCA), formalized in 2020 as the successor to the North American Free Trade Agreement (NAFTA), strengthens environmental and labor regulations, tightens rules of origin, and moves into new issues such as currency manipulation and digital trade. The Regional Comprehensive Economic Partnership—covering the ten Association of Southeast Asian Nations members plus Australia, China, Japan, New Zealand, and South Korea—came into effect in 2022 and began to stitch together the numerous overlapping trade agreements in Asia. Skeptical about the WTO's capacity to produce global agreements and respond to their particular needs, governments see PTAs as a practical alternative involving simpler negotiations, more tailored commitments, and quicker enactment.

PTAs may be easier to create than to operate, however. After all, actual implementation hinges on whether the contracting parties are closely entwined economically and have resources to enforce the rules. Moreover, PTAs can grow unwieldy with age, because the number of contracting parties commonly increases over time (Mansfield and Pevehouse 2013). Also, states can and do belong to multiple bilateral, subregional, regional, and transcontinental agreements simultaneously, resulting in a "spaghetti bowl" of commitments.

This has prompted two debates about PTAs. One is whether their net effect is to create trade or divert it. With PTAs, some trade is created in goods produced efficiently relative to the rest of the world, but some is diverted from efficient nonmembers due to the preferences states grant each other. If trade diversion surpasses trade creation, a PTA actually could reduce economic welfare.

A second debate is whether PTAs facilitate or hinder arrangements at the global level. Some observers see PTAs as a stepping stone: by involving only a subset of the world's states and allowing members to gradually improve their competitiveness, PTAs may pave the way for more intense liberalization. Other observers argue that PTAs are a stumbling block: larger economies can impose their will more freely, and interest groups may find it easier to lobby for their interests, inhibiting freer global trade. If true, then the proliferation of PTAs may actually amount to "termites" in the global trading system (Bhagwati 2008).

Monetary unions and regionalism. These debates touch on many trade arrangements, but they are particularly relevant for the European Union. The EU is not yet a complete political union akin to a "United States of Europe," but it is a regional monetary union that eliminates almost all internal trade barriers, harmonizes its member states' external economic policies, gives people access to labor markets and political participation across member states, and operates a shared currency. In the way it has evolved over the decades, the EU highlights trade arrangements beyond PTAs and also shows why many governments continue to prefer looser trade links.

As noted in Chapter 5, the EU's evolution from a customs union to a monetary union occurred in several phases. First, from 1958 to 1968, the six original member states eliminated internal tariffs, dismantled quantitative import restrictions, established a common external tariff and the Common Agricultural Policy, and resolved to negotiate as a single entity in international trade negotiations. During the 1970s and early 1980s, membership expanded but deeper integration stalled. From the late 1980s to the early 2000s, member states implemented the Single European Act, which amended the Treaty of Rome and culminated in a common currency called the euro.

This third phase was particularly complex. Although customs barriers were abolished in 1992, the free movement of labor took longer. Since 1993, with some exceptions, residents of EU member states have had the right to live and work in any other EU country. Most countries eliminated passport controls and adopted common visa regulations, but Denmark, Ireland, and the United Kingdom refused to do so. Even the countries that accepted the free movement of labor needed years to create a system of crediting each other's educational and professional qualifications.

Technical barriers to trade were contentious. For example, governments continued to cite health and safety standards to justify trade restrictions internally. Among technical barriers, competition policy was especially challenging. The Maastricht Treaty prohibited member states from favoring domestic companies for government contracts, but breaking long-standing monopolies or ending state aid to specific sectors proved to be politically difficult. In response, the European Commission became more active in investigating malfeasance, and the European Council became more dogged about examining corporate mergers.

Another challenge was the development of the euro as a new, shared currency. The 1992 Maastricht Treaty laid out the features and timetable for the euro, and the euro became operational for businesses in 1998 and for consumers in 2002. By reducing the transaction costs of trade and investment, the euro facilitated economic growth in EU countries and established itself as a safe currency for use around the world. The single currency symbolized regional unity but also a loss of national sovereignty, since participating states agreed to relinquish exchange rates and interest rates as domestic economic tools. That helps explain why several EU members—including Denmark, Sweden, and the United Kingdom—retained their national currencies instead of adopting the euro.

Europe's deep and broad economic integration is not matched by any other region. African countries have expressed interest in eventually creating a monetary union (discussed in Chapter 5), but they do not yet have a common market or shared currency. Several South American countries collaborate through Mercosur, which translates as Southern Common Market—but Mercosur remains a customs union, since there is not yet free movement of labor and capital. Other regions have been content with even more modest arrangements: free trade areas. For example, the Association of Southeast Asian Nations formed a free trade area in 1992. From its original membership (Brunei, Indonesia, Malaysia, Philippines, Singapore, and Thailand), the free trade area has expanded to Cambodia, Laos, Myanmar, and Vietnam. Another example is the USMCA (and its predecessor, NAFTA) involving Canada, Mexico, and the United States.

The Interaction of Trade and Other Policy Areas

Trade touches on labor, health, the environment, intellectual property, and other policy areas addressed by other governance regimes. For instance, since 1919 the International Labour Organization (ILO) has handled regulations concerning forced labor, child workers, migrants, job discrimination, collective bargaining, and other employment issues that underpin trade. Bodies such as the World Health Organization (WHO), Codex Alimentarius, and the World Organization for Animal Health work to ensure that international trade does not threaten the health of humans, plants, or animals. The UN Environment Programme and its associated treaties deal with environmental degradation from the production and transportation of traded goods. The World Intellectual Property Organization is an important venue for dealing with the intellectual property being traded in pharmaceuticals, media, technology, and the like.

In short, the WTO and other pieces of trade governance exist among several "regime complexes," that is, sets of overlapping and sometimes conflicting regimes (Johnson and Urpelainen 2012). A key feature of regime complexes is that there is no agreed way to assert a hierarchy when rules or decisions backed by different institutions conflict. Knowing this, actors can behave strategically, aiming for one forum to be influenced, revised, or undermined by decisions and politics in other forums (Alter and Raustiala 2018: 331).

Facilitating trade. Some regime complexes facilitate trade. Trade relies on the movement of goods and on shared expectations for how those goods will work. Therefore, it is useful to consider how the regimes for ocean shipping, air transport, and product standards—while not solely about trade—nevertheless make the conduct of trade easier.

Ocean shipping accounts for the vast majority of trade—about 60 percent by value, or over 90 percent by weight. Many important shipping norms date back to the nineteenth century or earlier. These include freedom of the high seas, innocent passage through territorial waters, flag-state jurisdiction over ships operating in international waters, and the right of the state to control entry of foreign ships. Over time, other practices have arisen through public and private international organizations.

The UN specialized agency for shipping is the International Maritime Organization (IMO), headquartered in London. Since its first meeting in 1959, the IMO has operated through an intergovernmental committee system that approves standards on issues such as safety, security, efficiency, pollution, and compensation. The IMO is mainly a standard-setting body, which leaves enforcement generally to states, sometimes aided by insurers or other private actors with economic interests. Relying on flag states for enforcement is problematic, however, because many ships sail under a "flag of convenience" marketed by states, such as Liberia and Panama, that promise minimal taxation and regulation. Therefore, traditional maritime powers (e.g., the United Kingdom, the United States) take on larger enforcement roles, and the IMO offers capacity-building programs for other states. Private initiatives are also important. For example, a specialized arm of the International Chamber of Commerce tries to track and reduce pirate attacks, counterfeiting, hijackings, fraud, and other crimes that jeopardize trade.

Air transport has adopted some of the norms of ocean transport and has developed practices of its own. States accept norms governing the prevention of accidents, damage, environmental harm, and crime. They also recognize freedom of air transport above the oceans but require state consent for passage over sovereign territory. Such norms and practices have developed through both the International Air Transport Association (IATA, a private body created by the airlines in 1945) and the International Civil Aviation Organization (ICAO, a UN specialized agency created in 1947).

Originally the IATA was supposed to set safety standards, but since the US-based company Boeing has dominated aircraft production for decades, the US government has taken on many tasks related to safety. Instead, the IATA focuses on facilitating fare-setting, ticket exchanges, and the flow of travelers and luggage. Meanwhile, ICAO recommends standards and practices concerning air infrastructure, navigation, inspection, border crossing, and accident investigation. It does not have regulatory authority to enforce these recommendations, but it is able to facilitate intergovernmental discussions and subtly pressure states through public "scorecards."

Beyond ocean and air transport, another fundamental piece of international trade is product standards. Here, the International Organization for Standardization (ISO) is central (Yates and Murphy 2019). As discussed in Chapter 3, the ISO is a nongovernmental umbrella organization composed of national standards organizations from more than 165 countries. Established in 1946 and headquartered in Switzerland, it collaborates with experts around the world to develop and disseminate standards for product safety and compatibility. The ISO is best known for criteria bearing its name, such as those for camera film or "green" building construction. Its work ranges widely, from smokestack scrubbers to credit card machines to baby seats. In 2021 alone, it published 1,619 standards. The ISO operates in any field other than electrical or electronic engineering, which is handled by a partner, the International Electrotechnical Commission. Together, these two institutions promulgate about 85 percent of the world's product standards, many of which alter companies' behavior (Prakash and Potoski 2014) and even become domestic law (Büthe and Mattli 2011).

This facilitates trade. ISO certification of goods and services reassures consumers about safety and compatibility, thereby increasing opportunities for compliant firms to do business around the world. But standard-setting is not a purely technical process; it is also political. Companies, governments, and other actors who participate in determining the standards are often best positioned to abide by them. Therefore, in addition to developing product standards, the organization spreads know-how and management practices, particularly through outreach and training programs to assist companies from developing countries.

Inhibiting trade. Existing arrangements for ocean shipping, air transport, and product standards facilitate trade; but the trade regime also intersects with some policy areas where the aim is to inhibit trade. One example is the regime complex for food security. Food security was portrayed as a human right at the 1996 World Food Summit, and it grew more prominent when world food prices hit historic highs in 2008 and then contributed to the Arab Spring protests of 2011. As noted in Chapter 11, the regime complex for food security includes not only the trade regime but also the regimes for agriculture and human rights.

The idea of food security shifts away from logistical questions of production and trade, instead raising normative questions about fair distribution and reliable access. States and their citizens are leery about depending on foreign suppliers to satisfy the fundamental and ongoing need for food. After all, food quantities and prices on international markets can fluctuate wildly due to weather conditions, natural disasters, genetic modifications, energy costs, pandemics, wars (as Russia's war in Ukraine has shown), and many other factors. When governments attempt to be more self-sufficient in agriculture to ensure food supply, they also forgo some of the efficiencies of international trade.

Sanctions are an even starker example of inhibiting trade to pursue other policy goals. Restricting trade for particular goods, industries, or countries is a key tool employed by the UN Security Council to address security threats. The UNSC has imposed sanctions to counter terrorism in Afghanistan, nuclear weapons development in Iran and North Korea, and civil war in Yugoslavia. In reaction to Russia's invasion of Ukraine in 2022, the US, EU, Japan, and other states coordinated in the UNSC to impose sanctions on Russia. The Belgium-based Society for Worldwide Interbank Financial Telecommunication (SWIFT) also banned several Russian banks from using its network to move money internationally.

Key Themes in Trade Governance

As one aspect of the global economy, trade reflects broader patterns in economic governance. In PTAs, in the GATT and WTO systems, and in the broader regime complexes that are relevant to international trade, the Global South has often been at a disadvantage. The leaders of trade governance are still largely states that have big market economies and are from the Global North. As Brazil, China, India, South Africa, and other developing countries have grown richer and more vocal, they have secured some changes in this system. However, governments and publics continue to debate whether trade is worthwhile in and of itself, or whether it is justified only as a means to an end such as development. Since companies, workers, civil society groups, and consumers all have a stake in international trade, the debate is not just between richer and poorer countries but also among a variety of NSAs. Whether WTO negotiations for new trade agreements can be jumpstarted will depend on whether the major trading powers, including the United States, EU, and China, decide to push for an agreement and whether the WTO under Ngozi's leadership can help bridge the differences among all stakeholders.

Governance of Finance

Finance is a second key area in economic governance. Contemporary financial governance involves long-standing international organizations such as the Bank for International Settlements (BIS) and the IMF, newer institutions such as the G-20, and new challenges such as digital currencies. To grasp how financial governance operates currently, it is necessary to understand how it operated in the past when the gold standard was the centerpiece.

Gold, the Float, and the Bank for International Settlements (BIS)

As noted above, in 1971 the US dollar was taken off the gold standard and allowed to "float" in value. People are willing to pay more for the currency of a country with a large, well-managed economy than for its opposite, and as a country's economy moves in one direction or the other, the value of its currency will generally rise or fall. Without the gold standard, these market forces make currencies volatile and tempt governments to intervene in exchange rates. Some governments prefer a "strong" currency, which is more likely to attract safe investors and hold its value. Other governments prefer a "weak" currency, which disincentivizes consumption of foreign products and makes a country's exports more affordable in foreign markets. To manipulate the valuation, governments can strategically buy or sell large amounts of a currency to shift its market price up or down.

Although governments may have an interest in making their currency strong or weak, companies and other actors often prefer stability. For financial stability, one of the most important international institutions has long been the Bank for International Settlements. Established in 1930, the BIS was the world's first public international financial institution. Created to coordinate central banks in the United States, Japan, and several European states, it was soon tasked with bailing out numerous collapsing currencies as the Great Depression spread around the world. Then it facilitated financial exchanges among various European central banks until the 1950s, when it was overshadowed by the loan-making capabilities of the recently created IMF.

The BIS remains crucial as a source of banking guidelines, however, particularly regarding bank reserves that are designed to ensure solvency. To aid in this regard, the Basel Committee on Banking Supervision was created within the BIS in 1974 by central bankers from ten countries. In 2023, the committee still included fewer than thirty countries. Yet because these countries and their central banks are important for global finance, other governments and institutions have strong incentives to follow the committee's guidelines (Young 2011: 39).

The International Monetary Fund (IMF)

Although the BIS has been influential in its niche, it pales in comparison to the IMF's global membership and multifaceted influence. The IMF's original purpose was to lend money to countries to weather short-term fluctuations in currency exchange rates. Member states made contributions in both gold and local currency, in line with quotas negotiated every five years.

Later, so-called special drawing rights were created to provide additional liquidity. To meet temporary balance-of-payments difficulties, members could withdraw funds according to the amount contributed, with a service fee on each transaction plus a charge based on the length of time the money was borrowed. These arrangements were intended to be brief, typically about twelve to eighteen months. After the United States unlinked its currency from gold in 1971 and refused to continue the Bretton Woods system's currency stabilization efforts, the IMF expanded its purview, doing more with development and longer-term assistance.

The structure of the IMF. The IMF is somewhat unusual in having a corporation-like structure. Although each member state has its own representative on the IMF's Board of Governors, the governors delegate much of the work to a smaller Executive Board, consisting of only twenty-four executive directors. Executive Board spots and vote shares are allocated according to states' financial contributions, known as "quotas." Seven states—the US, Japan, China, Germany, France, the United Kingdom, and Saudi Arabia—have individual executive directors, who together account for over 40 percent of the votes. Other member states are clustered into groups that must share the remaining votes and Executive Board spots.

This structure, whose purpose is to incentivize financial contributions, tends to privilege richer countries over poorer ones. Figure 8.4 shows how reforms in 2015 altered the quotas but still privileged specific states: although China's vote share increased, the United States retained the largest vote share and kept its ability to veto some key decisions. The largest vote-holders can shape the IMF's policy direction and even particular loans. For example, where a country's financial troubles are likely to cause harm to one of the individual Executive Board members, funds tend to be disbursed more quickly, in larger amounts, and with fewer conditions (Copelovitch 2010). In addition to this formal power, the United States wields informal influence due to the IMF's location in Washington, DC, and the organization's close relationship with personnel in the US Treasury Department (Stone 2011).

Many member states have complained about having little say compared with the US and IMF staff. The IMF has a strong and highly expert staff of about 2,500 people, many of whom have advanced degrees in economics from prestigious universities in Europe or North America. The staff is headed by the Managing Director, who often chairs Executive Board meetings. By tradition, the role of managing director has always been held by a European. The staff's expertise, credentials, and backing from rich countries gives their analysis and advice special weight, particularly when IMF personnel face officials from developing countries (Nelson 2017). Although the Executive Board is very active with regard to general policy issues, many of the decisions about loan programs for individual countries are

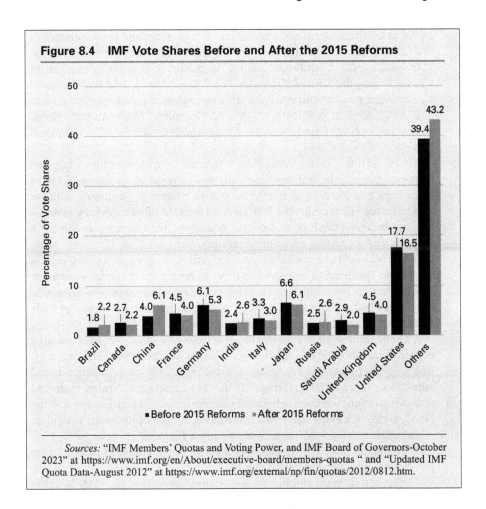

Figure 8.4 IMF Vote Shares Before and After the 2015 Reforms

Sources: "IMF Members' Quotas and Voting Power, and IMF Board of Governors-October 2023" at https://www.imf.org/en/About/executive-board/members-quotas " and "Updated IMF Quota Data-August 2012" at https://www.imf.org/external/np/fin/quotas/2012/0812.htm.

worked out in confidential negotiations between IMF personnel and the governments concerned.

Surveillance and crisis responses by the IMF. After the IMF's purpose abruptly shifted with the closing of the gold window, the organization became much more central to financial surveillance and responding to crises. In the late 1970s, the IMF introduced a surveillance process that involved annual consultations with member governments to evaluate exchange rate policies within the framework of general economic and policy strategies. This enabled the IMF to identify risks to stability and advise on policy adjustments that could stave off crises. The organization began offering programs to train government officials in data collection, bank management, and fiscal and monetary policy. In the mid-2000s the IMF failed to confront the United States and China about the consequences of their exchange rate policies and massive trade imbalances, but in 2011 the IMF added regular "spillover reports" to publicize how the economies of China, Japan, the United Kingdom, the United States, and the European Union affect other countries. The IMF's surveillance functions have grown, and three regular publications—*World Economic Outlook*, the *Global Financial Stability Report*, and the *Fiscal Monitor*—continue to be important parts of the process.

Although the IMF's surveillance functions have sometimes targeted richer countries, the organization's efforts to respond to financial crises often have had the biggest impact on poorer countries. Beginning with the 1982 Mexican debt crisis, the IMF took on the role of intermediary in negotiations between creditor and debtor countries, then became involved in bailouts and structural adjustment lending. Structural adjustment lending required recipients to institute economic policy reforms or achieve certain conditions (referred to as conditionality) in return for financial assistance. In addition to overcoming structural bottlenecks in countries' domestic economies and governmental policies, the conditions aimed to prompt trade liberalization and private-sector involvement.

The IMF also played a key role as Russia and other formerly socialist countries transitioned to market economies during the 1990s. The organization provided financial resources and technical advice to make external adjustment more orderly. Using IMF funds to liberalize foreign trade and reduce inflation, the most advanced economies in Central Europe and the Baltic states achieved rapid success. Russia, on the other hand, struggled. Although it received IMF assistance during a financial crisis in 1998, Russia's comeback was greatly aided by a fortuitous increase in prices for its petroleum and other natural resources.

Whether in transitioning or developing countries, the IMF's crisis responses were not always successful. After the 1997–1998 Asian financial crisis, the organization's interventions were sharply criticized. Even the IMF's major donor states acknowledged that not all crises were alike and the Washington Consensus was not always correct. Negative outcomes shook faith in the IMF and its liberal economic solutions, helping explain why the IMF's response to the 2008–2009 global financial crisis was muted at first. The organization made about $250 billion available for credit lines, then tripled that to $750 billion in 2009. Iceland became the first Western country to borrow from the IMF since 1976; substantial emergency loans were also made to Ukraine, Hungary, and Pakistan.

Eventually, the 2008–2009 crisis revitalized the IMF, which then took an active role in the subsequent crisis in the "eurozone." The IMF—alongside the European Union, the European Central Bank, and private banks—participated in summits and bailout packages in several countries that had adopted the euro as their shared currency (Henning 2017). The IMF also intervened in some political crises, such as when it provided $17 billion to the embattled pro-Western regime in Ukraine in 2014 after the ouster of pro-Russian President Viktor Yanukovych. Some observers criticized the IMF for taking sides, but others argued that the measures were essential for maintaining Ukraine's economy and sovereignty. In 2022 and 2023, the Executive Board approved $1.4 billion in emergency funding for Ukraine and then longer-term funding of more than $15 billion with requirements for a number of reforms, especially in the energy section.

During the Covid-19 pandemic, the IMF's surveillance functions and crisis response efforts coalesced. In 2020, having projected further shrinkage in the global economy and noting the types of countries likely to be hit hardest, the organization began targeting debt relief and credit lines to developing countries. As the world's richest states began producing vaccines and inoculating their citizens in 2021, the IMF's managing director joined the heads of the World Bank, World Health Organization, and WTO in calling for greater vaccine access for poorer countries. In addition, the IMF increasingly incorporates climate change into its financial advice, emphasizing the need for "resilience-building" so that states can better withstand both pandemics and climate-related disasters.

Reforming the IMF. IMF reforms tend to follow crisis situations. For example, after the Asian financial crisis in the late 1990s, the organization set up "fire alarms" to improve monitoring of the international financial system and better anticipate financial meltdowns. Although the IMF resisted calls to provide specific credit scores on countries, it did set up an additional credit line from which struggling governments could draw if they revealed previously confidential details of their national accounts (de Beaufort Wijnholds 2011: 125).

A decade later, after the 2008–2009 global financial crisis, the IMF reorganized its Exogenous Shocks Facility for low-income states and created a Short-Term Liquidity Facility for emerging-market countries. In 2010, given the G-20's elevation as a key part of global economic governance, the IMF's member states explored significantly increasing the quotas (and votes) of G-20 countries that were underrepresented on the IMF Executive Board. That resulted in the 2015 reforms depicted in Figure 8.4.

In some respects, the IMF has moved relatively quickly to reform itself. For example, it abruptly broke the long tradition of all-male managing directors in 2011, following a sexual harassment scandal. France's former finance minister, Christine Lagarde, became the first female Managing Director. When she left in 2019 to head the European Central Bank, she was succeeded by another woman, former World Bank acting president Kristalina Georgieva of Bulgaria. Having a woman at the helm may have tangible effects, such as pressuring governments to pay more attention to female labor force participation (Blackmon 2021). Both Lagarde and Georgieva brought to their positions past experience in IGO or governmental bureaucracies where expert knowledge in economics was essential. And, in Lagarde's case, she was France's finance minister during the eurozone crisis and when France assumed the presidency of the G-20 in 2011. Reform of the international monetary system was at the top of her agenda then and when she moved to the IMF.

Nevertheless, reform prospects are limited. Some critics charge that the IMF is too opaque and intrusive in imposing conditions on recipient countries. Others say the organization is not strict enough, inviting a moral hazard problem in which governments and investors engage in increasingly reckless behavior because they believe an IMF bailout will be forthcoming. Some observers push for the organization to do more about development or income inequality, but others call for the IMF to limit its attention to crisis management and balance-of-payments issues. With conflicting and contradictory outside demands, it is difficult for the IMF to make substantial changes.

The G-7, G-8, and G-20

The IMF is not the only finance-related body reflecting the Global North's traditional dominance and economic liberalism's ideational power. Both are evident in the G-7, an informal institution in which Canada, France, Germany, Italy, Japan, the United Kingdom, and the United States often have functioned as self-appointed leaders in global economic governance. Initially, heads of state and government met. However, within a few years they appointed so-called sherpas (reminiscent of Himalayan mountain guides) to handle preparations for annual summits, which expanded to include ministers of finance, trade, and foreign affairs. IGO heads and non-G-7 countries are often invited as guests.

The result is a communication process that runs year-round, helps leaders form personal relationships, and helps them learn from each other (Gstöhl 2007: 2). These features have proved valuable in managing crises, addressing new issues, prodding other institutions to act, and even establishing new institutions. For instance, the G-7 helped create the Financial Stability Forum to craft a set of financial codes based on practices in advanced countries (Drezner 2007: 136–145). In 1989, the G-7 created the Financial Action Task Force (FATF) which, as discussed in Chapter 7, combats money laundering, terrorist financing, and corruption by producing recommendations, peer reviews, and lists of non-compliant countries (Roberge 2011). As an independent entity with thirty-six members based at the headquarters of the OECD in Paris, the FATF is small and flexible enough to act quickly, and its standards in the financial area are well known (Findley, Nielson, and Sharman 2014).

Thus, despite being an informal institution without a written charter or permanent secretariat, the G-7 has been influential in global economic governance—raising concerns about the appropriateness of so much influence being wielded by an elite set of seven wealthy democracies. In 1997 the G-7 added Russia and began operating as the G-8, but Russia's membership was suspended after its 2014 incursion into Ukraine.

A third and larger entity is the G-20—which includes the G-7 members, the European Union, the African Union, and twelve additional developed and developing countries. As noted earlier, the group first convened in 1999 but did not become active until the 2008–2009 financial crisis. Since then, the G-20 has become a prominent forum and absorbed G-7 bodies such as the Financial Stability Forum, which was remade into the Financial Stability Board with a broader mandate, more institutionalized structure, and more diverse membership. Since 2008, the G-20 has met at least annually to address crises, economic growth, trade, and employment.

With a larger voice for developing countries, the G-20 has consistently advocated national prerogatives to promote growth, rather than only submitting to the rigors of market discipline. The G-20's informal structure includes rotating leadership among a larger, more diverse group of countries, which enhances its legitimacy. However, some states that are highly populated (e.g., Bangladesh, Nigeria, Pakistan) or economically influential (e.g., Iran, Israel, Switzerland) are still excluded. And, even with a cap of twenty members, the group's size and diversity can make consensus difficult (Cooper and Thakur 2013: 16).

The Eurozone and Regional Financial Governance

Whereas the G-20 tries to coordinate the macroeconomic policies of major countries located in different parts of the world, another approach in financial governance is to coordinate within a specific geographic region. As discussed in Chapter 5, the deepest experiment with regional financial governance has occurred in the eurozone: the nineteen EU member states that replaced their national currencies with a single common currency, the euro. This monetary union includes only a subset of the EU membership because Bulgaria, Croatia, the Czech Republic, Denmark, Hungary, Poland, Romania, Sweden, and (prior to exiting the EU) the United Kingdom opted to continue using their own currencies.

The eurozone's members vary in size, economic reputation, and depth of experience with capitalist democracy. Germany informally leads the eurozone and hosts the European Central Bank (ECB), which is governed by a board representing national central banks. In giving up their national currencies, eurozone members ceded substantial monetary power and relinquished their ability to manipulate their own currency values. As the EU's largest economy, Germany wields considerable sway in financial policy—but its preferences, such as a deeper concern with inflation than with unemployment, are sometimes at odds with the preferences of many fellow members.

These fissures proved problematic when the 2008–2009 global financial crisis hit. Eurozone governments dependent on borrowing in international markets were unable to meet debt obligations; weak and loosely regulated banks could not cover liabilities; and individuals confronted unemployment, declining wages, and shriveled investments. Meanwhile, Germany continued to enjoy trade surpluses due to its high productivity and wage restraint. Decreases in the euro's value made German exports even more competitive and simultaneously worsened other eurozone countries' balance-of-payments positions. Since German, French, and Scandinavian banks had made substantial loans to states in trouble, they were also vulnerable to what was happening elsewhere.

The result was a protracted crisis in the eurozone. By 2013, more than twenty summits—involving the major leaders, as well as representatives from the ECB, EU Commission, IMF, and private banks—had been convened to address the emergency. Greece required enormous bailouts. Cyprus, Ireland, Portugal, and Spain also experienced highly visible upheavals and were instructed to embrace austerity.

Germany became a particular target of criticism for its strict adherence to austerity and its pressure for others to do likewise. The ECB and IMF relaxed with time, calling for stimulus measures to invest in growth and reverse the high unemployment levels in many EU countries. Even in eurozone countries that did not suffer as much economically, there were political reverberations as upset citizens warmed to more nationalist or populist leaders. In short, the EU has its own internal divisions.

Due to the eurozone crisis, several major reforms were instituted. In 2012, the ECB was reorganized to become a bank regulator, with deposit insurance programs to augment national programs and authority to examine bank balance sheets. After the first review in 2014, it identified twenty-five failing banks and thirteen others that needed strengthening.

Despite reforms, the eurozone remains at an uncomfortable junction. It could intensify its activities and further reduce national sovereignty by becoming a true fiscal union with tax power held by a supranational authority. Alternatively, it could continue as a monetary union, but with a more selective membership. The Maastricht Treaty did not specify how countries could withdraw from the monetary union, but it did include eligibility requirements for joining, and thus there is at least a theoretical basis for expulsion. Lacking consensus about whether to intensify or contract—let alone authority for setting fiscal and monetary policies—the eurozone remains a monetary union with a bumpy past and uncertain future.

Private Governance in Finance

Not all financial governance occurs through intergovernmental bodies; some happens in the private sector. To manage markets, private companies or associations have worked together to establish industry-wide standards or norms of appropriate behavior. Such collaborations have grown since the 1980s, when many countries in the Global North started privatizing and regulating insurance, securities, telecommunications, and other industries. Examples of private governance include the International Organization of Securities Commissioners, established in 1983; the International Association of Insurance Supervisors, founded in 1994; and the International Accounting Standards Board, created in 2001.

Among the upsides of private governance in finance are bond-rating agencies such as Moody's or Standard and Poor's. They assess the creditworthiness of various institutions, then sell those assessments to investors. Their ratings (AAA, AA, B, etc.) constitute a transnational surveillance system for private investors and government authorities. When working well, bond-rating agencies perform essential governance functions such as establishing reporting rules, increasing transparency, and delivering neutral expertise.

The ratings are not always trustworthy, however. Several large financial institutions that were given high ratings in 2007 went bankrupt during the financial crisis in 2008, prompting governments to craft new regulations for bond-rating agencies. Concerned about ratings that did not signal trouble quickly enough, the US government passed the 2010 Dodd-Frank Act, which demanded more transparency about rating methodology, conflicts of interest, and accuracy over time. In contrast, concerned about ratings that were too hasty in questioning credit-worthiness, the EU threatened legal action against major bond-rating agencies that had downgraded various countries' sovereign debt. This illustrates that although private financial governance is prevalent and influential, it is not problem-free.

Sovereign Wealth Funds, Digital Currencies, and Private Finance

For the governance of finance, other challenges loom. One is sovereign wealth funds (SWFs): government-owned investment vehicles consisting of market instruments such as stocks, bonds, real estate, and precious metals. SWFs are generally funded by foreign-exchange reserves held in major world currencies, and they regularly invest in financial assets outside of the home country. SWFs have existed for decades but have attracted deeper international scrutiny because of their increased use by countries with large trade surpluses or savings rates (e.g., China, Singapore) and by countries with substantial oil or gas exports (e.g., Canada, Kuwait, Norway, Russia, Saudi Arabia, United Arab Emirates). Managing assets of over $1 trillion, the Norwegian Government Pension Fund is the world's largest SWF and is widely considered the most transparent and publicly accountable. This fund also tries to be socially conscious by prohibiting investments that are environmentally damaging or pose other problems.

For most SWFs, however, governance and risk management practices are opaque. Proponents argue that besides being crucial for domestic economic growth and stability, SWFs are also good for international markets because governments can take a longer-term view and ride out business cycles. Critics counter that SWFs blur the line between public and private investment and that their lack of transparency allows capital to be used for political or strategic purposes, making the funds more unpredictable and dangerous to host countries than private investment would be.

So far, governance of SWFs is thin. There is a voluntary intergovernmental body called the International Forum of Sovereign Wealth Funds, which began operating in 2009 and included more than thirty countries by 2023. This body encourages adoption of the Generally Accepted Principles and Practices (also known as the Santiago Principles) to harmonize governance and risk management across SWFs. However, it is merely an advisory and voluntary body, with little power over governments. Occasionally there is talk of governing SWFs in a more direct and mandatory way, perhaps from within the IMF or some other major organization, but this has not yet happened.

Beyond SWFs, digital currencies pose a second challenge for governing finance. Digital currencies are mediums of exchange that exist on computers, rather than physically. Often cryptography secures transactions and prevents fraud, so the term "cryptocurrency" is also used. Many digital currencies (e.g., Bitcoin) are decentralized, meaning the currency is issued and regulated by many actors, not by a central authority. Decentralized digital currencies use blockchains or other distributed ledger technologies to ensure that no single entity has a record of all transactions. Decentralization, pseudo-anonymity, and fast global transfers make digital currencies an alluring way for states, state-sponsored actors, and nonstate actors to dodge international regulations and oversight (Prasad 2021).

In June 2019, the FATF updated its recommendations about how its requirements should apply to digital currencies. Meanwhile, states have taken a variety of approaches. Some have imposed outright bans; others have implemented constraints, such as restricting how their financial institutions can facilitate transactions involving digital currencies; and others have constructed relaxed regulatory regimes, hoping to siphon business from stricter jurisdictions. A few states are even creating their own digital currencies. Although Sweden, the Bahamas, and some other governments have begun testing these on a moderate scale, China has gone furthest. In 2014, the Chinese government launched an internal group to develop e-CNY, a digital version of the existing renminbi. Seven years later, China's central bank and its Digital Currency Institute piloted the new currency in Shanghai and other major cities. Unlike Bitcoin and other decentralized cryptocurrencies, e-CNY is expressly under the control of the Chinese government.

Critics charge that innovations like the e-CNY are unfair monetary levers. For example, a central bank could program its digital currency to slowly lose value, thereby prompting people to spend rather than save. Many observers also fear digital currencies could be used as a tool for political repression, empowering governments to track and control their populations. Proponents counter that digitized national currencies should not be impeded, because they streamline transactions, link people who might not otherwise have access to institutionalized banking, and help governments uncover illegal activities such as tax evasion. The competing views make it unclear how or even whether global governance structures should attempt to handle centralized or decentralized digital currencies.

In addition to digital currencies and SWFs, a third challenge is private finance. This includes banking transactions (deposits and loans involving companies, private individuals, or governments), international remittances (portions of money earned in one country to assist family or friends in another country), and stock market transactions (investments involving brokerage houses, hedge funds, and the like). Other private actors that move funds around the world are insurance agencies, mortgage companies, financial advisors, bond-rating agencies, and currency-exchange companies. Both the monetary amounts and the number of participating financial institutions are massive.

Decades ago, private finance largely flowed from the Global North to the Global South. Over time, however, an ever-increasing portion of lending, investment, and speculation has been flowing from the South to the North, or staying within the South. Brazil, Russia, India, China, and South Africa have been especially active in lending, speculating, and investing in developing countries. They have argued that their recent experiences with development or economic transitions, coupled with their own remarkable growth, make them better attuned to which resources or practices would help developing countries the most.

China, in particular, blurs distinctions between private and public finance. In recent years, its government-linked banks have dominated the banking sector. On the 2022 list of the world's largest banks, China's "Big Four"—the Industrial and Commercial Bank of China, China Construction Bank, Agricultural Bank of China, and Bank of China—continue to be the world's four largest banks. It is hard for truly private banks to compete with government-linked banks because the government has the ability to print and manipulate the national currency. Many observers also worry that China's banks are not subject to sufficiently rigorous regulatory mechanisms, accounting standards, and transparency requirements. Given that global governance in this area is largely voluntary, it would be difficult to force China, or any other government, to drastically change its financial system.

Key Themes in Financial Governance

As with the governance of trade, financial governance exhibits the broader patterns of economic governance illustrated in this chapter's opening case study. There are North/South tensions, links with other areas of economic policy, and interactions between states and nonstate actors. The world has changed greatly since the 1940s—and in some ways, financial governance has changed too. Women and developing countries, for example, have assumed bigger leadership roles. However, critics of the current system warn that existing financial governance structures still do not fully incorporate countries from the Global South and may be insufficient for handling new challenges.

Governance of Development

Complex problems exist not only in the governance of finance but also in the governance of development. Traditionally, development was thought to be primarily economic, rather than encompassing broader processes of social and political change. The field was dominated by economists who prescribed ways to make economies grow, gauging development with measures such as GDP per capita (gross domestic product divided by a country's population). Over time, inputs from disciplines such as sociology, political science, and history expanded the notion of development to include institutional quality (Acemoglu and Robinson 2012), as well as human rights, gender, and environmental sustainability (Jolly et al. 2004). These differing perspectives have spurred debates—often in the UN—about the proper division of labor between states and nonstate actors, how best to promote and sustain development, and whether trade is a better development tool than aid. Economic development has broadened to "human development."

The actors involved in promoting human development are diverse. States clearly are important, since much of the assistance to developing countries during the Cold War was government-to-government bilateral aid, and this pattern has continued in the post–Cold War era. IGOs such as the World Bank, the IMF, regional development banks, the OECD, and a number of UN-affiliated bodies are highly relevant. In addition, numerous nonstate actors—including NGOs, civil society groups, foundations, MNCs, and even individual celebrities like Bill Gates and Angelina Jolie—play key roles. We start by looking at development aid that comes directly from governments and then turn to multilateral development aid that comes through international institutions.

States and Official Development Assistance

One of the oldest forms of aid is official development assistance (ODA): concessionary government-to-government financial aid directed to developing countries for their economic development and welfare. The "concessionary" stipulation means that at least part of the aid comes in the form of grants or below-market-rate loans. Since World War II, the vast majority of ODA has come from the thirty (largely Western) governments on the OECD's Development Assistance Committee (DAC). For instance, for Covid-19 vaccines alone, in 2021 over $6 billion was funneled from DAC members to developing countries (OECD 2022).

Critics question whether these large amounts of aid are truly generous or effective. For one thing, even record-breaking contributions during the Covid-19 pandemic are small compared with the size of rich countries' economies. In response to G-77 pressure in the 1960s, the UN had set a target that donor countries' yearly ODA should be 1 percent of that country's annual gross national income. When this did not come to fruition, the UN reduced the target to 0.7 percent. Yet in 2020, only five of the thirty DAC members (Sweden, Norway, Luxembourg, Denmark, and Germany) met this target. In absolute amounts, the United States was the largest donor at $35 billion, but this was less than 0.2 percent of US gross national income (OECD 2022).

Furthermore, donors may stipulate how aid can be used or may funnel aid according to their own policy goals. For example, the United States devoted one-fourth of its overall aid in 2020 to just ten countries: Israel, Jordan, Egypt, Tanzania, Kenya, Uganda, Mozambique, South Africa, Zambia, and Iraq. With Israel topping the list, it is obvious that US aid is not just about development, but also about other concerns. The United States is hardly alone in using financial aid to serve multiple policy goals. China, an increasingly important donor that is not an OECD member, often mixes its aid with direct investment, service contracts, labor cooperation agreements, long-term loans, and other instruments serving China's policy interests.

Scholars and practitioners have long debated aid's effectiveness (Dietrich 2021). Proponents such as Jeffrey Sachs (2005) believe people will move out of poverty if donors can make enough of a "big push." Critics such as William Easterly (2006) counter that aid creates dependency, market distortions, and more poverty. Other observers point out that rather than being all good or bad, the effectiveness of aid hinges on how well it is targeted. Perhaps it works best when funneled to narrower projects with readily measurable goals, or to states that are home to the "bottom billion" of the poor (Collier 2007). Years of empirical work suggest that aid does boost economic growth, but despite all the studies, there is little consensus on the relative costs or how aid leads to human development more broadly.

Multilateral Assistance through the World Bank Group and the IMF

Despite concerns about whether development aid is sufficiently generous or effective, governments continue to assist developing countries not only bilaterally but also multilaterally. A central player in multilateral development efforts is the World Bank Group, which encompasses the original post–World War II International Bank for Reconstruction and Development (IBRD) and four subsequently created bodies. These five institutions offer various forms of assistance to governments and businesses in developing countries.

The World Bank Group. Although the IBRD initially concentrated on postwar reconstruction in Europe, from the 1950s it pivoted to development in other regions. Using contributions from wealthy member states and capital raised in international financial markets, it extends low-interest loans to states for major development projects. The loans often fund projects such as social services (e.g., healthcare, education, housing), infrastructure (e.g., highways, electric facilities, telecommunications), and government restructuring, all of which are less likely to be financed by private banks. Unlike its private counterparts, however, the IBRD regularly attaches conditions in the form of policy changes that governments are asked to make to continue receiving money.

The IBRD operated alone until 1956, when the International Finance Corporation (IFC) became the first subsidiary organization in the World Bank Group. Working through more than 750 financial institutions, the IFC provides loans and services to promote the growth of private enterprises in developing countries. It operates as a "corporation," with over 180 member governments as shareholders whose votes parallel their paid-in capital. Over time, the IFC's financial autonomy in the World Bank Group has grown.

Another organization in the Group is the International Development Association (IDA), established in 1960. The IDA focuses on the world's poorest countries, whose low per capita income and lack of access to private capital markets qualifies them for IDA loans that carry no interest and can be repaid over several decades. By 2023, more than forty countries had successfully "graduated" from IDA eligibility, with only a handful relapsing. The IDA continues to lend to about seventy countries, about half of which are in Africa. Unlike other parts of the World Bank Group, the IDA depends on major donor countries to replenish its funds every few years.

Another subsidiary, the International Center for Settlement of Investment Disputes (ICSID), began operating in 1966. The ICSID is often referenced in bilateral investment treaties, which tend to funnel disputes between countries to this multilateral forum, rather than to domestic courts. In addition to supporting arbitration or conciliation proceedings, the ICSID offers research, publications, and advisory services.

The fifth and final part of the World Bank Group is the Multilateral Investment Guarantee Agency, established in 1988. To further encourage private-sector investments in developing countries, the MIGA offers insurance against losses. Coverage even includes losses from political risks such as expropriation, governmental currency restrictions, ethnic conflict, or civil war.

The World Bank Group's activities have changed over time, reflecting broader shifts in development thinking. In early decades, the emphasis was on large infrastructure projects. Then, under the leadership of Robert McNamara in the 1970s, the World Bank Group adopted a "basic needs" orientation, funding more projects related to health, education, and housing for the masses. Private-sector involvement became a central aim in the

1980s, followed by "good governance" in the 1990s. Under the leadership of James Wolfensohn, the World Bank Group ventured into politically charged discussions about government corruption as an inhibitor of development. This was dangerous territory, since it invited questions about the transparency or justness of the Group's own governance structure and its history of making disbursements even when there is evidence of corruption in its own projects (Weaver 2008: 108–113).

By the early 2000s, the World Bank Group had repositioned itself as a "knowledge bank" whose data, expertise, and advice set it apart from other funding sources. Under pressure from civil society, it had also moved away from most large infrastructure projects, which had been criticized as socially destructive and environmentally damaging. Increasingly, the World Bank Group has emphasized environmental sustainability, aid coordination, and community-driven development.

Development thinking is not the only thing that has changed; the scale has changed, too. By 2023 the IBRD had grown to encompass 189 member states, staff from 170 countries, and offices in 130 locations. From 1947 to 2023, the World Bank Group funded more than 12,000 projects. During the first year of the Covid-19 pandemic, the five organizations within the Group disbursed over $60 billion. Whether measured by membership, projects, or money, the World Bank Group is central to the governance of development.

The IMF. The IMF, though primarily concerned with finance, is also relevant to development because economic growth and stability are difficult for countries with financial troubles. Decades ago, as discussed earlier, the IMF expanded beyond currency convertibility to help countries with chronic balance-of-payments difficulties and heavy debt. Through structural adjustment programs (SAPs), such assistance has often been made conditional on policy changes that seek to prevent such problems from recurring.

Research is divided about the effects of structural adjustment and conditionality. There is evidence that SAPs have eased inflationary pressures and improved countries' balance of payments, but it remains unclear whether they have aided countries' economic growth. Numerous civil society groups have asserted that SAPs disproportionately hurt the poor by cutting public expenditures, reducing food subsidies, devaluing currencies, and harming the natural environment. Claims like these have led to loud critiques and even some mass demonstrations.

Heavy debt in developing countries has long been a problem. During the early 1980s, commercial banks were eager lenders, buoyed by funds from thriving OPEC countries that saw Western banks as safe places to deposit cash. The IMF and the World Bank added to developing countries' debt burden with SAPs and conditionality that often triggered adverse economic consequences. Falling commodity prices in the 1980s, combined with a steep rise in interest rates, made it impossible for some countries to service or refinance debts while meeting other obligations. Repayment crowded out opportunities for investment in the economy. Infrastructure suffered, spending on health-care and education was cut, and poverty increased.

The consequences of high debt levels and financial crises have been significant for many developing countries. In 1980, the debt of all develop-ing countries was $567 billion; by 1992, it had reached $1.6 trillion, and by 2000, $2.2 trillion. Excluding China, it reached $11.5 trillion in 2021, exac-erbated by government borrowing during the pandemic. Countries caught in a "debt trap" have included a significant number of the world's poorest African countries, along with middle-income countries in Asia and Latin America. In 1982, Mexico announced it could pay neither the interest nor the principal due on its foreign debt; in 2001, Argentina defaulted; shortly thereafter, Brazil and Turkey experienced crises. Some least-developed African states were spending four times more on debt servicing than on social services and education.

Under pressure from civil society groups to end ad hoc responses to individual crises and instead address the underlying commonalities, in 1996 the IMF partnered with the World Bank to launch the Heavily Indebted Poor Countries (HIPC) Initiative. Bringing together various public and pri-vate creditors, it proposed debt rescheduling or cancellation. The issue gained momentum with Jubilee 2000, a coalition of development-oriented NGOs, labor groups, and church leaders who called for developing coun-tries' debts to be wiped out with the turn of the millennium. The coalition dissolved after 2000, but its vision continued through the HIPC Initiative, whose eligibility requirements have loosened with time. Countries are eli-gible for debt rescheduling or cancellation if they face an unsustainable debt situation, are classified as low-income, have a track record of reforms and sound policies, and collaborate with domestic civil society groups to develop a poverty reduction strategy. By 2023 about forty countries, mostly in Africa, had reached the HIPC Initiative's completion point, and their debts were substantially rescheduled or entirely canceled.

In addition to collaborating on debt relief, the IMF has set up several in-house entities aimed at the poorest developing countries. In 1999, it established the Poverty Reduction and Growth Facility to offer low-interest loans; in 2015 it established the Catastrophe Containment and Relief Trust to provide grants to poor countries hit by natural disasters or public health crises. The IMF's mandate is to ensure financial stability for countries at all income levels, but increasingly it recognizes the particular challenges of developing countries.

Criticism and reforms. The World Bank Group and the IMF have faced questions about the fairness of their governance structures. In both, weighted voting systems give more formal influence to donors than to recipients. Major donors have individual seats, but other member governments share seats; for example, on the IMF's Executive Board, all the countries of sub-Saharan Africa are represented by just two seats. Although the vote shares in the World Bank and the IMF have been adjusted, especially in response to greater contributions from China, the United States is still by far the largest shareholder and the only state that can single-handedly block substantive decisions requiring an 85 percent supermajority. As mentioned previously, the IMF's Managing Director has always been European, while the World Bank Group's president has always been American. Although the IMF's approximately 2,500 employees and the World Bank Group's approximately 12,000 employees are from all over the world, many are economists who have been trained in Western universities (Nelson 2017).

Critics charge that the processes for selecting organizational heads are outdated, that emerging economies' formal influence is not yet commensurate with their economic contributions to the global economy, and that the United States is a declining hegemon that should not have so much formal power. Indeed, although the IMF and the World Bank Group are economic institutions, politics does intervene in the decisions over who gets financing and when. During the Cold War, for example, the United States blocked funding for Afghanistan, Chile, Cuba, Grenada, Laos, Nicaragua, and Vietnam.

Beyond fairness, both organizations face questions about their effectiveness. External critics argue that conditionality and structural adjustment programs disproportionately hurt people who are already marginalized (Foster et al. 2019). The World Bank Group's internal evaluators have acknowledged a "disbursement imperative" (Weaver 2007) and a "fear of risk" (Lowrey 2013) that push staff to focus on channeling funding rather than ensuring recipients' well-being. The IMF and the World Bank Group have altered their practices. Increasingly, the IMF encourages social safety nets, admits the wisdom of regulating capital flows, and recognizes that governments sometimes should take a proactive role in coordinating economic development. The World Bank Group downplays one-size-fits-all prescriptions, instead endorsing localized approaches and experimentation. Nevertheless, criticism persists (Humphrey 2023).

Regional Development Banks
Since the 1950s, several additional development banks have been created to be more sensitive to the needs of particular regions. These regional development banks tend to enjoy closer relationships with their constituencies than do global IGOs. With fewer members and often more similar needs, development programs can theoretically be more closely tailored to national and local situations. Four regional development banks in the Americas, Asia, Africa, and Europe are profiled before looking at two newer banks promoted by China.

The Inter-American Development Bank (IDB). The IDB, the oldest regional development bank, was founded in 1959 and is headquartered in Washington, DC. Of its forty-eight members, twenty-six are borrowing countries who hold just over 50 percent of the voting power, and the rest are donor countries who can block decisions only if they band together. Not all donors are in the Americas: the United States is the largest single shareholder, but other donors include China, Israel, Japan, South Korea, and many European countries. In contrast to the World Bank Group, donors do not clearly dominate IDB decisionmaking.

Like the World Bank, the IDB operates in a group with other entities emphasizing different elements of lending. The Multilateral Investment Fund promotes reforms in investment practices to stimulate private-sector involvement; the Inter-American Investment Corporation finances small- and medium-scale projects in the private sector; and the Fund for Special Operations lends to the least developed countries on concessional terms. Together, the entities in the IDB Group lend over $11 billion annually.

Throughout the 1960s and 1970s, the IDB Group was a leader in social sector lending for health and education projects as well as lending to smaller poor countries. In the 1980s and 1990s, it adopted some of the World Bank Group's agenda for economic liberalization. More recently, it still follows a broad approach of reducing poverty and inequality by financing micro-entrepreneurs and small-scale farmers, but it also tries to improve governance by working with civil society groups to promote democracy and regional integration.

The IDB Group has always had close relationships with states. By maintaining resident representatives in each borrowing country, the IDB group gains specialized information about the region's latest circumstances and needs. Working closely with states does have some challenges, however. For example, the bank president, who is always a Latin American, is closely scrutinized by the international banking community and generally must be acceptable to the United States, the largest shareholder.

The Asian Development Bank (ADB). The ADB focuses on Asia. Established in 1966 with headquarters in the Philippines, it has sixty-eight members: forty-nine from Asia and nineteen from outside the region. The ADB's approximately 3,000 employees work in offices around the world, including major banking centers like Frankfurt and London. Since its founding, the ADB has made loans totaling more than $20 billion, mostly to the public sector.

Within the ADB, Japan holds special influence. Like the World Bank, the ADB uses a weighted voting system linked to a country's capital contributions. Japan and the United States are the two largest shareholders, each controlling 12.75 percent of the vote. In addition, the organization's head has always been Japanese.

Japan has also been an instigator and major funder for new structures such as the Asian Development Fund, established in 2000 to offer grants or low-interest loans to the poorest member states. This fund promotes inclusive growth, social spending, regional integration, and environmental sustainability. Many projects are cofinanced with civil society groups. The emphasis on least-developed countries and collaboration with civil society is a significant departure from large, state-supported infrastructure projects.

Increasingly, however, Japan's dominance in the ADB is being challenged. China has increased its contributions to the bank and called for more funding for traditional infrastructure such as dams, roads, and railways. The ADB has responded by giving more attention to infrastructure but also underscoring the overall imperative of reducing poverty. Under its Strategy 2030, the ADB has articulated its commitment to achieving a "prosperous, inclusive, resilient, and sustainable Asia and the Pacific."

The African Development Bank (AfDB). Seeking to avoid dominance by any single state, the AfDB differs from its counterparts in Asia and the Americas. With headquarters in Côte d'Ivoire, the AfDB began operating in 1966, and initially its membership was restricted to African countries. In 1982 it started admitting nonregional members to augment its economic resources. By 2023, the fifty-four African members held about 60 percent of the voting power and the twenty-seven nonregional members held about 40 percent. The largest shareholder was Nigeria with about 9 percent. No state or even small set of states had veto power.

The AfDB has tried to bring a uniquely African perspective to development issues. Its president and almost all of its approximately 1,800 employees are African. Viewing itself as a purely economic institution, the AfDB originally established only economic conditions for its loans, believing that the imposition of political criteria constituted unwarranted interference in states' internal affairs. In the 1980s, however, AfDB began attaching more conditionality, suggesting that governments that did not move toward market systems would have difficulty obtaining future loans (Mingst 1990). Over time, project-based lending has been accompanied by lending to specific programs and sectors, with loans made to governments as well as private businesses. Like other regional development banks, the AfDB increasingly positions itself as a knowledge disseminator and incorporates climate change into its funding decisions (Mingst 2015).

The AfDB has faced some challenges not experienced by its counterparts in other regions. For example, in the 1990s it lost its credit rating just as the African continent was experiencing economic decline. This created a crisis. The AfDB responded with several restructurings aimed at strengthening top management, making the institution more responsive to clients, and increasing support for other actors in the development community. In another challenge, between 2003 and 2014, civil war in Côte d'Ivoire compelled the AfDB to operate from a temporary headquarters in Tunisia. Although its credit rating has rebounded and the staff are back in the Côte d'Ivoire facilities, the AfDB continues to operate on a relatively small scale compared with other regional development banks, limited in part by fewer resources.

The European Bank for Reconstruction and Development (EBRD). The EBRD was founded in 1991 to assist countries from the former Eastern bloc in their transitions from communism to capitalism. Over time, the geographic focus expanded beyond Eastern Europe into Central Europe and Central Asia. The EBRD monitors recipients' progress in price and trade liberalization, competition policy, enterprise restructuring, and establishing new legal frameworks. It has helped states move to full market economies while promoting safeguards for the environment and a commitment to sustainable energy.

The EBRD has seventy-one member states, plus the European Union and the European Investment Bank. In cooperation with commercial partners, it administers between 350 and 400 projects annually, totaling about €9 billion. Projects range from supporting agriculture and agribusiness in Moldova and Georgia to providing credit for small businesses in Serbia and Kazakhstan.

Several features distinguish the EBRD from other regional development banks. First, its borrowing from international capital markets allows it to operate with a greater range of financial instruments. Second, it actively promotes the private sector. Third, it is quite transparent, offering wide access to documents on its website, as well as a compliance channel that permits individuals or groups to report irregularities in the use of bank funds. Fourth, since the 2011 Arab Spring uprisings, the bank has developed programs to facilitate private investment in parts of the Middle East and North Africa. Perhaps most important, the EBRD was the first regional development bank to impose criteria that were explicitly political: borrowing countries must not only embrace capitalist economic development but also apply the principles of pluralism and multiparty democracy.

Asian Infrastructure Investment Bank (AIIB). Although the IDB, ADB, AfDB, and EBRD have important differences, they tend to share a commitment to the liberal economic paradigm. China has supported the creation of two newer development banks, which some observers believe pose challenges to the United States, the liberal economic order, and the older development banks. One of the new entities is the AIIB, created to finance infrastructure projects in Asia and Oceania. China was motivated partly by displeasure with the US-dominated World Bank and the Japan-dominated

ADB, both of which have deemphasized infrastructure projects in recent years and hesitated to increase China's vote share.

In 2014, twenty-two Asian countries became founding members of the AIIB. Despite public pressure from US President Barack Obama, in 2015 the United Kingdom became the first G-7 country to join the AIIB, followed by France, Germany, and Italy. In December 2015, when the founding agreement entered into force, the AIIB had fifty-seven members, including South Korea and Australia. With headquarters in Beijing, the AIIB began operating in 2016. China alone contributed half of the bank's $100 billion starting capital. At the time, this was a bit below the ADB's capital of $175 billion and far below the World Bank's $220 billion.

Although the AIIB's governance structure looks somewhat like that of the World Bank, there are notable differences. For example, instead of the World Bank's system of making many poorer countries share a single representative, the AIIB is led by a Board of Governors on which each member state has its own representative. Instead of the World Bank's resident Executive Board, the AIIB has a nonresident Board of Directors who meet intermittently and are not based in Beijing. Decisionmaking for lower-level activities is delegated to bank staff. Proponents say this increases efficiency; critics claim it decreases transparency. China argued that the AIIB could be a complement rather than a rival to the World Bank and the ADB. The new bank could strengthen China's regional and global influence, but it also addresses a genuine financing gap for infrastructure projects in Asia.

By 2023, the AIIB had 106 members and had funded about 140 projects in more than thirty countries. India is home to the largest number of projects, but the bank's flagship project is China's bilateral Belt and Road Initiative, which funds infrastructure to connect far-flung countries to China by sea and land. Several projects (e.g., in Ecuador, Egypt, Hungary, Rwanda, Turkey) are outside of Asia and Oceania, and the AIIB touts its commitment to climate finance in support of the 2015 Paris Agreement. Because the stable cash flow expected from infrastructure investments is attractive to long-term investors such as insurance companies and pension funds, the bank aims for half of its projects to be led by the private sector by 2030. Although the AIIB reflects the competition between China and the United States, it has been embraced by much of the rest of the world and received permanent observer status in the United Nations in 2018.

New Development Bank (NDB). A second recent addition is the NDB— formerly called the BRICS Development Bank because it was proposed and designed during a series of summits in 2012–2016 involving the original BRICS countries (Brazil, Russia, India, China, and South Africa). Several features distinguish the NDB from other multilateral development banks. First, environmental sustainability is explicit in its stated mission.

Second, to support capital markets in member states and protect borrowers from currency volatility, the NDB aims to issue the bulk of its loans in local currencies rather than euros or US dollars. Third, all five founding members have equal subscribed capital and equal voting power. Most decisions are made by majority agreement, and no individual state has veto power. Fourth, it is wholly owned and controlled by emerging economies. Thus far, the founding members have been lenders as well as borrowers, a significant departure from the historical divide between rich-country donors and poor-country recipients.

The NDB began operating in 2016 and immediately characterized itself as a leader in green financing. The bank's 2017–2021 strategic plan defined its key sectors of operation as clean energy, transport infrastructure, water resource management, economic cooperation and integration among member states, and sustainable urban development. By the end of its first three years, the NDB had approved 53 projects totaling $15 billion, with the greatest number of loans going to China and India. Russia's receipt of several large infrastructure loans raised concerns about whether the new bank was undermining Western sanctions against Russia. Critics also questioned the "greenness" of some NDB projects such as paving the trans-Amazonian highway through Brazil's rainforest. The NDB—which by early 2023 had approved ninety-six projects—has boasted that its loans are approved within just six months. Critics charge, however, that delivery of funds takes much longer and disbursed amounts are substantially lower than approved amounts.

While the AIIB is clearly dominated by China, the NDB's governance structure helps quell fears of Chinese dominance. Although the bank is headquartered in Shanghai, its president is elected from one of the founding members on a rotating basis for a five-year term. The founders have equal voting power, and when new members join they plan to evenly dilute their shares until they reach a minimum of 11 percent each, so they collectively maintain at least 55 percent of the voting power. Developed countries can join only as nonborrowing members with a maximum vote share of 7 percent each. As of early 2023, there were three new members, one prospective member, and no developed country members.

The UN and Development Ideas:
Tailoring, Data, Women's Roles, Sustainability

In addition to the multilateral development banks, the United Nations system is an important player in the governance of development. Although the UN Charter includes language about the promotion of economic and social well-being, it says little about how to pursue this, and historically the UN's budgetary allocations for development have been modest compared with those of bilateral donors or the World Bank Group. As a result, some of the UN's greatest contributions to development have been not in the form of material resources but in the form of ideas. Four specific contributions include tailoring approaches to development, gathering data and issuing reports, promoting women's roles in development, and introducing the concept of sustainability.

Tailored approaches to development. In the decades immediately after World War II, the UN differentiated itself from the World Bank by making technical assistance (i.e., the provision of training programs and expert advice) its primary contribution to development. The UN's role became somewhat more formalized when the General Assembly established the UN Conference on Trade and Development in 1964 and the UN Development Programme (UNDP) in 1965. UNCTAD has provided a dedicated forum for developing countries to discuss their challenges, and the UNDP has focused on how to overcome those challenges.

The UNDP, which was formed by merging the Expanded Program of Technical Assistance and the Special United Nations Fund for Economic Development, is considered the lead UN entity in the provision of technical assistance. Its in-country resident representatives are responsible for assessing local needs and priorities, coordinating programs, serving as liaisons between the UN and recipient governments, representing some of the UN's specialized agencies, and partnering with civil society organizations and other local stakeholders (Johnson 2014). The UNDP's resources are dwarfed by those of the World Bank and major bilateral aid donors. Unlike these entities, the UNDP emphasizes grants instead of loans, and therefore does not add to poor countries' debt burdens.

In his history of the UNDP, Craig Murphy (2006: 200–207) describes it as a "learning organization," particularly in regard to the central role of women in development, the value of micro-credit and empowerment of women, the linkages between human rights and development, the importance of democracy for economic sustainability, and the problems of structural adjustment programs and debt burdens. Murphy praises the UNDP for continually refining and spreading its ideas. The evidence," he adds, "is not just the popularity of the human development concept or the frequency with which the Programme is cited as being on the leading edge of UN reform; it is also in UNDP's frequent place in the stories other organizations [such as the World Bank] tell about their own learning" (Murphy 2006: 347).

In addition to the UNDP, the five regional commissions under ECOSOC aim to tailor development approaches to different areas of the world. The commissions have produced high-quality regional surveys and country plans used by national governments. Some commissions, such as those for Africa or western Asia, have been hampered by disputes among members or a lack of resources. Others have been very influential. For instance, as previously mentioned, ECLA played a vital role in establishing the IDB, challenging liberal economic thinking, and promoting the dependency school. Beginning in the 1950s, ECLA economists argued that the developing world was permanently mired in poverty and unable to grow given the inequality between the North and South. In their view, fundamental changes were necessary.

Virtually all of the UN specialized, functional agencies introduced in Chapter 3 have adopted some kind of development agenda, even if it was not part of their original mandate. The International Telecommunications Union and World Meteorological Organization, for example, offer capacity-building programs for developing countries in their respective areas of expertise. The WHO and the FAO have particularly important missions related to human development in poorer parts of the world (Chapters 3 and 11). The UN Industrial Development Organization fosters industrialization, while the UN Educational, Scientific and Cultural Organization (UNESCO) supports a variety of programs that target developing countries.

Development-related data and reports. The UN system has been essential in gathering and disseminating data to inform development planning (Ward 2004). Data collection is notoriously difficult in developing countries, which tend to lack technical expertise and well-funded statistical bureaus. UN involvement cannot completely solve these problems, but it does offer substantial improvements over having no data at all (Jerven 2021).

The UN has standardized social statistics and crafted a variety of development-related measures, such as the Gender Development Index, the Multidimensional Poverty Index, and the World Income Inequality Index. The UN's *Human Development Reports* provide updates on the now well-known Human Development Index that was introduced by the UNDP in the early 1990s along with analysis of key findings. Largely shaped by Indian economist Amartya Sen, the Human Development Index is a composite indicator that tracks per capita income, life expectancy, and education. This three-part indicator emphasizes that development is not just about economic growth, but is also about people's overall quality of life and their freedom to make their own choices (Sen 1999).

Promotion of women's roles in development. The earliest work of the UN Commission on the Status of Women (CSW) involved women's political rights, including their right to vote and hold office. Then in the 1960s and 1970s, the CSW pivoted to women's economic and social rights. A key instigator of this pivot was the Danish economist, activist, and UN consultant Esther Boserup, whose landmark book *Woman's Role in Economic Development* argued that as technology improves, men benefit economically, but women become increasingly marginalized (Boserup 1970). Her work was complemented by the ECA's data on women's essential roles in development. In 1975, the first UN-sponsored World Conference on Women, held in Mexico City, called for the UN to initiate programs to support research, training, and funding for strengthening women's roles in development. This led to the creation of the UN Development Fund for Women (UNIFEM) to support projects run by women and the International Research and Training Institute for the Advancement of Women (INSTRAW) to help women participate fully in development. Over the course of the Decade for Women (1976–1985), various UN specialized agencies and other international development actors integrated women's concerns into their programs. Women's participation in the labor force became a key area of research for the regional commissions and for the ILO, UNDP, and FAO. With the sponsorship of International Women's Year in 1975 and three more women's conferences in 1980, 1985, and 1995, the UN reshaped the development agenda with women in mind.

For many years, there were no data tracking women's economic position, but the UN began collecting such data in the 1980s, supported by key donor states in northern Europe. In 1990, the UN published *The World's Women*, the first data compilation and analysis of women's situation relative to men across a range of fields. The UN has established programs to assist women with agriculture, industry, small businesses, and microcredit. Activists have added minimum standards of social security, maternity protection, and workplace nondiscrimination to the UN's agenda.

In 2010, UNIFEM, INSTRAW, and other parts of the UN dealing with women's issues were merged to form the United Nations Entity for Gender Equality and the Empowerment of Women, known simply as UN Women. UN Women brings together multiple dimensions: human rights (gender equality as a basic right), politics (underrepresentation of women in decisionmaking), and economics (empowering women in the economy). With the help of UN Women and other initiatives, programs related to women's roles in development have been mainstreamed throughout the UN system.

Sustainable development. In addition to mainstreaming gender issues, the UN refined the concept of "sustainable development" (discussed further in Chapter 10). The concept had gained attention in the 1970s with the book *Limits to Growth* (Meadows et al. 1972). Juxtaposing the Earth's finite resources and exponential population increases, the book questioned how long economic growth could continue.

In the early 1980s, the meaning of "sustainable development" was still vague. In 1983, the UN General Assembly established the World Commission on Environment and Development, headed by Prime Minister Gro Harlem Brundtland of Norway and composed of eminent individuals from around the world. Recognizing that development had significant effects on the environment and was more than just economic growth, the commission was tasked with formulating a new development approach around the nascent concept of sustainable development.

In its 1987 report *Our Common Future*, the Brundtland Commission called for "development that meets the needs of the present without compromising the ability of future generations to meet their own needs" (World Commission on Environment and Development 1987: 8). Subsequently, that approach of balancing ecological concerns with the economic growth necessary to reducing poverty was adopted by a number of IGOs, as well as civil society groups and national development agencies. As discussed in Chapter 10, it also became the underlying theme for the 1992 UN Conference on the Environment and Development.

The UN and Goal-Setting for Development

The UN has shaped the governance of development through its work on tailored approaches, data and reports, gender equality, and sustainability, yet its broadest impact comes from goal-setting. The UN initially set goals for the development community in 1961 when the General Assembly designated the 1960s as the "United Nations Development Decade." In three subsequent Development Decades, the UN announced targets for various economic endeavors such as development aid, domestic savings, national income, and agricultural production. It also set goals related to broader human development (e.g., expanding education, reducing child mortality, eradicating smallpox, and increasing life expectancy) that became the operational responsibility of specialized agencies such as UNESCO, UNICEF, and the WHO.

The Millennium Development Goals (MDGs). Many of these goals were incorporated into the MDGs, adopted at the Millennium Summit in 2000. With a target of 2015, the eight MDGs were mutually reinforcing and intertwined, involving governments, IGOs, and NSAs. They included halving world poverty and hunger, reducing infant mortality by two-thirds, and achieving universal primary education. The goals were disaggregated into twenty-one targets and sixty performance indicators. An elaborate implementation plan involved ten global task forces, report cards for each developing country, regular monitoring, and a public information campaign to keep pressure on governments and international agencies. This was unprecedented: UN agencies and the Bretton Woods institutions had "aligned their operational activities behind a unifying substantive framework" for development (Ruggie 2003: 305).

The MDGs helped focus aid efforts and spur some new approaches. One was the Millennium Villages Project. Operated and funded by a mix of public and private actors, the project funneled development aid to fourteen African villages. The MDGs also inspired the Millennium Challenge Corporation, created by the US government to channel grants to developing countries that adopted "good governance" policies such as stopping corruption, strengthening the rule of law, supporting human rights, investing in health and education, and promoting private enterprise.

When the timeframe for the MDGs closed in 2015, several key goals had been met. Poverty rates and the number of people in extreme poverty fell in every developing region, including sub-Saharan Africa. The percentage of the population having completed primary education increased by 98 percent and infant mortality fell by 50 percent compared with 1990 levels.

Many improvements began even before the MDGs were articulated, however, so progress toward the goals did not necessarily mean progress because of them (McArthur 2014: 1). Moreover, some progress entailed unintended drawbacks, such as reliance on fertilizers to increase food production (Hinchberger 2011). Perhaps most important, much of the improvement was due to major gains in China and India (Liese and Beisheim 2011). Meanwhile, sub-Saharan Africa still lagged according to many indicators, including child and maternal health, urban–rural inequalities, and youth unemployment. Changes in climate were projected to hit the continent particularly hard. Hence, Africa's experience with the MDGs demonstrated that development is about more than poverty alleviation.

The Sustainable Development Goals (SDGs). In 2012, diplomats and experts began working on a new set of goals, the SDGs, to follow the MDGs in 2015–2030. In 2014, the year before the MDGs were set to expire, an UNCTAD report estimated that achieving a new set of goals by 2030 would require approximately $2.5 trillion per year. Bearing in mind some of the weaknesses of the MDGs—including the elite-driven process by which the MDGs were developed within the UN Secretariat—the UN Open Working Group worked with a task force of representatives from states, sixty UN agencies and other IGOs, and nonstate actors in a complex multistakeholder process (Kamau, Chasek, and O'Connor 2018). The result was a greatly expanded set of seventeen goals, shown in Figure 8.5.

These seventeen SDGs, also known as "Agenda 2030," were adopted by all UN member states at the September 2015 Summit of Heads of State and Government. "People, planet, prosperity, peace, and partnership" are at the center of the commitments that combine economic development goals with expanded pledges to foster social development, gender equality, and environmental sustainability by 2030. To make the SDGs more actionable, a follow-up resolution in 2017 endorsed 169 targets for outcomes or means of implementation, plus 232 specific data indicators. A key difference between the MDGs and the SDGs, however, is not just the number of goals and targets but that all countries—developed and developing—are expected to work toward the SDGs. This includes, for example, commitments by the Global North to combat inequality and promote environmentally sustainable consumption and production.

**Figure 8.5
The Sustainable Development
Goals (SDGs)**

1. No poverty
2. Zero hunger
3. Good health and well-being
4. Quality education
5. Gender equality
6. Clean water and sanitation
7. Affordable and clean energy
8. Decent work and economic growth
9. Industry, innovation, and infrastructure
10. Reduced inequalities
11. Sustainable cities and communities
12. Responsible consumption and production
13. Climate action
14. Life below water
15. Life on land
16. Peace and justice; strong institutions
17. Partnerships for the goals

From the outset, the SDGs' expansiveness generated debate. *The Economist* (2015: 63) complained, "Something for everyone has produced too much for anyone." To some observers, the SDGs are unwieldy, unprioritized, difficult to track (especially because of data unavailability in poorer countries), and even conflicting. For example, mosquito nets distributed to fight malaria are sometimes repurposed in developing countries as fishing nets that capture very small creatures, revealing tensions among SDG 2 (ending hunger), SDG 3 (improving health), and SDG 14 (sustainable aquatic ecosystems). Supporters counter that the SDGs have to be more complex than the MDGs because they were negotiated by a more diverse set of stakeholders and go beyond an exclusive focus on developing countries.

UN agencies have been making significant efforts to mainstream the SDGs in member states and throughout the UN system. These efforts are coordinated through the Sustainable Development Group, composed of the heads of various UN agencies and chaired since 2017 by UN deputy secretary-general Amina Mohammed, who had shaped the SDGs process as special adviser to former Secretary-General Ban Ki-moon. (Her term was renewed in 2022 for an additional five years.) There is an extensive communication effort aimed at the general public, repackaging the SDGs as the "Global Goals," with shortened descriptions and intuitive icons stamped on a variety of UN materials. In 2019, UN Secretary-General António Guterres appointed an initial group of SDGs advocates, including US actor Forest Whitaker, Queen Mathilde of Belgium, and Chinese entrepreneur Jack Ma. Through such celebrity efforts, the hope is to foster international and domestic demand for change.

Efforts toward the SDGs were severely challenged by the Covid-19 pandemic, which was particularly disruptive for women, the poor, and other marginalized people. In 2023, halfway through the SDGs' timeframe, very few goals were on track. UN Deputy Secretary-General Amina Mohammed warned, "Our ability to achieve the 2030 Agenda hangs in the balance." She added, "The Sustainable Development Goals will fail without... powerful private sector partnerships that invest in the transitions necessary to accelerate development progress and get the [goals] back on track" (UN 2023).

Development Partners: Civil Society Groups, Charitable Foundations, and Corporations

As the SDGs illustrate, development requires many partners. Numerous actors besides governments and IGOs are important. Indeed, many development activities occur through partnerships with nonstate actors such as civil society groups, charitable foundations, and corporations (Jönsson 2013).

Civil society groups. As noted in Chapter 6, "civil society" is sometimes used as shorthand for NGOs, but it actually encompasses an array of faith-based groups, Indigenous peoples, youth movements, and other entities that are not necessarily formally organized. Civil society groups get much attention for their roles as policy implementers and watchdogs, but they are also propagators of new concepts and practices. For example, civil society groups helped articulate and spread the concept of sustainable development, and they also pioneered micro-credit, which are small loans made to women and other people who have trouble qualifying for regular bank loans. In short, civil society groups are often innovators in the governance of development.

Across the IGOs involved in the governance of development, the pace and extent of engagement with civil society varies greatly, with the UN system generally much more open than the Bretton Woods institutions. Since the 1980s, there has been strong pressure from donor governments and civil society for the World Bank and IMF to open up more (O'Brien et al. 2000). As discussed further in Chapter 12, part of the reasoning is that civil society involvement improves IGO effectiveness and accountability.

The World Bank Group has steadily opened up since the early 1980s. Through the Bank Information Center, the Bretton Woods Project, and the Civil Society Policy Forum, it has facilitated interactions and partnerships with civil society groups. Starting in 2001, the World Bank Group's field offices hired civil society specialists to help with program design, implementation, and oversight. In 1990 civil society was involved in only about 20 percent of World Bank projects; within two decades, that number increased to more than 80 percent. Pressure from civil society also helped mainstream sustainability, gender, and independent inspections within the World Bank Group. Although governments are still formally charged with implementing World Bank projects, there are numerous channels for civil society participation.

In contrast, the IMF has had a rockier relationship with civil society groups. Under pressure in the 1990s, it initiated more regular meetings and consultations—including the Civil Society Policy Forum, which is co-hosted with the World Bank and meets during their spring and annual meetings. Nonetheless, the IMF is still known as an organization whose work is too opaque and technical to be truly accessible for civil society. In fact, a study of its operations in six sub-Saharan African countries indicated that the IMF's contact with domestic publics remained "skewed toward urban, professional, propertied, male, and culturally Western circles" (Scholte 2012: 187). Although the IMF has opened more in recent decades, its links to civil society are not especially broad or deep (Tallberg et al. 2013).

Charitable foundations. Another important set of actors in development governance are private charitable foundations. The largest single source of international philanthropy is the United States, where official development assistance from the national government is regularly surpassed by private philanthropic outflows. As discussed in Chapter 6, the unifying theme behind charitable foundations is that their main beneficiaries are people other than the donors themselves. Beyond this core similarity, however, philanthropic institutions vary greatly.

Philanthropy has long been associated with religious or social groups. In the past century, however, many of the world's most prominent charitable foundations have been built around the extraordinary fortunes of individual businesspeople, such as John D. Rockefeller, Henry Ford, and Bill Gates. As a result, funding for development is influenced not only by a relatively small set of rich countries but also by a small set of rich individuals.

Besides offering financial assistance to developing countries directly, charitable foundations shape development through related policy areas, such as health or agriculture. For instance, the Rockefeller Foundation helped finance the League of Nations' health office, laying the groundwork for the WHO. In the 1960s, the Ford Foundation dedicated substantial resources to funding research into high-yield agriculture, fueling a "green revolution" in India and elsewhere. Since the 1990s, the Bill and Melinda Gates Foundation has become a force for delivering large-scale vaccination programs, bolstering education, and improving access to clean water in developing countries.

Given their impact, charitable foundations are subject to scrutiny and criticism (Youde 2019). Because they tend to be affiliated with rich people or rich countries, they may exacerbate existing inequalities and serve as additional tools for actors in the Global North. Because they wield tremendous resources, they can prompt states to undertake activities that are not a national priority or to shirk in providing goods that ought to be delivered by governments. And, because they shape public policy but are not directly accountable to the general public, they may subvert democratic processes or local preferences. For all of these reasons, charitable foundations are important for development but are also controversial.

Corporations. Private-sector corporations are another important but controversial set of actors. Whereas the level of ODA from governments has been fairly steady since the 1980s, flows of private capital to developing countries have increased dramatically. Some of the primary beneficiaries were the "Asian Tigers," whose impressive development in the 1980s and 1990s was fueled by both their governments' mercantilist policies and corporations' large investment inflows.

In recent years, Africa has succeeded in drawing heavy Chinese investment through governmental and private-sector channels. Much of this has been directed toward extracting natural resources and building infrastructure. Some critics see this as quasi-colonialism since Chinese companies frequently rely on Chinese managers and labor, downplay environmental stewardship and labor rights, and undertake projects that serve Chinese rather than local interests (French 2014).

It is rare for private corporations to make investment decisions based on which people or places need it most. After all, the people or places in greatest need also tend to face political, economic, or social challenges that can make private investors nervous. Instead, corporations often direct their money to "safer" middle-income countries. Therefore, although Africa is the world's most capital-poor region, it receives only a relatively small portion of private capital flows—and most of what it receives is targeted at a handful of countries, including South Africa, Ghana, Morocco, Egypt, and Nigeria. This pattern plays out in the rest of the world, too, with only a small portion of private international finance going to the least-developed countries.

Although many governments go to great lengths to attract private investment, these capital flows can be fickle. After pandemics, natural disasters, political upheavals, and other shocks, corporations face strong temptations to reduce or even reverse their capital flows. This results in large fluctuations across time and across countries. Even though private capital flows have contributed to several development success stories and often surpass ODA, their volatility makes them a tricky tool for long-term development.

Increasingly, development is acknowledged to be a multifaceted task that relies on an array of actors, including corporations, charitable foundations, civil society groups, IGOs, and governments. Consequently, these actors have come together in various constellations to tackle particular aspects of development. As discussed in Chapter 11, one example is the Global Alliance for Vaccines and Immunizations, a public–private partnership that involves the Bill and Melinda Gates Foundation, the WHO, governments, pharmaceutical companies, civil society groups, and others. A similarly diverse set of actors may be necessary to make progress on the SDGs and other development initiatives (Andonova 2017).

Key Themes in Development Governance

At the heart of the governance of development is the aim to bridge the gap between the Global South and the Global North. This is more easily said than done because the gap involves not only wealth and power but also healthcare, education, housing, empowerment of women, and more. Given the policy overlaps and multiple actors in development, experts are divided about whether these moving parts work in tandem or at cross-purposes (Sachs 2005; Collier 2007; Easterly 2008). China and some other countries have made tremendous progress in recent decades, but many other areas (most notably parts of Africa and Latin America) remain disadvantaged. Much faith has been invested in the SDGs, for example, and the "whole of UN" approach to maximizing progress toward them. But the UN and other development governance actors continue to struggle with fragmented or duplicated efforts, lack of resources, and the difficulty of serving both donors and recipients.

Multinational Corporations: From Regulation to Partnering

MNCs span all three aspects of economic governance: trade, finance, and development. MNCs also span a wide range of industries and countries, as exemplified by the world's ten biggest companies according to *Fortune* magazine in 2022: Walmart, Amazon, State Grid, China National Petroleum, Sinopec Group, Saudi Aramco, Apple, Volkswagen, China State Construction Engineering, and CVS Health. Despite being a crucial part of the international economy, MNCs are not unequivocally beneficial. They may dodge taxes, bribe officials, damage the environment, abuse workers, and engage in other negative behaviors. Since the 1970s, governments and IGOs have experimented with both regulating and partnering with MNCs.

MNC Regulation Through IGOs

In 1974, the UN Commission on Transnational Corporations initiated an effort to regulate MNCs through a code of conduct that built on the idea of corporate social responsibility: "the economic, legal, ethical, and discretionary expectations that society has on businesses at a given point in time" (Carroll 1979: 500). The idea of corporate social responsibility stemmed from nineteenth-century concerns about the Industrial Revolution's harm to workers. Over time, concerns expanded to nonindustrial companies and nonworker issues, such as tax evasion and product safety. By the 1970s, many governments had implemented regulatory bodies to address problems at the local or national level, but other than this early UN effort which ended in 1994, few IGOs were dealing with corporations operating internationally.

An exception, then and now, is the OECD. With its small and relatively cohesive membership of wealthy market-based democracies, the OECD is well positioned to deal with MNCs, many of which have headquarters or substantial business operations in its member states. Since the 1970s, the OECD has been the locus for developing both nonbinding and binding regulations. For example, the OECD's 1976 Guidelines for Multinational Enterprises are a wide-ranging set of recommendations monitored by national contact points; the OECD's 1997 Anti-Bribery Convention is a legally binding agreement that requires adhering states to make bribery of foreign public officials a crime. Although in the 1990s a draft agreement on investment was not approved, OECD members have since agreed on voluntary guidelines giving MNCs the same treatment as domestic corporations so policies on labor, the environment, and bribery apply to both domestic and foreign companies. The OECD also has shaped economic policies beyond its own members. In 2021, 136 states agreed to an OECD plan for a 15 percent global minimum corporate tax rate that targets corporations' practice of placing their nominal headquarters in a "tax haven" country with low or no corporate taxes, even though much of their operations and revenues are in countries with higher taxes. Through this and other initiatives, the OECD continues to be a central player in regulating MNCs.

Another important regulator is the EU Commission, which is particularly vigilant in combating anticompetitive activities. Concerned about a monopoly in jet engines in 2001, it essentially vetoed a merger of two US-based companies, General Electric and Honeywell, on the grounds that the merger would eliminate competition. In a controversial case that dragged from 2004 to 2012, it fined Microsoft for making computer software that was purposefully incompatible with other companies' products. The Commission also has been energetic in defending people's internet privacy. Any company that provides services to EU citizens must abide by the EU General Data Protection Regulation, which restricts the transfer of personal information abroad. Soon after this regulation came into force in 2018, the Commission began levying fines on Google, Facebook, and other internet companies. Thus, the EU regulates the behavior of MNCs far beyond Europe.

Corporate Self-Regulation and NGO Monitoring

IGOs are not the only actors trying to regulate MNCs. MNCs also try to regulate themselves to avert or delay formal governmental regulations, appeal to customers or investors, or mollify concerned NGOs. Such self-regulation comes in three main forms. One centers on an individual company. Twitter, for example, developed rules for dealing with digitally manipulated media, false claims about elections and voting, and health misinformation. Many of those company rules were rescinded, however, after the entrepreneur Elon Musk acquired Twitter in 2022. A second form of self-regulation centers on a particular set of companies. In banking, for instance, over 100 financial institutions in more than thirty countries have adopted the Equator Principles to assess and manage environmental and social risks posed by the projects they fund. A third form of self-regulation involves multiple stakeholders. For example, the Clean Clothes Campaign is a network of labor unions, consumers, researchers, NGOs, and companies that promote adherence to a code of conduct to improve working conditions in the garment industry.

Self-regulation—whether involving one company, a set of companies, or multiple stakeholders—has disadvantages and advantages compared with regulation by states or IGOs (Papadopoulos 2013). Because corporations may prefer minimal standards serving their own interests, ceding regulatory space to them hardly seems democratic or ambitious. On the other hand, companies are often faster and nimbler than states or IGOs in reacting to different circumstances; in places where governments are disconnected from or unconcerned with ordinary people, companies' reactions even may be superior. It is hard to know whether the advantages outweigh the disadvantages, partly because the evidence on self-regulation is still mostly anecdotal.

NGOs have also stepped in as corporate monitors and whistle-blowers, as discussed in Chapter 6. One example is Transparency International, which annually releases a Corruption Perceptions Index used by the public and private sectors. Another example is Corporate Accountability International (previously known as Infact), which became famous in an infant formula campaign against Nestlé in the early 1980s and later spearheaded an anti-tobacco campaign that helped produce the WHO tobacco convention (discussed in Chapter 11). As corporate self-regulation has grown, monitoring by NGOs has grown, too.

Partnership and Collaboration: The UN Global Compact and the UN Guiding Principles

As the difficulties of regulation and self-regulation became clearer, governments and IGOs turned to collaborating with MNCs. UN personnel had long recognized the desirability of devising standards of corporate social responsibility. After the UN Commission on Transnational Corporations was disbanded in 1994, UN personnel persisted, eventually producing two collaborative initiatives: first the UN Global Compact, then the UN Guiding Principles on Business and Human Rights.

The Global Compact was proposed by UN Secretary-General Kofi Annan at the World Economic Forum in 1999 and began operating the next year. Its purpose is to stimulate collaboration between corporations and UN bodies, informed by research centers and civil society groups. One of its main designers, former Harvard professor John Ruggie, characterizes it as a global governance "experiment" involving a set of nested networks (Ruggie 2001, 2013). The Global Compact contains ten voluntary, nonbinding principles in four areas: human rights, labor, the environment, and anticorruption. By 2023, it had grown to over 12,000 corporate participants and other stakeholders, operating in more than 160 countries.

The Global Compact has had mixed results, however (Podrecca et al. 2022). Critics have noted that its large number of participants do not include some of the world's most important companies, and there are relatively few participants from some regions. Moreover, as a voluntary and nonbinding arrangement, it lacks mechanisms for enforcement. A corporation can be delisted if it fails to meet the deadline for reporting how it has integrated the voluntary principles into its business strategies and operations. Since corporations can choose which provisions to apply, however, they can claim progress even without overhauling their practices or tackling the most severe problems. As to whether the Global Compact has fundamentally altered norms of corporate social responsibility, the empirical evidence is inconclusive.

A second UN attempt to collaborate with MNCs has resulted in the UN Guiding Principles on Business and Human Rights. Approved by the Human Rights Council in 2011, the principles are built around a three-pillared "protect, respect, and remedy" framework in which states have a duty to protect human rights, corporations are responsible for respecting human rights, and people must have access to mechanisms for remedying violations of human rights. The framework contains thirty-one principles, overseen by a working group of five independent experts. The Guiding Principles have won acceptance from a wide variety of corporations, bridging some of the previous rifts between corporations' home and host countries.

As with the Global Compact, opinions about the Guiding Principles are mixed. On the one hand, they have been associated with increased human rights litigation in national courts and the drafting of due diligence laws in Germany and the EU. They were praised on their ten-year anniversary as a "breakthrough," a major first step in addressing and preventing human rights violations within complex global supply chains (European Coalition on Corporate Justice 2021). On the other hand, ready acceptance by corporations and governments may indicate the Global Principles are not sufficiently demanding. Critics point out that corporations do not have a mere "responsibility" to "respect" human rights—rather, they have an obligation to manifest human rights. NGOs such as Human Rights Watch have been particularly critical of the lack of enforcement mechanisms, and the UN Human Rights Council has expressed concern about threats and attacks on human rights defenders in businesses.

The Challenges of Economic Governance

Trade, finance, and development are three core aspects of economic governance, and they exhibit some common themes. First, there are the persistent tensions between the Global North and the Global South, and disparities between the rich and the poor raise difficult questions. Whose needs are most important? Who gets to lead? Do current governance structures mitigate inequalities or reinforce them? Second, economic issues intersect with each other and with many other policy areas, including food, health, the environment, and state and human security. As shown by the SDGs, making improvements is a complex undertaking. Third, economic issues are not for states and IGOs alone. Corporations, labor unions, civil society groups, Indigenous people, and many other nonstate actors are important, too.

Suggested Further Reading

Drezner, Daniel W. (2014) *The System Worked: How the World Stopped Another Great Depression*. New York: Oxford University Press.

Johnson, Tana, and Andrew Heiss. (2022) "Liberal Institutionalism." In *International Organization and Global Governance*, 3rd ed., edited by Thomas Weiss and Rorden Wilkinson. New York: Routledge, pp. 120–132.

Henning, Randall. (2017) *Tangled Governance: International Regime Complexity, the Troika, and the Euro Crisis*. New York: Oxford University Press.

Nelson, Stephen. (2017) *The Currency of Confidence: How Economic Beliefs Shape the IMF's Relationship with its Borrowers*. Ithaca, NY: Cornell University Press.

Park, Susan, and Jonathan R. Strand, eds. (2015) *Global Economic Governance and the Development Practices of the Multilateral Development Banks*. New York: Routledge.

Vreeland, James Raymond. (2015) *The International Monetary Fund (IMF): Politics of Conditional Lending*, 2nd ed. New York: Routledge.

9

Protecting
Human Rights

Case Study: Documenting War Crimes in Ukraine

Russia's invasion of Ukraine on February 24, 2022, posed a major challenge for global governance and for many international organizations, including the United Nations, the European Union, the Organization of Security and Cooperation in Europe (OSCE), and the Council of Europe. The invasion was a blatant violation of the UN Charter's prohibition on the use of force to settle disputes and a clear crime of aggression as discussed in Chapter 7. Within days, there was evidence of extensive war crimes and crimes against humanity committed by Russian troops.

In addition to condemnations by the UN General Assembly and European Union, the war led to an extraordinary mobilization by human rights experts and activists from the UN, International Criminal Court (ICC), OSCE, NGOs, and Ukraine itself to gather and document evidence of these crimes. Never before had there been such an effort while a war was under way and never before had there been the means for local civilians to video evidence and post on social media, for experts to use satellite images to capture and verify evidence, and for human rights activists to interview victims and observers in real time. Likewise, never before during a war had there been such rapid calls to hold the perpetrators accountable for these human rights violations and to consider in what type of international court or tribunal they could be brought to trial.

The list of war crimes and crimes against humanity committed by Russian military forces have ranged from bombing schools, hospitals, apartment buildings, electrical power infrastructure, and cultural sites to

(continued)

rape, torture, indiscriminate killings of civilians and summary executions, kidnapping children and taking them to Russia for adoption, the use of cluster munitions, and threats to nuclear power facilities. The names of Ukrainian towns and villages such as Bucha, Izium, and Mariupol gained notoriety for the widely publicized evidence of crimes committed. Russia and President Vladimir Putin are also being accused of the crime of aggression, and the prosecutor of the ICC issued an arrest warrant in March 2023 for Putin and Russian Commissioner for Children's Rights Maria Lvova-Belova for war crimes, specifically the unlawful deportation of children from Ukraine to Russia.

The effort to document these crimes in real time owes much to how the concepts of genocide, war crimes, crimes against humanity, and the crime of aggression have been developed over more than 150 years since the very first Geneva Convention on the treatment of wounded soldiers and prisoners of war was concluded in the 1860s. That effort also stems from the evolution of processes since the end of World War II and the Nuremburg and Tokyo war crimes trials to hold the guilty accountable in some way. These processes—especially the International Criminal Tribunals for Yugoslavia and Rwanda, the ICC, and the hybrid courts for Sierra Leone and Cambodia—have demonstrated the importance of document-

ing crimes. They have also contributed to refining definitions of what constitute these crimes. Only in 2018, for example, did ICC members conclude work on a definition of the crime of aggression—something that had proved elusive in innumerable UN debates.

For the crimes committed in Ukraine, there were a number of proposals by late 2022 for holding Russia and Russian military personnel accountable. Although the ICC prosecutor opened an investigation shortly after Russia invaded Ukraine, this was not a likely route because neither Russia nor Ukraine are ICC members (although in 2014 Ukraine accepted ICC jurisdiction for crimes committed on its territory). Any effort by the UN Security Council to create a tribunal would be blocked by Russia's veto. More likely is a special tribunal or court similar to those for Sierra Leone and Cambodia, where authorization would come from the UN General Assembly for the UN Secretary-General to negotiate an agreement with Ukraine to set up a court. Given the number of people with experience in setting up and running prior international criminal tribunals, much less time would be needed to establish rules of procedure and evidence than was the case in the past. It took four years to get the ICC operational (1998–2002), for example. These past tribunals dealt with genocide, war crimes, and crimes against humanity. The defini-

(continued)

tion of crime of aggression has not yet been prosecuted since agreement on the definition was only reached in 2018. To do so will require that a tribunal be designated an international court so that Putin, for example, would not have immunity as a head of state (Clancy 2022).

Subsequent sections of this chapter examine the evolution of international criminal law and justice and the broader processes of defining, promoting, monitoring, and enforcing international human rights and humanitarian norms along with the roles of IGOs and NGOs in the global governance of human rights.

The extraordinary and unprecedented effort to document war crimes and crimes against humanity while the war in Ukraine still rages highlights the dramatic increase in attention to human rights issues since the end of World War II. In 1989, Zbigniew Brzezinski (1989: 256) called this trend the "single most magnetic political idea of the contemporary time." Indeed, in spite of the tensions between the norms of sovereignty and nonintervention and human rights norms, that idea has spurred the development of a broad range of international rights norms and global human rights governance initiatives.

The Roots of Human Rights and Humanitarian Norms

The question of who should be protected—who is human—and how they should be protected has broadened over the centuries. Beginning with the nineteenth-century abolition of the slave trade, formerly enslaved people were granted nominal rights and protections. The rights of those wounded and taken prisoner during war were articulated with the first Geneva Convention in 1863. In the mid–twentieth century, colonialism came to an end as the norm of self-determination of colonial peoples took hold.

The Holocaust—Nazi Germany's campaign of genocide against Jews, the Roma, and other "undesirables"—was a powerful impetus to the development of the contemporary human rights movement. In the 1970s, human rights violations in the Soviet Union and Eastern Europe drew growing condemnation, as did the "disappearances" of individuals under authoritarian regimes in Chile and Argentina. South Africa's egregious policy of apartheid—the systematic repression and violence against the majority of the country's population solely on the basis of race—had a similar mobilizing effect. The dissolution of the Soviet Union, the downfall of other communist regimes, and the wave of democratization in the early 1990s liberated international efforts to promote human rights from the ideological conflict of the Cold War. The war in the former Yugoslavia and genocide in Rwanda created pressure for prosecuting those responsible for war crimes, crimes against humanity, and genocide. The increased numbers and activism of international and national human rights NGOs played a major role in efforts to address these issues and other situations of human rights abuses.

In addition, the revolution in communication technologies since the early 1990s has magnified the awareness of events involving human rights abuses by broadcasting images of genocide, ethnic violence, the use of child soldiers, and starving populations. In a twenty-four-hour news cycle, media report the abuses of governments. Meanwhile, nonstate actors, the internet, and social media are used to share information and mobilize responses.

In the 1990s, the expansion of democracy magnified the pressure for greater respect for human rights. Since the beginning of the twenty-first century, however, Freedom House (Repucci and Slipowitz 2022) has documented that with an increase in authoritarian governments, there has been a steady decline in freedom and checks on governments' power and human rights abuses. The rise of China as a major global power with different human rights priorities constitutes a further challenge to the realization of universal human rights standards. Still, the progress achieved in articulating human rights norms and establishing mechanisms of international accountability for how states treat their citizens remain in place. We turn to look briefly at the roots of human rights and humanitarian norms in major religions and in widely divergent philosophical traditions.

Religious Traditions

Hinduism, Judaism, Christianity, Buddhism, Islam, and Confucianism all assert the dignity of individuals and people's responsibility to their fellow humans. Hindus prohibit infliction of physical or mental pain on others. Jews support the sacredness of individuals, as well as the responsibility of the individual person to help those in need. Buddhism's Noble Eightfold Path includes right thought and action toward all beings. Islam teaches equality of races and racial tolerance. Although the relative importance of these values may vary, Paul Gordon Lauren (1998: 11) notes that "early ideas about general human rights . . . did not originate exclusively in one location like the West or even with any particular form of government like liberal democracy, but were shared throughout the ages by visionaries from many cultures in many lands who expressed themselves in different ways."

The Philosophers and Political Theorists

Like the world's religious thinkers, philosophers and political theorists have conceptualized human rights, although they differ on many specific issues and ideas. Philosophers from the liberal persuasion traditionally have emphasized individual rights that the state can neither usurp nor undermine. John Locke (1632–1704), among others, asserted that individuals are equal and autonomous beings whose natural rights predate both national and international law. Public authority is designed to secure these rights.

Key historical documents detail these rights, beginning with the English Magna Carta in 1215, the French Declaration of the Rights of Man in 1789, and the Bill of Rights in the US Constitution in 1791, which declared that no individual should be "deprived of life, liberty or property, without due process of law." Liberal theorists emphasize the importance of political and civil rights, including free speech, free assembly, free press, and freedom of religion; by custom, these rights have been referred to as first-generation human rights. To some theorists and many US pundits, these are not only the key human rights but also the only recognized human rights.

Theorists influenced by Karl Marx and other socialist thinkers have focused more on minimum material rights that the state is responsible for providing to advance the well-being of their citizens. Referred to as second-generation human rights, these include the right to education, healthcare, social security, and housing, although the amount guaranteed is unspecified. Without these rights, socialist theorists believe that political and civil rights are meaningless.

These religious traditions, philosophers, and political theorists influenced the work of those who drafted the first major statements of core human rights norms: the American Declaration of the Rights and Duties of Man, approved by the Ninth International Conference of the American States in 1948, and the Universal Declaration of Human Rights approved by the UN General Assembly, also in 1948.

Over time, the scope of these core norms has been expanded by the UN and regional organizations focusing on human rights for specific groups of people. These include Indigenous people, children, women, migrant workers, the disabled, refugees, and lesbian, gay, bisexual, transgender, and intersex (LGBTI) persons. Several UN resolutions also affirm certain collective rights, including the rights to development, a clean environment, and democracy. There is much more controversy over these newer third-generation human rights, raising the question of whether they truly are universal human rights or reflect Western bias.

Ongoing debate revolves around the relative priority of these three generations of rights. In Western liberal thinking, political and civil rights are clearly given higher status, whereas in many parts of the world, including China, priority goes to economic and social rights or to collective rights, such as the right to development. Just as the West has dominated economic relations, it has dominated human rights standard-setting. The majority of international and regional human rights governance mechanisms protects civil and political rights. The other two generations of human rights receive less attention, in part because it is more difficult to establish standards of compliance for economic, social, and collective rights. There is also ongoing debate about the universality of human rights norms.

The Debate over Universalism and Cultural Relativism

Are human rights truly universal—that is, applicable to all people, in all states, religions, and cultures? Are they inalienable—that is, fundamental to every person? Are they necessary to life? Are they nonnegotiable—so essential that they cannot be taken away? Or are rights dependent on culture?

Since the 1970s, some Muslims have questioned the notion of universal human rights. Two issues—the rights of Muslims versus non-Muslims and the rights of men versus women—have posed the most problems, reflecting conflicting interpretations of Islamic teachings and practice. One approach is to accept the notion of equality but offer reasons for why the principle of equality is not undermined by different rules protecting one group over another (Mayer 2013). Another approach is to proclaim the universality of human rights and reject the use of culture or faith to restrict those rights.

In the early 1990s, a number of Asian states argued that the principles in the Universal Declaration and other documents represented Western values being imposed on them and that the West was interfering in their internal affairs with its definition of human rights. They also argued that advocating the rights of the individual over the welfare of the community is unsound and contrary to some cultural traditions.

Some of the debate is clearly political, reflecting tensions between authoritarian states concerned about human rights intervention in their domestic affairs and Western democratic states eager to promote political change. The debate over universality versus cultural relativism is particularly sensitive, with respect to issues of religion, women's status, child protection, family planning, divorce, LGBTI rights, and practices such as female circumcision.

The Vienna Declaration and Programme of Action, adopted at the 1993 World Conference on Human Rights, stated: "All human rights are universal, indivisible and interdependent and interrelated." Regional arrangements "should reinforce universal human rights standards." Yet that declaration included the qualification that "the significance of national and regional particularities and various historical, cultural and religious backgrounds must be borne in mind." Thus, Stephen Hopgood (2013) has argued that although universalism has been the promise of the past, today it is ill adapted to the diversity of the multipolar world. This is even more true with debates about Western bias, the conditions under which local factors take precedence, whether civil and political rights are pushed at the expense of economic and social rights, and the implications of the increase in nationalist demagoguery, US decline, and China's rise as a potential hegemon (Braaten 2021).

These debates have led some human rights scholars to speculate about the future of universal human rights (Hopgood et al. 2018; Howard-Hassmann 2018). Is one encouraged, for example, as Brysk (2018) is by large popular protests such as the 2017 Women's March in the United States or by research showing the positive effects of human rights treaties (Creamer and Simmons 2020)? Or does one adopt a more pragmatic view that emphasizes universalism less and improvements in people's lives more (Hopgood et al. 2018)?

The Evolution of Humanitarian Norms

Just as human rights norms emerged and changed over time, so have humanitarian norms. Originating in the nineteenth century as warfare became increasingly destructive due to the technological capabilities of new weapons, humanitarian norms were created to save the lives of wounded soldiers and civilians and provide relief in an impartial way in conflict zones. The first multilateral treaty was the 1864 Geneva Convention for the Amelioration of the Condition of the Wounded, which required signatories to respect the neutrality of military hospitals and staff so they could provide medical care for wounded soldiers regardless of their nationality. This laid the basis for the International Committee of the Red Cross, created in 1863, and affiliated national committees to work anywhere in the world in the name of shared humanity. As Paul Lauren (2003: 61) notes, "the signing of this convention also demonstrated that it was war rather than peace—the care of soldiers rather than civilians—that stimulated and legitimized such active international interest in the rights of the individual." This original Geneva Convention led to subsequent efforts, such as the 1899 Hague Peace Conference (Chapter 3), to expand what came to be known as humanitarian law—that is, legal protections for victims of wars on land and sea (Lauren 2003: 62).

After World War II, the foundations of contemporary international humanitarian law were laid in four 1949 Geneva Conventions and two protocols concluded in 1977. These were designed to protect civilians, prisoners of war, and wounded soldiers as well as ban particular methods of war (e.g., bombing hospitals) and certain weapons that cause unnecessary suffering (e.g., poisonous gases). More recent conventions on land mines, cluster munitions, and chemical weapons (discussed in Chapter 7) are considered part of international humanitarian law. Together, these various conventions establish the legal basis for war crimes.

As discussed in Chapter 7, the humanitarian crises of the 1990s gave rise to efforts to establish the norm of responsibility to protect (R2P) in future situations. Scholars and practitioners have extensively debated R2P's status since the 2005 World Summit endorsed it and Security Council mandates for peace operations began to incorporate protection of civilians. Aiden Hehir (2019), however, concludes that R2P has become largely a "hollow norm" that has, in effect, been co-opted by states and is largely ineffective and unenforced except as it creates greater support for protection of civilian mandates in the Security Council.

We explore the relationship between humanitarianism and human rights in more detail later. At this point, it is important to look at the key role of states in protecting as well as abusing human rights and then the roles of IGOs and NGOs in globalizing human rights norms and establishing mechanisms for promoting, monitoring, and enforcing them.

The Key Role of States:
Protectors and Abusers of Human Rights

States, as realists posit, are primarily responsible for protecting human rights standards in their own jurisdictions. Yet as noted earlier, the development of international human rights law creates obligations and expectations that are in tension with the Westphalian norms of sovereignty and noninterference. Liberal democratic states have based human rights practices largely on political and civil liberties. Socialist and developing states have prioritized social and economic protections. Since the late 1970s, many countries in both categories have created national and subnational human rights institutions to promote and protect human rights domestically. These include national commissions, specialized commissions, and ombudsmen. Their purpose is to empower local actors and help embed human rights norms domestically (Kim 2013). In ratifying international human rights conventions, states accept responsibility for protecting their citizens against human rights abuses whether committed by state agents or private actors such as business enterprises under their jurisdiction, and for providing redress for those whose human rights have been violated.

Western states in the Global North led the way in drafting the UN Charter's human rights provisions, but Latin American states, a bloc of twenty out of the fifty countries at the 1945 San Francisco conference, also supported these measures. Along with other democratic states, they succeeded in getting the final Charter to reference human rights seven times, including listing promotion of human rights as one of the basic purposes of the UN and calling on the UN Economic and Social Council (ECOSOC) to set up a human rights commission.

Some Western states have attempted to internationalize their commitments to human rights by supporting human rights elsewhere. At US insistence, human rights guarantees were written into new constitutions in Iraq and Afghanistan. The EU has required candidate members to show significant progress toward improving their records on political and civil liberties prior to accession.

States are not just protectors and promoters, however; they are also the primary violators of human rights. Regime type and real or perceived threats are explanations for states' abuse of their own citizens. In general, authoritarian states are more likely to abuse political and civil rights, while many countries in the Global South, even liberal democratic ones, may be unable to meet basic obligations of social and economic rights or collective rights because of scarce resources. All states threatened by civil strife or terrorist activity, including democratic ones, are apt to use repression against domestic or foreign challengers. State security prevails over individual rights in such situations.

In fact, the International Covenant on Civil and Political Rights acknowledges that heads of state may revoke some political and civil liberties when national security is threatened. The United States, for example, has faced allegations of human rights violations concerning the continued detention at its base in Guantánamo Bay, Cuba of individuals linked to the September 11, 2001, attacks, and China has faced regular criticism for infringements of freedoms of assembly and expression and for its suppression of Uyghurs and Tibetans. Poor states or states experiencing deteriorating economic conditions often repress political rights in an effort by the elite to maintain power and divert attention from economic problems. In some cases, rights may be deliberately undermined or denied because of discrimination on the basis of race, creed, national origin, or gender, as in the case of women under the Taliban regime in Afghanistan. Finally, states with high degrees of fractionalization along ethnic, religious, or ideological lines often evidence the worst abuses.

International Human Rights Institutions and Mechanisms
The UN, other IGOs, and NGOs have played key roles in the process of globalizing human rights, establishing the norms, institutions, and activities for giving effect to the idea of universal rights. The international human rights movement—a dense network of human rights–oriented NGOs and dedicated individuals—has drafted much of the language of human rights conventions and mounted transnational campaigns to promote human rights norms. These groups and individuals and the processes by which they have persuaded governments to adopt human rights norms demonstrate the power of ideas to reshape definitions of national interests, a process best explained by constructivist theorizing.

NGOs and the International Human Rights Movement
As noted in Chapter 6, NGOs have long been active in human rights activities, with antislavery groups being among the first and most active. In the late eighteenth century, abolitionists in the United States (Society for the Relief of Free Negroes Unlawfully Held in Bondage), Great Britain (Society for Effecting the Abolition of the Slave Trade in Britain), and France (Société des Amis des Noirs) organized to end the slave trade. Although they were not powerful enough to effect an immediate international change, the British group pressed Parliament in 1807 to ban the slave trade for

British citizens. In 1815, the Final Act of the Congress of Vienna included an Eight Power Declaration that the slave trade was "repugnant to the principles of humanity and universal morality" (Lauren 1996: 27). Willingness to sign a statement of principles, however, did not mean states were ready to take specific measures to abolish the practice.

Over time, many human rights and humanitarian NGOs formed around specific issues either during or immediately following wars. As noted earlier, the International Red Cross was established in the 1860s to protect wounded soldiers, prisoners of war, and civilians caught up in war. During and after World War I, numerous NGOs formed to protect women and children from war's devastation and to ban the use of poisonous gas as a weapon. With World War II, humanitarian relief organizations grew in number. Groups such as Catholic Relief Services, originally formed in 1943 as War Relief Services, provided emergency aid to refugees fleeing conflict in Europe. Later its mandate expanded to include providing humanitarian relief to the poor, the displaced, and people suffering from natural disasters. CARE, Oxfam, and others followed.

In the late 1970s, a series of events gave rise to what became the international human rights movement. In 1975, the Helsinki Accords were signed to promote human rights in Eastern Europe and the Soviet Union, and the UN convened the first World Conference for Women in Mexico City. In 1976, riots in Soweto, South Africa, and the murder of black South African leader Steve Biko in 1977 and the large number of "disappearances" and other human rights abuses in Latin America, were widely publicized. US President Jimmy Carter made human rights a priority in US foreign policy for the first time, and Amnesty International was awarded the 1977 Nobel Peace Prize. These events gave a boost to the establishment of a new generation of human rights NGOs, such as Helsinki Watch, the Mothers (and Grandmothers) of the Plaza de Mayo, and a host of women's groups. With the Cold War's end and the increased number of democratic countries in the 1980s and 1990s, another generation of NGOs developed, including the Open Society Institute.

Today there are thousands of human rights groups at the international, national, and grassroots levels. Amnesty International and Human Rights Watch are by far the largest, best-known, and most influential. Over time, these NGOs together forged the international human rights movement, aided by the rise of investigative journalism and the attention it has brought to human rights issues (Neier 2012: 5). The information revolution has facilitated the movement's ability to transmit such information across borders, and UN-sponsored global conferences have enabled groups to connect in person and to form networks.

Despite their diversity, human rights NGOs perform a variety of functions and roles, both independently and in conjunction with IGOs, in international human rights governance. These include educating the public, providing expertise in drafting human rights conventions, monitoring violations, shaming violators, and mobilizing public support for changes in national policies. They may undertake operational tasks, such as providing aid for victims of human rights abuses and training police and judges. In addition, NGOs provided much of the momentum for the 1993 UN-sponsored World Conference on Human Rights (Vienna) and the 1995 Fourth World Conference on Women (Beijing).

As discussed in Chapter 6, one major strategy used by NGOs generally involves organizing transnational campaigns on specific issues. In the human rights field, there have been many such campaigns against apartheid, child labor, and sweatshops, as well as those promoting the rights of Indigenous people, women, and migrant workers. These campaigns have often involved local groups and transnational coalitions. With the rise of the internet and social media, individuals and groups are able to voice their grievances swiftly to a worldwide audience and solicit sympathizers to take direct actions. As constructivists have shown, these campaigns shape discourse and ideas, leading to learning across multiple constituencies and norm creation. NGO campaigns also can use human rights as weapons, instruments of conflict, and tools of power that can serve both liberal and "illiberal ends," as Clifford Bob's work has demonstrated (Bob 2019).

Another strategy used by NGOs involves framing issues in ways that attract support. For example, NGOs successfully framed the issue of antipersonnel landmines (discussed in Chapter 7) as a humanitarian rather than an arms control issue because of the high incidence of injuries to children and livestock from deadly mines that remain on or in the ground long after a conflict has ended. The result of the framing was the 1997 convention banning landmines (Thakur and Maley 1999). In an example of where a choice of framing resulted in a "lost cause," Charli Carpenter (2014: 122–153) compared the unsuccessful effort to pitch infant male circumcision as a violation of bodily rights with the more successful campaign to ban female genital mutilation.

As strong and vocal as human rights NGOs are, they do not always get their way. They also do not always get access to the forums where human rights documents are drafted. At the 1993 Vienna Conference, for example, NGOs were restricted from participating in the drafting of documents. Thus, NGOs are not equal partners with states in human rights governance. Much of their success has been due to opportunities presented by the League of Nations and the UN.

The League of Nations
The League of Nations Covenant made little mention of human rights, despite persistent efforts by some delegates to include principles of racial

equality and religious freedom. One fascinating story concerns the efforts by representatives of the Japanese government to convince negotiators, including US President Woodrow Wilson, to adopt a statement on human rights and racial equality. As a victorious and economically advanced power, Japan felt it had a credible claim that such basic rights would not be rejected. But the initiative was blocked when the US representatives recognized that such a provision would doom Senate passage of the peace treaty (Lauren 1996: 82–93). The Covenant did include, however, specific provision for protection of minorities and dependent peoples in colonies held by Turkey and Germany, the defeated powers of World War I. These were placed under the mandate system, whereby a designated victor nation would administer the territory and supervise it through the Mandates Commission until independence.

Despite having no right of inspections, the Mandates Commission acquired a reputation for being thorough and neutral. The United Kingdom administered Palestine, Transjordan, Iraq, and Tanganyika; France assumed the same role for Syria and Lebanon. They divided responsibility for the Cameroons and Togoland; Belgium administered Rwanda-Urundi; South Africa administered South West Africa; and Japan administered several Pacific islands. Between 1932 and 1947, pressure from the Mandates Commission led to independence for the Arab mandates of Lebanon, Syria, Iraq, and Transjordan, with Palestine being a glaring exception. The mandates in Africa (Cameroons, Togoland, and Rwanda-Urundi) and in the Pacific were transferred to the UN trusteeship system in 1946. South Africa continued to administer South West Africa until 1989, despite several legal challenges, and a long campaign through the UN led by African states led to its independence as Namibia.

The mandate system gave those under its supervision a greater degree of protection from abuses than they would have enjoyed otherwise. It reflected the growing sentiment that territories were not to be annexed after wars, that the international community had responsibilities over dependent peoples, and that the eventual goal was self-determination.

In addition, Woodrow Wilson's powerful promise of a right to self-determination brought groups from all over the world to the 1919 Paris Peace Conference. As a result, the rights of minorities and the corollary responsibilities of states were a major topic. Five agreements, known as the Minority Treaties, required beneficiaries of the peace settlement, such as Poland, Czechoslovakia, and others, "to assure full and complete protection" to all their inhabitants "without distinction of birth, nationality, language, race, or religion." These agreements also provided for civil and political rights. Later, the League made admission of new members contingent on a pledge to protect minority rights. Minority rights were a major agenda item for the League bodies, creating "significant precedents for increased international protection of human rights" (Lauren 2003: 114).

In other human rights activities, the League conducted a study of slavery after intensive lobbying by the British Anti-Slavery and Aborigines Protection Society and established the Temporary Slavery Commission, whose report led to the 1926 International Convention on the Abolition of Slavery and the Slave Trade. Although not listing specific practices or including monitoring provisions, the treaty was groundbreaking in setting the standard regarding slavery.

The League also established principles for assisting refugees and created the first organization dedicated to refugee relief, the Refugee Organization. Pressed by NGOs, it devoted attention to the issues of women's and children's rights and the right to a minimum level of health, and in 1924 approved the Declaration on the Rights of the Child. In the 1930s, the League Assembly discussed the possibility of an international human rights document, but no action was ever taken.

Rights of workers were an integral part of the agenda of the International Labour Organization (ILO), as discussed in Chapter 3, and between 1919 and 1939, the ILO approved sixty-seven conventions that covered issues like hours of work, maternity protection, minimum age, and old-age insurance. The ILO's mandate to work for the improvement of workers' living conditions, health, safety, and livelihood was (and remains) consistent with concepts of economic and social rights. Because it did not die with the League, the ILO's work provided a foundation for other UN human rights activities, including an important model for monitoring the standards.

The United Nations

A very different climate shaped the drafting of the UN Charter. US President Franklin Roosevelt's famous "Four Freedoms" speech in 1941 called for "a world founded upon four essential freedoms," and his vision of "the moral order" formed a normative base for the Allies in World War II (Roosevelt 1941). The chilling revelation of Nazi concentration camps helped make human rights an international issue. At the founding UN conference in San Francisco, a broad spectrum of groups—from churches to women's groups and peace societies, along with delegates from democratic states in the Latin America and elsewhere—pushed for including human rights language in the Charter. The Preamble reaffirmed "faith in fundamental human rights, in the dignity and worth of the human person, in the equal rights of men and women and of nations large and small." Although the seven references to human rights in the Charter were more weakly worded than advocates had hoped, they placed the promotion of human rights among the central purposes of the new organization.

The UN Charter incorporated a broad perspective of human rights, going far beyond the view of the League of Nations. Included in Article 1 is the statement that the organization would be responsible for facilitating cooperation in areas of a "humanitarian character" and "promoting and encouraging respect for human rights and for fundamental freedoms for all without distinction as to race, sex, language, or religion." Articles 55(c) and 56 amplify the UN's responsibility to promote "universal respect for, and observance of, human rights and fundamental freedoms for all" and the obligation of member states to "take joint and separate action in cooperation with the Organization for the achievement of the purposes set forth in Article 55."

Although these provisions did not define what was meant by "human rights and fundamental freedoms," they established that human rights were a matter of international concern and that states had assumed some as-yet-undefined international obligation relating to them. Despite the inherent tension between establishing international standards and Article 2(7)'s principle of noninterference in a state's domestic affairs, these provided the UN with the legal authority to undertake the definition and codification of human rights. The first step in this direction was made by the General Assembly passing the Universal Declaration of Human Rights (UDHR) on December 10, 1948, discussed below. Taken together, the UN Charter and the UDHR represented a watershed moment.

The evolving UN human rights system. In 1946 and 1947, ECOSOC established the Commission on Human Rights, the Commission on the Status of Women, and the Sub-Commission on the Prevention of Discrimination and Protection of Minorities. Between 1946 and 2006, the Commission on Human Rights was the hub of the UN system's human rights activity and largely responsible for drafting and negotiating the major documents that elaborate and define human rights norms, including the UDHR, the international covenants, and conventions on issues ranging from torture to the rights of the child and of migrant workers. It conducted studies and issued reports. In 1970, the commission gained the authority to review complaints of human rights violations and thereafter, its annual sessions included hearing complaints and individual petitions as well as addressing major human rights themes, such as racism and violations of human rights in Israeli-occupied Arab territories.

Beginning in the 1970s, the Commission on Human Rights became the subject of intense criticism for targeting countries such as South Africa, Israel, and Chile while ignoring other violators. Nonetheless, a study of the commission's actions from 1979 to 2001 found that "targeting and punishment were driven to a considerable degree by the actual human rights records of potential targets" (Lebovic and Voeten 2006: 863). Still, there was a growing tendency to avoid direct criticisms of states (Forsythe 2009) and to elect rights violators such as Sudan, Zimbabwe, and Saudi Arabia as members and Libya (another violator) as chair. Criticism of the commission intensified when the United States lost its commission seat for the first time in 2001.

In 2006, the General Assembly voted to replace the Commission on Human Rights with the Human Rights Council (HRC), which reports to the General Assembly and whose forty-seven members are elected by secret ballot by a majority of members of the General Assembly for three-year renewable terms with seats distributed among the five recognized regional groups. The HRC meets at least ten weeks throughout the year and may convene special sessions, as it has done on more than thirty occasions since 2006. Special sessions in 2014 addressed the human rights situation in Iraq in light of abuses committed by Islamic State of Iraq and Syria and the situation in occupied Palestine; a special session in 2021 focused on human rights in Myanmar after the coup there.

To address the problem of having human rights violators among the membership, the human rights records of all potential council members are subject to scrutiny under what is known as the Universal Periodic Review (UPR), and with a two-thirds vote the council can suspend members suspected of abuses. These provisions have not remedied the problem. The fact that HRC membership is based on "equitable geographical distribution" means that the Global South holds the majority of seats and political factors rather than human rights records tend to influence who gets elected (Freedman 2013: 67–69). When Fiji—known for having supported investigations into abuses in a number of countries—was decisively elected in 2021 to serve as president of the council, the head of Human Rights Watch perceived a "victory for those who believe the HRC should be used to defend human rights" (Cumming-Bruce 2021).

The HRC has retained many of the mechanisms of the former commission, including the system of Special Procedures whereby it can mandate a special rapporteur or working group to address special country situations or thematic issues such as child soldiers. These are discussed further in the section below on monitoring. Figure 9.1 shows the relationships between the HRC and other entities in the UN system. In 2008, the HRC established an Advisory Committee made up of eighteen human rights experts representing various regions who form a think tank that conducts studies and provides research-based advice for the council. It draws on information from NGOs, specialized agencies, other IGOs, member states, and national human rights institutions.

Some of the HRC's work has attracted public attention. In 2009 and 2014, for example, it authorized fact-finding missions following conflicts in Gaza between Israel and Hamas. Both found evidence of potential war crimes and crimes against humanity. In 2013, the HRC established the Commission of Inquiry on Human Rights in the Democratic People's Republic of Korea. With testimony from witnesses, the commission's 2014 report cataloged systematic human rights abuses by the North Korean regime against its own citizens. North Korea vehemently denied the allegations. In

438

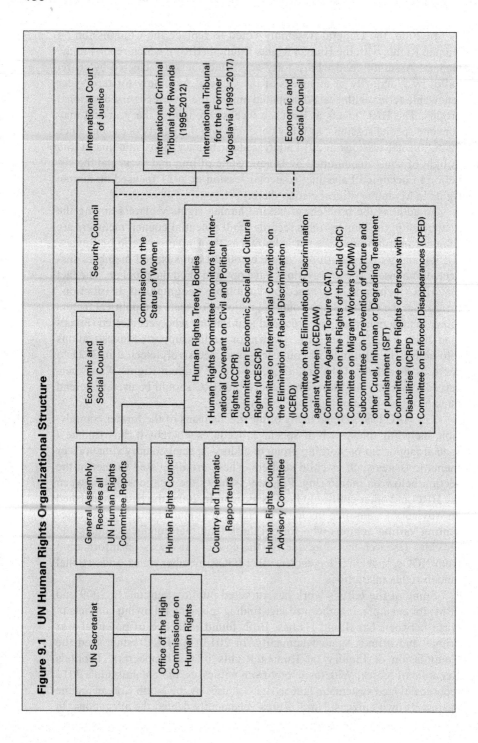

Figure 9.1 UN Human Rights Organizational Structure

International Court of Justice

International Criminal Tribunal for Rwanda (1995–2012)

International Tribunal for the Former Yugoslavia (1993–2017)

Economic and Social Council

Security Council

Economic and Social Council

Commission on the Status of Women

Human Rights Treaty Bodies
- Human Rights Committee (monitors the International Covenant on Civil and Political Rights (ICCPR)
- Committee on Economic, Social and Cultural Rights (ICESCR)
- Committee on International Convention on the Elimination of Racial Discrimination (ICERD)
- Committee on the Elimination of Discrimination against Women (CEDAW)
- Committee Against Torture (CAT)
- Committee on the Rights of the Child (CRC)
- Committee on Migrant Workers (ICMW)
- Subcommittee on Prevention of Torture and other Cruel, Inhuman or Degrading Treatment or punishment (SPT)
- Committee on the Rights of Persons with Disabilities (ICRPD
- Committee on Enforced Disappearances (CPED)

General Assembly Receives all UN Human Rights Committee Reports

Human Rights Council

Country and Thematic Rapporteurs

Human Rights Council Advisory Committee

UN Secretariat

Office of the High Commissioner on Human Rights

late 2014, prompted by the report, the Security Council took up the subject of North Korea's human rights violations and the report's recommendation that the Security Council refer the problem to the ICC. The issue was taken up by the Security Council again in 2015, 2016, and 2017, but China and Russia vetoed action. The very fact of putting the issue on the Security Council's agenda signifies how that body has become involved in human rights issues when violations are seen as a threat to international peace and security.

Despite these well-publicized actions, we must ask: is the HRC less politicized than its predecessor, the Commission on Human Rights? One empirical study of four years of council decisions found that the most controversial and polarizing resolutions were, indeed, sponsored by countries with blemished human rights records, including Cuba, Egypt, and Pakistan (Hug and Lukacs 2014). Indeed, common critiques include the persistence of politicization, repetitious statements, selectivity in how issues are treated, and voting in blocs (Freedman and Houghton 2017). There are "deep fault lines" between Northern and Southern countries on fundamental issues of international human rights law; the universality versus relativity of human rights; and third-generation rights issues, rights of LGBTI people, and racism and racial discrimination (Chane and Sharm 2016). Yet Joseph and Jenkin (2019: 77) suggest that the HRC has been misunderstood and argue that it is "a political body, so it is hardly surprising that the members act in a political way . . . [it] reflects the globe we live in today, not the Western-dominated globe of the colonial yesteryear."

The Office of the High Commissioner for Human Rights (OHCHR), created in 1993, is the UN focal point for human rights. While the UN High Commissioner for Human Rights (UNHCHR) is the most visible international advocate for human rights, the OHCHR is responsible for promoting human rights, mainstreaming them into the UN system, and informing and supporting relevant UN bodies. It serves as the secretariat for the HRC and supports the work of the Special Procedures (see Figure 9.1). Increasingly, the OHCHR has also assumed an operational role, providing technical assistance to countries in the form of training courses for judges and prison officials, electoral assistance, and advisory services on constitutional and legislative reform, among other things (Mertus 2009). Field offices in many countries help strengthen domestic institutions, promote compliance with international human rights standards, and report directly to the high commissioner on abuses. The UNHCHR sits on the UN Secretary-General's Senior Management Group. The office is heavily dependent on voluntary contributions from member states and institutional donors, however, since it receives only about 40 percent of its funding from the UN regular budget.

The effectiveness of the OHCHR depends partly on the legitimacy, personality, leadership skills, and initiatives of the high commissioner. Four of the eight commissioners to date have been women. The second commissioner

(Mary Robinson, former president of Ireland) and the fourth commissioner (Louise Arbour, former member of Canada's Supreme Court and chief prosecutor in the international ad hoc tribunals for Yugoslavia and Rwanda) elevated the effectiveness and prestige of the office. Likewise, South African judge Navanethem (Navi) Pillay, who served as fifth high commissioner from 2008 to 2014, was a strong and vocal commissioner who used her position in 2014 to press the Sri Lankan government to initiate an inquiry into human rights violations during its civil war and to condemn the anti-LGBT legislation passed by Nigeria and Uganda. In 2018, Michelle Bachelet, former president of Chile and first executive director of UN Women, became the seventh UNHCHR. She was followed in 2022 by Volker Türk, an Austrian with a long track record in the UN system, including working on refugee protection.

Although the former Commission on Human Rights and now the HRC have been the primary hubs for human rights activity in the UN, the General Assembly, by virtue of its central role for all issues, has also been important. Two of the assembly's main committees contribute to drafting human rights treaties. The Assembly must approve all UN human rights conventions. In the General Assembly's first session in 1946, India and other countries introduced the issue of South Africa's treatment of its Indian population, beginning debate over what became the UN's longest-running human rights issue: apartheid in South Africa. Colonialism was another prominent human rights issue during the UN's first twenty years. The General Assembly and almost all other UN bodies have condemned Israel's treatment of the Palestinians in the Occupied Territories, and the assembly has repeatedly condemned violations of human rights in North Korea, Iran, Syria, Afghanistan under the Taliban, and Myanmar, reflecting the majority of members at any given time.

Neither the Security Council nor the International Court of Justice traditionally had significant involvement with human rights issues. For the Security Council, this changed in 1990. During the Cold War years, the Council linked security threats with human rights violations in only two cases: the unilateral declaration of independence by a white minority regime in Southern Rhodesia (now Zimbabwe) in 1965, and the white minority apartheid regime in South Africa. Both were treated as situations that threatened international peace and security, and sanctions were applied under Chapter VII of the UN Charter.

Since 1990, the Security Council has repeatedly been faced with threats to peace connected with large-scale humanitarian crises and demands for intervention under Chapter VII. Ethnic cleansing, genocide, and other crimes against humanity led it not only to authorize interventions and peacekeeping as discussed in (Chapter 7) but also to include human rights activities in the mandates for peacekeeping operations and create two ad hoc war crimes tribunals (discussed below). Likewise, peacebuilding operations have increasingly needed to address human rights protection. Thus, the Security Council has come to embrace human rights norms and address not only specific situations where human rights violations create threats to peace and security (e.g., Myanmar in 2005 and 2017) but also broader issues, such as child soldiers, protection of civilians, and the role of women in promoting international peace and security.

The Rome Statute that created the ICC also gave the Security Council a role in referring situations involving war crimes and crimes against humanity to the court. This has been used in two cases—the situation in Darfur in 2005 and the situation in Libya in 2011. The Security Council is still hampered from addressing human rights issues when the interests of the P-5 or their allies are directly affected, however. In 2007, China and Russia vetoed a resolution on violations in Myanmar, claiming that such measures represented excessive interference in the country's domestic affairs. Yet in 2014 the Security Council unanimously condemned the violations of human rights and international humanitarian law by the Syrian government, a major step, given Russian and Chinese opposition to all previous draft resolutions on the Syrian conflict. Both, however, vetoed a 2014 draft resolution that would have referred the situation in Syria to the ICC and repeatedly blocked efforts to refer North Korea's human rights abuses to the ICC.

Where the ICC's role is clearly linked with human rights violations, it is highly unusual for the International Court of Justice (ICJ) to play any role in human rights governance given that it only takes cases involving disputes between states. It did confirm the principle of self-determination in the 1975 case regarding Western Sahara, noting that "self-determination requires a free and genuine expression of the will of the peoples concerned" (ICJ Advisory Opinion 1975). It concluded that South Africa had violated its continuing obligations toward South West Africa as a former League of Nations mandate under the UDHR (ICJ Advisory Opinion 1971). In 1993, the ICJ received the first case under the Genocide Convention. It concerned whether ethnic cleansing in Bosnia-Herzegovina constituted genocide. Indicative of the court's slow procedures, the case was decided only in 2007; a similar case involving Croatia and Serbia was begun in 2009 and concluded in 2015. In 2019, a case involving Myanmar's treatment of the Rohingya was filed with the ICJ.

As legal scholar Louis Henkin (1998: 512) noted, "The purpose of international concern with human rights is to make national rights effective under national laws and through national institutions." If that is true, then the task of IGOs like the UN is particularly problematic, because it poses the possibility of interfering in the domestic affairs of states, which violates one of the hallmark principles of state sovereignty. Nevertheless, the UN and regional organizations have undertaken a variety of functions in creating processes for states and nonstate actors to be key players in human rights governance, clearly establishing the legitimacy of such actions.

The Processes of Human Rights Governance

Over nearly eight decades, an international human rights regime has emerged that has articulated human rights norms and codified these standards in treaties, legal decisions, and practices. IGOs and NGOs have monitored the human rights records of states, compiled reports of abuses and compliance, promoted regime norms, and endeavored to enforce compliance when states have committed gross violations of those norms.

Setting Human Rights Standards and Norms

The prominent role of NGOs, transnational advocacy networks, and social movements in pushing for domestic laws and international treaties that set human rights standards has already been discussed. That role is well illustrated by the case of the anti-slavery movement.

NGOs. The nineteenth-century antislavery movement was one of the first examples of NGO activity that helped create the norm prohibiting slavery. With support from a diverse constituency in Great Britain—including religious groups, textile workers, rural housewives, and wealthy businessmen—the movement caught the attention of like-minded people in France and the Americas, forming the first transnational advocacy network. They used tactics such as letter-writing, petitions, popular theater, and public speeches. Networking across the Atlantic, they sent formerly enslaved people on public speaking tours and exchanged strategies and information (Hochchild 2005). In the twentieth century, the Anti-Slavery and Aborigines Protection Society lobbied the League of Nations and helped write the 1926 International Convention on the Abolition of Slavery and the 1956 Supplementary Convention on the Abolition of Slavery, Slave Trade, and Institutions and Practices Similar to Slavery. Subsequently, the group expanded its agenda to include practices such as child labor, trafficking in humans, and forced labor; in 1990 it changed its name to Anti-Slavery International. It and other NGOs continue to play key roles in setting human rights standards in many areas since slavery in various forms, including human trafficking, remains a significant problem.

The key role of the United Nations and treaty-making. The UN's core role in the international human rights regime is defining and elaborating what constitute internationally protected rights, initially in the UDHR and the Convention on the Prevention and Punishment of the Crime of Genocide, both concluded in 1948. Under the leadership of Eleanor Roosevelt, who chaired the Commission on Human Rights, these documents articulated a far-reaching rights agenda. In particular, the Universal Declaration elucidated novel principles that people have these rights by virtue of being human; that they apply universally; that human rights include political, civil, social, and economic rights; and that advancement of these rights involves legislation, public engagement, and monitoring. The drafting of the UDHR was noteworthy in that a number of women other than Eleanor Roosevelt played important roles in the process. One was Hansa Mehta, head of India's delegation to the commission, who was responsible for changing the language of Article 1 from reading that "all men" to "all human beings" are born free and equal (Singh-Rathore 2022). Mehta also ensured that the language made clear that women had equal entitlement to human rights.

The UDHR was preceded by the Latin American states' approval of the American Declaration on the Rights and Duties of Man eight months before—a further indication of their historical roles as human rights "protagonists" (Sikkink 2014). That declaration continues to serve as a "rallying banner for the young, the poor, and the oppressed in their quest for a more just world" (Ramcharan 2008: 1). The expectation was that these rights would be set forth in treaties (or conventions or covenants) for states to ratify according to their respective constitutional procedures.

Although other human rights conventions were approved in the 1950s, it took until 1966 for the General Assembly to approve the International Covenant on Economic, Social, and Cultural Rights and the International Covenant on Civil and Political Rights, which define these rights. Both became operative in 1976 after the necessary number of ratifications. Together with the UDHR, they are known as the "international bill of rights." That it took almost thirty years to define these legal standards suggests the difficulty of the task in a world where states jealously guard their national sovereignty. As shown in Table 9.1, not all states have ratified the covenants. The United States did not ratify the Covenant on Civil and Political Rights until 1992, for example, and has yet to ratify the Covenant on Economic, Social, and Cultural Rights. Other states have ratified the covenants but attached reservations, declarations, or interpretive statements that in some cases undercut the whole intent. This pattern is found with other human rights treaties, such as the Convention on the Elimination of Discrimination Against Women (CEDAW). As of 2023, of the 189 parties to this convention, 55 ratified with specific reservations, some on procedural issues and others on broader, more substantive issues, such as provisions that conflict with sharia law. The price of ratification, therefore, has often been highly qualified, weaker conventions.

The covenants and the other human rights treaties exemplify the UN's standard-setting role in human rights. Table 9.1 lists selected conventions by topic. These same standards are found in many national constitutions, legal documents, and court cases, as well as in regional human rights documents.

Table 9.1   Selected UN Human Rights Conventions

Convention	Opened for Ratification	Entered into Force	Ratifications (as of 2023)
General Human Rights			
International Covenant on Civil and Political Rights	1966	1976	173
International Covenant on Economic, Social and Cultural Rights	1966	1976	171
Racial Discrimination			
International Convention on the Elimination of All Forms of Racial Discrimination	1966	1969	182
International Convention on the Suppression and Punishment of the Crime of Apartheid	1973	1976	109
Rights of Women			
Convention on the Elimination of All Forms of Discrimination against Women	1979	1981	189
Human Trafficking and Other Slavery-like Practices			
UN Convention for the Suppression of the Traffic in Persons and of the Exploitation of the Prostitution of Others	1950	1951	82
Supplementary Convention on the Abolition of Slavery, the Slave Trade, and Institutions and Practices Similar to Slavery	1956	1957	124
ILO Convention Concerning the Prohibition and Immediate Action for the Elimination of the Worst Forms of Child Labor	1999	2000	187
UN Convention Against Transnational Organized Crime: Protocol to Prevent, Suppress and Punish Trafficking in Persons, Especially Women and Children	2000	2003	178
Refugees and Stateless Persons			
Convention Relating to the Status of Refugees	1951	1954	146
Protocol Relating to the Status of Refugees	1967	1967	147
Children			
Convention on the Rights of the Child	1989	1990	196
Optional Protocol to the Convention on the Rights of the Child on the Involvement of Children in Armed Conflict	2000	2002	173
Optional Protocol to the Convention on the Rights of the Child on the Sale of Children, Child Prostitution and Child Pornography	2000	2002	178
Other			
Convention on the Prevention and Punishment of the Crime of Genocide	1948	1951	153
Convention Against Torture and Other Cruel, Inhuman or Degrading Treatment or Punishment	1984	1987	173

(continues)

Table 9.1   continued

Convention	Opened for Ratification	Entered into Force	Ratifications (as of 2023)
Convention Concerning Indigenous and Tribal Peoples in Independent Countries	1989	1991	24
International Convention on the Protection of the Rights of All Migrant Workers and Members of Their Families	1990	2003	58
Optional Protocol to the Convention Against Torture and Other Cruel, Inhuman or Degrading Treatment or Punishment	2002	2006	91
Convention on the Rights of Persons with Disabilities	2006	2008	186
Optional Protocol for the Convention on the Rights of Persons with Disabilities	2006	2008	103
International Convention for the Protection of All Persons from Enforced Disappearance	2006	2010	70

Sources: International Labour Organization; University of Minnesota Human Rights Library; UN High Commissioner for Human Rights.

Regional human rights standards. Regional human rights bodies are also involved in the standard-setting process. Most have adopted similar standards, although the relative importance attached to different kinds of rights has varied. The European system is viewed as the most successful system of human rights protection in terms of the consensus attained and the strength of the procedures established. The 1961 European Social Charter incorporates economic and social rights, including protections against poverty and sexual harassment. The European Convention for the Protection of Human Rights and Fundamental Freedoms came into force in 1953 and has been amended several times to add rights. It has been ratified by all forty-six members of the Council of Europe. Among other provisions, it established the European Commission on Human Rights and the Court of Human Rights, discussed further below.

In the Americas, the human rights regime is embedded in the Organization of American States (OAS) and the American Convention on Human Rights (or Pact of San José). The American Convention on Human Rights was adopted in 1969 and came into force in 1978. Like the European system, it includes a commission and court, whose work is discussed later in this chapter. The convention highlights political and civil rights, but widespread abuses, including state-sanctioned disappearances in the 1970s and 1980s, undermined the regime. In the 1980s, as many countries democratized,

Latin America experienced a "norms cascade," a rapid shift toward recognizing the legitimacy of human rights norms in the regional and international conventions (Lutz and Sikkink 2000: 638). Two protocols have since been added to the convention, one of which addresses economic, social, and cultural rights; the other abolishes the death penalty. As discussed in Chapter 5, the OAS incorporated protection of democratic governments into its mandate in the 1990s and has taken a number of actions to enforce this.

In Africa, the African Charter on Human and Peoples Rights (or Banjul Charter, which was approved in 1981 and entered into force in 1986) is of special interest for two reasons. First, specific attention is given to third-generation rights—group and collective rights that are compatible with African traditions, including the rights to development, self-determination, and sovereignty over natural resources. Second, the charter includes a number of duties for individuals and people, such as not compromising the security of the state and preserving and strengthening national independence, territorial integrity, and "positive African cultural values." These provisions could be considered "clawback clauses" that qualify or limit human rights standards. In effect, they permit states to suspend fundamental rights with little protection and undermine the standards articulated in the African Charter (Mutua 1999: 358).

Conspicuously absent from the regional picture are Asian and Middle Eastern norms, standards, and institutions, although this is slowly changing in Southeast Asia. The Association of Southeast Asian Nations (ASEAN) Charter, approved in 2008, included human rights for the first time. In 2009, the ASEAN Intergovernmental Commission on Human Rights was established, followed in 2010 by the ASEAN Commission on the Promotion and Protection of the Rights of Women and Children and in 2012 by the ASEAN Declaration on Human Rights. Even though civil society groups were critical of flaws in the declaration, these are major steps in a region where any discussion of international human rights norms has been considered inconsistent with the norm of noninterference. As Langlois (2021: 153) notes, the creation of the ASEAN human rights regime has "opened the space for a new kind of discussion in the region about human rights: Human rights are now formally part of ASEAN's repertoire of discourse, institutions, and regional diplomacy . . . [and] as rights theorists of varying persuasions have argued . . . rights talk has performative and expressive features that lend themselves to emancipatory vision." However, the mix of authoritarian, military, and democratic governments in the region makes it unlikely that there will be major progress in developing regional standards.

States' commitment to and compliance with human rights treaties. Why do states sign and ratify international human rights treaties? On the question of why they ratify human rights agreements, Beth Simmons (2009: 28) identifies three categories of governments: the "sincere ratifiers," the "false negatives," and the "strategic ratifiers." The first and third are fairly self-evident; some governments genuinely support the rights covered by a particular treaty and expect to comply; others figure that by ratifying they may avoid criticism or improve their reputations (at least in the short run). The second case of "false negatives" is illustrated by United States, with its long-standing pattern of refusing (or being unable) to ratify a number of conventions, such as CEDAW and the Convention on the Rights of the Child, despite its support for these rights. The US federal system complicates implementation of international rights treaties because the national government's authority is constitutionally limited.

Some states ratify human rights conventions but then qualify that ratification with various types of reservations. Others sign conventions but never ratify. For example, the 1990 Convention on the Rights of Migrant Workers has been signed by sixty-nine countries but ratified by only fifty-eight as of 2022, more than a two decades after it came into force in 2003. When they ratify but attach reservations, states may hope to avoid criticism or improve their reputation. Although more than 170 governments have ratified the Convention Against Torture, a significant number of them did so with reservations; the same is true for CEDAW. Not surprisingly perhaps, there are significant regional variations in the patterns of ratification, with the European countries having the fewest reservations, given Europe's strong commitment to democratic values and Western cultural mores.

Does ratifying human rights conventions actually change state behavior? The ability of human rights conventions to contribute to changes in states' behavior depends largely on domestic politics. Compliance may take place through domestic courts and executive and legislative processes where civil society groups, including human rights NGOs, lawyers, and activists, work to translate treaty obligations into domestic law and practice and mobilize support for change (Simmons 2009: 129–149; Conrad and Ritter 2019). A recent study has shown linkages between social norms and compliance, particularly with CEDAW, where the greater the adherence to conservative norms on women's political participation, the lower a state's compliance with Article 7 dealing with women's voting rights (Benneker et al. 2020). One study found that state ratification of six core international human rights treaties led to changes in state practice if the issues were taken up by local NGOs that used the treaty obligations to pressure governments (Hafner-Burton and Tsutsui 2005). In short, increased NGO activity in a country, whether by local or transnational groups, or subnational human rights institutions such as provincial human rights councils and municipal ombudspersons, increases the likelihood that human rights conventions will have a positive effect on local human rights practices. National human rights institutions—state-mandated bodies, but independent of governments with broad constitutional or legal mandates to protect and promote human rights at the national level—have been found to be even more important for achieving political and legal changes in human rights due to their links with both national governments and civil society actors (Haglund and Welch 2021: 213–215).

As David Weissbrodt (2003: 89) aptly put it, "Getting countries to toe the mark is only possible when there is a mark to toe." Over time, the UN and some regional bodies have moved incrementally from articulating the standards to monitoring states' behavior.

Monitoring Human Rights

Monitoring the implementation of human rights standards requires procedures for receiving reports of state practice and complaints of violations from affected individuals or interested groups. It may also be accompanied by the power to comment on reports, appoint working groups, and vote on resolutions of condemnation. Publicity and public shaming are key tools.

UN procedures for monitoring. The UN has developed four different processes for monitoring human rights. The ILO set the first precedents beginning in 1926. In that system, states are required to submit periodic reports about the steps they have taken in law and practice under each ILO convention to which they are a party. These are subject to multiple reviews; governments may receive recommendations for steps to be taken; there are provisions for hearing complaints from workers' groups. Despite a provision for enforcement, the norm is to work with the country in question and offer technical assistance to facilitate compliance.

With only governments represented in the UN and in UN bodies, monitoring is much more problematic than in the ILO, where workers and management are included. Over time, new methods for monitoring were developed. In 1970, ECOSOC Resolution 1503 authorized the former Commission on Human Rights to undertake confidential investigations of individual complaints that suggest "a consistent pattern of gross and reliably attested violations." With this 1503 procedure, the commission significantly expanded monitoring to study specific civil rights problems, such as forced disappearances, torture, and religious discrimination. In 1980, the first so-called Special Procedure was established—the Working Group on Enforced or Involuntary Disappearances. This is the first way the UN currently monitors states' adherence to human rights standards. In 2006, the newly created HRC undertook a review of the Special Procedure, including all existing mandates for special rapporteurs, independent experts, and working groups. Their mandates range from issues such as the Palestinian territories, involuntary detentions, torture, and contemporary forms of slavery to disappearances. The mandates call for examining, advising, and publicly reporting on the human rights situation in a specific country or on a major thematic issue. Special rapporteurs may respond to individual complaints, conduct studies, and make country visits to investigate. Although the 1503 special procedure can handle only a fraction of the complaints received each year, it does provide means for pressuring offending governments as well as encouraging dialogue to address the complaints.

The Universal Periodic Reviews are the second way of monitoring UN members' human rights records. The purpose is to foster the improvement of human rights in every country by assessing states' human rights records and addressing violations. The UPR, like the ILO monitoring system, also aims to provide technical assistance to states, share best practices, and improve states' capacity for dealing with human rights challenges. The reviews are conducted by the UPR Working Group (the forty-seven HRC members) and any other UN member state that wishes to participate. The group reviews the national reports compiled by the states under review, plus information from independent human rights groups and experts within the UN system compiled by OHCHR, and information provided by other stakeholders, such as national human rights institutions and NGOs. There is then an interactive dialogue between states and other stakeholders. States themselves are responsible for implementing the recommendations and are held accountable for progress when reviewed again four and a half years later.

As of 2022, three cycles of the UPR had been completed. Although governments have been encouraged to draw on outside sources for information, the reports are largely state-driven. Time limits have tended to provide little opportunity for discussion and debate and, over time, the process has yielded growing numbers of recommendations leading to complaints from countries under review of being overwhelmed and to questions about the recommendations' usefulness and measurability.

The third mode for UN monitoring is through the ten treaty bodies created in connection with specific human rights treaties (see Figure 9.1). States that are parties to the conventions are required to periodically report their implementation progress to these bodies. The bodies are composed of independent experts elected by the parties to each treaty; the experts review the reports, engage in dialogue with governments, and issue concluding comments. Human rights NGOs frequently prepare their own "shadow reports," which provide an independent assessment of compliance that can put additional pressure on governments. National human rights institutions (and subnational institutions in some cases, such as the disabilities convention) can also provide reports independent of national delegations (Wolman 2014). UN agencies such as the UN Children's Fund in the case of the Committee on the Rights of the Child may also be important sources of information, and the OHCHR assists with follow-up and regional meetings for each treaty body to assist with the cumbersome reporting processes.

A fourth mode of UN monitoring is based on provisions for individual petitions and complaints in five treaties—the Covenant on Civil and Political Rights, CEDAW, and the conventions on racial discrimination, torture, and persons with disabilities. The violations of rights must be by a state party that has accepted the competence of the committee to review petitions. For example, only about one-third of the states that are party to the International Covenant on Civil and Political Rights and Convention Against Torture have accepted that provision. For the Convention on the Elimination of Racial Discrimination, only twelve parties permit petitions, and of those only a few are African states. No Asian states have accepted this provision. A further problem is the limited number of petitions that can be handled in a given year. Of the thousands of complaints relating to civil and political rights filed with the UN Secretary-General each year, only a small fraction can be considered by the committee.

In spite of efforts to reform the treaty body system, most recently in 2014 and 2020, the bodies are overburdened, making effective follow-up impossible. States, particularly small ones, are bogged down with multiple reporting requirements; late and incomplete reports are a persistent problem. Some reform proposals require new funding, which is unlikely. The absence of a human rights culture in many countries and limited follow-up by the treaty bodies hamper effectiveness. Studies show that the system has had a positive effect on the protection of human rights, however, by incorporating treaty norms into domestic law, particularly where countries were transitioning to democracy and where there were strong domestic constituencies for specific treaties, such as those on women, racial discrimination, and torture (Heyns and Viljoen 2020).

Does UN monitoring make a difference? One argument contends that over time, repeated condemnations can change attitudes, as happened with South Africa. But even that case is not entirely clear because the repeated condemnations were later coupled with sanctions. Another point of view holds that public monitoring, including naming and shaming, can antagonize states and harden their positions, leading to the opposite of the intended effect. One study compiled data on efforts by the UN, NGOs, and news media between 1975 and 2000 to name and shame the human rights practices of 145 states. The data showed that "governments put in the global spotlight for violations often adopt better protections for political rights afterward, but they rarely stop or appear to lessen acts of terror. Worse, terror sometimes increases after publicity" (Hafner-Burton 2008: 706).

Thus, although UN human rights monitoring has increased, its effect is limited, particularly if the state in question is a major power. The case of China illustrates the difficulties. Starting in 1993, China successfully blocked all action on resolutions dealing with its human rights situation (Kent 1999). Only in 2005, after ten years of effort, did the special rapporteur on torture make an official visit. When he found abuse "still widespread" and accused the Chinese authorities of obstructing his work (CBS News 2005), China attempted to get the rapporteur to alter the report. China files regular reports to the treaty bodies but continues to block efforts to examine its record except through the UPR. NGOs and other states have used that process to target China's actions in Tibet, against Muslim Uyghurs in Xinjiang Province, and its restrictions on freedom of expression. China vigorously objected to a 2015 report by the UN Committee Against Torture on its failure to reduce the use of torture since a previous review in 2008; its continuing use of secret prisons; its "unprecedented detention and interrogation" of more than 200 lawyers in 2015; and its failure to produce requested information (Cumming-Bruce 2015: A12). Much to the dismay of human rights activists, China was elected to the Human Rights Council in 2020. Not surprisingly, China strongly objected to the publication of another report after UNHCHR Michelle Bachelet's 2022 visit and report that China might have committed crimes against humanity in Xinjiang with its treatment of the Uyghur people. Bachelet released the report just minutes before leaving office, but China was successful in lining up the votes to block HRC debate on the report (Cumming-Bruce and Ramzy 2022). Clearly, if states believed that such reports did not have an effect, they would not object to their publication. Indeed, China often threatens retaliation against countries that criticize it.

Regional organizations' experiences with monitoring. Under the European Convention on Human Rights, the European Commission on Human Rights was originally responsible for monitoring the general human rights situation in member states and reviewing complaints from individuals before making referrals to the European Court of Human Rights. The commission was dissolved in 1998, however, when the European Court of Human Rights was enlarged and individuals were empowered to take complaints to it directly.

The 1978 Inter-American Convention on Human Rights established a dual commission and court system. The Inter-American Commission on Human Rights has monitoring responsibilities that include analyzing and investigating petitions from individuals who claim their rights have been violated by a member government. The commission did particularly notable work in the 1970s and 1980s, uncovering and publicizing abuses during the period of military dictatorships (Goldman 2009) It has long been active in issuing reports that outline human rights abuses and, like the UN, has appointed special, country, and thematic rapporteurs to gather and disseminate information on how different groups of people or rights are being protected. It may conduct country visits and issue recommendations. It can also receive petitions from individuals, groups of people, or NGOs. It also decides whether individual cases go to the Inter-American Court of Human Rights.

In Africa, the Commission on Human and Peoples' Rights is a quasi-judicial body that is tasked with promoting and protecting individual and collective rights that are enumerated in the African Charter on Human and Peoples' Rights. The commission can receive complaints from states, individuals, and NGOs; it can also issue rulings, as it did in 2010 regarding the eviction of the Endorois people from their homeland in Kenya and in 2016 to the Democratic Republic of Congo regarding violations of numerous rights related to development and the operations of a foreign mining company. It has had somewhat limited monitoring functions, but appointed a few special rapporteurs and, in 2021, a Commission in Inquiry to investigate serious crimes in the Ethiopian region of Tigray (Human Rights Watch 2022a). Civil society, however, is less well developed and engaged with the court mechanism.

The regional picture is mixed. Europe, where the human rights record is the best, is also the most economically developed, has the most democracies, and has the strongest civil societies, all strong predictors of better human rights practices. Where abuses are greater, the monitoring systems are weaker. Is it weak monitoring or underlying political and economic conditions that explain variations in human rights records among regions? In Asia and the Middle East, the lack of regional organizations with a human rights mandate means that human rights monitoring is left either to international institutions like the UN or to civil society and NGOs.

NGO monitoring: Amnesty International and Human Rights Watch. Given the unevenness of regional IGO monitoring, major international NGOs and local groups work to fill the gap. Amnesty International (AI), founded in 1961 and until 1981 the only NGO continuously monitoring human rights abuses, is perhaps the most well-known and respected human rights group, having received the 1977 Nobel Peace Prize. Emphasizing impartial and independent research about political prisoners—its initial focus—the AI secretariat in London had individual researchers following specific cases over time. That information was used by individual chapters for media and letter-writing campaigns to pressure governments on behalf of prisoners of conscience across all types of political systems. High-profile cases maintained the momentum of the organization as "keepers of the flame" (Hopgood 2006; Clark 2001). AI has earned a reputation for scrupulous neutrality by investigating and censuring governments of all types.

Beginning in the 1970s, Amnesty International mounted campaigns on broader cross-national issues such as torture and inhumane treatment of prisoners, the death penalty, violence against women, and, more recently, climate change, child rights, Indigenous people, and sexual and reproductive rights. A study of AI's background reports and press releases covering 148 countries between 1986 and 2000 found the organization concentrating on high-profile countries such as China, Russia, Indonesia, and the United States, while some of the most repressive states, including Afghanistan, Somalia, Myanmar, and Burundi, received less attention (Ron, Ramos, and Rodgers 2005). That is less true today. Although it might be in AI's interest to exaggerate rights abuses in some places to help raise money, there is no evidence for this (Hill, Moore, and Mukherjee 2013).

Human Rights Watch (HRW), founded in 1978 as Helsinki Watch after the 1975 Final Act of the Conference on Security and Cooperation in Europe, initially monitored progress in liberalizing Eastern Europe under the so-called Helsinki Accords. Transformed into HRW, its reach became global and its focus expanded to all types of human rights. It was Aryeh Neier, executive director and cofounder of HRW, who in 1992 proposed creating the ad hoc war crimes tribunal for Yugoslavia. Thanks to the reporting and research of Alison Des Forges, HRW's representative in Rwanda, the organization was able to alert the international community to the unfolding Rwandan genocide in 1994.

AI and HRW differ in that AI is a mass-membership organization with regional offices around the world and sections working in more than seventy countries. Advocacy, networking, attention to research, and mobilization of its constituencies are critical to its success. Relying on its professional staff working in more than 100 countries, HRW works with governments, armed groups, businesses, activists, and the UN, pushing for changes in laws, policies, and practices.

Some human rights NGOs are dedicated to specific issues, such as Indigenous people or the Dalits in India's caste system. Others are grouped in coalitions such as the International Lesbian, Gay, Bisexual, Trans, and Intersex Association (ILGA), which is the umbrella group for hundreds of LGBTI groups, discussed later in the chapter. Through such networks and aided by the proliferation of communication technologies since the 1990s, human rights NGOs can articulate a moral consciousness, empower domestic opposition, and pressure governments to pay attention to issues and situations (Risse, Ropp, and Sikkink 1999).

The experts that make up the UN human rights treaty bodies depend heavily on information compiled by NGOs, since many state reports are self-serving and rarely disclose treaty violations. Thus NGOs, with their unique local information bases, along with national and subnational human rights institutions, have undertaken the task of evaluating such reports, gathering additional information, pushing states for compliance, and publicizing abuses. The relationships between NGOs and the treaty bodies vary, however. The Committee on the Rights of the Child enjoys the closest working relationship with NGOs, which regularly review state reports, maintain dialogue with local NGOs, and help disseminate information. The Committee Against Torture calls on concerned NGOs only on an ad hoc basis, whereas the Committee on the Elimination of Discrimination Against Women does not formally solicit information from NGOs. Although NGOs may enjoy a unique capacity to engage in monitoring, part of their ability to carry out this function depends on the political space provided by each separate treaty body.

National human rights institutions created by many governments now have access to participate in the work of the HRC independent of official national delegations, while subnational institutions generally lack such access. The disabilities convention and the optional protocol to the torture convention, however, contain provisions that require state parties to set up, designate, or maintain mechanisms for implementation at subnational levels. This has led to subnational human rights institutions playing key roles as independent mechanisms for monitoring and reporting (Wolman 2014: 445–446).

Thus, IGOs and NGOs have developed capacities for monitoring, but their impact appears mixed. Does naming and shaming work as a strategy? Amanda Murdie and David Davis (2012) examined the effects of human rights organizations' shaming on state behavior. Drawing on data from over 400 human rights organizations on shaming governments between 1992 and 2004, the authors found that states targeted by NGOs do improve their human rights practices. Another study looked at the "hard case" of the United States and its use of torture, cruel, inhuman, and degrading treatment of prisoners after the September 2001 terrorist attacks. That study found that although the United States is a party to the torture convention, pressure campaigns against these violations by domestic and international actors were "mainly ineffective as long as the Bush administration was in office . . . because it used a compelling counter-norm, that of anti-terrorism to justify the use of torture and trump the legal prohibitions on the practice" (Sikkink 2013: 146). In short, more powerful countries are less susceptible to the effects of naming and shaming—a finding that certainly also holds for China.

Just as NGOs have been found to play key roles in monitoring states human rights behavior, they also play key roles promoting human rights by urging ratification of human rights conventions and enforcement of court judgments.

Promoting Human Rights
The challenge of promoting human rights lies in translating norms and rhetoric into actions that go beyond stopping violations and changing long-term attitudes and behavior. These efforts have been increasingly shared by the various actors in human rights governance.

UN role. The UN has played an increasingly active role in human rights promotion since the early 1990s. It has promoted democratization through its electoral assistance programs, not only in conjunction with postconflict peacebuilding missions such as in Kosovo, Iraq, Timor-Leste, and Afghanistan, but also at the request of states needing assistance in reforming electoral and judicial institutions. The UN Electoral Assistance Division, created in 1992, provides technical assistance to states regarding political rights and democratization.

Sometimes the UN role involves certifying electoral processes, as it did in the contested Côte d'Ivoire election in 2010; other times it relies on expert monitoring by personnel from the UN and regional organizations such as the OSCE and the OAS, or from NGOs like the Carter Center and the National Endowment for Democracy. Sometimes the UN shares that responsibility with states, as in Afghanistan in 2004–2005 and again in 2014, Iraq in 2005, and South Sudan in 2011. The UN provides technical assistance to states in developing credible, sustainable national electoral systems. In Afghanistan's 2014 presidential election, for example, the UN was responsible for overseeing the recount of all votes. Although international monitoring does not necessarily eliminate cheating or fraud, states gain legitimacy by having external monitors, and elections may be viewed as illegitimate if monitors are not present (Kelley 2008).

Since the early 1990s, second- and third-generation rights have been linked to development activities and programs across the entire UN system. Secretary-General Boutros Boutros-Ghali's *Agenda for Development* (1995), which emphasized the right to development, was incorporated into both the Millennium Development Goals and the Sustainable Development Goals. Since the mid-1990s, the World Bank has promoted "good governance" in its development programs, including attention to the recipient's political and civil rights record and the empowerment of women and civil society actors. The OHCHR has primary responsibility for overseeing the UN's promotional activities, supported by other UN agencies.

NGO roles. NGOs have been active in providing education on human rights in Cambodia, Central America, Kosovo, Afghanistan, and elsewhere. The Unrepresented Nations and Peoples Organization, for example, assists and empowers Indigenous people such as Australia's Aborigines, circumpolar groups in the Arctic, and Native Americans to represent themselves by providing training in international and human rights law, among other things. Cultural Survival, another NGO, has an extensive education program to raise awareness about Indigenous people, ethnic minorities, and human rights, helping shape the debate on the third-generation rights affecting Indigenous people. Amnesty International USA, the National Endowment for Democracy, and the Open Society Institute have sponsored the development of human rights educational curricula and lobbied state and local educational boards for their adoption.

Regional organizations. Regional human rights IGOs in Europe, Latin America, and Africa undertake relatively similar educational and promotional activities with respect to human rights. For women, for example, educational programs detailing specific rights have been created. There are training programs for judges, police, and teachers. Such promotional activities are by nature long-term investments in addressing human rights problems. They aim to mitigate abuses but not enforce compliance with international human rights norms and law.

Enforcing International Human Rights Norms and Law

Of the various governance tasks in human rights, enforcement is the most problematic, as countries generally have low stakes in enforcing other states' compliance and international institutions have limited capacity to compel compliance. The international community has increasingly undertaken enforcement activities in relation to war crimes, crimes against humanity, and genocide through special courts. States continue to enforce human rights norms through coercive measures, such as sanctions directed at other states, however. Meanwhile, to enforce compliance, individuals and groups may use national courts and, in some cases, regional courts such as the European Court of Human Rights and the Inter-American Court of Human Rights, as well as the ICC.

National courts. Two cases illustrate how judicial action through national courts may be used to enforce international norms. Under the US Alien Tort Claims Act of 1789, US federal courts have jurisdiction in civil cases filed by individuals of any nationality who are present in the country, for egregious acts committed in violation of the law of nations (i.e., international law) or a US treaty. In one case, *Doe v. UNOCAL* (US Ninth Circuit Court of Appeals 2002), the US-based oil company was accused of complicity in using forced labor provided by the Burmese military government and of rape and murder during the construction of a gas pipeline in Myanmar. The case was settled in 2005 when the company agreed to compensate Burmese villagers and improve the quality of life for people in the pipeline region. In 2013, the US Supreme Court, in *Kiobel v. Royal Dutch Petroleum*, announced in a unanimous decision that the Nigerian plaintiffs could not sue in US courts because they had a minimal presence in the United States and the human rights abuses had occurred abroad. This case may provide a "chilling effect" on efforts to use the Alien Tort Claims Act and US courts for relief of human rights violations abroad.

Another example of using national courts relying on international law to enforce human rights involves former Chilean dictator Augusto Pinochet.

Under a warrant issued by a Spanish judge seeking to extradite him, Pinochet was detained in the United Kingdom in 1998 for crimes allegedly committed while head of state. Although some of those crimes were committed against Spanish nationals living in Chile, Spain also claimed universal jurisdiction on the basis of crimes against humanity, which any country can legitimately do. The Judicial Committee of the UK House of Lords upheld Pinochet's arrest on the basis of international prohibitions against torture and murder and rejected his claim of sovereign immunity. Due to ill health, Pinochet was turned over to Chilean authorities. Although later stripped of his immunity and indicted, his death in 2006 ended the prosecution. Although controversial, the precedent has been set that under universal jurisdiction, individual leaders can be held accountable in other jurisdictions for major human rights violations committed against their own people, loosening the Westphalian hold on state sovereignty.

Coercive measures. Whereas national courts are used by individual plaintiffs, NGOs, or activist judges, governments and groups of states may take coercive actions. They may impose sanctions through the UN or regional IGOs, authorize other enforcement measures, or push the Security Council to refer a case involving war crimes, genocide, or crimes against humanity to the ICC. The campaign against apartheid in South Africa illustrates how governments may take unilateral coercive measures against other states. While the UN General Assembly called for international sanctions against South Africa for its apartheid policy, little happened until the 1980s. Responding to a public campaign of civil disobedience, the US Congress called for a review of US policy and for sanctions and, in 1986, approved the Comprehensive Anti-Apartheid Act over a presidential veto. The United Kingdom and other powerful states followed suit. The imposition of sanctions boosted the morale of apartheid opponents and inflicted pain on the South African business community and, through it, the government. The sanctions, along with the persistent campaign by the international community, were partly responsible for ending apartheid in the early 1990s and the installation of a majority democratic government in 1994.

A second instance illustrates the difficulty of sustaining sanctions. After China's crackdown on dissidents and the Tiananmen Square massacre in June 1989, the United States, Japan, and EU members instituted an arms embargo against China, suspended export credits and official visits, and got the World Bank and Asian Development Bank to cancel new lending to China. The coercive actions may have cost China over $11 billion in bilateral aid over a four-year period. However, in response to economic pressures, in 1994 the United States granted most favored nation status to China without human rights conditions attached (Donnelly 1998: 120–124).

Studies of foreign aid donors' use of sanctions to punish repressive states suggest that donors use negative sanctions for human rights abuses selectively and that an aid recipient's human rights record plays at best a limited role in aid allocation. Richard Nielson (2013) found, for example, that aid sanctions are used when the donor has few close ties with the violator, when violations negatively affect the donor, and when violations are widely publicized. Countries with strong human rights traditions, however, are "*less* likely to sanction rights violations," leading Nielson (2013: 800–801) to suggest that "supposedly moral policies may be adopted for amoral reasons: to pursue state interests."

UN enforcement. The UN's enforcement authority, as discussed in Chapters 4 and 7, is found in Chapter VII of the UN Charter. Under that provision, if the Security Council determines that human rights violations threaten or breach international peace, it has the authority to take enforcement actions. Since the early 1990s, the Council has imposed sanctions in many situations, some of which clearly involve human rights violations, such as sexual violence in conflict and using child soldiers. Whether it made an explicit linkage between those violations and a threat to international peace and security can only be determined by a close examination of the council debate and the text of the authorizing resolution(s).

Imposing UN sanctions against governments responsible for gross violations of human rights is still highly controversial. Arguing that human rights are not an appropriate subject for the Security Council, Russia and China have often vetoed draft resolutions that targeted human rights violators. In December 2022, however, both abstained on the very first resolution approved by the Council denouncing the Myanmar military's extensive violations of human rights following the 2021 coup. Invoking Chapter VI (not Chapter VII), the resolution expressed deep concern, condemned the military's execution of prodemocracy activists, and demanded "an immediate end to all forms of violence throughout the country" (Resolution 2669). As HRW's UN director noted, "China and Russia's abstentions signal that even the junta's few friends have lost interest in sticking out their necks to defend its atrocities. The building blocks put in place with this resolution offer a starting point for reinvigorating pressure on the junta among Security Council members and governments across the globe" (Human Rights Watch 2022b).

Sanctions are not the Security Council's only option for enforcement; it has also authorized the use of military force under Chapter VII to deal with conflicts that have produced egregious human rights violations. Ethnic cleansing in Bosnia and Kosovo, genocide in Rwanda and Darfur, famine and state collapse in Somalia, systematic rape and chaos in the DRC, and Qaddafi's threats against his own people in Libya in 2011 have all led to humanitarian interventions involving UN or regional peacekeeping forces to protect people and groups from abuse. As discussed in Chapter 7 and illustrated by the discussion of genocide later in this chapter, R2P is still a contested norm. When applied, however, it has demonstrated international will to use the UN to enforce human rights and humanitarian norms.

Overall, Walling (2020: 297) concludes that Security Council practices show that "accountability is considered an important component of international peace and security" and the integration of human rights into authorized peace operations has become "more of a norm rather than an exception." Still, she adds, there is "no consistent policy as to when gross and systemic human rights violations will be deemed a security threat by the council" (Walling 2020: 304).

A major step in human rights enforcement and toward providing accountability for war crimes, crimes against humanity, and genocide has come with the creation of two ad hoc tribunals, two hybrid courts, and the ICC.

Ad hoc war crimes tribunals. The desire to hold accountable individuals responsible for war crimes during World War II led to the establishment of the first war crimes tribunals. Because the Nuremberg and Tokyo trials were the victor's punishment, however, they were not regarded as precedents for future wartime crimes. In the 1990s, the idea of individual responsibility for war crimes, genocide, and crimes against humanity was revived in the face of the atrocities committed during conflicts in the former Yugoslavia and Rwanda. The UN Security Council used its Chapter VII authority to establish the International Criminal Tribunal for the Former Yugoslavia (ICTY) in 1993 in The Hague, Netherlands. The ICTY was followed by the International Criminal Tribunal for Rwanda (ICTR) in 1994 and later facilitated the creation of two other special courts. Each court began slowly, developing structures and procedures; gathering evidence; recruiting prosecutors, investigators, and judges; and working to gain the cooperation of states to arrest, try, and convict a number of individuals. In the process, the courts set precedents for the ICC and for human rights and international humanitarian law.

Over its twenty-three years, the ICTY employed more than fifty judges and three separate proceedings, plus more than 750 staff members from seventy-six countries. It addressed questions of authority, jurisdiction, evidence, sentencing, and imprisonment. As of its conclusion in 2017, the court had indicted 161 persons and sentenced 90; a number of cases were transferred to local courts in the former Yugoslavia, and thirty-seven cases were terminated or indictments withdrawn, including that of former Yugoslav president Slobodan Milosevic, who died during the trial in 2006. Nineteen individuals were acquitted. Radovan Karadžić, wartime leader of the Bosnian Serbs, was among those sentenced, and former Serb general Ratko Mladić was convicted of genocide in the killing of almost 8,000 Bosnian Muslim men and boys in Srebrenica in 1995. He lost his appeal in 2021. The ICTY formally ceased to exist in 2017, and the remaining appeal from Mladić and two retrials have been handled by the International Residual Mechanism for International Criminal Tribunals.

The ICTY's judgments elaborated on the Geneva Conventions, for example, by defining sexual violence and especially rape as a war crime—a first. They elaborated also on the elements of crimes of genocide and torture and the application of international humanitarian law to internal armed conflicts. The court considered fairness and impartiality of paramount importance, so even though the largest number of cases dealt with Serbs and Bosnian Serbs, it also convicted Croats, Bosnian Muslims, and Kosovar Albanians for crimes against Serbs and others. The ICTY's other accomplishments included developing procedures for establishing the relevant facts and providing victims a forum in which to be heard. Being seated in The Hague, however, the court's proceedings had less impact on people in the former Yugoslavia—a lesson that was heeded in later tribunals.

The Rwandan tribunal concluded its work at the end of 2015, having issued ninety-three indictments, sixty-two sentences, and fourteen acquittals. Its last action upheld guilty verdicts on six individuals. Then, in mid-2020, French police arrested Félicien Kabuga, a wealthy Rwandan who had been on the most wanted list for more than twenty years. He had been indicted by the ICTR for his role as the founder and director of the Radio Télévision Libre de Mille Collines that incited fear and hate as well as attacks on Tutsis during the genocide. As with the ICTY, residual functions of the ICTR have been assumed by the International Residual Mechanism, and Kabuga's trial began in late 2022 in The Hague. Up to this point, the ICTR's most important contributions to international criminal law were the convictions of three other prominent individuals for using TV, radio, and news media to incite and coordinate acts of genocide against the Tutsis. The conviction of Jean Kambanda, former prime minister of Rwanda, for the crime of genocide was the first conviction of a head of government.

Hybrid courts. In 2002 and 2008, two courts employing national and international law, procedures, and jurists were established by agreements between the UN and the governments of Sierra Leone and Cambodia to judge individual criminal responsibility for crimes against humanity and war crimes. In theory, such courts, because of their proximity, may have greater cultural sensitivity and hence more legitimacy. The Special Court for Sierra Leone tried individuals for crimes against civilians and UN peacekeepers during that country's civil war (1991–2002). Of ten people tried, nine were convicted and sentenced; two others died before proceedings commenced; another individual escaped. The most well-known defendant was Charles Taylor, the former Liberian president, who was convicted in 2012 of terrorism, participation in a joint criminal enterprise, planning attacks on three cities, war crimes, and crimes against humanity in aiding the two rebel groups in the Sierra Leone civil war. This made him the first former head of state found guilty by an international criminal tribunal. His trial was held in The Hague and he is serving his sentence in a UK prison. The Sierra Leone tribunal concluded its work at the end of 2013.

The Khmer Rouge Tribunal (Extraordinary Chambers in the Courts of Cambodia) has faced significant difficulties in its trials of individuals charged for their roles in the Khmer Rouge regime and the deaths of 1.7 million Cambodians by starvation, torture, forced labor, and execution between 1975 and 1979. The length of time that had passed since the crimes made gathering evidence difficult. Of the original five surviving Khmer Rouge leaders, two died before trial; three were convicted for crimes against humanity. The Cambodian government repeatedly tried to block the court proceedings. There were several problems with the conduct of the trial given the complicated process and hybrid mix of international and Cambodian legal systems and judges involved. One key (and positive) difference from the ICTY and ICTR was that the trials were held in the country itself, ensuring that Cambodians were more aware of them and of the crimes they brought to light.

These four ad hoc tribunals laid the groundwork for the world's first permanent international criminal court. The idea for such a court had been around since the Nuremburg and Tokyo war crimes trials after World War II, but it gained new support in the mid-1990s with the abundant evidence of the crimes and need for a system of accountability. As noted in the vignette at the beginning of this chapter, it is highly unlikely that war crimes cases stemming from Russia's invasion of Ukraine will or can be brought to the ICC. Far more likely is an ad hoc tribunal similar to either the Sierra Leone or Cambodian courts.

The International Criminal Court. In 1998, in light of the difficulties posed by the ad hoc nature of the tribunals for Yugoslavia and Rwanda and a long-standing movement to create a permanent international criminal court, UN members concluded the Rome Statute for the ICC. The Coalition for the International Criminal Court, an umbrella group of more than 2,000 NGOs, mobilized international support for the ICC and promoted ratification of the statute, and today continues with promotional activities. The ICC is officially recognized as an independent permanent judicial institution, but it reports its activities to the UN Secretary-General, has observer status in the General Assembly, and may address the Security Council. Under Article 13 of the Rome Statute, the Security Council may refer situations to the ICC, as it has done with two as of 2023—those of Darfur and Libya—although neither state is party to the statute.

The ICC began to function in 2002 and its first judges (eighteen) and prosecutors were chosen in 2003. As of 2023, 154 states had signed the

Rome Statute, and 123 states had ratified it. Among those who had not signed were the United States, China, and India, while Russia had signed but not ratified. Two states—the Philippines (2019) and Burundi (2017)—have withdrawn.

When inaugurated, the ICC was called "the most ambitious initiative in the history of modern international law" (Simons 2003: A9). It enjoys both compulsory jurisdiction and jurisdiction over individuals and nonstate entities, such as terrorist and criminal groups, whereas only states historically have been subjects of international law. The court has jurisdiction over "serious" war crimes that represent a "policy or plan," rather than just random acts in wartime. Abuses must be "systematic or widespread." Four types of crimes are covered: genocide (attacking a group of people and killing them because of race, ethnicity, religion), crimes against humanity (murder, enslavement, forcible transfer of population, torture), war crimes, and crimes of aggression (initially undefined). No individuals (save those under eighteen years of age) are immune from jurisdiction, including heads of state and military leaders. The ICC functions as a court of last resort in that it can hear cases only when national courts are unwilling or unable to deal with grave atrocities. Prosecution is forbidden for crimes committed before July 1, 2002, when the court came into being, and individuals must be present during the trial. Anyone—an individual person, government, group, or the UN Security Council—can bring a case before the ICC.

As of early 2023, there were thirty-one cases on the ICC docket related to war crimes or crimes against humanity in nine "situations"— all African cases, including individuals in the Central African Republic, Côte d'Ivoire, Sudan, the Democratic Republic of Congo, Kenya, Libya, Uganda, Rwanda, and Mali. Four states had referred cases, those in Côte d'Ivoire and Kenya were initiated by the ICC prosecutor, and two others were referred by the UN Security Council. There were investigations under way in seventeen situations, some of which had been referred to the court early in its existence, others such as Ukraine more recently.

The ICC initiated its first trials in 2009 after almost seven years of preparatory work ranging from the selection of initial judges and appointment of the chief prosecutor to developing the processes for investigations and selecting cases, establishing court regulations, and evaluating issues of jurisdiction and admissibility (Schiff 2008: 102–143). As of early 2023, the ICC had tried, convicted, and sentenced six defendants and acquitted four individuals. It had closed cases related to Sudan, Kenya, Libya, the DRC, and Côte d'Ivoire. Although all of these cases involved Africans, the ICC has pursued a number of investigations of situations and people in other parts of the world. Two indictments were particularly notable. In 2009, the ICC, in its first indictment against a sitting president, charged Sudan's Omar al-Bashir and three associates with war crimes and crimes against humanity in connection with the conflict in the Darfur region. Al-Bashir defied the court, but after being ousted in a coup in 2019, he was arrested. The government decided it would try him instead of turning him over to the ICC. In 2011, an indictment was issued against Uhuru Kenyatta and two other Kenyans for their role in interethnic violence after the 2007 presidential election. Kenyatta became president in 2013, and efforts to postpone the trial or change court procedures continued until late 2014, when the case was dropped for lack of evidence. Still, Kenyatta set an important precedent when he appeared in person before the court.

The prevalence of African cases at the ICC and the high-profile cases of al-Bashir and Kenyatta sparked a strong backlash against the ICC in Africa. The African Union, Organisation of Islamic Cooperation, and Arab League all accused the court of racism and neocolonialism. Al-Bashir openly defied the court, while some African leaders mounted a campaign to press African states to withdraw from the ICC. In 2016, it looked as if three African states would do so: South Africa, Burundi, and The Gambia. In the end, only Burundi withdrew. One particular concern relates to prosecution of senior state officials and whether there should be exemptions from ICC jurisdiction for sitting heads of state. Bower (2019: 89) argues that the contestation over this has not undermined the nonimpunity norm but empowered pro-norm constituencies such that "no actors openly deny that individuals should be held accountable for heinous international crimes."

It is significant that the ICC has functioned for more than twenty years despite US objections. Historically, the United States supported international accountability for war crimes but ended up opposing the ICC; President George W. Bush "unsigned" the Rome Statute in 2001. A major concern was the possibility that the ICC might prosecute US military personnel (for actions in Afghanistan) or even the US president.

In practice, the United States ended up taking an inconsistent approach. In 2005 it abstained on the Security Council resolution referring Darfur/Sudan to the court, but in 2011 it voted in favor of referring Libya. It sent US troops to assist in capturing Ugandan rebel leader Joseph Kony, who had been indicted by the court but was in hiding in remote areas of Central Africa. (The unsuccessful six-year mission ended in 2017.) In 2014, the United States pushed a Security Council draft resolution to refer Syria to the court, knowing that Russia would veto it, but also inserting language to block any investigation into the Golan Heights occupied by Israel, any prosecution of US soldiers, and any US financial support for the court. Under the Trump administration, the US rejected any cooperation, particularly after the court's Chief Prosecutor Fatou Bensouda initiated an investigation in 2020 of possible war crimes and crimes against humanity committed during the conflict in Afghanistan by the government, Taliban, or US forces. In fact, the United States placed sanctions on Bensouda herself, barring her from entering the United States and blocking her access to bank funds. These were lifted by President Joe Biden in 2021.

These international criminal proceedings raise a number of questions. For one, the operation of international courts is expensive. It is estimated that the Yugoslav tribunal cost $2 billion and the Rwandan tribunal cost $1–2 billion. The estimated cost of $2 billion for the ICC's few convictions raises questions as to whether this cost is justified.

In 2019, four former presidents of the ICC's Assembly of States Parties published a highly critical article calling for an independent investigation of the court's functioning. Although they noted that "We have never needed the Court more than today . . . the powerful impact of the Court's central message is too often not matched by its performance as a judicial institution . . . the quality of some of its judicial proceedings . . . results . . . [and] management deficiencies" (Raad Al Hussein et al. 2019). Longtime human rights activist Aryeh Neier (2019) reinforced his own critique of the ICC by noting that it had initiated proceedings against multiple heads of state but failed to convict any. He criticized its record in only securing 6 convictions in its first seventeen years of work in contrast to the 165 convictions of the ad hoc tribunals for the former Yugoslavia, Rwanda, and Sierra Leone. In response, the ICC's Assembly of States Parties created a Group of Independent Experts chaired by South African jurist Richard Goldstone. Its 2020 report focused on a number of areas in need of improvement, including the process for selecting judges, the ICC's working methods and culture, victim participation, and reparations (ICC 2020).

Using the ICJ for enforcement: The Rohingya and Myanmar. In 2019, a unique effort was initiated to use the ICJ to declare that Myanmar violated the provisions of the Genocide Convention and would have to cease these acts and implement its obligations to prevent genocide. The suit further asked the court to order provisional measures to stop Myanmar's genocidal conduct immediately. Since its independence in 1948, Myanmar has often been under military dictatorships, has seldom been free of insurgencies involving one or more of its ethnic minorities, and has regularly experienced human rights violations.

Starting in late 2016, one of the ethnic minorities, the Muslim Rohingya, who were concentrated in northern Rakhine State along the Indian Ocean coast, became the subjects of a major military crackdown in which numerous villages were burned, hundreds of people were killed, women were raped, and children were tossed into burning homes. This resulted in massive flights of people into neighboring Bangladesh over a three-week period beginning in 2017. Most of the 860,000 refugees ended up in camps and makeshift settlements across what is known as Cox's Bazar Peninsula.

The first references to the situation constituting genocide appeared in a report issued by the US Holocaust Memorial Museum and the NGO Fortify

Rights in November 2017 (Fortify Rights 2017), although earlier the HRC had raised alarm bells about the evidence of massive rights violations. That same month, the UN Security Council issued a statement (S/PRST/2017/22) condemning the widespread violence and mass displacement and calling for the Myanmar government to take all necessary steps to counter incitement to violence and provide greater access for humanitarian assistance. In early 2019, the HRC created a mechanism to gather evidence in preparation for international criminal proceedings.

In November 2019, The Gambia—the smallest state in Africa—filed suit in the ICJ on behalf of the Organisation of the Islamic Conference. The ICJ is the only court where a case can be brought against a state and is designated as the court for resolving disputes related to the Genocide Convention. This is where Bosnia and Croatia brought suits on genocide against Serbia in the early 2000s. Furthermore, Myanmar is not party to the Rome Statute, so the ICC has no jurisdiction. The Gambia's attorney general had worked as a lawyer for the ICTR for more than ten years and was intimately familiar with the Rwandan genocide and related legal cases.

Just two months after the case was initiated, the ICJ issued its first ruling. It did not determine whether Myanmar had committed genocide. That will take several years of court proceedings. The court did find that the Rohingya "appear to be a protected group," and it rejected Myanmar's claim that internal conflict between armed groups negated its obligations under the Genocide Convention. It also issued provisional measures ordering the Myanmar military to ensure that military and police forces not commit genocidal acts, to preserve all evidence of such acts, and to report to the court on its compliance (Rist 2020).

This ICJ ruling is considered a major breakthrough in international human rights law for the way it holds a state accountable for acts of genocide. Myanmar has been submitting reports as required but refuses to refer to the Rohingya by name and insists it is acting against an insurgency. Pending the court's ruling, the Security Council could take further action to enforce the ICJ provisional measures, but this is unlikely because China has blocked any council consideration of issues relating to Myanmar. It is also important to note that the ICC has its own preliminary investigation of specific individuals linked to the Myanmar genocide but is still hobbled by the fact that Myanmar is not a party to the Rome Statute.

This case shows the creativity of human rights activists in searching for ways to hold states and individuals accountable. A much more common route for accountability is the use of regional human rights courts.

Regional enforcement. With mandatory jurisdiction over forty-six member states and 675 million people, the European Court of Human Rights (ECHR) is the only regional court with specific enforcement mechanisms. Members agree to abide by a final court judgment in any case to which they are a party. Under a 2010 amendment, if they fail to do so, the court can initiate infringement proceedings. If the state's noncompliance is verified, the state can be declared in breach of its obligations under Article 46.

Over time, the ECHR's caseload has increased exponentially, with the majority of judgments occurring since 1998. Over 50,000 applications are submitted annually, although many are ultimately proclaimed inadmissible. Between 1958 and 2011, the court issued 14,940 binding rulings (Alter 2014: 73); from 2011 to 2020, it issued 10,815 judgments (ECHR 2023: 9). The subjects include controversial issues in political and civil rights such as challenges to the United Kingdom's policy of collecting and keeping fingerprint and DNA samples of all criminal suspects (even those later found innocent); Bulgaria's procedures for fair trials and sentencing; and Poland's permitting of US Central Intelligence Agency "black sites" where prisoners were mistreated and tortured during the US-led global war on terror.

States are obligated to inform the Council of Europe of actions taken to comply with the court's judgment. Sometimes that merely means paying compensation, which is relatively easy to enforce. When national laws or practices need to be changed, enforcement is more difficult. Bulgaria had to strengthen its laws after a 1998 decision found its legal procedures inadequate for investigating charges of wrongdoing by police and other officials. In only two cases as of 2022, however, has a state failed to comply with a court ruling. In such situations, the court conducts infringement proceedings to verify the noncompliance. In the very first such case, against Azerbaijan in 2019, a political activist who had been wrongly convicted had that conviction overturned and was awarded compensation. For the second case, which involves Turkey, infringement proceedings were initiated in 2022 and unresolved as of early 2023.

The Inter-American Court of Human Rights (IACHR) is very active, hearing appeals from the member states as well as from individuals. Like the European court, the numbers of petitions are significant—more than 30,000 between 2006 and 2021 (Inter-American Commission on Human Rights 2023). It issues several hundred requests to states each year to adopt "precautionary measures" where individuals are at risk of harm. Twenty-two of its thirty-five members have accepted compulsory jurisdiction. Between the court's founding in 1979 and 2011, it issued 239 binding rulings and 20 advisory opinions (Alter 2014: 73). In 2021, forty new cases were brought before the court—the highest number ever—and the court delivered twenty-seven judgments (Inter-American Court of Human Rights 2021). In a 2020 landmark ruling, the court found Ecuador responsible for failing to protect a student who experienced rape and sexual harassment at school. This was the first ruling to establish state responsibility for preventing sexual abuse against girls and adolescents in schools (Center for Reproductive Rights 2020).

The African Court of Human and Peoples' Rights became operational in 2006, following the entry into force in 2004 of the Protocol to the African Charter on Human and Peoples' Rights. It has its seat in Arusha, Tanzania, and is composed of eleven judges serving six-year terms. Between 2008 and 2022, the court handled 330 cases, finalizing 181 of them (African Court of Human and Peoples' Rights 2022). A 2013 judgment found Tanzania had violated several articles of the African Charter, including rights to freedom of association. The court directed Tanzania to take constitutional, legislative, and other measures to remedy the violations.

Global Human Rights and Humanitarian Governance in Action

Of the many human rights and humanitarian issues, we have chosen three—genocide and ethnic cleansing, violence against women, and LGBTI rights—to illustrate the strengths, successes, weaknesses, and failures of global human rights and humanitarian governance in action.

Genocide and Ethnic Cleansing

Despite the rhetoric of "never again," genocide continues to take the lives of millions. The Holocaust of World War II, with the deaths of six million Jews, Roma, and others, gave rise to the word and to a movement to make it an international crime. Genocides had occurred before then in the Belgian Congo in the late nineteenth century and Armenia in 1915. In 1944, the word "genocide" was coined by a Polish lawyer, Raphael Lemkin, who advocated for recognition of the crime and the UN General Assembly's approval of the Convention on the Prevention and Punishment of Genocide in 1948 (Frieze 2019). It became the first human rights treaty approved by the UN, one day ahead of the General Assembly's approval of the UDHR. The convention defines the crime of genocide, lists the prohibited acts, and calls for punishment of the perpetrators (see Figure 9.2 for key provisions).

The Genocide Convention was rapidly signed and ratified (except by the United States) and widely seen as a major advance in international human rights law. Yet how would it be interpreted and enforced? It does not specify how many people have to be killed to constitute genocide but only addresses the intention on the part of the perpetrators to destroy a group of people "in whole or in part." The convention created no permanent treaty body to monitor situations or provide early warnings of impending or actual genocide. For many years it seemed to have little effect. The international community ignored several situations that appeared to be genocide, such as the "killing fields" of Cambodia, where almost one-third of the country's population died in the mid-1970s.

Figure 9.2   The Genocide Convention (key provisions)

Article I. Genocide, whether committed in time of peace or in time of war, is a crime under international law which they undertake to prevent and punish.

Article II. Genocide means any of the following acts committed with intent to destroy, in whole or in part, a national, ethnical, racial or religious group, as such:
a. Killing members of the group;
b. Causing serious bodily or mental harm to members of the group;
c. Deliberately inflicting on the group conditions of life calculated to bring about its physical destruction in whole or in part;
d. Imposing measures intended to prevent births within the group;
e. Forcibly transferring children of the group to another group.

Article III. The following acts shall be punishable:
a. Genocide;
b. Conspiracy to commit genocide;
c. Direct and public incitement to commit genocide;
d. Attempt to commit genocide;
e. Complicity in genocide.

Article IV. Persons committing genocide or any of the other acts enumerated in Article III shall be punished, whether they are constitutionally responsible rulers, public officials or private individuals.

Article V. The Contracting Parties undertake to enact . . . the necessary legislation to give effect to the provisions of the present Convention and to provide effective penalties for persons guilty of genocide or any of the other acts enumerated in Article III.

The cases of Bosnia, Rwanda, Darfur, the Rohingya in Myanmar, the Uyghurs in China's Xinjiang Province, and Ukraine illustrate the dilemmas associated with applying the Genocide Convention. Did these cases constitute genocide? Was there a systematic attempt by one group to exterminate another group? Or were these just brutal civil wars or, in the case of the Uyghurs, a situation of massive forced labor? If genocide is committed, the parties to the convention are obligated to respond under Article I, but proving genocide is problematic, but not impossible, as the ICTY and ICTR showed for Bosnia and Rwanda. To be sure, few perpetrators leave behind conclusive evidence of their intent, which is key; that explains the effort by the international community to document Russian actions in Ukraine. Perhaps most important, in no cases have UN member states acted decisively and in a timely way to stop the killing.

During the Yugoslav civil war in the 1990s, the term "ethnic cleansing" was coined to refer to systematic efforts by Croatia, the Bosnian Serbs, and Serbia itself to remove people of another group from their territory, but not necessarily to wipe out the entire group or part of it as specified in the Genocide Convention. In Bosnia, Muslim civilians were forced by Serb troops to flee towns for Muslim areas within Bosnia or for neighboring countries. Some were placed in concentration camps. An estimated 60,000 Bosnian women were raped by Serb forces. Croatia expelled Serbs from its territory, and Serbia expelled Kosovar Albanians from Kosovo.

Starting in 1992, investigators from the UN Commission on Human Rights reported "massive and grave violations of human rights" against the Bosnian Muslim population. In the same year, the General Assembly condemned Serbia's ethnic cleansing of Bosnia's Muslims as a form of genocide, and the ICJ issued a unanimous order to Serbia in 1993 to follow the Genocide Convention.

In 2007, the ICJ concluded that although Serbia failed to prevent the 1995 Srebrenica genocide, it neither committed genocide nor conspired nor was complicit in the act of genocide (ICJ 2007). The judges pointed to insufficient proof of intentionality to destroy the Bosnians as a whole or in part. In 1999, however, Croatia had filed a suit against Serbia in the ICJ over the genocide claims, and Serbia filed a countersuit in 2010. The ICJ's 2015 decision was that neither Croatia nor Serbia had committed genocide against the other's population. Crimes were committed by both countries, but the intent to commit genocide had not been proven, the court decided (ICJ 2015). The ICTY convicted Bosnian Serb General Ratko Mladić of genocide in the Srebrenica massacre in 2017, as noted earlier. In short, legal opinions were divided as to whether the situation in the former Yugoslavia and particularly in Bosnia constituted genocide.

The evidence of genocide in Rwanda was much more definitive. In April 1994, after the death of the Rwandan and Burundian presidents in a mysterious plane crash, Hutu extremists in the Rwandan military and police began systematically slaughtering the minority Tutsis and moderate Hutus in a campaign of violence orchestrated by Radio Libres des Milles Collines. In a ten-week period, more than 800,000 were killed out of a total Rwandan population of seven million. Even before the plane crash, reports from NGOs and UN peacekeepers warned that there were plans to target the Tutsi population. In January 1994, General Roméo Dallaire's warnings of an impending genocide went unheeded at UN headquarters and his request for additional UN troops to augment his small, 2,500-member peacekeeping force was denied. He was forced to confine his activities to evacuating foreigners.

The international community was slow to recognize the significance of what was happening. Samantha Power (2002) traced the reasons for the US failure to act to self-serving caution and the belief at first that the killings were merely "random tribal slaughter." When evidence mounted to the contrary, it was ignored and officials avoided using the term "genocide," knowing full well that if it was invoked, they would be forced to take action under the terms of the Genocide Convention. Philip Gourevitch (1998) and Michael Barnett (2002) place harshest blame on the UN, particularly on Security Council members who preferred taking no military action and the

Secretariat, which misunderstood and ignored the problem. Other scholars have suggested that the genocide occurred so fast that the world could not have reliably known enough or had the time to prevent it (Kuperman 2001). Once recognized, there was little debate over whether it was genocide, however. As discussed earlier, the ICTR convicted key individuals for inciting and coordinating acts of genocide against the Tutsis, including former prime minister Jean Kambanda, four military officers, and, most recently, the head of Radio Milles Collines.

The situation in Darfur in Sudan, like the former Yugoslavia, is ambiguous as to whether it constituted genocide. Beginning in 2003, thousands of people fled their homes in the western region of Darfur in Sudan after attacks from government-backed Arab militias (the Janjaweed) on a rebel uprising. Exact figures are hard to come by, but estimates are that between 2003 and 2008, more than 300,000 people were killed in Darfur, 2.3 million were displaced, and another 250,000 fled, mostly to neighboring Chad. Large numbers of villages were destroyed, and more than three million people were dependent on international humanitarian aid. The situation drew the attention of celebrities such as George Clooney and sparked a "Save Darfur" media campaign to press governments to act. US Secretary of State Colin Powell, who labeled Darfur a case of genocide in 2004, was one of the rare official voices to speak out. With China and Russia opposing coercive measures against Sudan, the Security Council referred the situation to the ICC in 2005 and supported a small African Union (AU) monitoring force that was enlarged in 2007 into a joint UN-AU peacekeeping force (discussed in Chapter 7). As noted earlier, the ICC indicted six individuals, including former President al-Bashir, who was accused of genocide along with war crimes and crimes against humanity.

In neither of the other two cases here—the Rohingya and the Uyghurs—is there yet a judicial ruling on whether they constitute genocide. In the ICJ case against Myanmar, the court clearly holds Myanmar as a state accountable for possible acts of genocide, issuing provisional measures ordering the Myanmar military to ensure that its forces do not commit genocidal acts, preserve all evidence of such acts, and report on its compliance. The ICC had its own investigation of people linked to the Rohingya situation under way in 2023.

The situation of the Muslim Uyghur people in China's Xinjiang province is far less clear, and there is no legal action under way as of this writing. In November 2019, the *New York Times* (Ramzy and Buckley 2019) published evidence showing that more than one million ethnic Uyghurs, Kazakhs, and other Muslim minorities had been forcibly moved into internment camps. Satellite images also showed the camps. In addition, following Uyghur attacks against Han Chinese in 2014, President Xi Jinping called for eradicating radical Islam in Xinjiang. Reports subsequently showed that those interned were being subjected to reeducation designed to eradicate their religion, culture, and language and subjected to torture, solitary confinement, mass rape, and forced sterilization of women. Chinese government officials, however, have defended the camps as vocational education and training centers and spoken of the need to root out Islamist extremism to prevent terrorism. More recent evidence links them to forced labor. There has also been a major effort to resettle a large number of Han Chinese in Xinjiang.

In 2021 several Western governments, including the United States, Canada, United Kingdom, and Netherlands, declared that the situation in Xinjiang constituted genocide. HWR and AI have done the same. The 2022 report of UNHCHR Michelle Bachelet after her visit to China, however, referred to widespread and systemic abuse of human rights as well as "arbitrary and discriminatory detention" that may amount to crimes against humanity. Given her position as a UN official, she could hardly have said more. Most human rights activists think that the amount of evidence available makes a fairly clear case for calling the situation "genocide" (Chotiner 2022).

Finally, debate over whether Russia's invasion of and war in Ukraine constitute genocide reveals the limits of and problems with the Genocide Convention. It is a question that Ukraine posed to the ICJ three days after the invasion with a request for provisional measures similar to those approved for Myanmar. In that case, the ICJ asserted that it has jurisdiction and approved provisional measures in mid-March 2022.

Experts link the legal issues to what are called "fatal flaws" in the Genocide Convention. One is the way Rafael Lemkin made the Holocaust the archetype of genocide and "the crime of crimes," as if there were a hierarchy of criminality (Moses 2022). A second flaw was the wording "intent to destroy, in whole or in part, a national, ethnic, racial or religious group, *as such*" (emphasis added). As Moses (2022) notes, "'As such' requires that victims are targeted solely on the ground of their identity—for symbolic rather than material reasons, like warfare" which states did not regard as illegitimate. He added, "everyone understood that armed conflict affected civilians dramatically. . . . Killing masses of civilians was acceptable, if regrettable, when motivated by military goals: victory, not destruction." If proving genocide requires proving "intent to destroy . . . as such," it is exceptionally hard to do.

These cases demonstrate the challenges of proving that a genocide has occurred, as well as the difficulties of enforcing the international norm prohibiting genocide. This is unlikely to change soon.

Violence Against Women

The legal standards for proving violence against women are considerably less stringent than those for genocide, but this constitutes a far more pervasive and troubling human rights problem. Violence against women has been a problem for centuries, and no region of the world is immune to it. For a long time, it was largely hidden in the private sphere of family and communal life, where local authorities and national governments did not intervene and to which the international community turned a blind eye. Forced marriages at a young age, physical abuse by spouses (including disfigurement and rape), large dowry payments, female genital mutilation, and honor killings all occur within the home and family. The long-standing gendered division of labor has forced many women into sweatshop labor, sex work, and trafficking in their bodies; and, for millennia in civil and interstate wars, women have been raped, tortured, and forced into providing sexual services for troops. Similarly, women constitute a majority of the victims of human trafficking, which has grown exponentially with the opening of borders to the flows of capital, trade, and illicit industries with globalization. In 2022, UN Women reported that 65 percent of all trafficking victims globally were women and girls, and more than 90 percent of them were trafficked for sexual exploitation. Yet it is only since the 1990s that these abuses against women have come to be recognized as human rights issues (UN Women 2022).

Although the UN and its specialized agencies took up women's issues beginning in 1946, discussions of women's rights were not framed as issues of human rights until the 1980s and 1990s (Ruane 2011). The UN separated women's rights and human rights conceptually and bureaucratically, with the Commission on Human Rights located in Geneva and the Commission on the Status of Women located in New York.

NGO work on the issue of violence against women dates from 1976, when a group of women from developed countries organized the International Tribunal on Crimes Against Women, gathering two thousand women activists from forty different countries. The tribunal was a reaction to the first UN Conference on Women in 1975, which did not address the issue of violence against women. It heard testimonials from those who had suffered from domestic or community violence, such as rape and sexual slavery. It provided a major impetus to publicizing gender violence and networking, opening up an issue that had previously been regarded as private.

The turning points for linking human rights and women's rights came with the third and fourth UN Conferences on Women in 1985 and 1995 and the Vienna World Conference on Human Rights in 1993. Activist Charlotte Bunch's 1990 article "Women's Rights Are Human Rights" helped establish the conceptual link between the two. Both HRW and AI created women's rights projects in this period, joining the ninety or so human rights and women's NGOs in the Global Campaign for Women's Human Rights leading up to the 1993 World Conference on Human Rights, which endorsed the linkage.

A key element in that campaign was the focus on gender-based violence. Feminist organizations engaged in lobbying, brought lawsuits, networked across international and regional organizations, and demanded institutional changes (Htun and Weldon 2012). The campaign also organized the Global Tribunal on Violations of Women's Human Rights at the parallel NGO forum to the Vienna conference, hearing testimony from abused women and putting a human face on the related problems. The joint efforts of women's and human rights groups produced Article 18 of the Vienna Declaration and Programme of Action, which declared: "The human rights of women and of the girl-child are an inalienable, integral and indivisible part of universal human rights." Violence against women and other abuses in situations of war, peace, and domestic family life were identified as breaches of both human rights and humanitarian norms.

Particularly important to advancing attention to violence against women was the work of Latin American and Caribbean feminist activists who formed the Feminist Network Against Domestic and Sexual Violence. Htun and Weldon (2020: 40) credit these activists with getting the Inter-American Commission of Women to identify violence against women as a special concern in 1986. In 1993, the UN General Assembly approved the UN Declaration on the Elimination of Violence Against Women, calling for a special rapporteur on violence against women. The Latin Americans led the way again in 1994 in adopting the Inter-American Convention on the Prevention, Punishment and Eradication of Violence against Women (Convention of Belém do Pará). This was hard law, not just a declaration, and it included a provision for appointing a rapporteur to monitor compliance. Htun and Weldon's study (2020: 41) showed that by the mid-1990s, Latin American governments were "slightly more likely to have adopted policies on violence against women than European ones" and in the 2000s extended those with legislation recognizing a wide variety of forms and locations of violence.

The EU began promoting policies on violence against women after 1995 as a result of provisions in the Maastricht Treaty (1993) and the Treaty of Amsterdam (1997) that expanded EU legal competence into social policy and highlighted respect for human rights and the rule of law. The European Women's Lobby, with 2,700 affiliates, brought the issue to the public agenda through its Policy Action Center on Violence Against Women. This precipitated a response from the European Parliament's Women's Rights Committee. With enlargement to the east and the Schengen Agreement opening the EU's internal borders, trafficking in and violence against women became broader European issues. The European Commission was slow to take up the issues until pushed by activist women commissioners, but in 1997 the EU established the Daphne program to address gender violence, helping expand the capacity of states and local organizations to help victims (Montoya 2008).

A comparative study by Mala Htun and Laurel Weldon (2012) of seventy countries over four decades found that advocacy and mobilization by strong autonomous domestic feminist groups—feminist movements organized to raise women's status and challenge traditional gender roles, not women's movements organized for other purposes—best explained variations in states' policy development. Similarly, their findings point to the importance of gradual regional diffusion of norms addressing violence against women rather than ratification of CEDAW, leftist parties, women in government, or national wealth. It is noteworthy that action spread from Latin America and North America to Europe and later to parts of Africa, the Middle East, and Asia, where feminist activists in India had some early successes in the 1980s but China continues to lag (Htun and Weldon 2020: 38–51). Gradually, states began to take a variety of actions from creating government offices, funding domestic violence shelters, creating rape crisis centers, and adopting specialized legislation to training professionals who respond to victims and funding prevention and public education programs.

One of the most pernicious and persistent problems is that of rape and other violence against women during armed conflicts. This has been a significant focus of the UN Security Council's agendas on Women, Peace and Security and Protection of Civilians (Chapter 7). Rape, sexual slavery, and forced prostitution are all included in the Rome Statute's list of crimes against humanity. Rape has also been recognized as a war crime. The war in Bosnia in the 1990s and the genocide in Rwanda brought widespread recognition of the systematic use of sexualized violence, and the ICTR issued the first conviction for rape as a crime against humanity and a means of perpetrating genocide. Almost half of those convicted by the ICTY were also found guilty of crimes involving sexual violence, and the tribunal issued the first convictions of individuals for sexual enslavement as a crime against humanity and rape as a form of torture. In 2008, Security Council Resolution 1820 declared rape to be a "tactic of war to humiliate, dominate, instill fear in, disperse and/or forcibly relocate civilian members of a community or ethnic group" and a threat to international security. The following year, the Council created the Office of Special Representative of the Secretary-General on Sexual Violence in Conflict.

A number of other steps have now been taken across the UN system to address issues related to violence against women, including by UN peacekeepers. UN Women is the institutional home for coordinating work on gender equality and empowerment, including human rights and issues of gender-based violence. Among its most significant contributions is progress in reducing violence against women (UN Women 2023).

UN actions were augmented by the 2014 Global Summit to End Sexual Violence in Conflict which drew 123 government delegations along with 1,700 activists and survivors of conflict zones. Among the outcomes of the summit was the International Protocol on the Documentation and Investigation of Sexual Violence in Conflict, which set standards for collecting information, evidence, and witness protection.

The UN system undertook two separate approaches with regard to human trafficking, including of women and girls. Framed as a human rights issue, the action has involved setting standards and securing victims' rights to legal and rehabilitative remedies. The HRC has an anti-trafficking agenda, whereas the ILO has undertaken major studies of forced labor including trafficking. Historically framed as a transnational crime issue, trafficking has led to a series of international prohibitory conventions: the 1951 Convention for the Suppression of Traffic in Persons; the ILO's 1957 convention banning forced labor; the Optional Protocol to the Convention on the Rights of the Child on the Sale of Children, Child Prostitution, and Child Pornography (2002); and the Protocol to Prevent, Suppress, and Punish Trafficking in Persons, Especially Women and Children (2000), known as the Palermo protocol. The UN Office of Drugs and Crime (UNODC) is responsible for implementation, including drafting policies and providing training for law enforcement. Under both approaches, the UN, along with the International Organization for Migration, the OSCE, and concerned states support partnerships and capacity building to a variety of stakeholders.

In terms of articulating and promoting women's rights and an end to violence against women including trafficking of women and girls, the world has come a long way. The UN in particular (but not alone) has helped set legal standards through conventions and declarations; it has provided the forums for advocacy and action in the four women's conferences, the follow-ups to those conferences, and the 1993 World Conference on Human Rights. It has created entities within the UN system in addition to the HRC and CEDAW treaty body to promote, aid, and monitor observance and violations of women's rights, most notably UN Women and the UNODC's Expert on Human Trafficking. Yet cultural norms and long-running practices, along with human instincts, make the fulfillment of the promises of women's rights and rooting out gender-based violence in its many forms extremely difficult. The reality is that advances in legal protections do not always bring societal changes.

Our last case study is directly related to issues of gender identity, particularly the rights of those whose gender identities are not binary. This is a case where the struggle for recognition is very much still in progress and where even getting UN accreditation for the leading NGO took years of efforts.

The Quest for Recognition of LGBTI Rights

Rights based on sexual orientation and gender identity of LGBTI people have gained increasing acceptance in many parts of the world, even though they remain banned in some way in seventy countries. The quest for recognition of LGBTI rights illustrates the debate over whether they are universal rights.

The resistance has been greatest in Africa, the Middle East, and parts of Asia, particularly in many former British colonies where nineteenth-century colonial laws or traditional religious and social structures and attitudes are prevalent. In those cases, national laws permitting discrimination on the basis of sexual orientation with respect to employment, movement, housing, and government services are common and, more important, laws criminalize private consensual sexual activity. In eleven countries, this activity is punishable with the death penalty. In addition, harassment, assault, and even murder of LGBTI people continue to be widespread.

The International Lesbian, Gay, Bisexual, Trans, and Intersex Association (ILGA), an umbrella group of more than 1,800 LGBTI advocacy groups formed in 1978, has worked to internationalize the struggle for LGBTI rights. Getting access to the UN and other international bodies has taken time. Even HRW and AI were slow to endorse LGBTI rights. In its 1994 report on LGBTI rights, for example, Amnesty International noted rather cautiously that no international treaty explicitly defended these rights. Both groups are now active on LGBTI issues, however. In addition to efforts in the UN system, the ECHR and the Inter-American Human Rights Council have been active in addressing LGBTI rights.

The first advocacy efforts on behalf of LGBTI rights in the UN occurred in 1979, when ILGA applied for NGO consultative status with ECOSOC. It was 1993 before it was successful, and ILGA lost that status between 2002 and 2006. But ILGA did enjoy some successes. In 1990, the World Health Organization removed sexual orientation from the *International Classification of Diseases*—an initial success. In 1993, an ILGA representative was invited to address the Sub-Commission on Prevention of Discrimination and Protection of Minorities, and eventually ILGA achieved consultative status (ILGA 2013). In 1995, the first openly lesbian person addressed a UN body and called for states to adopt resolutions recognizing sexual diversity.

In the first decade of the 2000s, a number of states and groups of activists worked to include language that linked human rights and sexual orientation, pressure various UN bodies to prohibit discrimination against sexual minorities, and get the new HRC to address the issue. In 2008, Argentina took the lead in pressing the General Assembly to affirm that "human rights apply equally to every human being regardless of sexual orientation or gender identity" (ARC International 2008). Thereafter, a number of member states formed the UN LGBTI Core Group to promote LGBTI rights in the United Nations. As of 2022, it included thirty-eight UN member states, the EU, HRW, and OutRight Action International.

In 2007 legal scholars with the support of the International Commission of Jurists and the International Service for Human Rights decided to adopt a novel approach to setting standards. Rather than develop new rules to govern policies on LGBTI issues or propose a new convention, they drafted the Yogyakarta Principles on the Application of Human Rights Law in Relation to Sexual Orientation and Gender Identity by showing how existing human rights law applied to gay people (e.g., language on gender discrimination) also applies to sexual orientation. Likewise, treaties endorsing the right to privacy implicitly endorse the right to partnering between consenting adults (Principles 2 and 6), and CEDAW was interpreted to endorse nondiscrimination on the basis of sexual orientation (Mittelstaedt 2008: 362). Although the Yogyakarta Principles were readily accepted by some, they did not have a measurable effect on the politics of LGBTI rights for many states that oppose the idea. They certainly did not change the slow pace of efforts to address the issue.

Despite continuing opposition to including this human rights issue, UN officials continued to speak out. In 2010, Secretary-General Ban Ki-moon affirmed, "Where there is a tension between cultural attitudes and universal human rights, universal rights must carry the day" (United Nations UN News 2008)). In 2011, the HRC approved its first resolution on LGBTI rights, calling for the OHCHR to document discriminatory laws and practices against individuals based on their sexual orientation and gender identity. They found alarming patterns of human rights violations directed at LGBTI people, from discriminatory practices in the workplace, schools, healthcare, and other settings to criminalization of consensual same-sex relationships, as well as violent, hate-motivated attacks and killings. In 2013, OHCHR launched UN Free & Equal—a global public information campaign to promote equal rights and fair treatment of LGBTI people. Two years later, twelve UN agencies took the unprecedented step of issuing a joint statement calling for an end to homophobic and transphobic violence and discrimination and calling on states to do more on the issue.

Detailing this sequence of steps over several years shows what it took for the HRC finally to adopt its first resolution in 2016 (A/HRC/RES/32/2) deploring acts of violence based on sexual orientation and gender identity. The vote of twenty-three in favor, eighteen against, and six abstentions indicated how contentious the subject of LGBTI rights remains. The HRC appointed an Independent Expert on Sexual Orientation and Gender Identity (i.e., Special Procedure) to assess ways of overcoming violence and discrimination, to raise awareness, and to work with governments and relevant stakeholders to increase protections for LGBTI people. This expert reports annually to the HRC on specific topics such as "conversion therapies" (2020), data collection (2019), and decriminalization and antidiscrimination legislation (2017).

Despite opposition, the Free & Equal campaign and the work of the Independent Expert continue. The LGBTI Core Group has held events focused on ending violence and discrimination against LGBTI persons. In 2018, UNHCHR Michelle Bachelet, after noting that more than seventy countries still had laws in place subjecting LGBTI people to long prison sentences and even physical punishment, asserted, "It is essential that we defend and protect the LGBTI community, from every kind of violence and discrimination. There should be nothing 'controversial' about stopping people being murdered, or executed by agents of the State, simply because of who they are or whom they love. Tackling extreme violence does not require new norms." In 2019, the HRC took its first action aimed at discriminatory regulations, rules, and practices affecting some women athletes and the multiple forms of discrimination that women and girls face in sports settings. This led to a 2020 report on race and gender discrimination in sport (UN OHCHR 2020).

Looking at the regions where active human rights institutions have dealt with LGBTI issues, the European Council on Human Rights has approved a number of resolutions and reports over the years on LGBTI rights, discrimination, and the responsibilities of local authorities. In 2020, it criticized Poland in particular and the actions of a number of municipal authorities to declare themselves LGBT "ideology-free zones." Over many years beginning in the 1950s, first the European Commission on Human Rights, then its successor, the ECHR, have heard many cases relating to LGBTI persons. In addition to Poland, these have involved complaints against Russia, Romania, Croatia, Georgia, Bulgaria, Hungary, and Moldova. The EU has recognized sexual orientation as grounds of discrimination that is prohibited in EU law. Still, the scope of provisions does not cover social protection, healthcare, education, or recognition of marital or family status. The latter are subject to national regulations.

In the Americas, the Inter-American Commission on Human Rights decided in 2011 to appoint a rapporteur to strengthen monitoring, protection, and promotion of the rights of LGBTI persons. The OAS General Assembly has passed annual resolutions since 2008 relating to human rights, sexual orientation, and gender identity. In addition, in 2016, eight member states (Argentina, Brazil, Canada, Colombia, Chile, Mexico, the United States, and Uruguay) formed an OAS LGBTI Core Group to promote the issue.

Despite these efforts at global and two regional levels, ILGA's 2020 report, among other things, showed that at least forty-two UN member states still had legal barriers to freedom of expression on issues related to sexual and gender diversity (ILGA 2020: 5). Thus, the goal of securing legal protections through international human rights law remains elusive and UN member states, LGBTI activists, and NGOs continue their efforts to advance the cause.

The Globalization of Human Rights and the Role of the United States

For the final section of this chapter, we turn to the question of what role the United States has played in the development of international human rights law and governance as the dominant power in the world since the end of World War II and a leading actor in efforts to promote global governance and cooperation more generally. States remain key actors in the globalized world of human rights, although the UN and some regional IGOs along with NGOs, experts, and networks play critical roles in norm creation, monitoring, promotion, and in some cases enforcement. No one state has been as central as the United States.

Historically, the United States was a leader in supporting human rights and international mechanisms for accountability. Founded on liberal principles guaranteeing the political and civil rights of individual persons, it has long been a beacon for others. Yet its record is decidedly mixed. It has never recognized economic, social, and cultural rights, for example. It has failed to sign some human rights conventions. It has signed but not ratified others, including the International Covenant on Economic, Social, and Cultural Rights, CEDAW, the Convention on the Rights of the Child, and the Rome Statute of the ICC. In 2012, the US Senate failed to ratify the UN Convention on the Rights of Persons with Disabilities. The US human rights record since the terrorist attacks of September 2011 has been under particular scrutiny for its treatment of the suspected terrorists it detained. Although US abuses are not as widespread or as degrading as those in some other countries, they have tarnished America's reputation "because they were carried out by a powerful democratic state with great influence on other states" and because transnational campaigns and domestic pressure by the courts and civil society proved ineffective at changing US policy (Sikkink 2013: 145–146).

Consistent with liberal institutionalist theory, domestic structure and politics provide major explanations for US policy. The United States opposes or has attached reservations to treaties that it deems to be contrary to the US Constitution or inconsistent with its federal system of government, which leaves the death penalty, for example, as a prerogative for states. An understanding was attached to the Convention on the Elimination of All Forms of Racial Discrimination saying that the provisions would be implemented by the federal government to the extent that it had jurisdiction in such matters. In virtually every case, the United States also adds the declaration that the particular treaty is not self-executing—that is, it does not create rights that are directly enforceable (Buergenthal 1995: 290–298). Julie Mertus (2008: 2) has called the US approach a "bait and switch," arguing that "human rights are something the United States encourages for other countries, whereas the same standards do not apply in the same manner in the United States."

US exceptionalism is often given as an explanation for US ambivalence about committing itself to international human rights more fully. Conservative Republicans in the United States have long opposed giving up authority to what they view as unelected and unaccountable global bureaucracies. These sentiments trace from the defeat of the League of Nations in the Senate in 1919 down to the present.

Has US ambivalence toward the international human rights regime made a difference? At one level, the answer is "of course." When international institutions clash with a superpower that controls essential financial resources, it makes a difference. At another level, adherence to human rights norms is firmly established in a strong network of NGOs and democratic states, supported by public opinion. As constructivists argue, the norms are firmly implanted, and this explains why the deviant behavior of the United States has generated such vigorous debate and condemnation inside and outside the country. The jury may still be out on the long-term effect of this behavior, however, particularly as shifts in global power mean more influence for China and other emerging states that are far less devoted to human rights norms than is the United States.

* * *

There has been remarkable progress in human rights governance since World War II. Globalization of communication and ideas has been a powerful stimulus to the expansion of international human rights norms and humanitarianism, as has the activism of dedicated human rights advocates. Environmental issues and norms about protecting the environment, the subject of the next chapter, have become globalized in many of the same ways, with some activists even promoting the human right to a clean environment.

Suggested Further Reading

Barnett, Michael, ed. (2020) *Humanitarianism and Human Rights: A World of Differences?* New York: Cambridge University Press.

Bob, Clifford. (2019) *Rights as Weapons: Instruments of Conflict, Tools of Power.* Princeton, NJ: Princeton University Press.

Htun, Mala, and S. Laurel Weldon. (2018) *The Logics of Gender Justice: State Action on Women's Rights Around the World.* New York: Cambridge University Press.

Monshipouri, Mahmood, ed. (2020) *Why Human Rights Still Matter in Contemporary Global Affairs.* New York: Routledge.

Neier, Aryeh. (2012) *The International Human Rights Movement: A History.* Princeton, NJ: Princeton University Press.

Risse, Thomas, Stephen C. Ropp, and Kathryn Sikkink, eds. (2013) *The Persistent Power of Human Rights: From Commitment to Compliance.* New York: Cambridge University Press.

Schabas, William A. (2017) *An Introduction to the International Criminal Court,* 5th ed. New York: Cambridge University Press.

Simmons, Beth A. (2009) *Mobilizing for Human Rights: International Law in Domestic Politics.* New York: Cambridge University Press.

10

Preserving the Environment

Case Study: Climate Change and the Youth Movement for Climate Justice

The girl found herself before a crowd of government officials, business-people, journalists, and civil society activists who had convened to discuss environmental degradation. She may have been nervous, but mostly she was angry: a variety of adults had jeopardized the future of the planet and her generation. "You teach us . . . to clean up our mess, not to hurt other creatures, not be greedy," she reminded them. "Then, why do you go out and do the things you tell us not to do?" It was 1992, and twelve-year-old Severn Suzuki of Canada was representing the Environmental Children's Organization at the United Nations Conference on Environment and Development in Rio de Janeiro, Brazil (Suzuki 1992).

Nearly three decades later, there was a different girl and an uncannily similar scenario. It was 2018, and fifteen-year-old Greta Thunberg of Sweden was representing Climate Justice Now! at the 24th Conference of Parties for the UN Framework Convention on Climate Change. Like her predecessor, she may have been nervous, but mostly she was angry at the adults who still seemed to be dragging their feet on climate change. "You are not mature enough to tell it like it is," she scolded. "Even that burden you leave to your children" (Thunberg 2018).

Thunberg was not alone, nor was she powerless. On a single day in March 2019, she was joined by an estimated 1.6 million students who protested climate change inaction by walking out of classes in more than 130 countries. In addition to school strikes, energized young people turned to the courts. Within a few

(continued)

years, youth and other marginalized citizens in about forty countries had filed more than 1,500 environment-related lawsuits against governments and businesses.

Many lawsuits framed environmental degradation as a violation of young people's human rights. In several early cases, national courts ruled in environmentalists' favor—for example, by ordering the government of Colombia to reduce deforestation in the Colombian Amazon and by ordering the government of the Netherlands to cut carbon emissions. The European Court of Human Rights also proved sympathetic, fast-tracking a case that Portuguese youth brought against all of the EU countries plus Norway, Russia, Switzerland, Turkey, Ukraine, and the United Kingdom.

The youth movement for climate justice is a remarkable development. It has raised thorny issues about whether a healthy natural environment is a human right, whether governments have the authority to opt for inaction, and whether older people can be forced to make sacrifices for subsequent generations. How did things come to this?

The Evolution of Climate Science

As the Industrial Revolution spread in the 1800s, coal use skyrocketed in manufacturing, transportation, and other activities. Around the same time, scientists honed their understanding of Earth's natural greenhouse effect: how the planet's atmosphere admits and retains some (but not all) of the sun's heat, creating a climate conducive to plant and animal life. Researchers in Ireland and Sweden conjectured that this delicate balance eventually might be altered by humans' coal-fueled activities, which emitted greenhouse gases—including carbon dioxide (CO_2) and methane—that could collect in the atmosphere and further insulate the planet (Fleming 1998: ch. 6). However, the idea seemed so distant and far-fetched that most people dismissed it.

In the first half of the 1900s, automobiles and airplanes became common, and the world's population grew exponentially. Oil and natural gas joined coal as carbon-based fossil fuels driving industrialization and economic development. Some researchers continued to propose that greenhouse gas emissions from human activities might alter the Earth's climate, and by the 1960s there was a concerted effort to determine whether human-induced climate change was happening.

However, research programs were concentrated in a few countries in Europe and North America, and fundamental uncertainties persisted. Scientists disagreed whether the planet was warming or cooling. Even among scientists who fore-cast global warming, some mused that the change might bring net benefits—for example, by permitting agricultural production in previously frigid regions.

Although the vast majority of states did not have the resources and interest to investigate further, some international organizations did. Beginning in 1967, the World Meteorological Organization (WMO, a UN specialized agency) collaborated with the International Council of Scientific Unions (ICSU, a nongovernmental association of scientists, now known as the International Science Council) to research climate change. At the 1972 Stockholm Conference on the Environment, the UN established a new entity dedicated to environmental issues: the UN Environment Programme (UNEP). UNEP subsequently teamed up with the WMO and ICSU to sponsor climate conferences in 1979, 1980, and 1983.

Importantly, climate change was not the only atmospheric issue on which the WMO and UNEP were collaborating. Both organizations were also focusing on ozone depletion. In the 1970s, scientists had begun theorizing that everyday objects such as air conditioners and aerosol cans were releasing chemical compounds that could transform in the atmosphere, eventually thinning the ozone layer that protects Earth from the sun's harmful rays. Evidence for this grew over the years, and the WMO and UNEP helped governments negotiate a broad frame-work convention on ozone depletion (discussed later in the chapter) in 1985. Later that year, scientists confirmed a hole in the ozone layer over Antarctica, and by 1987 the public outcry propelled governments to negotiate a more specific and binding protocol to the earlier convention. This ozone context was crucial because it formed two difficult-to-shake expectations about how climate policy should mimic ozone policy: first prompt government action through scientific findings, then coordinate government action through a framework treaty followed by a protocol agreement.

In line with these expectations, UNEP bureaucrats again teamed up with WMO and ICSU personnel, hosting another climate conference in Villach, Austria, in 1985. The primary outcome was a 500-page report in which the authors laid out evidence that global warming was both real and problematic. The authors concluded that the scientific basis of climate change was understood well enough that scientists and policymakers should start formulating policies to deal with it.

Climate Inaction and Action

Although the 1985 conference boosted awareness, it did not prompt serious government policymaking. The report came from scientists, not from government officials or businesspeople who would need to change course. Because most countries lacked their own climate research programs, the scientists involved in the report tended to work in wealthy North American or Western European countries, not in the Global South or other areas necessary for a worldwide effort. Even in wealthy North American and Western European countries, the need for action was debated. If carbon emissions and fossil fuels were key culprits, the solution would require extensive economic and societal changes that could derail a host of other governmental goals—not only for the industrialized countries that were the primary historical contributors to greenhouse gases, but also for the developing countries that were aiming for greater future industrialization and consumption.

In short, no government had much enthusiasm for paying near-term economic and social costs nationally in hopes that this would avert long-term environmental dangers internationally. Although Western Europe today is recognized as a vocal proponent of environmental protection, its "Green" political parties were just beginning to form in the 1980s, and the European Environment Agency did not become operational until 1994. A global grassroots environmental movement was in its infancy and more focused on endangered species and pollution than on climate change.

Thus, instead of a single track of science-informed policymaking, discussions of climate change proceeded on distinct tracks: one focused on science, another focused on policy. In the scientific track, the focal point has been the Intergovernmental Panel on Climate Change (IPCC), established by the WMO and UNEP in 1988 (Johnson 2014). The IPCC relies on scientists and other experts who volunteer their time to scrutinize published research and periodically release massive reports. These reflect the work of three working groups: climate change science (Group I), climate change impacts (Group II), and climate change responses (Group III). Working Group I, which is grounded in the "hard" sciences, historically has been less politicized and contested than the other groups, whose work on impacts or responses draws from a more diverse set of disciplines and experts.

When covering IPCC reports, the media often focuses on Working Group I, where much of the deeper scientific consensus happens. Through the assessment cycles culminating in reports in 1990, 1996, 2001, 2007, 2014, and 2022, scientists have sharpened their evidence and expanded their agreement about climate change's scientific causes and effects. Glacial and polar ice melts, sea level rise, record heat, and extreme weather are now more definitively tied to manufacturing, transportation, agriculture, and other human activities, and the sense of urgency in the reports has steadily increased.

Compared with the scientific track, activity in the policy track has not been as centralized, reflecting the reality that climate-related policymaking takes place in a patchwork of forums that vary greatly in their geographic scope or policy focus. They may be global (such as the Global Environment Facility), regional (such as the European Union), national (such as the New Zealand Trading Emissions Scheme), or subnational (such as the Climate Alliance among US states). Moreover, because climate change holds implications for many policy areas, relevant activities also occur in nonenvironmental bodies dedicated to health, food, trade, human rights, labor, security, migration, and so on. In the UN system, for example, UNEP's climate work is regularly overshadowed by the World Bank (which administers large trust funds for climate mitigation or adaptation) and the UN Development Programme (which has fielded the world's biggest public opinion survey on climate change).

Adding to this complexity, other relevant forums exist in the private sector or the not-for-profit sector. For instance, voluntary climate regulations are often set within individual firms like Shell, industry organizations like the International Air Transport Association, or broad business groups like the World Business Council for Sustainable Development. In sum, climate-related policymaking has no clear leader and instead plays out in a regime complex involving actors operating at different geographic levels, in different policy areas, and in different sectors of society (Keohane and Victor 2011).

In addition to being less centralized, the policy track is less cumulative than the scientific track. It has not proceeded on a single path and sometimes has lost adherents. A foundational document in the policy track is the 1992 United Nations Framework Convention on Climate Change (UNFCCC). Although the UNEP Secretariat had played a key role in the negotiations on ozone in the 1980s, governments marginalized UNEP in the UNFCCC negotiations and opted to set up a separate Secretariat, located far from UNEP headquarters. Facing deep disagreements among themselves, governments also refrained from specifying implementation measures and instead focused on laying out broad principles, such as "common-but-differentiated responsibilities." All parties promised to take steps toward climate change mitigation, but the commitments were binding for only a short list of industrialized countries named in the treaty's Annex I.

Initially signed by more than 150 states, by 2023 the UNFCCC had been ratified by 198 states. The annual conferences of the parties (COPs) have been the sites for negotiations on implementation measures. A first step was the 1997 Kyoto Protocol, which obligated the UNFCCC's Annex I countries to start reducing their overall greenhouse gas emissions. It also outlined three "flexibility mechanisms"—emissions trading schemes, joint implementation, and the Clean Development Mechanism—by which

Annex I countries could collaborate with each other or with developing states to meet their obligations.

The United States refused to ratify the Kyoto Protocol, arguing that the system of common-but-differentiated responsibilities was unfair and futile: Annex I countries would pay significant economic and social costs for cutting their emissions, but because nothing kept emissions from China and other major developing countries from increasing, global emissions would not decline. The Kyoto Protocol still garnered enough ratifications to enter into force in 2005. EU member states created their own regulatory systems with legally binding targets and timetables and also launched the EU Emissions Trading System, which has been a key tool for reducing industrial greenhouse gas emissions. Nevertheless, in 2011, Canada withdrew from the Kyoto Protocol, and other states expressed their dissatisfaction with the protocol.

With the protocol's first commitment period scheduled to end in 2012, states explored alternatives. At the 2007 COP in Bali, states agreed that China and India should be included in any follow-up commitments. At the 2009 Copenhagen COP, the world's two biggest emitters, China and the United States, sketched a plan for bilateral action. By the 2014 COP in Lima, there was consensus that every country—rich or poor—should take steps to reduce the use of oil, gas, and coal and announce its intended cuts by mid-2015.

Rather than extending the Kyoto Protocol, governments replaced it with the Paris Agreement, which was finalized at the 2015 Paris COP and entered into force in 2016. Several factors were important to this process. One was that by November 2014, the United States and China had jointly announced emissions targets for themselves, setting an example for other countries and providing a sense of momentum. A second factor was several groups advocating for rapid action. These included the Alliance of Small Island States (AOSIS, a coalition of thirty-nine island and low-lying coastal states highly vulnerable to sea-level rise) and the Climate Action Network (a set of more than 1900 civil society groups in over 130 countries), which pressured governments to end the use of fossil fuels and to address the needs of those most vulnerable. A third factor was a sense of urgency that created a fundamental change in the geopolitics of climate change, "a shift in the perception of global warming from a distant warning to an immediate threat" (Davenport 2015: A1).

The Paris Agreement, which aims to limit global warming to below 2°C, contains provisions about abandoning fossil fuels by 2050, reducing deforestation, monitoring and reporting countries' implementation of their targets, and addressing loss and damage associated with climate change. It scraps the Kyoto Protocol's bifurcated approach of nonbinding promises for some countries and binding commitments for others, instead calling for all state-parties to make voluntary "nationally determined contributions" (NDCs). The NDCs are pledges to reduce a country's greenhouse gas emissions. Governments are supposed to ratchet up their pledges every five years, although the agreement does not stipulate any penalty for those that fail to meet or increase their NDCs. The agreement also contained provisions regarding reducing deforestation, monitoring and reporting on how countries reach their targets, and addressing the loss and damage associated with climate change.

Once again, US support of global action wavered, however. Knowing the Paris Agreement could not gain enough support in the US Senate to be ratified as a treaty, President Obama joined via an executive agreement, which meant US participation could be rescinded by a successor. In 2017, President Donald Trump announced the US's exit. In opposition to the Trump administration, California governor Jerry Brown and former New York City mayor Michael Bloomberg launched the America's Pledge initiative to coordinate and measure emissions-cutting activities by US states, cities, institutions, and businesses. In 2021, President Joseph Biden used a new executive order to rejoin the Paris Climate Agreement.

Another complication with the Paris Climate Agreement is that nothing prevents governments from picking unambitious targets. Indeed, countries' collective NDCs during the initial 2015–2020 cycle were not on track to avoid a 2°C increase in the global average temperature. A second five-year cycle, which was supposed to begin in 2020 and ratchet up all governments' NDCs, was delayed by the Covid-19 pandemic. Thus, although the Paris Agreement sought to move beyond the Kyoto Protocol, numerous environmentalists saw it as a step back.

With nearly 40,000 registered participants, the UNFCCC's 2021 COP broke records. Protesters descended on Glasgow, Scotland, to demand greater climate action. Many of the most passionate protesters were young women, while many of the most powerful decisionmakers were older men. US President Joseph Biden used the occasion to emphasize the return of US leadership in multilateralism, but several other world leaders (including China's Xi Jinping, Russia's Vladimir Putin, and Brazil's Jair Bolsonaro) did not attend at all. The single largest group of delegates was about 500 people linked to the fossil fuel industry. One noteworthy achievement of the conference was the first mention of "fossil fuels," subsidies for these fuels, and coal reduction in the outcome document. States also made some aspirational pledges about deforestation, methane emissions, and carbon offsets. As UN Secretary-General António Guterres commented, "The collective political will was not enough to overcome some deep contradictions . . . but we have some building blocks for progress" (UN Secretary-General 2021).

The UNFCCC's 2022 COP in Egypt produced more concrete achievements. In a continuation of multilateral attempts at climate change mitigation, states launched the Forest and Climate Leaders' Partnership to combat deforestation that contributes to climate change. Acknowledging that full mitigation might not be possible, states also explored climate change adaptation by planning Early Warnings for All, a system for forecasting, preparing for, and giving advance warning of climate-related natural disasters. Moreover, in a nod toward climate justice, wealthy countries agreed to contribute to a Loss and Damage Fund that would aid climate-vulnerable developing countries.

The Future of the Youth Movement for Climate Justice

For the youth movement for climate justice, however, all of this is too little, too late. Whether speaking in national legislatures, the UN, or the World Economic Forum, angry young people repeatedly cite scientific authorities (especially the IPCC's evidence) on the speed with which climate change is happening. In testimony to the US House of Representatives on Earth Day 2021, for example, Greta Thunberg warned, "If you compare the current so-called climate policies to the overall current best available science, you clearly see that there's a huge gap . . . How long do you think you can continue to ignore the climate crisis, the global aspect of equity, and historic emissions without being held accountable?" (Wade 2021).

The youth movement for climate justice certainly has numbers on its side. There are nearly two billion people between the ages of ten and twenty-four, making up the largest generation of youth in human history. Thunberg's school strikes in Sweden resonated with other young leaders, such as Licypriya Kangujam in India, Alexandria Villaseñor in the United States, and Elizabeth Wathuti in Kenya. Millions of students around the world have walked out of their classes to protest climate inaction. Even when the Covid-19 pandemic impeded some of the momentum, the movement found other ways to fight.

One of the most intriguing ways is through domestic or international courts. Youth have accused governments and businesses of not adhering to international conventions, domestic legislation, or constitutional provisions concerning a healthy natural environment. Constitutional provisions offer especially strong guarantees, and more than 100 countries have enshrined environmental rights in their constitutions. The coming years are likely to witness a deluge of lawsuits.

All of this raises high-stakes questions. Is a healthy natural environment a human right? Are governments liable if they do not act forcefully to address climate change? Can older people be forced to make sacrifices for younger or unborn generations? In raising such questions, the youth movement is rebelling against a long history of environmental problems getting worse while decisionmakers talk rather than act. By highlighting human rights, government liability, and intergenerational responsibility, many young people are trying to force a response.

General Challenges in Environmental Governance

As a pivotal contemporary topic, climate policymaking is worth understanding. It also offers broader insights. Indeed, the climate justice movement and young people's anger at climate inaction demonstrate at least five general challenges in environmental governance.

First, environmental governance partly hinges on scientists, whose methods conflict with the way that many people think. Scientists are trained to delve into the research opportunities presented by uncertainty or ignorance, but laypeople often expect authority figures to deliver immediate and unequivocal answers. They have a difficult time accepting the delays, debates, and corrections through which environmental scientists reach a shared understanding. For example, while today's young people rightly note that the majority scientific opinion about climate change has been set for years, older people find it hard to forget an earlier time when some scientists insisted that the planet was cooling or that global warming would be a net benefit. By the time scientists reach consensus, the window for policy responses may be closing. Even if the window remains open, scientific consensus on environmental circumstances does not necessarily tell policymakers how to navigate ethical dilemmas or painful trade-offs.

Second, environmental governance is rife with collective action problems in which individually rational decisions can produce a "tragedy of the commons"—that is, socially undesirable outcomes like atmospheric warming, deforestation, water pollution, or species loss (Hardin 1968). Delivering a collective good in such situations requires coordination mechanisms, but large or heterogeneous groups are hard to coordinate, and free-riders lurk. Moreover, since environmental issues regularly overlap with security, economic, or social considerations, decisionmakers tend to worry about getting doubly burned if they undertake costly changes that are not reciprocated. It is difficult for people to work together; human population growth, which is tied to many environmental problems, makes meaningful collective action even harder.

Third, environmental governance reveals tensions between rich and poor. Some tensions play out across national borders. People in developing countries blame the industrialized countries for exploiting the natural environment on their own paths to development, then trying to prohibit that for everyone else. People in industrialized countries counter that the dire repercussions are better understood now, and the damage to the shared planet cannot be reversed unless developing countries join them in behavioral changes. Meanwhile, other tensions play out inside national borders. More aggressive action to protect the natural environment is likely to result in job losses, higher prices, and other difficulties that tend to hit poor people hardest. Even if domestic policymakers could pinpoint everyone who needs help, they would have a tough time taking resources away from the well-off to deliver it. After all, the people who are most hurt by environmental problems may be the most disenfranchised. In many developing countries, for example, women are disproportionately harmed in natural disasters and are the household managers for food and fuel—but impoverished women have little political power domestically, let alone internationally.

Fourth, environmental governance often takes place in regime complexes containing numerous overlapping policy areas and institutions. Climate change is just one of many environmental issues that affect other areas like health, trade, human rights, labor, security, or migration (Diamond 2005). Moreover, environmental policy is less hierarchically institutionalized than trade, for example, where the World Trade Organization (WTO) is supposed to be the pinnacle institution in which global trade rules are set and to which regional or bilateral trade agreements are reported. Despite reforms in 2012, UNEP does not manage all environmental activities inside the UN system, let alone outside of it, but neither is it yet a full-fledged intergovernmental organization (IGO).

Fifth, environmental governance involves a variety of stakeholders. Governance structures at the global level do not necessarily supersede structures at the regional, national, or subnational levels. Public-sector institutions do not necessarily supplant institutions from the private sector or the not-for-profit sector. Organized groups do not necessarily trump looser social movements such as the youth movement for climate justice. Specialists are not necessarily representative of the general population. In 1992, UNEP solidified this diversity through its Nine Major Groups system, which provides platforms for local authorities, business and industry, nongovernmental organizations (NGOs), workers and trade unions, women, farmers, children and youth, the scientific and technological community, and Indigenous peoples. The result is a large and heterogeneous assemblage of governance actors, all with a stake in planet Earth (Hadden 2015).

For these five reasons—the zigzags of the scientific process, the prevalence of collective action problems, the tensions between rich and poor, the complexity of regimes, and the heterogeneity of stakeholders—environmental governance faces serious challenges.

UN Environmental Conferences, Commissions, and Summits

In national and international public policy, environmentalism is often viewed as a relatively recent issue, arising only in the mid-twentieth century. Evidence for this includes several developments in the 1960s: popular books like Rachel Carson's *Silent Spring* and Jacques Cousteau's *The Living Sea*, the Torrey Canyon oil spill off the coast of the United Kingdom, and the first photographs of Earth that astronauts took from outer space. Such developments made ordinary people more aware of the interdependence of living things, the dangers posed by industrialization, and the vulnerability of the planet as a single ecosystem. More citizens demanded that their governments make a concerted effort to protect the natural environment.

The demand for governmental action was also fueled by two trends that began long before the 1960s (Meyer et al. 1997). One was the gradual expansion of scientific knowledge, enabling the collection of data to monitor environmental trends. Another was the rise of environment-oriented associations—initially, national NGOs such as the Society for the Protection of Birds (1889) or the Sierra Club (1892), and then international NGOs such as the Society for the Preservation of the Wild Fauna of the Empire (1903) and the precursor to the International Union for the Conservation of Nature (IUCN, 1913). As scientists and civil society paid more attention to the natural environment, governments and the private sector did, too.

The UN Charter contains no mention of environmental protection. Nevertheless, UN-sponsored conferences and commissions have substantially contributed to the evolution of global environmental governance. This section describes some of the UN's most consequential contributions: the Stockholm Conference (1972), the Brundtland Commission (1983–1987), the Rio Conference (1992), the Johannesburg Conference (2002), and the Rio+20 Conference (2012).

The 1972 Stockholm Conference

In the 1960s, Sweden and other Nordic states proposed an international environmental conference, which came to fruition in Stockholm with the 1972 UN Conference on the Human Environment. Maurice Strong, a Canadian businessperson, served as the conference's secretary-general and had to deal with divergent views between the Global North and South.

The Global North, which often blamed environmental problems on poorer countries' rapid population growth, emphasized issues such as transborder pollution and biodiversity loss. The Global South, which often blamed environmental problems on rich countries' high-consumption lifestyles and overuse of natural resources, feared that environmental regulation could hamper economic growth and divert resources away from economic development. Many developing countries were reluctant to attend the conference. To reassure them, Strong made clear the conceptual links between development and the environment, arguing that environmental problems were a concern for everyone, not a plot to keep them underdeveloped.

The 1972 conference was a critical juncture. As noted earlier, it created UNEP to promote governmental cooperation and coordinate environmental activities. In addition, as discussed in Chapter 6, it set a precedent for running NGO forums in parallel with the intergovernmental meetings. It also tried to reconcile divergent North/South views and interests. The Stockholm Declaration, a soft-law statement of twenty-six principles, incorporated the view that states are obliged to protect the environment and not damage the environment of others. The declaration also stipulated that environmental policies should enhance developing countries' economic potential and not hamper the attainment of better living conditions. States agreed not to use environmental concerns as justification for discriminatory trade practices or as a way to decrease access to markets.

By establishing UNEP and permitting extensive involvement of NGOs and epistemic communities in policy efforts, the Stockholm Conference cemented environmental issues on national and international policy agendas. To signal their commitment and improve national capacity, many states began to create environmental bureaucracies (Aklin and Urpelainen 2014). In addition, notions such as Spaceship Earth and slogans such as "think globally, act locally" took hold in the popular consciousness.

The 1983–1987 Brundtland Commission

The Stockholm Declaration's linking of development and environmental protection was met with some skepticism by developing countries, which argued that environmental concerns ignored structural injustices in the international system and jeopardized their economic development. However, environmentalists continued to worry about championing economic growth when natural resources were already strained. In response to this tension, in 1983 the UN General Assembly established the World Commission on Environment and Development, chaired by Norway's former prime minister Gro Harlem Brundtland.

As discussed in Chapter 8, the Brundtland Commission sought to balance ecological concerns with the economic growth necessary to reduce poverty. In its 1987 report *Our Common Future*, it emphasized that the South could not develop in the same way the industrialized countries had, because humanity could not survive more radical transformations in the environment. Instead, the report promoted the concept of sustainable development: "development that meets the needs of the present without compromising the ability of future generations to meet their own needs" (World Commission on Environment and Development 1987: 8).

The report had far-reaching consequences. One was its concept of sustainable development, which was adopted by UNEP and later by the World Bank, the UNDP, NGOs, and many national development agencies. In addition to calling attention to long-term repercussions and acknowledging poverty as a source of environmental degradation, the concept encouraged people to ponder critical links among agriculture, trade, transportation, energy, and the environment (Esty 2001). A second far-reaching consequence was the commission's call for another global environmental conference to be held in 1992.

The 1992 Rio Conference

Twenty years after the Stockholm Conference, the 1992 UN Conference on the Environment and Development (UNCED) was held in Rio de Janeiro, Brazil. Also known as the Earth Summit or Rio Conference, it was a watershed for international environmental policy. It occurred as the Cold War was ending, and governments were striving to demonstrate that they could cooperate across East/West and North/South lines. The conference agenda was shaped by a series of key scientific findings from the 1980s: the discovery of the hole in the ozone layer over Antarctica, growing evidence of human-induced climate change, and richer data on fish depletion and biodiversity loss.

The Rio Conference was vast, both in the scope of the agenda and the number of participants. NGOs played key roles in the preparatory process and the meeting. The approximately 1,400 environmental groups accredited for the conference included not just large and well-financed NGOs such as the World Wide Fund for Nature (WWF) and IUCN, but also nascent grassroots groups with small budgets and few previous transnational linkages. NGOs participated at various stages, from information-gathering to decisionmaking to implementation. What began as a parallel informal process of participation set a precedent about stakeholders' right to engage.

In preparatory meetings, government representatives articulated their positions, resolved basic issues, and negotiated the texts of conference documents. At the conference itself, states were invited to sign two legally binding treaties, the Convention on Biological Diversity (CBD) and the UN Framework Convention on Climate Change (UNFCCC). Both treaties have suffered from the general challenges noted earlier, including collective action problems and tensions between rich and poor. For example, in attempting to appease the North and the South, the wording of the CBD obliged national governments to conserve biological diversity but also acknowledged their sovereignty over their domestic resources. All states ratifying the CBD committed themselves to making national preservation plans, and wealthy states further pledged to provide financial assistance for poorer states. But as with the UNFCCC, the CBD has relied on states for follow-through and enforcement, and many have been slow to act.

In several ways, the Rio Conference furthered the Brundtland Commission's concept of sustainable development. For instance, links between development and the environment were pushed in an 800-page nonbinding UNCED document called Agenda 21. The document reflected developmentalist views about state sovereignty over natural resources and the need to address inequalities in the international system, while also incorporating environmentalist views about the planet as a collective good and the need to be responsible stewards. In addition, it took the novel step of giving NGOs direct responsibility in dealing with environmental issues.

Links between development and the environment were further cemented in the 1993 creation of the Commission on Sustainable Development (CSD), headquartered in New York. For the next twenty years, the CSD monitored Agenda 21's implementation by receiving reports from states, other UN bodies, and NGOs. Since the reports' content, formatting, and timing were determined by the authors, there was no way to assess progress or make cross-national comparisons. Although the CSD eventually enjoyed some successes related to forests, oceans, and freshwater, it largely served as a "talk shop" (Kaasa 2007: 116–119).

Over time, the concept of sustainable development spread. For example, it was applied to the General Agreement on Tariffs and Trade (GATT) trading system and the gradual "greening" of World Bank programs. The Global Environment Facility (GEF) was structured to cover desertification and other environmental issues of particular concern to developing countries. Various subsequent conferences—including the UN's 1995 Social Summit, the 1995 Fourth World Conference on Women, and the 1996 Habitat II Conference—reinforced and publicized the concept. With the argument that all people are entitled to a healthy and productive life in harmony with nature, sustainable development also became linked to human rights.

The 2002 Johannesburg Summit

The 2002 UN World Summit on Sustainable Development (also known as Rio+10) met in Johannesburg, South Africa. Its purpose was to build on the Rio Conference's agenda, which had been ambitious but poorly executed. Participants hoped to curb poverty, pollution, and deforestation, all of which had accelerated during the 1990s. As discussed in Chapter 4, changing the meeting's name to a "summit" reflected some states' reluctance to continue the pattern of UN global conferences.

The divisions did not end there. The Europeans wanted targets and timetables, which the United States thought were unnecessary. Meanwhile, the Global South wanted more aid for economic growth. In contrast to the Rio Conference, few states held preparatory meetings to alleviate their disagreements, and many environmental activists felt marginalized. By the time the summit convened, there was increasing disillusionment with the concept of sustainable development. The term was criticized as empty buzzwords; some officials, especially in the developing world, even asserted that "sustainable" referred not to environmental stewardship but to continuity of economic growth (Esty 2001: 74).

Overall, the Johannesburg Summit was seen as disappointing compared with previous gatherings. Its main outcome was a plan of implementation containing some targets about access to clean water and proper sanitation, reduction of biodiversity loss, better use of chemicals, and more renewable energy. However, the plan left implementation to "action coalitions" of governments, citizen groups, and businesses, and it said little about deforestation and other important problems. Disappointment with the Johannesburg Summit led to the Earth System Governance Project, a social science research program that developed a roadmap for major institutional changes to be considered in a follow-up conference a decade later (Biermann 2012).

The 2012 Rio+20 Conference

The follow-up conference convened in Rio de Janeiro in 2012. Technically called the UN Conference on Sustainable Development, but more colloquially known as Rio+20, it aimed to cover two large topics: facilitating the "green economy" and strengthening the institutional framework for sustainable development. Again, there were months of preparatory meetings. These were partly animated by a growing recognition that environmental degradation had security implications, as competition over scarce resources could lead to interstate war, societal collapse, or state failure. In addition to persistent North/South disagreements about proposals such as technology transfer, this time many governments were distracted by the aftershocks of the 2008 global financial crisis and the ongoing calamity of Europe's sovereign debt.

Echoing earlier UN-sponsored mega-conferences, Rio+20 brought together thousands of stakeholders and hosted numerous parallel events. Several world leaders declined to attend, however. Activists had called for tough new measures, such as an international mechanism for corporate accountability and a timetable for governments to eliminate fossil fuel subsidies, but governments could not even agree on basic things like the meaning of the "green economy." The conference's final report, *The Future We Want*, did not contain many new commitments or enforcement mechanisms.

Instead, filled with weak terms such as "recognize" or "encourage," the report focused on reminding governments about their previous unfulfilled commitments (Ivanova 2013: 4).

The conference did bring about a few significant changes. For one thing, it endorsed UNEP reforms. Going forward, UNEP would have universal membership, more funding, and a bigger coordination role in various international environmental initiatives. In addition, conference negotiators agreed to replace the twenty-year-old CSD with the High-Level Political Forum on Sustainable Development (HLPF). The HLPF would convene every four years at the heads-of-state level under the General Assembly and annually under the UN Economic and Social Council. Reformers hoped this would be a more suitable counterweight to the World Bank and the WTO, which have substantially influenced international environmental policy despite being designed to deal with economic issues. The HLPF would take a central role in devising and overseeing the 2015–2030 Sustainable Development Goals, further discussed below.

Components of Global Environmental Governance

The UN's mega-conference approach may have outlived its usefulness, but it did pressure states to adopt national agendas, accept new behavioral norms, and engage with multiple stakeholders. The process incrementally shifted perceptions and behaviors (Haas 2002). Key components of global environmental governance include principles, agreements, and institutions, all shaped by a variety of actors—not just national governments but also epistemic communities, NGOs and civil society, the private sector, and subnational governments.

Key Principles

Two particularly important principles appear in the 1972 Stockholm Declaration. One is the principle of "no significant harm." Shaped by the 1941 Trail Smelter dispute between the United States and Canada, "no significant harm" means that states are responsible for ensuring that activities within their jurisdiction do not cause environmental damage to others. Second is the principle of "good neighbor" cooperation: if environmental problems do arise, states agree to cooperate in addressing them. Both principles have been in operation for decades and are generally recognized as customary international law—that is, obligations arising not from formal treaties but from established patterns of behavior.

Other principles are still emerging. The 1992 Rio Declaration contains several, including "polluter pays" (the party responsible for environmental damage should make amends for it); "preventive action" (states should take early steps to avoid environmental harm within their jurisdictions); and the "precautionary" principle (lack of scientific certainty should not preclude intervention against serious threats). In addition, the principles of sustainable development and intergenerational equity suggest that people of today must minimize harm and preserve the natural environment for people of the future. Several key environmental principles remain nonbinding "soft law."

Multilateral Environmental Agreements (MEAs)

By describing acceptable behaviors and establishing customary practices, soft law provides starting points for formulating "hard law" in multilateral environmental agreements (MEAs). MEAs are legally binding instruments by which two or more states commit to meeting environment-related objectives. They often take the form of treaties, to which states become parties via ratification or accession. MEAs can be bilateral (two states), regional (multiple states from a specific geographic area), or global. As of 2022, there were about 2,200 bilateral agreements and about 1,300 regional or global ones (Mitchell et al. 2020). Table 10.1 provides examples, including the UN High Seas Treaty, which opened for ratification in 2023.

Although some regional or global agreements are linked to specific organizations, others are free-standing. There is evidence that states may be more likely to participate in environmental treaties that contain dispute settlement provisions or assistance for building state capacity (Bernauer et al. 2013), but relatively few MEAs contain such mechanisms. Instead, the most common pieces are a secretariat, one or more specialized subsidiary bodies convening on an ad hoc basis, and a conference or meeting of the parties. Periodically, states that have ratified or acceded to a treaty convene to oversee the treaty and make any major decisions; day-to-day, many activities are handled by international bureaucrats who staff the treaty's secretariat. Between these two extremes are scientific bodies or other specialized subsidiaries that tend to meet more frequently than in annual or biannual COPs, but less continuously than secretariat staff. People serving on scientific bodies are usually nominated by state-parties—but, in line with professional norms, they are expected to provide independent assessments and be politically neutral.

The focus and scale of MEAs have differed over time. Before the 1970s, MEAs tended to be very specific, applying to one species or one part of the world. As scientists and policymakers learned more about ecological connectedness, MEAs began to reflect a more integrated approach, simultaneously covering multiple species and/or parts of the world. For example, the Convention on the Conservation of Migratory Species (CMS) encompasses a variety of wild animals, whether they migrate by land, water, or air. By the 1980s, there was growing recognition that some environmental

Table 10.1   Selected Global and Regional Multilateral Environmental Agreements (MEAs)

	Year Opened for Ratification	Year Entered into Force
Global MEAs		
International Convention for the Regulation of Whaling	1946	1948
Convention on International Trade in Endangered Species of Wild Fauna and Flora	1973	1975
Vienna Convention for the Protection of the Ozone Layer	1985	1988
Basel Convention on the Control of Transboundary Movements of Hazardous Wastes and Their Disposal	1989	1992
UN Convention on Biological Diversity	1992	1993
UN Framework Convention on Climate Change	1992	1994
UN Convention to Combat Desertification in Those Countries Experiencing Serious Drought and/or Desertification, Especially in Africa	1994	1996
Convention on Persistent Organic Pollutants	2001	2004
Minamata Convention on Mercury	2013	2017
UN High Seas Treaty	2023	—
Regional MEAs		
Convention for the Protection of the Mediterranean Sea against Pollution	1976	1987
Convention on Cooperation for Protection and Sustainable Use of the Danube River	1994	1998
ASEAN Agreement on Transboundary Haze Pollution	2002	2003
Agreement on the Conservation of Gorillas and Their Habitats	2007	2008
Agreement on Cooperation on Marine Oil Pollution Preparedness and Response in the Arctic	2013	2016

issues could affect all of planet Earth; this led to agreements such as the Vienna Convention for the Protection of the Ozone Layer (discussed earlier and below), ratified by all of the world's recognized states.

In addition to showing how MEAs' focus and scale have changed, the CMS Convention and Vienna Convention demonstrate two different models that allow an MEA to evolve. The CMS Convention illustrates an "appendix" model: the main text can remain unchanged while state-parties move species into and out of appendixes corresponding to different threat levels. The Vienna Convention illustrates a "framework" model: it articulates broad norms and aims, but it leaves details about implementation and enforcement to one or more separate protocols that may be updated or replaced over time.

By the early 1990s, the aim of protecting or conserving the environment was subsumed by broader discussions of sustainable use and sustainable development. As mentioned earlier, the 1992 Rio Conference was a watershed: it propelled the concept of sustainability and also formulated the global treaties on climate change and biodiversity. Subsequent MEAs have tended to reflect notions of sustainability and the connectedness of ecological processes.

IGOs and Related Institutions

In addition to intergovernmental treaties, global environmental governance relies on intergovernmental institutions. These play key roles such as setting standards, sponsoring MEA negotiations, monitoring governments' behavior, and occasionally enforcing environmental law. They bring together member states, NGOs, and other actors for discussions, funding, and implementation. Although the various aspects of environmental policy involve many intergovernmental institutions, four central institutions are spotlighted here: UNEP, the World Bank, the GEF, and the WTO.

United Nations Environment Programme. For decades, many IGOs have had an environmental component in their responsibilities. Examples include the WMO's examination of air pollution and the Food and Agriculture Organization's monitoring of fisheries. However, the UN system had no agency devoted to environmental issues until the 1972 Stockholm Conference created UNEP and designated Maurice Strong as its initial executive director. With headquarters in Nairobi, Kenya, UNEP was the first UN agency based in a developing country—a plus for the Global South but a negative for coordination with other UN bodies, whose main offices tend to be in New York, Geneva, and other cities in the Global North.

During its first forty years, UNEP was mandated to promote international cooperation, serve as an early warning system for environmental dangers, guide environmental programs in the UN system, and review program implementation. Pursuing this mandate required close collaboration with other IGOs. For instance, the WMO and the International Oceanographic Council proved important for monitoring atmospheric and ocean quality, respectively. Involvement in monitoring and assessments enabled UNEP to call attention to issues like marine pollution, chemical pollutants, and hazardous wastes.

Much of UNEP's early progress can be traced to Mostafa Tolba, the dynamic but divisive Egyptian microbiologist who succeeded Strong as executive director in 1975 and held that post until 1992. A signature achievement was the Regional Seas Programme, by which UNEP's early work with states bordering the Mediterranean Sea was incrementally replicated for seas in other regions. Another notable accomplishment involved ozone depletion, for which Tolba convened relevant parties, floated proposals, and applied pressure on the path to the adoption of the 1985 Vienna Convention. Eventually, UNEP was designated to provide secretariat services for eight global MEAs (the Vienna Convention, the CBD, the CMS, the Convention on International Trade in Endangered Species of Wild Fauna and Flora [CITES], the Minamata Convention on Mercury, the Rotterdam Convention on the Prior Informed Consent Procedure for Certain Hazardous Chemicals and Pesticides in International Trade, and the Stockholm Convention on Persistent Organic Pollutants) as well as seven regional MEAs.

Nonetheless, UNEP has been unable to spearhead a global response to climate change, meet states' needs for capacity-building resources, or even harmonize MEA reporting requirements (Ivanova 2021). Set up as a "program" rather than a full-fledged organization, for more than four decades UNEP had a modest number of staff, a secondary position reporting to the UN General Assembly via ECOSOC, and a relatively small budget (originally all raised through voluntary contributions). It was hampered by its location far from other UN centers, its limited engagement with high-level government officials beyond environment ministries, and its lack of leverage over states and UN specialized agencies. Yet it was expected to pursue an expansive environmental agenda, coordinate the activities of other IGOs, and be "catalytic" within the UN system (DeSombre 2006: 14–20; Ivanova 2010: 33).

The reforms endorsed at the 2012 Rio+20 conference brought more formal authority for UNEP to aid states with capacity-building and implementation, plus assessed contributions that provided greater financial stability (Ivanova 2013). The Governing Council was upgraded to become the UN Environment Assembly. UNEP adopted a results-based management system and reorganized its work into six key areas: ecosystem management, harmful substances, resource efficiency and sustainable consumption/production, postconflict and disaster management, climate change, and environmental governance. It also experimented with an alternative name, UN Environment, to emphasize its equal footing with specialized agencies. However, the organization still struggles with the enormity of global environmental governance, and key stakeholders complain that the 2012 reforms yielded lackluster results (Ivanova 2021). For instance, wealthy countries such as the United States and the United Kingdom still resist making larger voluntary contributions, charging that UNEP is either wasteful or captured by the interests of poorer countries.

The Global Environment Facility. Tensions between richer and poorer countries challenge UNEP and also help explain the creation and evolution of another entity, the GEF, which began operating in 1991 as a three-year pilot program sponsored by UNEP, UNDP, and the World Bank. At its core was a trust fund offering grants and concessional funding to cover additional costs associated with transforming countries' development projects into endeavors with global environmental benefits. Richer countries were asked to donate, with the funds distributed to poorer countries that were eligible for World Bank lending or UNDP technical assistance grants.

Instead of being situated in the wider UN system, the GEF was initially tucked within the World Bank Group. The bank spearheaded the selection of projects, administered the funding, and installed the director of its own Environment Department as the chair. This suited the richer countries that replenished the trust fund's resources. With the World Bank's weighted voting system, the richer countries had greater input into how their money was used and could pressure the GEF to focus on global issues such as climate change and biodiversity. This irked many poorer countries, whose sheer numbers would have commanded more clout with the one-country-one-vote approach of the UN system and who were more concerned with localized environmental problems such as soil degradation or urban air pollution.

Some of the tension was alleviated at the end of the pilot period in 1994. The GEF became a permanent institution, developing countries gained more say, and some of the World Bank's dominance decreased as UNEP and UNDP stepped up. UNEP solidified its responsibility for managing environmental projects, including working with the GEF's independent Scientific and Technical Advisory Panel. Meanwhile, UNDP cemented its leadership over technical assistance and capacity-building as well as running the GEF's small grants program for civil society groups. Despite being nominally separated from the World Bank Group, however, the GEF remained at the bank's headquarters in Washington DC, with the bank still serving as its trustee and administrator for funding.

The GEF's membership, institutional partners, and issue areas have expanded. As of 2023, the GEF Assembly included more than 180 states, meeting every three or four years to evaluate and update general policies. Between assembly meetings, a council of thirty-two member governments (sixteen from developing countries, fourteen from developed countries, and two from the former Soviet bloc) meets twice a year to consider projects and work programs. The GEF's three initial cosponsoring institutions are still heavily involved, but the partnering institutions have grown to include some NGOs (such as Conservation International), in addition to more IGOs (such as the Food and Agriculture Organization, the UN Industrial Development Organization, and the African Development Bank). Whereas the GEF in 1994 was the financial mechanism for only the CBD and the UNFCCC, it added the Stockholm Convention on Persistent Organic Pollutants in 2001, the UN Convention to Combat Desertification in 2003, and the Minamata Convention on Mercury in 2013. Most resources related to ozone depletion are funneled through the Montreal Protocol Multilateral Fund, but the GEF provides some supplemental funding for this issue area, too.

The GEF fills a critical niche. Its funding helps leverage additional money from other sources, and its small grants program aids civil society groups. By 2019, it had disbursed $18 billion in grants, supplemented by $94 billion in cofinancing for almost 5,000 projects in 170 countries. The majority of its funding supports climate change and biodiversity activities.

Nevertheless, criticism persists. The GEF relies on its implementing agencies for social safeguards, resulting in questionable effects on Indigenous people and other vulnerable groups. The GEF also continues to align with richer countries' preferences for addressing global environmental problems, leading to complaints about insufficient concern with priorities and stakeholders at the local level. As is evident with all development partnerships, working relationships within the GEF need to be constantly renegotiated.

The World Bank. Whereas the GEF and UNEP are explicitly environmental, other IGOs are pivotal in environmental policy even though their core work is in other policy areas. The World Bank, as a major funder for economic development, has been intensely pressured to ensure that its projects are compatible with environmental sustainability. It has responded by changing its operations—but to some observers, the changes do not go far enough.

For decades, many of the World Bank's biggest development projects involved highways, bridges, dams, and other infrastructure. Over time, an emerging transnational network of environmental advocates drew attention to the threat of environmental and social harm from projects such as Brazil's expansion into the Amazon basin, Indonesia's population relocation from Java to neighboring islands, and India's construction of dams. Opposition to dam construction was led by the International Rivers Network, which in the 1980s began campaigning against China's Three Gorges Dam, Malaysia's Bakun Dam, and India's Sardar Sarovar Dam, among others (Khagram 2000). Environmental coalitions argued that these projects diverted rivers, accelerated deforestation, altered ecosystems, forced people to move to environmentally fragile areas, and harmed Indigenous populations. Similar arguments were made about other infrastructure projects. Advocacy networks demanded that the World Bank incorporate environmental impact assessments in their lending decisions and include environmental safeguards in their funded projects.

The bank's response was incremental. From the 1970s onward, it appointed environmental advisers, but their concerns were not mainstreamed throughout the organization. By the end of the 1980s, World Bank officials were acknowledging environmental problems and working more closely with environmental groups. In 1993, again under pressure from civil society and governments, the bank established the Independent Inspection Panel to investigate specific projects in response to citizens' claims of harm. However, with a few exceptions such as Nepal's Arun III Dam, the investigations rarely led to projects being canceled.

Since 1993, the World Bank's attention to and funding for environmental concerns has increased. The number of staff addressing environmental issues has expanded. The bank's annual *World Development Report*, as well as many other reports and meetings, discuss sustainable development and reflect "green" language. Even so, internal and external observers questioned the bank's commitment to environmental sustainability (Buntaine and Parks 2013).

To address such skepticism, in 2016 the World Bank's Governing Board approved a multifaceted Environmental and Social Framework (ESF). The ESF includes an organizational vision on sustainable development, guidelines for staff to implement environmental and social policy, and a directive about risks and effects for disadvantaged or vulnerable people. However, the ESF's main targets are borrowing countries, which are expected to uphold ten standards relating to land, efficiency and pollution, natural resource management, risk assessments, financial intermediaries, transparency and disclosure, working conditions, health and safety, cultural heritage, and local communities. Fully in place as of 2018, the ESF attempts to boost project transparency through information disclosure and ongoing engagement with stakeholders.

Another important environmental hub in the World Bank is the Environment, Natural Resources, and Blue Economy Global Practice (ENB). As of 2021, the ENB oversaw a portfolio of more than 150 projects worth about $11 billion. Many projects combined climate change adaptation and mitigation with poverty-reduction efforts. But neither the ENB's work nor the ESF's guidelines have squashed complaints that bank-funded activities harm the natural environment.

The mixed results of the World Bank's reforms are not entirely surprising. Although some practices have changed, the real question is whether the World Bank has fundamentally altered its attitude toward development and whether new norms have been internalized. The bank employs fewer people in its environmental units than in its administrative or economic divisions. The organization's dominant culture still centers on economic analysis, and staff have had a difficult time making the case for environmental stewardship solely on an economic basis (Rich 2013). Consequently, whether environmental plans and concerns are actually integrated into projects often depends on the interests of individual country directors.

Similar problems confront regional development banks. Following the World Bank's lead, many have incrementally adopted environmental agendas, safeguards, and mechanisms. Some (such as the African Development Bank) have increasingly called attention to the threat that environmental issues like climate change pose to the world's poorest countries. But skeptics still question whether all development banks have really become "green"—or merely have been "greenwashed" with environmentally friendly words that are not backed by meaningful deeds (Weaver 2008: 21).

The GATT and the World Trade Organization. Like the World Bank and regional development banks, the apparatus surrounding the General Agreement on Tariffs and Trade was slow to embrace environmental initiatives. Environmental considerations seemed to bring trade distortions and hindrances, which were precisely what the GATT was meant to dismantle (Damian and Graz 2001: 600). The trade institution did have a Trade and Environment Working Group, but it focused on avoiding situations in which pollution control would impede trade.

Trade institutions such as the GATT and its successor, the WTO, have had to adjust to the fact that many governments pursue environmental policy in ways that affect trade policy. Indeed, the concept of sustainable development recognizes that production and consumption may need to be curtailed in the present to be available for future generations. Moreover, several of the multilateral environmental agreements listed in Table 10.1 include explicit provisions to restrict trade in order to protect parts of the natural environment.

Tensions among trade, development, and environmental objectives have resulted in legal disputes. One of the most famous was the "tuna/dolphin" case. Citing the 1972 US Marine Mammal Protection Act, the United States had prohibited the importation of Mexican tuna because the fish were snared with nets that also caught threatened (though not endangered) dolphins. In 1991, a GATT dispute panel ruled in favor of Mexico, declaring that environmental concerns over how a foreign industry operated could not be used to bar imports. The decision was never formally adopted by the GATT's governing body, but it enraged environmentalists and brought the trade institution much negative publicity. The United States and Mexico negotiated a bilateral settlement, and GATT rules continued to require states to treat similar products equally, without regard to the underlying production process.

Around the time of the tuna/dolphin flare-up, the United States and Mexico were negotiating with Canada to create the North American Free Trade Agreement (NAFTA). Environmentalists in Canada and the United States—concerned that liberalizing trade with Mexico, a developing country, would undermine environmental protection—demanded that NAFTA include explicit environmental provisions. The three countries struck a side agreement, and in 1994 they established a trilateral commission on environmental cooperation.

NAFTA's combination of trade and environmental considerations influenced the negotiations for the new WTO, which subsumed and expanded the GATT trading system (Johnson 2015). The 1994 agreement that established the WTO recognized the "objective of sustainable development, seeking both to protect and preserve the environment." The agreement maintained the GATT's requirement that states treat similar products equally, without regard to their underlying production process; however, it also recognized the validity of protecting plants and animals and conserving exhaustible natural resources. For such purposes, countries could restrict trade as long as the restrictions did not unfairly discriminate and were not actually a guise for advantaging their own industries. The WTO also encompassed numerous agreements beyond the original GATT, with some pertaining to environmental protection. For example, eco-labels and other documentation or packaging standards have been covered by the Technical Barriers to Trade Agreement, while invasive species and other threats to animal or plant health have been covered by the Sanitary and Phytosanitary Measures Agreement.

In addition to environmental provisions in its formal agreements, the WTO has a Committee on Trade and Environment, created under pressure from the EU and the United States (Johnson and Urpelainen 2020). Its deliberations have included ensuring market access for developing countries, addressing the permissibility of eco-labeling, and clarifying the relationship between multilateral environmental agreements and WTO rules (Johnson and Lerner 2023). On market access, developing countries have gained more opportunities to view and comment on standards being proposed in developed country markets for their exports. On eco-labeling, the WTO has not mandated environmental labeling that gives full information to consumers, but it has emphasized that such practices should not discriminate among trading partners (i.e., most favored nation treatment) or advantage domestically produced goods (i.e., national treatment). On MEAs, no specific provisions have been the subject of a WTO dispute, and several MEAs predate the creation of the WTO, so environmental law and trade law already coexist, even without a full clarification their relationship.

Since it began operating in 1995, the WTO's dispute resolution mechanism has dealt with several environment-related trade disputes. One particularly pivotal dispute was the "shrimp/turtle" case. India, Malaysia, Pakistan, and Thailand jointly filed suit against the United States, which had required domestic shrimpers to use special turtle-excluding devices and had banned the importation of shrimp that were not caught using such devices. The complainants did not dispute the US government's right (and obligation, under US law) to protect endangered sea turtles. Instead, they charged that the import ban discriminated between similar products on the basis of how those products were produced and that the United States was unfairly assisting particular countries with adopting the turtle-excluding devices. After the WTO ruled against the United States in 1998, the US changed its practices. Malaysia continued to assert that the United States was not in compliance, but a 2001 WTO ruling upheld the US's new practices.

The prolonged shrimp/turtle dispute ended up bolstering environmentalists in several ways. It showed that a country could satisfy the WTO's rules surrounding environmentally justified trade restrictions (Weinstein and Charnovitz 2001: 151–152). It reconsidered discussions of whether an import could be restricted because of its production process. It also established a precedent that WTO adjudicators could accept briefs containing information from NGOs or other stakeholders who are not parties to the suit itself.

The WTO is highly relevant for global environmental governance, yet it can hardly be considered a fully "green" institution. It remains wary of the precautionary principle: although WTO member governments can restrict trade temporarily if a serious threat arises, maintaining the restriction would require stringent scientific justification. The WTO does permit briefs from outside stakeholders but makes no guarantee that adjudicators will actually use them. It continues to hold many meetings behind closed doors. And although it has hosted discussions on environmental initiatives—such as implementing a border tax on carbon, reducing trade barriers on environmental goods, and dismantling fishing subsidies that incentivize overfishing—the discussions have been slow, rarely producing concrete policies. Like the World Bank, the WTO is an economic institution that certainly affects environmental policy, but does not always prioritize it.

A Variety of Other Actors

States are central to global environmental governance since they are the members of IGOs and the parties to MEAs. But global environmental governance also involves a variety of actors beyond national governments. These include epistemic communities, NGOs and civil society, the private sector, and subnational governments.

Epistemic communities. Throughout the history of environmental governance, a vital role has been played by epistemic communities—those networks of professionals (discussed in Chapter 6) that have an authoritative claim over expertise and policy-relevant knowledge within a particular domain (Haas 1992: 3). Although these professionals do not always come from a single discipline, they share some values, causal beliefs, applied competencies, and ways of validating knowledge (Johnson 2020: 10). The identity and nature of relevant epistemic communities can change. For example, whereas resource managers were once prominent in environmental policy, in recent decades ecologists and other scientists have been central.

That is why environmental policy is susceptible to the zigzags of the scientific process. Compared to scientists, policymakers and the general public are much less comfortable with uncertainty and incremental insights. As a result, environmental policy sometimes depends on the extent and pace of scientific consensus. The 1975 Mediterranean Action Plan, for example, was developed with the help of like-minded ecological experts from countries bordering the Mediterranean Sea. This epistemic community worked in tandem with government officials and provided data for a monitoring program (Haas 1990). In contrast, the IPCC is a truly global epistemic community that over time has reached large-scale consensus on how and why the climate is changing—but many governments justify a "wait and see" approach by citing earlier periods of scientific debate.

Epistemic communities are crucial for understanding problems and devising solutions, but they still face challenges. Their effectiveness hinges on being continually nurtured with resources, personnel, connections, and new research findings. Meanwhile, their legitimacy hinges on being representative of wide swaths of the world's population—a difficult thing since experts, whose knowledge sets them apart from the general population, may compound imbalances between elites and nonelites, rich and poor, North and South (Borland, Morrell, and Watson 2018).

Nongovernmental organizations and civil society. NGOs have played important roles in environmental affairs since the late nineteenth century. Since the emergence of environmental movements in the 1960s and the Stockholm Conference in 1972, environmental NGOs have expanded in number and scope. This is true for large international NGOs headquartered in developed countries and for small local NGOs based in developing countries. Environmental organizations now number in the tens of thousands, giving a voice to many ordinary citizens. NGOs such as Earthwatch, the Environmental Defense Fund, Greenpeace, the Nature Conservancy, the Sierra Club, the Rainforest Action Network, and the WWF have become well-known names.

Environmental NGOs embrace a variety of approaches and ideological orientations, with some preferring the status quo, others working for gradual change, and others seeking radical transformations. A few have even obtained remarkable levels of funding and decisionmaking access. For example, the European Environmental Bureau is a liaison office between the European Union and a network of more than 170 environmental citizens' organizations from more than thirty-five European countries. The bureau has offices in Brussels, receives funding from the European Commission, operates working groups on major issues, holds consultative status in EU institutions, and is in regular contact with the European Environmental Agency.

There are multiple avenues by which NGOs interact with other actors. One is education. Through epistemic communities, experts from NGOs may connect to counterparts from IGOs, government agencies, and elsewhere to educate people and change their behavior. For instance, the WWF has used its expertise to try to convince consumers and medical practitioners in Asia to stop using rhinoceroses and other endangered species for medicinal purposes. Similarly, the International Water Resources Association and several NGOs have pushed for policymakers to adopt a more integrated resource management perspective for water and rivers (Conca 2006: 123–140).

Another avenue is targeted criticism. Many NGOs strive for independence from governments and the private sector to maintain the ability to object to their behavior. Targeted criticism can be mild (e.g., Greenpeace's "Waste Trade Update" that tracks adherence to the Basel Convention on hazardous waste) or forceful (e.g., the Rainforest Action Network's campaign against Home Depot's sales of old-growth wood). Some groups even engage in direct, confrontational actions—which some people view as "eco-terrorism"—to stop purportedly unethical or illegal practices by governments or the private sector (Eilstrup-Sangiovanni and Bondaroff 2014). For instance, Sea Shepherd Conservation Society has attacked and disabled ships used for capturing whales.

A third avenue is the international policymaking process. NGOs often engage with environmental IGOs, particularly UNEP. They also work to influence MEA negotiations and monitor compliance. For instance, in cooperation with CITES' state-parties, the WWF and IUCN formed a monitoring network called Trade Records Analysis of Flora and Fauna in Commerce (TRAFFIC). In addition to training government officials and legal professionals, TRAFFIC performs on-site inspections.

Perhaps the most important avenue for NGO influence, however, is domestic policymaking at the national and local levels. In various ways, NGOs attempt to shape governments' environmental policies directly. One is through research, expertise, or training. For example, NGOs collaborated with the US Agency for International Development to train locals in antipoaching strategies in Zambia's national game preserves. Second, NGOs may collaborate with governments to package issues in ways that enhance the likelihood of compliance with treaty obligations or other commitments. Debt-for-nature swaps—that is, the acquisition of debt, usually by a conservation NGO, followed by the redemption of that debt in local currency to be used for conservation—are one example. Beginning in 1987, NGOs such as Conservation International and the Nature Conservancy arranged such swaps in Bolivia, Costa Rica, Ecuador, Madagascar, the Philippines, and Zambia, with local NGOs obtaining title to the conserved land. Third, NGOs may work through states' legislative or bureaucratic systems to sue a state for noncompliance or pressure a state to impose sanctions against noncomplying parties. The Earth Island Institute used this approach when it appealed to US courts to enforce the

1972 Marine Mammal Protection Act and protect dolphins from nets used in tuna fishing.

Nevertheless, it is important to remember that civil society is a broad umbrella that includes more than NGOs (Chapter 6). Indeed, the case study of young people demanding climate justice demonstrates that civil society operates not only through highly organized NGOs but also through many other groups, including less formal networks and social movements. As a result, measuring civil society's overall impact on environmental governance is difficult.

On the one hand, there is evidence that civil society groups have influenced treaty negotiations by reframing issues, changing negotiators' positions, or proposing language for treaty texts (Betsill and Corell 2008). Some groups seem to have played important roles in tracking governments' compliance with environmental treaties (Eilstrup-Sangiovanni and Sharman 2021) or "greening" international economic institutions such as the World Bank (Buntaine 2015). Civil society groups also have been savvy about using the Internet and social media to educate environmental constituencies, mobilize action groups, and reshape norms (Blondell, Colgan, and Van de Graaf 2019).

On the other hand, the primary responsibility for governance still lies with governments. Policymaking requires flexibility to engage in bargaining and compromise. Some formal NGOs may be so committed to particular ideologies or methods that they are ill-equipped for the give-and-take of governance, and other formal NGOs may be so concerned with maintaining cordial relationships with governments that they shy away from challenging the status quo (Stroup and Wong 2017). Less formalized portions of civil society sometimes escape such limitations, but they face constraints of their own. For instance, because they lack some of the privileges that governments and IGOs extend to full-fledged NGOs, their access to governance structures may be uneven, hinging on personal relationships and political will (Belfer et al. 2019).

The private sector. In addition to civil society, another governance actor is the private sector. The companies and markets making up the private sector are already known to be important for economic policy (Chapter 8). Increasingly, their importance is recognized for environmental policy too.

One area that has attracted much attention is private rule-setting: standards and guidelines that, unlike formal governmental regulations, are voluntarily developed and followed by companies themselves. Critics charge that privately set rules tend to be unambitious and lack means of enforcement. Proponents counter that private rule-setting benefits from specialized information held by companies and builds trust in a way that facilitates more ambitious rules over time.

Deforestation is a prominent example of an environmental issue that has spurred private environmental governance and rule-setting. Protecting endangered tropical forests has been on the international agenda since the 1970s, and the UN Conference on Trade and Development and the International Tropical Timber Organization have promoted certification that all tropical timber traded internationally comes from sustainably managed sources. Yet by the early 1990s, tropical deforestation had increased. Deforestation rates were doubling in the Amazon basin, and rapid deforestation in Indonesia eventually contributed to massive fires, air pollution, lower soil productivity, and threats to endangered species. Around the world, governments and businesses experiencing economic downturns were incentivized to increase timber exports. But flooding markets with timber drove down prices, inadvertently hurting exporting states and businesses and also prompting consumers (often in developed countries) to demand even greater quantities. In the lead-up to the 1992 Rio Conference, this mix of environmental and economic concerns prompted the WWF and other NGOs to initiate a multistakeholder dialogue involving labor unions, Indigenous peoples' groups, civil society, retailers, consulting firms, and the timber industry.

After more than a year of discussions in several countries, the stakeholders established the Forest Stewardship Council (FSC) in 1993. Based in Bonn, Germany, the FSC is an independent voluntary arrangement that aims for environmentally sound standards in the forest products industry and provides public information for consumers. A unique feature of the FSC is its structure. Members apply to join one of three chambers (economic, environmental, or social), and each chamber contains subchambers for representatives from the Global North and the Global South. Even though members from the North tend to be better resourced, weighted votes ensure that members from the South retain equal decisionmaking power (Dingwerth 2008: 617–619). To encourage compliance with decisions, the FSC combines two strategies: social pressure to persuade retailers and consumers to avoid wood from nonsustainable sources, plus certification to promote products made through sustainable practices (Dingwerth and Pattberg 2009: 712). The certification process requires highly detailed technical information not just about forest management practices but also about the wood's "chain of custody" as it moves from forest to consumer. The FSC logo is supposed to appear only on wood that is properly certified.

The results have been mixed. The FSC expanded the discussion of sustainable forestry to include land tenure, Indigenous people, and community rights. Several early studies found that it helped with reducing deforestation and wildfires (Hughell and Butterfield 2008), altering economic incentives (Conroy 2002: 215), conserving biodiversity (Newsom and Hewitt 2005), and preserving endangered species (Mannan et al.

2008). However, critics charge that the FSC has had more impact in the Americas than in Africa or Asia, favors big corporations over smaller businesses, is inconsistent in supporting Indigenous people and social concerns, and does not do enough to stamp out counterfeit certifications. To register disapproval, Greenpeace International declined to renew its FSC membership in 2018. Despite criticism, however, the FSC has been an innovation in private rule-setting and has served as a model for certification in other areas, such as fisheries (Abrams et al. 2018).

Another private set of standards is ISO 14001, established in the 1990s under the International Organization for Standardization (see Chapters 3 and 8). Designed to provide industrial plants with an environmental management system for internal operations, it uses a certification process that is expensive and intensive. Costing upward of $100,000, the process requires specialized training and documentation, with independent audits to verify compliance. ISO 14001 not only helps industrial plants meet national environmental guidelines but also encourages members to take additional steps in the interests of environmental stewardship.

Like the FSC, ISO 14001 has shown both achievements and shortcomings. Judging by the number of participants, it has been very successful. However, the vast majority of participants are in Europe or Asia, with far fewer in other parts of the world. These regional differences partly stem from firms' strategic responses to their home-country context. Firms are more likely to join ISO 14001 if they operate from countries with deep experience in management-based standards or if they heavily export to environmentally conscious consumers. They are less likely to join if they lack such conditions or face a domestic regulatory environment that is inflexible and adversarial (Potoski and Elwakeil 2011: 298).

In addition to setting voluntary rules, the private sector participates in public–private partnerships (PPPs). As noted in Chapter 8, PPPs do not simply replace state authority. Instead, they are hybrid relationships that retain some traditional foundations of public authority but incorporate private actors whose authority may be grounded in expertise or moral claims (Conca 2006: 211). Relatively rare in multilateral governance until after the end of the Cold War, PPPs became much more common from the 1990s onward, especially in policy areas such as environmental protection, global health, disaster responses, nutrition, and education (Andonova 2017: 14).

The World Commission on Dams, established by the World Bank and the IUCN in 1997, was an early model. It was an independent international body composed of twelve commissioners representing research institutes, hydropower companies, groups of affected people, multilateral development banks, river basin authorities, and governments directly involved with constructing large hydroelectric dams. Although it disbanded in 2001, it blazed a path for more experimentation with multistakeholder governance, as evidenced by the more than 4,000 PPPs that were registered with the UN Commission on Sustainable Development after the 2002 Johannesburg Summit.

PPPs continue to proliferate in environmental governance and are attractive to governments and IGOs for several reasons. They are a way to respond to stakeholders' demands for more participatory decisionmaking. They also tap into additional sources of funding and expertise. At the same time, PPPs can remain "soft, experimental" arrangements from which governments or IGOs could exit rather easily (Andonova 2010: 31).

Subnational governments. In international environmental policy, subnational governments are another relevant actor. In some situations, subnational governments reach out to each other directly, without working through national governments. For instance, US mayors and governors joined a coalition to mitigate climate change when the national government withdrew from the Paris Agreement.

In other situations, subnational and national governments work toward the same goal. In Australia, for instance, regional governments hold responsibility for making laws about many environmental matters, including the habitats of migratory birds. To protect migratory birds, Australia's national government engages in multilateral governance; in addition to signing five international treaties and reaching bilateral agreements with neighboring countries such as China and Japan, it works closely with subnational governments within Australia.

Subnational governments are relevant in developing countries, too. For example, India struggles with air pollution, which is correlated with health problems and economic difficulties. Some parts of the country are hit especially hard. Therefore, even though the national government sets nationwide goals and represents India to the rest of the world, subnational governments do much of the legwork, and some have very far to go. The same is true of Brazil in its struggles with water pollution. Agriculture, urbanization, and mining threaten Brazilian rivers and the health of its Indigenous people with chemical run-off, garbage, and mine tailings. The country also struggles with water shortages, like the crises that struck the city of São Paulo in 2013 and 2014. Subnational governments have been working with the national government to impose fines for environmental infractions, using the revenue to plant tree seedlings to bolster river ecosystems. For air pollution in India and water pollution in Brazil, what the national government can promise in international environmental negotiations is inextricably linked to what subnational governments can deliver at a more localized level.

As these examples suggest, multilevel policymaking is especially pertinent when relevant countries have federal systems of government. In a federal system, subnational governments and a national government share authority. Because federal systems are found in numerous countries that are environmentally impactful—including Australia, Brazil, Canada, Germany, India, Nigeria, Russia, and the United States—it is important to be cognizant of the needs, preferences, and activities of subnational governments and how authority is divided and shared in different systems.

The Sustainable Development Goals (SDGs)

All of these actors—states, IGOs, epistemic communities, NGOs and civil society, the private sector, and subnational governments—are relevant to the Sustainable Development Goals. As discussed in Chapter 8, the SDGs (also known as Agenda 2030, since they are supposed to be achieved by 2030) are a set of seventeen goals adopted by UN member states in 2015. Several focus explicitly on environmental issues such as clean water and sanitation, affordable and clean energy, sustainable cities and communities, responsible consumption and production, climate action, life below water, and life on land. The UN frames the initiative as a mix of global action, local action, and "people action."

The SDGs were crafted through high-level governmental negotiations, supplemented by multistakeholder dialogues. The goals emphasize environmental sustainability and demand action from both the Global North and the Global South. The UN's annual progress reports show some bright spots. For example, Asia-Pacific countries now have better data about their progress on SDG 7 (affordable and clean energy).

There is also much cause for concern, however. Some governments worry about the goals' "one-size-fits-all" approach; some IGOs fret about squabbling among member states; some epistemic communities warn that no real progress will be made without bigger structural changes; some civil society groups condemn the process as undemocratic; some companies suspect governments are simply offloading their own responsibilities; and some subnational governments lament a lack of political will among national leaders. In 2022, the midpoint of the SDGs' fifteen-year cycle, the mobilization of forces and the rate of progress were lagging, particularly for SDG 13 (climate action). The Covid-19 pandemic was an enormous setback for the SDGs because it prompted many states to focus on their domestic needs and prioritize shorter-term economic or health problems over longer-term environmental threats.

Regional Environmental Governance

Some issues, such as climate change, affect the whole planet and therefore involve negotiations at a global level. Even for climate change or other worldwide issues, however, one region may be more proactive or cohesive than another. Moreover, many environmental issues affect specific areas of the world and generate initiatives at a regional level. In fact, some of the earliest attempts at international environmental policymaking were regional rather than global, as shown in Table 10.1. Whether spurred by a need to fix local problems or a desire to help solve global problems, regional initiatives are often built on the belief that decisions are most effective when made at the lowest possible level (Betsill 2007: 12–13).

As noted in Chapter 5, regions can be difficult to define. This is certainly true for environmental issues, which do not necessarily follow political borders or even geographic proximity. For example, a region could be based on an ecological system (like the Mediterranean Sea or the Amazon rainforest), but it could also be based on the scope of transboundary flows (as occurs with fish stocks in the ocean or acid rain from the sky) or on some shared attribute (such as being a biodiversity hotspot or an arid area). As a result, where regional institutional mechanisms have been created for environmental governance, they do not always line up with IGOs that are oriented toward traditional political or geographic regions. Nevertheless, it is instructive to examine environmental governance in three regional institutions—the EU, the US-Mexico-Canada Agreement (USMCA), and the Association of Southeast Asian Nations (ASEAN)—that illustrate different approaches and degrees of institutionalization.

The European Union and the Environment

Among regional institutions, the EU stands out for its extensive environmental policies, its vocal support for addressing climate change, and its leadership in global environmental governance. The European Community's original Treaty of Rome never mentioned the environment. Only with the 1987 Single European Act, which called for accelerated integration of a single economic market, was the environment mentioned for the first time. Ten years later, in the Treaty of Amsterdam, signatories agreed that ensuring fair competition within the EU meant that environmental standards must be harmonized. With the 2007 Treaty of Lisbon, the EU committed itself to sustainable development, based on "a high level of protection and improvement of the quality of the environment" (Article 2.3). That commitment reflected strong public opinion in favor of environmental regulations, the emergence of green political parties in many EU member states, and the development of effective environmental agencies at national and local levels.

The EU's environmental approach rests on two key principles discussed earlier. One is "polluter pays," meaning that the party responsible for environmental damage should make amends for it. The other is the "precautionary principle," in which lack of scientific certainty should not preclude intervention against a serious threat. The EU most differentiates itself from other regional IGOs through its embrace of the precautionary principle.

Environmental policy is where member states have harmonized the most, with much policymaking competence moving from national governments to the EU level (Selin 2007: 64). Since 1985, environmental impact assessments and public consultations have been required for all public and private projects above a certain size. By 2011, EU environmental law had grown to more than 300 legislative acts, with more than 80 directives covering issues such as air, water, soil, waste disposal, biosafety, coastal zone management, and hazardous chemicals (Vogler 2011: 19). For example, the EU adopted increasingly strict directives on air pollution by vehicles, large factories, power stations, and aircraft; the phasing out of chlorofluorocarbons (CFCs); prohibitions against various forms of noise pollution; restrictions on genetically modified organisms (triggering trade disputes with the United States); and an energy tax on carbon dioxide emissions. The EU has also constructed a notion of environmental justice that is based on transparency and access to information, and it has set environmental standards for production, distribution, and consumption. The EU's first environmental action program was adopted in 1972, and its eighth environmental action program will last until 2030. Even though states are the implementers, much of this environmental policymaking has been initiated by the European Commission.

In environmental policymaking, several features may account for Europe's leadership and relative success. One is the attention paid to the citizenry. For instance, to help consumers make informed purchasing decisions, in 1992 the Council of Ministers initiated rules for granting EU eco-labels for environmentally friendly products. Since then, labeling products at each phase from production to consumption has become a prominent EU approach. There have also been efforts to engage civil society and the general public. An important entity is the European Environmental Bureau, which helps civil society groups form coalitions and gain access to EU institutions. Another important entity is the European Environment Agency, an independent EU body that became operational in 1994. Headquartered in Copenhagen, it was the first EU body that opened its membership to countries seeking to join the EU. Although the agency has turned out to be weaker than anticipated, it does report on states' climate change activities and collects other cross-national data that are shared with governments and the public.

A second possible reason for Europe's leadership and relative success is the blend of supranational guidance and national discretion. For example, major responsibility for environmental policy rests with the European Commission's Directorate-General for the Environment. However, that part of bureaucracy is less prestigious and less powerful than some other parts of the Commission, and some of its detailed work has been taken up by the Committee of Permanent Representatives, composed of the head or deputy head of each member state's mission in Brussels. A pattern of supranational guidance and national discretion also exists in the regulatory sphere, where the EU bureaucracy has often opted to issue directives instead of formal regulations. With directives, the EU lays out comprehensive long-term objectives but lets member states choose specific methods and pass the appropriate legislation. This provides space for national and local variation, while still establishing overall EU standards that help level the economic playing field.

Third, the EU has developed several mechanisms to back up environmental policies with financing and monitoring. For instance, the European Green Deal—reached in 2020 and laying out a vision of EU climate neutrality and zero pollution by 2050—is to be overseen by a new European Climate/Infrastructure/Environment Executive Agency and has been allocated more than €55 billion to be used by 2027. Among this agency's main funding distributors is the Financial Instrument for the Environment. Launched in 1992, it is the only EU financial instrument dedicated to environmental, climate, and clean energy issues; by 2022 its track record included more than 5,000 projects. As with earlier initiatives, the European Commission will monitor the European Green Deal's implementation and report on violations. The combination of financial "carrots" and monitoring "sticks" is a long-running formula that has helped the EU reduce noncompliance (Tallberg 2002: 610).

A final possible reason for Europe's environmental leadership and success is the Court of Justice of the EU (CJEU). More often than not, the CJEU has upheld EU environmental law. In a 2007 case, for example, it imposed a temporary measure on Poland to suspend work on a highway traversing an environmentally sensitive zone that had been protected by the EU's Directorate-General for the Environment. Eventually, an alternate route was found.

In many EU member states, it is clear that there has been a profound transformation—environmental protection is mainstreamed in policymaking and the public consciousness. One indication is the growth of Green Parties, which embrace environmentalism in their core political ideology. Since the 1970s, national Green Parties have gained more legislative seats and leadership roles in Germany and other EU member states. Since 2004, national Green Parties have formally collaborated through the European Green Party (also known as the European Greens), which facilitates cross-country policy coordination and fields candidates in European Parliament elections.

Environmentalism in the EU still faces political differences and implementation problems, however. Austria, Denmark, Germany, Finland, the Netherlands, and Sweden tend to be very strong supporters of environmental protection. Having adopted stringent standards at the national level, these countries also push for stringent standards at the EU level. In contrast, relatively less developed Western European states (such as Greece, Portugal, and Spain) and newer Eastern European members (such as the Czech

Republic, Hungary, and Poland) tend to have looser standards and fewer economic resources. EU enlargement certainly has given a boost to sustainable development, because states that join must meet its environmental standards and often receive help in the form of financial or technical assistance. But that does not mean all EU member states have the same will or wherewithal to protect the natural environment. Moreover, even EU leaders such as Germany have vulnerabilities, such as continued reliance on natural gas and coal. As a result, some observers worry that although Europe has led on environmental issues in the past, it might not do so far into the future.

The US-Mexico-Canada Agreement (USMCA) and the Environment

Although not as encompassing as Europe's supranational initiatives, there are also serious environmental initiatives among North American countries. The USMCA, ratified by its three parties in 2020, is a regional trade agreement that contains numerous provisions about the environment. In 2018, well before the text of the USMCA was finalized, the three countries concluded an Environmental Cooperation Agreement that enabled the public to participate in environmental monitoring and enforcement. Similar to citizens' domestic right to sue the US government to enforce national environmental laws, people in the three signatory countries were given the right to request an inquiry into whether the United States, Mexico, or Canada is fulfilling its domestic environmental laws.

In the final USMCA text, chapter 24 lays out additional environmental provisions. The chapter includes guidelines related to forestry, fisheries, invasive species, marine litter, and several other environmental issues. It requires all signatory states to construct domestic mechanisms to fulfill their obligations under certain multilateral environmental agreements, including CITES and the Montreal Protocol. It stipulates that projects with potentially major effects on the environment must undertake and release the results of environmental impact assessments. Chapter 24 also urges businesses to adopt voluntary practices such as the Equator Principles, a framework used by more than 130 financial institutions to assess and manage the environmental and social risks of projects they fund.

Such explicit links between trade and the environment are not new. The USMCA's predecessor, the North American Free Trade Agreement, also contained numerous environmental provisions. NAFTA was negotiated in the late 1980s and early 1990s, as GATT rulings were fueling concerns that freer trade could impede environmental protection and as the 1992 Rio Conference drew global attention to the natural environment. Since Mexico was much poorer and had lower environmental standards, environmentalists worried that Canada and the United States would relax their environmental standards in order to be economically competitive with Mexico.

To allay such fears of a "race to the bottom," NAFTA's final text included provisions to promote sustainable development and enforce environmental regulations. Each party was able to maintain its own level of environmental protection and ban imports produced in violation of those standards. The conditions for such bans were carefully specified: they could not be "applied in an arbitrary or unjustifiable manner" or "constitute a disguised restriction on international trade or investment."

Beyond the main treaty provisions, after a few years the three countries struck a side agreement to establish a North American Commission for Environmental Cooperation. Rather than setting shared standards, the commission encouraged compliance with domestic law and facilitated capacity-building. For instance, it developed an online training course for customs officials and border inspectors to crack down on illegal trading of ozone-depleting substances. More generally, the commission issued periodic overviews of environmental conditions in NAFTA's three countries.

When the USMCA replaced NAFTA, the environmental provisions were preserved and sharpened. To many observers, NAFTA had already been path-breaking in endeavoring to be "green," even when it did not function as well as hoped (Perez-Rocha and Trew 2014). Although it remains to be seen whether the USMCA improves on its predecessor's environmental record, it is clear that NAFTA's attention to the environment lives on in North America's newer trade agreement.

The Association of Southeast Asian States (ASEAN) and the Environment

Not all regions have embraced environmental governance. ASEAN provides an example of a regional IGO whose agenda includes environmental issues, yet environmental protection has never been the priority. Member states began cooperating on environmental policy in 1977, and by 1989 they were holding annual meetings of governmental environmental specialists. As in other geographic areas, the Rio Conference emboldened environmental NGOs to develop regional networks and demand access to IGO policymaking structures. The Asian Development Bank, UNEP, the UN Economic and Social Commission for Asia and the Pacific, and other external actors also encouraged regional environmental cooperation. Nevertheless, economic growth remained the main concern, especially as the Asian financial crisis of the late 1990s prompted states to set aside environmental goals and focus on economic recovery.

Over time, the region's increasingly urgent environmental concerns have led to calls for closer operational and technical cooperation, better harmonization of goals, and greater institutionalization. Consider Southeast Asia's haze problem, which stretches back decades. The dense haze over several countries has been exacerbated by deforestation and land practices in Indonesia, where subsistence farmers and large-scale operators have cleared land to produce paper, pulp, and palm oil. Ascertaining the scale of the problem is difficult because much of the activity is illegal, but it is estimated that 60 percent of Indonesia's forests have been burned or logged. The problem has been region-wide since 1997–1998, when thick toxic haze from burning forests started spreading from Indonesia to neighboring Malaysia and Singapore. This led to ASEAN's first regional environmental agreement, the 2003 Agreement on Transboundary Haze Pollution, which included a monitoring fund and penalties for noncompliance. Indonesia did not ratify the agreement until 2014, however, and continues to have one of the world's highest deforestation rates.

Haze is just one of many environmental problems in a region that is undergoing population growth, urbanization, and economic development, resulting in greater demands for food, water, land, and energy. It is a biodiversity hotspot with many endangered animals and plants. It is also experiencing changes in temperature, precipitation, and the frequency of extreme weather events.

In 2015, member states adopted several "blueprints" for the next decade. Among these is the ASEAN Socio-Cultural Community Blueprint 2025, which encompasses environment-related goals such as climate change mitigation and adaptation, sustainable production and consumption, and conservation of natural resources. But regional coordination to achieve these aims will be difficult because, as discussed in Chapter 5, ASEAN struggles with member states' varied capabilities, protection of sovereignty, and preference for nonbinding agreements (Elliott 2011).

Regional Environmental Disputes in International Courts
When states do not agree on what to do or renege on their promises, regional environmental disputes can be litigated in international courts. A prevalent issue is the development of river basins, such as along the Nile River (Egypt, Ethiopia, Sudan), the Indus River (Afghanistan, India, Pakistan), and the Rio Grande (Mexico, United States). Although states often sign agreements for allocating water supplies and protecting water quality, key players are sometimes marginalized. For example, the Mekong River Commission was formed in 1995 by the river's downstream states of Cambodia, Laos, Thailand, and Vietnam, with the upstream states of China and Myanmar relegated as mere "dialogue partners." Since then, China has constructed numerous upstream dams, affecting the downstream states' water flow and the livelihoods of farmers and fishers.

Even in arrangements that include all key players, states do not always fulfill their promises, so regional environmental disputes are sometimes handled in international courts. One dispute taken to the Permanent Court of Arbitration (PCA) involved the 1960 Indus Waters Treaty between India and Pakistan. Concerned by India's proposal to build a major hydroelectric project on a tributary river in the Indian-administered part of Jammu and Kashmir, Pakistan requested arbitration, protesting that the dam would hurt its water supply. In its 2013 decision, the PCA recognized India's right to divert water but also acknowledged Pakistan's right to a minimum water flow (PCA 2013). Most interesting from the perspective of environmental law, the court determined that a state is obligated to take "environmental protection" into consideration when its activities may harm a neighboring state.

In 1993, the International Court of Justice (ICJ) issued a similar ruling in its first environmental case, which involved a dam on the Danube River (Kumar 2013). Czechoslovakia and Hungary had signed a treaty in 1977 to construct a hydroelectric project. In the early 1990s, following the break-up of Czechoslovakia into the new states of Slovakia and the Czech Republic, Hungary cited the precautionary principle in suing Slovakia for environmental damage, while Slovakia accused Hungary of violating the original treaty (Deets 2009). In 1997, the ICJ ruled that both states had breached their treaty obligations and that their joint project needed to use current (not 1977) environmental standards to protect nature and water quality (ICJ Contentious Case 1997).

Since that initial environmental case, the ICJ and other courts have heard more cases involving environmental issues. For instance, in 2008 the ICJ ruled on a suit in which Ecuador claimed that Colombia's aerial spraying of toxic herbicides near their shared border was having adverse environmental and economic effects (ICJ Contentious Case 2008), and in 2014 the ICJ ruled on a case in which Australia accused Japan of not complying with a 1986 moratorium on commercial whaling (ICJ Contentious Case 2014). In 2023, the small Pacific island state of Vanuatu gained the support of the UN General Assembly to seek an ICJ advisory opinion on states' obligations to address climate change, potentially opening a legal avenue for pursuing enforcement action against states that fall short of their Paris Agreement commitments. And, as mentioned in the opening case study, the European Court of Human Rights has been sympathetic to cases in which young people have accused EU countries of violating human rights by not addressing climate change strongly enough.

Global Environmental Governance and Issues of Compliance and Effectiveness

As illustrated by discussions of the evolution, components, and regional variations of environmental governance, governing the natural environment is a challenge. This chapter has highlighted five major challenges: the zigzags of the scientific process, the prevalence of collective action problems, the tensions between rich and poor, the complexity of regimes, and the heterogeneity of stakeholders. To overcome these, scholars and practitioners have turned to journals such as *Global Environmental Politics* and *Global Governance* as forums to debate possible reforms.

Some people argue for greater centralization in a global environmental organization—a new and strong World Environment Organization (Biermann and Bauer 2005). Others counter that more attention and resources should be funneled to existing institutions and initiatives: perhaps UNEP could be bolstered further, or development institutions could take on greater roles. Still others recommend more grassroots construction of values and rules, facilitated by civil society groups (Conca 2006: 67–69); proponents of this option point to climate policy, where various subnational governments, epistemic communities, NGOs, businesses, and other nonstate actors have undertaken initiatives without waiting for national governments or IGOs. Such bottom-up alternatives may lack central coordination but come closer to governing the environment "democratically."

Beyond the issue of institutional reforms, there are broader questions to be addressed. To what extent have states implemented and complied with existing international arrangements? Especially for developing countries, failure to implement and comply is often a failure of state capacity, as has happened with deforestation in Indonesia. Even for environmental issues that require action from the private sector or subnational governments, compliance and implementation can hinge on national governments' enforcement capabilities. Thus, technical assistance and other enhancements to state capacity may be required.

More generally, are various environmental arrangements effective? For many years, the primary measure of effectiveness was states' implementation of and compliance with environmental conventions (Weiss and Jacobson 2000). Over time, however, effectiveness came to be seen as a more complex and multidimensional concept that also includes considerations such as equity, efficiency, or goal attainment (Young 1999). Establishing causation between governance structures and environmental effects is difficult, because both qualitative and quantitative analyses are needed to determine whether actors change their behavior, whether those behavioral changes have an effect on the natural environment, and whether those environmental effects can be traced to specific agreements, institutions, scientific findings, or principles.

So far, research shows mixed results about effectiveness. For example, one project summarized several environmental case studies and concluded that environmental regimes had a moderate or strong causal effect in terms of programmatic activities, data improvements, and reduction in uncertainty (Breitmeier, Underdal, and Young 2011). Effectiveness varied with regime features such as the distribution of power, the roles of "pushers and laggards," the influence of decision rules, and the degree of available knowledge. In contrast, another project considered numerous environmental regimes and determined that they resulted in environmental improvement only rarely (Ohta and Ishii 2014: 582).

Thus, the question of effectiveness is crucial but complicated. Fortunately, there are some environmental issues that, many observers agree, have been addressed well. The following discussion examines two: trade in endangered species and ozone depletion.

Success Story: Trade in Endangered Species

Estimated at over $19 billion annually as of 2023, international wildlife trade involves a variety of animals and plants used in foods, materials, furnishings, tools, medicines, and cosmetics. Caviar, alligator-skin boots, ivory carvings, rhino horn powders, and rosewood furniture are a few examples. In a global economy that can transform illegally harvested $10 snakeskins into $10,000 handbags, the incentives to pillage natural resources are significant.

The idea for an international treaty to deal with trade in endangered species was broached during a 1963 meeting of the IUCN. It came to fruition in 1973 as the Convention on International Trade in Endangered Species of Wild Fauna and Flora. By 2022, the treaty covered over 35,000 animal and plant species and had been ratified by 183 states plus the EU. In addition to pledging to strengthen their domestic efforts to manage trade in endangered species, the parties empower the Geneva-based CITES secretariat to monitor and publicize compliance. Noncompliant states can face trade sanctions.

CITES is commended not only for having "teeth" via trade sanctions but also for being a flexible mechanism. Using the "appendix" model described above, the main treaty can remain unchanged while states-parties move species into and out of three appendixes corresponding to different levels of threat and protection. For Appendix I, all commercial trade in wild specimens is prohibited, as these species are deemed in danger of extinction. For Appendix II, trade is permitted but strictly regulated, as these species are deemed sensitive due to decreased numbers, similar appearance to Appendix I species, or being captive-bred or cultivated versions of Appendix I animals or plants. For Appendix III, the species are not globally in danger of extinction, but particular states have asked for international cooperation in managing them, and therefore traders must present export permits and certificates of origin. Since Appendixes I and II involve more stringent controls, these are generally the most contentious deliberations when the parties meet triennially. Any state-party, regardless of whether it is a "range" state (i.e., its territory is within the natural range of a species), may propose that a species be removed, added, or relocated in the appendixes. If a two-thirds majority of states-parties support the change, it will be made even if range states resist.

For implementation, CITES works closely with NGOs and other actors. As mentioned earlier, the multistakeholder monitoring network called TRAF-FIC conducts inspections, investigates compliance with CITES rulings, and provides direct training for enforcement officers. Along with partners, CITES tries to address both the supply side and the demand side. On the supply side, it has assisted states such as Kenya and South Africa in expanding their antipoaching units and increasing domestic penalties. On the demand side, it has enlisted Chinese basketball player Yao Ming and other celebrities to speak against the demand for wildlife products like shark fins and ivory.

CITES was created outside of the UN system but, under a 1992 agreement, its COPs, secretariat, and trust fund are administered by UNEP. Given the links between wildlife trafficking and transnational crime, the CITES secretariat also works closely with the UN Office on Drugs and Crime (UNODC), which tracks illegal trade and provides support for local law enforcement through its Global Programme for Combating Wildlife and Forest Crime. Alongside the World Bank, the World Customs Organization, and the International Criminal Police Organization (INTERPOL), both CITES and the UNODC are part of the International Consortium on Combating Wildlife Crime.

For many years, CITES was widely praised as an effective international regime. Despite its ability to use trade sanctions to bolster its enforcement capabilities, it never came into direct conflict with the WTO. It collaborated with states and nonstate actors, adapted to changing scientific or policy circumstances, and used majority voting to surmount veto players. Its protection of particular species such as the South American vicuña and Nile crocodile has resulted in concrete progress.

The future may be tougher, however. CITES is focused on protecting animals and plants but has limited ability to protect habitats—a weakness underscored by recent pandemics, which have shown how quickly diseases in animals can spread to humans as their habitats increasingly overlap. Furthermore, the process of adding plants and animals to CITES's three appendixes is time-consuming, and some environmentalists worry that species still do not get protected quickly enough. CITES has been successful in the past, but its work may be harder going forward.

Success Story: Ozone Depletion

Effectiveness is more clear-cut with regard to ozone depletion. The ozone layer in the Earth's stratosphere absorbs most of the sun's ultraviolet radiation, which would otherwise threaten life forms near the Earth's surface. Thinning or holes in the ozone layer can cause a variety of problems, including skin cancer in humans and damage to crops.

As briefly discussed earlier, depletion of the ozone layer was thrust onto the international agenda in the mid-1970s, following a report in which two US scientists attributed its depletion to CFCs, chemicals widely used in refrigeration, aerosol propellants, foam manufacturing, and other human activities. Scientists and industry representatives debated the causal link—but within a decade, new data had confirmed a startling hole in the ozone layer over Antarctica, and many experts agreed it had been caused by the use of CFCs. This was a sensitive finding for governments, because the biggest producers and consumers of CFCs were in the United States and Europe, and usage in newly industrializing countries such as Brazil, China, India, and Mexico was rising at about 10 percent annually.

Remarkably quickly, international negotiations produced the 1985 Vienna Convention for the Protection of the Ozone Layer and the 1987 Montreal Protocol on Substances that Deplete the Ozone Layer. The negotiations were not easy, but states agreed that several sources of CFCs should be phased out worldwide. To facilitate this, industrialized states agreed to provide financial and technical assistance for developing countries (and, after the end of the Cold War, for countries transitioning away from communism). The Montreal Protocol has been amended several times, incrementally tightening states' commitments to permanent, quantitative emission limits on almost 100 ozone-depleting substances, including hydrochlorofluorocarbons and hydrofluorocarbons. Provisions were also included for international trading in emission entitlements. In 2018, UNEP reported that the ozone layer was on track to recover to pre-1980 levels by 2060.

The effectiveness of the international approach to ozone depletion can be attributed to at least five factors. First, the United States, Canada, Norway, and other industrialized states took the lead. Pushed by alarmed publics and civil society groups, these states pledged to change their own behavior in producing and consuming ozone-depleting substances. UNEP's dynamic executive-director, Mostafa Tolba, also provided leadership by consulting key stakeholders, applying pressure, and floating proposals of his own (Benedick 1998).

Second, scientists and large corporations contributed to the process. Scientists provided updates about the severity of the problem, often communicating their findings with language and pictures that were easy for policymakers and the public to grasp. Meanwhile, large CFC-producing corporations such as DuPont and Dow Chemical discovered suitable and affordable substitutes. Since these corporations produced many things and were not dependent on a single product, they were able to replace CFCs without jeopardizing their own survival. In contrast to climate change, key companies were already willing and able to change their behavior and did not spend decades demanding complete scientific consensus on whether CFCs were causing ozone depletion.

Third, the negotiations and procedures were handled expeditiously. The process was subdivided into smaller problems, and the resulting agreements were flexible. Following the "framework" model described earlier, the Vienna Convention articulated broad norms and aims, but it left details about implementation and enforcement to the Montreal Protocol, which could be adapted in response to changing scientific and policy circumstances. The parties agreed to compliance mechanisms that were independent of any formal dispute settlement procedures and also established an ad hoc working group of legal experts to encourage compliance in a nonjudicial, nonconfrontational, and conciliatory way.

Fourth, states at all development levels were required to phase out ozone-depleting substances, but developing countries were offered financial and technical assistance. At the 1990 Conference of Parties in London, states agreed to create the Multilateral Fund for the Implementation of the Montreal Protocol to alleviate the incremental costs of converting to substances that do not deplete the ozone layer. The fund's executive committee was set up with seven developed states and seven developing states, and its implementation committee provided technical assistance and additional funding to aid compliance. Following the end of the Cold War, the GEF offered similar assistance to formerly communist countries.

Fifth, the Ozone Secretariat, which is based in Canada and served by UNEP, has found ways to engage and balance various stakeholders. It became a hub for more than 100 national units serving developing countries' ministries, and it incorporated recommendations from the Technology and Economic Assessment Panel as it drafted protocol amendments and adjustments for consideration by states. Over time, the Ozone Secretariat acquired a solid reputation for technical expertise, transparency, and diplomatic skills. Despite being an active player behind the scenes, it positioned itself as a neutral tool for governments (Bauer 2006: 43–44).

Worldwide consumption of ozone-depleting substances has declined more than 75 percent since the Montreal Protocol came into force in the late 1980s, even though production has grown slightly in the developing world. Substitutes in refrigeration are now used and are effective. In reporting that the ozone layer was expected to recover to pre-1980s levels by 2060, scientists also reported that these results had made a large contribution to the reduction of the greenhouse gases implicated in climate change (Johnson and Urpelainen 2012; UNEP 2014). Despite questions about what will happen as the growing middle classes of India, China, and other developing countries demand more refrigerators and air conditioners, the ozone regime is widely regarded as a success story in global environmental governance. This stands in contrast to the inaction that often surrounds climate change.

These success stories related to ozone and trade in endangered species show that global environmental governance may be difficult, but it is not impossible (Conca 2015). True, environmental policy faces numerous challenges, but it is also a relatively young issue area in international politics. Moreover, it is an issue area in which many actors—states, IGOs, epistemic communities, civil society, the private sector, subnational governments—play a role. The key to the future is to get all of them to work in concert.

Suggested Further Reading

Conca, Ken. (2015) *An Unfinished Foundation: The United Nations and Global Environmental Governance.* Oxford: Oxford University Press.

Elliott, Lorraine, and Shaun Breslin, eds. (2011). *Comparative Environmental Regionalism.* London: Routledge.

Hadden, Jennifer. (2015) *Networks in Contention: The Divisive Politics of Climate Change.* New York: Cambridge University Press.

Ivanova, Maria. (2021) *The Untold Story of the World's Leading Environmental Institution: UNEP at Fifty.* Cambridge, MA: MIT Press.

Johnson, Tana, and Johannes Urpelainen. (2020) "The More Things Change, the More They Stay the Same? Developing Countries' Unity at the Nexus of Trade and Environmental Policy." *Review of International Organizations* 15:2: 445–473.

Park, Susan. (2010) *The World Bank Group and Environmentalists: Changing International Organization Identities.* London: Manchester University Press.

11

Promoting
Human Security

ALTHOUGH THE UNITED NATIONS WAS FOUNDED BY STATES TO PROTECT the territorial security of states, the opening words of the UN Charter make clear that the drafters were looking beyond this in writing "We the peoples . . ." Thus, while traditional concerns in international peace and security still dominate the work of the UN Security Council, the Council has increasingly met since 2000 on issues dealing with health (e.g., HIV/AIDS and Ebola), human rights (e.g., Darfur, Libya, Syria), and the environment (e.g., climate change) as well as protection of civilians and children in conflict zones and women's engagement in peace and security. In short, "Making human beings secure means more than protecting them from armed violence and alleviating their suffering" (Weiss, Coate, and Forsythe 2004: 278).

Canada played a key role in bringing the concept of human security to the Security Council's agenda by linking it to protection of civilians (POC) during armed conflict. This aligned with the Council's greater focus on humanitarian crises in the 1990s and became part of a series of resolutions on POC and other human security issues as well as of reports from the UN Secretary General (Dedring 2008). The link between health and human security was first made in a special session devoted to the challenge of HIV/AIDS in early 2000. The Security Council's broadened definition of security was underscored in late 2022 when for the first time in seventy-four years, it adopted a resolution on Myanmar, demanding an end to violence, release of political prisoners, expressing "deep concern" at the state of emergency imposed by the military, the blocking of humanitarian aid, and the "grave impact" on Myanmar's people (Resolution 2669). In short, the concept and the issues related to it have become a major focus in the UN system and for the Security Council for more than twenty years. But what is this expanded view of security all about?

The Concept of Human Security:
An Expanded View of Security

The Covid-19 pandemic, which spread around the world in 2020 in a matter of weeks, made clear the degree to which all of humanity is vulnerable to contagious pathogens. Simultaneously, the growing evidence of climate change has become increasingly obvious to those living in coastal zones, small island states, or areas where land degradation or rainfall amounts threaten agriculture and food security. From the UN's long role in articulating and promoting human rights norms, the people-oriented concept of sustainable human development developed in the 1980s and 1990s (discussed in Chapter 8). With this and the principle of responsibility to protect (R2P) approved by the World Summit in 2005 (Chapter 7) has come the shift to the broad concept of human security. As a result, since the 1990s, there have been significant shifts in the UN and in global governance more generally as a human security–oriented approach has cut across traditional divisions between peace and security or between economic and social issues. This comes at a time when the security of people and the planet are increasingly threatened.

When the term "human security" was first defined in the 1994 UNDP *Human Development Report*, some scholars argued that the concept lacked precision and was too expansive (Paris 2001; Krause 2004; Newman 2004). It is now widely accepted in the UN system as a useful way of conceptualizing a variety of threats that affect states, vulnerable groups, and individuals—threats that go beyond physical violence and specifically beyond the protection of states' territory and institutions. As the Commission on Human Security noted in its 2003 report, human security is "an alternative way of seeing the world, taking people as its point of reference, rather than focusing exclusively on the security of territory or governments" (Commission on Human Security 2003). Yet the concept of human security is not just a matter of perspective and protecting people; it is also about empowering people (Ogata and Cels 2003). It changes the concept of state sovereignty from absolute to conditional (Hama 2017: 15). This undermines the long-standing principle of nonintervention in the internal affairs of states by "blurring the distinction between what is domestic and what is international, by drawing attention to the potential link between domestic (human) insecurities and their external ramifications" (MacFarlane and Khong 2006: 229).

This evolution in thinking about security "has recognized the security needs of individuals and the responsibilities of states and organizations in attending to those needs (Jolly, Emmerij, and Weiss 2005: 34). It thereby has expanded interpretation of the principle of responsibility to protect well beyond issues of intervention in humanitarian crises (Chapter 7). It has been evident in the push to address arms control issues such as antipersonnel landmines and cluster munitions, which disproportionately injure civilians and livestock, as Javier Villacampa (2008) has pointed out. It is evident in the UN Security Council's attention to the Women, Peace and Security agenda and protection of civilians issues in conjunction with peace operations and in the increased efforts to investigate and prosecute war crimes (Hudson 2009).

The UN has played an important part in that evolution along with nongovernmental organizations (NGOs), civil society, private corporations, scientists, foundations, think tanks, other IGOs, as well as national and local governments. Human security issues often require multistakeholder approaches to empower individuals and communities to act on their own behalf and form partnerships to fill needs. Just as the various global governance actors have developed the new approach, so has the scholarly literature developed and expanded, especially from the securitization literature (Emmers 2017; Buzan and Hansen 2009; Murray 2022).

In this chapter, we focus on the role of the UN, other IGOs, and global governance actors in protecting human health and addressing the problems of food insecurity and the growing crisis of forced and voluntary migration of people. Health is one of the oldest areas of functional cooperation, predating both the UN and the League of Nations (discussed in Chapter 3); the Food and Agriculture Organization (FAO) came into existence to address food-related issues in 1944, before the UN itself was established. The first efforts to deal with those forcibly displaced in war, that is refugees, came at the ends of World Wars I and II. Migration more generally—whether forced or voluntary, triggered by climate-related changes or oppression or simply the desire to improve one's life—has been with humanity since time immemorial, but efforts to address the issues arising from migration are much more recent. What has changed is recognition that failure to address major threats to health and food security or the growing refugee and migration flows has a fundamental effect on human security, overlapping with more traditional security problems of violence, conflict, and war.

Human Security and the Governance of Health

Globalization has had a dramatic effect on the transmission, incidence, and vulnerability of people and communities to disease through migration, air transport, trade, tourism, and troop movements (including UN peacekeepers). The more people move locally, regionally, or intercontinentally, the more problems arise in containing outbreaks of cholera, influenza, HIV/AIDS, tuberculosis, West Nile virus, severe acute respiratory syndrome (SARS), avian (bird) influenza, H1N1 virus (a form of swine flu), Ebola, Covid-19, and future viruses. Pathogens can be carried in a matter of hours from one part of the world to another, long before symptoms may appear. Globalization has exacerbated the urgency and the scope of the threats that infectious diseases can pose to human security.

This was dramatically brought home to people the world over in 2020 with the emergence and worldwide pandemic caused by the Covid-19 virus. The issue is not only large-scale loss of life, but one of disease setting back development and weakening societies. As of 2022, the World Bank estimated that the pandemic pushed more than 70 million people back into extreme poverty, at the cost of more than 20 years of poverty reduction efforts (World Bank 2022). More than ever, there is significant need to fortify what former UN Secretary-General Ban Ki-moon once described as "collective global health security." That shift from thinking about international health to global health—from state-based and IGO governance to more "globality" and even supranational decisionmaking in new institutions with private actors and partnerships playing key roles—characterizes the changes that have taken place since the 1990s (Harman 2018: 720).

Developing International Responses to Health Issues: The Role of the World Health Organization

Quarantines and other rudimentary international rules to prevent the spread of disease date back hundreds of years, and institutionalized collaboration can be traced to 1851. Between 1851 and 1903, a series of eleven international conferences developed procedures to prevent the spread of contagious and infectious diseases. In 1907, the Office International d'Hygiène Publique was created with a mandate to disseminate information on communicable diseases, such as cholera, plague, and yellow fever. More than a decade later, at the request of the League of Nations Council, the International Health Conference met to prepare for a permanent International Health Organization. Instead, after the UN's creation, the World Health Organization came into being in 1948 as a UN specialized agency (see Chapter 3). The WHO secretariat is highly technical, with a director-general, other secretariat officials, and many delegates being medical doctors, public health experts, epidemiologists, and scientists. They and the medical and allied health communities form a strong epistemic community.

The WHO's main decisionmaking body is the World Health Assembly (WHA), composed of delegations from its 194 member states, each state with one vote. It meets annually to approve goals and priorities of the organization, appoint the director-general, and approve the budget. It is also empowered to adopt conventions and agreements. The Executive Board is a smaller group of thirty-four members that meet at least twice a year to set the agenda for the WHA and implement policies it has approved. By "a gentlemen's agreement," at least three of the five Security Council permanent members are supposed to be represented. The WHO Secretariat has several key roles: carrying out the programs the WHA has approved, providing technical guidance and support as a global hub of scientific and technical expertise, and coordinating responses to international health emergencies.

Although most UN agencies have offices in many countries, the WHO groups its member states into six regions (Africa, Americas, Southeast Asia, Europe, Eastern Mediterranean, Western Pacific), each with a regional office that enjoys a significant amount of autonomy. The regional offices select their own directors and control their own budgets, meaning that the WHO director-general does not have full control over these offices. They also oversee some 150 country offices. The result has created some problems, as discussed below.

Overall, the WHO employs more than 7,000 people in Geneva, 150 country offices, and the regional offices. The organization's budget comes largely from voluntary contributions from member states (in addition to states' assessed contributions), from the World Bank, and from private donors. These are known as "extrabudgetary funds" and are generally designated for specific purposes, such as polio eradication or HIV/AIDS programs; hence, the WHA (and Secretariat) has virtually no control over their use. To put this in some perspective, the extrabudgetary funds made up 20 percent of the WHO's annual expenditures in 1970; since 1990–1991, they have steadily exceeded assessed contributions, reaching 72 percent at one point (Youde 2012: 35). The WHO's overall budget was set at $5.84 billion for 2020–2021 and then augmented to address the Covid-19 pandemic.

Beyond the WHO, three UN funds and programs have mandates that encompass health—the UN's Children's Fund (UNICEF, child disease), UN Fund for Population Activities (UNFPA, women's reproductive health), and the UN Development Programme (UNDP, the right to health; ending tuberculosis and HIV/AIDs). The WHO is one of the eleven UN entities that are part of the UN Joint Programme on HIV/AIDS (UNAIDS) formed in 1996 in recognition that HIV/AIDS was not just a health issue. UNAIDS also includes national governments, corporations, religious organizations, grassroots groups, and NGOs. It tracks outbreaks, monitors responses, distributes strategic information, mobilizes resources, and reaches out to diverse groups. It complements the Global Fund.

These programs and funds frequently team up with the WHO, and all of them have received significant funding from the World Bank for their health-related work. They are increasingly involved in various partnerships with actors outside the UN system.

The WHO and Partnerships

Private funding and partnerships for addressing international health issues date from the early twentieth century when the US oil titan and philanthropist John D. Rockefeller established the Rockefeller Institute for Medical Research in 1901 and the Rockefeller University Hospital in 1910. He had a particular interest in supporting medical research and treatment. Since 2000, it has been Bill Gates, a founder of Microsoft, and his foundation, the

Bill and Melinda Gates Foundation, that has been the single biggest funder of global health programs ($592 million or 8 percent of WHO's funding in 2020–2021, second only to the United States) (WHO 2022). Foundation representatives attend WHA meetings, and Bill and Melinda themselves have been highly visible in promoting various health initiatives.

One of the most significant WHO partnerships is the Global Vaccine Alliance (GAVI) which started with a $799 million contribution from Gates in 1999 (a contribution that by 2020 totaled $4 billion) and focuses on providing vaccines for children in the poorest countries. GAVI's mission is inspired by the recognition that protecting successive generations of children with a series of basic vaccinations reduces child mortality and enables families, communities, and countries to be healthier, more stable, and prosperous. The GAVI partnership also includes UNICEF, which works with manufacturers to ensure a reliable supply of quality and affordable vaccines; the World Bank, which oversees economic and financing strategies and helps countries transitioning out of GAVI financial support; and many governments, other private foundations, corporations, and NGOs—a true multistakeholder arrangement. The WHO's role is to set the technical specifications for vaccines and prequalify them.

Another important WHO partnership is the Global Outbreak Alert and Response Network (GOARN), which involves over 600 partners, including technical and public health institutions, laboratories, and NGOs that work to detect and respond to potential epidemics. Its operational team is based at WHO, which also coordinates its resources and staffs its small secretariat. A fourth partnership is the Global Fund to Fight AIDS, Tuberculosis, Malaria and Covid-19 (commonly referred to as the Global Fund), which was created in 2002 and works primarily through partners in countries on these specific diseases. In 2020, Covid-19 Vaccines Global Access (COVAX) became the newest partnership, co-led by GAVI, the WHO, and the Coalition for Epidemic Preparedness Innovations. It has been at the core of the WHO's effort to create a global risk-sharing mechanism for pooling procurement and equitable distribution of Covid-19 vaccines. Figure 11.1 illustrates the variety of the WHO's partnerships.

WHO Activities

The WHO's activities include four major areas. The first, building on the work of predecessor organizations, is containing the spread of communicable diseases. In 1951, the WHO approved the International Sanitary Regulations, which were renamed the International Health Regulations (IHR) in a 1969 revision. These constitute the only international treaty that "explicitly regulates a state's obligations to the international community on the spread of infectious diseases." They also established the WHO as "the repository of all required disease surveillance information" (Youde 2010:

Figure 11.1 WHO Partnerships	
Partnership	Partners
Global Vaccine Alliance (GAVI)	WHO, World Bank, UNICEF, Gates Foundation
Global Outbreak Alert and Response Network (GOARN)	WHO and 600+ institutions and NGOs
Global Fund to Fight AIDS, Tuberculosis and Malaria (Global Fund)	Gates Foundation, World Bank, WHO, NGOs in-country partners
Ensuring Equitable Access to Covid-19 Vaccines (COVAX)	WHO, GAVI, Coalition for Epidemic Preparedness
UNAIDS	WHO, UNHCR, UNICEF, WFP, UNDP, UNFPA, UNODC, UN Women, ILO, UNESCO, and World Bank

147). Initially, the IHR required states to report outbreaks of four communicable diseases (yellow fever, cholera, plague, and smallpox) and take appropriate measures to contain any outbreak while minimizing interruption of international travel and commerce. Over time, governments failed to report outbreaks in a timely manner or underreported the number of cases, fearing condemnation and adverse economic consequences such as loss of tourism, although some failures were the result of limited resources.

Updating the diseases covered by the IHR has been challenging. Smallpox was removed in 1981, but other diseases needed to be added. Since the 1980s and 1990s, as a side effect of globalization, several new communicable diseases have emerged that were not covered under the IHR, including Ebola, West Nile virus, HIV/AIDS, SARS, avian flu, and swine flu. The last two both became pandemics for brief periods (2003 and 2009), provoking fears about the links between travel and spread of the disease. Older diseases thought to be under control, such as tuberculosis, have reemerged in different forms, with drug resistance becoming a major concern. Potential new threats to public health arose with incidents of bioterrorism, such as the Tokyo sarin nerve gas attack in 1995 and the US anthrax scare in 2001, along with concerns about use of nuclear, radiological, and chemical weapons. The latter has been a particular concern in the Ukraine war because of Russia's threats to use nuclear weapons and its cavalier treatment of nuclear power plants in Ukraine. On the plus side, the internet, cell phones, social media, and other technologies have facilitated faster and better information about outbreaks that states might once have been able to hide. This made it imperative to enable the WHO to receive reports of outbreaks from nonstate actors in addition to governments and to make determinations if an event constitutes a public health emergency of international concern (PHEIC).

The IHR provisions were revised in 2007 after negotiations that took over a decade. One key change was to include a wider range of public health risks so that rather than listing a set of specific diseases that should be reported to the WHO, the IHR now refer to all events "posing a serious and direct threat to the health of human populations" (Article 1.1). This makes the IHRs much more flexible and relevant to future public health threats. Particularly important is the WHO's ability to receive and act on information from nongovernmental sources. The IHR also require member states to assess their surveillance and response systems and implement plans to ensure core capacities. Although the WHO's constitution incorporates references to the human right to health, the revised IHR incorporate more explicit recognition of this right in connection with public health emergencies (Youde 2012: 118–131).

The revised provisions on who can report an emerging public health threat and on the WHO's ability to publicize potential problems, even over state objections, were intended to resolve the problems encountered during the SARS outbreak in 2002–2003, when China initially suppressed information on the outbreak, was slow to permit WHO officials to visit potentially affected areas, and failed to undertake preventative measures for several months. Although the epidemic killed fewer than 1,000 people, the potential for a global pandemic was widely recognized, and the economic repercussions on the most affected countries—China, Vietnam, Singapore, and Canada—were significant. Transparency proved to be a significant problem again in 2020 when the first cases of the new strain of coronavirus were detected in China and the Chinese government initially suppressed the information, as discussed further below.

The second area of WHO activity is eradication programs for certain diseases and working with state health authorities to improve health infrastructure. One of the WHO's greatest accomplishment was the successful eradication of smallpox in 1980—the only human disease to be fully eradicated (so far). Few people are aware today what a scourge smallpox was for millennia. It was endemic (i.e., always present) and caused high mortality rates along with its signature facial scarring in survivors across all continents. Between 1920 and 1978, the reported number of cases (certainly lower than the actual number) was 11.6 million. When the WHO launched its campaign in 1966, a vaccine had virtually eliminated smallpox in Europe and North America, and large-scale vaccination efforts produced rapid declines in South America, Africa, and Asia. India and Bangladesh were declared smallpox-free in 1975. The last reported case was found in Somalia in 1977, and in 1980 the WHO announced the full eradication of the disease—a remarkable achievement.

The current malaria and polio eradication campaigns build on that success and demonstrate how partnerships play an important role in the

WHO's activities. Rotary International and the Bill and Melinda Gates Foundation have been particularly important for the campaign against polio along with UNICEF, GAVI, and the US Centers for Disease Control and Prevention. The goal of polio eradication was close to realization in 2006, but local resistance to vaccination in Nigeria led to outbreaks that spread in neighboring countries, South Asia, and more recently, Syria and even New York City. After years of improvement, the campaign against malaria stalled with the Covid-19 pandemic. Between 2002 and 2020, however, the number of malaria deaths had dropped by 26 percent (Global Fund 2022).

The third major area of WHO activity involves standard-setting and norm creation, which often affects pharmaceutical and other industries. WHO has set standards for air pollution and drinking water because of their importance for public health. Because of developing countries' long-standing concern about the quality of imported drugs and desire for technical assistance in monitoring quality control to ensure that pharmaceutical companies were not exporting inferior drugs, the WHA approved guidelines for drug manufacturing in 1970. These cover such issues as labeling, potency, purity, and safety, as well as reporting adverse drug reactions. In 1977, the WHA approved the concept of "essential medicines"—a list initially of eight medicines deemed to satisfy core public health needs for which there should be safe, effective, affordable access. The list is revised as necessary every two years. The WHO has also addressed pricing for antiretroviral AIDS drugs in poor countries, the potential for an Ebola vaccine in 2014, and, in 2020–2021, vaccine distribution in the Covid-19 pandemic. These issues have put the WHO at the center of the contentious issue of corporate regulation, such as after the WHA's 1981 adoption of the Code of Marketing for Breast-Milk Substitutes, which called for states to adopt regulations banning marketing and advertising for infant formula that discouraged breast-feeding. The accessibility, quality, and affordability of drugs in developing countries remain on WHO's agenda, and these issues overlap with World Trade Organization (WTO)-related issues on intellectual property rights and generic drugs. These have also been major issues in the Covid-19 pandemic, particularly the ethically sensitive issue of major countries in the Global North prioritizing their citizens for vaccines over equitable global distribution.

Another area of WHO standard-setting was the effort to promote universal primary health care. This arose after the 1960s when so many former colonies became independent states and development became a central UN issue along with the promotion of a human right to health. In 1978, the WHO and UNICEF cosponsored a conference in Alma Ata, Kazakhstan, where delegates adopted the Alma Ata Declaration affirming commitments to a program called Health for All by 2000. Building on the concept of health as a public good, core parts of the declaration included access to essential medicines and nondiscrimination in care provision.

In recent years, the WHO has taken up several issues relating to noncommunicable diseases or what are also called lifestyle-related health issues—its fourth area of activity. Key among them is its campaign against smoking and tobacco. These issues (as illustrated in Chapter 6), are particularly contentious as they pit IGOs and states against large well-funded multinational corporations. Equally contentious have been the WHO's forays into other lifestyle issues, like obesity and alcoholic beverages. With this attention to lifestyle issues, the WHO has been criticized for overextending itself and diverting funds from core issues like communicable diseases.

To illustrate the WHO's core role in addressing communicable diseases—still a significant challenge to human security in this era of globalization—we look at its handling of the 2014 Ebola outbreak in West Africa and its responses to the Covid-19 pandemic. In contrast to the HIV/AIDS epidemic that began in the 1980s, where UN system responses evolved over many years, the speed with which Ebola spread in 2014 tested the WHO's ability to manage a major crisis in a region with relatively weak public health systems. This prompted significant reforms, which have since been tested severely with the Covid-19 pandemic. Looking at these two cases provides an excellent opportunity to understand how the WHO and the UN system as a whole have responded to two major health emergencies occurring within a five-year time period.

WHO, Ebola, and crisis management for human security. The 2014 outbreak of Ebola in West Africa revealed many of the challenges facing the global management of "problems without borders." On the one hand, it highlighted the relevance of the UN and the need for a global response as global resources and coordination were essential for stopping the epidemic. On the other hand, the outbreak revealed the limits of the WHO's capacity for rapid response, especially when its response depends on the capacity of states to report outbreaks. It also exposed how the way the WHO is funded can undermine its ability to manage a global health crisis.

In March 2014, the WHO was notified of an outbreak of Ebola virus disease in Guinea. By the end of that month, cross-border transmission was first reported. Five months later, in August, the WHO finally declared the situation an epidemic and a PHEIC under the IHR. The three countries most affected by the epidemic were Guinea, Liberia, and Sierra Leone, with isolated cases among international health care workers returning to Europe and the United States. The disease spread exponentially throughout 2014 with a death rate of 80 to 90 percent among those infected. Panic set in, along with fear that the overwhelmed countries would collapse; food supplies dropped; there were riots and attacks on healthcare workers; all commercial air service between the countries was stopped; and much economic activity had halted. By the end of 2015 when the epidemic was declared over in all three countries, almost 30,000 cases of Ebola had been reported with over 11,300 deaths.

With weak public health systems, persistent unemployment rates of close to 80 percent, literacy rates below 50 percent, and a chronic lack of medical personnel and hospitals, the affected countries needed outside help. All three countries were still recovering from civil wars in the 1990s. In the absence of responses from WHO's African regional center and Geneva headquarters, Doctors Without Borders (MSF) found itself the primary international medical group organizing assistance on the ground. It benefited from having well-organized stockpiles of protective gear and well-trained personnel available immediately. Still, in June 2014, MSF declared the epidemic "totally out of control." At that point, the situation was still seen as a health crisis, not a security issue.

Shortly after the WHO declared the epidemic a public health emergency in August, UN Secretary-General Ban Ki-moon appointed a senior UN system coordinator for Ebola and activated the UN crisis response mechanism, recognizing that he had no confidence in the WHO's ability to handle the crisis. In mid-September 2014, the epidemic finally gained global attention. For only the third time ever, the Security Council passed a resolution (2177) on a health issue, declaring Ebola a threat to international peace and security due to the "unprecedented extent of the epidemic in Africa." It called on member states to facilitate assistance, communicate and implement established safety and health protocols, and provide deployable medical capabilities, as well as to lift travel and border restrictions. The council meeting galvanized responses. Within weeks, the United States along with the United Kingdom, China, Cuba, and other countries deployed medical personnel and hospital units (including military medical brigades) to West Africa and the first ever UN emergency health mission, the United Nations Mission for Ebola Emergency Response (UNMEER was endorsed unanimously by the General Assembly in Resolution 69/1). These two UN resolutions marked a shift toward the "securitization" of global health (Burci and Quirin 2014).

UNMEER was tasked with overall planning and coordination of UN agencies, national governments, and other humanitarian actors, operating jointly under the WHO and the UN Secretariat. It focused heavily on contact tracing, safe burials, and community education while the UN system coordinator for Ebola worked with the World Bank president and others to raise funds to meet the estimated cost of almost $1 billion. The WHO was able to bring together representatives from Ebola-affected countries with development partners, civil society, regulatory agencies, and pharmaceutical companies as well as funding agencies to fast-track testing of vaccines for Ebola (Branswell 2020). It also worked to provide key information to states that were considering imposing a travel ban to and from those countries with infected patients. In July 2015, having achieved its core goals and with significant declines in transmission rates, UNMEER was disbanded.

There were multiple reviews inside and outside the WHO of its shortcomings in responding to the crisis. Among the factors cited were budget and staff cuts that had gutted the GOARN in particular; incompetent staff in the African regional office; the absence of a culture of rapid reaction to emergencies in the WHO; an executive director who deferred to national governments and regional offices; advisers who told headquarters that Ebola was a "small problem"; and concern that declaring a public health emergency might "hamper collaboration between WHO and the affected countries" (Garrett 2015: 97).

In early 2015, the WHO's Executive Board delivered a harsh assessment, stating that there was "a clear gap in the WHO's mission and structure . . . no clear lines of decision-making or dedicated funding in place [leading to] a slow, uncoordinated response to the Ebola outbreak" (Garrett 2015: 97). The board called for creating a reserve global health emergency workforce to be supported by a $100 million contingency fund, among other steps. Some critics suggested that the WHO can never be a crisis manager. Others urged the WHO to focus on basic public health programs. Still others argued that future epidemics are inevitable and the world must be prepared to deal with them effectively (Garrett 2015: 102–107).

In 2016, the WHO established a new Health Emergencies Programme to reform its response capabilities. It also launched an effort to provide more guidance on caring for people during disease outbreaks and yet another to address shortages of physicians and other experts prepared to provide that care. The reality is that there have been subsequent outbreaks of Ebola in the Democratic Republic of Congo, Guinea, and Uganda, but the biggest test of whether the WHO and the UN system had actually strengthened emergency response capabilities came with the 2020 Covid-19 pandemic.

The UN, the WHO, and the Covid-19 global pandemic. Barely five years after the West African Ebola crisis was largely contained, the world and the WHO were faced with a global pandemic with cases of a new, highly infectious coronavirus turning up on every continent in early 2020. No part of the world has gone untouched. Several vaccines have been developed and distributed, but "vaccine nationalism" meant this happened with considerable unevenness, particularly in developing countries. Furthermore, contagious variants of the virus have emerged, which has made it hard to predict the virus's future course. As of mid-2023, official records showed that more than 750 million people worldwide had been infected and more than 6.5 million had died, but the actual toll is assumed to be much worse (WHO 2023). The pandemic showed how little had changed in global health governance since Ebola and earlier outbreaks (such as SARS in 2002).

This case study provides a short overview of the outbreak and its course from early 2020 to early 2023, of how the WHO and other IOs, including the UN, have addressed the issues arising from this major health governance challenge.

The most notable features of the Covid-19 pandemic were the rapidity of its spread and the extent of its impact on the global and national economies and the lives of millions of people, especially women. By the end of 2020, an estimated 150 million people had been pushed back into extreme poverty, undoing years of poverty alleviation efforts and doubling the number of people rendered food insecure even in the United States. As the outbreak spread, international trade slowed, and national economies contracted or locked down. The global economy contracted by an estimated 4.3 percent, according to the World Bank (2021)—more than double the impact of the 2009 global financial crisis. Travel and trade were disrupted, with many countries adopting nationalistic responses that disrupted supply chains, closed borders, and prompted dire predictions of the end of globalization (Farrell and Newman 2020). As the Bill and Melinda Gates Foundation said in October 2020, "In the blink of an eye, a health crisis became an economic crisis, a food crisis, a housing crisis, a political crisis. Everything collided with everything else. . . . We've been set back about 25 years in about 25 weeks" (quoted in Harlan and Birnbaum 2020). In contrast to the case with Ebola in 2014, the global health governance "system" worked far better. As one scholar of global health governance has noted,

> COVID-19 had the potential to overwhelm and completely discredit the UN system. It has done neither. Global health security has never just been about the high-profile calls to action from the WHO or the UNSC; rather, it involves a diffuse system of governance that rests on the wider UN system, civil society, and the epistemic community of research and advocacy. COVID-19 has exposed the ability of such a diffuse and inclusive model of health security to adapt to and withstand global politics during a pandemic. (Harman 2020: 377)

Still, there were questions about the adequacy of the WHO's actions. Should it have declared a PHEIC when it received the first report from Wuhan? Were Dr. Tedros Ghebreyesus, WHO's director general and the WHO too deferential to the Chinese, accepting their explanations without more questioning? Did the WHO put sufficient pressure on China to permit its team of scientists to launch an immediate on-site investigation of the outbreak? Clearly the Chinese government's failure to be fully forthcoming with information about the outbreak, in accordance with the IHRs, was a critical problem. Even in 2022, the report of an international team of scientists assembled by the WHO to advise on the origins of the coronavirus indicated that more Chinese data were needed to determine how it spread to people (Mueller and Zimmer 2022: A9). Second, there was no consensus on the need for a PHEIC declaration initially. With regard to deference, the director-general of WHO, like the heads of other UN specialized agencies, has to be careful in how they handle member states, particularly the most powerful ones. The agencies depend on both their financial largesse and cooperation to function.

Over the weeks and months of 2020, the WHO and its partners such as UNICEF and the World Bank issued a steady stream of alerts, briefs, guidelines, manuals, webinars, and expert consultations on everything from mask-wearing and quarantines to findings on drugs found effective in treating the most severely ill patients. It launched a Covid-19 Solidarity Response Fund to raise donations for strengthening the capacity of low- and middle-income countries and to support the global response; with its partners, it set up a Solidarity Trial to generate data on treatments. With GAVI and other partners, the WHO set up the Access to Covid-19 Tools Accelerator to coordinate the research, development, manufacturing, and distribution of tests, treatments, and vaccines and, most particularly, to ensure equal access to them. In early April, the WHO established a UN Covid-19 Supply Chain Task Force, with other UN agencies (UNICEF, UNDP, UNFPA, UNHCR) to implement a global strategy for ensuring access to critical supplies, coordinate the capabilities of public and private actors to meet these needs, and ensure the flow of vital supplies and cargo (UN Covid-19 Supply Chain Task Force 2020).

To mobilize global cooperation on necessary scientific research, the WHO convened a virtual summit in early July 2020 to bolster Covid-related research and assess the evolving science on the virus. It also announced formation of the Independent Panel for Pandemic Preparedness and Response to evaluate responses to the pandemic and lessons learned, recognizing the need for accountability. In addition, it formed the COVAX Facility to negotiate prices, production, and distribution of vaccines to ensure equitable distribution—a goal that was never met because a number of developed countries hoarded vaccines for their own populations. WHO head Ghebreyesus cited this "vaccine inequity" as a major failure (WHO 2021).

The responses from the major UN organs were much weaker, particularly in comparison to those during the 2014–2015 Ebola outbreak. One plan, which operated between March and December 2020, the Covid-19 Coordinated Global Humanitarian Response Plan, called for UN agencies and NGOs to collaborate in delivering laboratory equipment and medical supplies to the most vulnerable countries, conduct public information campaigns on how to protect from the virus, and transport humanitarian workers and supplies to the places they were most needed. But funding proved woefully short (UN 2021).

In striking contrast to the 2014–2015 Ebola outbreak, neither the UN General Assembly nor the Security Council played significant roles in responding to the pandemic. Several UNGA resolutions and two special sessions calling for international cooperation and coordinated responses made no meaningful contribution. Neither did the Security Council, which was blocked by South Africa and China, who argued that the pandemic did not constitute a threat to peace and security and should be addressed in the WHO. The Council was also paralyzed by the tensions between the United States and China. The contrast to the situation in 2014–2015 when the United States helped put together a strong Security Council response to the Ebola epidemic illustrated how great power politics has become a much more significant problem for the UN.

Neither China nor the United States earned high marks for their actions during the pandemic. Many commentators criticized China for suppressing early information about the extent of the outbreak and confirmation of human-to-human transmission. It blocked WHO investigations into the virus's origins early on and even in January 2021 when a large team of WHO scientists was finally permitted to visit Wuhan, leading many to believe the Chinese were hiding key pieces of evidence. With its success in containing the outbreak by instituting a strict lockdown, heavy citizen surveillance, and quarantine of those infected, the Chinese Communist Party and President Xi Jinping created an official narrative that celebrated how the country had acted decisively in defeating the virus. China also used the pandemic to enhance its international status, distributing medical equipment ("mask diplomacy") and vaccines ("vaccine diplomacy") to affected countries and increasing its contribution to WHO by $50 million.

In contrast, US President Donald Trump attacked the WHO, blaming the pandemic on the WHO's "very China-centric" approach" (Walker 2020). This was not particularly surprising, given the Trump administration's persistent critiques of international institutions and the tensions in the United States between strong supporters of a major international role for the country and those who represent various strands of isolationist, antimultilateral opinions. As Covid-19 cases spread, the United States adopted "beggar thy neighbor" actions regarding supplies of essential protective and medical equipment and used its economic power to scramble for large supplies of these and vaccines under development. What stood out most was the failure of the United States to exhibit any leadership in mobilizing international cooperation in response to the pandemic, along with President Trump's freeze on US payments to the WHO and threat to withdraw entirely. To pull out of *the* global health organization, which the United States had helped create and long supported, in the midst of a pandemic made no sense because the United States relies on the WHO for access to global epidemiological and other necessary data for testing, vaccine development, campaigns to eliminate various diseases, identifying the seasonal flu viruses, and many other key functions.

In early 2021, the independent panel the WHO had created to assess responses to the outbreak was critical of the organization, of public health organizations around the world, and of governments for responding too slowly and ineffectively to the coronavirus despite years of warnings (and planning) about the likelihood of future pandemics. The panel noted, "There were lost opportunities to apply basic public health measures," including mask wearing, routine testing, and contact tracing. Responding to the WHO's long reluctance to support travel bans because they were thought to cause more harm than good, the panel declared that they would have "most likely been helpful in curbing transmission." The report also criticized the disparity in the vaccine rollout, noting, "Whether you happen to be born in Liberia, or New Zealand, or anywhere else, should not be the factor that determines your place in the vaccine queue." In addition, the panelists called attention to the "wide chasm" between what the WHO is expected to do and the amount of money it receives (Gebrekidan and Apuzzo 2021: A4).

Panel proposals included strengthening the IHRs and giving the WHO authority to conduct an independent investigation of a reported outbreak and perhaps even authority to compel (or funds to entice) a government to cooperate. Not surprisingly, the panel called for increasing funding for the WHO and decreasing the earmarking of funding for specific purposes, changing the decisionmaking process for a PHEIC to make it more transparent, and including more diverse expertise for considering the political and economic ramifications of health decisions. The key question will be what the WHO's member states are willing to change and to pay for.

Each major regional organization discussed in Chapter 5 also responded in various ways to the Covid-19 pandemic. We look briefly here at how some of those responses complemented the work of the WHO.

Regional organization responses to the pandemic. Starting in 2020, the European Union created an early warning response system for member states to share the steps they were taking to address the pandemic. It provided €132 million in support to research, additional funding for global aid and aid to member states to mitigate unemployment risks, and financial support to COVAX. Once vaccines were developed, the EU exported over a billion doses worldwide.

The Pan American Health Organization serves as the WHO regional office for the Americas. It created an incident management system at the regional and country levels to facilitate laboratory capacity, communication of risk, and other services, including technical documents to aid member states in developing their responses. The organization also provided equipment to some countries, training to community health workers in others, and a guide for reducing Covid-19 transmission among Indigenous and Afro-descendant groups.

The Association of Southeast Asian Nations (ASEAN) took a number of steps. These included creating the ASEAN BioDiaspora Virtual Centre for Big Data Analytics and Visualization—a tool that produces risk assessment reports, air travel data, and travel advisories; the ASEAN Emergency Operations Center Network for Public Health to facilitate information sharing; and an ASEAN Response Fund to aid member states. It also established a regional reserve of medical supplies for public health emergencies.

Like the EU, the African Union established a Covid-19 Response Fund to mitigate the socio-economic and humanitarian impact of the pandemic. It also created a diagnostic laboratory to test vaccine quality, produce diagnostic reagents, and undertake research on a new vaccine. The Africa Centre for Disease Control and Prevention took a number of steps, including creating a portal to provide information on travel restrictions, among other things. The African Union partnered with Mastercard Foundation to launch an initiative to improve access to vaccines; and, in 2022, it developed the Africa Joint Continental Strategy for Covid-19 Outbreak (Fagbayibo and Owie 2021).

Most global health experts and others who look at global trends predict that there will be other pandemics in the future. This means that the WHO, the UN system more broadly, and regional organizations will be called on to step up again. One small step was the decision by a special session of the WHA in 2021 to initiate work on a "pandemic treaty" to prevent and deal with future pandemics. A special intergovernmental body is charged with drafting and negotiating the text of what will be only the second WHO convention (the first being tobacco) by 2024.

Global Governance, International Organizations, and Food Security

Another major source of human insecurity—hunger and food insecurity—worsened during the Covid-19 pandemic and has become a persistent human security threat, challenging the World Food Programme (WFP), the FAO, hunger-related NGOs, major donor states, and the UN as a whole in their attempts to address it. With the war in Ukraine, the world has discovered how conflict in a region that produces high percentages of world food grains and fertilizer can affect global food security and require creative governance responses.

Food security is a crucial aspect of human security given the necessity of adequate nutrition to sustain human life. For that reason, food was the subject of the very first UN conference in 1943 (discussed in Chapter 3) and was presaged by the work of a short-lived League of Nations Nutrition Committee in the 1930s. It was also inspired by US President Franklin Roosevelt's 1941 State of the Union Address, in which he articulated four fundamental freedoms, one of which was freedom from want. Although the final 1943 conference document declared that each nation bore primary responsibility for ensuring that its people had adequate food, it concluded, "But each nation can fully achieve this goal only if all work together."

The FAO came into existence in October 1945 after the end of World War II. Thus, in the space of a decade from the League's work on nutrition in 1935 until the FAO came into being in 1945, hunger and malnutrition were defined as international problems. According to Jurkovich (2020: 18), it was "the growing belief that science could mitigate hunger through agricultural innovation" that made this possible, along with the leadership of the United States. When the Universal Declaration of Human Rights was approved in 1948, hunger gained the status of a human right essential to the right of health (Article 25). It was later incorporated into other international conventions, including the International Covenant on Economic, Social and Cultural Rights; the Convention on the Elimination of All Forms of Discrimination Against Women; and the Convention on the Rights of the Child in relation to pregnant and lactating women and children, respectively. In 2004, FAO members adopted a set of Voluntary Guidelines to Support the Progressive Realization of the Right to Adequate Food in the Context of National Food Security. The Commission on Human Rights established the post of Special Rapporteur on the Right to Food in 2000, and this post was carried forward in the transition from the Commission to the Human Rights Council in 2006. Thus, as Jurkovich (2020: 28) notes, "the human right to food is now firmly established in international law."

In exploring efforts to address food security, we look at the two primary UN food-related institutions—the FAO and the WFP.

The Food and Agriculture Organization

In the 1940s when the FAO was created, the general assumption was that the key to addressing hunger was the supply of food and people's ability to obtain enough food for a sufficient diet. Thus, the FAO's primary focus for many years was the availability of food or agricultural productivity, with a particular emphasis on increasing production. The Green Revolution of the 1950s, 1960s, and 1970s, for example, focused on the development and dissemination of high-yielding varieties of food grains (especially rice and wheat) to developing countries, producing large increases in productivity, especially in Mexico and India. In addition, key donor countries initiated major programs for bilateral food aid and established the WFP in 1961 as the primary multilateral institution for such aid.

Despite these initiatives, a major food crisis in the mid-1970s was triggered by a combination of rapid increases in food prices between 1973 and 1975 and record lows in food supply in 1974. The Sahel, Ethiopia, and Bangladesh suffered major famines. In response, the UN organized the first World Food Conference in 1974, which led to the creation of the International Fund for Agricultural Development (Chapter 3) to focus on increasing production and improving rural livelihoods in developing countries. It also established the UN Committee on World Food Security under the FAO as a forum for reviewing food security policies and the World Food Council to address coordination problems among states and IGOs.

By the 1980s, when Indian economist Amartya Sen published his major book *Poverty and Famine: An Essay on Entitlement and Deprivation*, thinking began to shift, however, partly as a result of critiques of the Green Revolution. Sen pointedly argued, "Starvation is the characteristic of some people not *having* enough food to eat. It is not the characteristic of there *being* not enough food to eat" (Sen 1981: 1). In short, access was key in his view, along with well-functioning markets and good public policies.

In the 1980s and 1990s, as periodic episodes of famine occurred, a number of NGOs became very active in operational and advocacy roles on food security, including CARE, World Vision, and Oxfam. By the early 2000s, WFP was working in partnership with many of these groups and with private donors and agricultural firms. When the UN convened the World Food Summit in 1996, NGOs actively participated. One outcome showed how the concept of food security had evolved, namely, the definition participants adopted: "Food security exists when all people, at all times, have physical, social and economic access to sufficient, safe and nutritious food which meets their dietary needs and food preferences for an active and healthy life" (FAO 1996). This wording was also consistent with the emerging concept of human security. The announced goal of halving hunger in the world by 2015 was announced and then reinforced in Millennium Development Goal (MDG) no 1. Although there was substantial progress toward this goal by the time the MDGs wrapped up in 2015 with the proportion of the world's population of undernourished decreased from 24 percent to 15 percent (primarily in Asia), much remained to be done. Hence, Sustainable Development Goal (SDG) no. 2 goal was set at the even more ambitious target of ending hunger, achieving food security and improved nutrition, and promoting sustainable agriculture.

Setting goals has not forestalled further crises in spite of steady, if slow, progress in reducing the numbers of food-insecure people in the world since 1990. A new global food crisis in 2007–2008 highlighted the difficulties of addressing food insecurity because it was triggered by price increases for key staple crops, high energy prices, and the global financial crisis in that same period. As Jennifer Clapp (2018: 712–713) explains, this crisis also revealed the degree to which food security has become deeply entwined with global economic forces, including agricultural trade rules handled by the WTO and lower levels of World Bank, donors' and developing countries' investment in agriculture, and more volatile agricultural markets and food prices. It should be noted that the UN food-related agencies do not have mandates to address any of these issues or hold governments to account on economic issues.

Again, the UN did what it often does in response to this crisis: created a high-level task force composed of representatives from more than twenty UN agencies and funds, including the World Bank and International Monetary Fund, plus the World Trade Organization. The task force convened another World Summit on Food Security in Rome in 2009. As a result of these initiatives, new norms were established to guide coordination of responses across the system, and the Committee on World Food Security set up in 1974 was reformed to include civil society representation. As Clapp (2018: 715) notes, the committee "now functions much more effectively as a forum for debating these issues, but . . . still lacks teeth to implement policy changes."

Thus, the concept of food security links to human rights (rights to freedom from hunger and an individual's right to food) and to development. It incorporates four dimensions: the availability of food, access to food, adequate nutrition, and the stability of food supply. It is measured using a mixture of data on national food production and household/individual levels of access to food. As illustrated in Figure 11.2, the FAO has created a Food Insecurity Experience Scale to measure the severity of need and the duration of need from seasonal to chronic and acute.

The reality today is that much of the public attention to the persistence of hunger and food insecurity relates to major food emergencies linked to wars, forced displacements of people, famines, major natural disasters, the Covid-19 pandemic, and the effects of climate change. These are the stories that grab the headlines and inspire people to give and make them more aware of the work of the WFP and humanitarian NGOs involved in food relief.

Figure 11.2 How the FAO Measures Levels of Food Insecurity

Food Insecurity by Intensity	Food Insecurity by Duration	Food Insecurity Experience Scale
Mild	*Seasonal:* when a person experiences a cyclical patten of inadequate access to food	Uncertainty regarding ability to acquire food
Moderate	*Chronic:* when a person is unable to meet minimum food requirements over a sustained period	Compromising on food quality and variety
Severe	*Acute:* inability to consume enough food places a person's life in immediate danger	Reducing food quantity, skipping meals
		No food for a day or more

Source: Food and Agriculture Organization, http://www.fao.org/hunger/en/.

The World Food Programme and
Responses to Food Emergencies

Where the FAO continues to focus on increased food production in relationship to agricultural development, the WFP has become *the* primary responder to food emergencies accompanying natural disasters, war, and famine. Some have called it the world's largest humanitarian organization. Its mission includes both short-term aid and assistance in more protracted situations as well as for development.

The scope of the need. At the beginning of 2023, some 205 million people around the world were estimated to go to bed hungry, with another 45 million in thirty-seven countries (more than half in Africa) facing starvation (WFP and FAO 2022). The top ten emergencies were Yemen, South Sudan, the Democratic Republic of Congo, Afghanistan, Venezuela, Ethiopia, Syria, northern Nigeria, and Haiti. Of greatest concern to WFP (and other humanitarian agencies) were the acutely malnourished children under the age of five.

The WFP's resources come entirely from voluntary contributions of money and surplus food from UN member states, other UN funds and agencies, and private donors; hence, these resources are often stretched beyond capacity. Eighty percent of the WFP's budget comes from ten major donor states, including the United States and the EU. In 2015, a shortfall forced it to cut the daily food allotments for Syrian refugees.

The WFP has field activities in more than eighty countries. These include delivering food supplies, running food-for-work programs where people build roads or irrigation systems in exchange for food, and providing school-based feeding programs so that children remain in school. They often risk their lives to carry out their mission in areas of conflict. The organization has ships, planes, and trucks to manage food deliveries. It partners with more than 3,000 local and international NGOs and community-based organizations to distribute food. In 2008, the WFP launched the "Purchase for Progress" program to stimulate agricultural and market development in developing countries in ways that would benefit small local farmers (i.e., closer to the actual needs), and it has pledged to procure 10 percent of its food purchases in this way. The program also strengthens local economies and contributes to SDG no. 2 (eradicate hunger) and no. 15 (responsible production and consumption). It operates in partnership with a number of major foundations, such as the Bill and Melinda Gates and Howard G. Buffett Foundations and has received funding from a number of governments as well. Through its training programs, the WFP has significantly increased the number of women who participate to 300,000 by the end of 2020 and benefited more than one million farmers in twenty-one countries. This reflects the reality that farming in developing countries is largely done by women.

The effects of the pandemic. The Covid-19 pandemic dramatically increased the problem of food insecurity in the world. As one commentator noted, "Make no mistake: Covid-19 has made the hungry hungrier and the poor poorer" (Sova 2021).

In 2020, the FAO reported global record grain production, so the challenges Covid-19 posed were not food supply per se. The globalization of food supply chains has made many more countries dependent on food imports than was the case in 2000, but there are also more exporting countries, which has made agricultural trade more resilient to swings in supply and demand. The sudden loss of employment and income for millions in rich and poor countries alike as a result of the pandemic was the key factor in the sharp rise in food insecurity. Where hunger had long been considered a largely rural phenomenon, cities in developing countries were affected (Sova 2021). The situation was particularly bad in countries that were struggling before the pandemic, such as Zimbabwe, Sudan, Yemen, and South Sudan, and countries such as Iran and Venezuela that have long depended on high oil prices to support their economies, yet the pandemic was accompanied by low oil prices. Where curfews or restrictions on movement were imposed to curb the spread of Covid-19, deliveries of seeds, tools, and food aid were affected. These disruptions inevitably affected food supplies for refugees, migrants, and people living in conflict zones.

In mid-2020, the FAO at the behest of the Italian government created a multistakeholder mechanism called the Food Coalition. Its purpose was to mobilize political, financial, and technical support for countries affected by the crisis; serve as a platform for exchange of knowledge and ideas; and prevent the pandemic from triggering a world food crisis (Food Ingredients First 2020).

In short, the pandemic significantly affected food security in many parts of the world, not just where the WFP has long operated in conflict and disaster zones. In recognition of its work in responding to the surge in global hunger amid the pandemic, the WFP was awarded the Nobel Peace Prize in October 2020. The Nobel Committee chair stated, "In the face of the pandemic, the World Food Program has demonstrated an impressive ability to intensify its efforts. . . . The combination of violent conflict and the pandemic has led to a dramatic rise in the number of people living on the brink of starvation." Noting the role of hunger as a weapon of war, the committee added, "It is one of the oldest conflict weapons in the world, that you can starve out a population to enter a territory" (Nobel Prize 2020).

The war in Ukraine and the 2022–2023 global food crisis. The Ukraine case clearly demonstrates the relationship between conventional security and human security. That recognition led WFP Executive Director David Beasley to warn "over the next nine months we will see famine, we will see destabilisation of nations and we will see mass migration" (*The Economist* 2022b: 20). With Russia and Ukraine together responsible for some 28 percent of the world market for wheat and significant sources for corn, barley, sunflower seeds for vegetable oil, and fertilizers, the war had immediate effects first on prices and then supplies, including the wheat the WFP gets from Ukraine. The FAO calculated that nearly fifty countries were dependent on one or both countries for percent (*The Economist* 2022b). Several Middle East and North African countries were particularly reliant on wheat imports from Ukraine and Russia.

The Russian blockade of Ukraine's Black Sea ports blocked its exports, missiles and bombs destroyed grain storage facilities, fighting caused loss of farmland, embargoes on Russian exports halted exports of its grain and fertilizers, and most Western suppliers of seed and chemicals pulled out of Russia. Not only did prices for grains and the fuel needed for farms and fertilizer go up, but the timing of the invasion also affected shipping of Ukraine's already harvested crops. The WFP and humanitarian aid organizations worried that the effects could be particularly catastrophic. UN Secretary-General António Guterres deplored the destructiveness of the war and warned that it was "an assault on the world's most vulnerable people and countries. . . . Now their breadbasket is being bombed" (WFP 2022).

The UN Security Council had first met on the issue of armed conflict and food security a year before the Ukraine war (March 2021) and approved Resolution 2417 on conflict-induced food insecurity, including famine, and condemned the use of starvation as a method of warfare. Security Council and other high-level meetings after Russia's invasion focused on increasing concerns about the Ukraine war's effects on global food security. A diplomatic solution was needed for Russia's blockade of Black Sea shipping routes for grain.

In late July 2022, diplomats and military officers from the UN, Russia, Turkey, and Ukraine hammered out details for a grain export shipping corridor from Ukraine through the Black Sea to the Mediterranean through the set of straits that Turkey controls. The resulting parallel agreements known as the Black Sea Grain Initiative were valid for 120 days. One was between Ukraine, Turkey, and the UN and the other was between Russia, Turkey, and the UN. The agreements authorized exports from three Ukrainian ports; specially created maritime corridors that had been demined; and inspections in Turkey of all merchant vessels going in either direction by the newly created Joint Coordination Centre, headed by a Turkish admiral. A separate agreement between Russia and the UN Secretariat called for the UN to facilitate the unimpeded export of Russian food and fertilizers—a key concern for Russia given sanctions against Russian banks and vessels and refusal of shipping companies to work with Russian clients. Russia subsequently suspended participation after a

Ukrainian attack on Crimea, then agreed to two extensions of the agreement, before pulling out in mid-2023, renewing attacks on Ukrainian port facilities, and threatening to attack civilian ships in the Black Sea. This triggered widespread criticism, rapid increases in wheat futures prices, and renewed diplomatic efforts to persuade Russia to return to the agreement. US Ambassador to the UN Linda Thomas Greenfield captured the sentiments of many when she said, "Russia is waging war on the world's food supply . . . Russia has zero, zero legitimate reason to suspend its participation in this arrangement" (Parks 2023).

A key question for this specific situation and for global governance of food security more generally is what is the significance of this example of ad hoc multilateralism? For one thing, Guterres saw the agreement as "probably the most important" achievement of his tenure and a "beacon of hope." For another, the agreement alleviated to some extent the acute shortages of food and fertilizers. It demonstrated the ability of Turkey's President Tayyip Erdoğan to work with Guterres in persuading Russia and Ukraine to cooperate (Crisis Group 2022).

Helpful as it was in freeing up some (but by no means all) shipments from Russia and Ukraine, the agreement neither shortened the war nor ended the global food crisis. It could not solve the problems caused by prolonged drought in the Horn of Africa or food shortages in South Sudan, Yemen, Afghanistan, Nigeria, and Haiti. Even more concerning was one warning that on top of the persistent problems of climate change, drought, and the pandemic, the Ukraine war's effects on food supply could lead to a true shortfall of food supply, which would clearly be a crisis because most past problems have been problems of distribution, not supply (Wallace-Wells 2022). Beyond the existential need for food for human survival lies a key global governance-related question: is there a human right to food?

Is There a Human Right to Food?

Historically, hunger and food were conceptualized as part of development. Simultaneously, on a separate track, the right to food was incorporated into the two core UN human rights documents: the Universal Declaration of Human Rights and the Convention on Economic, Social, and Cultural Rights. The same pattern held for health. It, too, was linked to development and incorporated into the same documents. While there was extensive advocacy and work related to political and social rights for many years, there was far less attention paid in the UN system or by human rights advocates to economic, social, and cultural rights (discussed in Chapter 9). Hunger was conceptualized "primarily as a humanitarian and development problem in which aid organizations either provide assistance directly to those in need or work with local communities to help them build capacity to provide their own food security" (Jurkovich 2020: 94). The weakness or states' lack of capacity was deemed the principal source of humanitarian crises and lack of development.

Human rights, on the contrary, "require state action to fulfill" (Jurkovich 2020: 94). Only since 1997 has the UN linked human rights with development, as borne out in the MDGs and the SDGs. This has not resulted in extensive human rights advocacy relating to hunger—a puzzle that Michelle Jurkovich (2020: chaps. 3 and 4) attributes to the absence of a human rights norm around hunger. That is, there is still no widespread belief that governments have a legal obligation under international human rights law to feed their people if they cannot feed themselves. Thus, the MDGs and SDGs around hunger have been aspirations with the primary responsibility for addressing food insecurity remaining with the UN food institutions in partnership with NGOs—international and local—along with private donors, civil society groups, national governments, and corporations. Eliminating hunger and addressing food crises is still heavily seen first as a humanitarian task and second as a development problem.

Still, food and food security along with health are fundamental humanitarian needs that the UN has long played a key role in meeting among the world's displaced people, whether they be refugees fleeing conflict and persecution, those forced from their homes by natural disasters, migrants whose land no longer supports agriculture, or people in search of a better life. The human security of the growing number of people on the move is a major governance issue for the UN system and other IGOs. In turning to look at efforts to address refugees and migration, however, we see that the landscape is somewhat different. There is a clear body of international law relating to those who are certified as refugees, although their rights are quite limited; most of the millions of people around the world migrating for a host of reasons are not covered by international law, however, leaving them dependent on humanitarian assistance and the willingness of other states to accept them.

International Organizations and the Global Refugee and Migration Crisis

Many factors can prompt people to migrate, from war and other violence, political repression, discrimination and gross human rights violations to economic deprivation, food insecurity, natural disasters, the effects of climate change, and the desire to improve one's life. As one of the foremost scholars in the field has noted, "International migration represents one of the most obvious contemporary manifestations of globalization. With growth in trans-boundary interconnections, there has been a rapid increase in human mobility across international borders." Not surprisingly, migration "has become increasingly politicized by states, and an issue "of great importance at the international level" (Betts 2011: 1). Figure 11.3 shows the rapid growth in numbers of international migrants since 1990. The largest number were in Europe (87 million), followed by North America (59 million), then North Africa and Western Asia (50 million). Just ten countries hosted half of all migrants, with the United States having the largest number at 51 million (UN Department of Economic and Social Affairs 2020: 6–8).

What gave migration greater visibility and urgency is how the issues of refugees—a specific category of migrants—and migrants more generally came together in 2014–2015. Thousands of refugees, asylum-seekers, and migrants from Central America arrived at the US southern border, and more than 900,000 refugees, asylum-seekers, and migrants arrived in Europe. These large-scale movements created a sense of crisis, particularly among the major powers of the Global North, since the migrants and refugees from the Global South were arriving at their borders rather than remaining in distant places. The situation in Europe was perceived by some as the greatest humanitarian tragedy since the end of World War II (UNHCR 2015; Ferris and Donato 2020: 76).

One of the biggest future challenges will be people forced or choosing to move from their places of origin because of multiple climate events, such

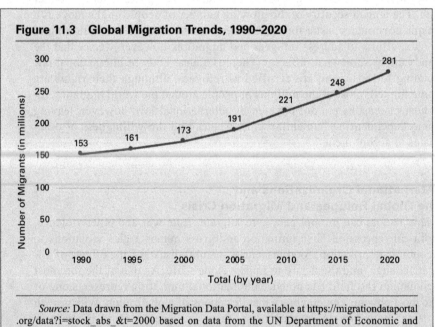

Figure 11.3   Global Migration Trends, 1990–2020

Source: Data drawn from the Migration Data Portal, available at https://migrationdataportal .org/data?i=stock_abs_&t=2000 based on data from the UN Department of Economic and Social Affairs.

as flooding, destructive storms, long-term changes to local ecosystems caused by seasonal weather patterns, sea level rise, drought, high heat, and desertification. Such climate-related migration threatens the economic stability, food security, and social stability of rural and urban areas and the very survival of low-lying island states worldwide (as discussed in Chapter 10). The connections between these climatic changes, violence, and conflict have already contributed to the massive increase in migrants of all types, including refugees and internally displaced persons (IDPs), that is, people forced to move or relocate in their own country because of violence, human rights violations, development projects, or natural disasters (but not poverty or unemployment). A 2015 study cited drought worsened by climate change as a contributing factor in the Syrian civil war, although the dominant narrative links the war to the Arab Spring (Fountain 2015).

In short, environmental changes constitute a major threat to human security and are already a significant driver of human migration. The World Bank has estimated that the number of people who may be displaced due to climate change-related disasters will reach 143 million by 2050 with most concentrated in sub-Saharan Africa, Latin America, and Southeast Asia (Podesta 2019). Contemporary climate changes, however, disproportionately affect those in the poorest regions of world. Not surprisingly, the countries with the highest numbers of IDPs as a result of natural disasters in 2021 were all in the Global South.

The term "environmental refugee" was first coined by Lester Brown in 1976 and has been used loosely since then. It has no legal standing, however, and creates confusion over the status of those affected and who bears some responsibility for assisting them (Brown, McGrath, and Stokes 1976). Referring to the 1951 Refugee Convention's definition of a refugee, Robert McLeman (2014: 204) notes, "The environment does not persecute; only humans are capable of this and so people made stateless by MSLR [mean sea-level rise] or by any other effects of climate change are by definition *not* refugees under international law." He further notes that the Guiding Principles on Internal Displacement, discussed below, do mention persons displaced by "natural or human-made disasters" as having a right to protection and assistance (McGrath 2014: 196). The reality is that climate change is creating a new way of becoming a stateless person, but drawing a clear distinction between forced versus voluntary migration in situations such as this is not always easy.

The scale and complexity of the crisis have only grown, continuing to challenge the UN system and some regional institutions. The problems are immense. Refugees were once thought to be a temporary problem at the end of World Wars I and II. Today, fueled on an unprecedented scale by violent conflicts, civil unrest, persecution, human rights abuses, economic disparities, natural disasters, weak states, and environmental degradation, the numbers of refugees, IDPs, and people who are forcibly displaced for other reasons barely begin to tell the story (and can be very difficult to pin down). The problems are greatest in the Middle East, South Asia, and Africa, yet hardly any part of the globe is untouched. Unlike in the past, the problem is no longer a short-term or temporary problem. As Figure 11.4 shows, there are three primary categories of persons forcibly displaced for which statistics are kept.

Until the Covid-19 pandemic erupted around the globe, the refugee and migration crisis was considered one of the greatest challenges for international cooperation and human security for the foreseeable future. Complicating matters, the long-standing distinction between refugees and migrants has become blurred, creating a "protection gap" for those who do not meet the strict legal definition of a refugee when the sheer numbers of those in need of humanitarian assistance are overwhelming the capacity of the two UN-related agencies created to address refugee and migration-related issues and the humanitarian NGOs that work alongside them. A further complication is that some of today's migrants are aided in their journeys by human traffickers and human trafficking as discussed in Chapter 9, is governed by human rights law and international criminal law, including the UN Office

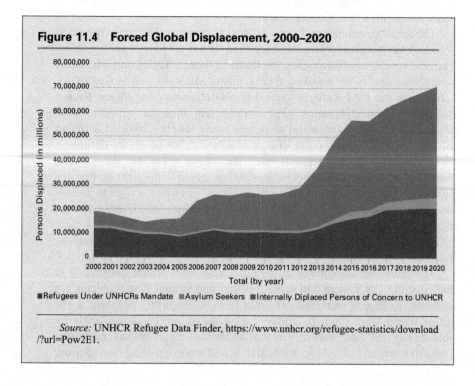

Figure 11.4   Forced Global Displacement, 2000–2020

Persons Displaced (in millions)

Total (by year)

■Refugees Under UNHCRs Mandate ■Asylum Seekers ■Internally Diplaced Persons of Concern to UNHCR

Source: UNHCR Refugee Data Finder, https://www.unhcr.org/refugee-statistics/download /?url=Pow2E1.

of Drugs and Crime (UNODC). The issue of trafficking also goes far beyond smuggling those who want to migrate across borders, however, and today's migration crisis often masks this illicit trade.

Our attention here is on two key UN-related institutions that deal with refugees and migration: the UN High Commissioner for Refugees (UNHCR) and the International Organization for Migration (IOM). In the process, we clarify definitions of the different populations they serve and the complex dimensions of the refugee and migration crisis.

The United Nations High Commissioner for Refugees

The UNHCR and the 1951 Convention Relating to the Status of Refugees (supplemented by the 1967 protocol) are the primary institutions defining refugees and organizing assistance to those who are forcibly displaced across borders. According to the convention, a refugee is a person who because of a "well-founded fear of being persecuted for reasons of race, religion, nationality, membership of a particular social group or political opinion, is outside the country of his nationality and is unable or, owing to such fear, is unwilling to avail himself of the protection of that country." The UNHCR's mandate is to protect people whom it certifies as refugees (its primary role) by providing refuge (a secondary role) until another state grants them asylum or they can return home (the third role: return or resettlement). The most significant right of a refugee is "non-refoulement"—the principle that refugees cannot be forced to return to their country of origin. Therefore, UNHCR provides administrative assistance and identity papers and protects refugees from forced repatriation and exploitation in the host state (two other roles). This legal protection mandate has become increasingly difficult to implement as the numbers have surged and what was envisaged as providing temporary assistance has become long-term or semi-permanent.

Originally, the 1951 convention only applied to Europe since UNHCR was only supposed to be in operation for three years to complete the task of resettling refugees from World War II. But it was made universal by the 1967 protocol and broadened through regional agreements, such as the 1969 Organisation of African Unity Convention Governing the Specific Aspects of Refugee Problems in Africa, which included those displaced by internal conflicts; the 1984 Cartagena Declaration on Refugees; the 1994 San José Declaration on Refugees and Displaced Persons, which also covered IDPs; and the 1980 European Agreement on Transfer of Responsibility for Refugees. These regional documents correspond more to actual causes of flight in particular regions and to the reality that it is "often impossible for asylum seekers to generate documented evidence of individual persecution required by the 1951 Convention . . . [since] most contemporary mass exoduses occur when political violence is of a generalized nature rather than a direct individual threat" (Loescher and Milner 2011: 191–192.

The UNHCR adapted its own mandate to address this reality starting in the 1970s and accelerating in response to the post–Cold War intrastate conflicts of the 1990s with their large humanitarian crises, including huge population displacements—internally and across borders—and what has become a growing problem of long-term displacement. As the primary humanitarian relief entity in the UN system until 1991, the UNHCR was forced to shift from legal protection to coordinating a range of assistance to large numbers of displaced persons and refugees. As part of these shifts, it adopted the human security concept as a way "to reconcile the security concerns of states, the protection needs of refugees, and the security needs of its staff." This demonstrated "the real security of states and the international community could only be achieved by providing security for 'people'" (Loescher, Betts, and Milner 2008: 57). With this change, UNHCR greatly expanded its cooperation with a number of other UN agencies, including the WFP, UNICEF, UNDP, Office for Coordination of Humanitarian Affairs (OCHA), and Department of Peace Operations, as well as the International Committee of the Red Cross, Save the Children, Doctors Without Borders (MSF), Lutheran World Federation, Oxfam, International Rescue Committee, the Danish and Norwegian Refugee Councils, and other NGOs plus local actors. As is true in many other parts of the UN system, partnerships have become key to strengthening what the UNHCR is able to do.

In mid-2022, the UNHCR was busier than ever before. It had more than 103 million persons "of concern"—the highest number since the end of World War II—with about a third of them refugees and half IDPs. The largest numbers of refugees were from Syria, Venezuela, Afghanistan, South Sudan, and Myanmar, and 86 percent of them were hosted by developing and least developed countries, which bear the brunt of the burden of assistance. Women and children make up the vast majority of the refugees and IDPs, with some 40 percent being under age eighteen (UNHCR 2023). Yet by mid-2022, only 162,400 refugees had returned to their countries of origin or were resettled in other countries, demonstrating the problem of protracted displacement. The latter is compounded by a "crisis of asylum" as states (including many in the EU along with the United States) have adopted restrictive asylum policies in recent years. There are also 5.6 million Palestinians that fall under the care of the UN Relief and Works Agency, which was created in 1949 specifically to serve their needs.

IDPs are not considered refugees under the 1951 convention. They present particular challenges because they remain within the boundaries of ostensibly sovereign states and thus are subject to domestic jurisdiction. The largest numbers (all over two million each) found in Syria, Democratic Republic of Congo, Yemen, Afghanistan, Nigeria, and Colombia.

Their numbers have increased dramatically because of intrastate conflict, ethnic cleansing, natural disasters, and the availability of more accurate data (see Figure 11.3).

Until the late 1990s, there was no international legal basis for providing assistance to IDPs. As a result of the work of two individuals—Roberta Cohen and Francis Deng—who framed the idea of protection for IDPs and brought attention to the issue, the 2005 UN World Summit endorsed the Guiding Principles on Internal Displacement. These affirm that national governments have primary responsibility for protection and assistance but that international assistance to IDPs is not to be considered interference in a state's internal affairs (Koser 2011).

Even before 2005, UNHCR had gradually taken on responsibility for assisting a significant portion of IDPs, and the UN had established a system of appointing different UN agencies, including the WFP, UNICEF, and the UN Educational, Scientific and Cultural Organization as lead actors in various areas of humanitarian action, such as supplying food, schooling for children, housing, sanitation, and healthcare. UNHCR retains the overall responsibility because of its role in registering all persons, providing assistance, and counseling on asylum applications.

In 2022, UNHCR had staff in 138 countries, providing protection and assistance to refugees, returnees, IDPs, and stateless people. Although it works with many partners, including other UN agencies, NGOs, and governments, it generally serves as the lead agency because of its responsibility for registering all persons. In many situations, UNHCR has been forced to construct and maintain refugee/IDP camps where it cannot arrange other modes of shelter and protection. In early 2021, there were 6.6 million refugees in camps. Long-term refugee camps such as in Kenya and Bangladesh become small cities with residents creating small businesses, rudimentary governance, radio stations, hospitals, and so on. But inhabitants are almost entirely dependent on international humanitarian assistance and live in what have been described as "dire conditions" with high degrees of physical and economic insecurity, including sexual and gender-based violence (Betts 2013: 146–149). Common issues in refugee camps include water supply, sanitation, waste dumps, lack of electricity, lack of access to education for refugee children and skills-building opportunities for youths, along with lack of access to basic health facilities.

Funding is a critical issue for UNHCR. Only about 2 percent of its budget is supported by a subsidy from the UN; the majority is funded by voluntary contributions from governments (of which the United States is the largest), corporations, foundations, and private individuals. The dramatic increases in numbers of refugees means a growing gap between needs and available funding. Since most NGOs depend on some of the same donors, there is significant competition for funds.

The International Organization on Migration

The total number of migrants in the world is far greater than the numbers of those categorized as refugees and IDPs. Yet until 2018, there was no formal multilateral institutional framework for coordinating states' responses to migration beyond the 1951 Refugee Convention and the 1967 protocol plus international human rights law. That changed with the approval in 2018 of the Global Compact for Migration (and a companion Compact for Refugees), discussed below, but there still was no migration organization in the UN system and only some elements of an international migration regime. The IOM only became a "related" organization in the UN system in 2016, when a summit meeting convened to address the large movements of refugees and other migrants in the latter half of 2015, including thousands each day crossing the Mediterranean in flimsy boats or trudging through the Balkans to seek refuge in European countries.

What became the IOM in 1989 started out in 1951 as the Provisional Intergovernmental Committee for the Movement of Migrants from Europe to facilitate settlement of the displaced in Europe after World War II and those fleeing communism. For many years, it was the entity that had responsibility for operational activities, including resettlement of refugees in countries that would receive them, whereas UNHCR was a nonoperational agency carrying out its original, more limited legal protection mandate for refugees. Over time, the IOM changed its focus and name, becoming an IGO in 1989. It now has 175 member states and 8 observer states, with its around 600 offices providing a range of services related to its mission of promoting "orderly and humane management of migration." The IOM works with governments and civil society to promote understanding of migration issues and the importance of protecting the human dignity and well-being of migrants. It compiles statistics on migration patterns, resettlement, voluntary returns, and counter-trafficking. It has also promoted consultation among informal groups of states about best practices and common standards (Bradley 2017; Pécoud 2018). In addition, it has become increasingly involved in humanitarian relief efforts.

Although "related" to the UN system, the IOM is not a specialized agency, and migration-related activities are pursued by several other UN agencies, including the International Labour Organization. There is no treaty, convention, or statute to give the IOM a clear, normative mandate. The agreement approved by the UNGA recognized the IOM as "an essential contributor in the field of human mobility, in the protection of migrants, in operational activities related to migrants, displaced people and migration-affected communities, including in the areas of resettlement and returns, and in mainstreaming migration in development plans" (UN General Assembly 2016). The IOM operates with considerable autonomy regarding its funding structure and reporting lines, but its director-general is a member of the UN Chief Executives Board and thus has a seat at the table for coordinating strategy and operations with other parts of the UN system (Bradley 2017; Thouez 2019). Its relationship with UNHCR and other actors in refugee and migration governance inside and outside the UN system, therefore, is still evolving.

Other Responses to the Global Refugee/Migration Crisis

Responses to the refugee/migration crisis reflect the different perspectives of countries in the Global North and South. Developing countries call for looking at protracted refugee situations, not just new arrivals, and at issues relating to migrants and refugees more generally. Developed countries tend to focus on ways to deter future arrivals and manage flows. There has been far less attention to the problem that many countries, including the United States and a number of EU members, have been trying to close their borders, contributing to the crisis (Ferris and Donato 2020: 79–81).

The European Union. Although 2015 was truly a crisis year for Europe, the flood of refugees and migrants continues. By comparison with situations in other parts of the world, these numbers hardly constitute a crisis. But it has become a crisis of political solidarity for the EU (Crawley 2016). The reasons for this lie in part in significant gaps in EU and member state migration policy and practice.

In seeking to understand the EU's responses, it is important to remember the distinction between federalism and intergovernmentalism in EU governance discussed in Chapter 5. The first refers to supranational policies instituted by EU institutions; the latter refers to issues and policy areas where member governments retain primary authority and any collective decisions require negotiation among the relevant member government authorities. The Justice and Home Affairs Council, which oversees migration and asylum policies, is largely intergovernmental. Although the 1985 Schengen Agreement led to the abolition of internal borders in the EU, external borders remained largely the province of member state control except as the 2004 Dublin Regulation and creation of Frontex (the European Border and Coast Guard Agency) provided some basis for handling asylum claims, coordinating border interventions, and assisting member states with screening, identifying, and fingerprinting migrants as well as with forced returns. Yet in 2013, legislation allowed member states to reinstate internal border controls in situations where the outer borders were not fully controlled. "Effectively the response to the needs of refugees was to reinstate the powers of the member states, to negate the principle of solidarity as between the member states, and to create a migration laissez-faire approach in which whoever builds the highest fence or stops the most asylum claims is the short-term winner" (Borg-Barthet and Lyons 2016: 232).

Efforts to enact an agreement on burden-sharing for relocations failed with several member states, including the United Kingdom, Denmark, Poland, and Hungary refusing to participate and others offering only limited places, whereas Germany accepted large numbers of refugees and migrants.

A number of problems have arisen since the 2015 crisis. For one thing, migrants and asylum seekers do not receive equal treatment in all member states. Second, the EU applies the rule associated with the 1951 UN Refugee Convention that the country of first arrival is responsible for receiving and processing applications. This has created hardship, especially for Greece, Spain, Malta, and Italy—the primary receiving states—and complications for implementation given the EU's open internal borders. It further encourages refugees to try to evade registration and reach their chosen country because there are significant variations in the acceptance rates of applications for asylum across the EU member states (Archibugi, Cellini, and Vitiello 2021: 492–493). The net result has been uneven burden-sharing and limited focus on human rights and upholding European values in the effort to "stem flows" and "secure borders" (Borg-Barthet and Lyons 2016: 234).

A further step the EU has taken is outsourcing its external border control through agreements with transit countries to limit the number of people arriving in Europe. Such agreements were struck with Turkey, Libya, and Morocco and involved significant payments for their cooperation. Although the approach has reduced the numbers of arrivals in recent years, none of these countries are noted for respecting human rights, especially those of refugees, migrants, and asylum seekers, which has put the EU in a position of depending on largely nondemocratic countries—a significant violation of its own values (Archibugi, Cellini, and Vitiello 2021: 494).

Finally, the refugee/migration issue has created a serious risk to the EU going forward. In all member states, it has fueled the rise of populist, nationalist, and even anti-EU politicians and political parties. Islamophobia and racism have increased, and migration is directly linked with security issues and the threat of terrorism (Crawley 2016: 20; Archibugi, Cellini, and Vitiello 2021: 498; *The Economist* 2022c: 49). In contrast, European states have been welcoming to Ukrainian refugees fleeing Russia's invasion either because they are white, they are overwhelmingly women and children, or because their presence is viewed as a temporary arrangement. Consequently, as *The Economist* (2022c: 49) put it, "Europe's approach to dealing with migration is a mess of national and EU policies. Southern Europeans resent rules that force potential refugees to apply for asylum in the first country they arrive at. . . . Northerners will agree only to a voluntary scheme, which has not worked well. That has eroded trust." The consequence, it adds, has been that "border controls that were once abolished within the bloc have made an unwelcome return in many countries [and] improvements since 2015 have largely focused on keeping migrants out."

One might have thought that if any group of countries could develop an effective multilateral set of responses to the refugee and migration flows, it would be the EU. That clearly was not the case in the 2015 crisis and continues to be a challenge for the EU (Ceccorulli 2021). We turn to look at what the UN has managed to accomplish by way of more global responses.

The UN and efforts to develop global responses. The inability of the EU member states to agree on cooperative responses demonstrates that IGOs are not always good at being flexible and nimble, even when the lives of thousands of humans are at stake. This is especially true when cooperation requires opening states' borders and communities to welcome refugees, asylum-seekers, and migrants who come from different countries and cultures.

Well before 2014–2015, there was growing recognition within the UN of the need for an international framework for governing migration. The 1994 International Conference on Population and Development in Cairo was the first recognition that migration can be beneficial for development. This led to the creation of the Global Commission on International Migration and the Global Forum on Migration and Development in 2002, which included seventeen UN agencies plus the IOM to further investigate the problem. The links between migration and climate change were recognized from the outset of the Intergovernmental Panel on Climate Change's work in the late 1980s. As a result, since the UN Framework Convention on Climate Change's (UNFCCC) conclusion in the early 1990s, migration has been treated as one of the possible outcomes of climatic events and changes. The 2010 Cancun Agreements by the UNFCCC Conference of Parties further mentioned migration and displacement in the context of adaptation and called for "Measures to enhance understanding, coordination and cooperation . . . at the national, regional and international levels" (UNFCCC 2010, Section II). The 2015 Paris Agreement (discussed in Chapter 10) also acknowledged the adverse effect of climate change on migration patterns and called for international advisory groups to recommend ways "to avert, minimize and address" such displacement (Chan 2015: 18). Yet as McLeman (2014: 59) notes, "Just as cultural, economic, environmental, political, and social factors operating at macro-, meso-, and micro-scales affect migration options, decisions, and behavior . . . they also affect adaptation options, decisions, and behavior." Some adaptive measures have been taken by small island states, some by urban coastal cities and regional authorities, and others by individuals and groups, but the UN's principal response thus far has been through the 2018 Global Compact for Migration.

In 2015, a small group of UN agency heads, plus the IOM, (still outside the UN) convened to focus on concrete solutions. The challenge was how to persuade governments to work toward a global framework for addressing both refugees and global migration policy. In December, the president of the General Assembly declared that the UN would convene a summit in September 2016 to address large movements of refugees and migrants in what was widely called "the global humanitarian and refugee crisis." In essence, the crisis forced the UN to do what it does best: convening its member states to discuss and engage on the issue. Still, it took time to persuade governments to accept the summit and the agenda of working toward a global framework for addressing issues involving refugees and global migration policy relating to labor migrants and migrants in what were called "vulnerable situations." This combined agenda marked the first time that the two sets of issues were addressed jointly at the UN.

The 2016 global summit and the global compacts. The September 19, 2016, Summit for Refugees and Migrants marked the first ever high-level meeting on these two related global issues. The summit's principal outcome was the adoption by the UNGA of the Global Compact on Refugees (GCR) and the Global Compact for Safe, Orderly and Regular Migration (GCM). As Elizabeth Ferris and Katharine Donato (2020: 2) note, "The Summit and the processes of developing the compacts occurred at a particular moment and in a particular political climate . . . [when] there seemed to be a collective yearning for coordinated, multilateral action to deal with the thorny issues of migration and refugee movements." Just six weeks after the summit, however, Donald Trump became the US president, having campaigned on an anti-immigration platform. Consequently, the United States, which had long been the leader on refugee and humanitarian issues, "crossed over to the other side and became a champion of restrictionist policies" (Ferris and Donato 2020: 2).

The negotiation processes for the compacts diverged from the beginning, with UNHCR taking the lead in negotiations for the compact on refugees and the ambassadors of Mexico and Switzerland facilitating negotiations on the compact on migration in a process that included regional and multistakeholder consultations as well as formal negotiations with member states. The Special Representative of the Secretary-General for Migration, Louise Arbour, and the IOM (by then in relationship with the UN) were also involved. The compacts were adopted by the UNGA in December 2018. The GCR was adopted by a vote of 181 in favor, 2 opposed (Hungary and the United States), and 3 abstentions. The GCM was more controversial, as the final vote shows: 152 in favor, 5 against (Czech Republic, Hungary, Israel, Poland, and the United States), and 12 abstentions. The United States withdrew entirely from the process in 2017 (Thouez 2019; Ferris and Donato 2020: chap. 5).

The compacts are not legally binding treaties or conventions; they are more statements about standards and practical cooperation, reflecting what governments were willing to agree to at that particular time. Some scholars consider them soft law with the potential to lead to hard law.

The GCR is considered the less ambitious of the compacts and has been described as an "incremental change" in the existing refugee regime (Ferris and Donato 2020: 113, 118). It emphasizes more equitable burden-sharing for hosting and supporting refugees and the need for enhanced refugee self-reliance. One innovation is the provision for hosting countries to be responsible for coordinating and facilitating support, including financing, thus giving them a bigger role. The GCR establishes a ministerial-level Global Refugee Forum to be convened every four years starting in 2019 to elicit pledges for funding and review progress toward achievement of objectives, plus high-level meetings every two years between forums for reviews. UNHCR is given the key role in implementation, including the development of indicators and measures of the effect of refugees on host states.

The GCM is more ambitious, particularly because there had never been an overall global framework for governing migration in its various forms. It views migration as beneficial, on balance. It includes twenty-three objectives with lists of concrete actions for implementation—some for states, some for other actors. These actions included measures to protect the human rights of migrants, reduce forced migration, improve migration management, enhance the safety of migrants, increase regional and international cooperation and burden-sharing, and collect accurate data for evidence-based policies. Gaps include lack of attention to "pull" factors in migration and to detention of children and the absence of enforcement or accountability mechanisms (Ferris and Donato 2020: 116–117). The GCM provides for reviews every four years beginning in 2022. The UN Network on Migration, created in 2018, serves as the coordinating body for the GCM; governments are expected to develop national responses for implementation; the IOM is tasked with working in coordination with other UN agencies; and the UN Secretary-General is to report to the UNGA on a biennial basis. No indicators are specified for measuring success.

Although both compacts created new mechanisms, the division of labor between the UNHCR and IOM was left unresolved. There is also concern that the GCR does not "come even close to addressing the operational deficits of the refugee regime" or filling the burden-sharing gap (Arnold-Fernández 2019: 191). It leaves to national governments the determination of how much freedom refugees have with regard to where they live, whether they can work, and what government and private services they can access.

The GCM is seen somewhat more positively as signaling member states' intent to "move away from reactive approaches to migration governance and identify concrete measures that benefit both migrants and states" (Devakumar et al. 2019: 2). As the first agreement negotiated under UN auspices on the subject of migration, that is no small accomplishment.

The principles it sets forth provide a basis for future advocacy and aim to bolster cooperation between states and strengthen regular migration pathways as well as address irregular migration and the protection of migrants' human rights. Antoine Pécoud (2021: 17) suggests that the GCM is a "depoliticized" document that creates no legally binding commitments but has spurred global debate on governing migration. Because the final vote showed that countries were deeply divided on the issue of migration, only time will tell whether either of the compacts makes a difference in the governance of refugees and migration.

The reality is that migration poses major governance challenges. Borders matter! They affect who is entitled to what protection. Refugees, whether individuals or groups, are entitled to a clear set of civil and political rights laid out in international law; those who are forcibly displaced—either within or across borders—by food insecurity, conflict or violence, economic deprivation, natural disasters, or climate changes have rights, but they are the rights enumerated in the Covenant on Economic, Social and Cultural Rights (discussed in Chapter 9) that are less widely accepted. Hence, as Alexander Betts (2013: 189) notes, "There is far more ambiguity and state variation in responses to survival migrants fleeing basic rights deprivations resulting from states' unwillingness and inability to protect." There is also considerable variation in the practice of the UNHCR, the IOM, and other international organizations as to who is entitled to what protection (Moretti 2021: 34–51).

The IOM and UNHCR are still sorting out answers to the questions of who does what and how best to coordinate their efforts, particularly in situations of large-scale or what is known as "mixed migration," where some people are entitled to UNHCR protections and others do not qualify. In situations like that involving the thousands of Rohingya forced to flee Myanmar, the fact that Bangladesh is not a party to the 1951 Refugee Convention meant that the IOM was in the lead and worked closely with the government of Bangladesh, which labeled the Rohingya "illegal migrants." Because the IOM lacks a protection mandate, it did not object to the Bangladesh government's security-driven response, confining Rohingya in camps without freedom of movement or many basic services and pushing for their swift return to Myanmar.

Cooperation between the IOM and UNHCR has generally been ad hoc—that is, worked out for specific settings and situations. In early 2019, however, the two organizations released a joint letter (notably not a more formal document) clarifying their roles and coordination arrangements for situations where both had legitimate reasons to be involved. Among other things, the IOM agreed to ensure that refugee law was respected and the relevant categorizations of persons "on the move" were respected. The UNHCR acknowledged the IOM's lead in supporting migrants. In situations of mixed movements, they committed to "work hand-in-hand in establishing and co-leading . . . for effective coordination" with the UNHCR taking the lead where there were large-scale movements predominantly composed of refugees (Moretti 2021: 34–51). Time will tell how well these two organizations are able to work together effectively in addressing the refugee and migration crisis.

A key actor in coordinating responses to refugee and migration crises as well as humanitarian crises caused by hunger, natural disasters, and conflicts is the UN OCHA, established in 1991 and headed by an under-secretary-general for humanitarian affairs who simultaneously serves as Emergency Relief Coordinator. The coordinator has specific responsibility for coordinating protection of and assistance to IDPs and chairs the Inter-Agency Standing Committee that oversees all humanitarian assistance.

Coordination: The Role of the OCHA

Clearly, human security–related issues have become a major part of the UN's work, and the various issues are deeply entwined with one another and require coordination. Often, in emergency situations such as the war in Ukraine, famine in northern Ethiopia and Somalia, or the 2020 East African locust infestation, OCHA appoints a humanitarian coordinator to oversee work on the ground by all the various entities, including local communities. Its role can involve negotiating safe access for aid delivery and coordinating the wide range of aid from food, water, sanitation, and medical assistance to shelter, as well as raising voluntary aid contributions. It relies for all but 5 percent of its budget on voluntary contributions, mostly from ten states and the EU, but securing adequate funding for human security and humanitarian needs is a persistent challenge.

OCHA and virtually all other aid organizations including NGOs have been severely challenged since the Taliban in Afghanistan placed restrictions on women working for all NGOs and UN agencies in late 2022. The prolonged economic and humanitarian crisis afflicting Afghanistan will be extremely difficult to address under these restrictions because women make up a large portion of the humanitarian assistance workforce. As William Byrd (2023) put it, "Afghanistan requires a change from humanitarian business as usual." Under the circumstances, even the UN Security Council has been engaged in debate over how to respond, how to finance, and how to coordinate and deliver aid. It is truly a challenge.

The Challenges of Protecting Human Security

The twentieth and twenty-first centuries have seen what seem like a growing number of human security crises. The media have long played a major part in raising awareness of these situations and the growth of the internet and social media since the late 1990s have contributed greatly to that and to the speed with which information (especially images) are widely available so that people in one part of the world see what is happening elsewhere. What has changed is the notion that security is not just about protecting states' borders and governments but is also about protecting fellow human beings experiencing humanitarian emergencies whether they stem from natural disasters, lack of food, changing climate, pandemics, or the violence of war and conflict.

Clearly the governance challenges for international organizations stemming from these threats are significant, and it has taken time for norms regarding state and IGOs' responsibility to develop. Yet the concept of human security has taken root not just among scholars but across the policy world, starting with the degree to which the UN Security Council has increasingly focused on human security-related issues since the early 2000s. Although the core institutions in health, refugees, and food security were established by the mid-1900s, their mandates and funding were limited, and funding remains a problem across all three issue areas. To address the growing migration crisis, in particular, new institutions have had to be created at the global and regional levels, but new norms and policies are only slowly being created. In all three issue areas, nonstate actors, especially NGOs, play major roles in filling gaps in meeting needs for protection and assistance.

In the final chapter, we look more broadly at some of these governance issues of limited capacity, legitimacy, accountability, and effectiveness as well as at the questions of what international organizations can and can't do well.

Suggested Further Reading

Anderson-Rodgers, David, and Kerry F. Crawford. (2023) *Human Security: Theory and Action*, 2nd ed. Lanham, MD: Rowman and Littlefield.

Betts, Alexander, ed. (2011) *Global Migration Governance*. Oxford: Oxford University Press.

Loescher, Gil, Alexander Betts, and James Milner. (2011) *The United Nations High Commissioner for Refugees (UNHCR): The Politics and Practice of Refugee Protection into the Twenty-First Century*, 2nd ed. New York: Routledge.

McKeon, Nora. (2015) *Food Security Governance: Empowering Communities, Regulating Corporations*. New York: Routledge.

Youde, Jeremy. (2012) *Global Health Governance*. Cambridge: Polity Press.

12

Challenges in
Global Governance

IN TODAY'S INTERCONNECTED WORLD, MANY PROBLEMS TRANSCEND national boundaries. Environmental degradation, infectious diseases, terrorism, refugees, food insecurity, nuclear proliferation, financial crises, human trafficking, and many other problems cannot be fixed by any state singlehandedly. This creates a need for global governance. Yet global governance can be difficult to achieve.

Why Global Governance Is Difficult

Throughout this book, we have uncovered multiple difficulties facing global governance. One difficulty is the number and variety of states. Today's nearly 200 states vary in their political systems, wealth, geography, population, and many other attributes, yet collectively they constitute the membership of traditional intergovernmental organizations (IGOs). IGOs handle the number and variety of member states in several ways. Some restrict membership to states with particular characteristics (as with the African Union or Organisation for Economic Co-operation and Development), others grant more formal control to very powerful states (as with the International Monetary Fund or UN Security Council), and others attempt to treat each member equally (as with the UN General Assembly or the Association of Southeast Asian Nations). Each approach has downsides: restrictive membership excludes some states; unequal formal control gives some members less say; and equal treatment ignores the fact that some states contribute more than others.

A second difficulty is the number and variety of nonstate actors (NSAs). States retain key roles in IGOs and continue to be especially protective of issues such as peace and security—yet much of what states and IGOs need for contemporary global governance is in the hands of NSAs.

567

For example, epistemic communities hold expertise and professional standards. Civil society, nongovernmental organizations (NGOs), transnational advocacy networks, and social movements offer know-how and grassroots connections. Private corporations have financial and technical resources. Consequently, very few IGOs or policy issues are untouched by NSAs today. NSAs can enhance global governance, but their proliferation can threaten state sovereignty or impose new expectations. That is why states sometimes push back against NSAs and why students of global governance continue to debate how much importance to accord to states versus nonstate actors.

A third difficulty facing global governance is the mixture of policy issues. Even though some IGOs—in particular, specialized agencies such as the World Health Organization (WHO) or the World Trade Organization (WTO)—are organized as if policy issues can be placed in separate silos, contemporary issues often involve multiple policy areas simultaneously. Human trafficking is an economically motivated problem that also violates core human rights; infectious disease is a health problem that also threatens development and human security; climate change is an environmental problem that has repercussions for migration and economic growth. To deal with the mixture of policy issues, responsibilities can be added to existing bodies (as occurred when the UN first undertook election monitoring and peace-building, initially handing the tasks to its Departments of Political Affairs and Peacekeeping Operations). Alternatively, new bodies can be created, as happened with the UN Joint Programme on HIV/AIDS, an organization that was launched by the WHO and several other organizations after it became clear that HIV/AIDS was a problem involving health, development, education, and more. Neither approach to multifaceted issues is flawless, however: giving responsibilities to an existing body can swamp its capabilities, whereas creating a new body can disrupt the chain of command.

The lack of a single solution to the mixture of policy issues is related to a fourth difficulty: a multitude of approaches that do not fit together elegantly. This multitude arises partly because groups of actors coalesce in various ways over time—as evidenced by the G-7 being overshadowed by the G-20 during the 2008 global financial crisis and by NSAs being more central to the Sustainable Development Goals (SDGs) than they were to the earlier Millennium Development Goals (MDGs). A multitude of approaches arises also because global governance exists alongside local or regional initiatives with different scopes and priorities, as illustrated by the fragmented responses to the Covid-19 pandemic in 2020. Due to ever-changing circumstances and the proliferation of relevant actors, approaches vary in being targeted or wide-ranging, centering on public-sector or private-sector entities, preserving or eroding state sovereignty. Frequently, relevant actors have such different interests that a single governance approach will not suffice. This occurs in internet governance, where states' concerns about national security, civil society groups' concerns about privacy, and businesses' concerns about profitability make it infeasible for the International Telecommunications Union to handle every aspect. Across issue areas, the multitude of approaches is likely to continue, with "an unattractive but adaptable multilateral sprawl" that delivers partial cooperation through "informal arrangements and piecemeal approaches" (Patrick 2014: 59).

Contributions of Global Governance Actors

Although global governance can be haphazard, it does quite well in several respects. Indeed, global governance actors have made significant contributions in at least six ways: shaping agendas; generating and spreading ideas; providing data; setting, promoting, and monitoring goals; undertaking adaptations and reforms; and developing new forms of governance.

Shaping Agendas

One of the largest contributions of global governance actors is in shaping agendas. Here, the United Nations stands out, since the General Assembly is a forum for the "peoples of the world." As noted in Chapter 4, the UN is a place where states and NSAs can raise new issues, thereby setting agendas for the UN, other IGOs, NSAs, and states. Since its creation, the UN has promoted self-determination and decolonization, pressured South Africa to abandon apartheid, negotiated the Law of the Sea Convention, recognized the unique position of small island states in the global climate change debate, called attention to the rights of migrant workers and the LGBTI community, and more. In most cases, it has taken years of hard work before the issue was an accepted part of the agenda.

According to some observers, the UN's role as an agenda-shaping forum sometimes has also been abused, such as when majorities repeatedly linked Zionism with racism in General Assembly resolutions beginning in the 1970s. But there is widespread recognition that the UN is a venue in which bold stands are taken. In 2012, the General Assembly recognized Palestine and admitted it as a nonmember observer state; in 2016, the General Assembly set in motion what became the Treaty on the Prohibition of Nuclear Weapons (Chapter 7). In 2022, when Russian and Chinese vetoes blocked the UN Security Council from acting on Russia's invasion of Ukraine, the General Assembly condemned Russia's actions, thus mobilizing global opposition.

The emergence of additional IGOs and the blurring of public/private distinctions provide additional forums where issues can be raised, resolutions put forward, and agreements reached. As noted in Chapter 1, the wider variety of forums means that states and NSAs have more opportunities to forum-shop to find a supportive venue. For example, development issues in

Asia can be discussed within the World Bank, the Asian Infrastructure Investment Bank, or the World Business Council for Sustainable Development. Environmental issues in Europe could be brought to the European Union, the UN Environment Programme, or scientific bodies. Health issues in Africa can be raised in the WHO, charitable foundations, or NGOs. In short, global governance actors have used many venues to raise issues.

Generating and Spreading Ideas

In addition to shaping agendas, global governance actors generate and spread ideas. The United Nations Intellectual History Project identified numerous ideas that have come from the UN—sometimes from member states or the Secretariat, other times from NSAs or from ad hoc bodies convened under the UN's auspices (Jolly, Emmerij, and Weiss 2009). With UN bodies providing forums for discussions, the resulting ideas can be promoted by Secretariat staff and epistemic communities, tested by civil society groups and businesses, funded by states and charitable foundations, monitored by the media and the public, and so on.

Some ideas advanced by the UN relate to security issues. For instance, peacekeeping is the idea that soldiers, police, or civilians could act on behalf of the international community by inserting themselves into conflict situations to stop fighting and to maintain a ceasefire. This is an innovation that was not explicit in the UN Charter. Another example is human security, the idea that people need to be protected from violence, economic deprivation, infectious diseases, human rights violations, and environmental degradation, as covered in Chapters 7–11. The UN has been instrumental in expanding the idea of security to include not just states but humanity overall.

Other ideas advanced by the UN go beyond security. For instance, the concept of sustainable development was articulated in the 1987 Brundtland Report, commissioned by the General Assembly. As discussed in Chapters 8 and 10, sustainability emphasizes that economic development must not occur without considering environmental impact, unintended consequences, and future generations' need for natural resources. Another example is human development. Just as security has been expanded to encompass human security, development also has been expanded to encompass people's broader social needs. As noted in Chapter 8, this idea represents an important shift away from measuring development only in terms of a state's gross domestic product compared with other states over time. The ideas of human development and sustainability are central in the SDGs.

Even when the UN and other IGOs are not the sources of specific ideas, they often refine and spread them. For instance, NGOs pushed for the idea of "human rights for all" to be included in the UN Charter in the 1940s, and NGOs continue to be key monitors of rights for vulnerable people. The UN has contributed to this idea by bringing together states and nonstate actors to improve the treatment of particular groups, including women and the LGBTI community. Something similar has happened with microfinance—supplying small amounts of financial assistance to individuals and groups who are cut off from regular banking systems. This idea emerged from the Grameen Bank experience, and the UN system has helped the idea spread to other nonprofit groups, for-profit banks, and even the World Bank.

Filling Knowledge Gaps and Providing Data

After global governance actors generate and spread ideas, they need data to translate the ideas into action. Data help describe problems, pinpoint knowledge gaps, identify potential solutions, and gauge outcomes. As new policy issues arise, new kinds of data need to be collected. For instance, as concern grew about the status of women, data illuminated the extent to which women were experiencing domestic violence, facing workplace discrimination, playing key roles in the economies of developing countries, and benefiting less than men from economic development.

For decades, the UN and Bretton Woods institutions have helped states gather economic information, but today there are many more producers, consumers, and subjects of data. IGOs continue to produce valuable data sets that track many countries over time. Yet data are also gathered and used by states, NGOs, epistemic communities, business associations, and others. Climate change is just one example: it took years of data collection and analysis by various actors, including the Intergovernmental Panel on Climate Change, to link human activity with environmental changes. As expectations have grown for assessing the impact of policy interventions, many actors now demand and supply data about a wide variety of policy areas.

Providing data is not always easy. Topics such as "decent work" or "quality of life" can be difficult to define and measure. Information about terrorist cells, child abuse, and violence against women can be difficult to uncover. Varying cultural norms and sensitivities can make governments defensive. However, as demonstrated by data sets such as Transparency International's Corruption Perceptions Index or the UN's Human Development Index, global governance actors continue to address such challenges in order to provide useful and multifaceted data.

Setting, Promoting, and Monitoring Goals

Another contribution of global governance actors is setting, promoting, and monitoring goals. States and NSAs participate in global governance because they perceive problems and seek improvements. Many are also adamant about monitoring progress toward these goals.

The UN and other IGOs are sometimes criticized for setting unattainable goals, such as eliminating extreme poverty. However, the UN Intellectual

History Project concluded that setting goals for economic and social development has been a "singular UN achievement" (Jolly, Emmerij, and Weiss 2009: 43). Beginning with the first "development decade" in 1960 and including the MDGs that spanned the years 2000 to 2015, the UN set and promoted more than fifty goals. For the MDGs, the UN conducted systematic monitoring and reporting on an annual basis. This process has continued for the SDGs (Chapter 8).

The issue of human rights provides another prominent example of goals set, promoted, and monitored by global governance actors. States have negotiated a long list of human rights treaties that provide the normative foundation of human rights for all. Through the Office of the High Commissioner for Human Rights (Chapter 9), the UN has established machinery not only for promoting human rights goals but also for monitoring states' human rights compliance. Many other actors assist in this endeavor: civil society groups, legal scholars, and other stakeholders are permitted to offer the OHCHR evidence of governmental abuses. In the area of human rights and elsewhere, goals have provided a focus for mobilizing various interests and generating pressures for action (Jolly, Emmerij, and Weiss 2009: 44).

Undertaking Reforms

A further contribution of global governance actors is undertaking reforms. Actors that do not change in the face of new circumstances will become irrelevant, decline, or die. Weeding out occurs more quickly and automatically for some than others. With their need to be profitable in market systems, businesses and media outlets in the private sector are particularly prone to decline and death if they fail to adjust adequately. Traditional media outlets such as *The Economist* or the *New York Times* have remade themselves in response to the emergence of the internet and social media by launching their own websites, podcasts, and other digital content.

NGOs, epistemic communities, charitable foundations, and other organizations in the not-for-profit sector are more protected from being wiped out by market forces. Nevertheless, they remain at risk of decline or irrelevance if they do not evolve with the times. For example, shifting from its original focus on political prisoners, Amnesty International increasingly has set its sights on drone warfare, treatment of terrorism suspects, and economic and social rights.

IGOs are sometimes portrayed as rigid and unresponsive, but they too must adapt and reform. For example, although the United States continues to have the highest vote share in the World Bank and the IMF, both IGOs have altered their voting structures over time to give more voice to rising economic powers, from Germany to Japan to China. Similarly, although the UN Security Council has had the same five permanent member states since its inception, the Council expanded its nonpermanent membership from six to ten states and continues to consider reforms to improve geographic representation (Chapter 4). Other parts of the UN system have adapted to changed circumstances more readily; for instance, the International Organization for Migration (IOM) became a UN-related agency in 2016.

Compared to global IGOs, regional IGOs have smaller and more homogeneous memberships and may be more responsive to new circumstances. For instance, the EU evolved from an economic union to a political and nascent security community, whereas the Organization of African Unity transitioned from its anticolonial underpinnings to an expansive African Union agenda in support of regional security, development, and democratization. Thus, although global governance actors are sometimes criticized for being resistant to change, the reality is that many successfully adapt and reform.

Developing New Forms of Governance

Beyond adapting and reforming, global governance actors have developed new forms of governance. Traditionally reliant on states, not all IGOs were quick to recognize the value of links with NSAs such as charitable foundations, epistemic communities, civil society groups, and firms. More recently, IGO personnel have realized NSAs' usefulness—whether for funding, specialized expertise, or getting local buy-in. As discussed in Chapter 6, IGO engagement with NSAs has become widespread since the 1990s.

As interactions among various global governance actors have grown, so have the forms of global governance, with public–private partnerships, private governance, networks, and rules-based governance as just a few examples. Yet these new forms are not all the same (Abbott and Snidal 2021). Some struggle to define themselves, have relatively few participants, and hold little authority. Others display a clear purpose, attract broad participation, and boast positive track records; they even may have been granted significant authority through formal or informal agreements with states. New forms of governance often involve experimentation, and some experiments thrive more than others.

Although much of the evidence is still anecdotal and circumstantial, these new forms of governance seem to make a difference. Perhaps most important, partnerships and other arrangements provide venues for learning, as lessons gleaned by one actor are often spread to others. For example, the EU's experience with subsidiarity shows that decisions may be superior when they are made at the lowest possible level. From watching coalitions of NGOs get issues such as landmines or species loss on the international agenda, states have recognized how framing can make issues more acceptable and how social media can be used to mobilize support.

Activities That Are Difficult for
Global Governance Actors

Global governance actors have made significant contributions, but that does not mean they are always successful. In fact, they are regularly criticized. Singularly or together, global governance actors have difficulty doing at least five things: dealing with states' internal struggles, enforcing international rules and decisions, coordinating a wide variety of actors, reacting quickly in a crisis, and managing long-term projects on behalf of broad goals.

Dealing with States' Internal Struggles

Global governance actors have trouble dealing with states' internal struggles, which may spill over borders. As noted in Chapters 4 and 7, the UN Charter upholds the nonintervention norm, but many transnational threats are rooted within states. When states are unwilling or unable to solve internal problems, those problems can spill into an international community that is ill-prepared to deal with them.

This is well illustrated by the Syrian civil war that began in 2011 and was complicated by the presence of the Islamic State of Iraq and Syria (ISIS). ISIS terrorized people, seized oil wells and bank assets, enforced its own version of Islamic law in territory it controlled, and declared itself a "caliphate" that aspired to spread throughout the Muslim world. The UN Security Council was unable to agree on much multilateral action other than sanctions and diplomatic efforts to achieve a ceasefire in the civil war. ISIS later lost much of its territory but the group—and the civil war it exploited—continue to exist.

Civil wars and terrorist groups are not the only internal problems that can cross borders. The same is true of inflation, communicable diseases, the "push" factors that can drive people to migrate, illicit drugs, pollution, and other issues. When a state is unwilling or unable to solve its own problems, global governance actors often cannot solve them either.

Enforcing International Rules and Decisions

Besides finding it hard to deal with states' internal struggles, global governance actors find it hard to enforce states' compliance with international rules and decisions. This certainly is true of NSAs, which generally lack the military or economic might of national governments. In cases of egregious human rights violations (e.g., war crimes and crimes against humanity), attempts at enforcement can include bringing individuals to justice through the International Criminal Court (ICC) or an ad hoc court. However, this process is slow and often thwarted by states that have little interest in delivering their citizens for prosecution or are not parties to the Rome Statute. Instead, NGOs and other actors regularly push for human rights compliance by "naming and shaming" particular states. This can be effective if the target state cares about its reputation for following the rules or faces strong domestic pressures to live up to its promises. If not, there are few remedies, and states are likely to persist in their noncompliance.

IGOs are also constrained by states. Although IGO staff can offer recommendations, they generally cannot make commitments on their member states' behalf. Even when states themselves make promises, as Thomas Weiss and Ramesh Thakur (2010: 21) have noted, "no ways exist to enforce decisions and no mechanisms exist to compel states to comply with decisions." When states fail to pay their assessed contributions or renege on other commitments, there is no international executive with a police force at its disposal; there is no international legislature with the ability to make domestic laws; there is no international judiciary with compulsory jurisdiction (Johnson 2020). The EU is a prominent exception in those areas of common policies where states have ceded sovereignty and where the decisions of the European Court of Justice are directly enforceable in member states. Even in the EU, however, policy areas such as migration and foreign policy remain intergovernmental and require unanimous approval from member states.

The enforcement power that some IGOs seem to have is largely reliant on states. For example, the UN Security Council can authorize economic sanctions and coercive military action only if the five permanent members (P-5) concur or do not exercise their vetoes. As discussed in Chapter 7, sanctions have been used extensively since the end of the Cold War, but enforcement through military action is still rare because states, mindful of their own national interests, are often reluctant to see the UN intervene. When the UN has undertaken military intervention, it has had to rely on NATO, coalitions of willing states, or major powers to provide the necessary military capability, since states have resisted granting the UN direct control over military resources. Although economic sanctions are more common than military action, states' (and other actors') incentive to cheat is ever present, and the possibility of leakage grows with the length of time the sanctions are in place. Thus, for both Security Council enforcement mechanisms, states might not back up their promises with sufficient resources, and their willpower might erode over time.

The problem is equally severe in nonsecurity issues. For example, the World Bank and the IMF can use "carrots" (financial rewards for taking certain actions) and "sticks" (withholding aid for failure to meet conditions). But as agreements are renegotiated, as influential donor states intervene on behalf of allies, and as recipients complain about perceived incursions into state sovereignty, such strict conditionality has been tough to uphold.

Enforcement becomes even more difficult when it goes against the national interests of a great power. For example, although the WTO's dispute settlement mechanism may seem powerful, its decisions merely authorize a complainant state to take retaliatory trade actions against a state that has been found guilty of violating trade rules. Therefore, it is states that apply economic pressures to wrongdoers, not the WTO itself, and these pressures often work much more effectively against states with small and undiversified markets than against the largest economies. Recent years exposed another way the WTO's dispute settlement mechanism is vulnerable to great power states. US presidents from Obama to Trump to Biden blocked appointments to the WTO Appellate Body to the point where it lacked personnel and became unable to handle appeals cases. In short, global governance actors find it very difficult to enforce states' compliance, especially if the state is a great power.

Coordinating a Wide Variety of Actors

Global governance actors also struggle to coordinate among themselves. Over the decades, many new forms of governance have been developed, and the quantity and variety of these entities have mushroomed. One observer has dubbed this "the new medievalism" to describe the breadth of arrangements and authorities operating without a clear hierarchy, as happened in the Middle Ages (Mathews 1997: 61).

There is widespread recognition that coordination among various institutions, funds, programs, and groups is crucial to avoid duplicating efforts or working at cross-purposes. Powerful donor states, in particular, regularly push various entities to team up and consolidate the activities for which they seek funding. Yet as numerous UN staff and NGOs have remarked, "Everyone is for coordination but nobody wants to be coordinated" (quoted in Weiss 2009: 81).

Lack of coordination, therefore, is a chronic problem. The problem is seen, for example, in the UN Economic and Social Council's long-standing inability to coordinate the multiple overlapping UN economic and social bodies (discussed in Chapter 4). Some critics blame the "spaghetti junction" of the UN organizational chart, lamenting that it leads to turf battles, competition for resources, or paralysis (Weiss 2009: chap. 3). However, lack of coordination goes well beyond IGOs. It is also seen in states' overlapping participation in regional trade agreements with conflicting rules (Chapter 8); in national, provincial, and local government officials' varying responses to climate change (Chapter 10); and in NGOs' haphazard responses to human security crises (Chapter 11). Although the states and nonstate actors involved in global governance have grown over time, coordination among them has not.

Reacting Quickly in a Crisis

Partly due to problems with coordination, global governance actors have difficulty reacting quickly in a crisis. Only the most powerful states generally have the necessary administrative, logistical, or financial resources—and even they sometimes struggle. Consider natural disasters like Typhoon Haiyan, which struck Southeast Asia in 2013, killed more than 6,000 people in the Philippines alone, and was one of the most powerful tropical cyclones ever recorded. China was criticized for failing to provide much financial assistance or to send its hospital ship to the Philippines. Although the UN humanitarian relief system and NGOs did help, much of the work was carried out by the US military.

Even the most powerful states were challenged by the Covid-19 pandemic. Well before the crisis became global in 2020, many in the medical community recognized that the WHO was poorly equipped to deal with emergencies. It depended on governments for information and resources, had undergone budget cuts that split the duties of its pandemic response department, and had struggled to contain the 2014 Ebola outbreak in West Africa. When Covid-19 was declared a pandemic, the WHO was hamstrung by two of its most influential member states as China withheld information and the United States withheld financial resources (Johnson 2020). The pandemic greatly challenged these states as well: China contained the virus with extreme measures that locked down entire cities for long periods, and the United States took a less restrictive approach that resulted in hundreds of thousands of American deaths. NGOs such as Doctors Without Borders quickly deployed to countries experiencing disease outbreaks but were overloaded as the crisis hit dozens of countries simultaneously.

Global governance actors find it difficult to handle not only communicable diseases and natural disasters but also human-made catastrophes like sudden, large refugee flows and civil wars. For example, the continuing stream of Middle Eastern and African refugees and migrants into Europe has taxed the UN High Commissioner for Refugees, the IOM, and EU's Frontex; swamped partner NGOs; and prompted much in-fighting among EU member-states. Civil wars are similarly difficult because multilateral military interventions—whether organized under the UN, AU, or NATO—require time for reaching agreement among member states, organizing seconded military units, transporting troops and equipment to the crisis area, and developing coordinated command and control structures. Consequently, global governance actors will continue to struggle with responses to natural disasters, pandemics, refugee flows, and civil wars.

Managing Long-Term Projects on Behalf of Broad Goals

A final activity that is difficult for global governance actors is managing long-term projects with broad goals. Given the number and variety of global governance actors, agreement and commitment can be difficult to sustain. Yet this is precisely what is needed for many issues because they only rarely involve short-term responses.

Consider the security realm. As discussed in Chapter 7, preventing the spread of nuclear weapons is a long-term project in which the International Atomic Energy Agency plays a key role. The IAEA's inspections are to be done indefinitely, with particular vigilance in states (e.g., Iran and North Korea) that are suspected of having weapons development programs. Another broad and long-term project is peacekeeping, which involves diverse personnel and tasks in complex conflict situations. These tasks can include disarming combatants, addressing humanitarian needs, consulting the local population, creating a new judicial system, rebuilding the local police, organizing elections, stopping sexual violence, addressing human rights violations, and, in a few cases, setting up an interim government. Success hinges on a sustained commitment to the overarching goal of a stable, secure state.

Managing broad and long-term projects is difficult in the nonsecurity realm, too. Economic and human development are decades-long undertakings that involve the World Bank, the UN, and many other global governance actors (Chapter 8). To achieve economic and human development, member states must stick to their commitments, a steady stream of the "right" resources must be provided, and recipients must put the resources to "good" use. Years may pass before any results are seen in reduced poverty levels and a more developed economy. As noted with regard to the mixed results of the MDGs, it remains to be seen to what extent the ambitious SDGs are achieved. As the number of actors involved in economic and human development has grown exponentially, along with the variety of different approaches, it has become harder to pinpoint exactly what worked. The reality is that no one knows precisely what combination of factors and steps will yield positive results in each unique setting.

Challenges for the Future: Beyond Effectiveness

In addition to finding some activities difficult, global governance actors face broader challenges. One basic challenge is effectiveness in addressing and resolving the world's problems. Effectiveness is notoriously difficult to evaluate because goals are often aspirational, and there is no single, accepted approach to assessment. Extreme poverty has not yet been eradicated, human rights are not yet respected for all people, and environmental degradation has not yet been reversed. Global governance may look ineffective if the focus is on unmet lofty goals, but it may seem effective if the focus is on incremental progress and improvements.

Beyond effectiveness, there are other challenges. To what extent is global governance accountable, legitimate, and just, and who will step up to provide leadership? These four challenges pertain not only to individual actors but also to global governance overall.

The Challenge of Accountability

Accountability is about who is responsible, for what, to whom, and by what mechanisms (Avant, Finnemore, and Sell 2010a: 363–364). It is critical at each stage of the policymaking process outlined in Chapter 6, from agenda-setting to decisionmaking to implementation (Woods 1999: 45). Through the various stages, who governs the governors? In a perfectly functioning domestic democracy, it is citizens—through electoral processes—who provide a semblance of accountability. Yet that is impossible at the international level, as discussed in Chapter 1.

Instead, accountability must be built into global governance in different ways (Grant and Keohane 2005). One way is to make global governance more representative, encompassing a wider variety of states and NSAs. Actors that have resisted this (e.g., the permanent members of the UN Security Council) continue to draw criticism for excluding large numbers of other interested actors. Another way to enhance accountability is to make actors' internal operations more transparent; for example, many IGOs publicly report on their meetings, spending, and decisions. A third way is to monitor implementation. NGOs, the media, and other nonstate actors play key roles in verifying whether states and IGOs are making progress in everything from respecting human rights to curbing nuclear weapons to protecting the environment.

Some steps have been taken in the right direction. For example, the G-7 has ceded some tasks to the more-representative G-20; the UN has developed many forms of budgetary control; and the World Bank has used an independent Inspection Panel to investigate individuals' or groups' allegations of harm from World Bank–funded projects. One study found that although many accountability mechanisms originated in particular types of IGOs—those with large budgets (e.g., the UN), influential donors (e.g., the World Bank), or strong democratic norms (e.g., the EU)—mechanisms quickly diffused across IGOs that interacted with each other. This may explain why even states that lack accountability mechanisms domestically have accepted those mechanisms in IGOs (Grigorescu 2010: 884).

Even so, improving accountability is difficult. Unanimous voting proved impractical as a decisionmaking procedure in the League of Nations. Today, consensus decisionmaking and closed meetings are common, but these can limit accountability since there is no public record of states' positions or discussions. States also regularly engage in selective consultations that exclude many interested parties. Sometimes a lack of transparency and openness is essential for decisionmakers to reach agreements without undue political pressure. Thus, the desire for greater transparency and openness must be balanced against the need for efficacy.

Accountability is not just a problem for states and IGOs. NGOs and other civil society groups are often assumed to be more closely connected to and representative of ordinary people. But they, too, often lack internal democratic mechanisms for the selection of leaders, and many are composed of a selective group of people. Rarely are there mechanisms to guarantee transparency and participation, especially for those most affected by their work or on whose behalf they make claims. More must be done to improve the accountability of NGOs and other civil society groups, because their organizational structures are often opaque, while their numbers and reach are extensive. Unfortunately, one of the most powerful accountability mechanisms is the need for money. This can make NGOs and civil society groups more responsive to donors than to beneficiaries and can prompt IGOs to pay the greatest attention to just a subset of their member states.

It is also difficult to ensure that firms and business associations are accountable to the international community. Because endeavors like the UN Guiding Principles on Business and Human Rights and the UN Global Compact operate on a voluntary basis (Chapter 6), companies are not required to participate and face few punishments if they fall short. Some arrangements—such as the Financial Action Task Force and OECD regulations regarding bribery—are obligatory and have teeth. However, many accountability efforts continue to depend on softer tactics, such as data collection, public naming and shaming, or consumer boycotts. Insufficient accountability for particular actors fuels perceptions of insufficient accountability for global governance overall.

The Challenge of Legitimacy

As noted in Chapter 1, the challenge of accountability is closely related to another challenge: legitimacy. Visible turmoil—from street protests at the G-20 meeting in Hamburg in 2017 to the UK's finalization of Brexit in 2020 and the WHO's continuing difficulty in securing Chinese data on the origins of Covid-19—have fueled claims that particular international institutions or even the overall "liberal world order" are illegitimate. Clearly, it is not feasible to institute democratic electoral processes at the international level. Nevertheless, global governance can be legitimated through other approaches.

One approach is to increase the number of states that operate democratically, so that more national governments participating in international decisionmaking have been elected by their citizens. This approach made substantial progress in 1991 as Russia and other formerly communist countries became democracies. The EU and the OECD both require members to be democracies. However, as demonstrated by democratic "backsliding" in places like Poland and Hungary (see Chapter 5), it is not easy for states to become and remain democratic, especially when populism and nationalism surge, globalization undermines some aspects of liberal democracy, and targeted sanctions against a state may strengthen rather than weaken a shift toward more authoritarian rule.

Another approach is multilayered governance, in which various structures and processes are opened to NSAs, including at the local level. This can allow many different voices to be heard, provide a broader sense of ownership, and give more people and groups a stake in policymaking (Dallmayr 2002: 154–155). In peacekeeping and peacebuilding (see Chapter 7), this requires more attention to local effects, including secondary impacts on employment structures or gender relations. In human rights (see Chapter 9), this entails activating local networks and helping develop national human rights institutions. In food governance, this means using more locally available food supplies and developing context-specific adaptations to climate change. Not all states or IGOs are equally open to NSAs, however. Moreover, as discussed in Chapter 6, the NSAs that participate most heavily in global governance may still be self-selected elites who are not sufficiently representative of or linked to ordinary citizens.

A third legitimation approach is to reduce how much global governance is seen as being under US and/or European control or is seen as a liberal economic project that is only compatible with the power and preferences of people and organizations in the Global North. Reforms in various IGOs reflect this approach. The IMF has incrementally reduced the United States' overwhelming vote share; the World Bank has formalized practices that prioritize hiring staff from developing countries; the UN has developed the "Major Groups" system to encourage participation by Indigenous communities and other marginalized people; the OECD has added members in Asia and Latin America. IGOs that have resisted reforms—such as the UN Security Council, where the P-5 continue to have veto power and permanent seats—face a legitimacy problem, since an institution is "unlikely to endure over time if powerful states or groups of states can simply flout the rules" (Woods 1999: 43). The US invasion of Iraq in 2003 and the Russian invasion of Ukraine in 2022 are examples of P-5 members using force in violation of the UN Charter. Clearly, global governance actors do not uniformly embrace values such as human development, poverty alleviation, sustainable development, and human security.

A fourth approach is to dispute claims of illegitimacy. For example, an examination of sixteen intergovernmental, nongovernmental, and hybrid institutions found that staff use words, statements, and arguments to defend themselves (Bexell, Jonsson, and Uhlin 2022). NGOs emphasize their democratic processes, whereas IGOs tout their technocratic methods. Such discourse does not necessarily convince the general public to view an institution positively, but it can prevent them from viewing it negatively.

Even used together, these four approaches—increasing the number of democratic states, listening more to local NSAs, reducing the dominance of states and ideas from the Global North, and refuting criticism—do not completely solve the challenge of legitimacy (Zweifel 2006: 14). Still, global governance structures are unlikely to be completely dismantled, for research has found that illegitimacy concerns are nuanced. From 2017 to 2019, a team of researchers surveyed thousands of people in five countries (Brazil, Germany, the Philippines, Russia, and the United States) about their views toward six major IGOs (the ICC, IMF, World Bank, WHO, WTO, and UN). The surveys were administered to ordinary citizens as well as to elites in government, civil society, businesses, research bodies, and the media. Most of the survey participants expressed moderately positive views toward the IGOs; in fact, many judged the IGOs' legitimacy to be higher than the legitimacy of their own national governments. However, elites regularly viewed IGOs even more positively than ordinary citizens did, and they underestimated the size of that gap. That is, elites seem willing to delegate more tasks to IGOs, but ordinary citizens are more comfortable with the status quo. This suggests that in the near future, global governance through IGOs will not die out, but it will not dramatically expand either (Dellmuth et al. 2022).

The Challenge of Justice

Legitimacy links to another challenge: justice. There are stark inequalities in power, wealth, and knowledge across and within states (Sen 2001), and global governance is unlikely to be deemed legitimate unless it combats these inequalities. Therefore, increased attention is being paid to the notion of global justice, which emphasizes that each human has equal value and deserves equal resources and moral consideration. In the same way that "human security" and "human development" focus on people rather than states, global justice wrestles with how to treat individuals fairly, regardless of their station or nationality (Dietzel 2019). This is in tension with conventional great power politics, where states matter more than individuals and powerful states matter most of all.

Numerous NSAs facilitate the global justice movement. Traditional media outlets cover events around the world, raising awareness of inequality and injustice (Boykoff 2006). Social media spreads user-generated content that conveys firsthand experiences (Christians 2019; Ba 2021). Activists press for accountability for war crimes and crimes against humanity through the International Criminal Court or hybrid tribunals. Legal scholars and other epistemic communities draw attention to international relations' prioritization of stability and predictability, sometimes at the cost of justice (Ray 1999). NGOs bridge gaps among political voices in the global community and reveal injustice (Macdonald and Macdonald 2022: 305–306).

Injustice can result from state behavior. For example, the United States has used unmanned aerial drones to strike suspected terrorists in the Middle East, sometimes resulting in civilian casualties. The US government has defended such strikes as occurring in "frontier areas," which under international law are considered locations with little or no state sovereignty. Although that defense may make it unnecessary to compensate a state for violating its sovereignty, it does not erase injuries and deaths among civilians (Nylan 2020: 628, 649). Another example is the EU's migration policy, which attempts to slow migration particularly from Africa and the Middle East. The rationale is that large inflows of foreigners with very different religious and cultural practices would destabilize European economies and societies (Ceccorulli 2021). However, blocking migration also makes life harder for people who are fleeing war, famine, or crime, and has resulted in the deaths of many trying to cross the Mediterranean to enter the EU.

Injustice also arises from IGO behavior. For example, sexual misconduct by UN peacekeepers taking advantage of refugees, women, and other vulnerable people has been a problem at least since the 1990s. It is difficult to address because only troop-contributing member states can discipline their own personnel. This limits the UN's ability to uncover such exploitation and provide justice to victims. Individuals can be hurt by IGO activities even while an IGO claims to be helping them (Reinold 2022).

Some progress on justice has been made—as noted in Chapter 9, with the example of recognizing violence against women as a violation of their rights. But it is unclear how or even whether global governance actors can fully overcome the challenge of justice. After all, injustice is linked to the very different histories and cultures around the world, yet global justice might not be attainable without a history or culture that unites the world (Dietzel 2019).

The Challenge of Leadership

Addressing the challenges of justice, legitimacy, and accountability will require leadership. Will that leadership come from a powerful state? From all states working collectively? From actors other than states?

For decades, the United States has been a leader in global governance. After World War II, it provided resources and a vision for the institutions, laws, and norms of the postwar "liberal world order." The Bretton Woods institutions, the UN system, and many other parts of that order are still in place, but US leadership is no longer undisputed. Significantly hampered by domestic political divisions and government paralysis, the United States is no longer an enthusiastic and reliable leader in global governance. Without US willingness and ability to bear the material and nonmaterial costs of leadership, the effectiveness of global governance might decline. Even if the United States continues to step up, global governance may not be seen as accountable, legitimate, or just, since the United States has a history of violating elements of the liberal world order while pursuing its own national interests.

The European Union has not fully substituted for US leadership in global governance and is unlikely to do so. Although some individual EU member states sent weaponry to Ukraine after Russia's 2022 invasion, the EU itself lacks military capabilities. Moreover, tensions in the EU over its supranational character—witness Brexit, the emergence of populist nationalism in several EU countries, and ongoing disagreements about immigration or national contributions—reduce its ability to function as a cohesive unit. In fact, despite boasting of providing a great deal of humanitarian assistance, the EU has struggled in responding to the Covid-19 pandemic, refugee flows, and Russia's invasion of Ukraine. Leadership is more than promoting democratic values, employing diplomatic and economic instruments, and influencing norms; sometimes it requires hard military power and executive authority, which the EU lacks.

China may aspire to a leadership role in a somewhat different world order, but it has not yet demonstrated its ability to fully replace US leadership. It no longer plays the low-key role it did in the 1980s and 1990s, when it was still transitioning from a developing country to a great power. In more recent years, it has used its economic might to build up its military capabilities, contribute to UN peace operations, and push for senior positions in various IGOs. It also has created new institutions, such as the Asian Infrastructure Investment Bank and the New Development Bank (Chapter 8). However, China resists some components of global governance, such as WTO rules against subsidies, WHO disease reporting requirements, World Bank loan conditionality, human rights protection, and the Permanent Court of Arbitration decision against its claims in the South China Sea. It continues to pursue "selective multilateralism," as evidenced by projects such as the Belt and Road Initiative (discussed in Chapters 5 and 8). Unenthusiastic about leading a global governance system it did not create, China increasingly seems to envision a new world order centered on itself.

Adequate global leadership will not necessarily come from states, which are often limited by their self-interest, domestic politics, and heterogeneous preferences. This means contemporary IGOs, whose members are states, are similarly limited (Weiss 2014). Indeed, multilateralism "has no magic that transforms states or enables them to create composite entities better endowed than themselves with political virtue" (Claude 1988: 108).

Some observers place hope in nonstate actors such as NGOs, epistemic communities, corporations, or charitable foundations. Such actors have authority based on "expertise, morality, competence, and other sources that are independent of the state" (Avant, Finnemore, and Sell 2010a: 357). Still, no NSA blends military, economic, social, and diplomatic power in the way that states do.

In today's world, leadership for global governance comes from multiple quarters and in multiple forms. No single actor dominates as the United States did after World War II. Instead, a variety of states, intergovernmental entities, nonstate actors, and even some prominent individuals will provide aspects of leadership. There is no assurance, however, that the resulting global governance will be effective, accountable, legitimate, or just.

The Need for Global Governance

In sum, a variety of actors have made many contributions to contemporary global governance. They have shaped agendas, spread ideas, provided data, promoted goals, undertaken adaptations and reforms, and developed new forms of governance. Yet many activities remain difficult. Global governance actors have trouble dealing with states' internal conflicts, enforcing international rules and decisions, coordinating a wide variety of actors, reacting quickly in a crisis, and managing long-term projects on behalf of broad goals. Global governance also faces broad challenges concerning effectiveness, accountability, legitimacy, justice, and leadership.

These challenges and difficulties have been magnified by antiglobalists, populists, and nationalists (Zürn 2018; Copelovitch and Pevehouse 2019). Antiglobalists worry about harm inflicted by globalization or global governance. Populists decry global governance as an endeavor carried out by and for elites to the detriment of ordinary people. Nationalists denounce global governance as an attempt to impose world government, restrict states' sovereignty, and reduce citizens' say in matters that affect them. The Global North more readily dismissed the complaints of antiglobalists, populists, and nationalists when they came from the Global South, but now such complaints are prevalent among their own citizens, too.

Even so, it is important to note that not all global governance actors are in crisis. For instance, a study of thirty-two international institutions from 1985 to 2020 found that only a few of them ever experienced severe criticism, and these unusual cases were the ones most reported in the news. There was an uptick in criticism during the antiglobalism backlash between 1995 and 2005, as well as some high-profile challenges to these international institutions between 2015 and 2020. However, criticism did not increase over time; it harmed institutions only when multiple stakeholders complained simultaneously; and the harm was short-lived. Within a few years of being criticized, many international institutions actually found that their material resources, scope of activities, or decisionmaking ability had increased (Sommerer et al. 2022).

Without various elements of global governance, the world would probably be worse off. When problems transcend national borders, it makes sense for solutions to do likewise. "Problems without passports" are evident throughout this book: nuclear weapons, terrorism, poverty, food insecurity, migration, natural disasters, pandemics, human trafficking, climate change, and more. There are also newer issues, such as artificial intelligence and ocean-floor mining. The debut of ChatGPT in 2022 made people more aware of the uses and abuses of artificial intelligence, and the International Seabed Authority's failure to craft regulations on ocean-floor mining in 2023 demonstrated tensions across environmental, economic, and security concerns. It is therefore unclear whether states, intergovernmental organizations, and nonstate actors will be able to solve the world's older and newer "problems without passports."

Global governance is admittedly imperfect, but still needed. Indeed, if the UN and other forms of global governance did not already exist, it is likely that people would reinvent them (Weiss 2018: 1). Because global governance involves "systems of rule at all levels of human activity—from the family to the international organization" (Rosenau 1995: 13), what matters is not only the ultimate outcome but also the underlying process. In other words, effectiveness is important, and so are accountability, legitimacy, justice, and leadership. Given the variety of global problems, there is a desperate need not to jettison global governance, but to update and reinvigorate its key institutions so they work better in the future (Weiss 2018).

Suggested Further Reading

Dellmuth, Lisa, Jan Aart Scholte, Jonas Tallberg, and Soetkin Verhaegen. (2022) *Citizens, Elites, and the Legitimacy of Global Governance.* Oxford: Oxford University Press.

Johnson, Tana. (2020) "Ordinary Patterns in an Extraordinary Crisis: How International Relations Makes Sense of the COVID-19 Pandemic." *International Organization* 74:1 (Spring): 1–21.

Weiss, Thomas G. (2018) *Would the World Be Better without the UN?* Cambridge: Polity Press.

Zürn, Michael. (2018) *A Theory of Global Governance: Authority, Legitimacy, and Contestation.* Oxford: Oxford University Press.

Zweifel, Thomas. (2006) *International Organizations and Democracy: Accountability, Politics, and Power.* Boulder, CO: Lynne Rienner.

Acronyms

A5	Arctic Five
AB	Appellate Body (WTO)
ADB	Asian Development Bank
AfCTA	African Continental Free Trade Area (AU)
AfDB	African Development Bank
AFTA	ASEAN Free Trade Area
AIIB	Asian Infrastructure Investment Bank
AMISOM	AU Mission in Somalia
AOSIS	Alliance of Small Island States
APEC	Asia-Pacific Economic Cooperation
AQIM	al-Qaeda in the Islamic Maghreb
ARF	ASEAN Regional Forum
ASEAN	Association of Southeast Asian Nations
AU	African Union
BIS	Bank for International Settlements
BIT	bilateral investment treaty
BRI	Belt and Road Initiative
BRICS	Brazil, Russia, India, China, and South Africa
BWC	Biological Weapons Convention
CAP	Common Agricultural Policy (EU)
CBD	Convention on Biological Diversity
CEDAW	Convention on the Elimination of All Forms of Discrimination Against Women
CFC	chlorofluorocarbon
CFSP	common foreign and security policy (EU)
CITES	Convention on International Trade in Endangered Species of Wild Fauna and Flora

CJEU	Court of Justice of the European Union
CMS	Convention on the Conservation of Migratory Species
COP	conference of the parties
COVAX	COVID-19 Vaccines Global Access
CSD	Commission on Sustainable Development
CSDP	Common Security and Defense Policy (EU)
CSW	Commission on the Status of Women (UN)
CTBT	Comprehensive Test Ban Treaty
CTBTO	Comprehensive Test Ban Treaty Organization
CTC	Counter-Terrorism Committee (UN)
CTED	Counter-Terrorism Executive Directorate (UN)
CWC	Chemical Weapons Convention
DAC	Development Assistance Committee (OECD)
DRC	Democratic Republic of Congo
DSG	Deputy Secretary-General (UN)
DSB	Dispute Settlement Body (WTO)
EBRD	European Bank for Reconstruction and Development
ECB	European Central Bank
ECHR	European Court of Human Rights
ECJ	European Court of Justice
ECLA	Economic Commission for Latin America (CEPAL in Spanish)
ECLAC	Economic Commission for Latin America and the Caribbean (UN)
ECOSOC	Economic and Social Council (UN)
ECOWAS	Economic Community of West African States
ECSC	European Coal and Steel Community
EEAS	European External Action Service
EEC	European Economic Community (now known as European Union)
ENB	Environment, Natural Resources, and Blue Economy Global Practice
EP	European Parliament
ESF	Environmental and Social Framework (World Bank)
EU	European Union
Euratom	European Atomic Energy Community
FAO	Food and Agriculture Organization
FATF	Financial Action Task Force
FDI	foreign direct investment
FSC	Forest Stewardship Council

FTAA	Free Trade Agreement of the Americas
G-7	Group of Seven
G-8	Group of Eight
G-20	Group of 20
G-77	Group of 77
GATT	General Agreement on Tariffs and Trade
GAVI	Global Alliance for Vaccines and Immunizations
GCC	Gulf Cooperation Council
GCM	Global Compact for Safe, Orderly and Regular Migration
GCR	Global Compact on Refugees
GDP	gross domestic product
GEF	Global Environment Facility
GOARN	Global Outbreak Alert and Response Network
HIPC	Heavily Indebted Poor Countries Initiative
HIPPO	High-level Independent Panel on Peace Operations
HLPF	High-Level Political Forum on Sustainable Development
HRC	Human Rights Council (UN)
HRW	Human Rights Watch
IAEA	International Atomic Energy Agency
IATA	International Air Transport Association
IACHR	Inter-American Commission on Human Rights
IBRD	International Bank for Reconstruction and Development (also known as World Bank)
ICANN	Internet Corporation for Assigned Names and Numbers
ICAO	International Civil Aviation Organization
ICAN	International Coalition to Abolish Nuclear Weapons
ICBL	International Campaign to Ban Landmines
ICC	International Criminal Court
ICG	International Crisis Group
ICISS	International Commission on Intervention and State Sovereignty
ICJ	International Court of Justice
ICRC	International Committee of the Red Cross
ICSID	International Centre for the Settlement of Investment Disputes (World Bank)
ICSU	International Council of Scientific Unions
ICTR	International Criminal Tribunal for Rwanda
ICTY	International Criminal Tribunal for the Former Yugoslavia
IDA	International Development Association

IDB	Inter-American Development Bank
IDP	internally displaced person
IFAD	International Fund for Agricultural Development
IFC	International Finance Corporation
IFOR	Implementation Force (NATO force in former Yugoslavia)
IFRC	International Federation of the Red Cross and Red Crescent Societies
IGO	intergovernmental organization
IHRs	International Health Regulations
ILGA	International Lesbian, Gay, Bisexual, Trans, and Intersex Association
ILO	International Labour Organization
IMF	International Monetary Fund
IMO	International Maritime Organization
INGO	international nongovernmental organization
INSTRAW	International Research and Training Institute for the Advancement of Women (UN)
INTERPOL	International Criminal Police Organization
IO	international organization
IOM	International Organization for Migration
IPCC	Intergovernmental Panel on Climate Change (UN)
IPI	International Peace Institute
IR	international relations
ISAF	International Security Assistance Force
ISIL	Islamic State of Iraq and the Levant
ISIS	Islamic State of Iraq and Syria
ISO	International Organization for Standardization
ITO	International Trade Organization
ITU	International Telecommunication Union
IUCN	International Union for the Conservation of Nature and Natural Resources (now known as IUCN–World Conservation Union)
JCPOA	Joint Comprehensive Plan of Action
LGBTI	lesbian, gay, bisexual, transgender, and intersex
MDGs	Millennium Development Goals
MEA	multilateral environmental agreement
Mercosur	Common Market of the South (Mercado Común del Sur)
MINUSMA	Multidimensional Integrated Stabilization Mission in Mali
MNC	multinational corporation

MONUC	UN Organization Mission in the Democratic Republic of Congo
MONUSCO	UN Organization Stabilization Mission in the Democratic Republic of Congo
MSF	Médecins Sans Frontières (Doctors Without Borders in English)
NAFTA	North American Free Trade Agreement
NAM	Non-Aligned Movement
NATO	North Atlantic Treaty Organization
NEPAD	New Partnership for Africa's Development
NDB	New Development Bank
NDCs	nationally determined commitments
NGO	nongovernmental organization
NPT	Nuclear Non-Proliferation Treaty
NSA	nonstate actor
OAS	Organization of American States
OAU	Organization of African Unity
OCHA	Office for Coordination of Humanitarian Affairs (UN)
OCHCR	Office of the High Commissioner for Human Rights (UN)
ODA	official development assistance
OECD	Organisation for Economic Co-operation and Development
OEEC	Organisation for European Economic Cooperation
OIC	Organisation of Islamic Cooperation
OPCW	Organisation for the Prohibition of Chemical Weapons
OPEC	Organization of the Petroleum Exporting Countries
OSCE	Organization for Security and Co-operation in Europe
P-5	five permanent members of the UN Security Council
P-5+1	P-5 plus Germany
PA	principal-agent
PBC	Peacebuilding Commission (UN)
PCA	Permanent Court of Arbitration
PCIJ	Permanent Court of International Justice
PHEIC	public health emergency of international concern
POC	protection of civilians
PPP	public–private partnership
PSC	Peace and Security Council (AU)

PTA	preferential trade agreement
R2P	responsibility to protect
SADC	Southern African Development Community
SAP	structural adjustment program (IMF)
SARS	severe acute respiratory syndrome
SCO	Shanghai Cooperation Organization
SDGs	Sustainable Development Goals
SEA	Single European Act (EU)
SIPRI	Stockholm International Peace Research Institute
SRSG	Special Representative of the Secretary-General (UN)
START	Strategic Arms Reduction Treaty
SWAPO	South West Africa People's Organisation (Namibia)
SWF	sovereign wealth fund
SWIFT	Society for Worldwide Interbank Financial Telecommunication
TAN	transnational advocacy network
TPNW	Treaty on the Prohibition of Nuclear Weapons
TRAFFIC	Trade Records Analysis of Flora and Fauna in Commerce
UAE	United Arab Emirates
UCG	unconstitutional change of government
UDHR	Universal Declaration of Human Rights
UIA	Union of International Associations
UN	United Nations
UNAIDS	UN Joint Programme on HIV/AIDS
UNASUR	Union of South American Nations
UNCED	UN Conference on the Environment and Development (Rio Conference)
UNCLOS	UN Convention on the Law of the Sea
UNCTAD	UN Conference on Trade and Development
UNDP	UN Development Programme
UNEF	UN Emergency Force
UNEP	UN Environment Programme
UNESCO	UN Educational, Scientific and Cultural Organization
UNFCCC	UN Framework Convention on Climate Change
UNFPA	UN Fund for Population Activities
UNHCHR	UN High Commissioner for Human Rights
UNHCR	UN High Commissioner for Refugees
UNICEF	UN Children's Fund
UNIFEM	UN Development Fund for Women
UNIFIL	UN Interim Force in Lebanon

UNIIMOG	UN Iran-Iraq Military Observer Group
UNITA	National Union for the Total Independence of Angola
UNITAF	United Task Force on Somalia (also known as Operation Restore Hope)
UNMEER	United Nations Mission for Ebola Emergency Response
UNMISS	UN Mission in South Sudan
UNOCHA	UN Office for the Coordination of Humanitarian Affairs
UNODC	UN Office on Drugs and Crime
UNOSOM	UN Operation in Somalia
UNPROFOR	UN Protection Force for Yugoslavia
UNSCOM	UN Special Commission for the Disarmament of Iraq
UNSG	UN Secretary-General
UNTAC	UN Transitional Authority in Cambodia
UNTAG	UN Transition Assistance Group in Namibia
UPR	Universal Periodic Review
UPU	Universal Postal Union
USMCA	US-Mexico-Canada Agreement
WEF	World Economic Forum
WFP	World Food Programme
WHA	World Health Assembly
WHO	World Health Organization
WMD	weapon of mass destruction
WMO	World Meteorological Organization
WPS	Women, Peace and Security Agenda (UN)
WSIS	World Summit on the Information Society
WTO	World Trade Organization
WWF	World Wide Fund for Nature

References

Abbott, Kenneth W., Philipp Genschel, Duncan Snidal, and Bernhard Zangl, eds. (2015) *International Organizations as Orchestrators*. New York: Cambridge University Press.

Abbott, Kenneth W., Jessica F. Green, and Robert O. Keohane. (2016) "Organizational Ecology and Institutional Change in Global Governance." *International Organization* 70:2 (Spring): 247–277.

Abbott, Kenneth W., Robert O. Keohane, Andrew Moravcsik, Anne-Marie Slaughter, and Duncan Snidal. (2000) "The Concept of Legalization." *International Organization* 54:3 (Summer): 401–419.

Abbott, Kenneth W., and Duncan Snidal. (1998) "Why States Act Through Formal International Organizations." *Journal of Conflict Resolution* 42:1 (February): 3–32.

———. (2021) *The Spectrum of International Institutions: An Interdisciplinary Collaboration on Global Governance*. New York: Routledge.

Abrams, Jesse, Erik Nielson, Diana Diaz, Theresa Selfa, Erika Adams, Jennifer Dunn, and Cassandra Mosely. (2018) "How Do States Benefit from Non-State Governance? Evidence from Forest Sustainability Certification." *Global Environmental Politics* 18:3 (August): 66–85.

Acemoglu, Daron, and James Robinson. (2012) *Why Nations Fail: The Origins of Power, Prosperity, and Poverty*. New York: Crown.

Acharya, Amitav. (1997) "Ideas, Identity, and Institution-Building: From the 'ASEAN Way' to the 'Asia-Pacific Way'?" *Pacific Review* 10:3: 319–346.

———. (2001) *Constructing a Security Community in Southeast Asia: ASEAN and the Problem of Regional Order*. New York: Routledge.

———. (2004) "How Ideas Spread: Whose Norms Matter? Norm Localization and Institutional Change in Asian Regionalism." *International Organization* 58:2 (Spring): 239–275.

———. (2007a) "The Emerging Regional Architecture of World Politics." *World Politics* 59 (July): 629–652.

———. (2007b) "Regional Institutions and Security in the Asia-Pacific: Evolution, Adaptation, and Prospects for Transformation." In *Reassessing Security Cooperation in the Asia-Pacific: Competition, Congruence, and Transformation*, edited by Amitav Acharya and Evelyn Goh. Cambridge: MIT Press, pp. 19–40.

———. (2012) *The Making of Southeast Asia: International Relations of a Region*. Ithaca: Cornell University Press.

————. (2014) *The End of American World Order*. Malden, MA: Polity Press.

————. (2016a) "Rethinking Demand, Purpose and Progress in Global Governance: An Introduction." In *Why Govern? Rethinking Demand and Progress in Global Governance*, edited by Amitav Acharya. New York: Cambridge University Press, pp. 1–27.

————. (2016b) "Regionalism Beyond EU-Centrism." In *The Oxford Handbook of Comparative Regionalism*, edited by Tanja A. Börzel and Thomas Risse. New York: Oxford University Press, pp. 109–130.

————. (2017) "The Myth of ASEAN Centrality?" *Contemporary Southeast Asia* 39:2: 273–279.

Acharya, Amitav, and Barry Buzan. (2017) "Why is There No Non-Western International Relations Theory?" *International Relations of the Asia-Pacific* 17:3 (September): 341–370.

Acharya, Amitav, and Alastair Ian Johnston. (2007) "Conclusion: Institutional Features, Cooperation Effects, and the Agenda for Further Research on Comparative Regionalism." In *Crafting Cooperation: Regional International Institutions in Comparative Perspective*, edited by Amitav Acharya and Alastair Ian Johnston. Cambridge: Cambridge University Press, pp. 244–278.

Adebajo, Adekeye. (2014) "UN Peacekeeping and the Quest for a Pax Africana." *Current History* 113:763 (May): 178–184.

Adler-Nissen, Rebecca, and Kristin Anabel Eggeling. (2022) "Blended Diplomacy: The Enlargement and Contestation of Digital Technologies in Everyday Diplomatic Practice." *European Journal of International Relations* 28:3: 640–666.

African Court of Human and Peoples Rights. (2023) "Statistics." https://www.african-court.org/wpafc/.

African Union. (2015) *Agenda 2063: The Africa We Want*. https://au.int/en/agenda2063/overview.

Akbarzadeh, Shadram, and Kylie Connor. (2005) "The Organization of the Islamic Conference: Sharing an Illusion." *Middle East Policy* 12:2 (May): 79–92.

Aklin, Michael, and Johannes Urpelainen. (2014) "The Global Spread of Environmental Ministries: Domestic-International Interactions." *International Studies Quarterly* 58:4 (December): 764–780.

Alden, Chris, and Daniel Large. (2015) "On Becoming a Norms Maker: Chinese Foreign Policy, Norms Evolution and the Challenges of Security in Africa." *China Quarterly* 221 (March): 123–142.

Aldrich, George H., and Christine M. Chinkin. (2000) "A Century of Achievement and Unfinished Work." *American Journal of International Law* 94:1 (January): 90–98.

Alger, Chadwick F. (2002) "The Emerging Roles of NGOs in the UN System: From Article 71 to a People's Millennium Assembly." *Global Governance* 8:1 (January–March): 93–117.

————. (2007) "Widening Participation." In *The Oxford Handbook on the United Nations*, edited by Thomas G. Weiss and Sam Daws. New York: Oxford University Press, pp. 701–715.

Al-Qassab, Abdulwahab, Khalil E. Jahshan, Tamara Kharroub, Imad K. Harb, Radwan Ziadeh, Nabeel A. Khoury, and Sheila Carapico. (2020) "The Arab Leagues Many Failures." Arab Center (October 8). https://arabcenterdc.org/resource/the-arab-leagues-many-failures/.

Alter, Karen J. (2013) "The Multiple Roles of International Courts and Tribunals in Enforcement, Dispute Settlement, Constitutional and Administrative Review." In *Interdisciplinary Perspectives on International Law and International Rela-*

tions, edited by Jeffrey L. Dunoff and Mark A. Pollack. New York: Cambridge University Press, pp. 345–370.

———. (2014) *The New Terrain of International Law: Courts, Politics, Rights.* Princeton: Princeton University Press.

Alter, Karen J., and Liesbet Hooghe. (2016) "Regional Dispute Settlement." In *The Oxford Handbook of Comparative Regionalism*, edited by Tanja A. Börzel and Thomas Risse. New York: Oxford University Press, pp. 538–558.

Alter, Karen J., and Kal Raustiala. (2018) "The Rise of Regime Complexity." *PS: Annual Review of Law and Social Science* (14): 329–348.

Anderson-Rodgers, David, and Kerry F. Crawford. (2023) *Human Security: Theory and Action*, 2nd ed. Lanham, MD: Rowman and Littlefield.

Andonova, Liliana B. (2010) "Public-Private Partnerships for the Earth: Politics and Patterns of Hybrid Authority in the Multilateral System." *Global Environmental Politics* 10:2 (May): 25–53.

———. (2017) *Governance Entrepreneurs: International Organizations and the Rise of Global Public-Private Partnerships.* New York: Cambridge University Press.

Ani, N. C. (2021) "Coup or Not Coup: The African Union and the Dilemma of 'Popular Uprisings' in Africa." *Democracy and Security* 17:3: 257–277.

Aniche, E.T. (2020) "From Pan-Africanism to African Regionalism: A Chronicle." *African Studies* 79:1: 70–87.

Annan, Kofi. (1999) *Annual Report of the Secretary-General to the General Assembly.* SG/SM/7136 GA/9596 (September 20).

———. (2000) "We the Peoples: The Role of the United Nations in the 21st Century." www.un.org/millennium/sg/report/full.htm.

———. (2005) *In Larger Freedom: Towards Development, Security, and Human Rights for All.* Report of the UN Secretary-General. www.un.org/largerfreedom/contents.htm.

Arbour, Louise. (2014) "The Relationship Between the ICC and the UN Security Council." *Global Governance* 20:2 (April–June): 195–201.

ARC International. (2008) "Joint Statement on Human Rights, Sexual Orientation and Gender Identity." (December 18). https://arc-international.net/global-advocacy/sogi-statements/2008-joint-statement/.

Archibugi, Daniele, Marco Cellini, and Mattia Vitiello. (2021) "Refugees in the European Union: From Emergency Alarmism to Common Management." *Journal of Contemporary European Studies* 30:3: 487–505.

Aris, Stephen. (2013) *Shanghai Cooperation Organization: Mapping Multilateralism in Transition.* New York: International Peace Institute.

Arnold, Christian. (2016) "Empty Promises and Nonincorporation in Mercosur." *Empirical and Theoretical Research in International Relations* 43:4: 643–667.

Arnold-Fernandez, Emily E. (2019) "National Governance Frameworks in the Global Compact on Refugees: Dangers and Opportunities." *International Migration* 57:6 (December): 188–207.

Atwood, J. Brian. (2012) *Creating a Global Partnership for Effective Development Cooperation.* Washington, DC: Center for Global Development.

Autesserre, Séverine. (2010) *The Trouble with the Congo: Local Violence and the Failure of International Peacebuilding.* New York: Cambridge University Press.

———. (2014) *Peaceland: Conflict Resolution and the Everyday Politics of International Intervention.* New York: Cambridge University Press.

Avant, Deborah D., Martha Finnemore, and Susan K. Sell. (2010a) "Conclusion: Authority, Legitimacy, and Accountability in Global Politics." In *Who Governs the Globe?* edited by Deborah D. Avant, Martha Finnemore, and Susan K. Sell. New York: Cambridge University Press, pp. 356–370.

———, eds. (2010b) *Who Governs the Globe?* New York: Cambridge University Press.

———. (2010c) "Who Governs the Globe?" In *Who Governs the Globe?* edited by Deborah D. Avant, Martha Finnemore, and Susan K. Sell. New York: Cambridge University Press, pp. 1–34.

Ayangafac, Chrysantus, and Jakkie Cilliers. (2011) "African Solutions to African Problems." In *Rewiring Regional Security in a Fragmented World*, edited by Chester A. Crocker, Fen Osler Hampson, and Pamela Aall. Washington, DC: US Institute of Peace, pp. 115–148.

Ayoob, Mohammed. (2020) "The UN and North-South Relations in the Security Agenda. *Global Governance* 26:2: 251–261.

Ba, Alice D. (2006) "Who's Socializing Whom? Complex Engagement in Sino-ASEAN Relations." *Pacific Review* 19:2: 157–179.

———. (2014) "Institutional Divergence and Convergence in the Asia-Pacific? ASEAN in Practice and Theory." *Cambridge Review of International Affairs* 27:2 (June): 295–318.

Ba, Oumar. (2021) "Global Justice and Race." *International Politics Reviews* 9:2 (December): 375–389.

Baldwin, David A., ed. (1993) *Neorealism and Neoliberalism: The Contemporary Debate*. New York: Columbia University Press.

Banjo, Damilola. (2022) "Trending UN News: Week Ending Oct. 14." *PassBlue*. https://www.passblue.com/2022/10/14/trending-un-news-week-ending-oct-14/.

———. (2023) "From a Paid Internship to a Nobel Peace Prize: The Amazing Journey of Beatrice Fihn." *PassBlue* (January 22). https://www.passblue.com/2023/01/22/from-a-paid-internship-to-a-nobel-peace-prize-the-amazing-journey-of-beatrice-fihn/.

Barber, Rebecca. (2019) "Uniting for Peace Not Aggression: Responding to Chemical Weapons in Syria Without Breaking the Law." *Journal of Conflict and Security Law* 24:1 (Spring): 71–110.

Barnett, Michael. (2002) *Eyewitness to a Genocide: The United Nations and Rwanda*. Ithaca: Cornell University Press.

———. (2011) *Empire of Humanity: A History of Humanitarianism*. Ithaca: Cornell University Press.

Barnett, Michael, ed. (2020) *Humanitarianism and Human Rights: A World of Differences?* New York: Cambridge University Press.

Barnett, Michael, and Raymond Duvall. (2005) "Power in Global Governance." In *Power in Global Governance*, edited by Michael Barnett and Raymond Duvall. New York: Cambridge University Press, pp. 1–32.

Barnett, Michael, Songying Fang, and Christoph Zürcher. (2014) "Compromised Peacebuilding." *International Studies Quarterly* 58:3 (September): 608–620.

Barnett, Michael, and Martha Finnemore. (1999) "The Politics, Power, and Pathologies of International Organizations." *International Organization* 53:4 (Autumn): 699–732.

———. (2004) *Rules for the World: International Organizations in Global Politics*. Ithaca: Cornell University Press.

———. (2005) "The Power of Liberal International Organizations." In *Power in Global Governance*, edited by Michael Barnett and Raymond Duvall. New York: Cambridge University Press, pp. 161–184.

Barnett, Michael, Hunjoon Kim, Madalene O'Donnell, and Laura Sitea. (2007) "Peacebuilding: What Is in a Name?" *Global Governance* 13:1 (January–March): 35–58.

Bauer, Steffen. (2006) "Does Bureaucracy Really Matter? The Authority of Inter-governmental Treaty Secretariats in Global Environmental Politics." *Global Environmental Politics* 6:1 (February): 23–49.

Baum, Matthew, and Philip Potter. (2008) "The Relationships between Mass Media, Public Opinion, and Foreign Policy: Toward a Theoretical Synthesis." *Annual Review of Political Science* 11:1: 39–65.

Beeson, Mark. (2019) "Asia's Competing Multilateral Initiatives: Quality versus Quantity." *Pacific Review* 32:2: 245–255.

———. (2020) "The Great ASEAN Rorschach Test." *Pacific Review* 33:3–4: 574–581.

Beisheim, Marianne, and Nils Simon (2018) "Multistakeholder Partnerships for the SDGs: Actors' Views on UN Metagovernance." *Global Governance* 24:4 (October–December): 497–515.

Belfer, Ella, James Ford, Michelle Maillet, Malcolm Araos, and Melanie Flynn. (2019) "Pursuing an Indigenous Platform: Exploring Opportunities and Constraints for Indigenous Participation in the UNFCCC." *Global Environmental Politics* 19:1 (February): 12–33.

Benedick, Richard Elliot. (1998) *Ozone Diplomacy: New Directions in Safeguarding the Planet*. Enlarged ed. Cambridge: Harvard University Press.

Benneker, Violet, Klarita Gërxhani, and Stephanie Steinmetz. (2020) "Enforcing Your Own Human Rights? The Role of Social Norms in Compliance with Human Rights Treaties." *Social Inclusion* 8:1: 184–193.

Bennett, A. LeRoy. (1995) *International Organizations: Principles and Issues*. 6th ed. Englewood Cliffs, NJ: Prentice Hall.

Bernauer, Thomas, Anna Kalbhenn, Vally Koubi, and Gabriele Spilker. (2013) "Is There a 'Depth Versus Participation' Dilemma in International Cooperation?" *Review of International Organizations* 8: 477–497.

Best, Jacqueline. (2017) "The Rise of Measurement-Driven Governance: The Case of International Development." *Global Governance* 23:2 (April–June): 163–181.

Betsill, Michele M. (2007) "Regional Governance of Global Climate Change: The North American Commission for Environmental Cooperation." *Global Environmental Politics* 7:2 (May): 11–27.

Betsill, Michele M., and Elisabeth Corell, eds. (2008) *NGO Diplomacy: The Influence of Nongovernmental Organizations in International Environmental Negotiations*. Cambridge: MIT Press.

Betts, Alexander. (2011) "Introduction: Global Migration Governance. In *Global Migration Governance*, edited by Alexander Betts. Oxford, UK: Oxford University Press, pp. 1–33.

———. (2013) "Regime Complexity and International Organizations: UNHCR as a Challenged Institution." *Global Governance* 19:1 (January–March): 69–81.

Bexell, Magdalena, Kristina Jonssön, Anders Uhlin, eds. (2022) *Legitimation and Delegitimation in Global Governance: Practices, Justifications, and Audiences*. New York: Oxford University Press.

Bhagwati, Jagdish.. (2008) *Termites in the Trading System: How Preferential Agreements Undermine Free Trade*. New York: Oxford University Press.

Bianculli, Andrea C. (2016) "Latin America." In *The Oxford Handbook of Comparative Regionalism*, edited by Tanja A. Börzel and Thomas Risse. New York: Oxford University Press, pp. 154–177.

Biermann, Frank. (2012) "Navigating the Antropocene: Improving Earth System Governance." *Science* 335 (March 16): 1306–1307.

Biermann, Frank, and Steffen Bauer, eds. (2005) *A World Environment Organization: Solution or Threat for Effective International Environmental Governance?* Aldershot: Ashgate.

Biermann, Frank, and Philipp Pattberg. (2012) "Global Environmental Governance Revisited." In *Global Environmental Governance Revisited*, edited by Frank Biermann and Philipp Pattberg. Cambridge: MIT Press, pp. 1–23.

Biermann, Frank, and Bernd Siebenhüner, eds. (2009) *Managers of Global Change: The Influence of International Environmental Bureaucracies*. Cambridge: MIT Press.

———. (2013) "Problem Solving by International Bureaucracies: The Influence of International Secretariats on World Politics." In *Routledge Handbook of International Organization*, edited by Bob Reinalda. New York: Routledge, pp. 149–161.

Biersteker, Thomas, Sue E. Eckert, and Marcos Tourinho, eds. (2016) *Targeted Sanctions: The Impacts and Effectiveness of United Nations Action*. New York: Cambridge University Press.

Bierstecker, Thomas J., Marcos Tourinho, and Sue E. Eckert. (2016) "Conclusion." In *Targeted Sanctions: The Impacts and Effectiveness of United Nations Action*, edited by Thomas J. Biersteker, Sue E. Eckert and Maria Tourinho. New York: Cambridge University Press, pp. 265–279.

Birnbaum, Michael. (2023) "How a Small Island Got World's Highest Court to Take on Climate Justice." *Washington Post* (March 29).

Blackmon, Pamela. (2021) "The Lagarde Effect: Assessing Policy Change under the First Female Managing Director of the International Monetary Fund (IMF)." *Global Society* 35:2: 171–190.

Blondell, Mathieu, Jeff Colgan, and Thies Van de Graaf. (2019) "What Drives Norm Success? Evidence from Anti-Fossil Fuel Campaigns." *Global Environmental Politics* 19:4 (November): 63–84.

Bob, Clifford. (2005) *The Marketing of Rebellion: Insurgents, Media, and International Activism*. New York: Cambridge University Press.

———. (2010) "Packing Heat: Pro-Gun Groups and the Governance of Small Arms." In *Who Governs the Globe?* edited by Deborah D. Avant, Martha Finnemore, and Susan K. Sell. New York: Cambridge University Press, pp. 183–201.

———. (2019) *Rights as Weapons: Instruments of Conflict, Tools of Power*. Princeton, NJ: Princeton University Press.

Bodin, Jean. (1967) *Six Books on the Commonwealth*. Oxford: Blackwell.

Borg-Barthet, Justin and Carole Lyons. (2016) "The European Union Migration Crisis." *Edinburgh Law Review* 20:2 (May): 230–235.

Borland, Robert, Robert Morrell, and Vanessa Watson. (2018) "Southern Agency: Navigating Local and Global Imperatives in Climate Research." *Global Environmental Politics* 18:3 (August): 47–65.

Börzel, Tanja A., and Thomas Risse. (2016) "Introduction: Framework of the Handbook and Conceptual Clarification." In *The Oxford Handbook of Comparative Regionalism*, edited by Tanja A. Börzel and Thomas Risse. New York: Oxford University Press, pp. 3–15.

———. (2019) "Grand Theories of Integration and the Challenges of Comparative Regionalism." *Journal of European Public Policy* 26:8, 1231–1252.

Bosch, Olivia, and Peter van Ham. (2007) "UNSCR 1520: Its Future and Contribution to Global Non-Proliferation and Counter-Terrorism." In *Global Non-Proliferation and Counter-Terrorism: The Impact of UNSCR 1540*, edited by Olivia Bosch and Peter van Ham. London: Chatham, pp. 207–226.

Boserup, Ester. (1970) *Woman's Role in Economic Development*. New York: St. Martin's Press.

Boucher, Alix and Caty Clemont. (2016) "Coordination of United Nations Sanctions with Other Actors and Instruments." In *Targeted Sanctions: The Impacts and*

Effectiveness of United Nations Action, edited by Thomas J. Biersteker, Sue E. Eckert and Maria Tourinho. New York: Cambridge University Press, pp. 119–149.

Boutros-Ghali, Boutros. (1992) *An Agenda for Peace: Preventive Diplomacy, Peacemaking, and Peacekeeping*. New York: United Nations.

———. (1995) *An Agenda for Development*. New York: United Nations.

Bower, Adam. (2019) "Contesting the International Criminal Court: Bashir, Kenyatta and the Status of the Non-impunity Norm in World Politics." *Global Security Studies* 4:1 (January): 88–104.

Boykoff, Jules. (2006) "Framing Dissent: Mass-Media Coverage of the Global Justice Movement." *New Political Science* 28:2 (June): 201–228.

Braaten, Daniel. (2021) "Human Rights: What Does the Future Hold?" *International Studies Review* 23:3 (September): 1164–1178.

Bradford, Ann. (2020) *The Brussels Effect: How the European Union Rules the World*. New York: Oxford University Press.

Bradley, Megan. (2017) "The International Organization for Migration (IOM): Gaining Power in the Forced Migration Regime." *Refuge* 33:1: 97–106.

Bradsher, Keith. (2023) "After Doling Out Huge Loans, China Is Now Bailing Out Countries." *New York Times* (March 27).

Branswell, Helen. (2020) "'Against All Odds' The Inside Story of How Scientists Across Three Continents Produced an Ebola Vaccine." *STAT* (January 7). https://www.statnews.com/2020/01/07/inside-story-scientists-produced-world -first-ebola-vaccine/.

Breitmeier, Helmut, Arild Underdal, and Oran R. Young. (2011) "The Effectiveness of International Environmental Regimes: Comparing and Contrasting Findings from Quantitative Research." *International Studies Review* 134 (December): 579–605.

Brewster, Rachel. (2013) "Reputation in International Relations and International Law." In *Interdisciplinary Perspectives on International Law and International Relations: The State of the Art*, edited by Jeffrey Dunoff and Mark A. Pollack. New York: Cambridge University Press, pp. 197–222.

Briceño-Ruiz, José. (2018) "Times of Change in Latin American Regionalism." *Contexto International* 40:3 (September/December): 573–592.

Brown, Lester, Patricia P. McGrath, and Bruce Stokes. (1976) "Twenty-Two Dimensions of the Population Problem." Worldwatch Paper 5. Washington, DC: Worldwatch Institute.

Brown, Mark Malloch. (2008) "The John W. Holmes Lecture: Can the UN Be Reformed?" *Global Governance* 14:1 (January–March): 1–12.

Browne, Stephen. (2022) "The UN in Crisis: Big Powers and Bad Influence." *PassBlue* (August 22). www.passblue.com/2022/08/22/the-un-in-crisis-big-powers -and-bad-influence/.

Brysk, Allison. (2018) *The Future of Human Rights*. New York: Polity.

Brzezinski, Zbigniew. (1989) *The Grand Failure: The Birth and Death of Communism in the Twentieth Century*. New York: Scribner's.

Buergenthal, Thomas. (1995) *International Human Rights in a Nutshell*. 2nd ed. St. Paul: West.

Bull, Hedley. (1977) *The Anarchical Society: A Study of Order in World Politics*. New York: Columbia University Press.

Bunch, Charlotte. (1990) "Women's Rights Are Human Rights: Toward a Re-Vision of Human Rights." *Human Rights Quarterly* 12:4: 486–500.

Buntaine, Mark. (2015) "Accountability in Global Governance: Civil Society Claims for Environmental Performance at the World Bank." *International Studies Quarterly* 59:1 (March): 99–111.

Buntaine, Mark T., and Bradley C. Parks. (2013) "When Do Environmentally Focused Assistance Projects Achieve Their Objectives? Evidence from World Bank Post-Project Evaluations." *Global Governmental Politics* 13:2 (May): 65–88.

Burci, Gian Luca, and Jakob Quirin. (2014) "Ebola, WHO and the United Nations: Convergence of Global Public Health and International Peace and Security." *ASIL Insights* 18:25 (November 14). www.asil.org/insights/volume/18/issue/25/ebola-who-and-united-nations-convergence-global-public-health-and.

Bures, Oldrich, and Stephanie Ahern. (2007) "The European Model of Building Regional Cooperation Against Terrorism." In *Uniting Against Terror: Cooperative Nonmilitary Responses to the Global Terrorist Threat*, edited by David Cortright and George A. Lopez. Cambridge: MIT Press, pp. 187–236.

Bush, Sarah. (2016) *The Taming of Democracy Assistance: Why Democracy Promotion Does Not Confront Dictators*. New York: Cambridge University Press.

Büthe, Tim, and Walter Mattli. (2011) *The New Global Rulers: The Privatization of Regulation in the World Economy*. Princeton: Princeton University Press.

Buzan, Barry and Lene Hansen. (2009) *The Evolution of Security Studies*. Cambridge: Cambridge University Press.

Buzan, Barry, Ole Waever, and Jaap de Wilde. (1998) *Security: A New Framework for Analysis*. Boulder: Lynne Rienner.

Byrd, William. (2023) "Afghanistan Requires a Change from Humanitarian Business as Usual." *Lawfare* (March 29). https://www.lawfaremedia.org/article/afghanistan-requires-change-humanitarian-business-usual.

Caballero-Anthony, Mely. (2014) "Understanding ASEAN's Centrality: Bases and Prospects in an Evolving Regional Architecture." *Pacific Review* 27:4 (September): 563–584.

———. (2022) "The ASEAN Way and the Changing Security Environment: Navigating Challenges to Informality and Centrality." *International Politics*. https://doi.org/10.1057/s41311-022-00400-0.

Campbell, John. (2021) "Ngozi Okonjo-Iweala: A Well-Qualified New Leader for the WTO." *Council on Foreign Relations* (February 17). https://www.cfr.org/blog/ngozi-okonjo-iweala-well-qualified-new-leader-wto.

Campbell, Susanna P. (2018) *Global Governance and Local Peace: Accountability and Performance in International Peacebuilding*. New York: Cambridge University Press.

Campe, Sabine. (2009) "The Secretariat of the International Maritime Organization: A Tanker for Tankers." In *Managers of Global Change: The Influence of International Environmental Bureaucracies*, edited by Frank Biermann and Bernd Siebenhüner. Cambridge: MIT Press, pp. 143–168.

Caporaso, James A. (1993) "International Relations Theory and Multilateralism: The Search for Foundations." In *Multilateralism Matters: The Theory and Praxis of an International Form*, edited by John Gerard Ruggie. New York: Columbia University Press, pp. 51–90.

Carpenter, Charli. (2014) *"Lost" Causes: Agenda Vetting in Global Issue Networks and the Shaping of Human Security*. Ithaca: Cornell University Press, 2014.

Carpenter, Charli, Sirin Duygulu, and Alexander H. Montgomery. (2014) "Explaining the Advocacy Agenda: Insights from the Human Security Network," *International Organization* 68:2 (May): 449–470.

Carr, Madeline. (2018) "Global Internet Governance." In *International Organizations and Global Governance*, edited by Thomas G. Weiss and Rorden Wilkinson. 2nd edition. New York: Routledge, pp. 744–755.

Carroll, Archie. (1979) "A Three-Dimensional Conceptual Model of Corporate Performance." *Academy of Management Review* 4:4 (October): 497–505.

Carson, Rachel. (1962) *Silent Spring*. Cambridge, MA: Houghton Mifflin.

CBS News. (2005) UN: China Torture Still Widespread." https://www.cbsnews.com /news/un-china-torture-still-widespread/.

Ceccorulli, Michela. (2021) "The EU's Normative Ambivalence and the Migrant Crisis: (In)Actions of (In)Justice." In *The EU Migration System of Governance: Justice on the Move*, edited by Michela Ceccorulli, Enrico Fassi, and Sonia Lucarelli. Cham, Switzerland: Palgrave Macmillan, pp. 33–56.

Center for Reproductive Rights. (2020) "Paola Guzmán Albarracín v. Ecuador." https://reproductiverights.org/case/paola-guzman-albarracin-v-ecuador-inter -american-commission-on-human-rights/.

Chan, Sewell. (2015) "Global Warming's Role in Mass Migration Is Addressed." *New York Times* (December 13).

Chane, Anna-Luisa and Arjun Sharma. (2016) "Universal Human Rights? Exploring Contestation and Consensus in the UN Human Rights Council." *Human Rights and International Legal Discourse* 10:2: 219–247.

Charnovitz, Steve. (1997) "Two Centuries of Participation: NGOs and International Governance." *Michigan Journal of International Law* 18:183 (Winter): 184–286.

Charron, Andrea and Clara Portela. (2016) "The Relationship between United Nations Sanctions and Regional Sanctions Regimes." In *Targeted Sanctions: The Impacts and Effectiveness of United Nations Action*, edited by Thomas J. Biersteker, Sue E. Eckert and Maria Tourinho. New York: Cambridge University Press, pp. 101–118.

Chayes, Abram, and Antonia Handler Chayes. (1995) *The New Sovereignty: Compliance with International Regulatory Agreements*. Cambridge: Harvard University Press.

Checkel, Jeffrey T., ed. (2005) *International Institutions and Socialization in Europe*. Special Issue: *International Organization* 59:4 (Fall).

Chesterman, Simon. (2015) "The Secretary-General We Deserve?" *Global Governance* 21:4 (September–December): 505–513.

Chotiner, Isaac. (2022) "Why Hasn't the U.N. Accused China of Genocide in Xinjiang?" *New Yorker* (September 13). https://www.newyorker.com/news/q-and -a/why-hasnt-the-un-accused-china-of-genocide-in-xinjiang.

Christians, Clifford. (2019) *Media Ethics and Global Justice in the Digital Age*. New York: Cambridge University Press.

Christy, David S. J. (2008) "Round and Round We Go." *World Policy Journal* 25:2 (Summer): 19–27.

Cirbirski, Antoine. (2022) "Has Europe's Hour Come?" Fondation Robert Schuman Policy Paper no. 625 (March22). www.robert-schuman.eu/en/doc/questions-d -europe/qe-625-en.pdf.

Clancy, Dawn. (2022) "UN Diplomats Negotiate First Steps to Try Russia for Crimes of Aggression." *PassBlue* (December 20). ww.passblue.com/2022/12/20 /diplomats-at-the-un-negotiate-the-first-steps-to-prosecute-russia-for-crimes-of -aggression/.

Clapp, Jennifer. (2018) "Food and Hunger." In *International Organizations and Global Governance*, edited by Thomas G. Weiss and Rorden Wilkinson. 2nd ed. New York: Routledge, pp. 707–718.

Clark, Ann Marie. (2001) *Diplomacy of Conscience: Amnesty International and Changing Human Rights Norms*. Princeton: Princeton University Press.

Claude, Inis L., Jr. (1964) *Swords into Plowshares: The Problems and Progress of International Organization*. 3rd ed. New York: Random House.

———. (1967) *The Changing United Nations*. New York: Random House.

————. (1988) "The Vogue of Collectivism in International Relations." In *States and the Global System: Politics, Law, and Organization*, edited by Inis L. Claude Jr. New York: St. Martin's, pp. 133–144.

Collier, Paul. (2007) *The Bottom Billion: Why the Poorest Countries Are Failing and What Can Be Done About It*. New York: Oxford University Press.

Commission on Global Governance. (1995) *Our Global Neighbourhood: Report of the Commission on Global Governance*. Oxford: Oxford University Press.

Commission on Human Security. (2003*) Human Security Now: Protecting and Empowering People*. New York: The Commission.

Conca, Ken. (2006) *Governing Water: Contentious Transnational Politics and Global Institution Building*. Cambridge: MIT Press.

————. (2015) *An Unfinished Foundation: The United Nations and Global Environmental Governance*. New York: Oxford University Press.

Conrad, Courtenay R. and Emily Hencken Ritter. (2019) *Contentious Compliance: Dissent and Repression under International Human Rights Law*. New York: Oxford University Press.

Conroy, Michael E. (2002) "Can Advocacy-Led Certification Systems Transform Global Corporate Practices?" In *Global Backlash: Citizen Initiatives for a Just World Economy*, edited by Robin Broad. Lanham, MD: Rowman and Littlefield, pp. 210–215.

Cooley, Alexander, and James Ron. (2002) "The NGO Scramble: Organizational Insecurity and the Political Economy of Transnational Action." *International Security* 27:1 (Summer): 5–39.

Cooley, Alexander, and Jack Snyder, eds. (2015) *Ranking the World: Grading States as a Tool of Global Governance*. New York: Cambridge University Press.

Cooper, Andrew F. (2004) "The Making of the Inter-American Democratic Charter: A Case of Complex Multilateralism." *International Studies Perspectives* 5:1 (February): 92–113.

Cooper, Andrew F., and Ramesh Thakur. (2013) *The Group of Twenty (G20)*. London: Routledge.

————. (2014) "The BRICS in the New Global Economic Geography." In *International Organizations and Global Governance*, edited by Thomas G. Weiss and Rorden Wilkinson. New York: Routledge, pp. 265–278.

Copelovitch, Mark S. (2010) *The International Monetary Fund in the Global Economy: Banks, Bonds, and Bailouts*. New York: Cambridge University Press.

Copelovitch, Mark, and Jon Pevehouse. (2019) "International Organizations in a New Era of Populist Nationalism." *Review of International Organizations* 14:1 (April): 169–186.

Cortright, David, and George A. Lopez. (2000) *The Sanctions Decade: Assessing UN Strategies in the 1990s*. Boulder: Lynne Rienner.

————. (2002) *Sanctions and the Search for Security*. Boulder: Lynne Rienner.

Court of Justice of the European Union (CJEU).

————. (2020) *European Commission v. Hungary*. C-286/12. ECLI: EU:C:2012:687.

————. (2022) *CJ v. Tesorería General de la Seguridad Social (TGSS)*. C-389/20. ECLI: EU:C:2022:120.

Cousens, Elizabeth, and David Harland. (2006) "Post-Dayton Bosnia and Herzegovina." In *Twenty-First-Century Peace Operations*, edited by William J. Durch. Washington, DC: US Institute of Peace, pp. 49–140.

Cousteau, Jacques-Yves, with James Dugan. (1963) *The Living Sea*. New York: Harper and Row.

Cox, Robert W. (1986) "Social Forces, States, and World Orders: Beyond International Relations Theory." In *Neorealism and Its Critics*, edited by Robert O. Keohane. New York: Columbia University Press, pp. 204–254.

———. (1992a) "Globalization, Multilateralism and Democracy." John W. Holmes Memorial Lecture. Academic Council on the United Nations System (ACUNS), Reports and Papers no. 2.

———. (1992b) "Toward a Post-Hegemonic Conceptualization of World Order: Reflections on the Relevancy of Ibn Khaldun." In *Governance Without Government: Order and Change in World Politics*, edited by James N. Rosenau and Ernst-Otto Czempiel. New York: Cambridge University Press, pp. 132–159.

Crawley, Heaven. (2016) "Managing the Unmanageable? Understanding Europe's Response to the Migration 'Crisis.'" *Human Geography* 9:2: 13–23.

Creamer, Cosette D. and Beth A. Simmons. (2020). "The Proof is in the Process: Self-Reporting Under International Human Rights Treaties." *American Journal of International Law* 114: 1: 1–50.

Crisis Group. (2023) "Who Are the Winners in the Black Sea Grain Deal?" (August 3). https://www.crisisgroup.org/europe-central-asia/eastern-europe/ukraine/who-are-winners-black-sea-grain-deal.

Crocker, Chester A., Fen Osler Hampson, and Pamela Aall. (1999) "Rising to the Challenge of Multiparty Mediation." In Crocker, Chester A., Fen Osler Hampson, and Pamela Aall, eds. (1999) *Herding Cats: Multiparty Mediation in a Complex World*. Washington, DC: US Institute of Peace, pp. 665–701.

———. (2004) *Taming Intractable Conflicts: Mediation in the Hardest Cases*. Washington, DC: US Institute of Peace.

Cronin, Bruce, and Ian Hurd. (2008) "Conclusion: Assessing the Council's Authority." In Bruce Cronin and Ian Hurd, eds. (2008) *The UN Security Council and the Politics of International Authority*. New York: Routledge, pp. 199–214.

Crossette, Barbara. (1999) "Kofi Annan Unsettles People, As He Believes U.N. Should Do." *New York Times* (December 31).

Cumming-Bruce, Nick. (2015) "Chinese Justice System Relies on Torture, U.N. Panel Finds." *New York Times* (December 10).

———. (2021) "Fiji Will Lead U.N. Rights Body, Over Russian and Chinese Opposition." *New York Times* (January 15).

Cumming-Bruce, Nick and Austin Ramzy. (2022) "U.N. Report on Rights Abuses in Xinjiang May Be Delayed Again." *New York Times* (August 25).

Cupitt, Richard, Rodney Whitlock, and Lynn Williams Whitlock. (1997) "The (Im)mortality of International Governmental Organizations." In *The Politics of Global Governance: International Organizations in an Interdependent World*, edited by Paul F. Diehl. Boulder: Lynne Rienner, pp. 7–23.

Daalder, Ivo H., and James G. Stavridis. (2012) "NATO's Victory in Libya: The Right Way to Run an Intervention." *Foreign Affairs* 91:2 (March–April): 2–7.

Dallmayr, Fred R. (2002) "Globalization and Inequality: A Plea for Global Justice." *International Studies Review* 4:2 (Summer): 137–156.

Damian, Michel, and Jean-Christophe Graz. (2001) "The World Trade Organization, the Environment, and the Ecological Critique." *International Social Science Journal* 170 (December): 597–610.

Dany, Charlotte. (2014) "Janus-Faced NGO Participation in Global Governance: Structural Constraints for NGO Influence." *Global Governance* 20:3 (July–September): 419–436.

Davenport, Coral. (2015) "Stung by Failure in Copenhagen in '09, 195 Nations Felt New Urgency." *New York Times* (December 14).

Davis, Kevin E., Benedict Kingsbury, and Sally Engle. "Indicators as a Technology of Global Governance." *Law and Society Review* 46:1 (March): 71–104.

Day, Adam. (2019) "Impact of UN Mission in South Sudan Complicated by Dilemmas of Protection." *IPI Global Observatory* (December 12). https://theglobalobservatory.org/2019/12/impact-un-mission-south-sudan-complicated-by-dilemmas-of-protection/.

de Beaufort Wijnholds, Onno. (2011) *Fighting Financial Fires: An IMF Insider Account.* Houndmills: Palgrave Macmillan.

de Coning, Cedric. (2019) "Are UN Peace Operations Effective?" *IPI Global Observatory.* (November 14). https://theglobalobservatory.org/2019/11/are-un-peace-operations-effective/.

Dedring, Jürgen. 2008. "Human Security and the UN Security Council." In *Globalization and Environmental Challenges. Reconceptualizing Security in the 21st Century,* edited by Hans Günter Brauch. New York: Springer, pp. 605–619.

Deets, Stephen. (2009) "Constituting Interests and Identities in a Two-Level Game: Understanding the Gabcikovo-Nagymaros Dam Conflict." *Foreign Policy Analysis* 5:1 (January): 37–56.

Dellmuth, Lisa, and Elizabeth Bloodgood. (2019) "Advocacy Group Effects in Global Governance: Populations, Strategies, and Political Opportunity Structures." *Interest Groups & Advocacy* 8:3 (September): 255–269.

Dellmuth, Lisa, Jan Aart Scholte, Jonas Tallberg, and Soetkin Verhaegen. (2022) *Citizens, Elites, and the Legitimacy of Global Governance.* New York: Oxford University Press.

DeSombre, Elizabeth R. (2006) *Global Environmental Institutions.* London: Routledge.

Devakumar, Delan et al. (2019) "Children and Adolescents on the Move: What Does the Global Compact for Migration Mean for their Health?" *The Lancet Child and Adolescent Health* 3:2 (February): 64–66.

DeVille, Ferdi, and Gabriel Siles-Brügge. (2019) "The Impact of Brexit on EU Policies." *Politics and Governance* 7:3: 1–6.

Diamond, Jarod. (2005) *Collapse: How Societies Choose to Fail or Collapse.* New York: Penguin.

Diaz-Maurin, François. (2022) "The 2022 Nuclear Year in Review: A Global Nuclear Order in Shambles." (December 26). https://thebulletin.org/2022/12/the-2022-nuclear-year-in-review-a-global-nuclear-order-in-shambles/#post-heading.

Diehl, Paul F. (2000) "Forks in the Road: Theoretical and Policy Concerns for 21st Century Peacekeeping." *Global Society* 14:3: 337–360.

———. (2008) *Peace Operations.* Malden, MA: Polity.

Diehl, Paul, and Alexandru Balas. (2014) *Peace Operations.* 2nd ed. Malden, MA: Polity.

Diehl, Paul, and Daniel Druckman. (2010) *Evaluating Peace Operations.* Boulder: Lynne Rienner.

Dietrich, Simone. (2021) *States, Markets, and Foreign Aid.* New York: Cambridge University Press.

Dietrichson, Elise and Fatima Sator. (2022) "The Latin American Women: How They Shaped the UN Charter and Why Southern Agency is Forgotten." In *Women and the UN: A New History of Women's International Human Rights,* edited by Rebecca Adami and Dan Plesch. New York: Routledge, pp. 17–38.

Dietzel, Alix. (2019) *Global Justice and Climate Governance: Bridging Theory and Practice.* Edinburgh: Edinburgh University Press.

Dingwerth, Klaus. (2008) "Private Transnational Governance and the Developing World: A Comparative Perspective." *International Studies Quarterly* 52:3 (September): 607–634.

Dingwerth, Klaus, and Philipp Pattberg. (2006) "Global Governance as a Perspective on World Politics." *Global Governance* 12:2 (April–June): 185–203.

———. (2009) "World Politics and Organizational Fields: The Case of Transnational Sustainability Governance." *European Journal of International Relations* 15 (November): 707–744.

Dobbins, James, Seth G. Jones, Keith Crane, Andrew Rathmell, Brett Steele, Richard Teltschik, and Anga Timilsina. (2005) *The UN's Role in Nation-Building: From the Congo to Iraq.* Santa Monica: RAND.

Dodds, Klaus, and Chih Yuan Woon. (2020) "Introduction: The Arctic Council, 'Asian States' and the 'Global Arctic.'" In *"Observing" the Arctic: Asia in the Arctic Council and Beyond,* edited by Chih Yuan Wood and Klaus Dobbs. Cheltenham: Edward Elgar, pp. 1–27.

Dominguez, Jorge I. (2007) "International Cooperation in Latin America: The Design of Regional Institutions by Slow Accretion." In *Crafting Cooperation: Regional International Institutions in Comparative Perspective,* edited by Amitav Acharya and Alastair Ian Johnston. New York: Cambridge University Press, pp. 83–128.

Donnelly, Jack. (1998) *International Human Rights.* 2nd ed. Boulder: Westview.

Dosch, Jörn. (2008) "ASEAN's Reluctant Liberal Turn and the Thorny Road to Democracy Promotion." *Pacific Review* 21:4: 527–545.

Doss, Alan. (2023) "Optimism from West Africa: Sierra Leone and Liberia Have Escaped the Conflict Trap." *PassBlue* (February 16). https://theglobalobservatory.org/2023/01/how-useful-are-the-uns-broad-protection-of-civilian-mandates/.

Doyle, Michael W. (1995) *UN Peacekeeping in Cambodia: UNTAC's Civil Mandate.* Boulder: Lynne Rienner.

Doyle, Michael W., and Nicholas Sambanis. (2006) *Making War and Building Peace.* Princeton: Princeton University Press.

Drezner, Daniel W. (2007) *All Politics Is Global: Explaining International Regulatory Regimes.* Princeton: Princeton University Press.

Duffield, John. (2003) "The Limits of 'Rational Design.'" *International Organization* 57:2 (Spring): 411–430.

———. (2007) "What Are International Institutions?" *International Studies Review* 9:1 (Spring): 1–22.

Durfee, Mary, and Rachael Lorna Johnstone. (2019) *Arctic Governance in a Changing World.* Lanham, MD: Rowman & Littlefield.

Easterly, William. (2006) *The White Man's Burden: Why the West's Efforts to Aid the Rest Have Done So Much Ill and So Little Good.* New York: Penguin.

The Economist. (2015) "Unsustainable Goals." (March 28): 63.

———. (2021) "The Palestinian Cause No Longer Binds the Arab World." (August 24).

———. (2022a) "Africa's Regional Club Is Less Effective at 20 Than It Was at Two." (February 12).

———. (2022b) "The Coming Food Catastrophe." (May 19).

———. (2022c) "A New Migration Crisis is Brewing in Europe." (November 17).

———. (2023) "China Is Paralyzing Global Debt-Forgiveness Efforts." (February 2).

Economy, Elizabeth. (2022) *The World According to China.* Medford, MA: Polity Press.

Effectiveness of Peace Operations Network (EPON). (2019) "Assessing the Effectiveness of the UN Mission in the DRC—MONUC/MONUSCO." Report 3/2019.

Norwegian Institute of International Affairs. https://effectivepeaceops.net/wp
-content/uploads/2019/09/EPON-MONUSCO-Report-Exec-Summary.pdf.

Eilstrup-Sangiovanni, Mette, and Teale N. Phelps Bondaroff. (2014) "From Advocacy to Confrontation: Direct Enforcement by Environmental NGOs." *International Studies Quarterly* 58:2 (June): 348–361.

Eilstrup-Sangiovanni, Mette, and J. C. Sharman. (2021) "Enforcers Beyond Borders: Transnational NGOs and the Enforcement of International Law." *Perspectives on Politics* 19:1 (March): 131–147.

Einaudi, Luigi R. (2020) "Conflict Between Theory and Practice: The Organization of American States." *Annals of the Fondazione Luigi Einaudi* 54 (December): 35–44.

Elliott, Lorraine. (2011) "East Asia and Sub-Regional Diversity: Initiatives, Institutions, and Identity." In *Comparative Environmental Regionalism*, edited by Lorraine Elliott and Shaun Breslin. London: Routledge, pp. 56–75.

Emmerij, Louis, Richard Jolly, and Thomas G. Weiss. (2001) *Ahead of the Curve: UN Ideas and Global Challenges*. Bloomington: Indiana University Press.

Esty, Daniel C. (2001) "A Term's Limits." *Foreign Policy* 126 (September–October): 74–75.

European Coalition on Corporate Justice. (2021) "Justice Delayed: 10 Years of UN Guiding Principles." European Coalition on Corporate Justice (June 16). https://corporatejustice.org/news/justice-delayed-10-years-of-un-guiding-principles/.

European Council. (2022) "Versailles Declaration of the EU Heads of State or Government." (March 11). https://portal.ieu-monitoring.com/editorial/versailles-declaration-of-the-eu-heads-of-state-or-government.

European Court of Human Rights (ECHR). (2023) *Analysis of Statistics 2022*. https://www.echr.coe.int/documents/d/echr/Stats_analysis_2022_ENG.

European Court of Justice (ECJ). (1964) *Flaminio Costa v. Enel*. Case 6/64 in the Court of Justice of the European Communities, *Reports of Cases Before the Court*.

———. (1979) *Cassis de Dijon*. Officially *Rewe-Zentral AG v. Bundesmonopolverwaltung für Branntwein*. Case 120/78 in the Court of Justice of the European Communities, *Reports of Cases Before the Court*.

———. (1995) *Union Royale Belge des Sociétés de Football Association, ASBL v. Bosman*. Court of Justice of the European Union, *Reports of Cases Before the Court*.

Evans, Gareth. (2012) "The Responsibility to Protect After Libya and Syria." Address to annual Castan Centre Human Rights Law Conference, Melbourne (July 20). www.gevans.org/speeches/speech476.html.

Evans, Paul. (2005) "Between Regionalism and Regionalization: Policy Networks and the Nascent East Asian Institutional Identity." In *Remapping East Asia: The Construction of a Region*, edited by T. J. Pempel. Ithaca: Cornell University Press, pp. 195–215.

Fabbrini, Sergio. (2020) "Institutions and Decision-Making in the EU." In *Governance and Politics in the Post-Crisis European Union*, edited by Ramona Coman, Amandine Crespy, and Vivien A. Schmidt. New York: Cambridge University Press, pp. 54–73.

Fagbayibo, Babatunde, and Udoke Ndidiamaka Owie. (2021) "Crisis as Opportunity: Exploring the African Union's Response to COVID-19 and the Implications for Its Aspirational Supranational Powers." *Journal of African Law* 65:S2: 181–108.

Farrell, Henry, and Abraham Newman. (2020) "Will the Coronavirus End Globalization as We Know It?" *Foreign Affairs* (March 16). https://www.foreignaffairs.com/articles/2020-03-16/will-coronavirus-end-globalization-we-know-it.

Fawcett, Louise. (2013) "The History of Regionalism." UNU-CRIS Working Paper W-2013/5. Bruges: UNU Institute.

Fearon, James, and Alexander Wendt. (2002) "Rationalism vs. Constructivism: A Skeptical View." In *The Handbook of International Relations*, edited by Walter Carlsnaes, Thomas Risse, and Beth Simmons. London: Sage, pp. 52–72.

Ferris, Elizabeth G., and Katharine M. Donato. (2020) *Refugees, Migration, and Global Governance: Negotiating the Global Compacts*. New York: Routledge.

Findley, Michael, Daniel Nielson, and J. C. Sharman. (2014) *Global Shell Games: Experiments in Transnational Relations, Crime, and Terrorism*. New York: Cambridge University Press.

Finnemore, Martha. (1996a) "Constructing Norms of Humanitarian Intervention." In *The Culture of National Security: Norms and Identity in World Politics*, edited by Peter J. Katzenstein. New York: Columbia University Press, pp. 153–185.

———. (1996b) *National Interests in International Society*. Ithaca: Cornell University Press.

———. (2003) *The Purpose of Intervention: Changing Beliefs About the Use of Force*. Ithaca: Cornell University Press.

Finnemore, Martha, and Michelle Jurkovich. (2014) "Getting a Seat at the Table: The Origins of Universal Participation and Modern Multilateral Conferences." *Global Governance* 20:3 (July–September): 361–373.

Finnemore, Martha, and Kathryn Sikkink. (1998) "Norms and International Relations Theory." *International Organizations* 52:4 (Fall): 887–917.

———. (2001) "Taking Stock: The Constructivist Research Program in International Relations and Comparative Politics." *Annual Review of Political Science* 4: 391–416.

Fleming, James. (1998) *Historical Perspectives on Climate Change*. New York: Oxford University Press.

Floyd, Steve. (2022) "Power Trials Commence at Grand Ethiopian Renaissance Dam Despite Stalled Negotiations and Regional Tensions." *Lawfare* (May 8). www .lawfaremedia.org/article/power-trials-commence-grand-ethiopian-renaissance -dam-despite-stalled-negotiations-and-regional.

Food and Agriculture Organization (FAO). (1996) "World Food Summit, Rome Declaration on World Food Security and Plan of Action." https://www.fao.org /3/w3613e/w3613e00.htm.

Food Ingredients First. (2020) "New Food Coalition Aims to Avert a 'Catastrophic' post-COVID-19 Food Crisis." Food Ingredients First (November 6). www .foodingredientsfirst.com/news/new-food-coalition-aims-to-avert-a-catastrophic -post-covid-19-food-crisis.html.

Forsythe, David P. (2005) *The Humanitarians: The International Committee of the Red Cross*. Cambridge: Cambridge University Press, pp. 85–110.

Forsythe, David P., with Baekkwan Park. (2009) "Turbulent Transition: From the UN Human Rights Commission to the Council." In *The United Nations: Past, Present, and Future—Proceedings of the 2007 Frances Marion University UN Symposium*, edited by Scott Kaufman and Alissa Waters. New York: Nova Science, pp. 85–110.

Fortify Rights and the United States Holocaust Memorial Museum Simon-Skjodt Center for the Prevention of Genocide. (2017) "They Tried to Kill Us All:" Atrocity Crimes against Rohingya Muslims in Rakhine State, Myanmar." (November). https://www.fortifyrights.org.

Fortna, Virginia Page. (2004) *Peace Time: Cease-Fire Arrangements and the Durability of Peace*. Princeton: Princeton University Press.

———. (2008) *Does Peacekeeping Work? Shaping Belligerents Choices After Civil War*. Princeton: Princeton University Press.

Foster, Timon, Alexander Kentikelenis, Bernhard Reinsberg, Thomas Stubbs, and Lawrence King. (2019) "How Structural Adjustment Programs Affect Inequality: A Disaggregated Analysis of IMF Conditionality, 1980–2014." *Social Science Research* 80 (May): 83–113.

Fountain, Henry. (2015) "Researchers Link Syrian Conflict to a Drought Made Worse by Climate Change." *New York Times* (March 2).

Franck, Thomas M. (1990) *The Power of Legitimacy Among Nations*. New York: Oxford University Press.

Freedman, Rosa. (2013) *The United Nations Human Rights Council: A Critique and Early Assessment*. New York: Routledge.

Freedman, Rosa and Ruth Houghton. (2017) "Two Steps Forward, One Step Back: Politicisation of the Human Rights Council." *Human Rights Law Review* 17:4 (December): 753–769.

French, Howard W. (2014) *China's Second Continent: How a Million Migrants Are Building a New Empire in Africa*. New York: Random House.

Friedman, Elisabeth Jay, Kathryn Hochstetler, and Ann Marie Clark. (2005) *Sovereignty, Democracy, and Global Civil Society: State-Society Relations at UN World Conferences*. Albany: SUNY Press.

Frieze, Donna-Lee. (2013) *Totally Unofficial: The Autobiography of Raphael Lemkin*. New Haven: Yale University Press.

Fröhlich, Manuel. (2013) "The Special Representatives of the UN Secretary-General." In *Routledge Handbook of International Organizations*, edited by Bob Reinalda. New York: Routledge, pp. 231–243.

———. (2014) "The John Holmes Memorial Lecture: Representing the United Nations—Individual Actors, International Agency, and Leadership." *Global Governance* 20:2 (April–June): 169–193.

Gadinis, Stavros. (2015) "Three Pathways to Global Standards: Private, Regulator, and Ministry." *American Journal of International Law* 109:1 (January): 1–57.

Gambill, Gary C. (2020) "The End of the Arab-Israeli Conflict." *Middle East Forum* (September 6). www.meforum.org/61485/the-end-of-the-arab-israeli-conflict.

Gardner, Kathryn L. (2007) "Task Force and International Efforts to Capture Terrorist Finances." In *Uniting Against Terror: Cooperative Nonmilitary Responses to the Global Terrorist Threat*, edited by David Cortright and George A. Lopez. Cambridge: MIT Press, pp. 157–186.

Garrett, Laurie. (2015) "Ebola's Lessons." *Foreign Affairs* 94:5 (September/October): 97.

Gebrekidan, Selam, and Matt Apuzzo. (2021) "W.H.O. Panel Cites a Chain of Global Failures." *New York Times* (January 20).

Ghébali, Victor-Yves. (2005) "The OSCE Between Crisis and Reform: Towards a New Lease on Life." Policy Paper no. 10. Geneva: Centre for the Democratic Control of Armed Forces.

Gilder, Alexander. (2023) "How Useful Are the UN's Broad Protection of Civilian Mandates?" *IPI Global Observatory* (January 18). https://theglobalobservatory.org/2023/01/how-useful-are-the-uns-broad-protection-of-civilian-mandates/.

Gill, Stephen. (1994) "Structural Change and Global Political Economy: Globalizing Elites and the Emerging World Order." In *Global Transformation: Challenges to the State System*, edited by Yoshikazu Sakamoto. Tokyo: UN University Press.

Gilpin, Robert. (1987) *The Political Economy of International Relations*. Princeton: Princeton University Press.

———. (2001) *Global Political Economy: Understanding the International Economic Order*. Princeton: Princeton University Press.

Ginsberg, Roy H. (2007) *Demystifying the European Union: The Enduring Logic of Regional Integration.* Lanham: Rowman and Littlefield.

Giumelli, Francesco. (2016) "The Purposes of Targeted Sanctions." In *Targeted Sanctions: The Impacts and Effectiveness of United Nations Action*, edited by Thomas J. Biersteker, Sue E. Eckert and Maria Tourinho. New York: Cambridge University Press, pp. 38–59.

Glennon, Michael J. (2003) "Why the Security Council Failed." *Foreign Affairs* 82:3 (May–June): 16–35.

Global Fund. (2022) "Malaria." www.theglobalfund.org/en/malaria/.

GLOBSEC Policy Institute. (2019) "Policy Paper: The Bumpy Road Towards the EU's Common Foreign Policy." GLOBSEC Policy Institute. https://www.globsec .org/what-we-do/publications/bumpy-road-towards-eus-common-foreign-policy.

Goldman, Robert K. (2009) "The Inter-American Human Rights System and the Role of the Inter-American Commission on Human Rights." *Human Rights Quarterly* 31:4 (November): 856–887.

Gourevitch, Peter, and David Lake. (2012) "Beyond Virtue: Evaluating and Enhancing Credibility of Non-Governmental Organizations." In *The Credibility of Transnational NGOs: When Virtue Is Not Enough*, edited by Peter A. Gourevitch and David A. Lake. New York: Cambridge University Press, pp. 3–34.

Gourevitch, Philip. (1998) *We Wish to Inform You That Tomorrow We Will Be Killed with Our Families: Stories from Rwanda.* New York: Farrar, Straus, and Giroux.

Gowan, Richard. (2011) "Multilateral Political Missions and Preventive Diplomacy." Special Report no. 299. Washington, DC: US Institute of Peace.

Grant, Ruth W., and Robert O. Keohane. (2005) "Accountability and Abuses of Power in World Politics." *American Political Science Review* 99:1 (February): 29–43.

Gray, Julia. (2018) "Life, Death, or Zombie? The Vitality of International Organizations." *International Studies Quarterly* 62:1 (March): 1–13.

Gregoratti, Catia. (2014) "UN-Business Partnerships." In *International Organization and Global Governance*, edited by Thomas G. Weiss and Rorden Wilkinson. New York: Routledge, pp. 309–321.

Grigorescu, Alexandru. (2005) "Mapping the UN–League of Nations Analogy: Are There Still Lessons to Be Learned from the League?" *Global Governance* 11:1 (January–March): 25–42.

———. (2007) "Transparency of Intergovernmental Organizations: The Roles of Member States, International Bureaucracies, and Nongovernmental Organizations." *International Studies Quarterly* 51:3 (September): 625–648.

———. (2010) "The Spread of Bureaucratic Oversight Mechanisms Across Intergovernmental Organizations." *International Studies Quarterly* 54:3 (September): 871–886.

Gruber, Lloyd. (2000) *Ruling the World: Power Politics and the Rise of Supranational Institutions.* Princeton: Princeton University Press.

Gstöhl, Sieglinde. (2007) "Governance Through Government Networks: The G8 and International Organizations." *Review of International Organizations* 2:1 (January): 1–37.

Gutner, Tamar. (2010) "When 'Doing Good' Does Not: The IMF and the Millennium Development Goals." In *Who Governs the Globe?* edited by Deborah D. Avant, Martha Finnemore, and Susan K. Sell. New York: Cambridge University Press, pp. 266–291.

Gutta, Nikhil. (2012) "Accountability in the Generation of Governance Indicators." In *Governance by Indicators: Global Power through Classification and Rankings*, edited by Kevin David, Angelina Fisher, Benedict Kingsbury, and Sally Engle Merry. New York: Oxford University Press, pp. 437–464.

Haack, Kirsten. (2014) "Breaking Barriers? Women's Representation and Leadership at the United Nations." *Global Governance* 20:1 (January–March): 37–54.

Haack, Kirsten, Margaret P. Karns, and Jean-Pierre Murray. (2022) "From Aspiration to Commitment: The UN's 'Long March' Toward Gender Equality." *Global Governance* 28:3 (July–September): 155–179.

———. (2023) "Where Are the Women Leaders in International Organizations and What Difference Do They Make?" In *Handbook on Governance in International Organizations*, edited by Alistair Edgar. Cheltenham: Edward Elgar.

Haack, Kirsten, and Kent J. Kille. (2012) "The UN Secretary-General and Self-Directed Leadership: Development of the Democracy Agenda." In *International Organizations as Self-Directed Actors: A Framework for Analysis*, edited by Joel B. Oestreich. New York: Routledge, pp. 29–59.

Haas, Ernst B. (1964) *Beyond the Nation-State: Functionalism and International Organization.* Stanford: Stanford University Press.

———. (1990) *When Knowledge Is Power: Three Models of Change in International Organizations.* Berkeley: University of California Press.

Haas, Peter M. (1990) *Saving the Mediterranean: The Politics of International Environmental Cooperation.* New York: Columbia University Press.

———. (1992) "Introduction: Epistemic Communities and International Policy Coordination." *International Organization* 46:1 (Winter): 1–35.

———. (2002) "UN Conferences and Constructivist Governance of the Environment." *Global Governance* 8:1 (January–March): 73–91.

Hadden, Jennifer. (2015) *Networks in Contention: The Divisive Politics of Climate Change.* New York: Cambridge University Press.

Hafner-Burton, Emilie. (2008) "Sticks and Stones: Naming and Shaming the Human Rights Enforcement Problem." *International Organization* 62:4 (Fall): 689–716.

Hafner-Burton, Emilie, and Kiyoteru Tsutsui. (2005) "Human Rights in a Globalized World: The Paradox of Empty Promises." *American Journal of Sociology* 110:5 (March): 1373–1411.

Haglund, Jillianne and Ryan M. Welch. (2021) "From Litigation to Rights: The Case of the European Court of Human Rights." *International Studies Quarterly* 65:1 (March): 210–222.

Hall, Brian. (1994) "Blue Helmets." *New York Times Magazine* (January 2): 22.

Hama, Hawre Hasan. (2017). "State Security, Societal Security, and Human Security." *Jadavpur Journal of International Relations* 21:1: 1–19.

Hampson, Fen Osler, with Michael Hart. (1995) *Multilateral Negotiations: Lessons from Arms Control, Trade, and the Environment.* Baltimore: Johns Hopkins University Press.

Hanchey, Jenna N. (2018) "Reworking Resistance: A Postcolonial Perspective on International NGOs." In *Transformative Practice and Research in Organizational Communication*, edited by Philip J. Salem and Erik Timmerman. Hershey, PA: IGI Global, pp. 274–291.

Hansen, Hans Krause and Tony Porter. (2017) "What Do Big Data Do in Global Governance?" *Global Governance* 23:2 (January–March): 31–42.

Hansler, Jennifer and Richard Roth. (2020) "UN Security Council Rejects US Proposal to Extend Iran Arms Embargo." *CNN Politics* (August 14).

Harb, Imad K. (2020) "The Arab League and the Libya Crisis." Arab Center (October 8). https://arabcenterdc.org/resource/the-arab-leagues-many-failures/.

Hardin, Garrett. (1968) "The Tragedy of the Commons." *Science* 162 (December 13): 1243–1248.

Hardt, Heidi. (2013) "Keep Friends Close, but Colleagues Closer: Efficiency in the Establishment of Peace Operations." *Global Governance* 19:3 (July–September): 377–399.

Harlan, Chico, and Michael Birnbaum. (2020) "Nobel Peace Prize Goes to World Food Program for Efforts to Combat Hunger." *Washington Post* (October 9).

Harman, Sophie. (2020) "COVID-19, the UN, and Dispersed Global Health Security." *Ethics & International Affairs* 34:3 (Fall): 373–378.

Hasenclever, Andreas, Peter Mayer, and Volker Rittberger. (2000) "Integrating Theories of International Regimes." *Review of International Studies* 26: 3–33.

Hawkins, Darren G., David A. Lake, Daniel L. Nielson, and Michael J. Tierney, eds. (2006) *Delegation and Agency in International Organizations*. Cambridge: Cambridge University Press.

Hawkins, Peter. (1997) "Organizational Culture: Sailing Between Evangelism and Complexity." *Human Relations* 50:4: 417–440.

Hehir, Aidan. (2019) *Hollow Norms and the Responsibility to Protect*. London: Palgrave Macmillan.

Heine, Jorge. (2013) "From Club to Network Diplomacy." In *The Oxford Handbook of Modern Diplomacy*, edited by Andrew F. Cooper, Jorge Heine, and Ramesh Thakur. Oxford: Oxford University Press, pp. 54–69.

Heins, Volker. (2008) *Nongovernmental Organizations in International Society: Struggles over Recognition*. New York: Palgrave Macmillan.

Heiss, Andrew, and Tana Johnson. (2016) "Internal, Interactive, and Institutional Factors: A Unified Framework for Understanding International Nongovernmental Organizations." *International Studies Review* 18:3 (September): 528–541.

Heiss, Andrew, and Judith Kelley. (2017) "Between a Rock and a Hard Place: International NGOs and the Dual Pressures of Donors and Host Governments." *Journal of Politics* 79:2 (April): 732–741.

Held, David. (2004) *Global Covenant: The Social Democratic Alternative to the Washington Consensus*. Cambridge: Polity.

Helleiner, Eric. (2014) "Southern Pioneers of International Development." *Global Governance* 20:3 (July–September): 375–388.

Hellquist, E. (2021) "Regional Sanctions as Peer Review: The African Union Against Egypt (2013) and Sudan (2019)." *International Political Science Review* 42:4: 451–468.

Hemmer, Christopher, and Peter J. Katzenstein. (2002) "Why Is There No NATO in Asia? Collective Identity, Regionalism, and the Origins of Multilateralism." *International Organization* 56:3 (Summer): 575–607.

Henkin, Louis. (1979) *How Nations Behave: Law and Foreign Policy*. 2nd ed. New York: Columbia University Press.

———. (1998) "The Universal Declaration and the US Constitution." *PS: Political Science and Politics* 31:3 (September): 512.

Henning, Randall. (2017) *Tangled Governance: International Regime Complexity, the Troika, and the Euro Crisis*. Oxford: Oxford University Press.

Hewitt, J. Joseph. (2008) "Trends in Global Conflict, 1946–2005." In *Peace and Conflict 2008*, edited by J. Joseph Hewitt, Jonathan Wilkenfeld, and Ted Robert Gurr. Boulder: Paradigm, pp. 21–26.

Heyns, Christof and Frans Viljoen. (2020) "What Difference Does the UN Human Rights Treaty System Make and Why?" (February). https://www.openglobalrights .org/what-difference-does-un-human-rights-treaty-system-make/.

Hill, Daniel W., Jr., Will H. Moore, and Bumba Mukherjee. (2013) "Information Politics Versus Organizational Incentives: When Are Amnesty International's 'Naming and Shaming' Reports Biased?" *International Studies Quarterly* 57:2 (June): 219–232.

Hinchberger, Bill. (2011) "Millennium Development Villages: A Lasting Impact?" *Africa Renewal* (December): 6–8.

Hirst, Monica. (1999) "Mercosur's Complex Political Agenda." In *Mercosur: Regional Integration, World Markets*, edited by Riordan Roett. Boulder: Lynne Rienner, pp. 35–48.

Hochchild, Adam. (2005) *Bury the Chains: Prophets and Rebels in the Fight to Free an Empire's Slaves*. Boston: Houghton Mifflin.

Holsti, Kalevi. (2004) *Taming the Sovereigns: Institutional Change in International Politics*. New York: Cambridge University Press.

Hopewell, Kristen. (2021) "When the Hegemon Goes Rogue: Leadership amid the US Assault on the Liberal Trading Order." *International Affairs* 97:4 (July): 1025–1043.

Hopgood, Stephen. (2006) *Keepers of the Flame: Understanding Amnesty International*. Ithaca: Cornell University Press.

———. (2013) *The Endtimes of Human Rights*. Ithaca: Cornell University Press.

Hopgood, Stephen, Jack Snyder, and Leslie Vinjamari, eds. (2017) *Human Rights Futures*. New York: Cambridge University Press.

Hossain, Ishtiaq. (2012) "The Organization of Islamic Conference (OIC): Nature, Role, and the Issues." *Journal of Third World Studies* 29:1: 287–314.

Howard, Lise Morjé. (2008) *UN Peacekeeping in Civil Wars*. New York: Cambridge University Press.

———. (2019) *Power in Peacekeeping*. New York: Cambridge University Press.

Howard-Hassmann, Rhoda E. (2018) *In Defense of Universal Human Rights*. New York: Wiley.

Howarth, Jolyon. (2020) "The CSDP in Transition: Towards 'Strategic Autonomy'?" In *Governance and Politics in the Post-Crisis European Union*, edited by Ramona Coman, Amandine Crespy, and Vivien A. Schmidt. New York: Cambridge University Press, pp. 312–330.

Htun, Mala, and S. Laurel Weldon. (2012) "The Civic Origins of Progressive Policy Change: Combating Violence Against Women in Global Perspective, 1975–2005." *American Political Science Review* 106:3 (August): 548–569.

———. (2020) *The Logics of Gender Justice: State Action on Women's Rights Around the World*. New York: Cambridge University Press.

Hudson, Natalie Florea. (2009) *Gender, Human Security, and the UN: Security Language as a Political Framework*. New York: Routledge.

Hufbauer, Gary Clyde, Jeffrey J. Schott, Kimberly Ann Elliott, and Barbara Oegg. (2007) *Economic Sanctions Reconsidered*. 3rd ed. Washington, DC: Peterson Institute for International Economics.

Hug, Simon. (2012) "What's in a Vote?" Paper prepared for presentation at the annual meeting of the American Political Science Association, New Orleans (August 30–September 2). www.un.org/Depts/dhl/resguide/gavote.htm.

Hug, Simon, and Richard Lukacs. (2014) "Preferences or Blocs? Voting in the United Nations Human Rights Council." *Review of International Organizations* 9:1 (March): 83–106.

Hughell, D., and R. Butterfield. (2008) "Impact of FSC Certification on Deforestation and the Incidence of Wildfires in the Maya Biosphere Reserve." Rainforest Alliance. www.rainforest-alliance.org/forestry/documents/peten_study.pdf.

Human Rights Watch. (2022a) "Ethiopia: Events of 2022." *World Report 2022*. https://www.hrw.org/world-report/2022/country-chapters/ethiopia.

———. (2022b) "UN Security Council: Historic Censure of Myanmar Junta." (December 21). https://www.hrw.org/news/2022/12/21/un-security-council-historic-censure-myanmar-junta.

Humphrey, Chris. (2023) *Multilateral Development Banks in a Fast-Changing World: From Bretton Woods to the BRICS*. New York, Oxford University Press.

Hurd, Ian. (2002) "Legitimacy, Power, and the Symbolic Life of the UN Security Council." *Global Governance* 8:1 (January–March): 35–51.

———. (2007) *After Anarchy: Legitimacy and Power in the United Nations Security Council*. Princeton: Princeton University Press.

———. (2008a) "Myths of Membership: The Politics of Legitimation in UN Security Council Reform." *Global Governance* 14:2 (April–June): 199–217.

———. (2008b) "Theories and Tests of International Authority." In *The UN Security Council and the Politics of International Authority*, edited by Bruce Cronin and Ian Hurd. New York: Routledge, pp. 23–39.

Hurrell, Andrew. (1995) "Regionalism in the Americas." In *Regionalism in World Politics: Regional Organization and International Order*, edited by Louise Fawcett and Andrew Hurrell. New York: Oxford University Press, pp. 250–282.

———. (2007) "One World? Many Worlds? The Place of Regions in the Study of International Society." *International Affairs* 83:1: 127–146.

Ikenberry, G. John. (2001) *After Victory: Institutions, Strategic Restraint, and the Rebuilding of Order after Major Wars*. Princeton: Princeton University Press.

Inboden, Rana Siu. (2021) "China at the UN: Choking Civil Society." *Journal of Democracy* 32:3 (July): 124–135.

Institute for Economics & Peace. (2023) *Global Terrorism Index 2023: Measuring the Impact of Terrorism*. Institute for Economics & Peace. https://www.economics andpeace.org/wp-content/uploads/2023/03/GTI-2023-web-170423.pdf.

Inter-American Commission on Human Rights. (2023) "Cases in the Court." https://www.oas.org/en/iachr/decisions/pc/cases.asp.

Inter-American Court of Human Rights. (2021) *2021 Annual Report*. https://www.oas.org/en/iachr/decisions/pc/cases.asp.

International Commission on Intervention and State Sovereignty (ICISS). (2001) *The Responsibility to Protect: Report of the International Commission on Intervention and State Sovereignty*. Ottawa: International Development Research Centre for ICISS.

International Court of Justice (ICJ), Advisory Opinions. (1949) "Reparation for Injuries Suffered in the Service of the United Nations." *ICJ Reports*, 174.

———. (1951) "Reservations to the Convention on the Prevention and Punishment of the Crime of Genocide." *ICJ Reports*, 15.

———. (1962) "Certain Expenses of the United Nations." *ICJ Reports*, 168.

———. (1971) "Legal Consequences for States of the Continued Presence of South Africa in Namibia." *ICJ Reports*, 144.

———. (1975) "Western Sahara (*Spain v. Morocco*)." *ICJ Reports*, 12.

———. (1999) "Difference Relating to Immunity from Legal Process of a Special Rapporteur of the Commission on Human Rights." *ICJ Reports*, 62.

———. (2004) "Legal Consequences Arising from the Construction of a Wall in the Occupied Palestinian Territories." *ICJ Reports*, 136.

———. (2010) "Accordance with International Law of the Unilateral Declaration of Independence in Respect of Kosovo." *ICJ Reports*, 403.

International Court of Justice (ICJ), Contentious Cases. (1969) North Sea Continental Shelf cases (*Federal Republic of Germany v. Denmark; Federal Republic of Germany v. Netherlands*). *ICJ Reports*, 3.

———. (1974) Nuclear-test cases (*New Zealand v. France*). *ICJ Reports*, 253.

———. (1980) Case concerning US diplomatic and consular staff in Tehran (*United States of America v. Iran*). *ICJ Reports*, 3.

————. (1984a) Case concerning Gulf of Maine area (*Canada v. United States of America*). *ICJ Reports*, 246.

————. (1984b) Case concerning military and paramilitary activities in and against Nicaragua (*Nicaragua v. United States*). *ICJ Reports*, 292.

————. (1986) Case concerning military and paramilitary activities in and against Nicaragua (*Nicaragua v. United States*). *ICJ Reports*, 14.

————. (1992) Questions of interpretation and application of the 1971 Montreal Convention arising from the aerial incident at Lockerbie (*Libyan Arab Jamahiriya v. United Kingdom*). *ICJ Reports*, 3.

————. (1997) Case concerning Gabcikovo-Nagymaros project (*Hungary v. Slovakia*). *ICJ Reports*, 1.

————. (2002) Case concerning land and maritime boundary between Cameroon and Nigeria (*Cameroon v. Nigeria*). *ICJ Reports*, 303.

————. (2007) Case concerning application of Convention on the Prevention and Punishment of the Crime of Genocide (*Bosnia and Herzegovina v. Serbia and Montenegro*). *ICJ Reports*, 43.

————. (2008) Application of Republic of Ecuador: Case concerning aerial herbicide spraying (*Ecuador v. Colombia*). *ICJ Reports*, 174.

————. (2014) Case concerning whaling in the Antarctic (*Australia v. Japan: New Zealand Intervening*). www.icj-cij.rg/docket/files/148/18136.pdf.

————. (2015) Application of the Convention on the Prevention and Punishment of the Crime of Genocide (*Croatia v. Serbia*). www.icj-cij.org/docket/files/118/18422.pdf.

International Criminal Court (ICC) Assembly of States Parties to the Rome Statute. (2020) "Review of the International Criminal Court and the Rome Statute System. (September 30). https://asp.icc-cpi.int/Review-Court.

International Lesbian, Gay, Bisexual, Trans, and Intersex Association (ILGA). (2013) "ECOSOC: LGBT Voices at the United Nations/ECOSOC Council Vote Grants Consultative Status to ILGA." ILGA. http://ilga.org/ilga/en/article/n5Geb HB1PY.

————. (2020) "State-Sponsored Homophobia Report 2020. https://ilga.org/state-sponsored-homophobia-report.

Ivanova, Maria. (2010) "UNEP in Global Environmental Governance: Design, Leadership, and Location." *Global Environmental Politics* 10:1 (February): 30–59.

————. (2013) "The Contested Legacy of Rio + 20." *Global Environmental Politics* 13:4 (November): 1–11.

————. (2021) *The Untold Story of the World's Leading Environmental Institution: UNEP at Fifty*. Cambridge: MIT Press.

Jackson, Nicole. (2006) "International Organizations, Security Dichotomies, and the Trafficking of Persons and Narcotics in Post-Soviet Central Asia: A Critique of the Securitization Framework." *Security Dialogue* 38 (September): 299–317.

Jacobson, Harold K. (1984) *Networks of Interdependence: International Organizations and the Global Political System*. 2nd ed. New York: Knopf.

Jacobson, Harold K., William M. Reisinger, and Todd Mathers. (1986) "National Entanglements in International Governmental Organizations." *American Political Science Review* 80:1 (March): 141–160.

Jahshan, Khalil E. (2020) "The Demise of the Arab League: A Sense of Déjà Vu." Arab Center (October 8). https://arabcenterdc.org/resource/the-arab-leagues-many-failures/.

Jain, Devaki. (2005) *Women, Development, and the UN: A Sixty-Year Quest for Equality and Justice*. Bloomington: Indiana University Press.

Jaknanihan, Arrizal. (2022) "Stiffening the ASEAN Spine in the South China Sea." *The Interpreter* (25 March). www.lowyinstitute.org/the-interpreter/stiffening -asean-spine-south-china-sea.

Jentleson, Bruce W.. (2012) "The John Holmes Memorial Lecture: Global Governance in a Copernican World." *Global Governance* 18:2 (April–June): 133–148.

Jerven, Morten. (2021) *The Wealth and Poverty of African States: Economic Growth, Living Standards, and Taxation since the Late Nineteenth Century.* New York: Cambridge University Press.

Jetschke, Anja and Patrick Theiner. (2020) "Time to Move On? Why the Discussion about ASEAN's Relevance Is Outdated." *Pacific Review* 33:3–4: 593–603.

Johnson, Tana.. (2014) *Organizational Progeny: Why Governments Are Losing Control over the Proliferating Structures of Global Governance.* New York: Oxford University Press.

———. (2015) "Information Revelation and Structural Supremacy: The World Trade Organization's Incorporation of Environmental Policy." *Review of International Organizations* 10:2 (June): 207–229.

———. (2016) "Cooperation, Co-optation, Competition, Conflict: International Bureaucracies and Non-governmental Organizations in an Interdependent World." *Review of International Political Economy* 23:5 (October): 737–767.

———. (2020) "Ordinary Patterns in an Extraordinary Crisis: How International Relations Makes Sense of the COVID-19 Pandemic." *International Organization* 74:1 (Spring): 1–21.

———. (forthcoming) "Formal International Institutions." In *The Oxford Handbook of International Institutions*, edited by Michael Barnett and Duncan Snidal. New York: Oxford University Press.

Johnson, Tana, and Andrew Heiss. (2022) "Liberal Institutionalism." In *International Organization and Global Governance*, edited by Thomas Weiss and Rorden Wilkinson. 3rd ed. New York: Routledge, pp. 120–132.

Johnson, Tana, and Joshua Lerner. (2023) "Environmentalism among Poor and Rich Countries: Using Natural Language Processing to Handle Perfunctory Support and Rising Powers." *Review of International Political Economy* 30:1 (February): 1–26.

Johnson, Tana, and Johannes Urpelainen. (2012) "A Strategic Theory of Regime Integration and Separation." *International Organization* 66:4 (October): 645–677.

———. (2020) "The More Things Change, the More They Stay the Same? Developing Countries' Unity at the Nexus of Trade and Environmental Policy." *Review of International Organizations* 15:2 (April): 445–473.

Johnston, Alastair Ian. (2003) "Socialization in International Institutions: The ASEAN Way and International Relations Theory." In *International Relations Theory and the Asia-Pacific*, edited by G. John Ikenberry and Michael Mastunduno. New York: Columbia University Press, pp. 107–162.

Johnston, Douglas. (1997) *Consent and Commitment in the World Community.* Irvington-on-Hudson: Transnational.

Johnstone, Ian. (2007) "The Secretary-General as Norm Entrepreneur." In *Secretary or General? The UN Secretary-General in World Politics*, edited by Simon Chesterman. Cambridge: Cambridge University Press, pp. 123–138.

———. (2008) "The Security Council as Legislature." In *The UN Security Council and the Politics of International Authority*, edited by Bruce Cronin and Ian Hurd. New York: Routledge, pp. 80–104.

———. (2011) "Managing Consent in Contemporary Peacekeeping Operations." *International Peacekeeping* 18:2: 168–182.

Jolly, Richard, Louis Emmerij, Dharam Ghai, and Frédéric Lapeyne. (2004) *UN Contributions to Developing Thinking and Practice.* Bloomington: Indiana University Press.

Jolly, Richard, Louis Emmerij, and Thomas G. Weiss. (2005) *The Power of UN Ideas: Lessons from the First 60 Years.* New York: United Nations Intellectual History Project, p. 34.

―――. (2009) *UN Ideas That Changed the World.* Bloomington: Indiana University Press.

Jonah, James O. C. (2007) "Secretariat Independence and Reform." In *The Oxford Handbook on the United Nations,* edited by Thomas G. Weiss and Sam Daws. Oxford: Oxford University Press, pp. 160–174.

Jones, David Martin, and Michael L. R. Smith. (2007) "Making Process, Not Progress: ASEAN and the Evolving East Asian Regional Order." *International Security* 32:1 (Summer): 148–184.

Jönsson, Christer. (1986) "Interorganization Theory and International Organization." *International Studies Quarterly* 30:1: 39–57.

―――. (2013) "International Organizations at the Moving Public-Private Borderline." *Global Governance* 19:1 (January–March): 1–18.

Joseph, Sarah and Eleanor Jenkin. (2019) "The United Nations Human Rights Council: Is the United States Right to Leave This Club?" *American University International Law Review* 35:1: 75–132.

Jurkovich, Michelle. (2020) *Feeding the Hungry: Advocacy and Blame in the Global Fight Against Hunger.* Ithaca: Cornell University Press.

Kaasa, Stine Madland. (2007) "The UN Commission on Sustainable Development: Which Mechanisms Explain Its Accomplishments?" *Global Environmental Politics* 7:3 (August): 107–129.

Kahler, Miles. (2009) "Networked Politics: Agency, Power, and Governance." In *Networked Politics: Agency, Power, and Governance,* edited by Miles Kahler. Ithaca: Cornell University Press, pp. 1–22.

Kaldor, Mary. (2003) "The Idea of Global Civil Society." *International Affairs* 79:3 (May): 583–593.

Kamau, Macharia, Pamela Chasek, and David O'Connor. (2018) *Transforming Multilateral Diplomacy: The Inside Story of the Sustainable Development Goals.* New York: Routledge.

Karlsrud, John. (2015) "The UN at War: Examining the Consequences of Peace-Enforcement Mandates for the UN Peace-Keeping Operations in the CAR, the DRC, and Mali." *Third World Quarterly* 36:1: 40–54.

Karns, Margaret P. (1987) "Ad Hoc Multilateral Diplomacy: The United States, the Contact Group, and Namibia." *International Organization* 41:1 (Winter): 93–123.

―――. (2009) "The Challenges of Maintaining Peace and Security in the 21st Century: The United Nations and Regional Organizations." In *The United Nations: Past, Present, and Future—Proceedings of the 2007 Francis Marion University UN Symposium,* edited by Scott Kaufman and Alissa Warters. New York: Nova Science, pp. 115–146.

―――. (2012) "The Roots of UN Post-Conflict Peacebuilding." In *International Organizations as Self-Directed Actors,* edited by Joel E. Oestreich. New York: Routledge, pp. 60–88.

Karns, Margaret P., and Karen A. Mingst. (2002) "The United States as 'Deadbeat'? US Policy and the UN Financial Crisis." In *Multilateralism and US Foreign Policy: Ambivalent Engagement,* edited by Stewart Patrick and Shepard Forman. Boulder: Lynne Rienner, pp. 267–294.

Katzenstein, Peter J. (2005) *A World of Regions: Asia and Europe in the American Imperium*. Ithaca: Cornell University Press.

Kaul, Inge. (2000) "Governing Global Public Goods in a Multi-Actor World: The Role of the United Nations." In *New Millennium, New Perspectives: The United Nations, Security, and Governance*, edited by Ramesh Thakur and Edward Newman. Tokyo: UN University Press, pp. 296–315.

Keck, Margaret E., and Kathryn Sikkink. (1998) *Activists Beyond Borders: Advocacy Networks in International Politics*. Ithaca: Cornell University Press.

Kelley, Judith. (2008) "Assessing the Complex Evolution of Norms: The Rise of International Election Monitoring." *International Organization* 62:2 (Spring): 221–255.

Kennedy, Scott. (2020) "The Biggest But Not the Strongest: China's Place in the Fortune 500 Global." https://www.csis.org.

Kent, Ann. (1999) *China, the United Nations, and Human Rights: The Limits of Compliance*. Philadelphia: University of Pennsylvania Press.

Keohane, Robert O. (1984) *After Hegemony: Cooperation and Discord in the World Political Economy*. Princeton: Princeton University Press.

———. (1993) "Institutional Theory and the Realist Challenge After the Cold War." In *Neorealism and Neoliberalism: The Contemporary Debate*, edited by David A. Baldwin. New York: Columbia University Press, pp. 269–300.

Keohane, Robert O., and Lisa L. Martin. (1995) "The Promise of Institutionalist Theory." *International Security* 20:1 (Summer): 39–51.

Keohane, Robert O., and Joseph S. Nye Jr. (1971) *Transnational Relations and World Politics*. Cambridge: Harvard University Press.

———. (1977) *Power and Interdependence: World Politics in Transition*. Boston: Little, Brown.

Keohane, Robert O., and David G. Victor. (2011) "The Regime Complex for Climate Change." *Perspectives on Politics* 9:1: 7–23.

Khagram, Sanjeev. (2000) "Toward Democratic Governance for Sustainable Development: Transnational Civil Society Organizing Around Big Dams." In *The Third Force: The Rise of Transnational Civil Society*, edited by Ann M. Florini. Tokyo: Japan Center for International Exchange, pp. 83–114.

Kille, Kent J. (2006) *From Manager to Visionary: The Secretary-General of the United Nations*. New York: Palgrave Macmillan.

Kim, Dongwook. (2013) "International Nongovernmental Organizations and the Global Diffusion of National Human Rights Institutions." *International Organization* 67:3 (Summer): 505–539.

Kim, Young Mie, Jordan Hsu, David Neiman, Colin Kou, Levi Bankston, Soo Yun Kim, Richard Heinrich, Robyn Baragwanath, and Garvesh Raskutti. (2018) "The Stealth Media? Groups and Targets behind Divisive Issue Campaigns on Facebook." *Political Communication* 35:4: 515–541.

Kindleberger, Charles P. (1973) *The World in Depression, 1929–39*. Berkeley: University of California Press.

———. (1986) "International Public Goods Without International Government." *American Economic Review* 76:1 (March): 1–13.

Klotz, Audie. (1995) *Norms in International Relations: The Struggle Against Apartheid*. Ithaca: Cornell University Press.

Koops, Joachim A., Norrie MacQueen, Thierry Tardy, and Paul D. Williams, eds. (2015) *The Oxford Handbook of UN Peacekeeping Operations*. New York: Oxford University Press.

Koga, Kei. (2018) "ASEAN's Evolving Institutional Strategy: Managing Great Power Politics in the South China Sea Disputes." *Chinese Journal of International Politics* 11:1 (January): 1–32.

Koremenos, Barbara, Charles Lipson, and Duncan Snidal. (2001) "The Rational Design of International Institutions." *International Organization* 55 (Autumn): 761–799.

Koser, Khalid. "Internally Displaced Persons," in *Global Migration Governance,* edited by Alexander Betts. Oxford: Oxford University Press, pp. 210–22.

Krasner, Stephen D. (1982) "Structural Causes and Regime Consequences: Regimes as Intervening Variables." In *International Regimes,* edited by Stephen D. Krasner. Ithaca: Cornell University Press, pp. 1–21.

———. (1993) "Westphalia and All That." In *Ideas and Foreign Policy,* edited by Judith Goldstein and Robert O. Keohane. Ithaca: Cornell University Press, pp. 235–264.

Krause, Keith, 2004. "The Key to a Powerful Agenda, If Properly Defined." Special Section: What Is "Human Security"? edited by J. Peter Burgess and Taylor Owen. *Security Dialogue* 35:3: 367–368.

Kreps, Sarah. (2020) *Social Media and International Relations.* New York: Cambridge University Press.

Kristoff, Madeline, and Liz Panarelli. (2010) "Haiti: A Republic of NGOs?" Peace Brief no. 23 (April 26). Washington, DC: US Institute of Peace. https://www.usip.org/sites/default/files/PB%2023%20Haiti%20a%20Republic%20of%20NGOs.pdf.

Ku, Charlotte, and Paul F. Diehl. (2006) "Filling in the Gaps: Extrasystemic Mechanisms for Addressing Imbalances Between the International Legal Operating System and the Normative System." *Global Governance* 12:2 (April–June): 161–183.

Kulish, Nicholas, and Somini Sengupta. (2013) "New U.N.'s Brigade's Aggressive Stance in Africa Brings Success, and Risks." *New York Times* (November 13).

Kumar, Shashank P. (2013) "The Indus Waters Kishenganga Arbitration (*Pakistan v. India*)." *American Society of International Law Insights* 17:13 (May 13).

Kuperman, Alan J. (2001) *The Limits of Humanitarian Intervention: Genocide in Rwanda.* Washington, DC: Brookings Institution.

Kurlantzick, Joshua. (2022) "ASEAN's Complete Failure on Myanmar: A Short Overview." Council on Foreign Relations (August 29). www.cfr.org/blog/aseans-complete-failure-myanmar-short-overview.

Laatikainen, Katie Verlin. (2006) "Pushing Soft Power: Middle Power Diplomacy at the UN." In *The European Union at the United Nations: Intersecting Multilateralisms,* edited by Katie Verlin Laatikainen and Karen E. Smith. New York: Palgrave Macmillan, pp. 70–91.

Lake, David A., and Matthew D. McCubbins. (2006) "The Logic of Delegation to International Organizations." In *Delegation and Agency in International Organizations,* edited by Darren Hawkins et al. Cambridge: Cambridge University Press, pp. 341–368.

Lall, Ranjit. (2023) *Making International Institutions Work: The Politics of Performance.* New York: Cambridge University Press.

Langlois, Anthony J. (2021) "Human Rights in Southeast Asia: ASEAN's Rights Regime After Its First Decade." *Journal of Human Rights* 20:2: 151–157.

Lasswell, Harold D. (1941) "The Garrison State." *American Journal of Sociology* 46 (January): 455–468.

Lauren, Paul Gordon. (1996) *Power and Prejudice: The Politics and Diplomacy of Racial Discrimination.* 2nd ed. Boulder: Westview.

———. (2003) *The Evolution of International Human Rights: Visions Seen,* 2nd ed. Philadelphia: University of Pennsylvania Press.

Laurenti, Jeffrey. (2007) "Financing." In *The Oxford Handbook on the United Nations*, edited by Thomas G. Weiss and Sam Daws. New York: Oxford University Press, pp. 675–700.

Lawson, Fred. (2012) *Transformations of Regional Economic Governance in the Gulf Cooperation Council*. Qatar: Center for International and Regional Studies, Georgetown University School of Foreign Service in Qatar.

Lebovic, James H., and Eric Voeten. (2006) "The Politics of Shame: The Condemnation of Country Human Rights Practices in the UNHCHR." *International Studies Quarterly* 50:4 (December): 861–888.

Lederer, Edith M. (2022) "UN Chief Warns World is One Step from 'Nuclear Annihilation." *APNews* (August 1).

Legrenzi, Matteo, and Marina Calculli. (2013) "Regionalism and Regionalization in the Middle East: Options and Challenges." New York: International Peace Institute.

Lehne, Stefan. (2022) "Making EU Foreign Policy Fit for a Geopolitical World." Carnegie Europe (April 14). https://carnegieeurope.eu/2022/04/14/making-eu -foreign-policy-fit-for-geopolitical-world-pub-86886.

Levin, Dan. (2014) "Report Implicates Chinese Officials in Smuggled Tanzanian Ivory." *New York Times* (November 6).

Liese, Andrea, and Marianne Beisheim. (2011) "Transnational Public-Private Partnerships and the Provision of Collective Good in Developing Countries." In *Governance Without a State? Policies and Politics in Areas of Limited Statehood*, edited by Thomas Risse. New York: Columbia University Press, pp. 115–143.

Lipson, Charles. (1984) "International Cooperation in Economic and Security Affairs." *World Politics* 37 (October): 1–23.

Loescher, Gil, Alexander Betts, and James Milner. (2008) *The United Nations High Commissioner for Refugees (UNHCR): The Politics and Practice of Refugee Protection Into the Twenty-First Century*. New York: Routledge.

Loescher, Gil, and James Milner. (2011) "UNHCR and the Global Governance of Refugees." In *Global Migration Governance*, edited by Alexander Betts. New York: Oxford University Press, pp. 189–209.

Lowrey, Annie. (2013) "World Bank, Rooted in Bureaucracy, Proposes a Sweeping Reorganization." *New York Times* (October 7).

Luck, Edward C. (2005) "How Not to Reform the United Nations." *Global Governance* 11:4 (October–December): 407–414.

———. (2007) "Principal Organs." In *The Oxford Handbook on the United Nations*, edited by Thomas G. Weiss and Sam Daws. Oxford: Oxford University Press, pp. 653–674.

———. (2016) "The Security Council at Seventy." In *The UN Security Council in the 21st Century*, edited by Sebastian von Einsiedel, David M. Malone, Bruno Stagno Ugarte. Boulder, CO: Lynne Rienner, pp. 195–216.

Lutz, Ellen L., and Kathryn Sikkink. (2000) "International Human Rights Law and Practice in Latin America." *International Organization* 54:3 (Summer): 633–659.

Lynch, Colum. (2014a) "They Just Stood Watching." *Foreign Policy* (April 7).

———. (2014b) "A Mission That Was Set Up to Fail." *Foreign Policy* (April 8).

Macdonald, Terry, and Kate Macdonald. (2022) "NGOs as Agents of Global Justice: Cosmopolitan Activism for Political Realists." *Ethics & International Affairs* 36:3 (October): 305–320.

Mace, Gordon. (1999) "The Origins, Nature, and Scope of the Hemispheric Project," in Gordon Mace, Louis Bélanger, and contributors, *The Americas in Transition: The Contours of Regionalism*. Boulder: Lynne Rienner, pp. 19–36.

Mace, Gordon, Jean-Philippe Thérien, Diana Tussie, and Olivier Dabène, eds. (2016) *Summits and Regional Governance: The Americas in Comparative Perspective.* New York: Routledge.

MacFarlane, S. Neil, and Yuen Foong Khong. (2006) *Human Security and the UN: A Critical History.* Bloomington: Indiana University Press.

MacLean, Ruth. (2022) "Explaining the 6 Coups Over the Past 18 Months in 5 African Countries." *New York Times* (February 1).

Maddy-Weitzman, Bruce. (2012) "The Arab League Comes Alive." *Middle East Quarterly* 19:3 (Summer): 71–78.

Madsen, Frank G. (2014) "Transnational Criminal Networks." In *International Organization and Global Governance*, edited by Thomas G. Weiss and Rorden Wilkinson. New York: Routledge, pp. 397–410.

Makinda, Samuel M., and F. Wafula Okumu. (2008) *The African Union: Challenges of Globalization, Security, and Governance.* New York: Routledge.

Malone, David M. (2006) *The International Struggle over Iraq: Politics in the UN Security Council, 1980–2005.* New York: Oxford University Press.

Mannan, S., K. Kitayama, et al. (2008) "Deramakot Forest Shows Positive Conservation Impacts of RIL." *ITTO Tropical Forest Update* 18:2: 7–9.

Mansfield, Edward D., and Helen V. Milner. (1999) "The New Wave of Regionalism." *International Organization* 53:3 (Summer): 589–627.

Mansfield, Edward D., and Jon C. W. Pevehouse. (2013) "The Expansion of Preferential Trading Arrangements." *International Studies Quarterly* 57:3 (September): 592–604.

Mariano, Karina Pasquariello, Regiane Nitsch Bressan, and Bruno Theodoro Luciano. (2021) "Liquid Regionalism: A Typology for Regionalism in the Americas." *Revista Brasileira de Política Internacional* 64:2: e004.

Mathews, Jessica T. (1997) "Power Shift." *Foreign Affairs* 76:1 (January–February): 50–66.

Mathiason, John. (2007) *Invisible Governance: International Secretariats in Global Politics.* Bloomfield, CT: Kumarian.

May, Christopher. (2018) "Global Corporations." In *International Organization and Global Governance*, edited by Thomas G. Weiss and Rorden Wilkinson. 2nd ed. New York: Routledge.

Mayer, Ann Elizabeth. (2013) *Islam and Human Rights: Tradition and Politics.* 5th ed. Boulder: Westview.

Mazower, Mark. (2012) *Governing the World: The History of an Idea, 1815 to the Present.* New York: Penguin Random House.

McArthur, John. (2014) "Seven Million Lives Saved: Under-5 Mortality Since the Launch of the Millennium Development Goals." Brookings Institution. www.brookings.edu/research/seven-million-lives-saved-under-5-mortality-since-the-launch-of-the-millennium-development-goals/.

McCandless, Erin. (2013) "Wicked Problems in Peacebuilding and Statebuilding: Making Progress in Measuring Progress Through the New Deal." *Global Governance* 19:2 (April–June): 227–248.

McCormick, John, and Jonathan Olsen. (2014) *The European Union: Politics and Policies.* Boulder: Westview.

McKeon, Nora. (2009) *The United Nations and Civil Society: Legitimating Global Governance—Whose Voice?* London: Zed.

———. (2015) *Food Security Governance: Empowering Communities, Regulating Corporations.* New York: Routledge.

McLeman, Robert A. (2014) *Climate and Human Migration: Past Experiences, Future Challenges.* New York: Cambridge University Press.

McNair, Brian. (2005) "What Is Journalism?" In *Making Journalists: Diverse Models, Global Issues*, edited by Hugo de Burgh. New York: Routledge, pp. 25–43.

Meadows, Donella, Dennis L. Meadows, Jørgen Randers, and William W. Behrens III. (1972) *The Limits to Growth*. New York: Universe.

Mearsheimer, John J. (1994–1995) "The False Promise of International Institutions." *International Security* 19:3 (Winter): 5–49.

Merrills, J. G. (2011) *International Dispute Settlement*. 5th ed. Cambridge: Cambridge University Press.

Mertus, Julie A. (2008) *Bait and Switch: Human Rights and U.S. Foreign Policy*. 2nd ed. New York: Routledge.

———. (2009). *The United Nations and Human Rights. A Guide for a New Era*. 2nd ed. London: Routledge.

Meyer, John W., David John Frank, Ann Hironaka, Evan Schofer, and Nancy Brandon Tuma. (1997) "The Structuring of a World Environmental Regime, 1870–1990." *International Organization* 51:4 (Autumn): 623–651.

Meyer, Peter J. (2014) *Organization of American States: Background and Issues for Congress*. Washington, DC: Congressional Research Service.

Miller, Rory. (2022) "The Gulf Cooperation Council and Counter-terror Cooperation in the Post-9-11 Era: A Regional Organization in Comparative Perspective." *Middle Eastern Studies* 58:3: 435–451.

Mingst, Karen A. (1987) "Inter-Organizational Politics: The World Bank and the African Development Bank." *Review of International Studies* 13: 281–293.

———. (1990) *Politics and the African Development Bank*. Lexington: University of Kentucky Press.

———. (2015) "The African Development Bank: From Follower to Broker and Partner." In *Global Economic Governance and the Development Practices of the Multilateral Development Banks*, edited by Susan Park and Jonathan R. Strand. London: Routledge, pp. 80–98.

Mingst, Karen A., Margaret P. Karns, and Alynna J. Lyon. (2022) *The United Nations in the 21st Century*. 6th ed. New York: Routledge.

Mitchell, Ronald, Liliana Andonova, Mark Axelrod, Jörg Balsiger, Thomas Bernauer, Jessica Green, James Hollway, Rakhyun Kim, and Jean-Frédéric Morin. (2020) "What We Know (and Could Know) about International Environmental Agreements." *Global Environmental Politics* 20:1 (February): 103–121.

Mitrany, David. (1946) *A Working Peace System*. London: Royal Institute of International Affairs.

Mittelstaedt, Emma. (2008) "Safeguarding the Rights of Sexual Minorities: The Incremental and Legal Approaches to Enforcing International Human Rights Obligations." *Chicago Journal of International Law* 9:1 (Summer): 353–386.

Monshipouri, Mahmood, ed. (2020) *Why Human Rights Still Matter in Contemporary Global Affairs*. New York: Routledge.

Montoya, Celeste. (2008) "The European Union, Capacity Building, and Transnational Networks: Combating Violence Against Women Through the Daphne Program." *International Organization* 62:2 (Spring): 359–372.

Moon, Chung-In, and Jongryn Mo. (2000) *Economic Crisis and Structural Reforms in South Korea: Assessments and Implications*. Washington, DC: Economic Strategy Institution.

Moravcsik, Andrew. (1997) "Taking Preferences Seriously: A Liberal Theory of International Politics." *International Organization* 51:4 (Autumn): 513–553.

———. (1998) *The Choice for Europe: Social Purpose and State Power from Messina to Maastricht*. Ithaca: Cornell University Press.

Moretti, Sebastian. (2021) "Between Refugee Protection and Migration Management: The Quest for Coordination between UNHCR and IOM in the Asia-Pacific Region." *Third World Quarterly* 42:1: 34–51.

Morgenthau, Hans. (1967) *Politics Among Nations*. 4th ed. New York: Knopf.

Moses, A. Dirk. (2022) "The Ukraine Genocide Reveals the Limits of International Law." *Lawfare* (May 16). https://www.lawfaremedia.org/article/ukraine-genocide-debate-reveals-limits-international-law.

Mozur, Paul. (2018) "A Genocide Incited on Facebook, with Posts from Myanmar's Military." *New York Times* (October 15).

Mueller, Benjamin and Carl Zimmer. (2022) "Mysteries Linger about Covid's Origins, W.H.O. Report Says. *New York Times* (June 9).

Mueller, Lukas Maximilien. (2021) "Challenges to ASEAN Centrality and Hedging in Connectivity Governance—Regional and National Pressure Points." *Pacific Review* 34:5: 744–777.

Mulder, Nicholas. (2022) "The Sanctions Weapon: Economic Structures Deliver Bigger Global Shocks Than Ever Before and Are Easier to Evade." *Finance and Development* (June): 20–23. https://www.imf.org/en/Publications/fandd/issues/2022/06/the-sanctions-weapon-mulder.

Murdie, Amanda M., and David R. Davis. (2012) "Shaming and Blaming: Using Events Data to Assess the Impact of Human Rights INGOs." *International Studies Quarterly* 56:1 (March): 1–16.

Murphy, Craig. (1994) *International Organization and Industrial Change*. New York: Oxford University Press.

———. (2000) "Global Governance: Poorly Done and Poorly Understood." *International Affairs* 75:4: 789–803.

———. (2006) *The United Nations Development Programme: A Better Way?* New York: Cambridge University Press.

Murphy, Hannah. (2010) *The Making of International Trade Policy: NGOs, Agenda-Setting and the WTO*. Cheltenham: Elgar.

Murray, Jean-Pierre D. (2022) "The Migration-Security Nexus in South-South Population Flows: Securitization of Haitian Migration in the Dominican Republic." Ph.D. diss., University of Massachusetts Boston.

———. (2023) "Caribbean International Relations." In *Understanding the Contemporary Caribbean*, edited by Henry F. Carey. Boulder: Lynne Rienner.

Mutua, Makau. (1999) "The African Human Rights Court: A Two-Legged Stool?" *Human Rights Quarterly* 21:2: 342–363.

Narine, Shaun. (2004) "State Sovereignty, Political Legitimacy, and Regional Institutionalism in the Asia-Pacific." *Pacific Review* 17:3: 423–450.

———. (2008) "Forty Years of ASEAN: A Historical Review." *Pacific Review* 21:4: 411–429.

Ndubuisi, Christian Ani. (2021) "Coup or Not Coup: The African Union and the Dilemma of 'Popular Uprisings' in Africa." *Democracy and Security* 17:3: 257–277.

Neier, Aryeh. (2012) *The International Human Rights Movement: A History*. Princeton: Princeton University Press.

———. (2019) "Indicting the International Criminal Court." *The Jordan Times* (May 19).

Nelson, Stephen. (2017) *The Currency of Confidence: How Economic Beliefs Shape the IMF's Relationship with its Borrowers*. Ithaca: Cornell University Press.

Newman, Edward. 2004. "A Normatively Attractive but Analytically Weak Concept." In Special Issue, "What Is Human Security?" edited by P. Burgess and T. Owen. *Security Dialogue* 35 (September): 358–359.

Newsom, D., and D. Hewitt. (2005) "The Global Impacts of SmartWood Certification: Final Report of the TREES Program for the Rainforest Alliance." Rainforest Alliance. www.rainforest-alliance.org/forestry/documents/sw_impacts.pdf.

Nichols, Michelle. (2020) "U.N. Warns 2021 Shaping Up to Be a Humanitarian Catastrophe." Reuters (December 4).

Nielson, Richard. (2013) "Rewarding Human Rights? Selective Aid Sanctions Against Repressive States." *International Studies Quarterly* 57:4 (December): 791–803.

Nobel Prize. (2020) "Press Release." https://www.nobelprize.org/prizes/peace/2020/press-release/.

Nolte, Detlev. (2021) "From the Summits to the Plains: The Crisis of Latin American Regionalism." *Latin American Policy* 12:1 (May): 181–192.

North Africa Post. (2022) "Arab League Expresses Solidarity with Morocco against Iranian Threats." (September 6). https://northafricapost.com/60524-arab-league-expresses-solidarity-with-morocco-against-iranian-threats.html.

Nyadera, Israel, Billy Agwanda, Murat Onder, and Ibrahim Mukhtar. (2022) "Multilateralism, Developmental Regionalism, and the African Development Bank." *Politics and Governance* 10: 2: 82–94.

Nylan, Alexandria. (2020) "Frontier Justice: International Law and 'Lawless' Spaces in the War on Terror." *European Journal of International Relations* 26:3 (September): 627–659.

Oatley, Thomas. (2001) "Multilateralizing Trade and Payments in Postwar Europe." *International Organization* 55:4 (Autumn): 949–969.

OAU. (2000) Declarations and Decisions Adopted By the Thirty-Sixth Ordinary Session of the Assembly of Heads of State and Government. AHG/Decl. 2 (XXXVI). https://au.int/sites/default/files/decisions/9545-2000_ahg_dec_143-159_xxxvi_e.pdf.

Obama, Barack. (2007) "Remarks of Senator Obama to the Chicago Council on Global Affairs." www.cfr.org/elections/remarks-senator-barack-obama-chicago-council-global-affairs/p13172.

O'Brien, Robert, Anne Marie Goetz, Jan Aart Scholte, and Marc Williams. (2000) *Contesting Global Governance: Multilateral Economic Institutions and Global Social Movements.* Cambridge: Cambridge University Press.

Oestreich, Joel E. (2012) "Introduction." In *International Organizations as Self-Directed Actors*, edited by Joel E. Oestrich. New York: Routledge, pp. 1–25.

Ogata, Sadako, and Johan Cels. (2003) "Human Security-Protecting and Empowering the People." *Global Governance* 9:3 (July–September): 273–282.

Ohanyan, Anna. (2012) "Network Institutionalism and NGO Studies." *International Studies Perspectives* 13:4 (November): 366–389.

Ohta, Hiroshi, and Atsuchi Ishii. (2014) "The Forum: Disaggregating Effectiveness." *International Studies Review* 15:4 (December): 581–583.

Olson, Mancur. (1968) *The Logic of Collective Action.* New York: Schocken.

O'Neil, Shannon K. (2022) "Why Latin American Lost at Globalization and How It Can Win Now." Council on Foreign Relations (August 25). www.cfr.org/article/why-latin-america-lost-globalization-and-how-it-can-win-now.

Organisation for Economic Co-operation and Development (OECD). (2022) "COVID-19-Related Activities in Official Development Assistance (ODA)." OECD. https://www.oecd.org/dac/financing-sustainable-development/development-finance-standards/vaccines-costs-oda.htm.

Organski, A.F.K. (1968) *World Politics*, 2nd ed. New York: Alfred A. Knopf.

Orsini, Amandine, Jean-Fréderic Morin, and Oran Young. (2013) "Regime Complexes: A Buzz, a Boom, or a Boost for Global Governance?" *Global Governance* 19:1 (January–March): 27–40.

Ostrom, Elinor. (1990) *Governing the Commons: The Evolution of Institutions for Collective Action*. Cambridge: Cambridge University Press.

Paats, Liise Margit. (2021) "EU Foreign and Security Policy: Overview and Challenges." *United Europe* (17): 49–55.

Padelford, Norman J. (1945) Unpublished letter to family and friends (June 26).

Papadopoulos, Yannis. (2013) "The Challenge of Transnational Private Governance: Evaluating Authorization, Representation, and Accountability." Working Paper no. 8 (February). Paris: SciencesPo/LIEPP (Laboratoire Interdisciplinaire d'évaluation des politiques publiques).

Paris, Roland. (2001) "Human Security: Paradigm Shift or Hot Air?" *International Security* 26:2: 87–102.

———. (2004) *At War's End: Building Peace After Civil Conflict*. New York: Cambridge University Press.

Park, Susan. (2010) *The World Bank Group and Environmentalists: Changing International Organization Identities*. London: Manchester University Press.

Park, Susan, and Jonathan R. Strand, eds. (2015) *Global Economic Governance and the Development Practices of the Multilateral Development Banks*. New York: Routledge.

Parker, Claire and Robyn Dixon. (2023) "Russia Comes Under Global Criticism for Grain Deal Pullout, Port Attacks." *Washington Post* (July 21).

Patrick, Stewart. (2014) "The Unruled World: The Case for Good Enough Global Governance." *Foreign Affairs* 93:1 (January–February): 58–73.

Pécoud. Antoine. (2018) "What Do We Know About the International Organization for Migration?" *Journal of Ethnic and Migration Studies* 44:10: 1621–1638.

———. (2021) "Narrating an Ideal Migration World? An Analysis of the Global Compact for Safe, Orderly and Regular Migration." *Third World Quarterly* 42:1: 16–33.

Pempel, T. J., ed. (2005) *Remapping East Asia: The Construction of a Region*. Ithaca: Cornell University Press.

Perez-Rocha, Manuel, and Stuart Trew. (2014) "NAFTA at 20: A Model for Corporate Rule." *Foreign Policy in Focus* (January 14). fpif.org/nafta-20-model -corporate-rule/.

Permanent Court of Arbitration. (2023) PCA Press Release—PCA Case No. 23-01: Proceedings under the *Indus Waters Treaty*. https://pcacases.com/web/sendAttach /47335.

Petersen, Mark and Carsten-Andreas Schulz. (2018) "Setting the Regional Agenda: A Critique of Posthegemonic Regionalism." *Latin American Politics and Society* 60:1 (Spring): 102–127.

Peterson, M.J. (2004) "Using the General Assembly." In *Terrorism and the UN: Before and After September 11*, edited by Jane Boulden and Thomas G. Weiss. (Bloomington: Indiana University Press), pp. 173–197.

Peterson, V. Spike. (2003) *A Critical Rewriting of Global Political Economy: Integrating Reproductive, Productive, and Virtual Economies*. London: Routledge.

Phelan, William. (2012) "What Is *Sui Generis* About the European Union? Costly International Cooperation in a Self-Contained Regime." *International Studies Review* 14:3 (September): 367–385.

Piiiparinen, T. T. K. (2016) "Secretariats." In *The Oxford Handbook of International Organizations* edited by J. K. Cogan, I. Hurd, and I. Johnstone. New York: Oxford University Press, pp. 839–857.

Podesta, John. (2019) "The Climate Crisis, Migration, and Refugees." Brookings Blum Roundtable on Global Poverty Report (July 25). www.brookings.edu /research/the-climate-crisis-migration-and-refugees/.

Podrecca, Matteo, Marco Sartor, and Guido Nassimbeni. (2022) "United Nations Global Compact: Where Are We Going?" *Social Responsibility Journal* 18:5 (June): 984–1003.

Popovski, Vesselin. (2011) "The Concepts of Responsibility to Protect and Protection of Civilians: 'Sisters, but Not Twins.'" *Security Challenges* 7:4 (Summer): 1–12.

Potoski, Matthew, and Elizabeth Elwakeil. (2011) "International Organization for Standardization 14001." In *Handbook of Transnational Governance: Institutions and Innovations*, edited by Thomas Hale and David Held. Cambridge: Polity, pp. 295–302.

Pouliot, Vincent. (2011) "Multilateralism as an End in Itself." *International Studies Perspectives* 12:1 (February): 18–26.

Power, Samantha. (2002) *"A Problem from Hell": America and the Age of Genocide.* New York: Basic.

Prakash, Aseem, and Matthew Potoski. (2014) "Global Private Regimes, Domestic Public Law: ISO 14001 and Pollution Reduction." *Comparative Political Studies* 47:3 (March): 369–394.

Prakathi, Mlungisi. (2018) "An Analysis of the Response of the African Union to the Coup in Burkina Faso (2015) and Zimbabwe (2017)." *Journal of Africa Union Studies* 7:3 (December): 129–143.

Prasad, Eswar. (2021) *The Future of Money: How the Digital Revolution Is Transforming Currency and Finance.* Cambridge: Harvard University Press.

Preston, Julia. (1994) "Boutros-Ghali Rushes in . . . in a Violent World: The U.N. Secretary-General Has an Activist's Agenda." *Washington Post* (January 10–16): 10–11.

Pretorius, Joelien. (2020) "A Legal Game-Changer: The Nuclear Ban Treaty and Legal Leverage for its Supporters." *Bulletin of the Atomic Scientists* (October 30). https://thebulletin.org/2020/10/the-nuclear-ban-treaty-and-legal-leverage -for-its-supporters/.

Price, Richard, and Nina Tannenwald. (1996) "Norms and Deterrence: The Nuclear and Chemical Weapons Taboo." In *The Culture of National Security: Norms and Identity in World Politics*, edited by Peter J. Katzenstein. New York: Columbia University Press, pp. 114–152.

Priebus, Sonja. (2022) "The Commission's Approach to Rule of Law Backsliding: Managing Instead of Enforcing Democratic Values?" *Journal of Common Market Studies* 60:6 (November): 1684–1700.

Princen, Thomas. (1995) "Ivory, Conservation, and Environmental Transnational Coalitions." In *Bringing Transnational Relations Back In: Non-State Actors, Domestic Structures, and International Institutions*, edited by Thomas Risse-Kappen. New York: Cambridge University Press, pp. 227–256.

Profitt, Tom. (2007) "Russia Plants Flag on North Pole Seabed." *The Guardian* (August 2). https://www.theguardian.com/world/2007/aug/02/russia.arctic.

Prügl, Elisabeth, and Jacqui True. (2014) "Equality Means Business? Governing Gender Through Transnational Public-Private Partnerships." *Review of International Political Economy* 21:6 (December): 1137–1169.

Puchala, Donald J., and Roger A. Coate. (1989) "The Challenge of Relevance: The United Nations in a Changing World Environment." Academic Council on the United Nations System (ACUNS), Reports and Papers no. 5.

Raad Al Hussein, Prince Zeid, Bruno Stagno Ugarte, Christian Wenaweser, and Tiina Intelmas. (2019) "The International Criminal Court Needs Fixing." *New Atlanticist* (April 24). https://www.atlanticcouncil.org/blogs/new-atlanticist/the -international-criminal-court-needs-fixing/.

Rachman, Gideon. (2011) "Think Again: American Decline. This Time It's for Real." *Foreign Policy* (January–February): 59–63.

Rade, Kees. (2022) "Diplomats Without Borders: A New Niche Service Aims to Mend Our Frayed World." *PassBlue* (August 10). https://www.passblue.com/2022/08/10/diplomats-without-borders-a-new-niche-service-aims-to-mend-our-frayed-world/.

Ramazini, Haroldo, Marcelo Passini Mariano and Julie De Souza Borba Gonçalves. (2021) "The Quest for Syntony: Democracy and Regionalism in South America." *Bulletin of Latin American Research* 41:2 (April): 305–319.

Ramcharan, B. G. (2000) "The International Court of Justice." In *The United Nations at the Millennium: The Principal Organs*, edited by Paul Taylor and A. J. R. Groom. New York: Continuum, pp. 177–195.

———. (2008) "The Universal Declaration of Human Rights at Sixty." Academic Council on the United Nations System (ACUNS). *In Memorandum* 76 (Fall): 1–3.

Ramani, Samuel. (2021) "The Qatar Blockade Is Over, but the Gulf Crisis Lives On." *Foreign Policy* (January 27).

Ramzi, Austin and Chris Buckley. (2019) "'Absolutely No Mercy': Leaked Files Expose How China Organized Mass Detentions of Muslims." *New York Times* (November 16).

Rathore, Khushi Singh. (2021) " Excavating Indian Women in the Early History of the UN." In *Women and the UN: A New History of Women's International Human Rights*, edited by Rebecca Adami and Dan Plesch. New York: Routledge, pp. 39–54.

Ratner, Steven R. (2013) "Persuading to Comply: On the Deployment and Avoidance of Legal Argumentation." In *Interdisciplinary Perspectives on International Law and International Relations: The State of the Art*, edited by Jeffrey Dunoff and Mark A. Pollack. New York: Cambridge University Press, pp. 568–590.

Raustiala, Kal, and David G. Victor. (2004) "The Regime Complex for Plant Genetic Resources." *International Organization* 58:2 (Spring): 277–309.

Ravndal, Ellen J. (2020) "A Guardian of the UN Charter: The UN Secretary-General at Seventy-Five." *Ethics & International Affairs* 34:3 (Fall): 297–304.

Ravenhill, John. (2001) *APEC and the Construction of Pacific Rim Regionalism.* Cambridge: Cambridge University Press.

———. (2007a) "In Search of an East Asian Region: Beyond Network Power." *Journal of East Asian Studies* 7: 387–394.

———. (2007b) "Mission Creep or Mission Impossible? APEC and Security." In *Reassessing Security Cooperation in the Asia-Pacific: Competition, Congruence, and Transformation*, edited by Amitav Acharya and Evelyn Goh. Cambridge: MIT Press, pp. 135–154.

———. (2008) "Fighting Irrelevance: An Economic Community 'with ASEAN Characteristics.'" *Pacific Review* 21:4: 469–487.

Ray, Aswini. (1999) "The Concept of Justice in International Relations." *Economic & Political Weekly* 34:22 (May): 1368–1374.

Rehman, Huma and Afsah Qazi. (2019) "Significance of Resolution 1540 and Emerging Challenges to its Effectiveness." *Strategic Studies* 39:2: 48–66.

Reimann, Kim D. (2006) "A View from the Top: International Politics, Norms, and the Worldwide Growth of NGOs." *International Studies Quarterly* 50:1 (March): 45–67.

Reincke, Wolfgang H. (1999–2000) "The Other World Wide Web: Global Public Policy Networks." *Foreign Policy* 117 (Winter) 44–57.

Reinold, Theresa. (2022) "Holding International Organizations Accountable: Toward a Right to Justification in Global Governance?" *Ethics & International Affairs* 36:2 (August): 259–271.

Repucci, Sarah and Amy Slipowitz. (2022) "Freedom in the World 2022: The Global Expansion of Authoritarian Rule. *Freedom House Report*. https:// freedomhouse.org/report/freedom-world/2022/global-expansion-authoritarian-rule.

Rich, Bruce. (2013) *Foreclosing the Future: The World Bank and the Politics of Environmental Destruction*. Washington, DC: Island Press.

Richmond, Oliver P. (2001) "A Genealogy of Peacemaking: The Creation and Re-Creation of Order." *Alternatives* 26:3 (July–September), pp. 317–348.

Riggs, Robert E., and Jack C. Plano. (1994) *The United Nations: International Organization of World Politics*. 2nd ed. Belmont, CA: Wadsworth.

Risse, Thomas. (2016) "The Diffusion of Regionalism." In *The Oxford Handbook of Comparative Regionalism*, edited by Tanja A. Börzel and Thomas Risse. New York: Oxford University Press, pp. 87–110.

Risse, Thomas, Stephen C. Ropp, and Kathryn Sikkink, eds. (1999) *The Power of Human Rights: International Norms and Domestic Change*. New York: Cambridge University Press.

———. (2013) *The Persistent Power of Human Rights: From Commitment to Compliance*. New York: Cambridge University Press.

Risse-Kappen, Thomas, ed. (1995) *Bringing Transnational Relations Back In: Non-State Actors, Domestic Structures, and International Institutions*. New York: Cambridge University Press.

Rist, Wes. (2020) "What Does the ICJ Decision on the Gambia v. Myanmar Mean?" American Society of International Law *Insights* 24:2 (February 27).

Roberge, Ian. (2011) "Financial Action Task Force." In *Handbook of Transnational Governance: Institutions and Innovations*, edited by Thomas Hale and David Held. London: Polity, pp. 45–50.

Roberts, Adam. (1999) "NATO's 'Humanitarian War' over Kosovo." *Survival* 41:2 (Spring): 102–123.

Rodrik, Dani. (2007) "The Global Governance of Trade as if Development Really Mattered." In *One Economics, Many Recipes: Globalization, Institutions, and Economic Growth*, edited by Dani Rodrik. Princeton: Princeton University Press, pp. 213–236.

Roemer, Ruth, Allyn Taylor, and Jean Lariviere. (2005) "Origins of the WHO Framework Convention on Tobacco Control." *American Journal of Public Health* 95:6 (June): 936–938.

Romaniuk, Peter. (2018) "Counterterrorism Cooperation and Global Governance." In *International Organization and Global Governance,* 2nd ed., edited by Thomas G. Weiss and Rorden Wilkenson. London: Routledge, pp. 498–510.

Romano, Cesare P. R. (1999) "The Proliferation of International Judicial Bodies: The Pieces of the Puzzle." *International Law and Politics* 31: 709–751.

Ron, James, Howard Ramos, and Kathleen Rodgers. (2005) "Transnational Information Politics: NGO Human Rights Reporting, 1986–2000." *International Studies Quarterly* 49:3 (September): 557–587.

Roosevelt, Franklin. (1941) "Address by the President." 87th Congress. *Congressional Record* 44: 46–47.

Rosenau, James N. (1992) "Governance, Order, and Change in World Politics." In *Governance Without Government: Order and Change in World Politics*, edited by James N. Rosenau and E. O. Czempiel. Cambridge: Cambridge University Press, pp. 1–29.

———. (1995) "Governance in the Twenty-First Century." *Global Governance* 1:1 (Winter): 13–43.

———. (1997) *Along the Domestic-Foreign Frontier: Exploring Governance in a Turbulent World*. Cambridge: Cambridge University Press.

Ruane, Abigail. (2011) "Pursuing Inclusive Interests, Both Deep and Wide: Women's Human Rights and the United Nations." In *Feminism and International Relations: Conversations About the Past, Present, and Future*, edited by J. Ann Tickner and Laura Sjoberg. London: Routledge, pp. 48–67.

Rudolph, Christopher. (2003) "Security and the Political Economy of Migration." *American Political Science Review* 97:4, 603–620.

Ruggie, John Gerard. (1982) "International Regimes, Transactions, and Change: Embedded Liberalism in the Postwar Economic Order." *International Organization* 36:2 (Spring): 379–415.

———. (1993) "Multilateralism: The Anatomy of an Institution." In *Multilateralism Matters: The Theory and Praxis of an Institutional Form*, edited by John Gerard Ruggie. New York: Columbia University Press, pp. 3–47.

———. (2001) "Global_Governance.net: The Global Compact as Learning Network." *Global Governance* 7:4 (October–December): 371–378.

———. (2003) "The United Nations and Globalization: Patterns and Limits of Institutional Adaptation." *Global Governance* 9:3 (July–September): 301–321.

———. (2013) *Just Business: Multinational Corporations and Human Rights*. New York: Norton.

Rüland, Jürgen, and Karsten Bechle. (2014) "Defending State Centric Regionalism through Mimicry and Localisation: Regional Parliamentary Bodies in the Association of Southeast Asian Nations (ASEAN) and Mercosur." *Journal of International Relations and Development* 17 (March): 61–88.

Ryder, Hannah, Anna Baisch, and Ovigwe Eguegu. (2020) "Decolonizing the UN Means Abolishing the Permanent Five: The Inequalities of the Past Can't Set the Rules of the Present." *Foreign Policy* (September 17).

Sachs, Jeffrey D. (2005) *The End of Poverty: Economic Possibilities for Our Time*. New York: Penguin.

Sanderson, John. (2001) "Cambodia." In *United Nations Peacekeeping Operations: Ad Hoc Missions, Permanent Engagement*, edited by Albrecht Schnabel and Ramesh Thakur. Tokyo: UN University Press, pp. 155–166.

Sandholtz, Wayne, and Kendall Stiles. (2009) *International Norms and Cycles of Change*. New York: Oxford University Press.

Satariano, Adam. (2019) "Russia Sought to Use Social Media to Influence EU Vote, Report Finds." *New York Times* (June 14).

Schabas, William A. (2017) *An Introduction to the International Criminal Court*, 5th ed. New York: Cambridge University Press.

Schechter, Michael. (2005) *United Nations Global Conferences*. New York: Routledge.

Schiel, R., J. Powell, and C. Faulkner. (2021) "Mutiny in Africa, 1950–2018." *Conflict Management and Peace Science* 38:4: 481–499.

Schiff, Benjamin N. (2008) *Building the International Criminal Court*. New York: Cambridge University Press.

Schillemans, Thomas, and Mark Bovens. (2011) "The Challenge of Multiple Accountability: Does Redundancy Lead to Overload?" In *Accountable Governance: Problems and Promises*, edited by Melvin J. Dubnick and H. George Frederickson. Armonk, NY: Sharpe, pp. 3–21.

Schimmelfennig, Frank. (2007) "Functional Form, Identity-Driven Cooperation: Institutional Designs and Effects in Post–Cold War NATO." In *Crafting Cooperation: Regional International Institutions in Comparative Perspective*, edited by Amitav Acharya and Alastair Ian Johnston. Cambridge: Cambridge University Press, pp. 145–179.

Scholte, Jan Aart. (2012) "A More Inclusive Global Governance? The IMF and Civil Society in Africa." *Global Governance* 18:2 (April–June): 185–206.

Security Council Report. (2014) "Security Council Working Methods: A Tale of Two Councils?" *Special Research Report.* www.securitycouncilreport.org/special -research-report/security-council-working-methods-a-tale-of-two-councils.php.

Selin, Henrik. (2007) "Coalition Politics and Chemicals Management in a Regulatory Ambitious Europe." *Global Environmental Politics* 7:3 (August): 63–93.

Sen, Amartya. (1981) *Poverty and Famines: An Essay on Entitlement and Deprivation.* New York: Oxford University Press.

———. (1999) *Development as Freedom.* New York: Knopf.

———. (2001) "A World of Extremes: Ten Theses on Globalization." *Los Angeles Times* (July 17).

Sénit, Carole-Anne, and Frank Bierman. (2021) "In Whose Name Are You Speaking? The Marginalization of the Poor in Global Civil Society." *Global Policy* 12:5 (November): 581–591.

Seth, Sanjay. (2011) "Postcolonial Theory and the Critique of International Relations." *Millennium: Journal of International Studies* 40:1: 167–183.

Sheeran, Scott, and Stephanie Case. (2014) *The Intervention Brigade: Legal Issues for the UN in the Democratic Republic of the Congo.* New York: International Peace Institute. https://www.ipinst.org/wp-content/uploads/publications/ipi_e_pub_legal _issues_drc_brigade.pdf

Shifter, Michael. (2012) "The Shifting Landscape of Latin American Regionalism." *Current History* (February): 56–61.

Shimizu, Kazushi. (2021) "The ASEAN Economic Community and The RECP in the World Economy." *Journal of Contemporary East Asian Studies* 10:1: 1–23.

Sikkink, Kathryn. (2009) "The Power of Networks in International Politics." In *Networked Politics: Agency, Power, and Governance*, edited by Miles Kahler. Ithaca: Cornell University Press, pp. 228–247.

———. (2013) "The United States and Torture: Does the Spiral Model Work?" In *The Persistent Power of Human Rights: From Commitment to Compliance*, edited by Thomas Risse, Stephen C. Ropp, and Kathryn Sikkink. New York: Cambridge University Press, pp. 145–163.

———. (2014) "Latin American Countries as Norm Protagonists of the Idea of International Human Rights." *Global Governance* 20:3 (July–Sept.): 389–404.

———. (2019 "Border Rules." *International Studies Review* 21:2 (June): 256–283.

Simmons, Beth A. (2002) "Capacity, Commitment, and Compliance: International Institutions and Territorial Disputes." *Journal of Conflict Resolution* 46:6 (December): 829–856.

———. (2009) *Mobilizing for Human Rights: International Law in Domestic Politics.* New York: Cambridge University Press.

———. (2019 "Border Rules." *International Studies Review* 21:2 (June): 256–283.

Simmons, P. J., and Chantal de Jonge Oudraat. (2001) "Managing Global Issues: An Introduction." In *Managing Global Issues: Lessons Learned*, edited by P. J. Simmons and Chantal de Jonge Oudraat. Washington, DC: Carnegie Endowment for International Peace, pp. 3–24.

Simons, Marlise. (2003) "World Court for Crimes of War Opens in The Hague." *New York Times* (March 12).

SIPRI. (2021) *Multilateral Peace Operations in 2021: Developments and Trends.* https://www.sipri.org/commentary/topical-backgrounder/2022/multilateral -peace-operations-2021-developments-and-trends.

Slaughter, Anne-Marie. (2004) *A New World Order*. Princeton: Princeton University Press.

Smith, Aaron, Laura Silver, Courtney Johnson, and Jingjing Jiang. (2019) "Publics in Emerging Economies Worry Social Media Sow Division, Even as They Offer New Chances for Political Engagement." Washington, DC: Pew Research Center.

Smith, Courtney B. (1999) "The Politics of Global Consensus Building: A Comparative Analysis." *Global Governance* 5:2 (April–June): 173–201.

———. (2006) *Politics and Process at the United Nations: The Global Dance*. Boulder: Lynne Rienner.

Smith, Jackie, Basak Gemici, Samantha Plummer, and Melanie Hughes. (2018) "Transnational Social Movement Organizations and Counter-Hegemonic Struggles Today." *Journal of World Systems Studies* 24:2: 372–403.

Smith, Jackie, and Dawn Wiest. (2012) *Social Movements in the World-System: The Politics of Crisis and Transformation*. New York: Russell Sage.

Snidal, Duncan. (1991) "Relative Gains and the Pattern of International Cooperation." *American Political Science Review* 83:3 (September): 701–726.

Solingen, Etel. (1998) *Regional Orders at Century's Dawn: Global and Domestic Influences on Grand Strategy*. Princeton: Princeton University Press.

———. (2008) "The Genesis, Design, and Effects of Regional Institutions: Lessons from East Asia and the Middle East." *International Studies Quarterly* 52:2 (June): 261–294.

Sommerer, Thomas, Hans Agné, Fariborz Zelli, and Bart Bes. (2022) *Global Legitimacy Crises: Decline and Revival in Multilateral Governance*. New York: Oxford University Press.

Souaré, I. K. (2014) "The African Union as a Norm Entrepreneur on Military Coups d'États in Africa (1952–2012): An Empirical Assessment." *Journal of Modern African Studies* 52:1: 69–94.

Sova, Chase. (2021) "COVID 19 and the Five Major Threats it Poses to Global Food Security." World Food Program USA (March 16). https://www.wfpusa.org /articles/covid-19-and-global-food-security/.

Spiro, Peter J. (1996) "New Global Potentates: Nongovernmental Organizations and the 'Unregulated' Marketplace." *Cardozo Law Review* 18 (December): 957–969.

Squire, Vicki, and Jef Huysman. (2017) "Migration and Security." In *Routledge Handbook of Security Studies*, 2nd ed., edited by Myriam Dunn Cavalty and Thierrh Balzacq. New York: Routledge, pp. 161–171.

Stapel, Sören. (2022) *Regional Organizations and Democracy, Human Rights, and the Rule of Law: The African Union, Organization of American States, and the Diffusion of Institutions*. Cham, Switzerland: Palgrave Macmillan.

Stedman, Stephen John, Donald Rothchild, and Elizabeth M. Cousens. (2002) *Ending Civil Wars: The Implementation of Peace Agreements*. Boulder: Lynne Rienner.

Steffek, Jens. (2013) "Explaining Cooperation between IGOs and NGOs: Push Factors, Pull Factors, and the Policy Cycle." *Review of International Studies* 39:4 (October): 993–1013.

Stevis-Gridneff, Matina. (2022) "As Europe Piles Sanctions on Russia, Some Sacred Cows Are Spared." *New York Times* (October 18).

Stiglitz, Joseph. (2002) *Globalization and Its Discontents*. New York: Norton.

Stone, Randall. (2011) *Controlling Institutions: International Organizations and the Global Economy*. New York: Cambridge University Press.

Strand, Håvard, and Håvard Hegre. (2021) "Trends in Armed Conflict, 1946–2022." *Conflict Trends* 3. Oslo: PRIO. https://cdn.cloud.prio.org/files/23f5796a-53e4 -454d-b877-883257c6f0e9.

Stroup, Sarah, and Wendy Wong. (2017) *The Authority Trap: Strategic Choices of International NGOs*. Ithaca: Cornell University Press.

Stubbs, Richard. (2019) "ASEAN Skeptics vs ASEAN Proponents: Evaluating Regional Institutions." *Pacific Review* 32:6: 923–950.

Suzuki, Sanae. (2020) "Exploring the Roles of the AU and ECOWAS in West African Conflicts." *South African Journal of International Affairs* 27:2: 173–191.

Suzuki, Severn. (1992) "Severn Cullis Suzuki at Rio Summit 1992." *YouTube*. https://www.youtube.com/watch?v=oJJGuIZVfLM.

Tallberg, Jonas. (2002) "Paths to Compliance: Enforcement, Management, and the European Union." *International Organization* 56:3 (Summer): 609–643.

Tallberg, Jonas, Thomas Sommerer, Theresa Squatrito, and Christer Jönsson. (2013) *The Opening Up of International Organizations: Transnational Access in Global Governance*. Cambridge: Cambridge University Press.

Tannenwald, Nina, ed. (2007) *The Nuclear Taboo: The United States and the Non-Use of Nuclear Weapons Since 1945*. New York: Cambridge University Press.

———. (2022) "Is Using Nuclear Weapons Still Taboo?" *Foreign Policy* (Summer): 36–38.

Tansey, Oisín. (2014) "Evaluating the Legacies of State-Building: Success, Failure, and the Role of Responsibility." *International Studies Quarterly* 58:1 (March): 174–186.

Taylor, Paul. (2000) "Managing the Economic and Social Activities of the United Nations System: Developing the Role of ECOSOC." In *The United Nations at the Millennium: The Principal Organs*, edited by Paul Taylor and A. J. R. Groom. New York: Continuum, pp. 100–141.

Tepperman, Jonathan. (2013) "Where Are You, Ban Ki-moon?" *New York Times* (September 24).

Terry, Fiona. (2002) *Condemned to Repeat? The Paradox of Humanitarian Action*. Ithaca: Cornell University Press.

Thakur, Ramesh. (2018) *The United Nations, Peace, and Security: From Collective Security to the Responsibility to Protect*. 2nd ed. New York: Cambridge University Press.

———. (2021) "2021 In Review. Always Immoral, Now Illegal. The Nuclear Ban Treaty Becomes Law." *Australian Outlook* (December 24). https://www.internationalaffairs.org.au/australianoutlook/always-immoral-now-illegal-the-nuclear-ban-treaty-becomes-law/.

Thakur, Ramesh, and William Maley. (1999) "The Ottawa Convention on Landmines: A Landmark Humanitarian Treaty in Arms Control." *Global Governance* 5:3 (July–September): 273–302.

Tickner, J. Ann. (2001) *Gendering World Politics: Issues and Approaches in the Post–Cold War Era*. New York: Columbia University Press.

Thouez, Colleen (2019) "Strengthening Migration Governance: the UN as 'Wingman.'" *Journal of Ethnic and Migration Studies* 45:8: 1242–1257.

Tieku, Thomas Kwasi. (2019) "Ruling from the Shadows: The Nature and Functions of Informal International Rules in World Politics." *International Studies Review* 21:2 (June): 225–243.

Tilly, Charles. (2004) *Social Movements, 1768–2004*. Boulder: Paradigm.

Tirman, John, ed. (2004) *The Maze of Fear: Security and Migration After 9/11*. New York: The New Press.

Tossell, J. (2020). *Consolidating Sudan's Transition: A Question of Legitimacy*. Clingendael: Netherlands Institute of International Relations. www.clingendael.org/sites/default/files/2020-02/Policy_Brief_Consolidating_Sudan_transition_February_2020.pdf.

True, Jacqui. (2011) "Feminist Problems with International Norms: Gender Main-streaming in Global Governance." In *Feminism and International Relations: Conversations About the Past, Present, and Future*, edited by J. Ann Tickner and Laura Sjoberg. London: Routledge, pp. 73–88.

Tussie, Diana, and Pia Riggirozzi. (2012) "The Rise of Post-Hegemonic Regionalism in Latin America." In *The Rise of Post-Hegemonic Regionalism: The Case of Latin America*, edited by Diana Tussie and Pia Riggirozzi. Dordrecht: Springer, pp. 1–16.

Union of International Associations. (UIA). (2023) "AboutUIA." https://uia.org/about.

United Nations (UN). (1992) "Letter Dated 29 November 1992 from the Secretary-General Addressed to the President of the Security Council." S/24868.

———. (1993) "The 'Second Generation': Cambodia Elections 'Free and Fair,' but Challenges Remain." *UN Chronicle* 30:5 (November–December): 26.

———. (1996) *The Blue Helmets: A Review of United Nations Peace-Keeping*. 3rd ed. New York: UN Department of Public Information.

———. (1999a) "Address of the Secretary-General to the UN General Assembly, 20 September." GA/9596.

———. (1999b) Press release. SG/SM/7263, AFR/196 (December 16). https://press.un.org/en/1999/19991216.sgsm7263.doc.html.

———. (2000) *Report of the Panel on United Nations Peace Operations* (Brahimi Report). A/55/305-S/2000/809 (August 21).

———. (2004) *A More Secure World: Our Shared Responsibility*. Report of the Secretary-General's High-Level Panel on Threats, Challenges, and Change. New York. https://www.un.org/peacebuilding/sites/www.un.org.peacebuilding/files/documents/hlp_more_secure_world.pdf.

———. (2005) *World Summit Outcome*. A/60/L.1, sec. 81. https://www.un.org/en/development/desa/population/migration/generalassembly/docs/globalcompact/A_RES_60_1.pdf.

———. (2008) *Peacekeeping Operations: Principles and Guidelines*. New York: UN Department of Peacekeeping Operations, Department of Field Support. https://police.un.org/en/united-nations-peace-operations-principles-and-guidelines-capstone-doctrine.

———. (2014) "Secretary-General's Remarks to Security Council High-Level Summit on Foreign Terrorist Fighters." (24 September). www.un.org/sg/statements/index.asp?nid=8040.

———. (2018) *Annual Report of the Secretary-General on the Work of the Organization*. https://www.un.org/annualreport/2018/.

———. (2021) "Global Humanitarian Response Plan COVID-19-Final Progress Report." https://reliefweb.int/attachments/825adbd0-ab76-3c0d-9770-5e9f4334476b/GHRP_ProgressReport_22FEB.pdf.

———. (2023) "Sustainable Development Goals 'Will Fail' without Private Sector Support', Deputy Secretary-General Tells High-Level Dialogue on Partnerships." (March 14), https://press.un.org/en/2023/dsgsm1839.doc.htm.

United Nations Covid-19 Supply Chain Task Force. (2020) https://interagencystanding committee.org/system/files/2020-05/COVID-19%20SupplyChainTaskForce_28.04.2020.pdf.

United Nations Department of Economic and Social Affairs. (2020) *International Migration 2020 Highlights*. https://www.un.org/development/desa/pd/sites/www.un.org.development.desa.pd/files/undesa_pd_2020_international_migration_highlights.pdf.

United Nations Development Programme (UNDP) and Arab Fund for Economic and Social Development. (2002) *Arab Human Development Report: Creating Opportunities for Future Generations*. New York: UNDP.

United Nations Environment Programme (UNEP). (2012) "United Nations Environment Programme Upgraded to Universal Membership Following Rio+20 Summit." UNEP. https://www.unep.org/news-and-stories/press-release/united-nations-environment-programme-upgraded-universal-membership.

———. (2014) "Ozone Layer on Track to Recovery: Success Story Should Encourage Action on Climate." UNEP. https://www.unep.org/news-and-stories/press-release/ozone-layer-track-recovery-success-story-should-encourage-action.

United Nations Framework Convention on Climate Change Conference of Parties, Cancun II (2010). Section II. https://unfccc.int/tools/cancun/index.html.

United Nations General Assembly. (2015) "Comprehensive Review of the Whole Question of Peacekeeping Operations in All Their Aspects." A/70/95-S/2015/446 (June 17): 12. https://peacekeeping.un.org/en/report-of-independent-high-level-panel-peace-operations.

———. (2016) "UN General Assembly Agreement Concerning the Relationship between the United Nations and the International Organization for Migration," Annex 1, Article 2, paragraph 2. A/70/976 (July 6). https://digitallibrary.un.org/record/837208?ln=en.

United Nations High Commissioner for Refugees (UNHCR). (2011) *Preventive Diplomacy: Delivering Results*. S/2011/552 (August 26). https://peacemaker.un.org/sites/peacemaker.un.org/files/SGReport_PreventiveDiplomacy_S2011552%28english%29_2.pdf.

United Nations Office of the High Commissioner for Human Rights. (2020) "A/HRC/44/26: Intersection of Race and Gender Discrimination in Sport—Report of the UN High Commissioner for Human Rights." (June 15). https://www.ohchr.org/en/documents/thematic-reports/ahrc4426-intersection-race-and-gender-discrimination-sport-report-united.

———. (2023) "Refugee Data Finder." UNHCR. https://www.unhcr.org/refugee-statistics/.

United Nations Secretary-General. (2010) "Remarks at Event on Ending Violence and Criminal Sanctions Based on Sexual Orientation and Gender Identity." https://www.un.org/sg/en/content/sg/statement/2010-12-10/secretary-generals-remarks-event-ending-violence-and-criminal.

———. (2021) "Secretary-General's Statement on the Conclusion of the UN Climate Change Conference COP26." (November 13). https://www.un.org/sg/en/content/sg/statement/2021-11-13/secretary-generals-statement-the-conclusion-of-the-un-climate-change-conference-cop26.

United Nations UN News. (2008) "Universal Decriminalization of Homosexuality a Human Rights Imperative–Ban." (December 10). https://news.un.org/en/story/2010/12/361672.

———. (2022) "Catastrophic Hunger Levels Leave 500,000 Children at Risk of Dying in Somalia." (September 13). https://news.un.org/en/story/2022/09/1126491.

UN Women. (2022) *Trafficking in Women and Girls: Crises as a Risk Multiplier: Report of the Secretary-General*. https://www.unwomen.org/en/digital-library/publications/2022/08/trafficking-in-women-and-girls-report-of-the-secretary-general-2022.

———. (2023) "Facts and Figures: Ending Violence against Women." https://www.unwomen.org/en/what-we-do/ending-violence-against-women/facts-and-figures.

US Ninth Circuit Court of Appeals. (2002) *Doe v. UNOCAL*. 395 F.3d 932.

US Supreme Court. (2013) *Kiobel v. Royal Dutch Petroleum.* 133 S. Ct. 1659.

US Trade Representative. (2013) *2013 Report to Congress on China's WTO Compliance.* www.ustr.gov/sites/default/files/2013-Report-to-Congress-China-WTO-Compliance.pdf.

Uvin, Peter. (1998) *Aiding Violence: The Development Enterprise in Rwanda.* West Hartford, CT: Kumarian.

Valbjörn, Morten. (2016) "North Africa and the Middle East." In *The Oxford Handbook of Comparative Regionalism,* edited by Tanja A. Borzel and Thomas Risse. New York: Oxford University Press, pp. 249–270.

Väyrynen, Raimo. (2003) "Regionalism: Old and New." *International Studies Review* 5:1 (March): 25–51.

Versailles Declaration. (2022) European Union. https://www.pubaffairsbruxelles.eu/eu-institution-news/the-versailles-declaration-10-and-11-march-2022/.

Villacampa, Javier Alcalde. (2008) "The Mine Ban Treaty, New Diplomacy and Human Security Ten Years Later." *European Political Science* 7:4 (December): 519–529.

Voeten, Erik. (2005) "The Political Origins of the UN Security Council's Ability to Legitimize the Use of Force." *International Organization* 59:3 (Summer): 527–557.

Vogler, John. (2011) "European Union Environmental Policy." In *Comparative Environmental Regionalism,* edited by Lorraine Elliott and Shaun Breslin. London: Routledge, pp. 19–36.

von der Schulenburg, Michael. (2014) "Rethinking Peacebuilding: Transforming the UN Approach." International Peace Academy Policy Papers. https://www.ipinst.org/wp-content/uploads/publications/ipi_e_pub_rethinking_peacebuilding.pdf.

von Einsiedel, Sebastian, with Louise Bosetti, James Cockayne, Cale Salih, and Wilfred Wan. (2017) "Civil War Trends and the Changing Nature of Armed Conflict." UN University Centre for Policy Research Occasional Paper 10 (March).

von Einsiedel, Sebastian, David M. Malone, and Bruno Stagno Ugarte, eds. (2016) *The UN Security Council in the 21st Century.* Boulder, CO: Lynne Rienner.

von Stein, Jana. (2013) "The Engines of Compliance." In *Interdisciplinary Perspectives on International Law and International Relations: The State of the Art,* edited by Jeffrey Dunoff and Mark A. Pollack. New York: Cambridge University Press, pp. 477–501.

Vreeland, James Raymond. (2015) *The International Monetary Fund (IMF): Politics of Conditional Lending,* 2nd ed. New York: Routledge.

Wade, Peter. (2021) "Greta Thunberg Warns Congress: You'll Have to Explain to Your Children Why You Didn't Act on Climate." *Rolling Stone* (April 22).

Walker, Molly. (2020) "Trump Mulls Halting Aid to WHO: 'They Called It Wrong' on COVID-19." *MedPageToday* (April 8).

Wallace-Wells, David. (2022) "How Bad Is the Global Food Crisis Going to Get? *New York Times* (June 7).

Walling, Carrie Booth. (2020) "The United Nations Security Council and Human Rights." *Global Governance: Special Issues: The United Nations at 75.* 26:2 (April–June): 291–306.

Walsh, Declan. (2023) "From Coast to Coast, Coups Bring Turmoil in Africa." *New York Times* (July 29).

Walter, Barbara F., Lise Morjé Howard, and V. Page Fortna. (2019) "The Extraordinary Relationship between Peacekeeping and Peace." *British Journal of Political Science* 51:4 (October): 1705–1722.

Waltz, Kenneth N. (1979) *Theory of International Politics.* Reading: Addison-Wesley.

Wang, Dong, and Friso M. S. Stevens (2021) "Why Is There No Northeast Asian Security Architecture? Assessing the Strategic Impediments to a Stable East Asia." *Pacific Review* 34:4: 577–604.

Wapner, Paul. (1996) *Environmental Activism and World Civil Politics*. Albany: SUNY Press.

Ward, Michael. (2004) *Quantifying the World: UN Contributions to Statistics*. Bloomington: Indiana University Press.

Weaver, Catherine E. (2007) "The World's Bank and the Bank's World." *Global Governance* 13:4 (October–December): 493–512.

———. (2008) *Hypocrisy Trap: The World Bank and the Poverty of Reform*. Princeton: Princeton University Press.

Weinberger, Naomi. (2002) "Civil-Military Coordination in Peacebuilding: The Challenge of Afghanistan." *Journal of International Affairs* 55:2 (Spring): 245–274.

Weinstein, Michael M., and Steve Charnovitz. (2001) "The Greening of the WTO." *Foreign Affairs* 80:6 (November–December): 147–156.

Weiss, Edith Brown, and Harold K. Jacobson, eds. (2000) *Engaging Countries: Strengthening Compliance with International Environmental Accords*. Cambridge: MIT Press.

Weiss, Thomas G. (2009) *What's Wrong with the United Nations and How to Fix It*. Cambridge: Polity.

———. (2014) "Reinvigorating the 'Second' United Nations: People Matter." In *Routledge Handbook of International Organizations*, edited by Bob Reinalda. New York: Routledge, pp. 299–311.

———. (2018) *Would the World Be Better Without the UN?* Cambridge: Polity Press.

Weiss, Thomas G., David P. Forsythe, and Roger A. Coate. (2004) *The United Nations and Changing World Politics*, 4th ed. (Boulder. CO: Westview Press), p. 278.

Weiss, Thomas G. and Pallavi Roy. (2016) "The UN and the Global South, 1945–2015: Past as Prelude?" *Third World Quarterly* 37:7, pp. 1147–1155.

Weiss, Thomas G., and Ramesh Thakur. (2010) *Global Governance and the UN: An Unfinished Journey*. Bloomington: Indiana University Press.

Weiss, Thomas G., and Rorden Wilkinson. (2014) "Rethinking Global Governance? Complexity, Authority, Power, Change." *International Studies Quarterly* 58:1 (March): 207–215.

Weissbrodt, David. (2003) "Do Human Rights Treaties Make Things Worse?" *Foreign Policy* 134 (January–February): 88–89.

Welsh, Jennifer. (2014) "Implementing the Responsibility to Protect: Catalyzing Debate and Building Capacity." In Alexander Betts and Philip Orchard eds. *Implementation and World Politics: How International Norms Change Practice*. Oxford: Oxford University Press, pp. 124–143.

Wendt, Alexander. (1995) "Constructing International Politics." *International Security* 20:1 (Summer): 71–81.

Whitfield, Teresa. (2007) *Friends Indeed? The United Nations, Groups of Friends, and Resolution of Conflict*. Washington, DC: US Institute of Peace.

Wickens, Corrine M. and Jennifer A. Sandline. (2007) "Literacy for What? Literacy for Whom? The Politics of Literacy Education and Neocolonialism in UNESCO and World Bank-sponsored Literacy Programs." *Adult Education Quarterly* 57: 4: 275–292.

Willetts, Peter. (2006) "The Cardoso Report on the UN and Civil Society: Functionalism, Global Corporatism, or Global Democracy?" *Global Governance* 12:3 (July–September): 305–324.

Williams, Paul D. (2007) "From Non-Intervention to Non-Indifference: The Origins and Development of the African Union's Security Culture." *African Affairs* 106 (April): 253–279.

———. (2011) *War and Conflict in Africa.* Cambridge: Polity.

———. (2018) *Fighting for Peace in Somalia: A History and Analysis of the African Union Mission (AMISOM), 2007–2017.* New York: Oxford University Press.

Williams, Paul D., M. D'Alessandro, L. Darkwa, A. Halal, and J. Machakaire. (2018) "Assessing the Effectiveness of the African Union Mission in Somalia (AMISOM)." EPON Report. Norwegian Institute of International Affairs. https://nupi.brage.unit.no/nupi-xmlui/bitstream/handle/11250/2597243/EPON-AMISOM-Report%201-2018.pdf?sequence=6.

Wolman, Andrew. (2014) "Welcoming a New International Human Rights Actor? The Participation of Subnational Human Rights Institutions at the UN." *Global Governance* 20:3 (July–September): 437–457.

Wong, Wendy H. (2012) "Becoming a Household Name: How Human Rights NGOs Establish Credibility Through Organizational Structure." In *The Credibility of Transnational NGOs: When Virtue Is Not Enough,* edited by Peter A. Gourevitch and David A. Lake. New York: Cambridge University Press, pp. 86–112.

Woods, Lawrence T. (1993) *Asia-Pacific Diplomacy: Nongovernmental Organizations and International Relations.* Vancouver: University of British Columbia Press.

Woods, Ngaire. (1999) "Good Governance in International Organizations." *Global Governance* 5:1 (January–March): 39–61.

World Bank. (2021) "Global Economy to Expand by 4% in 2021; Vaccine Deployment and Investment Key to Sustaining the Recovery." Press release (January 5).

———. (2022a) "FY 22 List of Fragile and Conflict-Affected Situations." https://thedocs.worldbank.org.

———. (2022b) "Free Trade Deal Boosts Africa's Economic Development." World Bank (June 30).

———. (2022c) "Global Progress in Reducing Extreme Poverty Grinds to a Halt." Press release. (October 5).

World Commission on Environment and Development. (1987) *Our Common Future.* Brundtland Commission Report. Oxford: Oxford University Press.

World Food Programme. (2022) "Countdown to Catastrophe Begins in Yemen as Funding for Food Assistance Dwindles." News release (February 24).

World Food Programme (WFP) and Food and Agriculture Organization (FAO). (2022) "Hunger Hotspots. FAO-WFP Early Warnings on Acute Food Insecurity: October 2022 to January 2023." *Outlook.* https://reliefweb.int/attachments/28f91fd2-2dbc-4e77-9e9e-70aff6c34a5c/WFP-0000142656.pdf.

World Health Organization. (2021) "Vaccine Inequity Undermining Global Economic Recovery." News release (July 22).

———. (2023) "WHO Coronavirus (COVID-19) Dashboard." https://covid19.who.int/.

Wroughton, Lesley. (2008) "Gates, Buffett Back WFP Plan to Help Poor Farmers." Reuters (September 25).

Yates, JoAnn, and Craig Murphy. (2019) *Engineering Rules: Global Standard-Setting Since 1880.* Baltimore: Johns Hopkins University Press.

Youde, Jeremy. (2010) *Biopolitical Surveillance and Public Health in International Politics.* New York: Palgrave Macmillan.

———. (2012) *Global Health Governance.* Malden, MA: Polity.

———. (2019) "The Role of Philanthropy in International Relations." *Review of International Studies* 45:1 (January): 39–56.

Young, Kevin. (2011) "The Basel Committee on Banking Supervision." In *Handbook of Transnational Governance: Institutions and Innovations*, edited by Thomas Hale and David Held. London: Polity, pp. 39–45.

Young, Oran R. (1967) *The Intermediaries: Third Parties in International Crises*. Princeton: Princeton University Press.

———. (1999) *The Effectiveness of International Environmental Regimes: Causal Connections and Behavioral Mechanisms*. Cambridge: MIT Press.

Yuan, Jing-Dong. (2010) "China's Role in Establishing and Building the Shanghai Cooperation Organization (SCO)." *Journal of Contemporary China* 19:67 (November): 855–869.

Zamęcki, Łukasz, and Viktor Glied. (2020) "Article 7 Process and Democratic Backsliding of Hungary and Poland. Democracy and the Rule of Law." *Modelling the New Europe* 34: 57–85.

Zartman, I. William, and Saadia Touval. (1996) "International Mediation in the Post–Cold War Era." In *Managing Global Chaos: Sources of and Responses to International Conflict*, edited by Chester A. Crocker and Fen Osler Hampson, with Pamela Aall. Washington, DC: US Institute of Peace, pp. 445–462.

Zürn, Michael. (2018) *A Theory of Global Governance: Authority, Legitimacy, and Contestation*. Oxford: Oxford University Press.

Zweifel, Thomas D. (2006) *International Organizations and Democracy: Accountability, Politics, and Power*. Boulder: Lynne Rienner.

Index

About the Book

ASTOUNDING, BUT TRUE . . . THE NEWEST EDITION OF *INTERNATIONAL Organizations* surpasses its predecessors!

The fourth edition of this award-winning text has been thoroughly revised and updated to capture nearly a decade of new developments affecting global governance: the Covid-19 pandemic, Russia's invasion of Ukraine, the rise of populist nationalism, implementation of the SDGs, the youth climate-justice movement, and much more. There is also an entirely new chapter on human security. As before, the authors provide a comprehensive, in-depth examination of the full range of international organizations.

Margaret P. Karns is professor emeritus of political science at the University of Dayton and a fellow at the Center for Governance and Sustainability at the University of Massachusetts Boston. **Tana Johnson** is associate professor of public affairs and political science at the University of Wisconsin–Madison. **Karen A. Mingst** is professor emeritus of political science at the University of Kentucky.